THE AVIATION FACTFILE

AIRCRAFT OF WORLD WAR II

THE AVIATION FACTFILE

AIRCRAFT OF WORLD WAR II

GENERAL EDITOR: JIM WINCHESTER

Grange
BOOKS

First published in 2004 for Grange Books
An imprint of Grange Books plc
The Grange
Kingsnorth Industrial Estate
Hoo, Nr Rochester
Kent ME3 9ND
www.grangebooks.co.uk

Reprinted in 2005

A catalogue record for this book is available from the British Library.

ISBN 1-84013-639-1

Produced by
Amber Books Ltd
Bradley's Close
74–77 White Lion Street
London N1 9PF
www.amberbooks.co.uk

Printed in Singapore

Contents

INTRODUCTION

On the eve of World War II in Europe in September 1939, the air forces of the world were largely equipped with biplane fighters, bombers and transport aircraft. By war's end six years later, biplanes were obsolete and five nations had flown jet or rocket-powered warplanes. The Munich Crisis in 1938 sounded the last warning before war, and gave all nations time to at least begin to rearm with modern equipment. Nonetheless, biplanes such as the Gloster Gladiator and Fiat CR.42 met in combat as late as 1942.

Britain's Royal Air Force moved into the modern era just in time. The early Spitfire and Hurricane were equal to or better than Germany's fighters,

Above: Although overshadowed by the Lancaster, the Halifax was an effective bomber.

bombers and dive-bombers, and were better employed tactically. Improved versions of the Spitfire jousted with new Messerschmitt Bf 109s in a see-saw struggle that lasted until 1945. The Typhoon and Tempest fighters became most effective in the low-level ground-attack role. Britain's bombers were more of a mixed bunch. After low-level daylight attacks proved ineffective and costly to squadrons of Blenheims, Wellingtons, Whitleys and others, Bomber Command switched to four-engined night bombers – the Stirling, Halifax and Lancaster – laying Germany's cities to waste.

Germany concealed the existence of the Luftwaffe until 1935, and many of its combat aircraft were developed under the guise of sport planes, mail planes or airliners. Only one all-new combat aircraft, the Focke-Wulf Fw 190, was introduced into large-scale Luftwaffe service during the war. Many promising projects were cancelled, and then restarted when the war situation deteriorated. Partly as a result, Germany never produced a successful strategic bomber. By 1945, Germany was fielding jet fighters, bombers and reconnaissance aircraft, and even a rocket fighter. Despite these technological innovations, these aircraft were unable to make a difference to the war's outcome.

Top: The transport workhorse of the war, the Douglas DC-3 served in every theatre.

Above left: De Havilland's 'Wooden Wonder', the Mosquito, performed several roles. It is pictured here in photo-reconnaissance colours.

Above: The Grumman F6F Hellcat was one of the US Navy's finest strike fighters. Its wings could be folded for carrier storage.

Japan's combat aircraft, particularly the A6M 'Zero' and G4M 'Betty' operated by the navy, surprised the Allies in 1941, particularly with their long range. This was achieved at the expense of armour or fuel tank protection, and the loss of experienced crews was to cost Japan dearly later in the war.

Below: More than 12,000 examples of the B-17 Flying Fortress were built. Many were lost in dangerous day bombing missions over Germany.

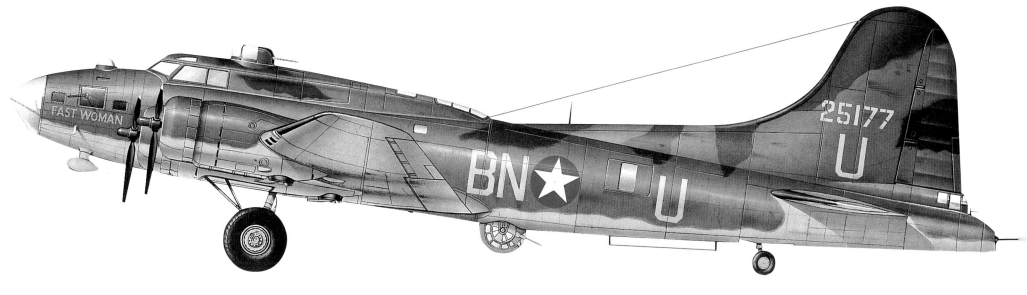

Production of improved models was hindered by bombing, but some of the war's best fighter designs, such as the Kawasaki Ki-100, emerged in Japan in 1944 and 1945. Sadly for Japan, many of their potential pilots had died in futile suicide attacks.

The USSR looked at aircraft largely as an adjunct of the infantry, building thousands of simple but tough aircraft such as the Il-2 'Sturmovik' and the Yak series of fighters. Added to this were thousands more US and British types supplied under the Lend-Lease scheme.

After the 1941 attack on Pearl Harbor, the USA quickly geared up production

of combat aircraft on a massive scale. America's industrial muscle turned out tens of thousands of fighters, bombers, transports and trainers. British experience helped the US refine its warplanes, notably the P-51 Mustang and B-17 Flying Fortress, which came to symbolise US airpower, despite the fact that the P-47 Thunderbolt and B-24 Liberator were built in greater numbers. The B-29 Superfortress, if not the warplane that won the war, was the one that brought it to a conclusion, and ushered in a whole new age of warfare.

Right: The Messerschmitt Bf 110 proved useful in the tank-busting role in the deserts of North Africa.

AICHI

D3A 'VAL'

● Naval dive-bomber ● Influenced by the He 70 ● Highly manoeuvrable

Having dropped the first Japanese bombs to fall on American targets during World War II, the D3A went on to sink more Allied warships than any other Axis aircraft. It was given the Allied codename 'Val' and its early success gave no hint of its troubled design history or the terrible losses that were to be suffered later in the war. During the initial stages of hostilities against America, the D3A was feared as a formidable dive-bomber.

▲ When the 'Val' entered service, Japanese crews originally found themselves with a highly competent aircraft. Unfortunately, it was to become increasingly vulnerable.

PHOTO FILE

AICHI D3A 'VAL'

◄ **Attack on Pearl Harbor**
This dramatic photograph depicts a D3A1 in action during the Japanese attack on Pearl Harbor. Exploding anti-aircraft shells surround this machine, but losses were comparatively light.

▼ **'Val' in plan**
A near-perfect plan view shows the He 70-inspired elliptical wing of the D3A. The dive brakes and undercarriage may also be seen.

▲ **Navy Type 99**
Known to the Japanese as the Navy Type 99 Carrier Bomber Model 11, the D3A1 was a highly accurate delivery platform, especially effective in diving attacks on ships. Later in the war, both D3A1 and D3A2 aircraft were used in desperate kamikaze attacks.

▲ **Second prototype**
Aichi produced two prototypes of the 11-Shi Navy Experimental Carrier Bomber, which was to become the D3A. This was the much-modified second aircraft.

◄ **Distinctive features**
This US Naval Intelligence photograph clearly shows the retracted dive brakes and tail-mounted arrester hook.

FACTS AND FIGURES

➤ An undesirable feature of the D3A prototype was its tendency to snap roll during tight turns.

➤ The 'Val' was the last Japanese carrier-based aircraft with spatted landing gear.

➤ Because of its agility, the D3A was sometimes flown as a fighter.

➤ During attacks on British ships in the Indian Ocean, 'Vals' placed 82 to 87 per cent of their bombs on target.

➤ Some aircraft were modified as D3A2-K Bomber Trainer Model 12s.

➤ With its extra fuel, the D3A2 could fly long-range missions over the Solomons.

PROFILE

'Val' in force over Pearl Harbor

Having identified a requirement for a new carrier-capable dive-bomber to replace its Aichi D1A2 biplanes, the Imperial Japanese Navy (IJN) issued a specification to Japanese industry during 1936.

Aichi answered with a monoplane design featuring a fixed, spatted undercarriage and a wing inspired by that of the He 70. Research had shown that the extra weight and complexity of retractable landing gear was not justified by the corresponding small increase in overall performance.

Initial flight tests revealed a number of serious problems, but after a major redesign, which included an increase in power, the aircraft was chosen over the Nakajima D3N1. At this stage a dorsal fin was added to rectify persistent directional stability problems, before carrier qualification began in 1940.

Involved in a number of naval actions, including the attacks on Pearl Harbor and the sinking of the British carrier HMS *Hermes*, the D3A1 was replaced from June 1942 by the D3A2, which featured increased fuel capacity, a propeller spinner and modified canopy. As World War II progressed, the 'Val' began to suffer horrendous losses and all but the smallest carriers had their aircraft replaced by the Yokosuka D4Y Suisei. In the final year of war, many D3As were expended in suicide attacks.

Externally, the main difference between the D3A1 and D3A2 was the use of a propeller spinner on the latter.

Belonging to the 33rd Kokutai, this D3A1 has its rear canopy removed, allowing the rear-seater a greater field of fire. This was a typical in-service configuration.

D3A2 Model 22 'Val'

Type: two-seat, carrier-based dive-bomber

Powerplant: one 969-kW (1,300-hp.) Mitsubishi Kinsei 54 14-cylinder, air-cooled radial engine

Maximum speed: 430 km/h (267 m.p.h.) at 6200 m (20,000 ft.)

Range: 1352 km (840 mi.) with bombload

Service ceiling: 10,500 m (34,500 ft.)

Weights: empty 2570 kg (5,654 lb.), maximum take-off 3800 kg (8,360 lb.)

Armament: two fixed forward-firing 7.7-mm (.303 cal.) Type 97 machine-guns and one flexibly-mounted 7.7-mm Type 97 machine-gun in the rear cockpit, plus 370 kg (814 lb.) of bombs

Dimensions:
span	14.37 m (47 ft. 2 in.)
length	10.20 m (33 ft. 6 in.)
height	3.85 m (12 ft. 8 in.)
wing area	34.90 m² (373 sq. ft.)

A prominent tubular sight mounted ahead of the windscreen enabled the pilot to aim the forward-firing machine-guns. They were useful weapons for ground-strafing but limited in air-to-air combat.

A further modification introduced on the D3A2 was a revised canopy profile. Even longer than the 'greenhouse' canopy of the D3A1, the new glazing featured an elongated rear section which was faired neatly into the rear fuselage. The frequent removal of this section in use meant that the canopy was not a reliable recognition feature of the D3A2.

D3A2 MODEL 22 'VAL'

Built by Showa Hikoki Kogyo, this late-production D3A2 was flown by the Meikoya Kokutai. Later in the war, 'Vals' flew only from the smaller carriers denied to the D4Y by its high landing speed.

Persistent problems with directional stability led Aichi to fit a dorsal fin to the 'Val'. This cured the stability problem, while cambered outer-wing leading edges cured an early tendency to snap roll in small radius turns.

An engine of increased power gave the D3A2 generally improved performance compared to the D3A1. Take-off power was 969 kW (1,300 hp.).

Mounted on a hinged crutch beneath the centre fuselage, the 250-kg (550-lb.) bomb was swung forwards and downward on release. Two 60-kg (132-lb.) bombs could be carried beneath the wings.

COMBAT DATA

MAXIMUM SPEED

Although it was carrier-based like the Douglas SBD-5 Dauntless, the D3A1 was very close to the Junkers Ju 87B-1 in overall design philosophy. With its fixed undercarriage, the 'Val' offered similar performance to the German design.

D3A1 'VAL'	385 km/h (239 m.p.h.)
SBD-5 DAUNTLESS	406 km/h (252 m.p.h.)
Ju 87B-1	390 km/h (242 m.p.h.)

RANGE

Exceptional range was an important feature of the SBD-5. Even on a bombing mission the aircraft had a range of 1794 km (1,100 mi.), which is very impressive when compared to the 600-km (370-mi.) range of the bombed-up Ju 87B-1. The D3A1 could reach 1470 km (913 mi.) only when unarmed.

D3A1 'VAL' 1470 km (840 mi.)

SBD-5 DAUNTLESS 1794 km (1,110 mi.)

Ju 87B-1 600 km (370 mi.)

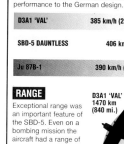

ARMAMENT

A heavy bombload and two hard-hitting 12.7 mm (.50 cal.) machine-guns in the engine cowling made the Dauntless a formidable attack aircraft. The D3A1 was deadly accurate, however.

D3A1 'VAL'
3 x 7.7-mm (.303 cal.) machine-guns
370-kg (814-lb.) bombload

SBD-5 DAUNTLESS
2 x 12.7-mm (.50 cal.) machine-guns
2 x 7.62-mm (.30 cal.) machine-guns
1021-kg (2,250-lb.) bombload

Ju 87B-1
3 x 7.9-mm (0.31-in.) machine-guns
700-kg (1,540-lb.) bombload

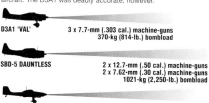

Naval Aichis

■ **B7A RYUSEI 'GRACE':** A powerful torpedo and dive-bomber, the B7A suffered a protracted development period and, by the time it was ready for service, all the IJN's carriers had been lost.

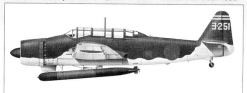

■ **D1A 'SUSIE':** Relying heavily on Heinkel's He 66 design, the D1A was the IJN's principal dive-bomber before the D3A entered service. Some 68 D1As were serving as trainers in 1941.

■ **E13A 'JAKE':** Designed as a reconnaissance floatplane, the E13A developed into a useful multi-role type and flew from land and shore bases throughout World War II.

AMIOT

143

● Twin-engined bomber ● 1930s design ● World War II service

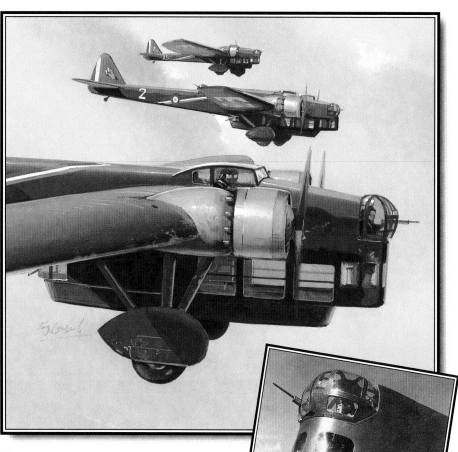

▲ *An undoubtedly apocryphal story relates that the Amiot 143 was chosen for production by the Armée de l'Air because it was the ugliest of the four competing designs.*

I n 1928 the Armée de l'Air announced its *Multiplaces de Combat* requirement for a new class of day- and night-bomber, reconnaissance and escort aircraft. In a competition to find a suitable design to fill the requirement, Amiot, Blériot, Breguet and SPCA built prototypes, from which Amiot's 140 was chosen. Placed in service as the 143 and 143M from the mid-1930s, the design was obsolete by 1939, but was active in the bombing role as late as 1941.

AMIOT 143

◄ **Amiot 150BE**
One of the final derivatives of the 143 was the 150BE scout/torpedo-bomber aircraft for the Aéronavale. The sole example crashed in 1939.

▲ **North African transport**
After France's defeat and the retirement of Amiot 143s from the bombing role, the aircraft were converted to transports by the Vichy air force and transferred to North Africa.

◄ **First in service**
These aircraft were attached to the 1er Groupe, 22^e Escadre at Chartres, the first unit to be equipped with 143s.

▼ **Vichy transport**
Bearing the distinctive red and yellow striped tail markings of a Vichy aircraft, this 143M was operated in Morocco by GT III/15 in 1942.

▲ **Early production**
The first 30 aircraft had a 17.95-m (59-ft.) fuselage which was shorter than that of subsequent aircraft. From the 41st aircraft, Lewis 7.7-mm (.303 cal.) machine-guns were replaced by MAC 1934 7.5-mm (0.3-in) guns.

FACTS AND FIGURES

➤ During 1936 one 143M was fitted with Gnome-Rhône 14N radials for high-temperature trials in Indo-China.

➤ An Amiot 142, powered by two liquid-cooled Hispano-Suiza engines, was built.

➤ As well as home-based units, a bomber group in Marrakesh had 143Ms in 1939.

➤ One daylight raid was made by 143s, when 12 aircraft attacked bridges at Sedan on 14 May 1940; most were lost.

➤ During night operations GB I/38 and II/38 lost just four 143s in 197 sorties.

➤ The last Amiot 143s were grounded in North Africa in February 1944.

PROFILE

Armée de l'Air's valiant defender

Left: Amiot 143-01, the first prototype, flew in August 1934 and was engaged in bombing and firing trials the following year.

Amiot's less-than-attractive aircraft was a typical example of an interim monoplane bomber design of the 1930s, which was rendered obsolete by the rapid advances in aircraft design brought about by the onset of war.

Initially, an order for 40 Amiot 140s was placed, but the advent of a more powerful, supercharged Gnome-Rhône 14Kdrs/Kgrs engine meant that this was amended to a similar number of the improved 143. From the 41st example

production switched to the 143M, which had further improved 649-kW (870-hp.) 14 Kirs/Kjrs engines, a lengthened fuselage and different machine-guns. The last 25 examples were built to 143 BN4 night-bomber and 143 B5 day-bomber standard. Production of 140/143/143Ms amounted to 178 aircraft, and deliveries to the Armée de l'Air were complete by 1939.

From 3 September 1939 the type was used for night reconnaissance and leaflet-dropping raids over enemy

territory. Apart from the equally antiquated Farman 222, the air force had no other aircraft with sufficient range. Even after the German invasion of France in May 1940, 143s were making bombing sorties over targets such as bridges and railway marshalling yards in Belgium, France and Germany.

From 1941, the Vichy government made use of the type in the transport role and mainly in North Africa, where 143s continued flying until the Axis was defeated in Tunisia in 1943.

Above: Amiot 143M No. 118 belonged to the 4e Escadrille, 35e Escadre based at Bron. Although outdated, the Amiot 143 had a useful range compared to other French bombers.

143M

On 3 September 1939, 143M No. 78 was serving with GB II of the 35e Escadre de Bombardement, which undertook night reconnaissance operations from Pontarlier. By 10 May 1940, when France was invaded, GB II/35 had re-equipped with Breguet 691s.

143M

Type: five-seat night-bomber and reconnaissance aircraft

Powerplant: two 649-kW (870-hp.) Gnome-Rhône 14Kirs/Kjrs Mistral Major 14-cylinder radials

Maximum speed: 310 km/h (192 m.p.h.) at 4000 m (13,000 ft.)

Climb rate: 14 min 20 sec to 4000 m (13,000 ft.) at 8610-kg (18,942-lb.) weight

Normal range: 1200 km (745 mi.)

Service ceiling: 7900 m (26,000 ft.)

Weights: empty 6100 kg (13,420 lb.); maximum take-off 9700 kg (21,385 lb.)

Armament: four 7.5-mm (0.3-in.) MAC 1934 machine-guns, plus up to 800 kg (1,760 lb.) of bombs on external racks and 800 kg (1,760 lb.) of bombs in an internal bomb-bay

Dimensions:
span	24.53 m	(80 ft. 5 in.)
length	18.26 m	(59 ft. 10 in.)
height	5.68 m	(78 ft. 6 in.)
wing area	100 m²	(1,076 sq. ft.)

While the Amiot 140, 143 and 143M production standard aircraft were powered by versions of the Gnome-Rhône 14K Mistral Major, various versions were proposed with alternative powerplants. Principal among these was the Hispano-Suiza-engined 142, which used the supercharged, liquid-cooled 12-cylinder Hispano-Suiza 12Y.

The 143 had an all-metal fuselage. The thick-section wing comprised five sections built up on three Duralumin tube girder spars with tube girder ribs. Duralumin sheet was rivetted to this to form the skin. The outermost wing sections contained six fuel tanks (from the 41st aircraft) with a total capacity of 2719 litres (718 gal.). In earlier aircraft, fuel tanks were jettisonable.

The rectangular-section fuselage was made up of open-sectioned formers with fore and aft stringers covered with Duralumin sheet.

Originally envisaged with a crew of four, the 143M had a fifth crewmember for the night–bomber role. The navigator/bombardier and radio operator were situated in the ventral gondola.

Bombload capacity was limited to 800 kg (1,760 lb.) internally, in varying combinations from four 200-kg (440-lb.) to 64 12.5-kg (27.5-lb.) bombs. A further 800 kg (1,760 lb.) could be carried on external outer wing racks.

Although lightly armed by the standards of World War II, the 143 had a defensive armament which was arranged to protect the aircraft from attack from every direction. Apart from nose and dorsal turrets and a flexible ventral mounting, 143s often carried a fourth 7.5-mm (0.3-in.) MAC 1934 machine-gun which fired through the floor of the forward fuselage.

ACTION DATA

MAXIMUM SPEED

By 1939 the obsolescence of the Amiot 143 had become increasingly apparent. Although its maximum speed was not far short of that of the Dornier Do 17, the 143's cruising performance when carrying a load was considerably less and made it vulnerable to fighter attack.

143M	310 km/h (192 m.p.h.)
H.P.54 HARROW Mk II	322 km/h (200 m.p.h.)
Do 17E-1	347 km/h (215 m.p.h.)

SERVICE CEILING

In terms of its range and altitude ability, the 143M was one of the Armée de l'Air's better bomber types. This led to the type's use in raids on the Rhine during 1939.

143M	H.P.54 HARROW Mk II	Do 17E-1
7900 m (26,000 ft.)	6950 m (22,800 ft.)	5100 m (16,700 ft.)

ARMAMENT

Although the Amiot had a useful bombload – better than that of the contemporary Handley Page Harrow and over twice that of the Do 17 – it was a far more vulnerable aircraft. The Do 17 was able to use its speed to good effect in the early years of the war.

143M	4 x 7.5-mm (0.3-in.) machine-guns / 1600-kg (3,520-lb.) bombload
H.P.54 HARROW Mk II	4 x 7.7-mm (.303 cal.) machine-guns / 1361-kg (3,000-lb.) bombload
Do 17E-1	2 x 7.92-mm (0.31-in.) machine-guns / 750-kg (1,650-lb.) bombload

Amiot's inter-war designs

■ **110C.1:** A single-seat design, the 110 was built to a French lightweight fighter requirement. Two were produced; one later became a racer.

■ **122-BP3:** This large biplane bomber/escort had a crew of three and entered service in 1929. Eighty were built for the Armée de l'Air.

■ **340:** Based on the long-range postal 341, the 340 was a three-seat bomber flown in 1937. It featured an all-metal fuselage.

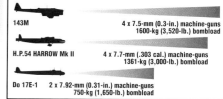

■ **351:** The 350 series bombers were derived from the 340. By June 1940, 86 Amiot 351s and 354s had been completed for the Armée de l'Air.

ARADO

AR 196

● Catapult-launched reconnaissance floatplane ● Eyes of the fleet

A highly successful design, the little Arado 196 was the eyes of the Kriegsmarine. Not only did it perform the hazardous role of spotting for the guns of the fleet, it performed daring air–sea rescues in the English Channel and lonely coastal patrols over Biscay. The Ar 196 served on Germany's capital ships and cruisers and in all European maritime theatres of war. It was one of the finest floatplane designs of its time.

▲ Most Ar 196 floatplanes served from land bases in occupied Norway, France and Denmark, but the aircraft is best remembered as the catapult-launched light spotter of the German navy.

ARADO AR 196

Trials on the water ▶
The prototypes of the Ar 196 were recognisable by the twin-bladed propeller. This was replaced by a variable-pitch three-bladed type, and the airframe was slightly modified in production aircraft.

Lone patrol ▶
Although designed to spot for the fleet's guns, the Ar 196 was used for many tasks, such as dropping agents and attacking Allied maritime patrol planes.

▲ Seal hunter
One of the Ar 196's great moments was the capture of HMS Seal in 1940. The British submarine had been damaged by a mine during a patrol off the coast of Norway. Two Ar 196s, operating from Aalborg in Denmark, attacked the crippled submarine and managed to inflict enough damage to prevent it submerging. It was then captured by the Kriegsmarine.

▲ Plane sailing
Most Ar 196s had twin floats, as trials of a single-float version with small outrigger floats had proved it to be tricky to operate on water.

◀ On the slipway
This Ar 196 served with 2./SAGr 125, and was moored in Suda Bay, Crete. The unit carried out anti-submarine patrols against the Royal Navy.

FACTS AND FIGURES

➤ The Arado beat a rival Focke-Wulf design in the competition to replace the Heinkel He 50 as the fleet floatplane.

➤ Ar 196s also served in coastal units with Bulgaria, Finland and Romania.

➤ Twin floats were chosen because pilots liked the stability given during taxiing.

➤ The Ar 196 was almost used in a floatplane record-breaking attempt, but the Reich Air Ministry banned it.

➤ *Bismarck* launched its Ar 196 to drive off a shadowing RAF Catalina in 1941.

➤ Ar 196 operations ranged from the Arctic Circle to the Black Sea.

Eyes of the German fleet

Arado began designing the Ar 196 in 1936, to replace the obsolete Heinkel He 50 reconnaissance floatplanes then in service with the fleet. Unlike the floatplanes of most navies, the Ar 196 was a thoroughly modern design, with metal frame construction for most of the aircraft. It also packed a very powerful punch; two Ar 196s even managed to

capture a Royal Navy submarine in 1940 after blasting it with their cannon and machine-guns.

The Ar 196 completed trials just as the war was beginning. The first warship to take the aircraft to sea was the *Admiral Graf Spee*, and all the other Kriegsmarine capital ships and heavy cruisers subsequently received them, including the

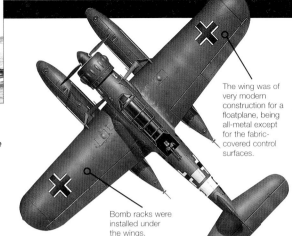

The Arado was the last fighting floatplane to be built in Europe. This example was captured by the Royal Navy and was evaluated by the Marine Aircraft Experimental Establishment.

Bismarck. The Ar 196 was produced in several variants, and was built by Fokker and SNCA for Germany.

The wing was of very modern construction for a floatplane, being all-metal except for the fabric-covered control surfaces.

Bomb racks were installed under the wings.

Ar 196A-3

Type: two-seat shipboard and coastal patrol aircraft

Powerplant: one 716-kW (960-hp.) BMW 123K nine-cylinder radial

Maximum speed: 310 km/h (193 m.p.h.) at 4000 m (13,120 ft.)

Combat radius: 1070 km (665 mi.)

Service ceiling: 7000 m (23,000 ft.)

Weights: empty 2990 kg (6,592 lb.); loaded 3730 kg (8,223 lb.)

Armament: two 20-mm (0.79-in.) cannon in the wings; one or two 7.92-mm (0.31-in) guns in the rear cockpit and front fuselage; two 50-kg (110-lb.) bombs

Dimensions:
span	12.40 m	(40 ft. 8 in.)
length	11.00 m	(36 ft. 1 in.)
height	4.45 m	(14 ft. 7 in.)
wing area	28.40 m²	(306 sq. ft.)

AR 196A-5

This aircraft served with 2./Seeaufklärungsgruppe 125 which operated from shore bases in the eastern Mediterranean and the Aegean Seas during 1943.

Power was provided by a 716-kW (960-hp.) BMW radial engine. The mounts were one of the aircraft's weak spots – engines were known to break off when moving across choppy water.

The cannon armament was unusually powerful for a floatplane, enabling it to take on RAF Whitley bombers over the Bay of Biscay or shoot up enemy ships.

Final production versions carried two MG 81 machine-guns in the rear cockpit, but most versions carried a single 7.92-mm (0.31-in.) MG 15.

The Arado had a roomy, modern, enclosed cockpit, in contrast with its British opponents, which were generally open to the elements and far more uncomfortable for their crews.

The Ar 196 had a conventional steel tube frame with a forward metal skin covering and a fabric covering for the rear fuselage. The airframe was a sound design, and was barely changed after completing prototype trials.

To ease handling on the water the floats were equipped with rudders. They also contained fuel tanks, and could store emergency survival kit.

COMBAT DATA

MAXIMUM SPEED

Floatplanes are not very fast, since their huge floats create immense amounts of drag in flight. However, the Arado's clean, modern design meant that it was one of the fastest of its type, with considerably more performance than its British and American equivalents.

Ar 196	310 km/h (193 m.p.h.)
OS2U KINGFISHER	265 km/h (165 m.p.h.)
SEAFOX	200 km/h (125 m.p.h.)

RANGE

Scout planes were designed to extend the horizon of the mother ship out to 100 or 200 km (62 to 125 mi.). The ability to loiter for long periods was more important than out-and-out range, and the Ar 196 could remain on station for more than four hours.

OS2U KINGFISHER 1300 km (808 mi.)

Ar 196 1070 km (665 mi.)

SEAFOX 700 km (435 mi.)

SERVICE CEILING

The Arado could climb much higher than either the American Kingfisher or the British Seafox. This was of inestimable advantage when searching for ship-sized targets, as the crew of the German machine could keep watch over a greater area of sea than observers in either of their opponents.

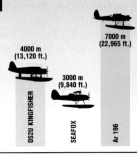

OS2U KINGFISHER	SEAFOX	Ar 196
4000 m (13,120 ft.)	3000 m (9,840 ft.)	7000 m (22,965 ft.)

Prowling the oceans

■ **SCOUTING FOR THE FLEET:** The Arado Ar 196 was designed to scout for raiders like the battlecruiser *Gneisenau*. In effect, it gave the warship's lookouts the ability to search for targets at distances of several hundred kilometres.

■ **COMMERCE RAIDING:** The Kriegsmarine's main task was to interrupt Britain's seaborne trade. Battleships, cruisers and disguised commerce raiders used their Arados to locate Allied convoys or individual merchant ships, checking to see if they were escorted. The location of a target would be transmitted to the mother ship, which would then steam to intercept, sinking the hapless merchantman by gunfire.

ARADO

AR 232

● Heavy transport ● Two sets of undercarriage ● Unique design

By the autumn of 1938, it was clear that the Luftwaffe needed a new medium transport aircraft to replace its ageing Ju 52/3ms. Both Arado and Henschel received specifications for an aircraft capable of raising and lowering itself to truck-bed height for loading. Henschel's twin-boom machine proved unsuccessful, allowing Arado to go ahead with production of one of the most distinctive transport aircraft of World War II.

▲ Even though the Ar 232 had two sets of undercarriage and rough-field capability, landing supplies at the front line was always dangerous. This one has crashed on a supply flight late in the war.

ARADO AR 232

▼ Rough landing
The 11 pairs of wheels were designed to cope with ditches up to 1.5 m (5 ft.) wide.

▲ Engine shortage
Flown for the first time in the summer of 1941, the Ar 232 V1 was powered by two BMW 801 engines, the same powerplant as in the Fw 190. The priority given to fighters saw them replaced with four less-powerful BMW 323 nine-cylinder radials.

Last plane out
The Ar 232's finest hour was in the winter of 1942/43, when it flew supply missions to support the beleaguered Sixth Army in Stalingrad. This aircraft gained the distinction of being the last transport to fly out of the city before the garrison surrendered to Soviet forces.

◀ Sole survivor
Having survived the war, this Ar 232 was brought from Flensburg to the Royal Aircraft Establishment at Farnborough and test flown. Pilots found the handling qualities were good.

Post-war service
Because of the carrying capacity of the four-engined variant, immediately after the war the sole surviving Ar 232 was pressed into service repatriating prisoners of war from both sides.

FACTS AND FIGURES

➤ Ar 232B-08 (V11) operated in Norway with its under-fuselage wheels replaced by an 8-metre long ski.

➤ During the early summer of 1941, the Ar 232 V1 flew for the first time.

➤ Performance of the twin- and four-engined aircraft was very similar.

➤ Arado used an Ar 232 during the Ar 234 test programme and passed the aircraft on to the RAF at the end of World War II.

➤ During 1942, both the V1 and V2 aircraft saw extensive service over the USSR.

➤ All but one of the Luftwaffe's Ar 232s were destroyed by enemy action.

PROFILE

The military 'Millipede'

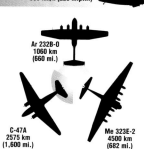

Left: One of eight Ar 232B-0 pre-series transports which equipped the 'Arado Staffel' transport wing.

No more than 30 Ar 232s seem to have been completed and the type saw only limited service.

Both the Ar 232 V1 and V2 prototypes were fitted with two BMW 801 radial engines as demanded by the original specification. It was immediately apparent, however, that Fw 190 production would place huge, more urgent demands on the limited supply of this powerplant. Hence, Arado was instructed to complete the V3 and subsequent aircraft with four lower-powered BMW-Bramo 323R engines.

A unique feature of the Ar 232 was its multi-wheel undercarriage arrangement. Normal operations were carried out with the tricycle main gears, but for loading and taxiing over rough ground, these units were partially retracted, allowing the aircraft to be loaded directly from a truck-bed and manoeuvred on its 11 pairs of under-fuselage wheels.

Eight pre-series Ar 232B-0 aircraft were completed, the first

of them also being known as the Ar 232 V4. Four B-0s joined the surviving Ar 232As in special missions over the Soviet Union, flying from bases in Finland and Norway during 1944. One aircraft crashed near Moscow while on a covert mission.

Ironically, the Allies made extensive use of the one surviving Ar 232 in transporting personnel and captured aircraft to the UK, immediately after the cessation of hostilities.

Above: The twin-engined Ar 232 V2 is seen in flight. This aircraft served until late 1944, before being lost in action.

Ar 232B-0

Type: heavy transport aircraft

Powerplant: four 895-kW (1,200-hp.) BMW-Bramo 323R-2 radial piston engines.

Maximum speed: 340 km/h (211 m.p.h.) at 4600 m (15,100 ft.)

Range: 1060 km (660 mi.)

Service ceiling: 8000 m (26,250 ft.)

Weights: empty 12,802 kg (28,164 lb.); loaded 21,135 kg (46,595 lb.)

Armament: one 13-mm (0.51-in.) MG 131 machine-gun in the nose; one or two similar weapons at the rear of the fuselage; one 20-mm (0.79-in.) cannon in a power-operated dorsal turret

Dimensions: span 33.50 m (109 ft. 11 in.)
length 23.52 m (77 ft. 2 in.)
height 5.69 m (18 ft. 8 in.)
wing area 142.60 m² (1,535 sq. ft.)

Extensive glazing in the nose offered the pilots excellent visibility on approach to landing zones. This was a major advance over previous designs, although the aircraft was vulnerable to attack. A single forward-firing 13-mm (0.51-in.) machine-gun was located in the extreme nose, with 500 rounds, and above the cockpit a power-operated turret housed one 20-mm (0.79-in.) cannon.

The Ar 230 was designed for twin-engined layout, but demand for the Fw 190 fighter meant that there were insufficient powerplants to allocate. Four lower-powered BMW-Bramo 323R-2 Fafnir engines were fitted instead. Moving from a two- to a four-engined layout required a larger wing span, although handling characteristics were found to be unaffected by the change.

The semi-monocoque fuselage pod was attached to a shoulder-mounted wing and the tail surfaces were carried on a single circular-section boom which projected from the upper fuselage. This design proved highly successful and allowed unrestricted loading around the rear of the airframe. The rear loading ramp could not be opened in flight to drop supplies.

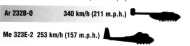

Although few Arado 232s reached operational service, their contribution to airlift operations was significant. Their missions ranged from evacuation of wounded to transporting special operations troops across Russia.

The main undercarriage was of the tricycle type and was used during normal ground operations and take-offs and landings. During loading and unloading the gear retracted upwards, thereby lowering the fuselage.

The 11 pairs of idler wheels were fitted with low-pressure tyres and mounted on independently-sprung suspension legs. They could cope with soft, rough terrain and ditches up to 1.5 m (5 ft.) across.

A rear loading ramp offered sufficient clearance to permit direct loading onto trucks, thereby reducing the loading and unloading times. Defence at the rear was provided by a single machine-gun.

AR 232A-O

The Luftwaffe required a large transport aircraft almost as soon as World War II started. Although it was a successful design, events prevented the Ar 232 from achieving its full operational potential.

German World War II transports

■ **Fw 200 CONDOR:** Developed from the maritime patrol aircraft, the Condor transport had turrets and bomb equipment removed.

■ **Ju 52:** Designed as a pre-war airliner, the Ju 52 was the main transport aircraft for the Luftwaffe and served on every major front.

■ **Ju 290:** A late-war design which was pressed into service as a transport despite being designed as an patrol bomber.

■ **Me 323:** Basically a powered version of the 321 glider, the Gigant was capable of carrying small tanks but proved extremely vulnerable.

COMBAT DATA

MAXIMUM SPEED

Because of their slow speed, the Me 323 and Ar 232 often required an escort of fighters to support any supply mission. Although faster, the C-47 carried far less cargo so more aircraft were needed to deliver the equivalent payload.

Ar 232B-0   340 km/h (211 m.p.h.)
Me 323E-2   253 km/h (157 m.p.h.)
C-47A   365 km/h (226 m.p.h.)

RANGE

Based on a pre-war airliner, the C-47 featured exceptional range. Because of its wartime design – and complications that arose during its manufacture – the Ar 232 had poor range when compared to other Allied and German transports.

Ar 232B-0 1060 km (660 mi.)
C-47A 2575 km (1,600 mi.)
Me 323E-2 4500 km (682 mi.)

PAYLOAD

The Luftwaffe's transport fleet at the start of the war was regarded as the largest in the world. Later designs of transport were capable of carrying small tanks and troops; the Arado proved to be more suitable than the C-47 for moving outsized loads.

Ar 232B-0 21,135 kg (18,000 lb.)
Me 323E-2 45,000 kg (35,000 lb.)
C-47A 11,794 kg (8,000 lb.)

ARADO

AR 234

● First jet bomber ● Fast reconnaissance aircraft ● Brief success

The Arado Ar 234 'Blitz' (Lightning) was the world's first jet bomber, although initially it was conceived as a fast reconnaissance aircraft. When it appeared in 1943 this advanced aircraft was unique in the aviation world. However, while it possessed speed and versatility, it was far from viceless and, although early operations showed promise, this potentially devastating new weapon was 'too little, too late' for the Third Reich.

▲ *The first operations by Ar 234s were reconnaissance sorties by two aircraft based in France in 1944. These were judged a success and bombing missions followed in the Ardennes later in the year.*

ARADO AR 234

▼ Rocket assistance
Two Walter rocket-assisted take-off (RATO) units were fitted to improve performance. These were used on the first reconnaissance missions in 1944.

▲ Parachute malfunction
The RATO units were jettisoned after take-off, although their landing parachutes had a tendency to malfunction.

Trolley undercarriage ▶
The trolley undercarriage generally worked well, only rarely refusing to detach on take-off. A major disadvantage, however, was the aircraft's vulnerability after a skid landing.

▼ Night-fighter version
Some of the least-known sorties were the night-fighter missions flown experimentally by Kommando Bonow with two Ar 234s from March 1945.

▲ Four-engined 'Blitz'
The 13th prototype, with four BMW 003A-1 engines, was the basis for the stillborn Ar 234C version.

FACTS AND FIGURES

➤ Development of the Jumo engines was slow, so the prototype 'Blitz' did not fly until 15 June 1943.

➤ The 'Blitz', with conventional landing gear, made its maiden flight on 10 March 1944.

➤ At least a third of the 210 Ar 234Bs built failed to reach operational units.

➤ Ar 234s were operational for six months before one was shot down by an RAF Tempest pilot.

➤ Twin- and four-engined versions were built using Junkers and BMW engines.

➤ Ar 234s were the first combat aircraft to use rocket-assisted take-off, or RATO.

The world's first jet bomber

On the cutting edge of aircraft design when it appeared in 1943, the Ar 234 'Blitz' was intended to fulfil a Luftwaffe requirement for a high-speed reconnaissance aircraft. Delivered during the winter of 1941/42, the prototype's first flight was delayed by the slow arrival of its Junkers turbojets.

The first reconnaissance sorties were flown in late-1944, many taking the 'Blitz' over the United Kingdom. Its speed made the evasion of enemy fighters straightforward.

Production examples were designated Ar 234B. Bombing duties began on Christmas Eve 1944 when a successful raid took place on Allied supplies in the Belgian town of Liège. Perhaps the type's most vital missions were against the Allied assault on the Ardennes, especially during the battle for Remagen in 1945.

However, 'Blitz' operations had ceased by March, the Ar 234 having arrived too late and in too small numbers to have the impact which the Luftwaffe had desired.

A number of Ar 234s were captured by the Allies in the closing stages of the war in Europe.

For level bombing the pilot used an autopilot system. This allowed him to disconnect the control stick and use a bombsight between his feet. Though very advanced, this was a risky manoeuvre if there were enemy fighters in the area.

Although it had the straight-line speed to outrun the Allies' piston-engined fighters, the Ar 234 was unmanoeuvrable at low speeds.

Plans and actual prototypes for several experimental Ar 234s existed at the end of World War II. One involved fitting a swept 'crescent' wing to a 'Blitz' to improve performance. This design was adopted by the British company Handley Page and fitted to the Victor bomber in the 1950s.

Ar 234B-2

Type: single-seat twin-turbojet tactical reconnaissance bomber

Powerplant: two 8.8-kN (1,975-lb.-thrust) Junkers Jumo 004B-1 Orkan turbojet engines

Maximum speed: 742 km/h (460 m.p.h.) at 6000 m (20,000 ft.)

Range: 1630 km (1,010 mi.)

Service ceiling: 10,000 m (33,000 ft.)

Weights: empty 5200 kg (11,440 lb.); maximum take-off 9800 kg (21,560 lb.)

Armament: up to 1995 kg (4,400 lb.) of bombs

Dimensions:
span	14.44 m (46 ft.)
length	12.64 m (41 ft.)
height	4.29 m (14 ft.)
wing area	27.3 m² (294 sq. ft.)

AR 234B-2

Delivered to KG76 in 1944, this Ar 234 undertook bombing missions in the Ardennes over the winter. It was captured by the Allies at Achmer in May 1945.

For shallow diving attacks a periscope sight was fitted above the pilot's seat.

Although the prototype first flew with BMW engines, these proved less reliable than the Junkers Jumos fitted to production aircraft. These early turbojets had a life of just 25 hours. A lack of fuel hampered operations in the closing stages of the war.

The Ar 234 was reportedly pleasant to fly, though its directional stability was poor. Fully laden and without RATO gear, it required up to 380 m (1,250 ft.) to become airborne.

A primitive but effective ejection seat was fitted in the cockpit.

This 'Blitz' carries an SC1000 'Hermann' 907-kg (2,000-lb.) bomb under the fuselage.

Prototype Ar 234s used a trolley undercarriage because of a lack of room in the fuselage – fuel tanks were more important. Later variants were redesigned to include landing gear.

Two fixed aft-firing Mauser MG151/20 20-mm (0.79-in) cannon were fitted to some aircraft. These were aimed with the dive-bombing periscope which could be turned aft.

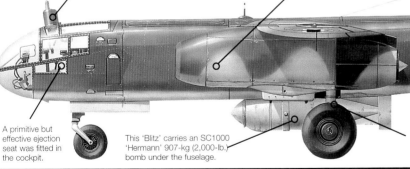

Arado 'Blitz' take-off

TROLLEY UNDERCARRIAGE: Early Ar 234 prototypes were not fitted with conventional undercarriages and used a three-wheeled trolley. On the first flights this was jettisoned once the aircraft was 60 m (200 ft.) off the ground.

PARACHUTE BRAKE: Unfortunately, parachute problems resulted in a number of trolleys being destroyed. Instead it was decided to jettison the trolley on take-off, but still using a parachute to bring it to a stop.

LANDING SKID: On landing, retractable skids were deployed. One was fitted under the fuselage, the others being outriggers; one each under the engine nacelles. These prevented the wings from touching the ground on landing.

COMBAT DATA

MAXIMUM SPEED

At Hitler's insistence a bomber version of the new Messerschmitt jet fighter was built to assist the attempts to stop the Allied advance through Europe. As a fighter design it was faster than the Arado. The piston-engined Mosquito was the Allies' fastest bomber.

Ar 234B-2	742 km/h (460 m.p.h.)
Me 262A-2a	870 km/h (540 m.p.h.)
MOSQUITO B.Mk IV	612 km/h (380 m.p.h.)

RANGE

The Mosquito was conceived as a long-range reconnaissance aircraft and its size gave it good range performance. Similarly, the 'Blitz' was a reconnaissance aircraft modified for the bombing role. The smallest of the three was the Me 262. While its range compared well with other fighters like the P-51 Mustang, as a bomber it was lacking. The early jet engines used by the Ar 234 and the Me 262 had very high fuel consumption and were unreliable.

Ar 234B-2	Me 262A-2A	MOSQUITO B.Mk IV
1630 km (1,010 mi.)	845 km (524 mi.)	1963 km (1,217 mi.)

BOMBLOAD

As a light bomber the Ar 234 could deliver around two tons of bombs. Later versions of the Mosquito could match this load in an enlarged bomb-bay, at the expense of top speed. Had the war continued, plans for larger versions of the 'Blitz' would undoubtedly have been manufactured.

Ar 234B-2	Me 262A-2A	MOSQUITO B.Mk IV
2000 kg (4,400 lb.)	500 k (1,100 lb.)	907 kg (2,000 lb.)

ARADO

AR 240

● Multi-role ● Remotely controlled armament ● Advanced design

Renowned for its advanced and unusual aircraft designs, Arado was quick to draw up a proposal to satisfy a new Reichsluftfahrtministerium (RLM) development order. This called for a multi-role machine, armed with a new weapons system consisting of machine-guns firing from remotely-controlled barbettes. The resulting Ar 240 was plagued by problems, however, and was eventually cancelled.

▲ As the subject of a comprehensive redesign, the Ar 240 suffered from so many problems that the entire project was scrapped. The design was highly advanced, however.

ARADO AR 240

▲ **Pre-production aircraft**
Ar 240A-01 (V5) is the central aircraft of this group of three pre-production machines.

▲ **Operational reconnaissance**
Both the Ar 240A-01 (illustrated) and the A-02 were issued to JG 5 in Finland. Three more pre-production aircraft were built, all of which flew operationally.

▲ **New aerodynamics**
Even at the pre-production stage fundamental problems were being tackled. Both the V5 and V6 aircraft featured an entirely new wing of revised section but similar planform.

▲ **Third prototype**
V3 was an attempt to solve the problems of the initial prototypes and was radically altered.

Finnish combat trials ▶
Finland's harsh climate served to accentuate the shortcomings of the basic Ar 240 design.

FACTS AND FIGURES

➤ After cancellation of the Ar 240, Arado nonetheless continued development with the Ar 240 V7 to V12.

➤ Reconnaissance, dive-bomber and anti-bomber versions were planned.

➤ All Ar 240s flew badly and suffered innumerable minor problems.

➤ AGO Flugzeugwerke was to have been responsible for building a series of pre-production Ar 240A-0 machines.

➤ Ar 240A-02 and -01 flew reconnaissance missions over the Murmansk railway.

➤ The Ar 240Cs were intended to be high-speed bombers and night-fighters.

Germany's misguided Kampfzerstörer

Early in 1938, Arado began work on its E 240 project. A highly advanced machine, the E 240 not only used a new weapons system, but also utilised the latest aerodynamic devices, cockpit pressurisation and a unique tail-mounted airbrake which acted a little like an umbrella.

Flown initially as the Ar 240 V1 and V2, the aircraft proved impossibly unstable and emerged after a major redesign in V3 form.

Although not entirely devoid of the evil handling characteristics of the earlier machines, the V3 was used on operational trials in a reconnaissance role. Several missions were flown at high speeds and altitudes over Britain. The Ar 240 V4 followed, equipped for dive-bombing and with the dive brake which had been deleted from the V3 reinstated. Successful trials of the V4 were completed, but it was felt that the reconnaissance aircraft was most important. The V5 and V6 prototypes were completed as Ar 240A-01 and -02 pre-production aircraft.

Below: Among the changes intended to make the Ar 240 V3 a workable aircraft was the deletion of the dive brake and repositioning of the pressure cabin to the extreme nose.

Above: Complex aerodynamics and unreliable, fragile systems served to make the Ar 240 a failure.

Again, service trials were performed, but the programme was halted in December 1942. Arado doggedly continued development, however, testing the Ar 240C-01 as late as 1943.

Ar 240A-01

Type: high-speed reconnaissance aircraft

Powerplant: two 877-kW (1,176-hp.) Daimler-Benz DB 601E 12-cylinder inverted, in-line piston engine

Maximum speed: 620 km/h (384 m.p.h.) at 6000 m (20,000 ft.)

Climb rate: 11 min to 6000 m (20,000 ft.)

Range: 2000 km (1,240 mi.) maximum, with 600-litre (159-gal.) auxiliary fuel tank

Service ceiling: 10,500 m (34,400 ft.)

Weights: empty 6200 kg (13,640 lb.), maximum take-off 9450 kg (20,790 lb.)

Armament: two fixed forward-firing 7.92-mm (0.31-in.) MG 17 machine-guns and four 7.92-mm machine-guns in remotely controlled barbettes

Dimensions:
span	13.33 m	(43 ft. 9 in.)
length	12.80 m	(42 ft.)
height	3.95 m	(12 ft. 11 in.)
wing area	31.30 m²	(337 sq. ft.)

Although apparently similar to the wings used previously, the flying surfaces of the Ar 240A-0 were entirely new and of laminar flow section.

AR 240A-02

Both the Ar 240A-01 and -02 were issued to Jagdgeschwader (JG) 5 and based in the Petsamo area in North Finland. They were used on operational reconnaissance missions.

Originally, the Ar 240 project hinged around a system of remotely-controlled gun barbettes and their potential for bomber-destroying.

When the pre-production aircraft were built, Arado again deleted the unique 'umbrella' dive brake. Reconnaissance was considered a more important mission than dive-bombing, hence the completion of the A-0 aircraft for the former role.

In an attempt to cure the appalling handling of the Ar 240 V1 and V2, the cockpit section was moved forward from its original, more conventional position.

As reconnaissance machines, each of the Ar 240A-0 aircraft carried a vertically-mounted Rb 50/30 camera in the rear of each engine nacelle. Annular cooling intakes were fitted in place of the conventional spinners used on earlier machines.

Arado made many attempts to solve the Ar 240's inherently poor flying qualities. This included auxiliary fins above and below the tailcone of the A-0s.

COMBAT DATA

MAXIMUM SPEED

Arado's Ar 240 was fast enough to avoid interception by Allied fighters during its limited operational career, but could not match the later Mosquito PR.Mk 34 or Lockheed F-5G.

Ar 240A-0	620 km/h (384 m.p.h.)
MOSQUITO PR.Mk 34	684 km/h (424 m.p.h.)
F-5G LIGHTNING	673 km/h (417 m.p.h.)

SERVICE CEILING

Both the Ar 240A-0 and Mosquito PR.Mk 34 had similar altitude capabilities, but were not as high-flying as the Lightning. Reconnaissance types often relied on their altitude for safety.

F-5G LIGHTNING 13,565 m (44,500 ft.)

Ar 240A-0 10,500 m (34,400 ft.)

MOSQUITO PR.Mk 34 10,973 m (36,000 ft.)

MAXIMUM RANGE

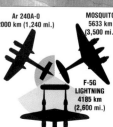

Even with auxiliary fuel the Ar 240A-0 was short-ranged by comparison with the Mosquito and Lightning. Had further operational use been made of the Arado this would have limited the type's usefulness to tactical reconnaissance missions, further adding to the problems that the design presented to its crews.

Ar 240A-0 2000 km (1,240 mi.)

MOSQUITO 5633 km (3,500 mi.)

F-5G LIGHTNING 4185 km (2,600 mi.)

Reconnaissance in World War II

DE HAVILLAND MOSQUITO PR: Successive marks of photo-reconnaissance (PR) Mosquito, such as the PR.Mk XVI, offered increased performance and capability.

MITSUBISHI Ki-46-II 'DINAH': This PR version of the Ki-46 initially proved immune to Allied interception, but as improved fighters were introduced losses mounted.

NORTH AMERICAN P-51 MUSTANG: PR conversions of most P-51 variants were completed, as well as many new-build aircraft. The RAF used its Mk IAs for low-altitude work.

SUPERMARINE SPITFIRE PR: Spitfires were used by the RAF and US Army Air Force for both high- and low-altitude missions. This PR.Mk XIX has a long-range fuel tank.

ARMSTRONG WHITWORTH

ALBEMARLE

● Bomber design ● Wood/metal construction ● D-Day glider-tug

Designed by Bristol and manufactured by A.W. Hawkesley Ltd, the Albemarle evoked little enthusiasm when it first appeared as a medium bomber. Constructed at a time when a shortage of light alloy was anticipated and when fears that Britain's aircraft factories would be devastated by the Luftwaffe were at their height, the Albemarle used steel and wooden components provided by small sub-contractors outside the aircraft industry.

▲ Based on a Bristol design intended to meet an RAF bomber requirement, the Albemarle entered service as a transport and glider-tug for British special forces.

PHOTO FILE

ARMSTRONG WHITWORTH **ALBEMARLE**

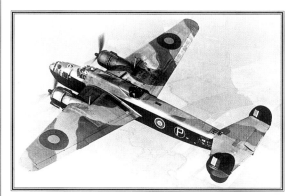

▼ **Glider-towing over Sicily, 1943**
No. 297 Squadron, RAF, was one of two units to make the first use of the Albemarle as a glider-tug.

▼ **Bristol design**
The Albemarle began life as the Bristol Type 155, designed to Spec. B.18/38.

▲ **Special Transport Mk I**
The last Mk I built became the ST.Mk I prototype. Principal changes included deletion of the rear fuselage fuel tank and bomb release gear to make space internally, and a reduction in armament.

▼ **Easily dismantled and transported**
The Albemarle was easily dismantled and moved aboard 18.3-m (60-ft.) 'Queen Mary' road trailers.

▲ **Production**
Production of the Albemarle ended in December 1944, after 602 aircraft had left the Brockworth factory of A.W. Hawkesley Ltd.

FACTS AND FIGURES

➤ Production of Albemarle sub-assemblies was entrusted to numerous contractors, including car and furniture makers.

➤ Russia took delivery of 10 RAF Albemarles for the transport role.

➤ The first Albemarle flew in 1939 but crashed before the second aircraft flew.

➤ Vickers 'K' guns of 7.7-mm (.303 cal.) calibre were employed; either four in a Boulton Paul turret, or two under a sliding hood.

➤ The Albemarle's tricycle undercarriage was of Lockheed design.

➤ As many as 1000 sub-contractors were employed on the Albemarle project.

PROFILE

Wood and metal special transport

Bomber design had advanced at such a pace during the years of the Albemarle's development that the aircraft was destined never to enter service as a bomber.

Instead it was found to be more useful in transport and glider-tug duties for Britain's special forces. The Albemarle's first action came in 1943 with the invasion of Sicily, when it was used to tow gliders full of troops to the battlefield.

Another famous episode for the RAF's Albemarles came in June 1944, when four squadrons of the aircraft towed the Horsa gliders that took Allied airborne troops to France for the first time during Operation Overlord, the invasion of occupied Europe. Later the same year, two squadrons provided glider-tugs during the assault on the Rhine bridges at Arnhem.

The anticipated light alloy shortage did not occur and Britain's aircraft factories escaped relatively unscathed by German attack. Thus the Albemarle 'experiment' was not to have the significance it might otherwise have had.

The Soviet Union was the only other Albemarle operator, although it has been suggested that the country was only interested in the aircraft's engines, which, it is thought, were later copied for local use.

Albemarle production ended in December 1944 after 602 of an ordered 1060 had been built.

Left: The first Albemarles were operational with No. 295 Squadron, RAF, in 1942. Nos 296 and 297 followed in 1943.

Above: Although the alloy shortage failed to materialise, Albemarle production soon proved justified in the type's role.

Albemarle ST.Mk V

Type: special forces transport

Powerplant: two 1186-kW (1,590-hp.) Bristol Hercules XI radial piston engines

Maximum speed: 426 km/h (264 m.p.h.) at 3200 m (10,500 ft.)

Range: 2092 km (1,300 mi.)

Service ceiling: 5486 m (18,000 ft.)

Weights: empty est. 6800 kg (14,960 lb.); maximum take-off 16,556 kg (36,423 lb.)

Armament: four 7.7-mm (.303 cal.) machine-guns in a Boulton Paul dorsal turret or two 7.7-mm machine-guns amidships

Dimensions:
span	23.47 m (77 ft.)
length	18.26 m (59 ft. 11 in.)
height	4.75 m (15 ft. 7 in.)
wing area	74.65 m² (803 sq. ft.)

ALBEMARLE ST.Mk V

On the night before D-Day, 6 June 1944, No. 297 Squadron dropped troops and supplies behind enemy lines. The following day, Albemarles from No. 297 towed Horsa gliders across the Channel.

Test pilot John Grierson described the Albemarle as an average aircraft, '... with no virtues and no vices'. The first 32 built were intended for use as reconnaissance bombers, with a crew of two pilots, a navigator and a radio operator. However, the Albemarle was never operated in this role.

The only defensive armament fitted to the Albemarle was four 7.7-mm (.303 cal.) machine-guns in a Boulton Paul turret. When firing forwards, a fairing in front of the turret lowered automatically. Some aircraft modified as special forces transports dispensed with the turret in favour of a two-gun armament covered with a sliding hood.

Albemarles often wore standard Bomber Command markings. The black and white striping on the fuselage and wings was an identification aid for Allied aircraft during the D-Day landings.

Most Albemarles were powered by two 1186-kW (1,590-hp.) Bristol Hercules XI two-row radial engines. Two aircraft, a GT.Mk II and a Mk IV, were fitted with American Wright Double Cyclones. When the Soviet air force acquired Albemarles, it is believed they were valued mostly for their engines, which are thought to have been copied later.

The Albemarle consisted of a steel structure with spruce formers and plywood covering. Much of the wing structure was wooden with a plywood covering. The wing centre-section was also covered in plywood.

For glider-towing a Malcolm-type quick-release hook was fitted to the extreme rear of the fuselage. The release mechanism was controlled by the pilot.

RAF special forces transports and tugs

ARMSTRONG WHITWORTH WHITLEY: Employed as a paratroop trainer from 1940 , this bomber design saw action in 1941, dropping troops over Malta. Although not used operationally as glider-tugs, Whitleys equipped a glider training unit.

DOUGLAS DAKOTA: The Allies' standard transport throughout World War II, the C-47/Dakota also filled a Horsa glider-tug role, especially with the RAF and USAAF during the D-Day landings in 1944.

SHORT STIRLING: By 1944 this, the first of the RAF's four-engined bombers, had been relegated to transport and glider-towing duties. First used on D-Day, Stirlings were active in these roles until March 1945.

COMBAT DATA

ENGINE POWER

Heinkel's He 111Z was specially designed as a glider-tug and effectively consisted of two He 111 bombers joined together with an extra engine added. This gave it a huge power advantage over other glider-tug types.

ALBEMARLE ST.Mk V	He 111Z-1 ZWILLING	C-47A SKYTRAIN
2372 kW (3,180 hp.)	5033 kW (6,750 hp.)	1790 kW (3,940 hp.)

MAXIMUM TAKE-OFF WEIGHT

The comparatively massive He 111Z Zwilling weighed almost twice as much as other glider-tug types. The C-47 and Albemarle were of similar size, although the Albemarle, as a bomber design, was the heavier aircraft.

ALBEMARLE ST.Mk V	He 111Z-1 ZWILLING	C-47A SKYTRAIN
16,556 kg (36,423 lb.)	28,600 kg (62,920 lb.)	11,793 kg (25,945 lb.)

ARMAMENT

The C-47 carried no defensive armament, while the Albemarle retained part of its defensive machine-gun fit as installed in the original bomber design. The He 111Z carried no fewer than eight cannon and machine-guns.

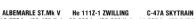

ALBEMARLE ST.Mk V   4 x 7.7-mm (.303 cal.) machine-guns

He 111Z-1 ZWILLING   4 x 7.9-mm (0.31-in.) machine-guns
1 x 20-mm (0.79-in.) cannon, 3 x 13-mm (0.51-in.) cannon

C-47A SKYTRAIN   none

ARMSTRONG WHITWORTH

WHITLEY

● Early heavy bomber ● Maritime patrol and special operations

A long with the Vickers Wellington and Handley Page Hampden, the Whitley was one of the RAF's three principal bomber types at the start of World War II. Though the oldest of the three, it was to become the first British aircraft to drop bombs over both Germany and Italy. It was also the first to be equipped with radar for submarine hunting. It also went on to fill several other roles, including paratrooping aircraft on special operations.

▲ Having been designed as a heavy bomber, the Whitley found success flying in the maritime patrol role, towing gliders, dropping paratroops and special agents and as a civilian freighter.

ARMSTRONG WHITWORTH WHITLEY

▼ **Maritime operations**
The Mk VII was slightly slower than the bomber versions because of its higher weight and the drag from its ASV Mk II radar antennas.

▲ **On the flightdeck**
There were a few initial criticisms of the Whitley and most of these centred on the cockpit layout. Some controls were difficult to operate.

▲ **Engine testbed**
This Mk I was used without armament to test the Rolls-Royce Merlin for later versions.

▲ **Glider tug**
Whitley Mk Vs were used for the training of glider tug pilots. Three squadrons served operationally.

Night bomber ▶
With docile landing characteristics and long range, the Whitley was an ideal night bomber.

FACTS AND FIGURES

➤ Ordered from the drawing board in June 1935, the prototype first flew on March 17, 1936 from Whitley Aerodrome.

➤ A box-like shape was chosen for the fuselage to make manufacture simple.

➤ A new wooden wing was designed to save materials, but was never flown.

➤ On the first night of World War II during the so-called Phony War, 10 Whitleys flew over Germany, dropping propaganda leaflets.

➤ As initially fitted, the Merlin engines were unusually noisy and needed modification.

➤ A four-gun rear turret improved rearward defence from the Mk IV onwards.

The right Mark for the right job

Designed to a 1934 requirement and first flown in March 1936, the Whitley was originally powered by Armstrong Siddeley Tiger radial engines. These were used on the 160 Mks I, II and III; later models switched to Merlin in-line engines, which boosted top speed by 84 km/h (52 m.p.h.).

There were only 40 Mk IVs, but nearly 1500 of the Mk V, which remained in production from 1939 until 1943. The Mk IV had introduced a powered tail turret with four machine guns,

and the Mk V had a slightly longer fuselage to extend the tail gunner's field of fire.

Whitleys carried out the majority of the controversial leaflet raids during the first year of the war and joined the night bombing offensive in 1940, taking part in the first raid on Berlin in August. The Whitley remained in front-line service with Bomber Command until the spring of 1942.

Some Mk Vs had been transferred to Coastal Command early in the war for use in maritime

patrol and another 146 were built as Mk VIIs with long-range search radars capable of detecting submarines. These were active from March 1941 over the Atlantic; a Whitley crew made the first U-boat kill with ASV radar in November. They remained in service until early 1943.

Whitleys were used as paratroop trainers and glider tugs from 1940, while 12 Mk Vs were converted to freighters in 1942 and used by British Airways.

Left: Obvious on this Whitley Mk V is the flat glass panel for the bombardier. Less apparent is the extended rear fuselage.

Above: With long range and search radar, the Whitley joined coastal command in 1942. No. 502 Squadron had previously sunk U-206 with a Mk VII on 30 November 1941.

Whitley Mk V

Type: bomber, reconnaissance and anti-submarine aircraft

Powerplant: two 895-kW (1,200-hp.) Rolls-Royce Merlin X inline piston engines

Maximum speed: 367 km/h (228 m.p.h.) at 5395 m (17,700 ft.)

Range: 2540 km (1,500 mi.)

Initial climb rate: 244 m/min (800 f.p.m.)

Service ceiling: 5395 m (17,700 ft.)

Weapons: five 7.7-mm (.303 cal.) machine guns; up to a 3168-kg (6,985-lb.) bomb load (usually fourteen 227-kg/500-lb. bombs).

Weights: Empty 8759 kg (19,310 lb.); maximum take-off 15,164 kg (33,431 lb.)

Dimensions:
span	25.60 m	(84 ft.)
length	22.10 m	(72 ft. 6 in.)
height	4.57 m	(15 ft.)
wing area	105.63 m²	(1,137 sq. ft.)

WHITLEY MK IV

Serving with No. 10 Squadron in the summer of 1939, this Mk IV shows the higher visibility of pre-war markings. Before going into action the underwing serial numbers were removed.

Problems with the change to Merlin engines included a drop in the efficiency of the cabin heater. This had to be rectified for long-range, high-altitude night missions.

The first prototype had straight wings, but the second prototype and all production aircraft had a small amount of dihedral on the outer wing panels.

A bombardier and nose-gunner occupied the extreme end of the nose, which contained a single 7.7-mm (.303 cal.) Browning machine gun.

Rolls-Royce Merlin IV engines gave a 84 km/h (52 m.p.h.) speed improvement over the Whitley Mk I.

A limited field of fire was presented to the rear gunner by the twin tailfins. From the Mk V onward the rear fuselage was extended to solve this problem.

Rolls-Royce worked with the Royal Aircraft Establishment to solve the problem of noisy engines. Investigation of the propellers and exhausts was necessary.

When retracted, the main wheels protruded below the level of the undercarriage doors. This minimised damage in the event of a wheels-up landing.

Unsure of the effect of flaps, the manufacturer fitted the wing at a high angle to the fuselage. This gave a low landing speed and distinctive nose-down flying attitude.

The power-operated Nash and Thompson rear turret, introduced on the Mk IV, relieved the gunner from having to manually turn the turret when tracking a target.

World War II Whitley actions

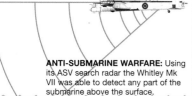

ANTI-SUBMARINE WARFARE: Using its ASV search radar the Whitley Mk VII was able to detect any part of the submarine above the surface.

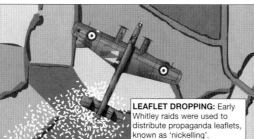

LEAFLET DROPPING: Early Whitley raids were used to distribute propaganda leaflets, known as 'nickelling'.

AGENT INSERTION: Whitleys were often used for air dropping agents behind enemy lines.

BOMB LOAD

As the Luftwaffe's most important bomber, even the most developed forms of the He 111 suffered from limited bomb load. With the B-18 not seeing combat, the large bomb load of the Whitley so early in World War II was impressive.

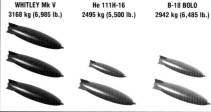

WHITLEY Mk V	He 111H-16	B-18 BOLO
3168 kg (6,985 lb.)	2495 kg (5,500 lb.)	2942 kg (6,485 lb.)

AVRO

ANSON

● Airliner design ● Maritime reconnaissance ● Training

▲ The prone bomb-aimer's position in the nose of the Anson Mk I had a sliding panel in the floor for operation of the Wimperis Mk VIIB bombsight.

Developed to meet an RAF Coastal Command requirement for a land-based reconnaissance aircraft, the Anson was derived from the Avro 652 six-seat airliner. Flown for the first time in March 1935, it entered service a year later. Although the Hudson had started to replace it by the start of World War II, the Anson continued to carry out reconnaissance missions until 1942. It also became one of the Allies' most widely used trainers.

AVRO ANSON

▼ Radar training
In 1944 the Royal Navy received Ansons, fitted with radar scanners, for training observers to use radar.

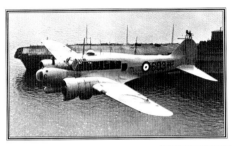

▲ Cadet gunners
By 1943 the Anson's primary task was training. Prospective air gunners were taught day and night gunnery skills using the Boulton Paul turret.

Trainer for Rhodesia ▶
The post-war Anson Mk 20 was built as a trainer for Rhodesia. The RAF also used a small number.

◀ Pre-war exports
The RAF was not the only armed force to realise the potential of the Anson. This example was one of three acquired by Finland in 1938. Other export users of the Mk I included Australia, Estonia, Ireland and Greece.

Dutch survivors ▶
No. 321 was one of two RAF squadrons manned by Dutch aircrew who escaped during the German invasion. The aircraft has a Dutch insignia on the fin.

FACTS AND FIGURES

➤ Avro's Anson was based on the Avro 652 six-seat airliner for Imperial Airways which first flew on 7 January 1935.

➤ The Anson beat the competing DH.89M Rapide for the RAF order.

➤ On 5 September 1939 the Anson first saw combat, attacking a German U-boat.

➤ During the Dunkirk evacuation an Anson of No. 500 Squadron shot down two of three attacking Bf 109 fighters.

➤ Retired in 1968, after 32 years, the Anson was the longest-serving RAF type.

➤ Anson production totalled 11,020 airframes, including licence production.

PROFILE

From maritime patroller to trainer

When it first entered service in 1936, the Anson was the RAF's fastest twin-engined aircraft and the force's first monoplane with a retractable undercarriage. For military service a forward-firing machine-gun, one in a dorsal turret, plus a bomb-bay for two 45-kg (100-lb.) and eight 9-kg (20-lb.) bombs, were added.

Although its performance was rather tame by the standards of 1940, the type could turn inside the Bf 109 and continue turning for much longer. This ability enabled Anson crews to claim six of the German fighters in combat. From 1941 it was also used by a number of air-sea rescue squadrons.

In addition, the Anson was used as a trainer from an early stage in its career, and in 1940 it was chosen as the standard twin-engined aircraft for training pilots in Canada.

The Anson was used by at least 20 air forces, and after the war many were converted to civil transports. More than 11,000 were built, nearly 3000 of them in Canada with Wright, Jacobs or Pratt & Whitney engines. Production continued until 1952, and the type remained in RAF service until 1968.

Above: Tasked with land-based maritime reconnaissance of the English Channel, North Sea and the Western Approaches, the Mk I was a vital tool in protecting British shipping.

Below: Demand for the Anson was so great that licence production, supervised by Federal Aircraft Ltd, was set up in Canada The 50 purchased by the US Army Air Force were designated AT-20s. They differed from British Mk Is in having Jacobs L-6BM engines and Canadian equipment.

Anson Mk I

Type: advanced trainer

Powerplant: two 261-kW (350-hp.) Armstrong Siddeley Cheetah IX seven-cylinder air-cooled radial engines

Maximum speed: 303 km/h (188 m.p.h.) at 2130 m (7,000 ft.)

Climb rate: 229 m/min (750 f.p.m.) at sea level

Range: 1270 km (787 mi.)

Service ceiling: 5790 m (19,000 ft.)

Weights: empty 2438 kg (5,361 lb.); maximum take-off 3629 kg (7,984 lb.)

Armament: two 7.7-mm (.303 cal.) machine-guns and up to 163 kg (360 lb.) of bombs

Dimensions:
span	17.22 m (56 ft. 6 in.)
length	12.88 m (42 ft. 3 in.)
height	3.99 m (13 ft. 1 in.)
wing area	43.00 m² (463 sq. ft.)

ANSON MK I

Carrying the training colour scheme of temperate land upper camouflage and trainer yellow lower surfaces, this Mk I was one of 850 from the sixth RAF production batch.

With a normal crew of three, the cockpit was fairly spacious. The pilot had solo controls and a Reid and Sigrist Mk I blind flying panel. A navigator/bomb aimer, with a plotting table and instrument panel, sat behind the pilot. The wireless operator/gunner sat at the rear of the cabin.

The only major design changes from the prototype were a 25 per cent increase in tailplane span and a reduction in elevator area. After stability trials in January 1936, the rudder area was also increased.

During the bomb run, the bomb aimer would move to a prone position in the nose. A sliding panel in the floor allowed the bombsight to be operated.

Defensive armament included a manually-operated Armstrong Whitworth turret fitted with a 7.7-mm (.303 cal.) Lewis Mk 3A machine-gun and five drums of ammunition. When not in use, the gun barrel was lowered into a slot in the top of the fuselage.

N9765

Power for the Mk I was provided by two Armstrong Siddeley Cheetah IX engines within seven-lobed NACA cowlings.

Originally designed as a low-wing airliner, the Anson had a welded steel tube fuselage covered with fabric and wooden wings.

The Anson Mk I had a fixed tailwheel and retractable main undercarriage. The manually-operated mainwheels, which required 164.5 turns of a handle to raise, were replaced by hydraulically-operated gear on later models.

COMBAT DATA

CRUISING SPEED

As it was derived from a small airliner of the mid-1930s, the Anson had a respectable, though not particularly fast, top speed. The Si 204 was equipped with more powerful engines than both the Anson and Ki-54.

ANSON Mk I	254 km/h (188 m.p.h.)
Si 204D	340 km/h (210 m.p.h.)
Ki-54a 'HICKORY'	240 km/h (148 m.p.h.)

ARMAMENT

Although the reconnaissance variants of the Siebel Si 204 were often fitted with radar, they were generally unarmed. The Anson and Tachikawa Ki-54 were both armed, and the latter could carry twice the load and defensive armament of the British aircraft.

ANSON Mk I	2 x 7.7-mm (.303 cal.) machine-guns / 163-kg (360-lb.) bombload
Si 204D	none
Ki-54a 'HICKORY'	4 x 7.7-mm (.303 cal.) machine-guns / 408-kg (900-lb.) bombload

RANGE

The Anson's range made it suitable for maritime reconnaissance until it was replaced by the Lockheed Hudson, another type derived from an airliner. The 'Hickory' had the least range, although it carried a larger weapons load. This aircraft was developed initially as a trainer; a maritime version entered service later.

ANSON Mk I	Si 204D	Ki-54a 'HICKORY'
1270 km (787 mi.)	1800 km (1,118 mi.)	960 km (595 mi.)

RAF World War II trainers

■ **AIRSPEED OXFORD:** As the first twin-engined monoplane advanced trainer in RAF service, the Oxford was used for all aspects of aircrew training, including gunnery.

■ **DE HAVILLAND TIGER MOTH:** As the most numerous and famous British elementary trainer during World War II, the Tiger Moth equipped 44 Flying Training Schools in 1939.

■ **MILES MAGISTER:** Known as the 'Maggie', this classic Miles design was the first monoplane trainer to be used by the RAF. Employed in elementary training, it was fully aerobatic.

■ **MILES MASTER:** In 1938 the Master gained the largest ever contract for a trainer at the time. Used for advanced training, the Master had a top speed of 364 km/h (226 m.p.h.).

AVRO
LANCASTER

● Heavy bomber ● Dam-buster ● Delivered largest bomb of WWII

AVRO LANCASTER

◄ 'Window'
An electronic warfare Lancaster drops metal strips known as 'Window' to jam German radar.

Tail-end Charlie ►
Usually the first victim of a night-fighter, rear gunners had an unenviable task and low survival rate.

◄ Low level
The Lancaster was not just a night-bomber. One of the first Lancaster missions was a daylight raid on the MAN works at Augsburg, flown at low level.

▼ Power turrets
The RAF fitted fast-acting power turrets to enable its bombers to defend themselves. Apart from an underside blindspot, the Lancaster was no easy meat for a fighter.

▲ Bridge buster supreme
The tough Bielefeld Viaduct survived many RAF attacks, but was finally smashed by Lancasters of the famous No. 617 Squadron, using 9979-kg (10-ton) 'Grand Slam' bombs.

Britain's greatest bomber of World War II was the Avro Lancaster, providing the backbone of the RAF's night assault on Germany. This four-engined heavy bomber carried and delivered a bigger bombload than any other bomber in the European theatre. From its first minelaying mission in 1942 to its final bombing sortie of 1945, the 'Lanc' was a formidable fighting machine. One aircraft even survived 140 combat missions over Germany.

▲ Lancaster crews liked their aircraft, considering it superior to the previous Halifaxes and Stirlings. A total of 59 Royal Air Force squadrons flew the Lancaster on 156,000 combat sorties.

FACTS AND FIGURES

➤ The Lancaster on display at the RAF Museum at Hendon near London flew 137 combat missions over Europe.

➤ The first Lancaster, a rebuilt Manchester, flew on 9 January 1941.

➤ The Lancaster could drop the massive 9979-kg (10-ton) 'Grand Slam' bomb.

➤ To bomb Japan, a long-range version with a 5455-litre (1,360-gal.) 'saddle' fuel tank atop its fuselage was tested but not needed.

➤ One 'Lanc' was rebuilt with the Bristol B.17 dorsal gun turret.

➤ France's Aeronavale was still flying maritime Lancasters into the 1950s.

Britain's finest night-bomber

The Lancaster won immortality with the 'Dambusters'. Royal Air Force No. 617 Squadron, under Wing Commander Guy Gibson, used the new bomber for their 21 March 1943 low-level attacks on German dams using drum-like 4196-kg (9,230-lb.) bombs designed by Sir Barnes Wallis.

But the Lancaster was much more than a one-mission wonder. Developed from the unsatisfactory twin-engined Avro Manchester, it was one of the few warplanes in history to be 'right' from the start. It was so well-designed that only minor changes were made as production surged ahead through World War II. While Flying Fortresses and Liberators pounded Hitler's 'Fortress Europe' during the day, the Lancaster ruled the night. It was vulnerable to German fighters from below, but it was also fast and heavily armed, and it usually got through to the target.

The Lancaster served well in post-war years, sometimes in civil duties. The final military user was Canada. Today, the Royal Air Force still maintains one flying Lancaster, alongside Spitfires and Hurricanes, in the Battle of Britain Memorial Flight.

The Lancaster possessed all the features desired by the RAF. It had a good ceiling, long range and enormous load capacity. And combat experience showed that it was tough, reliable and had reasonable defensive armament.

Lancaster B.Mk I

Type: seven-seat heavy bomber

Powerplant: four 1223-kW (1,750-hp.) Merlin 24 inverted inline piston engines

Maximum speed: 462 km/h (286 m.p.h.) at 3500 m (11,480 ft.)

Range: 2700 km (1,674 mi.) with 6350-kg (13,970-lb.) bombload

Service ceiling: 7467 m (24,492 ft.)

Weights: empty 16,783 kg (36,923 lb.); loaded 30,845 kg (67,859 lb.)

Armament: early production model, nine 7.7-mm (.303 cal.) Browning machine-guns plus up to 6350 kg (14,000 lb.) of bombs

Dimensions:
span	31.09 m (102 ft.)
length	21.18 m (69 ft.)
height	6.25 m (20 ft.)
wing area	120.49 m² (1,296 sq. ft.)

LANCASTER B.Mk I

'S-Sugar' served with No. 83 Squadron during 1942. It went on to fly 137 combat missions and is preserved in the Royal Air Force Museum.

The crew consisted of pilot, navigator, flight engineer, bomb-aimer/nose gunner, mid-upper gunner/radio operator and rear gunner.

The radio operator doubled as the mid-upper gunner, firing a pair of Browning 7.7-mm (.303 cal.) machine-guns from a powered turret.

The Lancaster's undercarriage retracted backwards into the inner engine nacelles. It was of simple but immensely tough construction.

The twin-tail layout gave the Lancaster great stability. The extra control surfaces could take massive damage and still leave the bomber flyable enough to get home.

The sting in the tail was provided by a four-gun turret. The tail gunner was the most isolated and vulnerable member of the crew.

The key to the Lancaster's success was its capacious bomb-bay, which could hold up to seven tons of bombs and, with modification, could house the massive 10-ton 'Grand Slam' semi-recessed under the fuselage.

Most Lancasters were powered by the same kind of Merlin engines as used in Spitfires, Hurricanes, Mosquitoes and Mustangs.

COMBAT DATA

CRUISING SPEED

LANCASTER 340 km/h (211 m.p.h.)

B-17 FLYING FORTRESS 400 km/h (248 m.p.h.)

B-24 LIBERATOR 350 km/h (217 m.p.h.)

Since American bombers were expected to operate by day they were much more vulnerable to enemy defences than the Lancaster. Every step was taken to reduce that vulnerability, from heavy armour and armament to a higher speed than their British equivalents.

RANGE

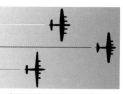

LANCASTER 4000 km (2,480 mi.) with 2000-kg (4,400-lb.) load

B-17 FLYING FORTRESS 5000 km (3,100 mi.) with 1000-kg (2,200-lb.) load

B-24 LIBERATOR 3500 km (2,170 mi.) with 2500-kg (5,500-lb.) load

The Lancaster had exceptional range when carrying a heavy load. The B-17 could go farther, but could not deliver as powerful a punch. A 'bombed-up' B-24 could not match the other two four-engined aircraft. However, with a light load and extra fuel it could go the farthest of them all, regularly mounting anti-U-Boat patrols into the middle of the Atlantic.

NORMAL BOMBLOAD

LANCASTER	B-17 FLYING FORTRESS	B-24 LIBERATOR
6350 kg (13,970 lb.)	2725 kg (5,995 lb.)	3629 kg (7,984 lb.)

Lancasters routinely operated with heavier bombloads than their contemporaries, and could carry the massive 9979-kg (21,954-lb.) 'Grand Slam' bomb. The B-17 Flying Fortress had a maximum bombload almost as high as the Lancaster, but rarely carried such weight, the USAF preferring to use surplus power to lift extra armour and defensive guns.

The Dambusters Raid

It was one of the most spectacular missions of World War II. By the dead of night, RAF bombers mounted an attack on the Ruhr dams, whose associated power stations served Germany's greatest industrial complex. Smashing the Möhne and Sorpe Dams with the revolutionary bouncing bomb, designed by Sir Barnes Wallis, the chosen crews of No. 617 Squadron performed a low-level night attack of unbelievable precision. But although it disrupted German war production for some months, the raid had little permanent effect, and it cost the lives of 56 of the cream of British and Commonwealth aircrew.

The bomb used to attack the dams was a rotating cylinder, 127 cm (50 in.) in diameter and weighing 4196 kg (9,231 lb.). Bouncing across the water to hit the dam, the bomb then sank down the inner side of the structure, detonating well below the surface of the lake.

Precision flying was essential. The aircraft had to release its weapon between 370 and 410 m (1,214 and 1,345 ft.) from the target, while flying at exactly 402 km/h (249 m.p.h.) and at a height of 18.3 m (60 ft.) above the water.

AVRO

MANCHESTER

● Night bomber ● Father of the Lancaster ● Maritime patrol

Overshadowed by the immortal Lancaster that replaced it in service, the Manchester was plagued by the unreliability of its Rolls-Royce Vulture engine. First flown in 1940, the Manchester had a brief operational career, and the aircraft's last combat mission was flown in mid-1942. The real fame of the aircraft was that, with the marriage of its airframe and four Rolls-Royce Merlin engines, it became the Avro Lancaster.

▲ *The Manchester might have been a useful design, having a potent defensive and offensive armament, but the Vulture engine spent more time under repair than in service.*

AVRO MANCHESTER

▼ Night raider
A Manchester Mk IA from No. 207 Squadron, which was based at RAF Waddington.

▲ First of the few
This Manchester is a Mk I with a central tail fin. The fin was later deleted and the tail span increased by another 3 m (10 ft.), as in the Lancaster.

▲ Short span
Like many of the first RAF night bombers, the Manchester had a short wing span to fit pre-war hangars.

▲ Son of Manchester
With four reliable and powerful Merlin engines, most of the Manchester's ills were cured. The Lancaster immediately replaced its ancestor in squadron service.

▲ Waiting for the night
A Mk IA Manchester awaits another night of bombing operations. A Westland Lysander army co-operation aircraft is parked behind it.

◄ Well protected
One of the best points of the Manchester was the good coverage of its defensive armament, with tail, nose and dorsal gun turrets.

FACTS AND FIGURES

➤ Flying Officer L. T. Master of No. 50 Squadron won a Victoria Cross while flying a Manchester.

➤ Manchesters took part in the first ever 1000-bomber raid, against Cologne.

➤ The first Lancaster was in fact a Manchester III with four Merlin engines.

➤ The first 13 Manchesters built were destroyed in a German air raid on the Metropolitan Vickers factory.

➤ Manchesters dropped 1855 tonnes (1,825 tons) of bombs and incendiaries.

➤ The original company designation of the Manchester was the Avro 609.

PROFILE

Killed by the Vulture engine

Had the Manchester been powered by a viable engine, its career might have been far longer. However, it was stuck with the dubious Rolls-Royce Vulture, a mighty V-24 in-line engine that failed to deliver the power intended, and also suffered from chronic reliability problems. The engine was also intended for a rival Handley Page design which was later cancelled.

The first Manchester prototype flew in July 1939, and a second in 1940. The Air Ministry ordered 200, and then 400. After flight trials, the wing span was increased by three metres and a central fin was added between the two endplate fins (later deleted in the Mk IA). The first squadron, No. 207, was formed in November 1940 and carried out its first mission in February 1941. Nine bomber squadrons received the aircraft, and one flight of Coastal Command. The Manchester was not really a success in combat, suffering from a number of airframe faults as well as endless failures of the Vulture engine. The last

Bomber Command operation with the aircraft took place over Bremen on 25/26 June 1942. Only 202 Manchesters had been built, of which about 40 per cent were lost on operations and 25 per cent in accidents.

Were it not for the Manchester, Avro might not have built the Lancaster, probably the best night bomber of the war. The type also gave Bomber Command useful ideas about how its future bomber aircraft should look.

Left: No. 207 Squadron had the dubious privilege of first taking the Manchester to war, over Brest harbour on 25 February 1941.

Above: The first Manchester bomber is seen in December 1940. Unfortunately, this example and several others were destroyed in an enemy air raid a few days later.

MANCHESTER MK IA

One of the first Manchesters into action, this No. 207 Squadron aircraft enjoyed a brief operational career. The RAF roundel with its white band was abandoned later in the war as it was too visible at night.

The nose of the Manchester was almost identical to that of the later Lancaster, and was one of the better parts of the design. The pilot and flight engineer sat side by side in the cockpit, with an astrodome behind for the navigator to take measurements of the stars for astro-navigation. The controls were well laid out, and the aircraft was not hard to fly.

All operational Manchesters were painted in the standard matt black lower (to reduce detection by enemy searchlights) and camouflage upper (to blend in with the terrain when viewed from above).

EM was the marking for No. 207 Squadron, the first Manchester operator. Later in the war the squadron flew Lancasters, and then their replacement, the Avro Lincoln.

EM◉U — L7316 — I

The nose gunner/bomb aimer sat in a powered turret with a pair of Browning 7.7-mm (.303 cal.) machine-guns. At night, the nose gunner rarely had to use his guns.

After flight trials, wing span was increased by 3.05 m (10 ft.). This wing was a sound design, being well able to accept a new engine configuration and absorbing massive battle damage.

The capacious bomb bay was one of the most useful Manchester features. It could accept the large RAF 1818-kg (4,000-lb.) 'Cookie' bomb that became a standard load for British bombers at night.

The rear gunner fired four Browning machine-guns. He was usually the most vital gunner, as night-fighters tended to attack from below and behind. He would call out evasive actions to the pilot if the aircraft came under attack.

Manchester Mk I

Type: twin-engined medium bomber

Powerplant: two Rolls-Royce Vulture 24-cylinder engines rated at 1312 kW (1,760 hp.)

Maximum speed: 426 km/h (264 m.p.h.) at 5180 m (17,000 ft.)

Combat radius: 2623 km (1,625 mi.) with 3674-kg (8,100-lb.) load

Service ceiling: 5850 m (19,200 ft.)

Weights: empty 13,350 kg (29,370 lb.); loaded 25,401 kg (55,880 lb.)

Armament: two 7.7-mm (.303 cal.) machine-guns in the nose turret and mid-upper turret, four 7.7-mm machine-guns in the rear turret; 4695 kg (10,330 lb.) of bombs or incendiaries

Dimensions:
span	27.46 m	(90 ft 1 in.)
length	21.13 m	(69 ft. 4 in.)
height	5.94 m	(19 ft. 6 in.)
wing area	105.63 m²	(1,137 sq. ft.)

COMBAT DATA

BOMB LOAD

The Manchester's ability to deliver a respectable bomb load came at a cost to its performance. It could carry more than the Vickers Wellington, however. The Lancaster, which is widely regarded as the best four-engined night bomber of World War II, corrected all the mistakes of its Manchester forebear.

MANCHESTER Mk I
4695 kg (10,330 lb.)

WELLINGTON Mk III
2041 kg (4,490 lb.)

LANCASTER Mk I
6350 kg (13,970 lb.)

MAXIMUM SPEED

Though the Manchester was capable of a high speed compared to similar twin-engined bombers, its Vulture powerplants were unreliable and often resulted in the aircraft being lost because of mechanical failure. Rapid progress in engine development led to Bristol powerplants being installed in the Wellington.

MANCHESTER Mk I 426 km/h (264 m.p.h.)

WELLINGTON Mk III 378 km/h (234 m.p.h.)

LANCASTER Mk I 462 km/h (286 m.p.h.)

RANGE

Bombing missions during the war required that RAF aircraft be capable of crossing Europe to attack targets in Germany. Although the Manchester could reach these objectives, many were lost. The Lancaster, which improved the striking power of Bomber Command, owed much of its design to the earlier Manchester.

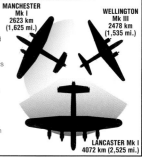

MANCHESTER Mk I 2623 km (1,625 mi.)

WELLINGTON Mk III 2478 km (1,535 mi.)

LANCASTER Mk I 4072 km (2,525 mi.)

RAF bombers of 1939

■ **HAMPDEN Mk I:** The only RAF medium bomber at the start of the war, its poor defensive armament saw the aircraft reduced to second-line duties with Coastal Command squadrons.

■ **HARROW Mk II:** The first monoplane bomber to enter service with the Royal Air Force, the Harrow was introduced before World War II, but was quickly replaced by the Wellington.

■ **WELLINGTON Mk IC:** One of the first aircraft capable of bombing Germany, the Wellington was the work-horse of Bomber Commands during the raids early in World War II.

BACHEM

BA 349 NATTER

● Rocket-powered ● Wooden construction ● Point defence

By the spring of 1944 the mounting pressure placed on the Luftwaffe's fighter force by the continuous stream of Allied bombers had reached a critical point. Germany could not survive unless the effect of these raids was rapidly reduced. A radical solution was sought, and the German air ministry issued a request for a machine which combined the capabilities of an interceptor aircraft and a missile. Bachem proposed the rocket-powered Ba 349 Natter (Adder).

▲ After a number of pilotless Natter launches, the first manned flight took place on 28 February 1945. It ended fatally, but was followed by three successful tests.

BACHEM BA 349 NATTER

Museum piece ▶
One Ba 349 survived Allied evaluation after the war. It is now in the Smithsonian in Washington, DC.

▼ Fifty prototypes built in three months
Unpowered gliding trials began in November 1944. They were so successful that powered launching began the following month.

First manned flight ▶
Oberleutnant L. Siebert died during the first manned flight. After launch the canopy blew off, probably knocking him out.

▼ Rocket armament
The Ba 349's primary weapons were the 24 Hs 217 rockets housed in the nose.

▼ On the gantry
Natters blasted off from a 6-m (20-ft.) vertical gantry. Three channelled rails guided the wings and the lower fin.

FACTS AND FIGURES

➤ Erich Bachem had first proposed his rocket-powered interceptor in 1939 but received little official encouragement.

➤ For the first unpowered flight, the Natter was carried to 5500 m (18,000 ft.) beneath an He 111.

➤ Unmanned test launches were carried out with a dummy pilot in the cockpit.

➤ The improved Ba 349B had a rocket motor of increased endurance, but only three were produced before VE Day.

➤ To fire the salvo of unguided rockets the pilot ejected the Natter's nosecone.

➤ To prevent them falling into Allied hands all but four of the Ba 349s were blown up.

PROFILE

Germany's desperate defender

Four companies submitted designs to meet the German air ministry's demand for a small point interceptor and Bachem's Ba 349 was eventually chosen for evaluation. This was mainly due to the intervention of SS leader Heinrich Himmler, who was looking for ways to increase his influence in the armed forces.

With Germany's industry suffering from Allied raids it was necessary for the Natter to be built from wood and be of simple construction, allowing rapid and economical production.

The final Ba 349 design was essentially that of a manned surface-to-air missile. Launched from a vertical rail, the Natter would continue to climb vertically, controlled by an autopilot, using its main rocket engine and additional power from rocket boosters. As the aircraft reached a bomber formation, the pilot would resume control and make a firing pass using unguided rockets. The aircraft would then descend to an altitude of 1400 m (4,600 ft.) and the nose section would separate from the fuselage. The pilot would release

himself and descend, along with the fuselage, by parachute.

Of 36 airframes built, only 10 reached operational status. These never saw combat, however, but were blown up as American land forces approached their base.

Left: A pilotless Ba 349 is prepared for the first vertical launch on 18 December 1944.

Above: This Ba 349A is mounted on a trailer which was used to transport the aircraft to the launching ramp. In the foreground is one of the Schmidding solid-fuel booster rockets, four of which were attached to the rear fuselage.

Ba 349A Natter

Type: single-seat semi-expendable interceptor

Powerplant: one 19.62-kN (3,748-lb.-thrust) Walter HWK 509C-1 bi-fuel rocket motor, plus four 4.9-kN (2,640-lb.-thrust) Schmidding 109-533 solid-fuel rockets

Maximum speed: 998 km/h (619 m.p.h.) at 5000 m (16,400 ft.)

Initial climb rate: 11,400 m/min (36,415 f.p.m.)

Combat radius: 40 km (25 mi.) at 12,000 m (39,400 ft.)

Weights: loaded 2200 kg (4,850 lb.)

Armament: 24 x 73-mm (2.9-in.) Hs 217 Föhn rockets

Dimensions: span 3.60 m (11 ft. 10 in.)
length 6.10 m (20 ft.)
wing area 2.75 m² (30 sq. ft.)

Above the nose was a ring sight for the nose-mounted rocket armament, which was covered by a jettisonable plastic fairing before launch. Twin 30-mm (1.18-in.) MK 108 cannon were proposed but never fitted.

Protection for Natter pilots was of major importance, with sandwich-type armour being fitted on all four sides. Instrumentation in the cockpit was spartan. Plans to fit an ejection seat were rejected because of space constraints.

The main engine was a variant of that fitted to the Messerschmitt Me 163 interceptor. For vertical launch four booster rockets were added, which burned during the first 10 seconds of flight.

Cruciform fins on the rear fuselage carried the control surfaces. Elevators and rudders, operating differentially, provided roll control.

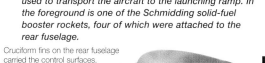

The fuselage was constructed of wood. The only metal parts were control push rods, hinges and load-supporting attachment points.

Originally it was envisaged that the Natter would make ramming attacks on bomber formations once it had expended its rockets. This would have necessitated fitting an ejection seat for the pilot, but the idea was abandoned and a jettisonable nose was fitted instead.

BA 349A NATTER

This example is one of an estimated 20 Ba 349As completed by early 1945. Ten of these aircraft were set up for operations at Kirchheim, close to the Wolf Hirth production factory.

COMBAT DATA

MAXIMUM SPEED

Powered by the same engine as the Messerschmitt Me 163, the Natter's lighter and more streamlined form gave it an edge in performance, pushing the aircraft close to the sound barrier. The Bolkhovitinov BI was the world's first rocket-powered fighter and had startling performance.

Ba 349B-1a NATTER 998 km/h (619 m.p.h.)
Me 163B-1a KOMET 960 km/h (595 m.p.h.)
BI 1000 km/h (620 m.p.h.)

CLIMB RATE

With its main rocket engine plus booster rockets the Natter had an amazing rate of climb from the vertical position. The g forces sustained were so great that the aircraft had to be controlled by autopilot during the ascent.

Ba 349B-1a NATTER 11,400 m/min (36,415 f.p.m.)
Me 163B-1a KOMET 5000 m/min (16,400 f.p.m.)
BI 4980 m/min (16,335 f.p.m.)

ENDURANCE

Both the Natter and the Me 163 were designed as point interceptors and had exceptionally short endurance. This meant that they were only capable of making one firing pass on an enemy formation.

Ba 349B-1a NATTER 4 min 22sec
Me 163B-1a KOMET 7min 30sec
BI 15 min

Operational Natter missions

1 LAUNCH: If the Natter had ever been used operationally it would have been launched from a vertical rail to accelerate rapidly to its operational height guided by an autopilot.

2 INTERCEPTION: On reaching the enemy bomber formation the Natter pilot would eject the nose cone and fire a salvo of unguided rockets.

3 DESCENT: When the rocket fuel was exhausted the Natter would make an unpowered descent to 1400 m (4,600 ft.).

4 TOUCHDOWN: The pilot would then jettison the nose section using explosive bolts and release himself from the fuselage. Both the pilot and the rear fuselage would then descend to the ground by parachute.

BELL

P-39 AIRACOBRA

● Tricycle undercarriage ● Mid-engined design ● Soviet service

A revolutionary design, the Airacobra had its engine located behind the pilot and was one of the world's first single-seat fighters to feature a tricycle landing gear. But due to the pace of fighter development in the early 1940s the P-39 was rapidly outclassed. It fought well against heavy odds in the early days of World War II in the Pacific and later won high praise from Russia, which used its cannon to destroy German ground targets.

▲ The most remarkable feature of the P-39 was its mid-mounted engine, which drove the propeller via a long driveshaft. The main reason for adopting this layout was so that the aircraft could carry the massive 37-mm (1.46-in.) cannon.

BELL P-39 AIRACOBRA

P-39 in the Pacific ▶
The Airacobra performed well in the Pacific against Japanese opposition. It was mainly used for ground-attack missions.

▼ Car door
Another unusual feature of the P-39 was the side-opening, car-style door.

◀ Cannon armed
The barrel for the mighty 37-mm (1.46-in) cannon protruded through the propeller spinner.

▼ Post-war racer
At the end of World War II, several P-39s were snapped up at rock-bottom prices and modified for air racing.

▲ USAAF fighter
When the US entered the war in 1941, the P-39 was the best fighter they had available. A few flew in Europe with the USAAF, but they were outclassed by German fighters and were replaced by Spitfires.

FACTS AND FIGURES

➤ The Airacobra was the first US single-seat fighter with a nosewheel to enter service.

➤ The prototype Bell XP-39 made its first flight on 6 April 1939.

➤ Russian forces took delivery of about 5000 P-39s during World War II.

➤ Although designed as a fighter, Soviet forces used the P-39 for ground attack, with great success.

➤ The RAF ordered 675 Airacobras, but only one squadron was ever equipped.

➤ P-39s were operated by the Italian Co-Belligerent Air Force during 1944.

PROFILE

Mid-engined attacker

One of many pre-war innovations explored by the Bell Aircraft Company, the Airacobra appeared to be fast and heavily armed when it was first produced. Its engine, 'buried' in the fuselage behind the pilot's seat, was fitted with an extension shaft to the propeller running under the cockpit. A tricycle undercarriage and a 37-mm (1.46-in.) cannon were also incorporated.

When war came in 1939, RAF tests revealed that the P-39's overall performance did not match that of British fighters. This and the fact that the Airacobra's unusual systems could prove unreliable caused it to be rejected for service.

In the Pacific, the USAAF had to use any available fighters and the outclassed Airacobras were thrown into war sorties against the Japanese during 1942/43. American pilots also flew it during the early combat operations in the Middle East.

Bell improved the aircraft, and when US fighter groups re-equipped with other types many Airacobras were passed to the Red air force, where the 'Little Shaver' proved very popular. 'Shaving' was Russian pilot slang for ground strafing, and the P-39 soon earned great respect as a destroyer of German tanks and vehicles.

Airacobra pilots stencilled dozens of tiny stars on their machines to show how adept the 'Lend-Lease' American fighter was at this deadly and dangerous task. The P-39 was also flown by Italian and French pilots during the war.

Above: Although its performance could not match that of fighters such as the Spitfire, the P-39 had respectable figures and good manoeuvrability.

Left: If the RAF had only retained the P-39 with its original turbocharged engine, it might have found a winner. Instead, it was discarded due to chronic unreliability.

P-39N Airacobra

Type: single-seat fighter and ground-attack aircraft with tricycle undercarriage

Powerplant: one 895-kW (1,200-hp.) Allison V-1710-63 liquid-cooled engine

Maximum speed: 642 km/h (400 m.p.h.)

Range: 1207 km (750 mi.)

Service ceiling: 11,735 m (38,500 ft.)

Weights: empty 2566 kg (5,645 lb.); loaded 3702 kg (8,145 lb.)

Armament: one 37-mm (1.46-in.) plus two 12.7-mm (.50 cal.) MGs in nose and four 7.62-mm (.30 cal.) MGs in wings; bombload of up to 227 kg (500 lb.)

Dimensions:
span	10.36 m	(34 ft.)
length	9.19 m	(30 ft.)
height	3.78 m	(12 ft.)
wing area	19.79 m²	(213 sq. ft.)

Chief armament of the P-39 was the 37-mm (1.46-in.) M4 cannon, fed by a belt-type magazine holding 30 rounds. British Airacobras had a 20-mm (0.79-in.) cannon instead.

The pilot sat in an extremely well-protected cockpit, surrounded by armour to protect him from bullets. This was especially useful in the ground-attack role.

A large percentage of the 9,558 Airacobras built wore the Soviet red star. These were usually assigned to the elite Guards regiments.

The engine was mounted immediately behind the pilot's seat, and a long shaft ran under the seat, through the cockpit to a gearbox below the propeller shaft.

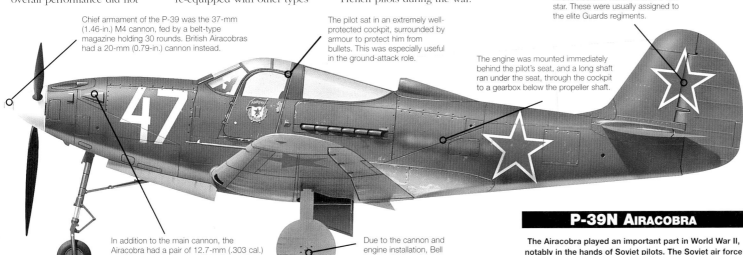

In addition to the main cannon, the Airacobra had a pair of 12.7-mm (.303 cal.) machine-guns in the top of the forward fuselage. The P-39Q could carry two more 12.7-mm guns in underwing pods.

Due to the cannon and engine installation, Bell had to design a tricycle undercarriage, the first in an operational fighter.

P-39N AIRACOBRA

The Airacobra played an important part in World War II, notably in the hands of Soviet pilots. The Soviet air force not only found the type ideal for tank busting but also in the air-to-air role.

COMBAT DATA

MAXIMUM SPEED

The late-model P-39N restored some of the lost performance of the early P-39s by having a more powerful engine. It was no better than a Bf 109, however, and grossly inferior to the excellent Yak 9.

P-39N AIRACOBRA 642 km/h (400 m.p.h.)

Bf 109G 623 km/h (386 m.p.h.)

Yak 9 700 km/h (434 m.p.h.)

SERVICE CEILING

Soviet fighters were almost invariably better at low altitude, and the P-39 was thus markedly superior to the Yak 9 at altitude. It was equivalent to the Bf-109G, which was a good performer at height.

P-39N AIRACOBRA 11,735 m (38,500 ft.)

Bf 109G 11,750 m (38,550 ft.)

Yak 9 10,950 m (35,900 ft.)

ARMAMENT

The P-39's cannon was a single-shot killer, even to tanks. The use of a single, large cannon and two smaller guns was popular with Soviet and German designers but not the British or Americans.

P-39N AIRACOBRA
4 x 7.62-mm (.30 cal.) MGs
2 x 12.7-mm (.50 cal.) MGs
1 X 37-mm (1.46-in.) cannon

Bf 109G
2 x 7.92-mm (0.31-in.) MGs
2 x 20-mm (0.79-in.) cannon
1 x 30-mm (1.18-in.) cannon

Yak 9
2 x 12.7-mm (.50 cal.) MGs
1 x 23-mm (0.9-in.) cannon

Modified Airacobras

■ **NAVAL XFL-1:** The XFL-1 Airabonita was a naval variant with a tailwheel, strengthened fuselage and arrester hook. It was not adopted by the US Navy due to unsuccessful trials.

■ **V-TAIL:** An experimental trial of tail surfaces combining elevator and rudder functions was not used in service, as it reduced the P-39's excellent handling.

■ **SQUARE TAIL:** This trials XP-39E's square-cut wing and tailfin was also not adopted. Powered by an Allison V-1710-47, its tail bore a strong resemblance to that of a Mustang.

■ **AIR RACER:** This P-39, registration N40A, was owned privately and based in Orange County, California. It was painted red and white with blue trim, and flew frequently.

BELL

P-63 KINGCOBRA

● Close-support fighter ● Huge exports ● Airacobra development

Created as an improved version of the Bell P-39 Airacobra, the P-63 Kingcobra retained the tricycle landing gear of the earlier type, a nose cannon and an engine mounted behind the pilot driving the propeller through a long shaft. Like the P-39, it also had a car-type door for access to the cockpit. Unfortunately, the P-63 never measured up to the top wartime fighters, like the P-51, Bf 109 and Zero.

▲ Although not one of the most successful wartime fighters, the Kingcobra operated successfully in the close-support and attack roles. It saw most service with Soviet forces and was formidably armed and armoured.

BELL P-63 KINGCOBRA

▼ **Silver Kingcobra**
Of the few P-63s which remained in the United States, some were used for test and training duties. The majority of the rest went to the USSR.

▲ **Nose guns**
Most P-63s had twin 12.7-mm (.50 cal.) machine-guns installed in the upper engine cowling.

▼ **Experimental variants**
Two XP-63Ns were flown with 'butterfly' tails. One was modified after the war to L-39-1 standard and flew swept-wing tests for the US Navy.

▲ **Lend-Lease to Russia**
Fitted with underwing drop-tanks, this P-63A flying with the Soviet air force is typical of the 2400, or more, delivered under the Lend-Lease programme.

Allison power ▶
Removal of the engine access panels from this preserved P-63A reveals the 12-cylinder Allison V-1710 engine mounted behind the cockpit.

FACTS AND FIGURES

➤ A Kingcobra on display in San Antonio, Texas, survived use as a frangible bullet target during 1946.

➤ More than 3300 Kingcobras, in half a dozen versions, were produced.

➤ The first Kingcobra prototype made its initial flight on 7 December 1942.

➤ During the Korean War, some American pilots said that they had encountered P-63s flown by North Koreans.

➤ Both prototypes were lost in mishaps early in the flight test programme.

➤ About 2400 Kingcobras were turned over to the Soviet Union.

PROFILE

Close-support over Europe

A US Army Air Force (USAAF) order for two prototypes in June 1941 launched the P-63 Kingcobra. Further prototypes followed before deliveries of the first production version began in October 1943.

It quickly became clear that the P-63 was not advanced enough for front-line service, and the majority of Kingcobras were delivered to the Soviet Union under the Lend-Lease programme. A significant number also went to Free French forces, and a single example was

delivered to the RAF. Several were used as flying testbeds.

The P-63 was a low-wing design which served American forces well in a training capacity but was never used by them in combat. The Kingcobra was not an easy aircraft to fly, however, especially in the circuit pattern around an airfield, and pilots never bestowed on it the affection they extended to the Mustang, Thunderbolt and Hellcat.

Kingcobras were given a variety of second-line duties. In one of the most unusual, known

as Project Pinball, modified, armoured Kingcobras acted as manned targets for gunnery exercises by fighters shooting frangible bullets.

Above: At least 300 P-63s were delivered to the Free French Armée de l'Air. This is a P-63C with its distinctive ventral fin.

Below: All aircraft up to the P-63A-5 were fitted with a centre-section rack but had no wing racks. The four 12.7-mm (.50 cal.) machine-guns were supplemented by a 37-mm (1.46-in.) cannon in the nose.

P-63A KINGCOBRA

One of a large number of P-63A and P-63C Kingcobras supplied to the Soviet air force during World War II, this P-63A-9 was fitted with an M10 (instead of an M4) hub cannon and additional armour.

P-63A Kingcobra

Type: fighter and ground attack aircraft

Powerplant: one 988-kW (1,325-hp.) Allison V-1710-93 liquid-cooled 12-cylinder Vee piston engine driving a four-bladed propeller

Maximum speed: 660 km/h (409 m.p.h.) at 7620 m (25,000 ft.)

Cruising speed: 608 km/h (377 m.p.h.)

Range: 724 km (450 mi.)

Service ceiling: 13,106 m (43,200 ft.)

Weights: empty 2892 kg (6,932 lb.); maximum take-off 4763 kg (10,479 lb.)

Armament: one 37-mm (1.46-in.) cannon and four fixed forward-firing 12.7-mm (.50 cal.) machine-guns, plus up to three 237-kg (520-lb.) bombs or six rocket projectiles dependent on the sub-variant

Dimensions:
span	11.68 m	(38 ft. 4 in.)
length	9.96 m	(32 ft. 8 in.)
height	3.84 m	(12 ft. 7 in.)
wing area	23.04 m²	(248 sq. ft.)

Unlike other fighters, the P-63 did not have a hinged or sliding canopy. The pilot entered the cockpit via a car-type door on the port side.

An Allison V-1710 engine drove the four-bladed propeller of the P-63A via a long extension shaft. This ran forwards through the cockpit and between the pilot's legs.

This large intake above the rear fuselage fed air to the carburettor. Placing the engine behind the pilot seemed, on paper, to offer many advantages. Instead it created a number of engineering problems and did not provide the hoped-for performance benefits.

Twin 12.7-mm (.50 cal.) machine-guns were mounted in the upper nose.

269778

The powerful nose armament was completed by the 37-mm (1.46-in.) cannon, which fired through the spinner. Sub-types up to the P-63A-8 carried only thirty 37-mm rounds.

Streamlined fairings covered the underwing machine-guns. Starting with the P-63A-6, underwing hardpoints were fitted.

Aircraft fitted with only the centreline hardpoint could carry a single 237-kg (520-lb.) bomb. Alternatively, a 341-litre (90-gal.) or 796-litre (200-gal.) fuel tank could be fitted. Later aircraft carried more weapons; the A-9 and A-10 variants complementing this with 28 extra rounds of 37-mm (1.46-in.) ammunition.

The P-63 had a taller, more angular tail than the P-39 Airacobra. The P-63's configuration, including its laminar flow wing, was largely tested on the experimental XP-39E.

COMBAT DATA

MAXIMUM SPEED
The P-63A was much faster than the P-40N Warhawk, since the Curtiss fighter was nearing the end of its development potential. The P-63 was much slower than, arguably, the greatest US fighter of World War II, the North American P-51D Mustang.

P-63A KINGCOBRA	660 km/h (409 m.p.h.)
P-51D MUSTANG	721 km/h (447 m.p.h.)
P-40N WARHAWK	609 km/h (378 m.p.h.)

RANGE
North American achieved exceptional range with the P-51, while Curtiss always struggled with the P-40 design. The P-63 was optimised for the ground attack role and, as such, was unlikely to be required to fly long-range escort or fighter missions. It had adequate range for the close-support role.

P-63A KINGCOBRA 724 km (450 mi.)

P-51D MUSTANG 2092 km (1,297 mi.)

P-40N WARHAWK 386 km (250 mi.)

ARMAMENT
Both the P-40 and P-51 adopted ground attack as a secondary role and were therefore able to carry fewer bombs than the P-63A. The Kingcobra also featured a powerful spinner-mounted cannon.

P-63A KINGCOBRA
1 x 37-mm (1.46-in.) cannon
4 x 12.7-mm (.50 cal.) machine-guns

P-51D MUSTANG
6 x 12.7-mm (.50 cal.) machine-guns

P-40N WARHAWK
6 x 12.7-mm (.50 cal.) machine-guns

681-kg (1,500-lb.) bombload

454-kg (1,000-lb.) bombload

227-kg (500-lb.) bombload

Bell fighters of the 1940s

■ **P-39 AIRACOBRA:** Designed as a highly manoeuvrable fighter, the radical P-39 proved to be a disappointment. It matured into an effective ground attack aircraft, however.

■ **P-59 AIRACOMET:** Planned as a contemporary of the Gloster E.28/39 and He 178, the P-59 did not in fact fly until after the Me 262 and Meteor. It was America's first jet fighter.

■ **XP-77:** Using pre-war racing aircraft design as a basis, Bell produced this lightweight wooden fighter prototype. It failed to achieve acceptable performance.

BLOHM UND VOSS

BV 138

● Flying-boat ● Air-sea rescue ● Maritime patrol

The Blohm und Voss BV 138 was crucial to Germany's naval war effort. It was the brainchild of Dr Ing Richard Vogt, and although it suffered from initial structural weaknesses the BV 138 had a successful career as a maritime patrol aircraft and anti-ship bomber. Despite extensive problems with the initial design, the BV 138 eventually proved to be a capable machine and was later adapted for minesweeping.

▲ *Although it finally emerged as a useful design, the BV 138 had a problematic start and came close to being abandoned. It served from the Black Sea to the fringes of the Arctic Circle.*

BLOHM UND VOSS **BV 138**

▲ **Sweeping circle**
With its guns removed, the BV 138MS (nicknamed the mouse-catching aircraft) was used to sweep canals for mines.

▲ **Water jump**
Early BV 138s had alarming handling on water. Hull drag was excessive, making take off a prolonged business.

▼ **First missions**
The Luftwaffe was so short of floatplanes that it impressed the first two BV 138s into service for the Norwegian campaign.

▲ **Black Sea patrol**
BV 138s flew patrols in the Black Sea as late as 1944 from bases in Romania, with protection from Romanian escort fighters.

Back to the drawing board ▶
The Ha 138V2 was the second prototype. With enlarged tail surfaces it handled better than the original aircraft but still suffered from vibration problems. A complete redesign was recommended by the Air Ministry technical office.

FACTS AND FIGURES

➤ A BV 138 was one of the last planes to leave Berlin on 1 May 1945, taking off from a lake with wounded troops.

➤ In 1941 a BV 138 shot down an RAF Catalina over the North Sea.

➤ Convoy PQ-18 was the first to fight off shadowing BV 138s with Sea Hurricanes.

➤ This seaplane was nicknamed 'Der Fliegende Holzschuh' (The Flying Clog) when it appeared as a prototype in 1937.

➤ The prototype, known then as the Ha 138, first flew on 15 July 1937.

➤ As late as the summer of 1944 BV 138s flew anti-ship missions in the Black Sea.

PROFILE

Germany's hunchback

The BV 138 was handicapped by not being strong enough to withstand the battering of prolonged operation on the open seas, and the prototype had to be extensively redesigned after showing severe instability on the water. After major modifications, the aircraft entered squadron service in 1940, initially proving unreliable. However, the aircraft's problems were later solved and it went on to provide good service, flying important naval reconnaissance missions against Allied convoys, especially in the Atlantic and Barents Sea. Two

BV 138s even operated from the frozen wastes of Novaya Zemlya with the support of U-boats.

In addition to shore bases, BV 138s flew from seaplane tenders, some modified with catapults for launch. All BV 138s were able to use assisted take-off rockets and some carried FuG 200 Hohentwiel radar for shadowing convoys. The BV 138 could even fight off Allied fighters, as one crew showed by downing a Blenheim over Norway. The final version was fitted with a giant electromagnetic ring for triggering magnetic mines.

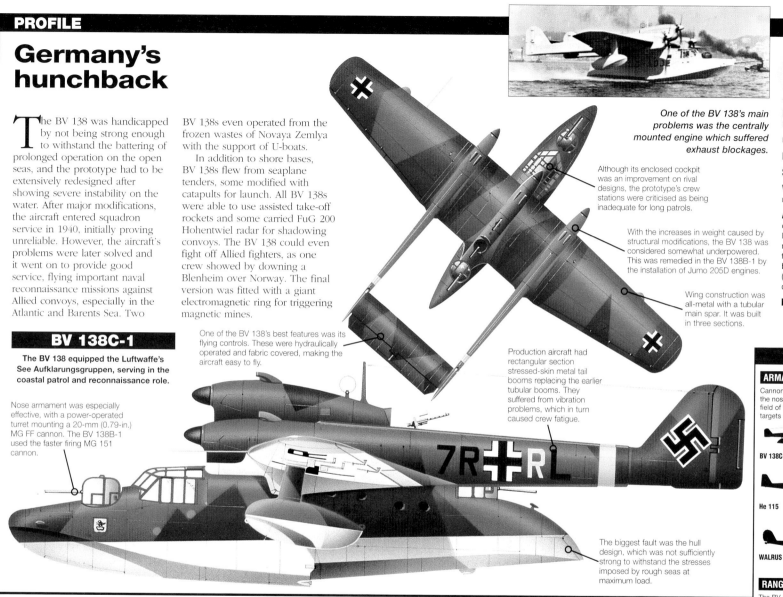

One of the BV 138's main problems was the centrally mounted engine which suffered exhaust blockages.

Although its enclosed cockpit was an improvement on rival designs, the prototype's crew stations were criticised as being inadequate for long patrols.

With the increases in weight caused by structural modifications, the BV 138 was considered somewhat underpowered. This was remedied in the BV 138B-1 by the installation of Jumo 205D engines.

Wing construction was all-metal with a tubular main spar. It was built in three sections.

One of the BV 138's best features was its flying controls. These were hydraulically operated and fabric covered, making the aircraft easy to fly.

Production aircraft had rectangular section stressed-skin metal tail booms replacing the earlier tubular booms. They suffered from vibration problems, which in turn caused crew fatigue.

The biggest fault was the hull design, which was not sufficiently strong to withstand the stresses imposed by rough seas at maximum load.

BV 138C-1

The BV 138 equipped the Luftwaffe's See Aufklarungsgruppen, serving in the coastal patrol and reconnaissance role.

Nose armament was especially effective, with a power-operated turret mounting a 20-mm (0.79-in.) MG FF cannon. The BV 138B-1 used the faster firing MG 151 cannon.

7R+RL

BV 138C-1

Type: reconnaissance flying-boat

Powerplant: three 656-kW (880-hp.) Junkers Jumo 205D inline piston engines

Maximum speed: 285 km/h (177 m.p.h.) at sea level

Cruising speed: 235 km/h (146 m.p.h.)

Range: 5000 km (3,107 mi.)

Service ceiling: 5000 m (16,400 ft.)

Weights: empty 11,770 kg (25,948 lb.); maximum take-off 17,650 kg (38,912 lb.)

Armament: one 20-mm (0.79-in.) MG 151 cannon in the bow turret, one 13-mm (0.51-in.) MG 131 machine-gun at the rear centre engine nacelle and one 7.92-mm (0.31-in.) MG 15 firing through starboard hatch; three 50-kg (110-lb.) bombs under starboard wingroot, or six 50-kg (110-lb.) bombs or four 150-kg (330-lb.) depth charges (BV 138C-1/U1)

Dimensions:
span	27.00 m	(88 ft. 7 in.)
length	19.90 m	(65 ft. 3 in.)
height	5.90 m	(19 ft. 4 in.)
wing area	112 m² (1,206 sq. ft.)	

COMBAT DATA

ARMAMENT

Cannon armament made attacking a BV 138 a hazardous task, as the nose gunner occupied a powered turret and had an excellent field of fire. In comparison the He 115 and the Walrus were easy targets for a fighter pilot and neither usually carried bombs.

BV 138C-1 — 1 x 20-mm (0.79-in.) cannon, 1 x 7.92-mm (0.31-in.) MG, 1 x 13-mm (0.51-in.) MG, 4 x 150-kg (330-lb.) bombs

He 115 — 2 x 7.92-mm (0.31-in.) MGs, 2 x 250-kg (550-lb.) bombs

WALRUS — 2 x 7.7-mm (.303 cal.) MGs, up to 345 kg (760 lb.) of bombs

RANGE

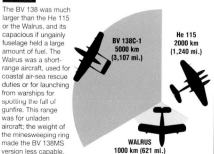

The BV 138 was much larger than the He 115 or the Walrus, and its capacious if ungainly fuselage held a large amount of fuel. The Walrus was a short-range aircraft, used for coastal air-sea rescue duties or for launching from warships for spotting the fall of gunfire. This range was for unladen aircraft; the weight of the minesweeping ring made the BV 138MS version less capable.

BV 138C-1 5000 km (3,107 mi.)

He 115 2000 km (1,240 mi.)

WALRUS 1000 km (621 mi.)

BV 138 missions

AIR-SEA RESCUE: At the start of the war the Luftwaffe was notably more efficient than the RAF at rescuing its shot-down aircrew. Pilots had excellent survival equipment.

PICK-UP: One of the last BV 138 sorties of the war was to a lake in Berlin. The pilot picked up 10 wounded soldiers and escaped back to Denmark.

CONVOY PATROL: BV 138s spotted the location of Allied convoys, giving position reports to U-boat Wolf Packs. The British replied by using Sea Hurricanes in defence, rocket-launched from ships.

MINE SWEEP: Using a powerful magnetic signal, the BV 138MS could set off enemy mines which were often dropped in canals.

BLOHM UND VOSS

BV 222 WIKING

● Airliner design ● Huge capacity ● Transport and patrol service

Deutsche Lufthansa (DLH) ordered three Blohm und Voss BV 222 Wiking (Viking) aircraft in September 1939 to fill a requirement for a new 24-berth transatlantic airliner. The first of these made its initial flight in September 1940; by then World War II had started and DLH no longer had a use for the type. Possible military roles were investigated and the following July BV 222 V1 made its first supply flight, the first of many sorties for the Luftwaffe.

▲ *During 1942 BV 222s were engaged on supply missions to North Africa. From Greek and Italian bases the aircraft flew to Tobruk or Derna, and often returned carrying casualties.*

Responsive controls ▶
Flight tests proved that the BV 222 handled well in flight. The only drawbacks were slight directional instability and a tendency to porpoise whilst taxiing.

▲ Diesel power
The long-range reconnaissance BV 222C was powered by six Jumo 207C diesel engines.

▼ Submarine support
In May 1943 BV 222 V5 was transferred to south-west France for U-boat support duties.

▲ Defensive sting
After two BV 222As were lost to Allied fighters in 1942, the bow gun position (seen here) was removed and more powerful armament installed including unusual wing-mounted turrets.

Diverted to the Luftwaffe ▶
Rolled out in August 1940, the prototype BV 222 carried a civilian registration. The aircraft was acquired by the Luftwaffe and began operations in July 1941.

FACTS AND FIGURES

➤ Production time of a complete BV 222 airframe (less engines and equipment) totalled 35,000 man hours.

➤ Slow and vulnerable, a number of BV 222s were shot down by RAF fighters.

➤ Towards the end of World War II, Wikings reverted solely to transport roles.

➤ By the end of 1942 Wikings had carried more than 1400 tonnes (1,377 tons) of cargo, 17,000 troops and 2400 casualties in the Mediterranean.

➤ Seven BV 222s survived the war; two were flown to the US for evaluation.

➤ In October 1943 a Wiking shot down an RAF Lancaster bomber over the Atlantic.

Giant German flying boat

Powered by six BMW-Bramo Fafnir 323R radial engines, the giant Wiking was the largest flying-boat to see service during the war.

The first prototype (BV 222 V1) made its first cargo flight to Norway in July 1941 and later flew supplies to the Afrika Korps in North Africa. The subsequent V2 and V3 were armed with machine guns in various positions on the fuselage and wings for defence. By late 1942, five more pre-production Wikings had entered service

and, with the first three aircraft, equipped the specially-formed Luft-Transportstaffel (See) 222.

With interest in the BV 222 as a long-range reconnaissance aircraft growing, a number of the flying-boats were refitted, receiving search and rear-warning radar equipment and powered gun turrets. Soon they were in service from bases in the Bay of Biscay, for Atlantic U-boat co-operation flights.

Meanwhile, in April 1943, BV 222 V7 made its first flight, powered by six Junkers Jumo

Above: The stabilising floats retracted to lie flush with the outer wing panel. This example has its floats lowered in preparation for landing.

207C diesels. This became the prototype for the BV 222C, which entered production at the Blohm und Voss plant near Hamburg. Five were delivered to maritime patrol units in 1943; four others remained uncompleted.

Above: BV 222A-0 V8 is seen here testing its engines on a launching ramp. It was shot down by RAF Beaufighters on 10 December 1942.

BV 222C Wiking

Type: long-range transport and maritime reconnaissance flying boat

Powerplant: six 746-kW (1,000-hp.) Junkers Jumo 207C in-line diesel engines

Maximum speed: 390 km/h (242 m.p.h.) at 5000 m (16,400 ft.)

Range: 6095 km (3,787 mi.)

Service ceiling: 7300 m (23,950 ft.)

Weights: empty 30,650 kg (67,572 lb.); maximum take-off 49,000 kg (108,027 lb.)

Armament: (BV 222C-09) three 20-mm (0.79-in.) MG 151 cannon and five 13-mm (0.51-in) MG 131 machine guns

Dimensions:
span	46.00 m	(150 ft. 11 in.)
length	37.00 m	(121 ft. 5 in.)
height	10.90 m	(35 ft. 9 in.)
wing area	255 m²	(2,745 sq. ft.)

The flight crew consisted of two pilots, two flight engineers, a navigator and a wireless operator. To help the pilot on longer missions an autopilot system was fitted to a three-section elevator. The pilot controlled the outer and inner sections with the autopilot controlling the central section.

Armament was upgraded a number of times although, even with its most powerful arrangement, the aircraft was still vulnerable to fighters. Upgraded BV 222As had the unusual arrangement of two turrets mounted in the wings aft of the outer engine nacelle each armed with a single 20-mm (0.79-in) cannon.

BV 222A-0 WIKING

This BV 222 flew transport sorties from Petsamo, Finland during the early months of 1943. The yellow bands signify that the aircraft was operating in the Eastern Front theatre.

The main passenger/cargo portion of the hull was very spacious thanks to the lack of bulkheads. The bulkheads were fitted between the keel and the floor.

Of all-metal construction, the two-step hull was covered by corrosion-resisting alloy sheet which varied from 3 mm to 5 mm (⅛ to ¼ in.) in thickness. It was divided into two sections, the lower for passengers/cargo and the upper for the flight crew.

The all-metal wings were supported by a single, immensely strong, wing spar measuring 145 cm (4 ft. 9 in.) in diameter. The spar was sub-divided to contain six fuel tanks.

The fin and rudder were large and, after initial problems, provided good directional stability. The rudder was operated by two interconnected tabs driven by the main circuit. The elevator was mounted near the base of the fin.

COMBAT DATA

MAXIMUM SPEED

With six engines, the BV 222 was by far the most powerful of the German World War II seaplanes. This power translated into a healthy maximum speed for an aircraft of this type. It was faster than the RAF's closest equivalent, the Short Sunderland.

BV 222C WIKING	**390 km/h (242 m.p.h.)**
BV 138B	**289 km/h (180 m.p.h.)**
Ju 52/3mW	**262 km/h (163 m.p.h.)**

OPERATIONAL RANGE

Designed for the long-range maritime patrol role, the BV 222C had much greater range than the BV 138 and Ju 52 floatplane which were intended to patrol coastal waters. The BV 222C actually had a shorter range than the BV 222A as fuel capacity was decreased with the installation of the Junkers Jumo diesel-powered engines.

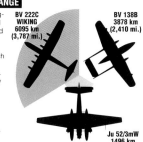

BV 222C WIKING 6095 km (3,787 mi.)

BV 138B 3878 km (2,410 mi.)

Ju 52/3mW 1496 km (930 mi.)

CREW CAPACITY

As the largest flying boat to reach operational status in any country during World War II, the BV 222 was capable of carrying a large crew. Eight of the crew were gunners.

BV 222C WIKING 14

BV 138B 5

Ju 52/3mW 3

Blohm und Voss seaplanes

■ **BV 138:** The first flying-boat design to be built by the company, the BV 138 was used in a variety of roles during World War II including reconnaissance and mine-sweeping.

■ **Ha 139:** Designed to meet a requirement for a transatlantic mailplane, the Ha 139 was pressed into Luftwaffe service late in 1939. Three examples were operated until 1942.

■ **Ha 140:** In 1935 design work began on the Ha 140 which was to compete directly with the Heinkel He 115 as a torpedo and reconnaissance floatplane. It did not win the orders.

■ **BV 238:** The giant BV 238 was to have been built in both sea and landplane versions. Only one example flew and this was sunk at its moorings by USAAF P-51 Mustangs.

BOEING

B-17 FLYING FORTRESS

● Long-range heavy bomber ● Backbone of the US 8th Air Force

Boeing's Flying Fortress was one of the most important bombers in history. B-17s fought in every theatre of World War II, but won immortality in their epic daylight battles against the Luftwaffe in which thousands of young American flyers lost their lives transforming the impotent United States Army Air Force of early 1943 into a force of devastating, destructive power just 12 months later.

▲ The Flying Fortress was America's main strategic weapon in Europe during World War II. From the summer of 1943, huge numbers of Boeing's great silver bird were to be found on English airfields.

PHOTO FILE

BOEING B-17 FLYING FORTRESS

◀ **Mass production**
Nowhere was America's huge industrial might more visible than in the aircraft factories which turned out hundreds of B-17s each month.

Daring missions ▶
During the long bomb-run into the target area the bomb-aimer controlled the B-17. Losses were extremely high as the aircraft was forced to fly straight and level.

▼ **A hard-fought battle**
The Fortress was tough, but over Germany it was pitted against some of the most experienced fighter pilots in the world, and losses were heavy.

◀ **The young man's war**
It was a rare B-17 pilot who was older than 30: most of the men who took the big bombers into battle were barely into their 20s.

▲ **Silver machines**
The B-17 soldiered on after World War II in some oddball roles. This is a rescue aircraft with a lifeboat carried under the fuselage.

FACTS AND FIGURES

➤ A B-17 shot down by Japanese Zeroes on the way to Pearl Harbor was the first American combat loss in World War II.

➤ The Boeing 299, the Flying Fortress prototype, first flew on 28 July 1935.

➤ 12,731 B-17s were built, with production of the B-17G model reaching 8680.

➤ At the height of the war in Europe, B-17s occupied more than 25 airfields in the south and east of England.

➤ More than 47,000 US 8th Air Force crew died in daylight raids over Germany.

➤ A search and rescue SB-17 flew the first American sortie of the Korean War.

PROFILE

Castles in the sky

In the mid-1930s, Boeing engineers suggested a big bomber to the US Army Air Corps. The best American bomber at the time was an inadequate, twin-engined adaptation of the DC-3 transport. The decision to go ahead with the B-17 Flying Fortress was a courageous leap forward: it gave the United States an embryonic bomber force by the time of the attack on Pearl Harbor. Early B-17s did not have enough guns and were not available in sufficient numbers, but as the war progressed the Flying Fortresses took command of the skies.

B-17 crews faced unspeakable horror, pressing ahead into Luftwaffe fighters and flak while blinded by smoke, beaten by turbulence, plagued with mechanical mishaps and paralysed by numbing cold. On the first Berlin mission, B-17 crewmen killed in the air numbered the same as Germans killed on the ground by bombs (about 400). As the bombing campaign wore on casualties aboard the B-17s remained high, but the bombing became more effective.

Right: B-17s were used to make precision daylight attacks on German industrial centres.

Left: Hit by flak, a burning B-17 falls away from the protection of its fellows.

B-17G Flying Fortress

Type: nine-/10-seat long-range bomber

Powerplant: four 895-kW (1,200-hp.) Wright R-1820-97 Cyclone turbocharged radial piston engines

Maximum speed: 462 km/h (287 m.p.h.) at 7690 m (25,230 ft.)

Range: 3220 km (2000 mi.) with 2725-kg (6,007-lb.) load

Weights: empty 16,391 kg (36,136 lb.); loaded 29,710 kg (65,499 lb.)

Armament: 13 12.7-mm (.50 cal.) machine-guns in twin turrets, plus single dorsal and fore and aft beam positions; 8000-kg (1,7640 lb.) maximum bombload

Dimensions:
span	31.62 m	(103 ft. 9 in.)
length	22.66 m	(74 ft. 4 in.)
height	5.82 m	(19 ft. 1 in.)
wing area	131.92 m²	(1,420 sq. ft.)

The 'Mighty Eighth' Force was the premier user of the B-17 Flying Fortress.

B-17F 'FAST WOMAN'

'Fast Woman' was one of the first American B-17s to arrive in Britain during World War II. Attached to the 359th Bomb Squadron of the 303rd Bomb Group, it was based at Molesworth in Huntingdonshire.

The Norden bombsight with which the B-17 was equipped was reputed to be able to 'drop a bomb into a pickle barrel' from 4000 m (13,125 ft.).

Boeing were among the pioneers of stressed-skin design, and the B-17 was among the earliest all-metal monoplane heavy bombers to enter service.

Fortresses were defended by as many as 13 heavy machine-guns. The vulnerable undersides were covered by a ball turret and by the two waist gunners.

The B-17 was immensely strong. Aircraft managed to return to base with severe battle damage, and the big bomber could still fly even with large sections of the huge vertical tail shot away.

The B-17 was powered by reliable Wright Cyclone radial engines. They were turbocharged, which enabled the Fortress to operate at higher altitudes than its European contemporaries.

The bomb-bay was relatively small, and although the B-17 could fly with an eight-tonne bombload it generally carried a quarter of that amount on operations.

B-17s were not originally fitted with tail guns. A tail gunner's position was added to the B-17E and all subsequent models.

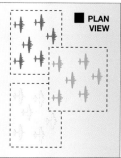

■ SIDE VIEW

3rd COMBAT BOX (7900 m/25,920 ft.)) Each box contained 18 bombers, which could amass more than 200 heavy machine-guns.

LEAD COMBAT BOX (7600 m/24,934 ft.)) The formation commander flew in the lead bomber, with responsibility for navigation and ordering simultaneous release of bombs.

2nd COMBAT BOX (7300 m/23,950 ft.) Combat boxes manoeuvred in unison, always keeping in close formation for mutual support against fighters.

COMBAT DATA

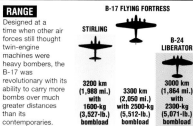

RANGE

Designed at a time when other air forces still thought twin-engine machines were heavy bombers, the B-17 was revolutionary with its ability to carry more bombs over much greater distances than its contemporaries.

B-17 FLYING FORTRESS

STIRLING	B-17 FLYING FORTRESS	B-24 LIBERATOR
3200 km (1,988 mi.) with 1600-kg (3,527-lb.) bombload	3300 km (2,050 mi.) with 2500-kg (5,512-lb.) bombload	3000 km (1,864 mi.) with 2300-kg (5,071-lb.) bombload

DEFENCES

Originally relatively lightly armed, the Flying Fortress entered combat in armour plate and with an all-round machine-gun fit. A box of 18 bombers could bring tens or even hundreds of guns to bear on an attacker coming from any direction.

STIRLING 8 x 7.7-mm (.303 cal.) machine-guns

B-17 FLYING FORTRESS 13 x 12.7-mm (.50 cal.) machine-guns

B-24 LIBERATOR 10 x 12.7-mm (.50 cal.) machine-guns

Layered defences

Every B-17 aircraft contributed to the defence of the whole formation. Each squadron of six aircraft moved in unison in formations called boxes, and squadrons were layered and staggered horizontally and vertically, to allow simultaneous release of bombs.

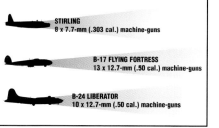

■ PLAN VIEW

BOEING

B-29 SUPERFORTRESS

● Long-range bomber ● Largest of World War II ● Assault on Japan

Boeing's talent for turning out huge aircraft paid a super dividend with the Superfortress: the B-29 became the 'big stick' of the final campaign of World War II. Feared by those who fell beneath its shadow, this giant brought war home to Japan's cities and people and ushered in the atomic age. The B-29 also fought in Korea, it was converted into a key post-war transport and tanker, and was even copied without permission by the Russians.

▲ *Sting in the tail: in Korea, B-29 gunners were so good at shooting down enemy aircraft that it became the second highest-scoring Allied type, after the F-86 Sabre.*

BOEING B-29 SUPERFORTRESS

◀ **Fire from the sky**
In the last days of World War II B-29s poured a deluge of incendiary bombs onto Japanese cities, which were built largely of wood. The resulting conflagration consumed most of the residential areas.

◀ **The bomb ends the war**
Dropping the atomic weapons brought the war to a swift conclusion, saving many lives in the process.

X-plane ▶
mother ship
Several B-29s and the improved B-50 were modified for special missions. Among the most important was carrying early supersonic X-planes to altitude.

▲ **Bomber over Korea**
Just as the B-29 had flattened Japan, the Superfortress relentlessly crushed Communist resistance in Korea.

▼ **Atomic bomber**
Immortalised in song, 'Enola Gay' was the Superfortress which dropped the first atomic bomb on Japan, hitting the port city of Hiroshima on 6 August 1945.

▲ **Flying gas station**
In its KB-29 form the Superfortress was the world's first true service tanker aircraft, pioneering the inflight refuelling that has become vital to modern air combat.

FACTS AND FIGURES

➤ On the night of 9-10 March 1945, 324 B-29s attacked Tokyo at low level in the most destructive air raid in history.

➤ $3 billion had been invested in the B-29 before the first aircraft flew – more than any other aircraft project to that time.

➤ Russia's Tupolev design bureau copied the B-29 as the Tu-4 bomber.

➤ After the war, KB-29s were the USAF's first aerial refuelling tankers.

➤ Crew members travelled from nose to tail of the B-29 through a 'personnel tunnel' above the bomb-bay.

➤ B-29s were used to drop the first atomic bombs on Japan, and in post-war tests at Bikini atoll.

PROFILE

The first strategic bomber

The B-29 was the first pressurised bomber to enter service, and was therefore able to operate over vast distances and at safe heights to deliver huge bombloads onto the enemy.

Originally designed to bomb Germany from America during World War II, the B-29 entered service only at the end of the European war. This massive, revolutionary bomber was transferred to the fight against Japan, where it devastated cities in huge firebomb raids.

Without the reach of the B-29, America would have had to fight for much longer to recover the Pacific islands from Japan. And it was the B-29 that delivered the final, catastrophic blow in the form of two atomic bombs, dropped onto the cities of Hiroshima and Nagasaki.

Post-war, the B-29 joined the Royal Air Force as the Washington, and inspired the Russian Tu-4. Its final battle was in Korea, where it carried out night bombing raids and shot down many enemy aircraft.

The Superfortress represented one of the biggest technological leaps ever achieved by one aircraft type. Even today, its technology turns up in Russia's nuclear bombers.

In RAF service the B-29 served as a nuclear bomber, and as a secret reconnaissance aircraft which probed Soviet airspace for electronic signals.

B-29 Superfortress

Type: 10-/11-seat long-range strategic bomber

Powerplant: four 1641-kW (2,200-hp.) Wright R-3350 Cyclone 18 turbocharged radial piston engines

Maximum speed: 576 km/h (358 m.p.h.)

Range: 5230 km (3,250 mi.)

Service ceiling: 9170 m (30,085 ft.)

Weights: empty 31,815 kg (70,140 lb.); loaded 56,245 kg (123,999 lb.)

Armament: two 12.7-mm (.50 cal.) machine-guns in each of four remotely-controlled turrets and three 12.7-mm guns or two 12.7-mm guns and one 20-mm cannon in the tail; bombload 9072 kg (20,000 lb.)

Dimensions:
span	43.05 m	(141 ft. 3 in.)
length	30.18 m	(99 ft. 2 in.)
height	9.02 m	(29 ft. 7 in.)
wing area	161.27 m²	(1,736 sq. ft.)

It took 11 men to fly the B-29 on operations. There were two pilots, a bombardier, navigator, flight engineer, radio operator, radar operator, central fire control gunner, left gunner, right gunner and tail gunner.

Most B-29s had a sophisticated radar under the belly which allowed them to bomb accurately even through cloud.

WASHINGTON B.MK 1

The mighty Superfortress was a war-winning weapon, and went on to become one of the main forces in the Cold War. The RAF operated the type in the late 1940s and early 1950s, calling it the Washington.

The gunners all sat in the rear compartment, looking out for enemy fighters through domed windows and firing the guns via an early computer system.

WF 545

WF545

The forward cabin was connected to the rear cabin by a crawlway. In the back sat the gunners, and there were also bunks for resting on long missions.

Two enormous weapons bays carried the B-29's bombload. Each bay had winches inside to hoist the bombs up into the aircraft.

Under its tail the Superfortress had a retractable tail bumper, which protected the rear fuselage when the aircraft took off.

Sitting alone in the tail compartment, the tail gunner had two machine-guns and a 20-mm (0.79-in) cannon at his fingertips.

Superfortress superbomber

B-29 SUPERFORTRESS: The B-29's two bays held over 9000 kg (19,842 lb.) of bombs, the biggest standard load of any wartime bomber.

B-17 FLYING FORTRESS: Although it theoretically could carry 7900 kg (17,417 lb.) of bombs, the B-17 rarely flew combat missions with more than 2300 kg (5,071 lb.).

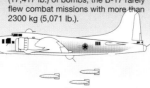

AVRO LANCASTER: The RAF's main bomber had a normal combat load of about 6300 kg (13,889 lb.).

HEINKEL He 177: In theory, Germany's heaviest bomber could carry 6000 kg (13,230 lb.), but in practice 2000 kg (4,400 lb.) was a more realistic load.

COMBAT DATA

MAXIMUM SPEED

The Boeing B-29 was a revelation when it first flew. Easily the biggest bomber of World War II, it flew faster than any of its predecessors, and at altitude it could outpace most of the Japanese fighters which were its principal foes.

B-29 SUPERFORTRESS	576 km/h (358 m.p.h.)
LANCASTER	462 km/h (287 m.p.h.)
B-24 LIBERATOR	467 km/h (290 m.p.h.)

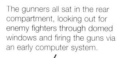

BREDA

BA.65

● Attack aircraft ● Spanish Civil War service ● North African use

Despite its heavy armament, the Ba.65 was not a success in the ground-attack role for which it was intended. Although comparable in size, weight and power to the earliest Spitfires, it was much slower and far less manoeuvrable. In service from the late 1930s, the Ba.65 found a few export customers, but was used principally by the Regia Aeronautica assisting Nationalist forces in Spain and fighting British forces in North Africa.

▲ *Flown for the first time in 1935, the Ba.65 was one of a number of Italian designs that were outmoded and unsuitable for combat tasks by the time Italy entered World War II in 1940.*

BREDA BA.65

▼ **Nationalist Spanish Ba.65**
Thirteen Ba.65s equipped the 65ª Squadriglia of the Aviazione Legionaria, the Italian air contingent supporting the Fascist forces in the Spanish Civil War.

▲ **Engine problems in the desert**
After Italy's entry into World War II, Ba.65s were committed to the North African campaign, where they came up against British forces. Serviceability, or lack of it, in the sandy desert conditions proved to be the type's biggest problem.

▲ **Natural metal**
This Ba.65bis, seen at the factory, has been fitted with a hydraulically-operated turret of unusual design, mounting a single 12.7-mm (.50 cal.) machine-gun. The Ba.65 was a descendant of the Ba 64 two-seat ground-attack type.

▲ **First batch**
The 81 aircraft for Italy were powered by 522-kW Gnome-Rhône radials.

◄ **101ª Squadriglia**
This Ba 65 carries 101ª Squadriglia markings. Eight squadrons were equipped with the aircraft in 1939.

FACTS AND FIGURES

➤ The last operational Italian Ba.65s were lost during the British offensive in Cyrenaica in early 1941.

➤ Iraqi Ba.65s saw limited action against the British during the 1941 insurrection.

➤ In June 1937 one Ba.65 was flown with a Pratt & Whitney R-1830 engine.

➤ Regia Aeronautica Ba.65s made reconnaissance flights during the invasion of Abyssinia.

➤ Caproni-Vizzola built 57 of a batch of 137 aircraft for the Regia Aeronautica.

➤ Ba.65s in Fascist service were used over Santander, Teruel and the River Ebro.

PROFILE

Civil War and desert veteran

Derived from the earlier Ba 64 and flown for the first time in 1935, the Ba.65 was produced in both single- and two-seat versions. Most were two-seaters, and some had a Breda L turret and 7.7-mm (.303 cal.) machine-gun fitted at the rear of the cockpit, in addition to the four wing-mounted weapons. The final Ba.65bis variant had an open cockpit-mounted gun.

The first Ba.65s, powered by Fiat engines, were supplied to the Iraqi air force in 1937. The first aircraft for the Italian air force were Gnome-Rhône-powered. Other exported Ba.65s were delivered to Chile, Hungary, Portugal and Paraguay, but plans to sell a Pratt & Whitney-powered version to Nationalist China foundered.

From August 1937 the Ba.65 served in substantial numbers with the Italian legionary air force fighting alongside the Nationalists in the Spanish Civil War. However, it was used only for reconnaissance missions during that conflict.

By the time Italy joined World War II in June 1940, the Italian air force had 154 Ba.65s in front-line service. They were used mainly in North Africa, but their poor manoeuvrability and lack of speed made them easy prey for Allied fighters.

Left: Portugal took delivery of 10 two-seat Ba.65s, powered by Fiat radials and fitted with the Breda L turret, in November 1939.

Above: The basic Ba.65 was a single-seater, and was intended for interceptor, light bomber and attack/reconnaissance roles.

Ba.65/A.80

Type: single-seat ground-attack aircraft

Powerplant: one 746-kW Fiat (1,000-hp.) A.80 RC41 18-cylinder air-cooled radial engine

Maximum level speed: 430 km/h (267 m.p.h.)

Range: 550 km (340 mi.)

Service ceiling: 6300 m (20,660 ft.)

Weights: empty equipped 2400 kg (5,280 lb.); maximum take-off 2950 kg (6,490 lb.)

Armament: two 12.7-mm (.50 cal.) and two 7.7-mm (.303 cal.) machine-guns, plus up to 500 kg of bombs in the internal bomb-bay and on wing racks

Dimensions:
span	12.10 m (36 ft. 8 in.)
length	9.30 m (30 ft. 6 in.)
height	3.20 m (10 ft. 6 in.)
wing area	23.50 m² (253 sq. ft.)

Initial examples of the Ba.65 were single-seaters, but most were two-seaters with an observer/gunner and machine-gun in the rear cockpit.

An internal fuselage bomb-bay usually carried 300 kg (660 lb.) of bombs; an additional 200 kg (440 lb.) was carried on wing racks. A maximum load of 1000 kg (2,200 lb.) was theoretically possible.

BA.65

No. 5 (Fighter) Squadron of the Iraqi air force, formed in 1938, was equipped with Ba.65s. They were among a number of Italian aircraft delivered in the late 1930s, including Savoia-Marchetti SM.79s.

This Ba.65 is a Fiat-engined example, like the bulk of production aircraft. The first 81 delivered to the Regia Aeronautica employed 522-kW (700-hp.) French Gnome-Rhône K-14 radials. Chile's 20 examples were powered by Piaggio P.XI C.40s.

A conventional cantilever low-wing monoplane, the Ba.65 had a fuselage and wing structure of chrome-molybdenum steel alloy tubing covered with Duralumin sheet, except for the trailing edges of the wing which were fabric-covered. The wing incorporated trailing-edge flaps and Handley Page leading-edge slats. The single fin and rudder were strut- and wire-braced.

ACTION DATA

MAXIMUM SPEED

Although the Ba.65 was appreciably faster than similar types like the Ju 87 (by more than 100 km/h/60 m.p.h.) and was able to carry heavier bombloads, it suffered at the hands of more agile Allied fighters in the North African campaign.

BA.65/A.80	430 km/h (267 m.p.h.)
Ju 87A-1	320 km/h (198 m.p.h.)
Hs 123A-1	341 km/h (211 m.p.h.)

RANGE

Breda Ba.65s lacked the range of the Junkers Ju 87 and Henschel Hs 123. This limited their operational usefulness when deployed against British and Allied forces in North Africa. However, the type could carry a much larger load.

BA.65/A.80 550 km (340 mi.)

Ju 87A-1 1000 km (952 mi.)

Hs 123A-1 860 km (535 mi.)

ARMAMENT

Compared to contemporary attack types, the Ba.65/A.80 was defensively well-armed, with four forward-firing machine-guns. To defend the rear of the aircraft, later versions had a rearward-facing gun. This was turret-mounted in some examples.

BA.65/A.80
2 x 12.7-mm (.50 cal.) machine-guns
2 x 7.7-mm (.303 cal.) machine-guns
500-kg (1,100-l.b) bombload

Ju 87A-1
2 x 7.9-mm (0.31-in.) machine-guns
250-kg (550-lb.) bombload

Hs 123A-1
2 x 7.9-mm (0.31-in.) machine-guns
200-kg (440-lb.) bombload

Breda designs of the 1920s, 1930s and 1940s

■ **A 7:** This two-seat, parasol-winged monoplane served in small numbers with Italian air force reconnaissance units from 1929.

■ **Ba 27:** This fighter, which resembled the Boeing P-26, flew in 1934. Its metal structure led to the nickname *Metallico* (Metal One).

■ **Ba 88 LINCE:** Originally a speed record-breaking aircraft, the Lince (Lynx) suffered severely impaired performance in military trim.

■ **Ba 201:** Evaluated during 1941, the Ba.201 single-seat dive-bomber was first thought to be a licence-built Junkers Ju 87.

BREGUET

690

● Little-known World War II bomber ● Early Breguet monoplane

I n October 1934 the French air ministry issued a specification for a new fighter. As well as serving as a two-seat day or night-fighter, it was to be capable of carrying the commander of a fighter formation. The Breguet 690 prototype was rejected because it was more than 1000 kg (2,200 lb.) heavier than the maximum 3500 kg (7,700 lb.) specified. Despite its weight, though, it was faster than its rivals and was subsequently developed as the 691 two-seat attack aircraft.

▲ One of the best French aircraft at the outbreak of World War II, the Breguet 690, originally designed as a fighter, ended up as an attack aircraft. Built in three major versions, its operational career was cut short by the Nazi occupation of France.

BREGUET 690

Quick into service ▶
By May 1940 several units, mainly belonging to Groupement 18, were equipped with the Bre. 693.

▼ Beaufighter forerunner
A trio of Bre. 693s in flight illustrate the distinctive lines, reminiscent of the later Bristol heavy fighter.

▼ Franco-American Breguet
More powerful Pratt & Whitney Twin Wasp radials marked the Breguet 695. This variant was the last major production version and entered service in 1940. In all 50 were built and they ended up being operated by GBA 151 of the Armée de l'Air Armistice (Vichy French Air Force) until late 1942.

▲ Italian trainers
In 1943 the few 690s that remained were transferred to the Regia Aeronautica in Italy for use as operational trainers.

Rush order ▶
Built to a Triplace de Chasse (three-seat fighter) specification, the first Breguet 690 was a very clean-looking aircraft when it was rolled out in April 1938. Before it had even flown, a production order for 100 examples was given by the French air ministry.

FACTS AND FIGURES

➤ Although design of the 690 began in 1935, the prototype did not fly until 1937, because of a lack of suitable engines.

➤ The change from the fighter to ground attack role resulted in the 691.

➤ Engines could be removed, overhauled and replaced in one hour 30 minutes.

➤ The second major variant, the 693, was powered by Gnome-Rhône engines instead of Hispano Suizas fitted to 691s.

➤ Production ceased when German forces over-ran the factory at Villacoublay.

➤ Breguet 695s, despite more powerful engines, were not popular with pilots.

Promising attack bomber

A fter making its first flight in March 1938, the Breguet 690 was ordered for the French air force as the 691-AB2 attack bomber. Early models had 522-kW (700-hp.) Hispano-Suiza 14AB10/11 engines, but later aircraft of the 78 production run had 597-kW (800-hp.) 14AB12/13s.

In 1940 the 691 version was superseded in production by the 693, which was fitted with 522-kW (700-hp.) Gnome-Rhône 14M6/7 engines. About 130 were built before the German occupation, along with 33 examples of the 695, which was powered by 615-kW (825-hp.) Pratt & Whitney Twin Wasp Juniors. Breguet had also produced a new fighter design, the 692, to meet a two-seat fighter specification issued at the end of 1936. This was then developed as the 697 and the intended production version, designated the Breguet 700, would have been armed with two cannon and two or four machine-guns.

Two prototypes were ordered, and there were plans to start production of the 700 alongside the 693 and 695 attack aircraft, but these were halted by the German invasion of May 1940. Subsequently, some of the 693s and 695s captured by the Germans were transferred to Italy and used by the Italian air force as crew trainers.

Above: A clean, squat fuselage, mid-mounted wing and twin tails were distinctive 690 features.

An endearing feature of the 693, especially to the technicians, was its ease of maintenance. An entire engine could be removed, overhauled and quickly replaced.

Fabric-covered metal control surfaces were a feature of the 690. In flight the aircraft had pleasant handling and was quite agile for its size.

A simple and rugged structure meant that the Bre. 693 could sustain heavy battle damage and still return to base. This was demonstrated on several occasions.

Bre.693

Type: two-seat attack bomber

Powerplant: two 522-kW (700-hp.) Gnome-Rhône 14M-6/7 radial engines

Maximum speed: 490 km/h (304 m.p.h.)

Cruising speed: 299 km/h (185 m.p.h.)

Range: 1350 km (837 mi.)

Service ceiling: 5000 m (16,400 ft.) (est.)

Weights: empty 3010 kg (6,622 lb.); loaded 4900 kg (10,780 lb.)

Armament: one 20-mm (0.79-in.) Hispano Suiza cannon and three 7.5-mm (0.3-in.) Darne machine guns plus up to 400 kg (880 lb.) of bombs

Dimensions:
span	15.73 m (51 ft. 7 in.)
length	9.67 m (31 ft. 9 in.)
height	3.19 m (10 ft. 5 in.)
wing area	29.20 m² (314 sq. ft.)

BRE 693

This aircraft belonged to GBA (Groupe Bombardement d'Assaut) II/54. Based at Roye during May 1940, this unit flew sorties against the advancing Germans in the Tongeren area.

A single-seat cockpit was located in the nose. Pilots enjoyed flying the 693 which was remarkably capable in the air, especially at low level. This performance was improved by the substitution of more reliable engines.

Production attack bombers had the navigator's station replaced by a small internal bomb bay which could accommodate 50-kg (108-lb.) bombs.

Located just behind the wing was a second cockpit for a gunner/radio operator who had a single 7.5-mm (0.3-in.) MAC machine-gun for defence. The two fuselage mainframes separated the crew compartments.

Aircraft flying with the Armée de l'Air carried their unit colours on the rear fuselage. Breguet 693 No. 1013 of GBA II/54 wore these very distinctive markings in June 1940.

COMBAT DATA

MAXIMUM SPEED

Despite the excellent performance of the Breguet 690, the French air ministry selected the Potez 63 instead; the latter aircraft proved less effective in combat although it was marginally faster. The Messerschmitt Bf 110 was primarily a fighter and thus quicker.

BREGUET 693 490 km/h (304 m.p.h.)

POTEZ 63 440 km/h (273 m.p.h.)

MESSERSCHMITT Bf 110C 562 km/h (348 m.p.h.)

RANGE

A problem that plagued the Luftwaffe was the inadequate range of its fighters, including the Bf 110. This gave them little combat time over enemy territory. French aircraft such as the Breguet 690 and Potez 63 had a much greater radius of action.

BREGUET 693 1350 km (837 mi.)

POTEZ 63 1500 km (930 mi.)

Bf 110C 850 km (527 mi.)

ARMAMENT

Armament was crucial to the survivability of bombers during World War II. The Potez 63 had no hard-hitting cannon and many of these aircraft were easily shot down by German fighters in 1940. Bre. 690s proved to be tougher opposition.

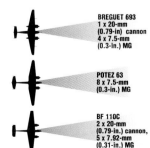

BREGUET 693 1 x 20-mm (0.79-in) cannon 4 x 7.5-mm (0.3-in.) MG

POTEZ 63 8 x 7.5-mm (0.3-in.) MG

BF 110C 2 x 20-mm (0.79-in.) cannon, 5 x 7.92-mm (0.31-in.) MG

Breguet 690 operators

■ **ARMÉE DE L'AIR:** Belonging to Groupement 18, this was one of many 690s on strength that braved the German onslaught in May 1940. These aircraft were based at La Ferte Gaucher.

■ **ARMÉE DE L'AIR ARMISTICE:** Remaining aircraft were assigned to newly formed Vichy units in late 1940. This Pratt & Whitney engined Bre. 695 flew with GBA 1/51 at Lezignan.

■ **REGIA AERONAUTICA:** When the Germans took total control of France in 1942, the few remaining Bre. 690s were transferred to Italy. These only served until the armistice in 1943.

BRISTOL

BLENHEIM MK IV

● Twin-engined light bomber ● European, Asian and Middle Eastern service

Its performance was startling in the early 1930s, but the Blenheim proved inadequate for the demands of World War II combat. By 1941 the bomber was clearly obsolescent, but it had been designated a 'super-priority' type and thousands more were built. The Mk IV remained in service for a further two years with Bomber Command, and survived even longer in North Africa and the Far East. More than 600 were built in Canada, mainly for training.

▲ Despite its early obsolescence in its intended role, with its slow speed and modest weapon load, Blenheim production reached 3297. Some were built by Rootes and Avro.

BRISTOL BLENHEIM MK IV

▼ Groupe 'Lorraine'
Equipped with 21 Blenheim Mk IVs, this unit of Free French personnel operated in Syria and the Western Desert in 1941 and 1942. During six months in 1942, 388 day sorties were flown.

▲ RAF bomber of the early war years
An RAF Blenheim Mk IV was the first British aircraft to cross the German border, making a reconnaissance flight on 3 September 1939. The following day Blenheims made the first Bomber Command raids.

◄ Training in Canada
The bulk of Canadian-built Blenheims were engaged in training navigators and gunners for the duration of the war.

▼ Operational Training Units
Although they flew their last operations with Bomber Command in August 1942, Mk IVs continued to serve with training units.

◄ Mk IV formation
The nearest of these three Mk IVs has a Frazer-Nash remotely-controlled turret under the nose. This would normally carry two 7.7-mm (.303 cal.) Browning machine-guns to defend against attack from below.

FACTS AND FIGURES

➤ Ten Mk IVs were built in Finland in 1944 and undertook forestry and survey work until as late as 1956.

➤ Other wartime operators of the Mk IV included Finland, Greece and Portugal.

➤ One Mk IV was experimentally fitted with a radar in a hemispherical nose radome.

➤ The only surviving airworthy Blenheim is a Bolingbroke trainer restored to flying condition and based at Duxford.

➤ The intended replacement for the Mk IV, the Mk V was slower but better armed.

➤ Blenheim IV production accounted for just over half of all Blenheims made.

PROFILE

RAF light bomber veteran

After they had outlived their usefulness in Europe, RAF Blenheims were particularly active in the Middle East. Despite their turrets, they were no match for enemy fighters.

One of the main drawbacks of the Blenheim Mk I was its very cramped navigator's compartment. A new nose with improved accommodation was one of the principal improvements offered by the Mk IV, which replaced the Mk I in production from late 1938.

All but the first 80 Mk IVs had more powerful engines and additional fuel tanks in the wings, which improved their range. Deliveries to RAF squadrons started in March 1939, and after World War II began some were fitted with rear-firing machine-guns in a remotely-controlled turret under the nose. A fighter variant had a four-gun pack under the fuselage.

Blenheim Mk IVs carried out the RAF's first bombing raid of the war, and from late 1940 flew many missions over Germany. There was also a Mk V (briefly known as the Bisley), which was even slower than the earlier models but was used by 10 RAF squadrons in North Africa and the Far East.

Mark IVs were built under licence in Finland, and more than 600 were produced in Canada under the name Bolingbroke. Most were completed as navigation and gunnery trainers; others could be fitted with ski landing gear and used for maritime reconnaissance duties.

Although painted to resemble a Blenheim Mk IV, the only Blenheim that is still airworthy is, in fact, a Bolingbroke Mk IV-T trainer.

Blenheim Mk IV

Type: three-seat light bomber

Powerplant: two 675-kW (905-hp.) Bristol Mercury XV nine-cylinder air-cooled radial piston engines

Maximum speed: 428 km/h (265 m.p.h.) at 3595 m (11,800 ft.)

Range: 2350 km (1,460 mi.)

Service ceiling: 8310 m (27,250 ft.)

Weights: empty 4441 kg (9,770 lb.); loaded 6532 kg (14,370 lb.)

Armament: five 7.7-mm (.303 cal.) machine-guns and 579 kg (1,274 lb.) of bombs

Dimensions:
span	17.17 m (58 ft. 4 in.)
length	12.98 m (42 ft. 7 in.)
height	3.00 m (9 ft. 10 in.)
wing area	43.57 m² (469 sq. ft.)

BOLINGBROKE MK IV

Aircraft 9140 carries the maritime patrol markings of No. 115(BR) Squadron, Royal Canadian Air Force (RCAF), with which it operated from Patricia Bay, British Columbia, in August 1943.

The Blenheim/Bolingbroke's three crew consisted of a pilot, navigator/observer and a gunner for the dorsal turret.

Most 'long-nosed' Blenheims were fitted with a dorsal turret, containing two 7.7-mm (.303 cal.) machine-guns, for self-defence. Late-build Mk IVs had a remotely-controlled Frazer-Nash aft-firing, two-gun turret beneath the nose.

In Canada the Fairchild Aircraft Company built 676 Blenheim IVs. Those with RCAF serials 9001 to 9201 were constructed with American instruments and equipment and were known as Bolingbroke Mk IVs.

Due to the harsh winter conditions, Bolingbroke Mk IVs were fitted with de-icing boots on their wings and tail surfaces.

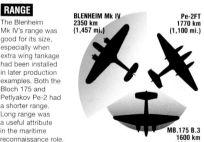

The tried and tested Bristol Mercury nine-cylinder radial powered most Blenheims, although when engine supplies from England were under threat a small number were built in Canada with Pratt & Whitney Twin Wasp Juniors as the Bolingbroke Mk IV-W.

The small fuselage bomb-bay of the Mk IV bombers had a 454-kg (1,000-lb.) capacity. A further 145 kg (320 lb.) could be carried under the wings. The Bolingbrokes used for maritime patrol in Canada were equipped with dinghies.

The markings carried by home-based RCAF units were often at variance with those employed by RAF aircraft in the same role. This aircraft has an unusually small roundel on the fuselage and has its serial number painted under the port wing.

A single Bolingbroke Mk III was fitted with Edo floats for evaluation, but was later reconverted to a landplane.

COMBAT DATA

MAXIMUM SPEED

One of the main handicaps facing the Blenheim was its relatively slow top speed. It was at least 100 km/h slower than other light bombers of the period. Fighter speeds increased markedly within a short space of time in the early years of the war and rendered bombers like these, which appeared to be fast enough when they were designed, outdated.

BLENHEIM Mk IV	428 km/h (265 m.p.h.)
Pe-2FT	534 km/h (360 m.p.h.)
MB.175 B.3	540 km/h (335 m.p.h.)

RANGE

The Blenheim Mk IV's range was good for its size, especially when extra wing tankage had been installed in later production examples. Both the Bloch 175 and Petlyakov Pe-2 had a shorter range. Long range was a useful attribute in the maritime reconnaissance role.

BLENHEIM Mk IV 2350 km (1,457 mi.)

Pe-2FT 1770 km (1,100 mi.)

MB.175 B.3 1600 km (995 mi.)

ARMAMENT

In addition to its speed disadvantage, the Blenheim suffered from a shortage of defensive guns. The Pe-2 was not only fast, but was well armed. Even the Bloch 175 boasted nine guns and an equivalent bombload to the Blenheim.

BLENHEIM Mk IV	Pe-2FT	MB.175 B.3
5 x 7.7-mm (.303 cal.) machine-guns 579-kg (1,284-lb.) bombload	2 x 20-mm (0.79-in.) cannon 2 x 12.7-mm (.50 cal.) machine-guns 2 x 7.62-mm (.30 cal.) machine-guns 1000-kg (2,200-lb.) bombload	2 x 20-mm (0.79-in.) cannon 7 x 17.5-mm (0.69-in.) machine-guns 600-kg (1,320-lb.) bombload

Blenheims at war

FIRST BOMBER COMMAND RAIDS: On 4 September 1939 Blenheim Mk IVs of Nos 107 and 110 Squadrons made a raid on the German fleet at Schillig Roads.

IN THE WESTERN DESERT: Although vulnerable to fighter attack, Blenheims were employed by Middle East Command against Axis ground forces in the early 1940s.

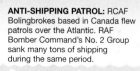

ANTI-SHIPPING PATROL: RCAF Bolingbrokes based in Canada flew patrols over the Atlantic. RAF Bomber Command's No. 2 Group sank many tons of shipping during the same period.

BRISTOL

BEAUFIGHTER

● Rocket-armed fighter ● Anti-shipping ● Torpedo strike

Dubbed 'Whispering Death' by the Japanese, the heavily-armed Bristol Beaufighter could be tricky to handle, especially in low-speed flight. It was nevertheless one of the most lethal warplanes of its era and was a Royal Air Force stalwart in the battle against Germany's night offensive over Britain. The powerful, slab-winged Beaufighter went on to become one of the most potent anti-shipping strike aircraft of the war.

▲ Beaufighter crews had great confidence in their aircraft, which had a combination of long range, fair speed, massive strength and the heaviest gun armament of any Allied fighter.

BRISTOL **BEAUFIGHTER**

▲ New tail
The early Beaufighters experienced some instability when carrying a torpedo, but this was corrected by fitting a dihedral tailplane. The Beaufighter proved to be a very stable weapon launching platform.

▲ Rocket raid
Armed with eight rockets, the Beaufighter blasted coastal targets throughout Norway.

▲ Bristol factory
Over 5500 Beaufighters were built, not only by the Bristol Aeroplane Company, but also at factories in Australia.

Radar nose ▶
The TF.Mk X version carried a nose thimble centimetric radar for detecting surface ships. It was the first radome fairing ever fitted to an aircraft.

▲ Torpedo bomber
By 1944, many Beaufighters were used as anti-shipping torpedo aircraft. They brought German coastal shipping in Europe to a standstill.

FACTS AND FIGURES

➤ The first 50 Beaufighters built claimed 60 aerial victories in night battles over Britain in 1941.

➤ The Beaufighter prototype's maiden flight took place on 17 July 1939.

➤ First flight of a Merlin-powered Beaufighter occurred on 26 July 1940.

➤ RAF Beaufighters attacked Japanese forces at Myitkyina in occupied Burma on the Emperor's birthday.

➤ Australian Beaufighters sank more than 700 Japanese vessels in 1945.

➤ Between 1939 and 1944, a total of 5564 Beaufighters were manufactured.

PROFILE

The 'Whispering Death'

A snub-nosed battleship of a plane which first appeared in 1939, the twin-engined Beaufighter was immensely strong and surprisingly manoeuvrable. Although early Hercules-engined Beaufighters were a little underpowered, the more powerful engines of later models made them fast and snappy.

The Beaufighter was roomy enough to carry the bulky first generation of AI (airborne intercept) radar, and when radar-equipped fighters joined the RAF, they became a strong reason for the Luftwaffe abandoning its night assaults on London.

Eventually, the 'Beau' fought on all fronts. Rockets were added to the type's potent gun armament in 1943 and in combination with air-launched torpedoes made the beefy aircraft a superb long-range fighter, fighter-bomber and anti-shipping machine. Beaufighters destroyed German shipping running down the coast from Norway. Australian Beaufighters did a similar job with Japanese shipping, and it was their victims that gave the aircraft the name 'Whispering Death', a reference to the distinctive noise made by the sleeve-valve radial engine.

Left: When all eight rockets were fired at once, the effect was devastating. A rocket salvo was equivalent to the broadside from a cruiser's main guns.

Above: Beaufighters were formed into specialised strike wings, with a mixture of torpedo- and rocket-armed aircraft able to destroy any target at sea.

Beaufighter TF.Mk X

Type: two-seat low-level strike fighter

Powerplant: two 1320-kW (1,770-hp.) Bristol Hercules XVIII radial piston engines

Maximum speed: 488 km/h (330 m.p.h.) at 400 m (1,312 ft.)

Range: 2366 km (1,470 mi.)

Service ceiling: 4570 m (29,000 ft.)

Weights: empty 7076 kg (15,507 lb.); loaded 11,431 kg (25,200 lb.)

Armament: six forward-firing 7.7-mm (.303 cal.) machine-guns and one flexible 7.7-mm Vickers 'K' machine-gun in dorsal position, four forward-firing 20-mm (0.79-in.) cannon, plus one torpedo and two 113-kg (230-lb.) bombs or eight 41-kg (90-lb.) air-to-surface rockets

Dimensions:
span	17.63 m (58 ft.)
length	12.70 m (42 ft.)
height	4.83 m (16 ft.)
wing area	46.73 m² (503 sq. ft.)

BEAUFIGHTER MK VI

The Beaufighter Mk VI was the first of the type to be supplied to the US Army Air Force (USAAF), serving in the Middle East and Mediterranean with the 1st Tactical Air Command.

The observer's rear bubble could mount a single Vickers 'K' machine-gun for defence. The rear fuselage contained a store of food and water for emergency survival.

The tail was modified in the Beaufighter Mk II because the liquid-cooled Merlin engine caused the aircraft's centre of gravity to change, leading to instability problems.

The Hercules radial was a solid and reliable design, which had 'sleeve valves' that were built around the sides of the engine cylinders.

A tough wing was another great strength of the Beaufighter design, which was able to carry rocket rails or a 113-kg (250-lb.) bomb. It could also survive heavy combat damage.

Crew entered the Beaufighter through hatches in the underside of the fuselage. These could also be used as an emergency exit, in addition to a knock-out window in the canopy.

KV912

COMBAT DATA

RANGE

The Ju 88 was designed as a bomber and had long range. The Pe-2 was originally intended as a long-range fighter like the Bf 110; it could fly further than most single-seat fighters but not as far as dedicated long-range strike aircraft. The Beaufighter's performance was somewhere between the two, with good range for a strike aircraft.

BEAUFIGHTER TF.Mk X 2366 km (1,470 mi.)
Ju 88A-4 2730 km (1,693 mi.)
Pe-2 bis 1160 km (719 mi.)

MAXIMUM SPEED

The Beaufighter was not powerful enough to outrun single-engined fighters, but it could hold its own with a Bf 110 or Ju 88. The Pe-2 was a much faster machine, but mainly because it carried less fuel and had a sleeker design.

BEAUFIGHTER TF.Mk X 488 km/h (330 m.p.h.)
Ju 88C-2 470 km/h (291 m.p.h.)
Pe-2 bis 540 km/h (334 m.p.h.)

ATTACK ARMAMENT

The Beaufighter had devastating armament, more powerful than its contemporaries. Although its bombload was comparatively low on paper, it rarely acted as a bomber. The single torpedo or eight rockets were more than capable of destroying a ship.

BEAUFIGHTER TF.Mk X
4 x 20-mm (0.79-in.) cannon; 6 x 7.7-mm (.303 cal.) MGs, 500-kg (1,100-lb.) bombload

Ju 88C-2
3 x 20-mm (0.79-in.) cannon; 3 x 7.92-mm (0.31-in.) MGs, 1000-kg (2,200-lb.) bombload

Pe-2 bis
1 x 20-mm (0.79-in.) cannon; 1 x 12.7-mm (.50 cal.) MG; 2 x 7.62-mm (.30 cal.) MGs 1000-kg (2,200-lb.) bombload

Beaufighter variants

■ **BEAUFIGHTER Mk I:** The first Beaufighters were used as night-fighters and long-range strike fighters. They fought with distinction in North Africa and in the Mediterranean.

■ **BEAUFIGHTER Mk II:** Shortages of the Bristol Hercules radial engine meant that the Beaufighter Mk II was refitted with the Rolls-Royce Merlin. All Mk IIs served as night-fighters.

■ **TORPEDO BEAUFIGHTER Mk VI:** The first torpedo Beaufighter, known as a 'Torbeau', was the Mk VI. This used uprated Bristol Hercules VI engines and could carry bombs.

■ **TF.Mk X IN USAAF:** The TF.Mk X was one of the only British aircraft used by the USAAF in World War II. The earlier Mk VI had also been used by them in the Middle East.

■ **AUSTRALIAN Mk 21:** The Beaufighter Mk 21 was basically an Australian-built TF.Mk X, performing anti-shipping strike missions with the aid of its own nose-mounted radar.

CAPRONI BERGAMASCHI

CA 310 SERIES

● Developed from a transport plane ● Nearly bought by the RAF

Seeking to improve the military potential of the Ca 309, which had been used operationally in North Africa, Caproni Bergamaschi developed the Ca 310 Libeccio (south-west wind). The aircraft was highly impressive in the pre-war years and attracted significant foreign orders, including 300 from Great Britain and 200 from France. However, the onset of World War II meant the aircraft were diverted to the Italian air force, which had already ordered significant numbers.

▲ A light bomber and reconnaissance aircraft, the Ca 310 was developed in parallel with the Ca 309, but featured a retractable undercarriage and slightly more powerful engines.

▼ Order cancelled
Count Gianni Caproni sought to export his design and for a time it looked like the RAF would purchase the type. Italy's entry into the war put an end to this potentially lucrative order.

▲ Fighting for Franco
Despite being overshadowed by more famous types, the Ca 310 nevertheless took part in the Spanish Civil War during the late 1930s.

Low production ▶
The first flight of the Ca 310 took place in February 1937. A total of only 161 of this variant was built, followed by small numbers of sub-types, culminating in the Ca 316.

◀ South-west winds in Africa
Wearing Italian civil registrations, this group of Libeccios is seen being guarded by a local tribesman in Libya. Civilian Ca 310s were operated extensively in the Italian colonies in Africa during the years leading up to World War II.

Spanish colours ▶
Ca 310s delivered to Nationalist Spanish units wore a distinctive mottled-green and brown camouflage. This one served with 15th Escuadrilla of Grupo 18, Spanish Nationalist air force.

FACTS AND FIGURES

➤ Ca 310 series aircraft were exported to Croatia, France, Germany, Norway, Sweden, Hungary and Yugoslavia.

➤ Fitted with Piaggio C.35 radial engines, the Ca 310 first flew on 20 February 1937.

➤ Hungarian aircraft were returned to Italy for service with the Regia Aeronautica.

➤ Spruce wood was used in construction of the wings, but the outbreak of war resulted in supplies being reduced.

➤ Ca 311s, 313s and 314s continued in service after Italy capitulated in 1943.

➤ A Ca 313G (for Germany) took approximately 23,000 man-hours to build.

Multi-role Italian twin

Improving on the Ca 309 by adding retractable landing gear and more powerful engines produced one of Italy's most versatile warplanes of World War II. First flying in 1937, the Ca 310 was destined to fly bombing, reconnaissance, anti-shipping, ground-attack, transport and training missions throughout the war.

In its original version the Ca 310 flew with the air forces of Norway, Peru, Yugoslavia and Italy and was tested as a civil transport with twin floats.

By the outbreak of World War II the aircraft had been developed into a number of improved variants. The Ca 311 had an extensively glazed nose for bomb aiming and reconnaissance. This was followed by the Ca 312 which had more powerful Piaggio engines and was ordered by Belgium and Norway, although these aircraft were not delivered before the German invasion.

French and British interest centred on the Ca 313, which also served with Sweden in such varied roles as transport and torpedo bomber. The more powerfully armed Ca 314 was the final and most important variant in the Italian air force. It was built in a number of sub-variants including the Ca 314C, which carried two additional 12.7-mm (.50 cal.) machine-guns for ground-attack duties.

Left: Despite the Ca 310's low-wing configuration, the undercarriage featured long, stalky oleo legs.

Right: Deliveries to the Regia Aeronautica began in 1937 and were completed some two years later. The most extensively built version of the Libeccio family was the Ca 314 convoy escort and patrol aircraft, fitted with in-line engines.

Ca 314A

Type: convoy escort and maritime patrol aircraft

Powerplant: two 544-kW (730-hp.) Isotta-Franschini Delta RC 35 in-line piston engines

Maximum speed: 365 km/h (245 m.p.h.)

Cruising speed: 320 km/h (198 m.p.h.)

Range: 1690 km (1,048 mi.)

Service ceiling: 6400 m (21,000 ft.)

Weights: empty 4560 kg (10,032 lb.); loaded 6620 kg (14,564 lb.)

Armament: two 12.7-mm (.50 cal.) machine-guns in the wings and one 7.7-mm (.303 cal.) gun in a dorsal turret, plus up to 320 kg (705 lb.) of bombs

Dimensions:
span	16.65 m (54 ft. 7 in.)
length	11.80 m (38 ft. 8 in.)
height	3.70 m (12 ft. 2 in.)
wing area	39.20 m² (422 sq. ft.)

Ca 310 LIBECCIO

Prior to the outbreak of World War II, the Ca 310 enjoyed some export success. Norway was one nation which purchased four aircraft. These were all destroyed during the German invasion in 1940.

On top of the fuselage was a single turret, housing just one 7.7-mm (.303 cal.) machine-gun. Like many Italian aircraft, the weakness of the Libeccio lay in its poor defensive armament and slow speed. The Norwegian machines suffered severely at the hands of Luftwaffe fighters.

In service, the Libeccio series had more than its fair share of problems. Leaking hydraulics and unreliable electrics were notable among these and the aircraft was prone to catching fire. However, it was also a sturdy machine and could absorb a tremendous amount of punishment.

Depending on the variant, various engines could be specified. Ca 310s were powered by twin 350-kW (470-hp.) Piaggio P.VII C.35 radial engines driving two-bladed, variable-pitch propellers.

Tall undercarriage oleos gave the Ca 310 a dramatic raked stance on the ground. These retracted rearward into the engine nacelles with the tyres remaining exposed to facilitate 'belly' landings.

Fabric was used quite extensively in the construction of the Ca 310, particularly on the control surfaces. Many air arms which acquired the type bedecked their aircraft with large national insignia or flashes on the rudder.

COMBAT DATA

MAXIMUM SPEED

Italian aircraft of World War II, especially bombers, were seldom known for their high performance. Exceptions to the rule were the S.M.79 and the large four-engined Piaggio P.108B.

Ca 310 LIBECCIO	365 km/h (226 m.p.h.)
P.108B	429 km/h (266 m.p.h.)
S.M.79-1	429 km/h (266 m.p.h.)

OPERATIONAL RANGE

Despite their other shortcomings, these three aircraft had decent endurance, a factor much needed in the Mediterranean theatre. With only a small number built, Ca 310s did not feature prominently in the air campaign, unlike the excellent SIAI-Marchetti S.M.79s.

Ca 310 LIBECCIO 1649 km (1,022 mi.)

P.108B 3519 km (2,182 mi.)

S.M.79-1 1899 km (1,177 mi.)

BOMBLOAD

Most Italian bombers, such as the Ca 310, were limited by small bomb loads, though the P.108B could carry up to 3500 kg (7,700 lb.) if required. The S.M.79 was most often used as a torpedo bomber.

Ca 310 LIBECCIO 400 kg (880 lb.)	P.108B 3500 kg (7,700 lb.)	S.M.79-1 1250 kg (2,750 lb.)

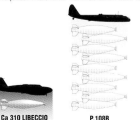

Italian bombers of World War II

FIAT BR.20 CICOGNA: Blessed with decent performance, the BR.20 Cicogna (Stork) had the distinction of being the only mass-produced, Italian twin-engined bomber of World War II.

CANT Z.1007: One of several three-engined designs, the Z.1007 Alcione (Kingfisher) was marred by lack of a suitable powerplant and a weak structure, which was prone to deforming.

SIAI MARCHETTI S.M.81 PIPISTRELLO: A forerunner of the more famous S.M.79 Sparrowhawk, this sturdy aeroplane was used extensively as a bomber/transport in the Mediterranean theatre.

CONSOLIDATED

PB2Y CORONADO

● Maritime reconnaissance ● Anti-shipping ● Transport

▲ This PB2Y has had its armament removed and was used in the transport role. The specialist PB2Y-5H was used as a casualty evacuation aircraft with accommodation for 25 stretchers.

S oon after Consolidated's famous PBY Catalina had flown, plans were drawn up to build a larger maritime patrol flying-boat with a greater weapons capacity and higher speed. The resulting XPB2Y-1 competed successfully against the Sikorsky XPBS-1 and after a number of modifications it entered production as the PB2Y Coronado. The type saw limited service in World War II with the US Navy and 10 examples were used by the RAF, mainly as transports.

CONSOLIDATED PB2Y CORONADO

▼ **Experimental squadron**
All six PB4Y-2s built were operated by VP-13 Squadron, US Navy, for experimental duties. Each could carry 5443 kg of bombs.

◄ **Principal production version**
The US Navy procured a total of 210 PBY-3s which were used in the Pacific theatre. These are early examples without radar.

Single-fin prototype ►
In competition with the Sikorsky XPBS-1, the XPB2Y-1 first flew in December 1937 and was regarded as the more suitable aircraft for production. A lack of lateral stability was rectified by replacing the single fin with two endplates.

▼ **Lend-lease Coronado**
Ten PB2Y-3Bs were diverted to the RAF as Coronado GR.Mk Is. After brief service with Coastal Command they were used as transports with No. 231 Squadron.

▲ **Searching for ships**
Later-model PB2Ys were fitted with a dorsal Air to Surface Vessel (ASV) radar. This could detect targets in bad weather or at night.

FACTS AND FIGURES

➤ Named XPB2Y-1, the Coronado prototype first flew on 17 December 1937, powered by Pratt & Whitney XR-1830-72 engines.

➤ With five defensive gun positions, a crew of nine was needed to man the PB2Y.

➤ The PB2Y-3R transport version featured faired-over turrets and R-1830-88 engines.

➤ The first squadron to operate the Coronado was VP-13, which received its first PB2Y-2 on 31 December 1940.

➤ The PB2Y-3 featured self-sealing fuel tanks and protective armour.

➤ Production PB2Ys had a much deeper hull than the prototype to improve handling.

PROFILE

Patrol boat from San Diego

Left: A number of PB2Y-3s were converted to PB2Y-5 standard. Alterations included fitting more powerful R-1830-92 engines, increased fuel capacity and provision for RATO (rocket-assisted take-off) gear.

With heavy defensive armament, long range and a large weapons load the PB2Y had the potential to be one of the US Navy's most important patrol flying-boats of World War II. However, production preference was given to the twin-engined PBY Catalina of which thousands were built compared to a mere 226 production PB2Ys.

The prototype, designated XPB2Y-1, underwent evaluation in early 1938 and was selected over the XPBS-1, but a number of shortcomings needed to be addressed before production could begin. The most serious problem was lateral instability which was solved by modifying the tail unit. The tailplane was given significant dihedral, and endplates similar to those on the B-24 bomber were fitted. The nose profile was also changed to a more rounded appearance.

The main production version was the PB2Y-3, which saw little operational service during the War. Ten PB2Y-3Bs supplied to the RAF as Coronado GR.Mk Is were mostly used for hauling freight across the Atlantic.

Later versions were fitted with air to surface vessel (ASV) radar and other variants included the PB2Y-3R transport and the PB2Y-5H casevac aircraft. All Coronados had been withdrawn from service by VJ Day.

Above: This photograph shows the sharp dihedral of the Coronado's tailplane and its associated endplates. The aircraft were wheeled to the water using a trolley system.

PB2Y-3 Coronado

Type: long-range flying-boat patrol bomber

Powerplant: four 895-kW (1,200-hp.) Pratt & Whitney R-1830-88 Twin Wasp radial piston engines

Maximum speed: 359 km/h (223 m.p.h.) at 6095 m (20,000 ft.)

Range: 3814 km (2,365 mi.)

Service ceiling: 6250 m (20,500 ft.)

Weights: empty 18,568 kg (40,850 lb.); maximum take-off 30,844 kg (67,857 lb.)

Armament: two 12.7-mm (.50 cal.) machine-guns in each of bow, dorsal and tail turrets, and one 12.7-mm machine-gun in each of two beam positions, plus up to 5443 kg (11,975 lb.) of bombs, depth bombs or torpedoes in bomb bays

Dimensions:
span	35.05 m (115 ft.)
length	24.16 m (79 ft. 3 in.)
height	8.38 m (27 ft. 6 in.)
wing area	165.36 m² (1,780 sq. ft.)

To protect the PB2Y from enemy fighter attack the aircraft was equipped with nose, dorsal and tail turrets each with a pair of 12.7-mm (.50 cal.) machine-guns. Single 12.7-mm machine-guns were also fitted to the fuselage sides on flexible mounts.

The PB2Y-5 was fitted with more powerful R-1830-92 engines giving the aircraft much improved performance at low altitudes. The fuel capacity was also increased.

PB2Y-5 CORONADO

Little use was made of the PB2Y Coronado in World War II. This example was used mostly for transport purposes before it was retired along with the rest of the fleet in 1944-45.

After the single fin arrangement on the XPB2Y-1 was found to be inadequate, a new tail unit with rounded endplate fins was fitted. The fins and rudders were similar to the units fitted to the B-24 Liberator.

This PB2Y-5 shows a mixture of darker non-specular sea blue merging into pale grey-blue with white undersurfaces, the camouflage scheme carried by PB2Y-5s in the later stages of World War II.

A two-step hull provided the aircraft with good handling in water. The stabilising wingtip floats retracted to form the wingtips in flight.

COMBAT DATA

MAXIMUM SPEED

Although the H6K was an earlier design than the other two types it had the edge in speed. Speed was less important than endurance and to increase fuel economy all three types generally operated at a speed of about 250 km/h (155 m.p.h.).

PB2Y-3 CORONADO	**359 km/h (223 m.p.h.)**
H6K5 'MAVIS'	**385 km/h (238 m.p.h.)**
SUNDERLAND Mk V	**343 km/h (213 m.p.h.)**

ARMAMENT

The Coronado had a massive bombload compared to the other two types, making it capable of attacking more than one target. All three types had formidable defensive armament.

PB2Y-3 CORONADO 8 x 12.7-mm (.50 cal.) machine-guns 5443-kg (11,975-lb.) bombload	**H6K5 'MAVIS'** 4 x 7.7-mm (.303 cal.) machine-guns 1 x 20-mm cannon 1600-kg (3,520-lb.) bombload	**SUNDERLAND Mk V** 8 x 7.7-mm (.303 cal.) and 2 x 12.7-mm (.50 cal.) machine-guns 907-kg (2,000-lb.) bombload

RANGE

As the best flying-boat of the early years of World War II, the H6K had exceptional range, allowing it to operate deep into the Pacific Ocean on reconnaissance and anti-shipping missions. Both the Sunderland and the Coronado had modest range in comparison but could still operate 10-hour missions.

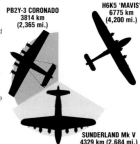

PB2Y-3 CORONADO 3814 km (2,365 mi.)

H6K5 'MAVIS' 6775 km (4,200 mi.)

SUNDERLAND Mk V 4329 km (2,684 mi.)

World War II maritime patrol aircraft

■ **CONSOLIDATED LIBERATOR:** Operated by both RAF Coastal Command and the US Navy, the Liberator helped close the 'U-boat gap' in the middle of the Atlantic Ocean.

■ **FOCKE-WULF Fw 200 CONDOR:** With unprecedented range, the Fw 200 was a major threat to Allied shipping in the early years of World War II.

■ **LOCKHEED HUDSON:** As the first US-built aircraft to be used operationally by the RAF in World War II, the Hudson filled an urgent requirement for a maritime patrol bomber.

■ **SHORT SUNDERLAND:** Operating in the Atlantic and the Pacific, the Sunderland flew reconnaissance sorties as well as anti-shipping and anti-submarine missions.

CONSOLIDATED

B-24 LIBERATOR

● Heavy bomber ● Long-range maritime patrol ● Transport

▲ The B-24 was a product of American bombing philosophy, which called for precision attacks from high altitude by well-defended aircraft using the Norden bombsight.

Consolidated's B-24 Liberator is often compared unfavourably to the more famous B-17 Flying Fortress. But the B-24 was newer, more efficient and much more versatile than the Boeing design; and with nearly 20,000 aircraft completed, more Liberators were built than any other military aircraft in American history. It was a good bomber, serving on every front, but its most valuable work may have been the war against the U-boats.

CONSOLIDATED B-24 LIBERATOR

◀ **Not so lucky**
After raiding southern Germany, this B-24 fought a running battle with Luftwaffe fighters all the way through Italy, crashing just after the crew bailed out.

▶ **Snarling beasts**
Garishly painted B-24s were used as 'lead ships', acting as markers on which the huge Eighth Air Force bomber formations would assemble before setting off on raids over Europe.

▲ **Blasted but alive**
Although not as strong as the B-17, the Liberator was tough enough to bring its crews home in spite of severe damage.

◀ **Nose turret**
Late-model B-24s, from the 'G' onward, were fitted with powered nose turrets after experience had shown that Luftwaffe fighter pilots often attacked head-on.

▼ **Tactical strike**
After the Allied landings in France in 1944, Liberators were used to bomb tactical targets in support of the advancing armies. Railways, bridges and troop concentrations were heavily attacked.

▼ **Work of art**
'Alley Cop' was the nickname for this B-24, which sported typically bright nose art. USAF bombers were rarely camouflaged after 1943, going into action in a natural metal finish.

FACTS AND FIGURES

➤ Liberators were manufactured by Consolidated, Douglas, Ford and North American.

➤ The all-silver B-24 prototype made its first flight on 29 January 1940.

➤ The Luftwaffe used a captured B-24 for special covert operations.

➤ A B-24 crew crashed near Gyantse in Tibet while flying over the Himalayas on a supply mission to China.

➤ Winston Churchill used a modified B-24 as his personal transport.

➤ 19,256 Liberators and Privateers were manufactured between 1940 and 1945.

America's long-range bomber

The B-24 Liberator was built around the Davis wing; a long, thin, large-area structure mounted high on the fuselage. Its twin bomb-bays used 'roller shutter' doors which retracted within the fuselage when opened, reducing drag. The twin tail, like the wing, was a Consolidated trademark. All this resulted in an excellent long-range bomber which had other applications; there were cargo, tanker, patrol, training and reconnaissance variants. Some were armed with even more guns as bomber escorts.

A B-24 caught on the ground at Hickam Field, Hawaii, on 7 December 1941 produced the first American casualties of the war. Liberators fought in the Pacific and China-Burma-India theatres. From the Middle East they attacked their most famous target – Romania's Ploesti oilfields. They also joined with the B-17 in the Eighth Air Force's three-year aerial campaign over Europe. The B-24 was never as popular with its crews as the B-17, as it was quicker to catch fire in battle

and sometimes suffered hydraulic problems, but it was in some ways a better aircraft, with more modern systems.

The mighty armada of B-24s went to pasture in just a few years. Soon after the war, Liberators began to disappear from the skies. Today, only a couple of surviving examples are airworthy.

Left: Although the Liberator did not carry as many bombs as some other Allied aircraft, it had exceptional performance and massive defensive armament.

Below: The need for tight formation flying was vital for daylight bombing, where mutual cover meant survival.

Some late-model B-24s could carry bombs on racks under the inner wing. Anti-submarine versions in RAF service carried rockets.

B-24D Liberator

Type: heavy bomber with a crew of 10

Powerplant: four 895-kW (1,200-hp.) Pratt & Whitney R-1830-43 Twin Wasp radial piston engines

Maximum speed: 488 km/h (300 m.p.h.)

Range: 2896 km (2,850 mi.)

Service ceiling: 9900 m (32,500 ft.)

Weights: empty 15,413 kg (34,000 lb.); maximum 27,216 kg (60,000 lb.)

Armament: one 12.7-mm (.50 cal.) nose gun (some with additional 12.7-mm fixed nose guns), two more each in dorsal turret, tail turret, retractable ball turret, and waist positions, plus maximum internal bombload of 3629 kg (8,800 lb.)

Dimensions:
span	33.52 m (110 ft.)
length	20.22 m (66 ft. 4 in.)
height	5.46 m (17 ft. 11 in.)
wing area	97.36 m² (1,048 sq. ft.)

B-24D LIBERATOR 'TEGGIE ANN'

'Teggie Ann' was the command ship for the 'Liberandos', the 376th Bomb Group. This unit was severely mauled following attacks on the Romanian oilfields at Ploesti in 1944.

The very-long-span wing gave the B-24 long range and excellent performance at high altitude.

USAF B-24s based in North Africa were painted in a desert pink camouflage.

The tricycle undercarriage was another modern feature of the B-24.

240664
100

The bombardier sat in the glazed nose compartment, aiming his bombs with a Norden sight.

100 TEGGIE ANN

The rear gunner fired a pair of 12.7-mm (.50 cal.) machine-guns from a powered turret. This was replaced by manually controlled guns in the B-24L.

The deep fuselage was designed to allow the 3600-kg (4-ton) bombload to be stored vertically, with a catwalk giving the crew access to the rear fuselage.

COMBAT DATA

MAXIMUM SPEED

The World War II generation of big four-engined bombers was reasonably fast by pre-war standards, but speed alone was never going to get them away from marauding enemy fighters. The American solution to survival was to fly in large formations that were able to bring hundreds of guns to bear on interceptors.

B-24D LIBERATOR	488 km/h (300 m.p.h.)
HALIFAX	500 km/h (310 m.p.h.)
He 177	472 km/h (290 m.p.h.)

BOMBLOAD

Although the B-24 had, like other American bombers, a smaller load on paper than its contemporaries, some variants could carry up to six tons of weaponry. The Heinkel, by contrast, rarely carried more than half its stated capacity, and sometimes much less. The B-24 could carry its load higher and farther.

B-24D LIBERATOR 3629 kg (8,800 lb.)
HALIFAX 5900 kg (13,000 lb.)
He 177 6000 kg (13,200 lb.)

SERVICE CEILING

American bomber tactics called for precision strikes from high altitude. The B-24 had a long, very efficient wing, together with extremely powerful turbocharged two-row radial engines, and it customarily operated at greater heights than its European rivals. This lessened its vulnerability to fighters in the Pacific, where Japanese aircraft had to struggle to reach such high operating altitudes.

9900 m (32,500 ft.)
7300 m (24,000 ft.)
7000 m (23,000 ft.)
HALIFAX
B-24D LIBERATOR
He 177

Closing the Atlantic Gap

BRITAIN'S SURVIVAL LIFELINE: Britain depended on America for war material and food to support its densely packed population, and those supplies came by convoy across the Atlantic.

CONVOY ESCORTS: Although most convoys were escorted by warships, the most effective weapon against the U-boat threat was continuous air cover.

THE ATLANTIC GAP: In the first years of conflict, aircraft lacked the range to cover the whole crossing, leaving a gap in the mid-Atlantic in which convoys were vulnerable.

WOLF PACKS: U-boats based in western France could be intercepted by British flying-boats in the first stage of their journeys, but once clear they were free to attack the convoys in mid-Atlantic.

CLOSING THE GAP: The deployment of very-long-range variants of the Liberator meant that the window of vulnerability was closed, and the U-boat menace was considerably reduced.

B-17 FLYING FORTRESS
SUNDERLAND
B-24 LIBERATOR
CONVOYS
U-BOATS

CONSOLIDATED
PBY CATALINA

● Amphibian and flying-boat ● Long-serving naval patrol bomber

I t was old when World War II began. It was slow and could be uncomfortable, but the Consolidated PBY Catalina was one of the classic designs; rarely has an aircraft proved so useful to so many people. A deadly adversary to an enemy submarine or warship, the PBY is better remembered as the angel of mercy which achieved thousands of rescues in all circumstances throughout the war.

▲ The Catalina operated in every theatre of the Pacific war, from the balmy southern waters to the frozen oceans of the North. This crew is seen in the Aleutians.

CONSOLIDATED PBY CATALINA

◄ Slow but sure
Although slow and cumbersome, the PBY was immensely tough and had a great range, essential for long maritime patrols.

Flight deck ►
On long missions, pilots might be expected to occupy the flight deck for up to 20 hours at a time.

▼ Shipboard operations
Catalinas often operated from seaplane tenders, being hoisted aboard by cranes for maintenance and restocking.

▲ Observation blisters ►
The large 'greenhouses' on each side of the rear fuselage could mount heavy machine-guns and were perfect for rear observation.

◄ Assisted take-off
The Catalina had good take-off performance, but for launching at high weights or in tight spots it could use strap-on rockets for extra boost.

FACTS AND FIGURES

➤ In October 1935 the Catalina prototype made a non-stop flight of 5633 km (3,500 mi.) from Coco Solo to San Francisco.

➤ In the 1930s, civil PBYs were used for scientific exploration of New Guinea and later the Indian Ocean.

➤ Over 1000 Catalinas were manufactured in Russia.

➤ The 'Black Cats' squadron hunted Japanese ships at night; in addition to bombs and depth charges they unleashed empty beer bottles, which made an eerie whistling descent.

➤ The Catalina was so slow that critics joked that its navigator needed a calendar rather than a stopwatch.

PROFILE

'Black Cats' over the Pacific

Here was aviation at its essence. The high-wing, twin-engine Catalina was not speedy, not flashy, not graceful, but it was more practical than anyone realised when the first ship took to the skies on 28 March 1935. With its braced parasol wing and seagoing hull, the PBY Catalina became famous and was built in larger numbers than any other flying-boat in aviation history.

The PBY revolutionised long-range patrol in the US Navy. The well-loved 'Cat' ranged outward at great distance to stalk the enemy's fleet or to attack his submarines, and British Catalinas ferreted out the elusive German warship *Bismarck*. A PBY spotted the periscope of a Japanese submarine at Pearl Harbor. On all the world's oceans, Catalinas fought valiantly. Some were among the first American aircraft to carry radar. They were amphibians, flying from land or sea. Also produced in Canada and Russia, the Catalina often shed its warlike duties to become a Samaritan, bringing salvation to those in peril.

Ranging far and wide, the Catalina was instrumental in denying Axis forces the use of the sea. It was a Catalina which tracked down the Bismarck *during the hunt for the battleship, which ended in its sinking.*

The large unobstructed plank-like wing gave the Catalina excellent endurance and benign handling. The outrigger stabilising floats hinged upwards to form the wingtip fairing in flight.

PBY-5A Catalina

Type: seven-/nine-seat long-range maritime patrol bomber

Powerplant: two 895-kW (1,200-hp.) Pratt & Whitney R1830-92 Twin Wasp radial piston engines

Maximum speed: 288 km/h (175 m.p.h.) at 2135 m (6,500 ft.)

Range: 4900 km (3,045 mi.)

Service ceiling: 4480 m (18,100 ft.)

Weights: empty 9485 kg (21,000 lb.); loaded 16,066 kg (35,420 lb.)

Armament: two 7.62-mm (.30 cal.) machine-guns in bow, one 7.62-mm machine-gun firing aft from the hull step, and two 12.7-mm (.50 cal.) machine-guns in beam position; up to 1814 kg (4,000 lb.) of bombs or depth charges

Dimensions:
span	31.70 m (104 ft.)
length	19.47 m (63 ft. 10 in.)
height	6.15 m (20 ft. 2 in.)
wing area	130.06 m² (1,400 sq. ft.)

OA-10 CATALINA

During the war the US Air Force took over a large number of Catalinas for use in the air-sea rescue role, designated OA-10. These gave valuable service long after the end of the conflict.

Most late-production PBYs had search radar, with an antenna in a teardrop fairing above the flight deck. Other aerials were carried under the wings.

The basic crew of the Catalina comprised eight. In the extreme nose was an observer/bomb aimer, behind which sat the two pilots. Behind them was a compartment for the radio operator and navigator.

Catalinas were powered by a pair of Pratt & Whitney Twin Wasp radial piston engines. Sturdy and reliable, the Twin Wasp's output was boosted from 615 kW (820 hp.) in early examples to nearly 900 kW (1,200-hp.) in the final production PBY-5s.

Catalinas were built either as pure flying-boats or, as here, as amphibians, with a retractable tricycle undercarriage. The main wheels pulled up into wells above the hull line, and were left exposed.

The flight engineer's station was in the centre of the aircraft beneath the wing, while the aft cabin usually housed two gunner/observers. Weapons were carried under the wing.

COMBAT DATA

CRUISING SPEED

The Catalina was old, noisy and slow, especially when compared with its contemporaries. But it was tough and reliable, and could land and take off in anything short of a hurricane.

H6K 'MAVIS'	260 km/h (211 m.p.h.)
PBY CATALINA	188 km/h (175 m.p.h.)
BV 138	230 km/h (171 m.p.h.)

RANGE

The big patrol 'boats' may not have been fast, but they could cover a lot of ocean. A typical flying-boat at the beginning of World War II could stay aloft for up to 24 hours, and often crew fatigue was the limiting factor on mission length.

PBY CATALINA 4900 km (3,045 mi.)
H6K 'MAVIS' 6700 km (4,163 mi.)
BV 138 5000 km (3,107 mi.)

World War II maritime patrollers

■ **KAWANISHI H6K 'MAVIS':** The H6K was Japan's main long-range flying-boat at the start of World War II. Based on a Sikorsky design, it was very tough and seaworthy.

■ **SHORT SUNDERLAND:** Much larger than the PBY, the Sunderland was Britain's main maritime patrol machine. It was adapted from a civil design, and first flew in 1937.

■ **CANT Z.506:** Italy specialised in floatplanes rather than flying-boats, and the three-engined Cant was one of the largest of its kind. It held numerous pre-war seaplane speed records.

■ **BLOHM UND VOSS BV 138:** Known as 'Die fliegende Holzschuh', the twin-boom three-engined BV 138, or 'Flying Clog', saw action from the Mediterranean to the Arctic.

CURTISS

P-40 WARHAWK

● Single-seat fighter ● Desert fighter-bomber ● 'Flying Tiger' in China

D espite criticisms of its inferiority to Spitfires, Messerschmitts, Zeroes and Mustangs, the P-40 was important – if not critical – to victory in World War II. As the most numerous US Army fighter at the time of Pearl Harbor, the P-40 bred a generation of fighter pilots and won fame with General Chennault's 'Flying Tigers', who took it to the limit against superior Japanese forces.

▲ The P-40 was immortalised by the 'Flying Tigers' of the American Volunteer Group in China, who used the type with great success against the previously all-conquering Japanese.

PHOTO FILE

CURTISS **P-40 WARHAWK**

▲ Still flying
This P-40 has been restored, and flew at a British air show in 1984. The shark mouth marking was used by No. 112 Squadron RAF, which flew ground-attack missions in Egypt in 1942.

▲ Lucky escape
A Zero fighter almost claimed this P-40, flown by John Wood of the USAAC, over Guadalcanal. The P-40 was better able to withstand a hit than a Zero, but was inferior to it in most other respects.

◄ Kittyhawk
The first Tomahawks lacked performance, but the improved Kittyhawk Mk III had a more powerful Allison engine and enlarged tailfin.

▲ Desert airstrip
Tactical air support meant using rough strips just behind the front line. The rugged P-40 did well in the severe conditions of the desert, where sand was a constant problem as engines wore out.

Scramble ▶
Pilots race for take-off as enemy aircraft approach. The P-40 was an excellent attack aircraft, but never really did well as an interceptor fighter.

◄ Loading up
The Warhawk family carried six powerful 12.7-mm (.50 cal.) machine-guns, which were excellent weapons for the ground-attack role as well as for air combat.

FACTS AND FIGURES

➤ The prototype for the P-40 series was flown in October 1938.

➤ At Pearl Harbor on 7 December 1941, 73 P-40s were among 152 US Army aircraft destroyed by the Japanese attack.

➤ Production of all P-40s totalled 16,802, including 13,738 for US forces.

➤ The 'Flying Tigers' in China were credited with 286 aerial victories while losing 23 American P-40 pilots.

➤ P-40s served with Australia, Britain, China, the USSR and South Africa.

➤ When World War II ended, the US had only one P-40 group still in service.

PROFILE

Close air support in the Warhawk

Known by many names, including Hawk, Kittyhawk, Tomahawk and Warhawk, 31 variants of the P-40 battled on every continent. The definitive P-40N entered production in 1943, and reached US Army Air Force squadrons in March 1944.

By then, the P-40 was not a world-class pursuit ship. To some extent it was purposely assigned to secondary theatres so that more advanced warplanes (P-38, P-47, P-51)

could fly where the US perceived its first priorities. But none of this meant much to American pilots slogging in the Aleutians, Australians in New Guinea, or South Africans in Libya; they took this solid, rugged fighter and made the most of what they had.

It was plenty. The P-40 excelled when primitive maintenance, terrible weather and heavy odds were the order of the day. It was not in the category of a Bf 109 or Zero

Like many imperfect or obsolete fighters, the P-40 came in very useful as a ground-attack machine. The Desert Air Force used the type extensively, often working alongside the equally rugged Hawker Hurricane.

as a dogfighter, but was superb at providing close support to ground troops. When production ended in September 1944 the P-40 had served almost everywhere and had been used for just about everything.

Early P-40s had a pair of 12.7-mm (.50 cal.) machine-guns on top of the fuselage, but these were often deleted in RAF aircraft.

RAF Desert Air Force P-40s all wore a two-tone brown camouflage scheme.

The only parts of the P-40 which were fabric-covered were the control surfaces. This was to save weight and to make flying easier.

P-40N Warhawk

Type: single-seat interceptor and fighter-bomber

Powerplant: one 1015-kW (1,360-hp.) Allison V-1710-81 inline piston engine

Maximum speed: 609 km/h (378 m.p.h.) at 3210 m (10,530 ft.)

Range: 386 km (240 mi.)

Service ceiling: 11,630 m (38,160 ft.)

Weights: empty 2724 kg (6,045 lb.); loaded 4018 kg (8,858 lb.)

Armament: six 12.7-mm (.50 cal.) machine-guns in wing; provision for 227-kg (500-lb.) bomb or 197-litre drop-tank under fuselage

Dimensions:
span	11.42 m	(37 ft. 6 in.)
length	10.20 m	(33 ft. 6 in.)
height	3.77 m	(12 ft. 4 in.)
wing area	21.95 m²	(236 sq. ft.)

TOMAHAWK MK IIB

This Curtiss Tomahawk Mk IIB served with No. 112 Squadron RAF, based at Sidi Haneish, North Africa, in the autumn of 1941. The squadron later received Kittyhawks and took part in the Italian campaign.

The 'shark mouth' was one of the most characteristic of all Warhawk markings. No. 112 Squadron aircraft was the first to wear it.

The canopy was later improved to give better visibility. The front windscreen was bulletproof and the cockpit was armoured.

For an average performer, the P-40 had a good level of equipment fit, with effective cockpit heating, heat ducting to the guns, armour and self-sealing fuel tanks.

AN413

The Allison V-1710 engine was fitted with a supercharger. The cowling was later changed, with an enlarged air scoop.

Wing armament was four Browning 7.7-mm (.303 cal.) guns. This was later changed to six 12.7-mm (.50 cal.) machine-guns, with 235 rounds per gun.

The fuselage hardpoint could carry a single 227-kg (500-lb.) bomb or a 197-litre (43-gal.) fuel tank.

The fuselage was of modern construction, with all-alloy framework covered by an 'Alclad' skin. Additional fuel was contained in a fuselage tank.

The Kittyhawk Mk II (P-40F) had a lengthened fuselage. With the rudder hinge behind the elevator hinge, the pilot had increased manoeuvrability and better control.

COMBAT DATA

MAXIMUM SPEED

The original P-40 was as fast as its contemporaries, but it lacked the agility and acceleration of the Zero. It could dive very fast, however, and the American Volunteer Group in China used it to make quick slashing attacks on the Japanese, accelerating away to avoid a dogfight.

HURRICANE Mk II	540 km/h (336 m.p.h.)
TOMAHAWK Mk IIB	555 km/h (345 m.p.h.)
A6M5 ZERO	540 km/h (336 m.p.h.)

SERVICE CEILING

Allison-engined aircraft often had very good performance at low level, but unless boosted by a powerful supercharger they tended to be somewhat sluggish at high altitude. The early P-40s were no exception, and high-level performance was far from ideal.

HURRICANE Mk II 10,000 m (33,000 ft.)

A6M5 ZERO 11,000 m (36,000 ft.)

TOMAHAWK Mk IIB 9200 m (30,200 ft.)

ARMAMENT

Originally fitted with 12.7-mm (.50 cal.) machine-guns, the Tomahawks in British service usually carried 7.7-mm (.303 cal.) Brownings like other RAF fighters to ease logistic problems. Later aircraft switched back to 12.7-mm weapons, and although the aircraft could carry cannon these were never fitted.

TOMAHAWK Mk IIB 6 x 7.7-mm (.303 cal.) machine-guns

A6M5 ZERO 2 x 20-mm (0.79-in.) cannon 2 x 7.7-mm (.303 cal.) machine-guns

HURRICANE Mk II 8 x 7.7-mm (.303 cal.) machine-guns

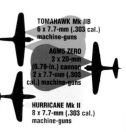

Warhawk development

■ **CURTISS P-36 HAWK:** First flown in 1935, the radial-engined Hawk was an intermediate step between the great Hawk biplanes and the P-40.

■ **P-40B:** Fitting an Allison inline engine to the P-36 produced a better fighter, which was used by the Flying Tigers in China.

■ **TOMAHAWK:** Early P-40s were known as Tomahawks in RAF service, and flew with distinction in the desert campaigns of 1941 and 1942.

■ **KITTYHAWK:** Later P-40s with bigger engines were known as Kittyhawks. This example is a P-40F with a Rolls-Royce Merlin engine.

■ **WARHAWK:** The final P-40s were known as Warhawks, a name which the US Air Force applied to the whole Hawk series. This is a P-40N of 1943.

CURTISS

SB2C HELLDIVER

● Dive-bomber ● Carrier strike ● US Navy

Disadvantaged from the start by having to replace the highly capable SBD Dauntless, the Helldiver never quite won a similar place in the hearts of US naval aviators. It took time to prove itself in action and eventually became an effective carrier-launched dive- and torpedo-bomber in the war against the Japanese. But the SB2C did not win the reliability battle soon enough for some commanders and picked up the derogatory nickname 'Beast'.

▲ The Helldiver was a hard-hitting aircraft which gained many combat successes, but pilots hated it. The designation SB2C was said to stand for 'son of a bitch, second class' by aircrews.

CURTISS SB2C HELLDIVER

▼ **Hook down to land**
Ready to land, this SB2C pilot has lowered the tail hook of his aircraft. When landing, Helldivers often revealed their poor handling to careless pilots.

▲ **Weapons away**
Helldivers were built to carry a large 907-kg (2,000-lb.) bomb internally, or two 725-kg (1,600-lb.) bombs.

Rear gunner ▶
In combat, the Helldiver's rear gunner slid back the hood to fire a pair of 7.62-mm (.30 cal.) Browning machine-guns.

▼ **Big bird**
Even with its wings folded, the Helldiver was a big aircraft. This was due to the requirement for an internal bomb-bay.

▲ **Fleet strike force**
By 1944 hundreds of SB2Cs were in service with the carrier battle groups of the US Pacific Fleet.

FACTS AND FIGURES

➤ From an order for 450 Helldivers for the Royal Navy, only 26 reached Britain. None of them were used operationally.

➤ In total, 5516 Helldivers were delivered to the US Navy during World War II.

➤ One of the prototype SB2Cs fell to pieces in a dive-bombing trial.

➤ The Helldiver specification was influenced by the Luftwaffe's success with the Ju 87 Stuka dive-bomber.

➤ SB2Cs first went to war with carrier squadron VB-17 on USS *Bunker Hill*.

➤ The USAAF used the SB2C as a trainer and target-towing aircraft.

Dive-bomber from hell

Taking its name from an earlier Curtiss type, the Helldiver was a powerful, modern dive-bomber designed to undertake a variety of combat missions. It was also tentatively required by the US Marines and the Army Air Forces which compromised the SB2C, giving the manufacturers the demanding task of creating a 'multi-role' aircraft in the middle of a war. There was no time to perfect the requirement and when the Army did not order the aircraft in quantity, it was left to the Navy

to sort out the teething troubles. A long list of 'fixes' was required, which delayed the Helldiver's deployment for some months.

But the job was done, and from November 1943 when Helldivers pounded the Japanese island garrison of Rabaul until the end of the war the Navy used the Helldiver in every major surface action as an integral part of its carrier air groups. Cannon armament, a relative rarity on World War II American aircraft, was fitted to the SB2C-1C, the

Below: The Royal Navy tested the Helldiver, but rejected it immediately because of its appalling handling, which was said to be even worse than the Fleet Air Arm's Barracuda.

Above: The SB2C was not a good marketing tool for Curtiss. The company boss, Guy Vaughan, called it 'one of the biggest crosses we had to bear'.

last suffix indicating the heavier, more powerful guns. One of the most effective models was the SB2C-4 which introduced the distinctive 'cheese grater' split flaps to aid stability during a dive.

SB2C Helldiver

Type: three-seat dive-/torpedo-bomber

Powerplant: one 1268-kW (1,900-hp.) Wright R-2600-8 Cyclone air-cooled engine

Maximum speed: 452 km/h (294 m.p.h.)

Range: 1786 km (1,200 mi.)

Service ceiling: 7530 m (29,100 ft.)

Weights: empty 4990 kg (10,978 lb.); loaded 7550 kg (16,610 lb.)

Armament: two 20-mm (0.79-in.) cannon or four 12.7-mm (.50 cal.) machine-guns in wings and two 7.62-mm (.30 cal.) machine-guns in rear cockpit; up to 907 kg (2,000 lb.) of bombs in internal bay

Dimensions:
span	15.20 m	(49 ft. 6 in.)
length	11.20 m	(36 ft. 8 in.)
height	5.10 m	(13 ft. 2 in.)
wing area	39.20 m²	(422 sq. ft.)

Tail buffeting was a constant problem, and despite a redesign it never entirely disappeared.

SB2C HELLDIVER

In June 1944, the US Navy changed the colour scheme of all its aircraft to overall gloss dark blue. The Helldiver served from 1943 to 1949 with the USN.

One early source of trouble was the Wright Cyclone engine and its Curtiss Electric four-bladed propeller. Many of the propellers, like this one, had the spinner removed in service. The carburretor intake was in the top of the cowling.

The gunner was protected by a large sheet of armour. Between him and the pilot was the radio bay, the life raft, the autopilot controls and a large fuel tank.

Engine oil and hydraulic fluid tanks were fitted behind the engine, with an oil cooler at the bottom of the engine bay.

Upper surface divebrakes were fitted to the wing, and the the trailing-edge flaps were split. The leading-edge slat opened simultaneously with undercarriage operation.

Unlike earlier dive-bombers, the SB2C had a large internal bomb-bay with displacement gear for the bombs and hydraulic doors over the bay. The wingroot contained additional fuel tanks.

The arrester hook was connected to a large hydraulic damper to reduce the impact of catching the deck wire.

The Battle of Leyte Gulf

3 DECOY FORCE: A third decoy force was sent in from the north to distract the Americans. Task Force 38 eventually gave chase. The decoy was not noticed for some time.

PHILIPPINE ISLANDS

Japanese aircraft sink US carrier *Princeton*

Force 'A'

SB2Cs attacked from here

■	Japanese Naval Forces
■	US Pacific Fleet

Force 'C'

2 AMERICAN AIR RAIDS: Japanese efforts to thwart American landings failed after SB2Cs attacked and sank a battleship and damaged a cruiser.

1 JAPANESE STRIKE FORCES: The Japanese Plan Sho-1 operation was intended to stop American landings at Leyte. The First Striking Force ('A' and 'C') sailed from Brunei; a second fleet came from the north.

BRUNEI

ACTION DATA

RANGE

An important feature of a carrier-based aircraft was its range performance due to the fact that it operated over water. The D4Y3 traded range for a higher top speed, while the Barracuda had a superior range but a comparatively low top speed.

SB2C HELLDIVER 1786 km (1,107 mi.)

D4Y3 'JUDY' 1520 km (942 mi.)

BARRACUDA Mk II 1850 km (1,147 mi.)

MAXIMUM SPEED

Dive-bombers were vulnerable to attack from enemy fighters due to their low speeds. The D4Y3 had fairly good speed and was a steamlined design compared to the SB2C, with its bulbous radial engine.

SB2C HELLDIVER 452 km/h (280 m.p.h.)

D4Y3 'JUDY' 575 km/h (357 m.p.h.)

BARRACUDA Mk II 367 km/h (228 m.p.h.)

DE HAVILLAND

DH.98 MOSQUITO

● **Unarmed high-speed bomber** ● **Versatile 'Wooden Wonder'**

We think of Mosquitoes fighting the Luftwaffe or pressing relentlessly to bomb their targets, but it was probably the most useful Allied aircraft of World War II. Fighter, bomber, night-fighter, attack aircraft, torpedo-bomber, transport – these are just a few of the roles that de Havilland's design performed with miraculous success. The Mosquito was all the more impressive as it was mostly made of wood. The RAF virtually ignored the aircraft at first, but it became one of its most valuable planes.

▲ *The key to the Mosquito's success was its light wooden construction and the power of its twin Merlin engines, which gave it the speed to outfly almost every other bomber and fighter of the war.*

PHOTO FILE

DE HAVILLAND DH.98 MOSQUITO

▼ Reconnaissance Mosquito
This brightly-painted PR.Mk 16 was an unarmed photographic aircraft. These Mosquitoes performed the hazardous task of gathering intelligence from enemy territory, relying on speed for safety.

▲ Loading up
The usual load for a tactical strike was 113-kg (250 lb.) or 227-kg (500-lb.) bombs, but the Mosquitoes of Bomber Command later carried a modified 1814-kg (3,690-lb.) 'Cookie'.

◄ Bomber crews
The Mosquito B.Mk IV became a very important part of the bomber offensive, target-marking for the larger Lancaster and Halifax force.

▼ Desert mission
These FB.Mk VI bombers patrolled the Suez Canal while based in the Middle East. The hot, dry desert climate presented little problem, but the aircraft had structural weaknesses when based in the Far East, due to the humidity affecting the wood glue.

▲ Speedster
Mosquito bombers carried their bombs internally; nothing was allowed to break the aircraft's smooth aerodynamic lines. Later variants had a bulged bay for larger weapons.

FACTS AND FIGURES

➤ The prototype 'plywood' Mosquito made its first flight on 25 November 1940.

➤ 7781 Mosquitoes in 43 versions were manufactured in England (6439), Canada (1134) and Australia (208).

➤ Mosquitoes were flown by air forces of 12 Allied nations during World War II.

➤ A Mosquito became the first twin-engined aircraft to land on a ship on 25 March 1944 aboard the carrier HMS *Indefatigable*.

➤ The last Mosquito built was a night-fighter, delivered on 28 November 1950.

➤ Mosquitoes were among the first aircraft to carry bombing radar.

Mosquito – the wooden wonder

The Mosquito came from obscurity and rose to glory. Official interest was lukewarm when de Havilland made a private proposal for a fast, twin-engined, two-man bomber. But its performance was so outstanding that it went into production.

The Mosquito was fast and nimble, and performed well in an attack on Gestapo headquarters in Oslo which was thwarted by dud bombs. High-speed, precision air strikes became the stock-in-trade for the Mosquito, which also adapted quickly to other roles and missions.

Almost four dozen versions of the Mosquito carried out every wartime duty, from whisking spies behind the lines to photo-mapping enemy territory. Precision-bombing of special targets persisted throughout the war – Amiens prison, Gestapo headquarters in the Hague, V-1 'buzz bomb' launching sites. Each time, the Mosquito demonstrated its unique ability to strike fast, hit hard, and get away clean.

More than a dozen overseas air forces used Mosquitoes in the years after the war.

The Mosquito could fly almost unchallenged over occupied Europe, day or night, and deliver devastating attacks from rooftop height. The bomber versions were as fast and agile as fighters, and could generally escape from an enemy attacker.

Mosquito B.Mk IV

Type: high-speed light bomber

Powerplant: two 918-kW (1,230-hp.) Rolls-Royce Merlin 21 inline piston engines

Maximum speed: 612 km/h (379 m.p.h.) at 6400 m (21,000 ft.)

Range: 3000 km (1,860 mi.)

Service ceiling: 10,500 m (34,450 ft.)

Weights: empty 6400 kg (14,080 lb.); loaded 10,200 kg (22,440 lb.)

Armament: maximum internal bombload four 227-kg (500-lb.) bombs;

Dimensions:
span	16.51 m (54 ft.)
length	12.43 m (41 ft.)
height	4.65 m (15 ft.)
wing area	42.18 m² (454 sq. ft.)

Like the fuselage, the wing was of wooden construction. The main parts were screwed, glued and pinned together, with a fabric covering. This had the unexpected advantage that enemy gunfire often passed through without doing much damage.

MOSQUITO B.MK IV

No. 105 Squadron was the first unit to operate the Mosquito B.Mk IV. The squadron carried out many daytime attack missions, but later received 'Oboe' equipment and flew at night instead.

The beautiful curved tail profile of the Mosquito was a classic de Havilland feature, present in pre-war aircraft like the DH.88 as well as the post-war Chipmunk trainer.

Although pilots liked the Mosquito, it was a very tricky machine to escape from. The pilot had a small door to get out of, and the navigator exited through a small hatch.

Mosquitoes had a huge number of different noses. The B.Mk IV had a glazed nose for a bomb-aimer to lie in.

The outer fuselage consisted of two plywood skins separated by spruce blocks.

Weapons were carried internally in a small bomb-bay. Rockets could be carried externally beneath the wings.

The Mosquito's Merlin engines were constantly uprated to keep the aircraft out in front. The propellers both turned the same way, which gave the Mosquito a pronounced 'swing' on take-off that occasionally surprised unwary pilots.

The glazed nose was common to both bomber and reconnaissance versions of the Mosquito.

COMBAT DATA

MAXIMUM SPEED

Several aircraft flying during World War II proved to be extremely versatile. The well-known Ju 88 was larger than the Mosquito, but was considerably slower and was much more vulnerable to enemy fighters. The less-well-known Soviet Pe-2 was more of a match for the Mosquito, and like the other two aircraft was also developed into a potent fighter and fighter-bomber.

MOSQUITO B.Mk IV	612 km/h (379 m.p.h.)
Ju 88A-4	435 km/h (270 m.p.h.)
Pe-2	580 km/h (359 m.p.h.)

RANGE

The Mosquito's sleek aerodynamic shape translated into excellent range, even at the high speeds and altitudes adopted on many of its missions. It could fly much further than both of its contemporaries, and led to the type's employment as a long-range reconnaissance machine.

Pe-2 1150 km (713 mi.)

MOSQUITO B.Mk IV 3000 km (1,860 mi.)

Ju 88A-4 1800 km (1,115 mi.)

DEFENSIVE ARMAMENT

The Mosquito bomber's relative invulnerability to interception meant that it needed no defensive armament, nor extra crew to man the guns. Although the Russian Pe-2 was almost as fast, it carried machine-guns. The slower German Ju 88 was vulnerable to fighters and carried a heavy defensive armament.

MOSQUITO B.Mk IV no guns

Ju 88A-4 up to 8 x 7.92-mm (0.31-in) MGs

Pe-2 4 x 7.62-mm (.30 cal.) MGs

Arming the Mosquito bomber

The Mosquito was designed primarily as a light bomber. Early variants did not have a heavy warload, but the aircraft's speed meant that it could attack targets that would have been suicide for heavier, more conventional aircraft. It also proved to be extremely good at pinpoint low-level attacks, where accuracy of delivery was more important than sheer tonnage of high explosive dropped.

EARLY WARLOAD: For pinpoint raids the Mosquito was generally armed with four 227-kg (500-lb.) high-explosive bombs.

BULGED BOMB-BAY: The bulged bomb-bays of later bomber variants of the Mosquito meant that they could carry the brutally simple 1814-kg (4,000-lb.) demolition bomb.

FIGHTER-BOMBER: Although fitted with a heavy gun armament, many fighter Mosquitoes were still capable of carrying bombs. A typical warload was two 227-kg (500-lb.) and two 112-kg (240-lb.) weapons.

DEWOITINE

D.520

● Interceptor ● Fought in Tunisia ● Flown by ace pilot Pierre Le Gloan

Dewoitine's D.520 was an inspired design, into which its builders hoped to install an engine of around 1000 kW (1,500 hp.). Although there was no suitable powerplant available, this elegant fighter performed well, and was one of the few modern craft available when France was invaded in 1940. Even with inadequate power, pilots took great delight in its agility and fine handling qualities. The D.520's short career ended after the liberation campaign in 1944.

▲ Many D.520s
were taken by the Germans with the fall of France in 1940, and were used as fighter trainers. Others flew on with Vichy forces, fighting against the RAF.

DEWOITINE D.520

▲ First test
This D.520 was restored to working order and taken over by the Musée de l'Air in Paris. The cowling panels were removed to allow access to the engine.

▲ Squadron memorial
After the war around 30 D.520s survived to form an instructor's squadron, No. 704. This was finally disbanded in 1947.

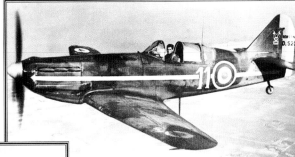

Moroccan warrior ▶
This D.520 was flown by Sergeant Hardouin at Casablanca, Morocco. The mask badge on the tail was the unit emblem of 5ᵉ Group III/6.

▼ Last in action
This D.520 was one of the last surviving examples seized by the Germans. It was restored to action and then used by GCB 1/18 in April 1945.

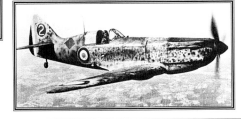

▲ Light fighter
With its mixed cannon and machine-gun armament, small size and fine agility, the D.520's design philosophy was similar to that of Russian fighters, and proved a match for the Bf 109E.

FACTS AND FIGURES

➤ The open cockpit prototype of the Dewoitine D.520 took to the air for the first time on 2 October 1938.

➤ World War II users of the D.520 included France, Bulgaria, Italy and Romania.

➤ French ace Pierre Le Gloan gained 18 of his 22 kills while flying the D.520.

➤ Famed test pilot Marcel Doret forgot to lower the undercarriage and wrecked the D.520 prototype in 1938.

➤ In 1940, French industry produced 300 D.520 fighters in a single month.

➤ French fighter groups flying the D.520 were credited with 147 aerial victories.

Dogfighting for France

Dewoitine had considerable experience with advanced stressed-skin monoplane construction in the 1930s. The Dewoitine D.520 which appeared on the eve of World War II was a rakish, low-wing monoplane, resembling its predecessor, the D.513. Forward of the cockpit, however, was a wing with a new shape and a cleaner-looking engine installation.

By May 1939, the French air arm had ordered 200 D.520s. Later, the purchase was increased to 710 and again (under Vichy rule) to 740.

With major improvements, the production D.520 of 1939 became the most capable fighter of French design used in the early days of the war. French pilots fought valiantly and the D.520 acquitted itself well against the Luftwaffe. In 1942, the Luftwaffe seized 411 D.520s and passed many to allied countries. After serving with the Vichy air arm (in some cases in locations as distant as Syria), these attractive fighters were

again in the hands of free French pilots in late 1944 when they flew their final combat sorties against the last German pockets in southern France.

Flying examples of the D.520 are very rare, as few were made and even fewer survived the war. Many were used as fighter trainers by the Luftwaffe in 1944.

D.520

Type: single-seat fighter

Powerplant: one 697-kW (935-hp.) Hispano-Suiza 12Y 45 inline piston engine with Szydlowski supercharger

Maximum speed: 535 km/h (332 m.p.h.)

Initial climb rate: to 4000 m (13,120 ft.) in 5 minutes 48 seconds

Range: 890 km (950 mi.)

Service ceiling: 10,500 m (39,440 ft.)

Weights: empty 2036 kg (4,479 lb.); maximum take-off 2677 kg (5,889 lb.)

Armament: one 20-mm (0.79-in.) HS 404 rapid-fire cannon and four wing-mounted 7.5-mm (0.3-in.) MAC 34 M39 machine-guns

Dimensions: span 10.20 m (34 ft.)
length 8.60 m (28 ft.)
height 2.57 m (8 ft.)
wing area 15.97 m² (172 sq. ft.)

The wing armament consisted of two 7.5-mm (0.3-in.) machine-guns, with 675 rounds of ammunition for each. The middle section of the wing also contained a small fuel tank.

A small baggage compartment was located aft of the cockpit, with an access door on the port side.

The D.520's engine was reliable if slightly underpowered. The rival French M.S.406 was powered by a similar engine.

D.520

Displaying the red and orange 'Vichy stripes' adopted at Gabes, Tunisia, by D.520 Escadrilles, this aircraft fought against the Allied invasion of North Africa.

The cockpit was a long way aft of the long engine cowling, making landing and taxiing a tricky business for the inexperienced pilot.

The Hispano-Suiza cannon fired through the airscrew, with the engine acting as a recoil buffer. This powerful weapon was superior to the Bf 109's MG FF.

The main undercarriage retracted inwards, with the wheels fitting into wells in the fuselage.

The forward fuselage contained the main fuel tank, which gave the D.520 its long nose shape. The 60-round cannon magazine was located between the tank and the engine in the upper nose section.

The black panther badge belonged to 40 Escadrille, Group de Chasse II/7.

COMBAT DATA

ARMAMENT

Experiments in 1938 showed that two cannon were better than eight machine-guns. The cannon in the Bf 109 was a modified anti-aircraft gun, and it suffered poor muzzle velocity and had a low rate of fire. The Hispano-Suiza cannon was a much better weapon and was well respected.

D.520
1 x 20-mm (0.79-in.) cannon
4 x 7.5-mm (0.3-in.) MGs

HURRICANE Mk I
8 x 7.7-mm (.303 cal.) MGs

Bf 109E
2 x 20-mm (0.79-in.) cannon
2 x 7.9-mm (0.31-in.) MGs

MAXIMUM SPEED

The sleek Bf 109 with its powerful fuel-injected DB 601 engine could outrun a Hurricane or D.520 with ease, especially in a dive. The Dewoitine was slightly underpowered in comparison. Although the Hurricane had a superb engine, the powerful Rolls-Royce Merlin, it was a larger and less streamlined machine than its rivals.

HURRICANE Mk I 550 km/h (342 m.p.h.)

Bf 109E 575 km/h (357 m.p.h.)

D.520 534 km/h (332 m.p.h.)

RANGE

Another advantage of the Bf 109's fuel-injected engine was increased efficiency, especially at altitude, giving greater range. Luckily for the British and French air forces in 1940, they were generally on the defensive, and were often taking on Bf 109 pilots who were flying at the limit of their range.

HURRICANE Mk I 740 km (477 mi.)

Bf 109E 1000 km (620 mi.)

D.520 890 km (552 mi.)

Fighters of the 1940 campaign

■ **HAWKER HURRICANE:** Despite lacking cannon armament, the Hurricane was manoeuvrable and rugged, and was the RAF's most numerous fighter during the battles in France in 1940.

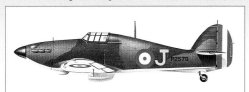

■ **MESSERSCHMITT Bf 109E:** Arguably the best fighter in the world in 1940, the Bf 109E was popular with German pilots, some of whom retained the 'Emil' even after the Bf 109F appeared.

■ **MORANE-SAULNIER M.S.406:** The main fighter of the French air force in 1940, the M.S.406 was an inferior design to the D.520 and Bf 109, but played an important part in resisting the Luftwaffe.

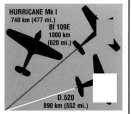

DORNIER

Do 18

● Wal successor ● Maritime patrol flying-boat ● Search and rescue

With its origins in the Wal series of flying-boats which Dornier had been developing since 1922 and which had culminated in the military Do 15, the Do 18 was developed to provide both a replacement for the Do 15 and a transatlantic mail carrier for the German airline Lufthansa. Using the new, fuel-efficient Junkers Jumo 205 diesel engine, the Do 18 proved to have outstanding range, but its main military use was for air-sea rescue.

▲ For its transatlantic mail-carrying role, the Do 18 carried two pilots, a radio operator and a flight engineer. Four fuel tanks holding 3920 litres (862 gal.) and a mail compartment were amidships.

PHOTO FILE

DORNIER Do 18

▼ Junkers-type flaps
The large 'double-wing' flaps, of Junkers design, can clearly be seen here.

▲ Over the Baltic
D-ABYM was the V3 third prototype of the Do 18. Redesignated Do 18E, it flew a 30-hour 21-minute test flight over the Baltic before been delivered to Lufthansa.

▲ Launching trolley
After being removed from the water, the Do 18 was craned onto a launching trolley and pushed down a slipway for relaunch.

▲ Catapult launch
Lufthansa extensively used seaplane tenders, equipped with Heinkel catapults, before World War II.

Military developments ▶
Here, the first prototype (V4) of the military Do 18D is seen operating from rough seas. The lower fuselage sponsons aided stability.

FACTS AND FIGURES

➤ Unarmed rescue Do 18N-1s in Red Cross markings were allegedly used by the Luftwaffe for clandestine operations.

➤ Just over 100 Do 18s, including 70 Do 18Gs, were built, the last in 1939.

➤ In transatlantic service Do 18Es made a number of record-breaking flights.

➤ The first German aircraft shot down by the British in World War II was a Do 18 attacked by an Royal Navy Skua.

➤ The Do 18's compartmentalised Stümmel sponsons were a Dornier trademark.

➤ In the training role the Do 18H-1 was fitted with dual controls.

Early wartime search and rescue

First flown in March 1935 with two Jumo 5 diesel engines, the Do 18 was one of the most refined flying boats of its era. Its wide hull and sponsons made it extremely stable on the water, while internal watertight compartments meant that it was difficult to sink.

As well as operating its four Do 18Es on the southern Atlantic mail route, Lufthansa used the single Do 18F to set a new distance record for seaplanes in March 1938. The aircraft

flew 8390 km (5,213 mi.) after being catapult-launched from the tender *Westfalen*.

The Luftwaffe's Do 18D entered service in 1936 and served with maritime reconnaissance units during the Polish and Norwegian campaigns before being used as an air-sea rescue aircraft during the Battle of Britain in 1940. With just two 7.9-mm (0.31-in.) machine-guns, however, it proved to be too poorly armed for military service. New engines and heavier

armament were installed to produce the Do 18G. The Do 18H was a training version.

During 1941 many Do 18Gs were converted to Do 18Ns for the air-sea rescue role. This was the Do 18's main task for the remainder of its career.

Above: Although this aircraft carries a civilian registration, it is actually the pre-production Do 18D-01. The position of the bow 7.9-mm (0.31-in.) machine-gun is clearly visible.

Left: As a maritime patrol aircraft the Do 18 was very vulnerable to enemy fighters and its front-line career came to an end in August 1941.

Do 18G-1

Type: four-seat maritime patrol and reconnaissance flying-boat

Powerplant: two 656-kW (880-hp.) Junkers Jumo 205D six-cylinder in-line diesel engines

Maximum speed: 267 km/h (166 m.p.h.) at 2000 m (6,562 ft.)

Climb rate: 1000 m (3,280 f.p.m.) in 7 min 48 sec

Range: 3500 km (2,175 mi.)

Service ceiling: 4200 m (13,780 ft.)

Weights: empty 5980 kg (13,184 lb.); maximum take-off 10,795 kg (23,800 lb.)

Armament: one 13-mm (0.51-in.) machine-gun, one 20-mm (0.79-in.) cannon and two 50-kg (110-lb.) bombs

Dimensions:
span	23.70 m	(77 ft. 9 in.)
length	19.38 m	(63 ft. 7 in.)
height	5.32 m	(17 ft. 5 in.)
wing area	98 m²	(1.055 sq. ft.)

Do 18G-1

This aircraft flew in the search and rescue role during 1941/42, after the type had been retired from combat duties. It was on the strength of 6. Seenotstaffel, based in the central Mediterranean area.

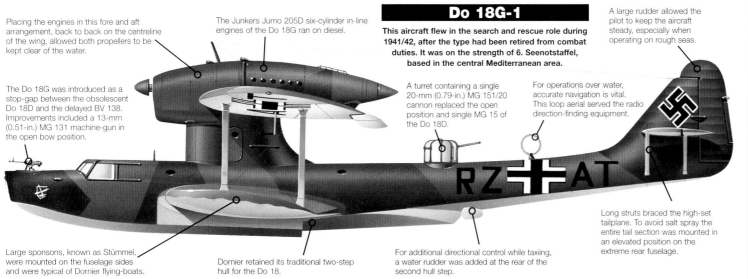

Placing the engines in this fore and aft arrangement, back to back on the centreline of the wing, allowed both propellers to be kept clear of the water.

The Junkers Jumo 205D six-cylinder in-line engines of the Do 18G ran on diesel.

A large rudder allowed the pilot to keep the aircraft steady, especially when operating on rough seas.

The Do 18G was introduced as a stop-gap between the obsolescent Do 18D and the delayed BV 138. Improvements included a 13-mm (0.51-in.) MG 131 machine-gun in the open bow position.

A turret containing a single 20-mm (0.79-in.) MG 151/20 cannon replaced the open position and single MG 15 of the Do 18D.

For operations over water, accurate navigation is vital. This loop aerial served the radio direction-finding equipment.

Large sponsons, known as Stümmel, were mounted on the fuselage sides and were typical of Dornier flying-boats.

Dornier retained its traditional two-step hull for the Do 18.

For additional directional control while taxiing, a water rudder was added at the rear of the second hull step.

Long struts braced the high-set tailplane. To avoid salt spray the entire tail section was mounted in an elevated position on the extreme rear fuselage.

COMBAT DATA

MAXIMUM SPEED

The Do 18 had a top speed which was comparable to that of the Allies' Catalina, but almost 100 km/h less than that of the Heinkel He 115. Speed, however, was not the most important attribute of a maritime patrol aircraft.

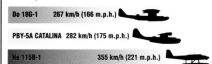

Do 18G-1	267 km/h (166 m.p.h.)
PBY-5A CATALINA	282 km/h (175 m.p.h.)
He 115B-1	355 km/h (221 m.p.h.)

RANGE

All three types had similar range, in the region of 3500 km. The Catalina was marginally the better performer, but all three aircraft were able to operate far from their bases. The amphibious PBY-5A had the added flexibility of being able to operate from land and water.

Do 18G-1
3500 km
(2,175 mi.)

PBY-5A CATALINA
3782 km
(2,350 mi.)

He 115B-1
3350 km
(2,082 mi.)

ARMAMENT

In terms of its weapons load, the Catalina was the most capable patrol flying-boat of World War II. In its PBY-5A version it carried four defensive guns and could lift more than 1.5 tons of bombs and/or depth charges. The He 115 was also a well-armed aircraft.

Do 18G-1	PBY-5A CATALINA	He 115B-1
1 x 13-mm machine-gun 1 x 20-mm (0.79-in.) cannon 100-kg (220-lb.) bombload	1 x 12.7-mm machine-gun 3 x 7.62-mm machine-guns 1816-kg (4,004-lb.) bombload	1 x 12.7-mm (.50 cal.) machine-gun 3 x 7.62-mm (.30 cal.) machine-guns 1250-kg (2,756-lb.) bombload

World War II search and rescue

■ **DORNIER Do 24:** Having been designed to satisfy a pre-war Dutch civilian requirement, the exceptional Do 24 went on to replace the Do 18 in the search and rescue (SAR) role.

■ **GRUMMAN JF DUCK:** Operating mainly around the US coast, the Duck served as a utility and SAR amphibian with the US Navy and Coast Guard.

■ **SUPERMARINE WALRUS:** Despite its antiquated appearance, the Walrus was one of the UK's primary SAR aircraft and flew with distinction during the Battle of Britain.

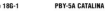

DORNIER
Do 24

● Search and rescue ● Transport missions ● Mine-sweeping

Designed to fill a requirement for the Royal Netherlands Naval Air Service, the Do 24 was a three-engined all-metal flying-boat which came to excel in the air-sea rescue role. Exported to the Dutch before the start of World War II, the aircraft was to serve both sides during the conflict. Although very few modifications were introduced during the production run, such was the enduring nature of the design that it continued to serve until the late 1970s.

▲ *A German pilot and his crew prepare to board their Dornier Do 24 at the start of a long-range patrol that may see them rescue pilots, search for submarines and observe enemy activity.*

PHOTO FILE

DORNIER Do 24

▼ Post-war service
Twelve Do 24T-3s were supplied to Spain in June 1944. Remarkably these aircraft remained in service into the 1970s in the search and rescue role.

▲ Mine-sweeper
The Do 24MS was a special variant fitted with a degaussing loop and on-board generators for mine-sweeping duties.

Dependable Dornier ▶
Crews soon came to marvel at the capabilities of their aircraft. This early Do 24 is being put through its paces during rough water tests. The aircraft proved to be extremely reliable.

▼ Safe and sound
Here a Do 24 retrieves a downed bomber crew from the Atlantic Ocean. Search and rescue was one of the main roles of the Do 24.

▲ Royal Dutch Navy
Designed to meet a requirement for the Royal Dutch Navy, many of the Do 24s were quickly armed and pressed into Luftwaffe service after the outbreak of World War II, and were used for patrol flights.

FACTS AND FIGURES

➤ In the rescue role Dornier Do 24s served in the Arctic, Mediterranean, English Channel and the Pacific.

➤ Five aircraft were operated by the RAAF for operations against the Japanese.

➤ During the evacuation of Crete, aircraft flew with more than 24 passengers.

➤ One Do 24 lost its entire tail unit during a rescue attempt. The crew sealed the aircraft and simply taxied back to base.

➤ Twelve aircraft were supplied to Spain in 1944 for search and rescue duties.

➤ A Do 24 was used as a testbed for an advanced wing design in 1983.

PROFILE

Slender-wing saviour

The Do 24 was an excellent search-and-rescue aircraft which first flew in July 1937. It was soon delivered to the Dutch navy for service evaluation, and after acceptance of the type the Dutch acquired 11 factory-built examples and also licence-built another 25 aircraft powered by three Wright R-1820 engines and designated Do 24Ks.

At the outbreak of World War II Germany had only one airworthy prototype. However, with the defeat of Holland all semi-completed Do 24Ks were shipped to Germany and were fitted out for air-sea rescue duties. Under the supervision of the German company, Weser-Flugzeugbau, production also continued in Holland. During the next four years about 170 BMW-Bramo-powered Do 24Ts were produced. These served with Luftwaffe rescue units in the Atlantic and Mediterranean.

Before being overrun by the Japanese the Dutch used a number of Do 24s successfully in the East Indies. The aircraft

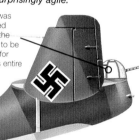

Above: An early Jumo-powered example awaits its next call to rescue. Crews found the Dutch design more capable than their own aircraft.

were later passed to the Royal Australian Air Force. Spain also acquired Do 24s and used these after World War II. A number of these remained in service for almost 30 years.

Above: Despite the large size of the Do 24 the aircraft was surprisingly agile.

Do 24T-1

Type: air-sea rescue and transport flying-boat

Powerplant: three 746-kW (1,000-hp.) BMW-Bramo 323R-2 nine-cylinder radial engines

Maximum speed: 331 km/h (205 m.p.h.)

Range: 4700 km (2,915 mi.)

Service ceiling: 7500 m (24,600 ft.)

Weights: empty 9400 kg (20,680 lb.); maximum take-off (overload) 18,400 kg (40,480 lb.)

Accommodation: two pilots and four crew

Armament: one 7.9-mm (0.31-in.) MG 15 machine gun in bow and stern turrets and one 20-mm (0.79-in.) Hispano Suiza 404 cannon in dorsal turret

Dimensions: span 27.00 m (88 ft. 7 in.)
length 22.05 m (72 ft. 4 in.)
height 5.75 m (18 ft. 10 in.)
wing area 108 m² (1,162 sq. ft.)

Early Do 24 variants were not fitted with a nose turret but, after combat losses, an enclosed turret with a 7.9-mm (0.31-in) machine gun was installed. Cockpit visibility was reasonable but was improved by the addition of large side windows.

Mounted high above the fuselage the wing provided the Do 24 with excellent lift, particularly when taking-off.

Rear defensive firepower was provided by a fully enclosed turret. The high-set tail of the Do 24 allowed the aircraft to be towed up onto the beach for repairs. One Do 24 had its entire tail blown off but survived.

Protruding from the lower fuselage on either-side were large winglets which helped stabilise the aircraft in rough seas. On two particular variants a large loop was attached around the fuselage of the aircraft for the mine-sweeping role.

Despite its slim profile the Do 24 was able to accommodate huge loads within its fuselage. During the evacuation of the Greek islands the aircraft airlifted more than 24 troops each with 30 kg (66 lb.) of equipment, before the advancing Allied army could capture them.

Do 24T-2

The skull emblem identifies this Do 24 as belonging to 8. Seenotstaffel, which operated in the Black Sea under Seenotbereichskommando XI during 1942. These aircraft were transferred from Mamaia, Romania, to Varna in Bulgaria.

COMBAT DATA

MAXIMUM TAKE OFF WEIGHT

With one of the largest take-off weights of any World War II flying-boat, the Do 24 proved itself capable of airlifting huge loads consisting of both troops and cargo. Earlier Dornier designs like the Do 18 simply could not match the Do 24's ability.

Do 24T-1 — 18,400 kg (40,480 lb.)
Do 18G-1 — 10,795 kg (23,749 lb.)
He 115B-1 — 10,400 kg (22,880 lb.)

MAXIMUM RANGE

Because of its long-range the Do 24 was ideal for search and rescue and reconnaissance duties. The Do 18 and He 115 also had respectable endurance. Like the Do 24, the He 115 served on both sides during World War II, the RAF operating a few captured He 115s on covert missions in the Mediterranean theatre.

Do 24T-1 4700 km (2,915 mi.)
Do 18G-1 3500 km (2,170 mi.)
He 115B-1 3350 km (2,077 mi.)

MAXIMUM SPEED

Equipped with three BMW engines, the Do 24 was capable of reaching a relatively high speed. However, Heinkel's He 115 was able to out-perform the Do 24 because of its lightweight fuselage and streamlined design.

Do 24T-1 331 km/h (205 m.p.h.)
Do 18G-1 267 km/h (166 m.p.h.)
He 115B-1 355 km/h (220 m.p.h.)

Flying boats of World War II

■ **CATALINA:** Operated by the US Navy and the Royal Navy Consolidated's Catalina was the Allies' main flying-boat for rescue work, serving both in the European and Pacific wars.

■ **SUNDERLAND:** Developed from the Shorts Empire flying-boat, the Sunderland allowed the RAF to search the whole of the Mediterranean for German submarines.

■ **WALRUS:** First flown in June 1933, the Supermarine Walrus was used for rescue duties and mine-spotting. The aircraft was small enough to be operated from battleships.

DOUGLAS

A-20 BOSTON/HAVOC

● Multi-role light bomber ● Low-level strike attack

D uring World War II the Douglas A-20 Havoc, called Boston by the RAF, fought on every continent and in every theatre of the war. It was not the fastest plane in its class, but it was extremely tough, handled well and was a popular and effective fighting machine, especially in the low-level attack role. Pilots knew they could fly the A-20 much like a fighter, inflicting considerable damage on their adversaries in the process.

▲ The A-20 was greatly feared by the enemy as it combined speed, agility and a hard-hitting weapon load. It successfully fulfilled many roles that it was never designed to undertake.

DOUGLAS A-20 BOSTON/HAVOC

Slim profile ▶
The narrow fuselage of the A-20 is apparent when seen from ahead. The shape gave speed and agility, but restricted the movement of the navigator and gunner.

▼ Boston bomber
The RAF was one of many satisfied foreign users. The Boston Mk III was used as a light bomber, but other Bostons served as radar night-fighters.

▲ Formation flying
Swarms of A-20s ranged at will over north-west Europe both before and after the invasion of Normandy.

Precision ▶ bomber
Bombing with deadly accuracy, Bostons and Havocs were used to attack communications targets in France and Belgium.

▲ Rocket-launcher
The hard-hitting Boston Mk III could be armed with 27-kg (60-lb.) rockets. The great strength of all the A-20 variants was their versatility in accepting almost any armament.

FACTS AND FIGURES

➤ The prototype for the A-20 Havoc series, the DB-7, first flew on 23 January 1939.

➤ One A-20 was evaluated by the US Navy as the BD-1, and eight reached the Marine Corps, designated BD-2.

➤ The first American A-20s used in combat flew from England in 1942.

➤ Russia received 3,125 A-20s, Britain 1,800 and the United States 1,962.

➤ The final A-20 was rolled out at Santa Monica on 20 September 1944.

➤ An F-3A Havoc photo ship was the first Allied aircraft to land at Itazuke, Japan, after the August 1945 surrender.

PROFILE

The all-purpose attack bomber

When designers Jack Northrop and Edward Heinemann designed the Douglas DB-7 in 1938, the idea of a twin-engined attack bomber with tricycle gear seemed futuristic. Although considered very advanced when it was purchased by Britain in 1940, it was no match for top fighters like the Spitfire and Bf 109. Known as the Boston in RAF service, it was used as a bomber and as a carrier for Turbinlite, a searchlight used to illuminate Luftwaffe warplanes by night for RAF Hurricanes to stalk.

As the A-20 Havoc the aircraft entered service with US Forces as a heavily-armed attack bomber. Havocs saw a lot of service. They ranged far and wide over the Pacific, strafing and bombing in the war against Japan, and supplied devastating fire support for the Normandy landings of June 1944. They were also popular with the Soviet air force, which was the largest user of the type. The P-70 night-fighter version and the F-3 Havoc reconnaissance craft were used mostly for training and saw limited combat.

Havocs flew some extremely dangerous missions. This raid on a Japanese anchorage in New Guinea resulted in the loss of one of the attacking A-20s.

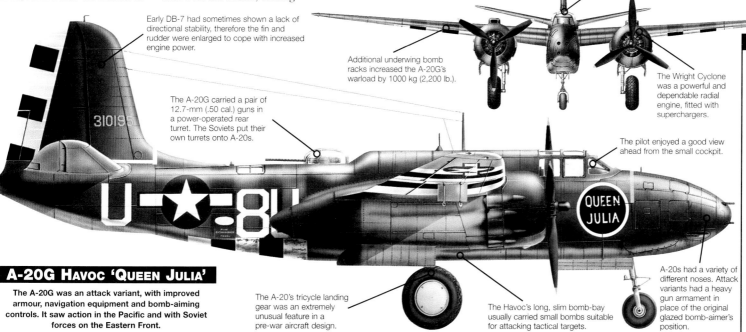

Early DB-7 had sometimes shown a lack of directional stability, therefore the fin and rudder were enlarged to cope with increased engine power.

Emergency flight controls were fitted to the rear crew compartment of early A-20s.

Additional underwing bomb racks increased the A-20G's warload by 1000 kg (2,200 lb.).

The A-20G carried a pair of 12.7-mm (.50 cal.) guns in a power-operated rear turret. The Soviets put their own turrets onto A-20s.

The Wright Cyclone was a powerful and dependable radial engine, fitted with superchargers.

The pilot enjoyed a good view ahead from the small cockpit.

A-20s had a variety of different noses. Attack variants had a heavy gun armament in place of the original glazed bomb-aimer's position.

A-20G HAVOC 'QUEEN JULIA'

The A-20G was an attack variant, with improved armour, navigation equipment and bomb-aiming controls. It saw action in the Pacific and with Soviet forces on the Eastern Front.

The A-20's tricycle landing gear was an extremely unusual feature in a pre-war aircraft design.

The Havoc's long, slim bomb-bay usually carried small bombs suitable for attacking tactical targets.

A-20G Havoc

Type: two-/three-seat light-attack bomber

Powerplant: two 1193-kW (2,625-hp.) Wright R-2800-23 Double Cyclone radial piston engines

Maximum speed: 546 km/h (340 m.p.h.) at 3780 m (12,400 ft.)

Range: 1754 km (1,087 mi.)

Service ceiling: 7865 m (25,800 ft.)

Weights: empty 7250 kg (14,950 lb.); loaded 12,338 kg (27,144 lb.)

Armament: six forward-firing 12.7-mm (.50 cal.) machine-guns in nose; two 12.7-mm machine-guns in power-operated dorsal turret; one manual 12.7-mm machine-gun in the ventral position; up to 1814 kg (3,990 lb.) of bombs

Dimensions:
span	18.69 m (61 ft.)
length	14.63 m (48 ft.)
height	5.36 m (18 ft.)
wing area	43.11 m² (464 sq. ft.)

COMBAT DATA

MAXIMUM SPEED

The Douglas DB-7 from which the A-20 was developed was one of the fastest bombers in service at the beginning of World War II. The Bristol Blenheim was, like the Douglas design, intended to be a light, fast bomber, but proved far more fragile. The Dornier Do 17 was classed as a medium bomber, but had similar performance to the smaller American machine.

A-20B HAVOC 475 km/h (295 m.p.h.)
Do 17Z 425 km/h (264 m.p.h.)
BLENHEIM Mk IV 470 km/h (291 m.p.h.)

RANGE

The A-20's range was sufficient for most tactical purposes, although the advanced Douglas design had less of a reach than its British equivalent. But the Blenheim had been developed from a record-breaking light transport, and had exceptional long-distance performance.

A-20B HAVOC 1600 km (992 mi.)
Do 17Z 1100 km (682 mi.)
BLENHEIM Mk IV 2500 km (1,550 mi.)

BOMBLOAD

Early versions of the Havoc had a relatively small weapons load, although the Dornier, classified as a medium bomber, could carry very little more. By the end of the war A-20s were routinely carrying nearly two tons of bombs.

A-20B HAVOC 907 kg (2,000 lb.)
Do 17Z 1000 kg (2,200 lb.)
BLENHEIM Mk IV 454 kg (1,000 lb.)

Havocs around the world

■ **FRANCE:** The first user of what was to become the Boston and then the Havoc was the French air force. Some were operated by the Vichy air force and others diverted to the RAF after the defeat of France in 1940.

■ **ON THE EASTERN FRONT:** The Soviets flew more A-20s than anybody else, receiving more than 3000 under Lend Lease. This Soviet navy A-20B served with the Northern Fleet in the Arctic late in 1943.

■ **DEFENDER OF THE EMPIRE:** British and Commonwealth air forces operated large numbers of Douglas bombers. This Boston Mk III was in action in March 1943 in New Guinea with No. 22 Squadron, Royal Australian Air Force.

DOUGLAS
A-26 INVADER

● Twin-engined bomber ● European and Pacific service

P erhaps better known for its post-war exploits, the Douglas A-26 Invader first served in the European and Pacific theatres of World War II from September 1944. Designed by Ed Heinemann to replace the A-20 Havoc, the A-26 was very similar to the Havoc in configuration. The roles of bomber, night-fighter and ground-attack aircraft were envisaged for the type, but it was for air-to-ground roles that production aircraft were ordered.

▲ Almost too late for combat during World War II, the Invader was destined for service during the Korean War and even flew, in refurbished form, during the Vietnam conflict.

PHOTO FILE

DOUGLAS A-26 INVADER

◀ XA-26 prototype
In an olive drab finish and fitted with large propeller spinners, the XA-26 prototype 41-19504 runs its engines. The serial '219504' was erroneously painted on its fin.

Wheels up on Okinawa ▶
This eight-gun Invader of the 89th Bomb Squadron, 3rd Bomb Wing, made a belly landing on Okinawa after one of the last strikes of the war on 11 August 1945.

Early gun nose ▶
This 'gun nose' B-model has four 12.7-mm (.50 cal.) machine-guns on the starboard side and two to port.

▼ Flak damage
A direct hit by German flak took off the port wing of this A-26B over Europe.

▼ First Invaders in Europe
In heavily overcast conditions at Beaumont-sur-Oise, A-26Bs of the 552nd Bomb Squadron, 386th Bombardment Group, share the apron with B-26 Marauders in May 1945.

FACTS AND FIGURES

➤ In all, 67 A-26s were lost in operations in the European theatre. Seven air-to-air victories by A-26s were confirmed.

➤ Douglas 'mocked-up' a 14-gun version of the A-26B; it failed to enter production.

➤ A-26s were known as B-26s in 1948, after the last Martin Marauders were retired.

➤ Unlike other bomber types, most A-26s were retained after 1945, and many became staff transports and target tugs.

➤ As well as A-20s, the A-26 was also used to replace B-25 Mitchells in some units.

➤ Of 2452 Invaders built, 2446 were A-26Bs and A-26Cs.

PROFILE

Just in time for the war

X A-26 41-19504, the Invader prototype, first took to the air on 10 July 1942. This aircraft had the glazed nose of the projected A-26C bomber variant. The A-26A night-fighter would have had a radar set in the nose, with four 20-mm cannon in a ventral pack.

For attack missions, the A-26B had six 12.7-mm (.50 cal.) machine-guns in its nose, remotely-controlled dorsal and ventral turrets, each with two 12.7-mm machine-guns, and up to 10 more in underwing and under-fuselage packs.

The night-fighter was cancelled, but the A-26B and A-26C models were rushed into production. The first Invaders in combat were four A-26Bs used in New Guinea, where the aircraft proved unpopular on low-level sorties. Clearly, all the type's 'bugs' had yet to be ironed out.

In September 1944 the 553rd Bomb Squadron at Great Dunmow, England received 18 machines. Their results were more promising. Eventually, 11,567 missions were flown, delivering 18,344 tonnes (18,054 tons) of bombs. One aircraft was even

credited with a probable 'kill' of an Me 262 jet fighter.

In the Pacific, air-to-ground and anti-shipping strikes were typical. Three USAAF bomb groups used A-26s against targets in Okinawa, Formosa and mainland Japan; A-26s were active near Nagasaki when the second A-bomb was dropped on 9 August 1945.

Left: With eight extra machine-guns guns in four underwing two-gun packs, the two A-26s nearest the camera are a glazed-nose A-26C (in the foreground) and an A-26B.

Above: A mixed complement of A-26s within the squadrons of a bomb group was not unusual. The 386th Bombardment Group operated both A-26Bs and Cs.

A-26C Invader

Type: three-seat light attack bomber

Powerplant: two 1419-kW (2,000-hp.) Pratt & Whitney R-2800-79 Double Wasp radial piston engines

Maximum speed: 600 km/h (372 m.p.h.)

Initial climb rate: 619 m/min (2,030 f.p.m.)

Range: 2253 km (1,400 mi.)

Service ceiling: 6735 m (22,100 ft.)

Weights: empty 10,365 kg (22,803 lb.); maximum take-off 15,876 kg (34,927 lb.)

Armament: six 12.7-mm (.50 cal.) machine-guns (two each in nose, dorsal and ventral positions), plus 1814 kg (4,000 lb.) of bombs internally

Dimensions:
span	21.34 m (70 ft.)
length	15.62 m (51 ft. 3 in.)
height	5.56 m (18 ft. 3 in.)
wing area	50.17 m² (540 sq. ft.)

A-26B INVADER

Stinky was an A-26B built at Douglas's Tulsa, Oklahoma plant. Attached to the 552nd Bomb Squadron, 386th Bombardment Group, it was based at Beaumont-sur-Oise in April 1945.

As well as a pilot, A-26s were crewed by a bombardier/navigator, who normally sat next to the pilot but also had a work station in the nose, and a gunner.

Poor visibility was a problem on early-build Invaders. The original heavily-framed canopy was hinged at the front and was difficult to open into the airstream during an in-flight emergency. Later aircraft had a two-section 'clam shell' canopy, hinged at the sides and meeting in the middle. These greatly improved visibility and made emergency exits easier.

Pratt & Whitney's R-2800 Double Wasp 18-cylinder radial engine powered the A-26 Invaders. During the production life of the B model, the oil cooler air intakes were redesigned, which accounted for 80 per cent of the later improvement in the aircraft's performance. The inside of the engine cowlings were painted in an olive drab anti-dazzle finish to reduce glare problems encountered by pilots.

Nose gun armament fitted to the B-model Invader varied from batch to batch. Six or eight 12.7-mm (.50 cal.) machine-guns were typical. Some carried cannon.

A bomb bay with capacity for up to 1814 kg (4,000 lb.) of bombs filled the space between the cockpit and the gunner's position. Large two-piece bomb bay doors were even longer, stretching from the cockpit almost as far as the ventral turret.

The Invader's gunner reached his position via a bomb bay entry hatch and remotely controlled the dorsal and ventral turrets, each of which held two 12.7-mm (.50 cal.) machine-guns. In the 'gun-nose' C-model, the navigator also served as a gun loader for the nose armament.

COMBAT DATA

MAXIMUM SPEED

Among the improvements introduced with the A-26 was an increased top speed. The A-26C had a speed advantage of close to 100 km/h (62 m.p.h.) over its predecessor, the A-20 Havoc. The Havoc's contemporary, the B-26 Marauder, was slower still.

A-26 INVADER	600 km/h (372 m.p.h.)
A-20G HAVOC	510 km/h (316 m.p.h.)
B-26	454 km/h (281 m.p.h.)

CEILING

The Invader had a lower service ceiling than the A-20, of about 6700 m (22,000 ft.), just 300 m (1,000 ft.) more than that of the B-26. The Invader's initial operations in the Pacific theatre were at low level. Bomb-release altitudes were higher in Europe.

A-26C INVADER 6735 m (22,100 ft.)	A-20G HAVOC 7865 m (25,800 ft.)	B-26 MARAUDER 6400 m (21,000 ft.)

RANGE

One of the greatest improvements to come with the Invader was range. The A-26C had a 400–500 km (250–350 mi.) advantage over the types it was to replace. This added to the versatility of the type, and was especially useful in the 'over-water' operations carried out in the Pacific.

A-26C INVADER 2253 km (1,400 mi.)

A-20G HAVOC 1754 km (1,087 mi.)

B-26 MARAUDER 1851 km (1,148 mi.)

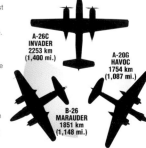

Douglas's famous wartime designs

■ **A-20/P-70 HAVOC:** Immediate predecessor of the Invader, the A-20 was built in bomber and attack versions; the P-70 was a night-fighter.

■ **C-47 SKYTRAIN:** Known by the RAF and Commonwealth as the Dakota, the C-47 was the Allies' standard wartime transport aircraft.

■ **DB.7 BOSTON:** The RAF employed a bomber variant of the A-20 known as the Boston and a night-fighter version called the Havoc.

■ **SBD DAUNTLESS:** This carrier-borne scout bomber served the US Navy in large numbers in the Pacific theatre.

DOUGLAS
SBD DAUNTLESS

● Carrier-borne dive-bomber ● Hero of the Pacific war

▲ Deck and air crew prepare for a mission. No aircraft did more to win the Pacific war than the SBD Dauntless: it sank more Japanese ships than any other type.

I f it had done nothing else but fight at Midway – where a handful of carrier pilots turned the tide of the Pacific war – the Douglas SBD Dauntless would be counted among important aircraft of the 20th century. But the SBD did more than wreck the Japanese fleet in that battle on 4 June 1942. From its conception in 1938 until late 1944 the SBD showed itself to be the most important American dive-bomber ever built.

DOUGLAS SBD DAUNTLESS

▲ Dauntless 'Leathernecks'
Although best known as a US Navy warplane, the Dauntless also served in large numbers with the US Marine Corps, operating from land bases.

Dive attack ▶
The leader of a section of SBDs rolls into the attack. Dive strikes were usually made from an altitude between 4500 and 6000 m (15,000 and 20,000 ft.), with the dive angle reaching about 70°. This gave great accuracy.

▲ In North Africa
Atlantic Fleet SBDs got their first taste of major action in November 1942, during the Allied landings in North Africa, known as Operation 'Torch'.

▲ Difficult Dauntless
Despite its successes, the SBD Dauntless was underpowered, vulnerable and, above all, exhausting to fly for any length of time.

Carrier launch ▶
An SBD gets the signal to take off from its carrier. The air wing was carefully arranged on the deck in the order in which the aircraft were due to fly.

FACTS AND FIGURES

➤ Pilot Lieutenant Robert Dixon signalled 'Scratch one flat-top' after his attack on the Japanese carrier *Shoho*.

➤ The first Dauntless, a modified XBT-2, was test-flown on 22 April 1938.

➤ At the battle of Midway, Dauntlesses sank Japan's four main aircraft-carriers.

➤ One US Navy Dauntless gunner was credited with shooting down seven Mitsubishi Zero fighters in two days.

➤ SBDs sank more Japanese shipping than any other US aircraft in the Pacific.

➤ The last Dauntless, an SBD-6, was rolled out on 22 July 1944.

PROFILE

Douglas' deadly dive-bomber

The Douglas SBD Dauntless pounded the Japanese at Coral Sea, Midway and in the Solomons, and supported US Navy and Marine Corps actions until late 1944. This was a fair achievement for an aircraft that was underpowered, vulnerable, short on range and exhausting to fly. For all its flaws, the Dauntless, designed by Jack Northrop and Ed Heinemann, was a dramatic success.

Pilots of the SBD Dauntless sat high in a relatively 'clean' aircraft optimised to hurl bombs at targets while flying straight down into the enemy's midst. The pilot aimed the aircraft, and a crutch-like trapeze threw forth a centreline bomb that narrowly cleared the propeller arc before boring downwards. The SBD roared, rattled and required constant attention on stick, throttle and rudder, but pilots took pride in mastering it and praised its achievements as a dive-bomber.

The US Army Dauntless, the A-24, was outfought on Java in 1942 and was later used mostly for training. By the end of the war, Navy Dauntlesses were replaced by the Curtiss SB2C Helldiver, but this aircraft never won the affection routinely bestowed on its predecessor.

Above: Three SBD-5s return from a mission. The furthest aircraft has its aft defensive guns deployed from the rear cockpit.

Above: Until mid-1942, US aircraft wore highly visible red and white rudder stripes.

Left: In the dive the Dauntless used 'Swiss cheese' divebrakes to keep the speed down.

SBD-5 Dauntless

Type: two-seat carrier-based scout and dive-bomber

Powerplant: one 895-kW (1,200-hp.) Wright R-1820-60 Cyclone air-cooled radial piston engine

Maximum speed: 410 km/h (254 m.p.h.) at 3050 m (10,000 ft.)

Initial climb rate: 518 m/min (1,700 f.p.m.)

Range: 730 km (453 mi.) on a bombing mission; 1244 km (771 mi.) on a scouting mission

Service ceiling: 7400 m (24,275 ft.)

Armament: two 12.7-mm (.50 cal.) fixed machine-guns in the nose and two 7.62-mm (.30 cal.) manually aimed machine-guns in the rear crewman's position, plus up to 725 kg (1,600 lb.) of bombs under the fuselage and 295 kg (650 lb.) of bombs under the wings

Dimensions:
span	12.66 m (42 ft.)
length	10.09 m (33 ft.)
height	4.14 m (14 ft.)
wing area	30.19 m² (325 sq. ft.)

SBD-4 DAUNTLESS

Clutching a bomb to its belly, this Dauntless served with the US Marine Corps in July 1943, flying in New Guinea. The US Navy and USMC SBDs exacted a huge toll on the Japanese shipping fleet.

Power for the Dauntless came from the trusty Wright R-1820 Cyclone engine. Even at 746 kW (1,000 hp.) in the SBD-3/4 this was not really enough, so the SBD-5 introduced an uprated Cyclone offering 895 kW (1,200 hp.).

The pilot had a telescopic bombsight projecting through the windshield. This tended to fog over because of the change in temperature during the dive.

In the rear cockpit sat the radio operator. It was also his task to operate the rear defensive armament, which consisted of a pair of 7.62-mm (.30 cal.) Browning machine-guns. In transit these weapons were stowed in the fuselage behind hinged doors. On entering the combat zone, the rear canopy was stowed in the fuselage and the guns deployed from their bay, giving the gunner a wide field of fire.

The bomb armament consisted of a single weapon of up to 726 kg on the centreline, with 295 kg of bombs under the wings.

The centreline bomb was carried on a special double-armed cradle. When the bomb was released by the pilot, the cradle swung forwards so that the bomb would clear the propeller arc.

The wings had a strange brake assembly which extended on both the upper and lower surfaces. On the undersides the brake surfaces were located right the way across the fuselage. All the surfaces had large holes in them, hence the name 'Swiss cheese' divebrakes, to avoid buffeting problems.

COMBAT DATA

MAXIMUM SPEED

The Dauntless was a neat design, but the lack of power did not give it a blistering turn of speed. However, compared to its early-war rivals it was well placed. Its intended replacement in the US Navy, the Curtiss SB2C Helldiver, was not much faster at about 470 km/h (291 m.p.h.).

SKUA Mk II	362 km/h (224 m.p.h.)
SBD-5 DAUNTLESS	410 km/h (254 m.p.h.)
D3A1 'VAL'	385 km/h (239 m.p.h.)

BOMBLOAD

Compared to its rivals the Dauntless carried an exceptional load, due largely to the high stressing of the centreline cradle. This in turn allowed it to carry bombs of true ship-killing size. The small wing bombs gave added firepower, notably in attacks against land targets.

SBD-5 DAUNTLESS 1020 kg (2,245 lb.)
D3A1 'VAL' 370 kg (814 lb.)
SKUA Mk II 330 kg (725 lb.)

RANGE

One area where the Dauntless did not perform well was range, certainly compared to its main rival in the Pacific, the D3A. This gave Japanese carrier commanders a slight advantage: they could position their ships so that the D3As could just reach the Americans, but were themselves out of range of the Dauntless force.

SBD-5 DAUNTLESS 1244 km (771 mi.)
D3A1 'VAL' 1470 km (911 mi.)
SKUA Mk II 1223 km (758 mi.)

Battle of Midway

PACIFIC TURNING POINT: Japan's complex plan to dominate the Pacific hinged on drawing into battle and destroying the US Navy carrier force. But the Americans knew that they could turn the tables on Admiral Yamamoto if they could find the Japanese and strike first. The manoeuvring came to a climax on 4 June 1942, north-east of the island of Midway.

1 Japanese launch strike at Midway at 0430.

2 Midway-based US aircraft attack at 0730.

4 US Navy torpedo planes attack unsuccessfully at 0928, followed by Dauntless dive-bombers which smash the carriers *Kaga, Akagi* and *Soryu* between 1025 and 1030.

5 Sole surviving carrier *Hiryu* launches against American carriers at 1331; attacked by SBDs from *Enterprise* at 1700 and fatally damaged.

6 *Yorktown* hit by *Hiryu* strike and abandoned. The hulk was sunk by a Japanese submarine three days later.

3 Main US Navy carrier strikes launched between 0800 and 0900.

DOUGLAS
TBD DEVASTATOR

● Carrier-based torpedo-bomber ● All metal ● World War II service

This American torpedo-bomber is mainly remembered for a tragic reason – at Midway an entire squadron of Douglas TBD Devastators was lost in a matter of minutes. The Devastator was a perfectly acceptable aircraft by pre-war standards, but it came on the scene when change was occurring rapidly. By the time men and machines were pitted in combat in the Pacific, the TBD was no longer an effective warplane.

▲ *Although the Devastator represented the state of the art in the mid-1930s, it was to be tragically outclassed during the battles in the Pacific in the early 1940s.*

DOUGLAS TBD DEVASTATOR

◄ First squadron equipped
VT-3 was the first unit to receive the Devastator, in October 1937. Three more squadrons received the aircraft in 1938, and in 1942 all four saw action against the Japanese.

▲ First Devastator – the XTBD-1
Flown in April 1935, the first TBD had a lower cockpit canopy. This was raised on production aircraft to improve visibility on take-off and landing.

▲ Devastator floatplane
The first production TBD was fitted with Edo floats, as the TBD-1A, and was test flown from Newport, Rhode Island, in 1939.

Hydraulic wing folding ▶
TBDs were the first US naval aircraft with hydraulically-powered wing folding. The upward fold of the wings was also unusual.

California ▶ factory
These TBDs are seen under construction at Douglas' Santa Monica factory. The left-hand aircraft carries the markings of the US Navy's VT-2 unit.

▲ Aboard *Enterprise* before Midway
Only four of these TBDs from torpedo-bomber squadron VT-6 returned from their next mission.

FACTS AND FIGURES

➤ One of the first Technicolour films about US naval aviation was *Dive Bomber* of 1941, which featured VT-3 TBDs.

➤ TBD carrier trials began in December 1935 aboard USS *Lexington*.

➤ Devastators ended their careers as communications and training aircraft.

➤ The Devastator was the US Navy's first all-metal, low-wing aircraft and its first carrier-based monoplane.

➤ The first TBD was delivered to the Navy just nine days after its maiden flight.

➤ Douglas built 129 production TBD-1s while also developing the SBD Dauntless.

PROFILE

First Navy all-metal monoplane

Donald Douglas' fine aircraft company developed the TBD Devastator in 1934 to give the US Navy a much-needed torpedo-bomber which was able to fly from aircraft-carrier decks. The low-wing, tailwheel-equipped Devastator was able to carry a torpedo or bomb beneath its fuselage, or smaller bombs under its fuselage and wings.

The crew of three, consisting of pilot, gunner and navigator/torpedo officer operator, faced a great deal of danger. From the very beginning of World War II, it was obvious that the Devastator was outclassed.

On 4 June 1942 at Midway, no fewer than 35 Devastators were shot down. They included all of the US Navy's Torpedo Squadron Eight (VT-8). Sole survivor Ensign George Gay, having succumbed to Japanese fire and bobbing in a life raft, had a horrific view as Japanese guns blasted his colleagues out of the sky. Many were victims of withering fire from the ships' guns; others were shot down by fighters.

Soon afterwards, the Devastator was withdrawn from combat units – left behind by a war that was moving faster than it did – and relegated to training duties.

Above: Seen over Wake Island in February 1942, this TBD from the Enterprise *carries a fresh coat of sea green and pale grey paint. In May a US Navy dispatch ordered the red national insignia and tail markings to be removed.*

Below: This pre-war view shows Devastators of VT-5. By early 1942 TBDs from this unit, stationed aboard USS Yorktown, *were raiding Japanese targets in the Gilbert Islands.*

TBD-1 Devastator

Type: three-seat torpedo-bomber

Powerplant: one 671-kW (900-hp.) Pratt & Whitney R-1830-64 Twin Wasp radial piston engine

Maximum speed: 332 km/h (205 m.p.h.) at 2440 m (8,000 ft.)

Cruising speed: 206 km/h (128 m.p.h.)

Range: 670 km (415 mi.)

Service ceiling: 6005 m (19,700 ft.)

Weights: empty 2804 kg (6,169 lb.); maximum take-off 4624 kg (10,173 lb.)

Armament: one 7.62-mm (.30 cal.) forward-firing machine-gun and one 7.62-mm gun on flexible mount, plus one 454-kg (1,000-lb.) torpedo or up to 680 kg (1,500 lb.) of bombs

Dimensions:
span	15.24 m	(50 ft.)
length	10.67 m	(35 ft.)
height	4.60 m	(15 ft.)
wing area	39.20 m²	(422 sq. ft.)

TBD-1 DEVASTATOR

TBD-1 0322 carries the pre-war markings of Torpedo Squadron 6 (VT-6), one of four units equipped with the Devastator from 1937.

The R-1830 variant of Pratt & Whitney's well-known Twin Wasp powered the TBD. This powerplant was also widely used in other types, such as the C-47 Skytrain.

Devastators were manned by three crew: a pilot, a navigator/torpedo officer and a gunner. The latter sat at the rear of the cockpit 'glasshouse' and fired a 7.62-mm (.30 cal.) machine-gun. A forward-firing machine-gun was also fitted in the inner port wing.

Although the TBD was built with wing flotation bags to allow the crew time to escape the aircraft if it ditched, these were removed in wartime. This ensured that the TBD would sink, taking its advanced Norden bombsight with it.

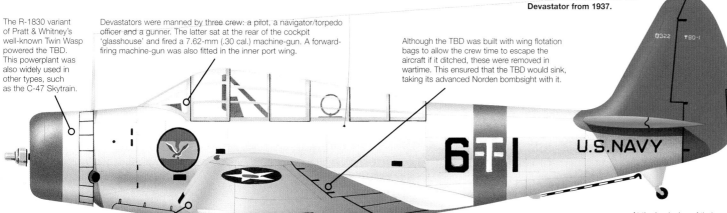

Although the TBD boasted a powered wing-folding mechanism, it lacked sufficient power to move the wings in a strong cross wind. This required assistance from the ground handlers.

The TBD's usual load was a 454-kg (1,000-lb.) torpedo carried under the fuselage. An alternative often used in 1942 against Japanese targets in the Gilbert and Marshall Islands was up to three 227-kg (500-lb.) bombs or a dozen 45-kg (100-lb.) bombs, six under each wing.

At the beginning of their service TBDs suffered a number of crashes after pilots, who were not used to folding wings, failed to check that their wings were locked in position.

COMBAT DATA

MAXIMUM SPEED

The Avenger, which also suffered losses during the Battle of Midway, had a top speed some 100 km/h (60 m.p.h.) higher than the TBD. This, combined with its better defensive armament, made it less vulnerable to Japanese fighters.

TBD-1 DEVASTATOR	**332 km/h (205 m.p.h.)**
TG-2	**204 km/h (126 m.p.h.)**
TBF-1 AVENGER	**436 km/h (270 m.p.h.)**

RANGE

Range was very important for a torpedo-bomber, allowing it to fly missions over longer distances from the carrier, and therefore reducing the risk to the ship. The TBD's range was more than twice that of the TG-2.

TBD-1 DEVASTATOR	**1152 km (714 mi.)**	
TG-2	**531 km (329 mi.)**	**TBF-1 AVENGER** 1955 km (1,212 mi.)

ARMAMENT

In a similar way that the Devastator was a huge improvement over the TG-2, so the Grumman Avenger was a much better armed aircraft, both defensively and offensively. It carried more machine-guns and had a high-capacity weapons bay.

TBD-1 DEVASTATOR	2 x 7.62-mm (.30 cal.) machine-guns 1 torpedo or 680 kg (1,500 lb.) of bombs
TG-2	1 x 7.62-mm (.30 cal.) machine-gun 1 torpedo
TBF-1 AVENGER	2 x 7.62-mm (.30 cal.) machine-guns 1 x 12.7-mm (.50 cal.) machine-guns 1 torpedo or 726 kg (1,600 lb.) of bombs

US Navy aircraft at Midway

■ **CONSOLIDATED PBY CATALINA:** Catalina patrol bombers based at Midway and with a 4500-km (2,790-mi.) range gave the Navy prior warning of the approaching Japanese fleet.

■ **DOUGLAS SBD DAUNTLESS:** Carrier-based Dauntless dive-bombers inflicted the bulk of the damage on the Japanese fleet, helping to sink four of its carriers.

■ **GRUMMAN F4F WILDCAT:** Fighter escort for the bombers was provided by carrier-based Wildcats. In all, 79 were deployed aboard three carriers: Enterprise, Hornet and Yorktown.

■ **GRUMMAN TBF AVENGER:** Some of the Navy's first Avengers were deployed in Midway and flew missions against the Japanese in which they suffered huge losses.

DOUGLAS
C-47 SKYTRAIN

● Worldwide service ● Transport and glider tug ● Still flying

Based on the DC-3, the Douglas C-47 Skytrain became the most widely used transport of the war. This familiar and versatile military transport hauled cargoes, dropped paratroops and towed gliders. No airfield was too close to the front or too rough for the versatile Skytrain. Eisenhower called the C-47 one of the four most important weapons of the war, along with the bazooka, the Jeep and the atomic bomb.

▲ Many crewmembers owed their lives to the strength of the C-47, when the aircraft were caught by enemy fighters or anti-aircraft fire. Equally, many troops were saved by supplies and reinforcements delivered by the Skytrain.

PHOTO FILE

DOUGLAS C-47 SKYTRAIN

▲ Skytrain gathering
Many hundreds of aircraft were involved in operations from the UK. Here, closely parked C-47s prepare for a mission in support of the D-Day invasion forces.

▲ Floating transport
A single XC-47C was built with floats and a few aircraft were converted to this configuration in the field.

▲ 'Gooney Bird'
US Army Air Force personnel nicknamed the C-47 'The Gooney Bird'.

▼ Last of the line
Douglas built 10,691 C-47s, this aircraft being the last manufactured at the Long Beach factory. Some aircraft were built in Japan and the USSR.

▲ Supply drop
Troops in every theatre, from Europe through Africa to the Pacific, regarded the C-47 as a lifeline. All types of equipment, food and medical supplies were dropped by parachute to the front line.

FACTS AND FIGURES

➤ On 10 July 1943 Skytrains dropped 4381 Allied paratroopers during the invasion of Sicily.

➤ The prototype for the DC-3/C-47 made its maiden flight on 17 December 1935.

➤ More than 1000 C-47s participated in the D-Day invasion.

➤ Skytrains were fine glider tugs and were used to haul glider-borne troops into battle in France and Burma.

➤ Some C-47s were flown with floats, instead of their wheeled undercarriage.

➤ Skytrains were built in Japan by Nakajima and in the USSR by Lisunov.

Unsurpassed military transport

The qualities which made the DC-3 a fine airliner made the C-47 a superb military transport, which served in every theatre of the war. The twin-engined C-47 was rugged and reliable, and could fly from primitive airfields in the midst of the war zone, carrying cargo, troops or towing gliders.

The Skytrain was in many respects the most versatile military aircraft ever built and flew in a number of very important operations. The most memorable C-47 mission was the dropping of paratroopers in Normandy in the hours before the 6 June 1944 invasion of Europe by Allied armies.

But the C-47 was everywhere: in Burma, an enterprising Skytrain pilot poked a Browning automatic rifle out of his cockpit and shot down a Japanese Zero fighter. In the Aleutian Islands C-47s equipped with skis brought supplies to American soldiers by landing on and taking off from ice-covered surfaces.

Many Skytrains survived being hit by gunfire and being attacked by fighters, and were deemed the 'most survivable' of all Allied transport aircraft.

Left: Gliders were too valuable to be used only once and therefore a system of retrieval was devised. The glider's towline was held above the ground between two poles and snatched by a long hook trailing from a low-flying C-47 Skytrain.

Above: Although it was an exceptional airlifter, the C-47 was not very easy to load. All cargo had to be hauled through the left-hand side cargo doors.

C-47A Skytrain

Type: cargo, troop or paratroop transport and glider tug

Powerplant: two 895-kW (1,200-hp.) Pratt & Whitney R-1830-92 Twin Wasp radial engines

Maximum speed: 365 km/h (226 m.p.h.) at 2285 m (7,500 ft.)

Range: 2414 km (1,597 mi.)

Service ceiling: 7070 m (24,000 ft.)

Weights: empty 8256 kg (18,163 lb.); maximum take-off 11,794 kg (25,947 lb.)

Accommodation: up to 28 paratroops or 14 stretchers or 4536 kg (9,979 lb.) of cargo

Dimensions:
span	29.11 m	(95 ft. 6 in.)
length	19.43 m	(63 ft. 9 in.)
height	5.18 m	(17 ft.)
wing area	91.69 m²	(987 sq. ft.)

C-47A SKYTRAIN

During the D-Day landings 'Buzz Buggy' flew from a British base with the 81st Troop Carrier Squadron of the 436th Troop Carrier Group.

A three-man crew of pilot, co-pilot and radio operator flew the C-47. The radio operator sat in a separate compartment behind the cockpit and the aircrew entered by the small forward door.

Folding wooden seats along the cabin sides could accommodate up to 28 fully equipped paratroops. As well as cargo, standard internal fittings allowed 18 stretchers to be carried.

Two large cargo doors allowed cabin access, one opening forwards and the other backwards. A small door inset into the forward freight door was used for in-flight paratroop dropping.

Two Pratt & Whitney R-1830 14-cylinder air-cooled radial piston engines, each of 30-litre (6.5-gal.) capacity, drove the Hamilton Standard propellers of all the standard production Skytrains.

Douglas designed the C-47 with a structure of metal stressed-skin and multiple spars, which produced a wing which was very resistant to fatigue.

All Allied aircraft taking part in the D-Day operations were painted with these black and white 'invasion stripes' as a recognition aid.

Skytrain versatility

This highly versatile aircraft flew many types of mission, but its primary role was as a transport and glider tug.

DROPPING PARATROOPS: Several daring airborne raids would not have been possible without large numbers of C-47s; 28 troops could be dropped in quick succession.

GLIDER TUG: Several hundred gliders were used in the D-Day assault on Normandy. Packed with troops and equipment, the glider was released near the landing zone.

WACO CG-4A HADRIAN: Using gliders, the Allies were able to increase the capacity of their transport fleet quickly and cheaply.

FREIGHTER: Loading freight, especially heavy wheeled equipment into the C-47 was difficult because of the aircraft's tailwheel undercarriage.

COMBAT DATA

PAYLOAD

Being a larger aircraft than the C-47, the Curtiss C-46 was able to carry more cargo. The capabilities of the C-46 were well suited to the Pacific theatre and most never saw the difficult combat action of the C-47. The Ju 52/3mg3e had a poor payload.

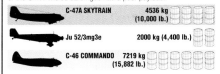

C-47A SKYTRAIN	4536 kg (10,000 lb.)
Ju 52/3mg3e	2000 kg (4,400 lb.)
C-46 COMMANDO	7219 kg (15,882 lb.)

SERVICE CEILING

At higher altitudes an aircraft possesses better range. This is an important factor for long-distance flights or those over mountainous terrain.

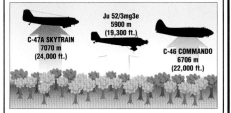

Ju 52/3mg3e 5900 m (19,300 ft.)
C-47A SKYTRAIN 7070 m (24,000 ft.)
C-46 COMMANDO 6706 m (22,000 ft.)

RANGE

Flying over 'the hump' into China was the main mission of the C-46, which had an extremely long range. The Junkers Ju 52/3mg3e served in a very similar, but more tactical, role to the C-47. Its range was much less than its American equivalent, however, and the Ju 52 was not a great glider tug. The Ju 52 was the only one with defensive guns.

Ju 52/3mg3e 1100 km (682 mi.)
C-47A SKYTRAIN 2414 km (1,597 mi.)
C-46 COMMANDO 7219 km (3,150 mi.)

FAIREY

FIREFLY

● Carrier-based ● Night-fighter ● Attack and reconnaissance

FAIREY FIREFLY

◀ In the Pacific
Displaying the large white and blue Pacific theatre markings of the period, a Firefly sets off in search of Japanese surface vessels during the closing stages of World War II.

Aboard HMS Pretoria Castle ▶
As the pilot walks away, deck hands prepare to remove a crashed Firefly, the victim of a failed arrester hook.

Radar-equipped ▶
Carrying American ASH radar in a pod under its nose, the Firefly F.Mk I became the FR.Mk I. Firefly night-fighters used a modified version of the same radar and were designated NF.Mk I. The NF.Mk I was a conversion, unlike the purpose-built NF.Mk II.

▼ Night fighter
Equipped with a bulky AI.Mk X radar, the NF.Mk II Firefly featured an extended forward fuselage to retain the same centre of gravity for the aircraft.

▲ Trials flying
With the brightly painted yellow under-surfaces of a trials machine, this early Firefly Mk I is seen on a test flight. Minor differences compared to later machines include the unfaired cannons and low profile cockpit canopy.

Fighter-reconnaissance aircraft had been part of the Royal Navy's inventory since the mid-1920s, when machines like the Fleetwing and Osprey were conceived. The first monoplane in this class was the Fairey Fulmar of 1940 and it was to replace this aircraft that another Fairey product, the Firefly, was designed. Perhaps better known for its post-war service, the Firefly served from 1943 and was active on raids against the *Tirpitz* and in the Pacific.

▲ Like other carrier-borne aircraft the Firefly had folding wings to facilitate storage aboard ship. These were heavy and had to be manhandled into position by deck crews before each flight.

FACTS AND FIGURES

➤ Fireflies were the first FAA aircraft to fly over, and the first British aircraft to land on, the Japanese mainland in 1945.

➤ The Firefly was the second Fairey naval design to bear the name.

➤ FAA NF.Mk Is were used to intercept He 111s carrying V-1 flying bombs in 1944.

➤ The Firefly's first air-to-air victory was on 2 January 1945 when a No. 1770 Squadron pilot downed a Japanese Nakajima Ki-43.

➤ Post-war, a number of Firefly Mk Is were converted to pilot and observer trainers.

➤ FAA Fireflies raided Japan prior to the planned invasion of the mainland.

PROFILE

Fairey's fearsome Firefly

Among the Firefly's features that made it such an advance over the Fulmar were its more powerful Rolls-Royce Griffon engine, 20-mm (0.79-in.) cannon armament, a higher top speed and a set of Fairey-Youngman flaps. The latter greatly improved low-speed handling and all-round manoeuvrability.

The Firefly prototype flew on 22 December 1941 and the following year 200 Firefly F.Mk I were ordered for the Fleet Air Arm (FAA). Between 1943 and 1946 850 Mk Is were built, including a batch by General Aircraft.

Following the F.Mk I into service was the FR.Mk I fighter-reconnaissance version, with American ASH air-to-surface vessel radar fitted. (F.Mk Is converted to FR standard were known as F.Mk IAs.) The only Firefly Mk IIs built were 37 NF.Mk II night-fighters, with AI.Mk X radar. When it was decided to convert FR.Mk Is for the role (as NF.Mk Is with modified ASH radar), further Mk II production was cancelled.

The Mk I was operational for the first time in July 1944, when aircraft from No.1770 Squadron aboard HMS *Indefatigable* attacked gun positions and

Above: Despite its size, the Firefly was a fairly nimble aircraft. This example has a radar pod bracket fitted.

auxiliary vessels during raids on the German battleship *Tirpitz*. In the Far East, FAA Fireflies attacked Japanese oil refineries on Sumatra in January 1945. After joining the British Pacific Fleet, three Firefly squadrons took part in raids on the Caroline Islands during June.

Below: Deck crews hurriedly fold the wings of rocket-firing FAA Fireflies after a strike against Japanese oil refineries on Sumatra. These attacks disrupted enemy fuel supplies.

Firefly F.Mk I

Type: two-seat reconnaissance fighter and fighter/bomber

Powerplant: one 1290-kW (1,730-hp.) Rolls-Royce Griffon IIB piston engine

Maximum speed: 509 km/h (316 m.p.h.) at 4265 m (14,000 ft.)

Range: 2092 km (1,300 mi.)

Service ceiling: 8535 m (28,000 ft.)

Weights: empty 4423 kg (9,731 lb.); maximum take-off 6359 kg (13,990 lb.)

Armament: four 20-mm (0.79-in.) Hispano cannon in wings, plus provision for up to eight 27-kg (60-lb.) rockets or two 454-kg (1,000-lb.) bombs on wing racks

Dimensions:
span	13.56 m	(44 ft. 6 in.)
length	11.46 m	(37 ft. 7 in.)
height	4.14 m	(13 ft. 7 in.)
wing area	30.47 m²	(326 sq. ft.)

The Firefly prototype and the early production aircraft were distinguished by their shallower windscreen and more confining cockpit canopy. Later machines, like this one, had larger canopies to improve the pilot's view.

The aircraft's observer was accommodated in the rear cockpit. When ASH radar was fitted, as on the FR.Mk I and NF.Mk I, the radar screen was situated here for operation by the observer. The NF.Mk II, of which only 37 were built, had such a heavy radar set that the aircraft's centre of gravity was upset, necessitating the fitting of a longer nose.

ROYAL NAVY
Z2035

Rolls-Royce's then new Griffon engine was installed in the Firefly, greatly improving performance over that of the Fulmar. This drove a three-bladed propeller on early production aircraft.

In common with other British fighters of the second half of World War II, the Firefly had an armament fit consisting of four 20-mm (0.79-in.) Underwing racks were used to carry rockets.

Fairey-Youngman flaps fitted to the Firefly greatly improved the aircraft's handling at the slow flight speeds associated with aircraft carrier approaches.

FIREFLY F.MK I

Firefly Mk I Z2035 was delivered in May 1944 and employed as a Fleet Air Arm torpedo training aircraft before being assigned to No. 730 Squadron, a communications unit, at Ayr, Scotland.

ACTION DATA

MAXIMUM SPEED

Of the various Fairey types employed by the FAA in the air-to-surface role during World War II, the Firefly Mk I was by far the fastest. Intended to fill a fighter role, the Griffon-powered Firefly needed a good turn of speed.

FIREFLY F.Mk I	509 km/h (316 m.p.h.)
BARRACUDA Mk II	367 km/h (228 m.p.h.)
SWORDFISH Mk II	222 km/h (138 m.p.h.)

SERVICE CEILING

Service ceiling was also an area in which the Firefly had a definite edge. It had a 3000 m advantage over the Fairey Barracuda and an even larger margin over the Fairey Swordfish. Height was an important advantage for an interceptor like the Firefly.

FIREFLY F.Mk I	BARRACUDA Mk II	SWORDFISH Mk II
8535 m (28,000 ft.)	5060 m (16,700 ft.)	3260 m (10,700 ft.)

RANGE

In terms of range the differences between the types were less pronounced. A slow, torpedo-carrying aircraft, the old Swordfish biplane had a good range, about 50 per cent more than that of the more modern Barracuda, another anti-shipping aircraft.

FIREFLY F.Mk I 2092 km (1,300 mi.)

BARRACUDA Mk II 1104 km (685 mi.)

SWORDFISH Mk II 1658 km (1,030 mi.)

FAA fighter-reconnaissance types

FAIREY FLEETWING: In 1926 the FAA saw the need for a spotter-reconnaissance aircraft with a limited ability as a fighter. The sole Fleetwing (N235) was among several prototypes built to meet the FAA requirement, but failed to achieve an order; losing out to the Osprey.

HAWKER OSPREY: A deck-landing variant of the RAF's Hart bomber, the Osprey entered service in 1932. A number were completed with floats and were joined by the single-seat Nimrod (derived from the Fury) in 1933. The last examples were retired in 1939.

FAIREY FULMAR: The Firefly's immediate predecessor, the Fulmar entered service in 1940 as the FAA's first eight-gun fighter. Active for almost the entire war, this carrier-based type was also used as a night-fighter from shore bases. A drawback was its lack of speed.

FAIREY

FULMAR

● Carrier-based fighter ● Fleet reconnaissance ● Night-fighter

Designed in the 1930s, when Britain's Fleet Air Arm desperately needed new warplanes, the Fulmar was handicapped by Royal Navy demands for twin-seat fighters. Underpowered, and with modest manoeuvrability and rate of climb, the Fulmar could be easy prey for a seasoned enemy fighter pilot. Yet, with heavy armament and a robust structure, the Fulmar did achieve notable success, particularly in the Mediterranean theatre.

▲ *Spending the majority of its operational service life flying from Royal Navy aircraft-carriers in the Mediterranean, the Fulmar gained notable victories against both Italian and German opposition.*

FAIREY FULMAR

▼ Reconnaissance work
With its excellent endurance, the Fulmar was used as a carrier-borne spotter. In 1941, Fulmars successfully located and trailed the Bismarck.

▲ Bomber origins
The Fulmar was developed from the P.4/34 day bomber project which was abandoned in 1936.

▲ Catching a wire
Rudder and elevator control was poor at low speeds, making carrier landings difficult. Fulmars also had a tendency to crab bodily to the left during take-off.

▲ Ubiquitous Merlin
Powered by the popular Merlin engine, the Fulmar had spritely performance for a two-seater. This example is serviced during the defence of Ceylon.

Saving Malta ▶
In August 1942, Fulmars on HMS Victorious protected 14 merchant ships carrying vital supplies to Malta.

FACTS AND FIGURES

➤ The first of two Fulmar prototypes completed its maiden flight on 13 January 1937.

➤ About 100 Fulmars were converted to night-fighters, but with limited success.

➤ Fulmars were involved in catapult launch tests from merchant ships.

➤ Altogether, Fulmars served with 20 squadrons and with eight fleet aircraft-carriers and five escort carriers.

➤ The first prototype Fulmar is preserved at the Fleet Air Arm Museum in England.

➤ The last of 600 Fulmars to be built was delivered to the FAA in February 1943.

PROFILE

Defender of the Malta convoys

Developed from the P.4/34 light bomber project, which was eventually abandoned, the Fulmar filled the Royal Navy's desperate need in the late 1930s for a modern monoplane fighter.

Because of a lack of precision navigational instruments, the FAA deemed it necessary for their new fighter to have a second seat to accommodate a navigator, and thus ensure a return to an aircraft-carrier in any weather. Although slower and more cumbersome than its single-seat land-based counterparts, the Fulmar was an excellent aircraft considering the design constraints.

Entering service in 1940, the Fulmar Mk I was soon in action protecting the vital supply convoys to the beleaguered island of Malta. During autumn 1940, Fulmars from No. 806 Squadron were especially busy, managing to shoot down 10 Italian bombers as well as downing six enemy fighters, while giving cover to the famous Swordfish raid on Taranto.

Below: By mid-1941, the Fulmar equipped eight operational FAA squadrons. This example is leaving HMS Victorious on a dawn patrol.

Above: As the best FAA fighter of 1940–42, the Fulmar had good range and firepower, but lacked the speed and agility of single-seat fighters.

In addition to fighter duties, Fulmars were also engaged in the fleet reconnaissance role, most notably against the *Bismarck*, and a number of the later, more powerful Mk IIs were modified to become night-fighters.

Fulmar Mk I

Type: two-seat carrier-based fighter

Powerplant: one 805-kW (1,080-hp.) Rolls-Royce Merlin VIII 12-cylinder Vee piston engine

Maximum speed: 398 km/h (247 m.p.h.) at 2745 m (9,000 ft.)

Patrol endurance: 4 hours, with reserve

Initial climb rate: 366 m/min (1,200 f.p.m.)

Service ceiling: 6555 m (21,500 ft.)

Weights: empty 3955 kg (8,700 lb.); maximum take-off 4853 kg (10,677 lb.)

Armament: eight 7.7-mm (.303 cal.) machine-guns in wings

Dimensions:
span	14.14 m (46 ft. 5 in.)
length	12.24 m (40 ft. 2 in.)
height	4.27 m (14 ft.)
wing area	31.77 m² (342 sq. ft.)

FULMAR MK I

From the first production batch, this example is a Fulmar Mk I fitted with the Merlin VIII engine. These aircraft were employed on the Malta convoys and first saw action in September 1940.

Like the successful Spitfire and Hurricane fighters, the Fulmar was powered by the Rolls-Royce Merlin engine. The Mk II was upgraded with the more powerful Merlin 30.

Unlike the P.4/34, the Fulmar had a non-continuous cockpit canopy. A dinghy was added, as with all naval aircraft, for use in the event of the aircraft ditching.

The rear cockpit housed the navigator/wireless operator who was given the task of finding the Fulmar's floating home in even the worst weather. The second pair of eyes was also very useful during reconnaissance sorties.

The tailplane was raised by 20.3 cm (8 in.) from the prototype, but elevator and rudder control was still fairly heavy. Engine power had to be high during landing so that the slipstream could increase elevator and rudder effectiveness.

As with all British fighters of the period, the Fulmar was equipped with a tailwheel-type undercarriage arrangement. The main gear retracted inwards and the tailwheel was fixed.

Modifications from the P.4/34 included reducing the wingspan by 40.6 cm (16 in.) and fitting folding wings for stowing in the confined space aboard aircraft-carriers.

Fairly aerodynamically clean, the Fulmar was structurally strong thanks to its origins as a conventional bomber or dive-bomber. The Fulmar was noted for its ability to take significant punishment and still return home.

ROYAL NAVY
N1860

COMBAT DATA

MAXIMUM SPEED

Although all three types were powered by the Rolls-Royce Merlin engine, the Fulmar's extra weight and size, incurred by its two-seat design, gave the aircraft mediocre performance. This enabled it to tackle bombers but it was noticeably outclassed by other fighters.

FULMAR Mk I 398 km/h (247 m.p.h.)

SEA HURRICANE Mk IIC 550 km/h (341 m.p.h.)

SEAFIRE Mk III 581 km/h (360 m.p.h.)

ARMAMENT

Entering service earlier than these other two naval fighters, the Fulmar had only machine-guns to fight with. The Sea Hurricane and Seafire benefited from cannon armament which had greater destructive power, making a 'kill' more likely.

FULMAR Mk I 8 x 7.7-mm (.303 cal.) machine-guns

SEA HURRICANE Mk IIC 4 x 20-mm (0.79-in.) cannon

SEAFIRE Mk III 4 x 7.7-mm (.303 cal.) machine-guns 2 x 20-mm (0.79-in.) cannon, 227-kg (500-lb.) bombload

RANGE

Designed from the outset as a naval aircraft, the Fulmar had excellent range and endurance, making it ideal for reconnaissance as well as fighter duties. The Seafire and Sea Hurricane were both developed from land-based fighters, and could not cover such a wide area of ocean.

FULMAR Mk I 1136 km (704 mi.)

SEA HURRICANE Mk IIC 740 km (459 mi.)

SEAFIRE Mk III 748 km (464 mi.)

Royal Navy Merlin-powered aircraft

■ **HAWKER SEA HURRICANE:** Originally used aboard CAM (Catapult Aircraft Merchantmen) ships, the Sea Hurricane went on to serve successfully on conventional aircraft-carriers.

■ **SUPERMARINE SEAFIRE:** Entering service in 1942, the Seafire was a capable naval fighter, but it was notoriously difficult to land because of its narrow-track undercarriage.

■ **DE HAVILLAND SEA MOSQUITO:** Again a modified land-based aircraft, the Sea Mosquito TR.Mk 33 was used as a carrier- or shore-based long-range strike aircraft.

■ **DE HAVILLAND SEA HORNET:** As the only two-seat version of the Hornet to be produced, the Sea Hornet was the FAA's standard carrier-borne fighter from 1949 to 1954.

FAIREY

SWORDFISH

● Carrier-based torpedo-bomber ● Anti-submarine ● Taranto attacker

It was a most unlikely warplane. A fabric and wire biplane in an age of high-speed monoplanes, the Fairey Swordfish was obsolete before it even entered service. But although it was lumbering and slow, this classic warplane was no anachronism. As a carrier-based torpedo-bomber it amassed a combat record second to none, from the historic attack on the Italian fleet at Taranto to its final years as a radar- and rocket-equipped anti-submarine patroller.

▲ Swordfish crews carried out some of the most devastating attacks of the war and achieved many firsts, including the first torpedo attack on a fleet in home port at Taranto in 1940.

FAIREY SWORDFISH

▲ Floatplane Swordfish
The floatplane version of the Swordfish was an effective aircraft, but the drag from the floats and weight of a torpedo limited its speed quite drastically.

▲ Strike mission
Swordfish from HMS Courageous begin an anti-shipping strike. Torpedo attacks required enormous nerve, as the weapon had to be released at close range in the face of heavy gunfire.

▲ Memorial flight
Swordfish still fly with the Royal Navy's Historic Flight, and are star attractions at air shows.

▲ Sub-chaser
Equipped with radar and rockets, the Swordfish was a lethal foe to U-boats, especially when flying from small escort carriers.

Slow mover ▶
A loaded Swordfish could barely make 180 km/h (112 m.p.h.). But it was very stable and could deliver a torpedo accurately.

▲ Open cockpit
With little weather protection Swordfish crews were prone to the elements.

FACTS AND FIGURES

➤ The prototype Swordfish flew on 17 April 1934, when it was known as the T.S.R.II.

➤ At the outbreak of World War II, the Royal Navy's Fleet Air Arm had 13 Swordfish squadrons.

➤ On 13 April 1940 a Swordfish made the Fleet Air Arm's first U-boat kill.

➤ The Swordfish Mk III carried an airborne radar scanner between its mainwheels.

➤ 2391 Swordfishes were built between 1934 and 1944, 1699 by Blackburn.

➤ The last front-line Swordfish squadron disbanded on 21 May 1945.

PROFILE

The victor of Taranto

On 11 November 1940, 21 Swordfish torpedo-bombers from the carrier HMS *Illustrious* ripped the heart out of the Italian fleet at Taranto, sending two battleships, a cruiser and a destroyer to the harbour bottom and effectively taking Italy's navy out of the war.

The Swordfish entered service with Britain's Fleet Air Arm (FAA) in 1936, where it became known as the 'Stringbag'. It was

originally used with great success as a torpedo-bomber, making the crucial hit on the *Bismarck*, among other feats; but by 1942 it was simply too slow for the job. In an heroic but futile attack on the battlecruisers *Gneisenau* and *Scharnhorst*, five out of six Swordfishes were downed and the flight leader posthumously awarded the Victoria Cross.

But the big biplane still had plenty to offer, and remained in

production until 1944. Assigned instead to anti-submarine, mine-laying, bombing and reconnaissance duties, the Swordfish also tested, and used, the FAA's first air-to-ground rocket projectiles.

A large notch was cut out of the upper wing to increase crew visibility upwards.

Most Swordfish wore a grey-green sea camouflage scheme, but some were painted white for Arctic operations.

The radio operator/air gunner was not always carried. He enjoyed an excellent field of fire, but the single Vickers 'K' 7.7-mm (.303 cal.) machine-gun would have deterred very few enemy fighter pilots.

SWORDFISH MK II

The Fairey Swordfish was the most successful British torpedo-bomber of the war, sinking more ships than all the Royal Navy's battleships put together.

A single forward-firing 7.7-mm (.303 cal.) Vickers gun was fitted in the upper fuselage, synchronised to fire through the propeller disc.

The pilot communicated with his crew by a very primitive but effective system of voice pipes, known as 'Gosport tubes'.

The structure of the Swordfish was from an earlier age, with fabric covering and wire bracing. But it was surprisingly strong, and could tolerate a rocket-assisted take-off.

The Pegasus radial engine proved extremely reliable, and was known to keep running even when one cylinder head was blown away by gunfire.

The Swordfish carried standard 457-cm (18-in.) torpedoes. A hit by one of these weapons was enough to fatally damage the steering gear of the *Bismarck*.

A large arrester hook was standard fit in all Swordfish.

Swordfish Mk II

Type: two-/three-seat torpedo-bomber/reconnaissance biplane

Powerplant: one 559-kW (750-hp.) Bristol Pegasus XXX nine-cylinder radial piston engine

Maximum speed: 222 km/h (138 m.p.h.)

Range: 1658 km (1,028 mi.)

Service ceiling: 3260 m (10,690 ft.)

Weights: empty 2132 kg (4,690 lb.); loaded 3406 kg (7,493 lb.)

Armament: one forward-firing 7.7-mm (.303 cal.) Vickers machine-gun in fuselage and one 7.7-mm Lewis or Vickers 'K' gun mounted in rear cockpit; one 730-kg (1,600-lb.) torpedo, or depth charges, mines or bombs up to 680 kg (1,500 lb.), or eight rocket projectiles

Dimensions:
span	13.87 m (45 ft.)
length	10.87 m (36 ft.)
height	3.76 m (12 ft.)
wing area	56.39 m² (607 sq. ft.)

COMBAT DATA

MAXIMUM SPEED

Roughly contemporary with the Swordfish, the US Navy's Devastator was a modern low-wing monoplane, as was the Imperial Japanese Navy's 'Kate', which flew some two years after the British 'Stringbag'. Both the other bombers were very much faster than the Swordfish.

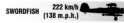
SWORDFISH 222 km/h (138 m.p.h.)

TBD DEVASTATOR 330 km/h (205 m.p.h.)

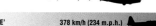
B5N 'KATE' 378 km/h (234 m.p.h.)

RANGE

In spite of its size, the Swordfish's slow speed and light weight did not place much demand on the engine, and the archaic biplane had a very good range. This was to stand in its favour late in its career, when aircraft based on light carriers could mount anti-submarine patrols over convoys for hours at a time.

B5N 'KATE' 1990 km (1,234 mi.)

SWORDFISH 1658 km (1,028 mi.)

TBD DEVASTATOR 700 km (434 mi.)

WARLOAD

SWORDFISH	TBD DEVASTATOR	B5N 'KATE'
one torpedo or 680 kg (1,600 lb.) of bombs	one torpedo or one 454-kg (1,000-lb.) bomb	one torpedo or 800 kg (1,760 lb.) of bombs

High lift from its biplane wings and sturdy construction meant that the Swordfish could carry almost 30 per cent of its empty weight in weapons. It could hold its own with the much more advanced Japanese 'Kate', and could carry a heavier load than the USA's surprisingly ineffective Devastator.

Torpedo attackers of World War II

■ **DOUGLAS TBD DEVASTATOR:** The Devastator was a much more advanced aircraft than the Swordfish but was much less successful.

■ **NAKAJIMA B5N 'KATE':** The best torpedo bomber of the early years of World War II, the B5N ripped the heart out of the US Navy at Pearl Harbor.

■ **FAIREY ALBACORE:** Designed to replace the Swordfish, the Albacore was a more modern aircraft built on the same general principles.

■ **GRUMMAN TBF AVENGER:** Tough and very versatile, the highly successful Avenger's combat debut took place at Midway in June 1942.

■ **FAIREY BARRACUDA:** Never performing as well as expected, the ugly Barracuda was nevertheless an effective torpedo- and dive-bomber.

FIAT
CR.42

● Italian fighter ● Manoeuvrable biplane ● Unequal-span wings

By the late 1930s most of the leading warplane producers were abandoning open-cockpit, fabric-covered biplane designs in favour of stressed-skin monoplanes with a retractable landing gear. But in Italy, Celestino Rosatelli of Fiat believed there was still a role for a highly manoeuvrable biplane fighter. Fiat thus produced the CR.42 Falco, the best fighter available to either side in North Africa from the start of the war until the arrival of the RAF's Hawker Hurricane.

▲ An ignominious end for a CR.42 of 95ª Squadriglia of the Corpo Aereo Italiani. Poor training and a lack of support equipment had contributed to low CR.42 availability.

FIAT CR.42

Effective camouflage ▶
The Italian air force adopted a new dappled, two-tone brown camouflage for its Fiat CR.42s operating in North Africa.

▼ Foreign sales
Sixty-eight CR.42s were ordered by the Hungarian air force in 1941. Falcos took part in the campaign against Yugoslavia.

With the Swedish air force ▶
One of Sweden's 72 CR.42s of J 11/3 Division, operating from Save in 1942.

▼ Aegean theatre
Italian CR.42s operated in 1941 from the Isle of Scarpanto.

Hungarian Fast Corps ▶
Flying in the Soviet Union during late 1941, this CR.42 was flown by 1/3 Sqn, 1/II Group of the Hungarian Fast Corps.

FACTS AND FIGURES

➤ Although the prototype CR.42 did not fly until January 1939, it entered service with the Italian air force the following November.

➤ A robust, clean and fast design, it was already obsolete when it entered service.

➤ The CR.42 was the last biplane fighter produced by Fiat.

➤ Fifty CR.42s provided the Italian fighter element operating from Belgium against England during 1940/41.

➤ Overall production of all CR.42 versions totalled 1784.

➤ One CR.42 was built in 1940 as a twin-float seaplane.

PROFILE

Last of the Fiat biplane fighters

After World War I, the Fiat company commenced production of a series of biplane fighters. These aircraft became the mainstay of the Italian air force's fighter squadrons. By the early 1930s, the CR.32 was in service. This was to be the main fighter in Franco's forces during the Spanish Civil War in 1936.

By the late 1930s, most of the world's major air forces were gradually re-equipping with low-wing monoplane fighters. Fiat still believed that there was a place for the biplane and designed the CR.42, with the prototype making its maiden flight in January 1939. It was instantly ordered into production for the Italian air force. With a number of export orders following, some 1784 had been built by 1943.

In service with the Regia Aeronautica, CR.42s were used as day fighters and escort fighters in the Mediterranean theatre and as night-fighters for home defence.

By 1942, Fiat had managed to raise the top speed to 518 km/h (322 m.p.h.) but the design still fell short in other respects. Biplane fighter production was at an end.

Below: A standard Italian air force fighter in the markings of 95ª Squadriglia, 18º Gruppo. It had a bright yellow engine cowling and spinner on the three-bladed propeller.

Above: A converted two-seat trainer version of the CR.42, painted overall silver with the markings of the post-war Sezione Autonoma Collegiamenti.

CR.42 FALCO

This CR.42 carries the markings of the 97ª Squadriglia, 9º Gruppo 'Caccia Terrestre', of the Regia Aeronautica's 4º Stormo based at Benina in Libya during 1940.

CR.42 Falco

Type: single-seat biplane fighter

Powerplant: one 626-kW (840-hp.) Fiat A.74 R1C.38 14-cylinder, two-row radial piston engine

Maximum speed: 420 km/h (261 m.p.h.)

Initial climb rate: 732 m/min (2,402 f.p.m.)

Combat range: 775 km (482 mi.)

Service ceiling: 10,500 m (34,450 ft.)

Weights: empty 1782 kg (3,929 ft.); maximum take-off 2295 kg (5,060 lb.)

Armament: two fixed forward-firing Breda-SAFAT 12.7-mm (.50 cal.) machine-guns, plus up to 198 kg (437 lb.) of bombs

Dimensions:
span	9.70 m	(31 ft. 10 in.)
length	8.27 m	(27 ft. 2 in.)
height	3.59 m	(11 ft. 9 in.)
wing area	22.40 m²	(241 sq. ft.)

The wing was manufactured from light alloy and steel, with a fabric covering. Ailerons were fitted only to the top wings.

The pilot's open cockpit was situated aft of the cut-out in the trailing edge of the upper wing to give better all-round vision.

CR.42s were powered by a Fiat A.74R1C.38 radial air-cooled, geared and supercharged engine.

The fixed main landing gear had two oleo-pneumatic legs.

CR.42s featured a sesquiplane with rigidly-braced wings constructed in two sections, joined at the centreline and supported above the fuselage.

The steel-tube fuselage structure was welded and faired to an oval section and covered with metal panels from the cockpit forwards. The rear section was fabric-covered.

A faired, non-retractable tailwheel was situated at the end of the lower fuselage. A fuel tank was situated in the rear fuselage behind a fireproof bulkhead.

COMBAT DATA

MAXIMUM SPEED

Clearly, in terms of its speed performance the biplane had had its day by 1940. Hawker's Hurricane, which equipped RAF fighter squadrons in large numbers, was a full 100 km/h (62 m.p.h.) faster. The Luftwaffe's Messerschmitt Bf 109 was faster still.

CR.42	420 km/h (261 m.p.h.)
HURRICANE Mk I	520 km/h (323 m.p.h.)
Bf 109E-7	578 km/h (359 m.p.h.)

ARMAMENT

With only two machine-guns, the CR.42 was also out-gunned by the monoplane fighters of the day. However, as a biplane the Fiat was a comparatively manoeuvrable machine.

CR.42 FALCO	2 x 12.7-mm (.50 cal.) machine-guns
HURRICANE Mk I	8 x 7.7-mm (.50 cal.) machine-guns
Bf 109E-7	1 x 20-mm (0.79-in.) cannon, 4 x 7.9-mm (0.31-in.) MGs

RANGE

The range advantage enjoyed by the German Messerschmitt Bf 109 was useful in the type's escort role during the Battle of Britain. The Fiat's range was much less but actually slightly superior to that of early models of the RAF's Hurricane.

CR.42 FALCO 775 km (482 mi.)

Bf 109E-7 1094 km (680 mi.)

HURRICANE Mk I 740 km (460 mi.)

CR.42s in three liveries

■ **BELGIUM:** Serving with the Belgian air force in May 1940, this CR.42, one of 15 in service, had Italian-style camouflage markings but a Belgian roundel and white cocette.

■ **NORTH AFRICA:** This Italian air force CR.42 carries the colours of the 20ª Squadriglia, 46º Gruppo Assolto, 15º Stormo that served in North Africa in the summer of 1942.

■ **BATTLE OF BRITAIN:** An Italian air force CR.42 from the 18º Gruppo 'Caccia Terrestre', based in Belgium and operating over southern England during the Battle of Britain in 1940.

FIAT

G.55 CENTAURO

● Fastest Italian fighter ● Daimler-Benz powered ● Post-war service

ust as a powerful in-line engine transformed the Macchi MC.202 into the MC.205, the same powerplant resulted in the Fiat G.55 – a speedy derivative of the sluggish G.50 Freccia. The G.55 Centauro (Centaur) was produced in limited numbers before the armistice in September 1943, but production continued in German-held parts of Italy. Most Centauros served with the Italian forces that fought alongside the Luftwaffe until 1945.

▲ Similar in appearance to the Macchi 202 and 205, the Fiat G.55 Centauro was an excellent Italian fighter which was unique in being adopted for the torpedo-bombing role.

FIAT G.55 CENTAURO

▼ German powerplant
Originally intended to be powered by a Fiat A38, the G.55 was fitted with a licence-built Daimler-Benz DB 605 V12 engine.

▲ Maximum velocity
Two G.56s, with DB.603 engines, were built. This would have been the fastest Italian fighter of the war, but production was cancelled.

Postwar service ▶
Production was resumed after the end of the war and the G.55 served with the Aeronautica Militare Italiana (AMI) until the early 1950s.

◀ Two-seat Centaur
A two-seat derivative, known as the G.55B, was also built but did not fly until 1946. Ten were supplied to the AMI, and a further 15 were purchased by Argentina.

Allied to the Luftwaffe ▶
After the Armistice a small number of G.55s continued to fly with the Aviazione Nazionale Repubblicana (Fascist Republic Air Arm) alongside the Germans.

FACTS AND FIGURES

➤ Built in direct competition with the Macchi MC.205 and Reggiane 2005, the G.55 was the best aircraft.

➤ Centauros first saw action during the defence of Rome in 1943.

➤ One of the two Fiat G.56s survived the war and was used as a testbed.

➤ Heavy bombardment by the Allies in 1944 meant that Fiat was not able to supply enough G.55s to the front line.

➤ A Fiat test pilot, Serafino Agostini, flew a British prisoner of war to safety in a G.55.

➤ Torpedo bombing saved the Centauro and enabled post-war production.

PROFILE

Fiat's flying Centaur

Left: An elegant design, the G.55 was also sturdy and its airframe could withstand very high g manoeuvres during dogfights.

Despite their pre-war success with powerful in-line engines installed in Schneider Trophy racing seaplanes, Italian fighter manufacturers concentrated on radial engines for their fighters of the 1930s. Consequently, when war began in 1939 the Regia Aeronautica's fighter units were ill-equipped. Aircraft like the Fiat G.50 were underpowered and suffered at the hands of more modern Allied types. In addressing this problem,

manufacturers developed new variants of these machines, fitted with more powerful German engines. The Daimler-Benz DB.605, which powered the Luftwaffe's Messerschmitt Bf 109G and late-model Bf 110s, was put into production by Fiat as the RA.1050 Tifone (Typhoon). This engine was installed in both the Macchi MC.205 and a reworked Fiat G.50, the G.55.

The resulting aircraft vie for the title of the best Italian fighter of the period. First flown in

April 1942, the G.55 was an all-metal aircraft armed with three 20-mm (0.79-in.) cannon and two machine-guns and carried a modest bombload. Very few were delivered before the Italian surrender in 1943, but continued production allowed a small number to see service with the fascist Aeronautica Nazionale Repubblicana, fighting alongside the Luftwaffe.

Above: Surviving G.55s were pressed into service with the fledgling air arm of the Fascist Republic in 1944. Many of them were destroyed or damaged during Allied air attacks.

G.55/I Centauro

Type: single-seat fighter and torpedo-bomber

Powerplant: one 1100-kW (1,475-hp.) Fiat RA 1050 Tifone (Daimler-Benz DB 605A) inverted V12 liquid-cooled piston engine

Maximum speed: 630 km/h (391 m.p.h.)

Range: 1200 km (744 mi.)

Service ceiling: 12,700 m (41,700 ft.)

Weights: empty 2630 kg (5,786 lb.); loaded 3520 kg (8,180 lb.)

Armament: three 20-mm (0.79-in.) Mauser MG 151/20e cannon and two fuselage-mounted Breda SAFAT 12.7-mm (.50 cal.) machine-guns, plus two 160-kg (352-lb.) bombs on underwing racks

Dimensions:
span	11.85 m	(38 ft. 10 in.)
length	9.37 m	(30 ft. 9 in.)
height	3.13 m	(10 ft. 3 in.)
wing area	21.11 m²	(227 sq. ft.)

Powering this sleek fighter was a Fiat RA 1050 Tifone inverted V12 engine. A licence-built version of the Daimler-Benz DB.605, this gave the G.55 superb performance.

A high mounted cockpit offered superb visibility for the Centauro pilot and was similar to that found on the rival MC.205 Veltro. The heavily framed canopy hinged to starboard for entry and exit.

G.55S CENTAURO

Designed to replaced the tri-motored SM. 79s in the torpedo bombing role, the G.55S saved the design from extinction, though this variant had failed to enter service in wartime.

Common characteristics of many Italian World War II fighters were fragile tail surfaces. The Centauro did not suffer from such problems and in the air possessed viceless handling.

Centauros were to be seen in a variety of colour schemes. This example wears a distinctive two-tone mottled camouflage.

A wide-track undercarriage gave the G.55 excellent ground handling. Both main oleos were immensely strong and hydraulically actuated, retracting inward for flight.

When the aircraft was fully laden with a 930-kg (2,046 lb.) torpedo, pilots felt the G.55S to be slow and lumbering, though it was by no means an easy target for enemy fighters.

To provide adequate ground clearance for the massive torpedo, the tail wheel oleo had to be extended and strengthened.

COMBAT DATA

MAXIMUM SPEED

Sleek and fast, the Fiat G.55 and Reggiane Re.2005 were arguably two of the best fighters of World War II. The Reggiane Re.2001 Falco was slightly slower because of the drag induced by the its larger powerplant.

G.55 CENTAURO	630 km/h (391 m.p.h.)
Re.2005 SAGITTARIO	630 km/h (391 m.p.h.)
Re.2000 FALCO I	529 km/h (328 m.p.h.)

OPERATIONAL RANGE

The range of Italian late-war fighters was adequate, with the G.55 having one of the greatest endurances. It was, however, poorer than that of the US Fifteenth Air Force's North American P-51 Mustangs, which began arriving in the Mediterranean theatre of operations in large numbers during the spring of 1944.

G.55 CENTAURO 1200 km (744 mi.)

Re.2000 FALCO I 1400 km (868 mi.)

Re.2005 SAGITTARIO 1250 km (775 mi.)

NORMAL TAKE-OFF WEIGHT

Lighter than the Re.2005, the Centauro also had slightly better handling, in the air and on the ground. Both were heavier still than the radial-engined Falco which owed much to American fighter design, particularly that of the Republic P-43 Lancer.

G.55 CENTAURO 3520 kg (8,180 lb.)

Re.2005 SAGITTARIO 3610 kg (7,942 lb.)

Re.2000 FALCO I 2595 kg (5,709 lb.)

Daimler-Benz powered late-war fighters

■ **KAWASAKI Ki-61 HIEN 'TONY':** This superb fighter was unique in Japanese service in being powered by a liquid-cooled in-line engine.

■ **MACCHI MC.205 VELTRO:** Based on the MC.202 Folgolore, the Veltro (Greyhound) was capable of meeting the P-51 on even terms.

■ **REGGIANE Re.2005 SAGITTARIO:** Only 48 examples of Reggiane's most capable fighter ever saw operational service, with Gruppo 22°.

■ **MESSERSCHMITT Bf 109K:** Among the last variants of this famous aircraft, the K was more powerful but less agile than earlier Bf 109s.

FIESELER

FI 156 STORCH

● Observation aircraft ● Short take-off and landing

A brilliant design, the Fi 156 Storch was so perfect at what it did that even if it was designed today, 60 years after its first flight, it could not be improved. The best observation and army co-operation aircraft of World War II, it had an almost unbelievable short take-off and landing capability, reflected in an uncanny ability to operate out of restricted spaces and to perform a wide variety of liaison tasks.

▲ Storch missions
varied from the humdrum air-taxi job of ferrying Wehrmacht officers to the front line to the dramatic rescue of Benito Mussolini from mountain-top captivity.

PHOTO FILE

FIESELER FI 156 STORCH

▲ Crash landing
The light construction of the Storch meant that battle damage usually brought it down. The best defence of the Storch was to fly as low and as slow as possible to avoid fighters.

▲ Alpine Storch
The Storch was especially useful to the Swiss, because the mountainous terrain was often only accessible to short take-off planes.

Ski Storch ▶
Croatian forces found the Storch a useful machine when fitted with skis. It was also easy to manhandle when on the ground.

▲ Czech made
The Storch was so good that after the end of World War II large numbers were produced in both Czechoslovakia and France.

Light weight ▶
This view shows just how tiny a Storch was. The aircraft weighed less than a modern family car.

▲ Multi-role
The Fi 156C-5 was able to carry an underfuselage drop-tank or an optional camera, and had an improved Argus 10P engine.

FACTS AND FIGURES

➤ The prototype Fi 156 Storch flew on or around 24 May 1936.

➤ In 1943, an Fi 156 rescued Italy's Benito Mussolini by landing and taking off in less than 100 metres (330 ft.) at high altitude.

➤ The last plane to take off before the fall of Berlin in May 1945 was a Storch.

➤ The Fi 256 was a concept similar to the Storch which would have served as a four-place civil aircraft.

➤ Between 1937–45, the Luftwaffe accepted just short of 2900 Storchs.

➤ Numerous Storchs are still flying today, appearing as warbirds at air shows.

PROFILE

The plane that flew everywhere

Gerhard Fieseler, an ace of the Great War with 22 victories, combined with designers Reinhold Mewes and Erich Bachem to create a most remarkable aircraft with the high wing, flaps and stalky landing gear needed to land and take off almost anywhere.

No Allied warplane measured up to the Storch, which in a stiff breeze could land in a matter of metres. But apart from its obvious qualities as a liaison and spotter craft, the Fi 156 was incredibly versatile. It was so manoeuvrable at speeds of less than 55 km/h (35 m.p.h.) that it could elude much faster fighters; it could be rigged to drop small bombs, and one was even tested against a U-boat with 135-kg (300-lb.) depth charges. There was seemingly nothing the Storch could not do.

In the end, the Fi 156 even landed and took off in a Berlin under siege from advancing Russian armies. The Storch outlived the Third Reich, and remained in production in Czechoslovakia and France long after the war.

Morane-Saulnier of France had produced the Fi 156 during World War II. After the end of the war, it built the MS.500, 501 and 502. A projected five-seat version was not produced.

The long, straight wing, with its flaps and slats, could keep the Storch airborne at almost any airspeed, and it could 'hover' when flying into a breeze.

Although the Storch looked flimsy with its braced construction and fabric covering, it was in fact a very sturdy aircraft.

Fi 156C Storch

Type: three-seat liaison, observation and rescue aircraft

Powerplant: one 179-kW (240-hp.) Argus As 10C-3 inverted Vee-8 air-cooled piston engine

Maximum speed: 175 km/h (108 m.p.h.)

Range: 385 km (239 mi.)

Service ceiling: about 6800 m (22,300 ft.)

Weights: empty 930 kg (2,046 lb.); loaded 1325 kg (2,915 lb.)

Armament: provision for one 7.92-mm (0.3-in.) MG 15 machine-gun with four spare 75-round magazines

Dimensions:
span	14.25 m	(47 ft.)
length	9.90 m	(32 ft.)
height	3.00 m	(10 ft.)
wing area	26.00 m²	(280 sq. ft.)

FI 156C-3 STORCH

This Storch served with a Kurierstaffel of the Luftwaffe in the communications role.

The secret of the Storch's remarkable performance was its wing. The slotted ailerons and flaps were advanced features when the Storch was designed in the 1930s.

The Fi 156E-0 had a tandem wheeled undercarriage with a pneumatic rubber track linking each wheel.

The Storch carried a 7.92-mm machine-gun for defence, but very few crews ever managed to shoot their way out of trouble.

Most Storchs had a tailskid, as the landing and take-off were so short that a tailwheel was not really a necessity.

The Storch featured 'long travel' undercarriage legs, rather like a modern trail bike, that could cope with the bumpy landing on rough strips.

With a high-mounted wing and a canopy that protruded outside the airframe, the Storch was an excellent spotter plane. But it was very vulnerable to enemy small-arms fire.

COMBAT DATA

CRUISING SPEED

High speed is not a prerequisite for army co-operation aircraft. Aircraft like the Storch are at their most effective when flying slowly: in a light breeze the Storch could take off in less than 70 m (230 ft.), and could land in about one-third of that distance.

Fi 156C STORCH	130 km/h (80 m.p.h.)
L-4 GRASSHOPPER	121 km/h (75 m.p.h.)
AUSTER Mk V	180 km/h (112 m.p.h.)

LOADED WEIGHT

Fi 156C STORCH
1325 kg (2,915 lb.)

L-4 GRASSHOPPER
533 kg (1,173 lb.)

AUSTER Mk V.
840 kg (1,848 lb.)

Observation craft do not need to carry weapons or heavy cargo, and are generally of very light construction. In spite of its frail appearance, the Storch was more solidly-built than its British or American equivalents.

RANGE

Endurance is more important than range in an observation aircraft. Although its range was negligible, the Storch was usually based very close to the front line, and flew so slowly that it could stay in the air for two or three hours at a time.

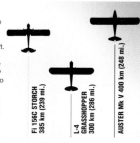

Fi 156C STORCH 385 km (239 mi.)

L-4 GRASSHOPPER 300 km (286 mi.)

AUSTER Mk V 400 km (248 mi.)

World War II Army co-operation

■ **HENSCHEL Hs 126:** Larger than the Storch, the Henschel served as a spotter and reconnaissance aircraft in the first years of World War II.

■ **FOCKE-WULF Fw 189:** Replacing the Hs 126, the Fw 189 'Uhu' became the Luftwaffe's most important 'eye in the sky' on the Eastern Front.

■ **WESTLAND LYSANDER:** Closer to the Henschel than the Storch, the Lysander won fame landing British agents in occupied Europe.

■ **POLIKARPOV U-2:** This archaic Russian biplane served with distinction in roles as varied as air ambulance and harassment bomber.

■ **PIPER L-4 GRASSHOPPER:** America built thousands of light liaison aircraft. By far the most successful was the long-serving L-4.

FOCKE-WULF

Fw 190A

● Interceptor ● Ground-attack aircraft ● Bomber destroyer

Kurt Tank's superb Focke-Wulf Fw 190 first saw combat over the English Channel in September 1941. The new fighter was a shock to the RAF, being faster and more agile than the Spitfire. Known as the 'Butcher Bird', the Fw 190 went on to become a dominant force in aerial combat in Europe, performing with equal distinction as a fighter and as the Luftwaffe's most important ground-attack machine.

▲ Luftwaffe ace Josef 'Pips' Priller climbs from his Fw 190. Allied pilots had a healthy respect for the aircraft in the hands of such experienced combat fliers.

FOCKE-WULF **Fw 190A**

◄ Conversion trainer
This two-seat trainer was developed to help former Stuka pilots convert from the lumbering Ju 87 to the vastly more powerful Fw 190.

▲ Squadron line-up
A squadron prepares to take on the RAF from its French base. The Fw 190 came as a very unwelcome surprise to the RAF, and gave German pilots the edge over Mk V Spitfires in 1941 and early 1942.

▲ Dogfighter
The Fw 190 was a hard opponent in a dogfight, with heavy armament, excellent manoeuvrability and high speed.

Stripdown time ▶
The Fw 190's compact and complex BMW radial engine could often be troublesome to service in the field.

▼ Pairs formation
Pilots needed to give each other support in battle. The Fw 190 cockpit allowed good visibility for crews to check behind, and they always flew as a tactical combat pair.

◄ Broken nose
In spite of its wide-track undercarriage, the Fw 190 could be difficult for an inexperienced pilot to land. By the end of the war, such accidents had become common.

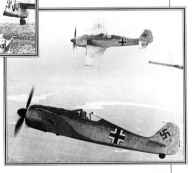

FACTS AND FIGURES

➤ On 14 October 1943, Fw 190s decimated US bombers attacking Schweinfurt and Regensburg, shooting down 79.

➤ The prototype Fw 190 made its first flight on 1 June 1939.

➤ Fw 190s could carry a huge range of weapons, from bombs and rockets to aerial torpedoes.

➤ The long-nosed Fw 190D, or 'Dora', series performed superbly after being introduced in mid-1944.

➤ Later models of the Fw 190 carried 30-mm (1.18-in.) cannon and air-to-air rockets.

➤ The Fw 190A-8/R8 was a heavily armoured variant designed to destroy American bombers by ramming them.

PROFILE

The 'Butcher Bird'

Conceived in 1937 as a complement to the Bf 109, Focke-Wulf's Fw 190 became a potent threat to Allied air power in every region where the Luftwaffe fought. Fw 190s inflicted cruel punishment on Flying Fortress and Liberator crews, and were almost impossible to defeat until the long-range P-51 Mustang finally became available in 1944 to escort bombers to their targets.

As a fighter-bomber and anti-tank aircraft, the Fw 190 was Germany's best air-to-ground fighter.

The Fw 190A-8 was used extensively in Defence of the Riech operations during 1944. Heavily armed with four cannon and two machine-guns it wreaked havoc upon US daylight bombers. The long-nosed Tank Ta 152 versions of the Fw 190 reached air speeds as high as 760 km/h (472 m.p.h.), and might have altered the outcome of the war if more than 93 had been built before hostilities ended.

No one who fought in the hotly contested skies of Europe will forget the feats of Fw 190 pilots such as Oberleutnant Otto Kittel, the Luftwaffe's fourth-ranking ace, who scored most of his 267 victories in the type. It is truly one of the great fighters of all time.

The Fw 190 carried out many combat tasks. It even replaced the Ju 87 Stuka as the Luftwaffe's tank-busting machine.

The flaps of the Fw 190 were electrically-operated, which was a first for a fighter aircraft of the 1940s.

The Fw 190-A1 was armed with two 20-mm (0.79-in.) MG FF cannon and two MG 17 machine-guns in the wings, with two more MG 17s above the engine.

Fw 190A-8

Type: single-seat fighter and fighter-bomber

Powerplant: one 1567-kW (2,100-hp.) BMW 801D-2 14-cylinder radial piston engine

Maximum speed: 654 km/h (406 m.p.h.)

Combat radius: 800 km (497 mi.) on internal fuel

Service ceiling: 11,400 m (37,400 ft.)

Weights: empty 3170 kg (6,989 lb.); loaded 4900 kg (10,803 lb.)

Armament: two 7.92-mm (0.31-in) MG 17 machine-guns; four 20-mm (0.79-in.) MG 151/20 cannon; one 500-kg (1,100-lb.) and two 250-kg (550-lb.) bombs or one 300-litre (67-gal.) drop-tank

Dimensions:
span	10.50 m	(34 ft. 5 in.)
length	8.84 m	(29 ft.)
height	3.96 m	(13 ft.)
wing area	18.30 m²	(197 sq. ft.)

The first Fw 190s were powered by the BMW 801C-1 engine, rated at 1200 kW (1,600 hp.). Early examples of the compact 18-cylinder radial were prone to overheating.

Fw 190A-1

The first operational Fw 190 unit was 6 Staffel, JG 26 'Schlageter'. Flying out of the Pas de Calais, the squadron took the new fighter into action for the first time early in September 1941.

The 190's cockpit was a major improvement over the Bf 109. It had all-electric-powered systems, excellent visibility and good armour plating. The light controls made it easy to fly.

The cut-down fuselage made it easy for the pilot to see to the rear.

The wide-track undercarriage was much more stable than that of either the Spitfire or the Bf 109.

The small size of the Fw 190 was a big advantage in a dogfight, where being seen first was a problem. This aircraft carries a standard Luftwaffe grey/green camouflage scheme.

The aircraft depicted was flown by Oberleutnant Walter Schneider, Staffelkapitän of 6./JG 26. Schneider was killed in December 1941.

COMBAT DATA

ARMAMENT

The Fw 190's armament was characteristically much heavier than that of British or American aircraft. Goaded by the bitter experience of being on the receiving end of German gun power, the British were now fitting cannon to most of their fighters, while the otherwise superb Mustang was woefully undergunned.

Fw 190A-8
4 x 20-mm (0.79-in.) cannon
2 x 7.92-mm (0.31-in) machine-guns

SPITFIRE Mk IX
2 x 20-mm (0.79-in.) cannon
4 x 7.7-mm (.303 cal.) machine-guns

P-51B MUSTANG
4 x 12.7-mm (.50 cal.) machine-guns

MAXIMUM SPEED

Fw 190A-8	654 km/h (406 m.p.h.)
SPITFIRE Mk IX	657 km/h (408 m.p.h.)
P-51B MUSTANG	700 km/h (435 m.p.h.)

The speed of the Fw 190 spurred Britain to fit a more powerful engine into the Spitfire, the resulting Spitfire Mk IX bringing performance up to the German fighter's levels. Both were soon to be outclassed by the American P-51 Mustang, which turned out to be the most outstanding fighter of the European theatre.

SERVICE CEILING

The Fw 190 was almost unbeatable at medium altitudes, between 4000 and 8000 m (13,000 and 26,000 ft.). However, at high altitudes its performance fell off considerably, and at 10,000 m (33,000 ft.) it was vulnerable to Spitfires and Mustangs. US bombers operated as high as possible to avoid the Fw 190 threat.

Fw 190A-8 11,400 m (37,400 ft.)
SPITFIRE Mk IX 12,750 m (42,000 ft.)
P-51B MUSTANG 12,750 m (42,000 ft.)

Weapons variations

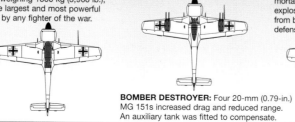

GROUND ATTACK: One 250-kg (550-lb.) and four 50-kg (110-lb.) bombs was a standard attack mission load.

HEAVY BOMBER : The SC1000 bomb, weighing 1800 kg (3,968 lb.), was the largest and most powerful carried by any fighter of the war.

BOMBER DESTROYER: Four 20-mm (0.79-in.) MG 151s increased drag and reduced range. An auxiliary tank was fitted to compensate.

FORMATION DESTROYER: WfrGr 21 mortars were designed to launch high-explosive shells into a bomber formation from beyond the range of the bomber box's defensive fire.

TANK-BUSTER: Two 30-mm (1.18-in) Mk 103 cannon were capable of destroying enemy tanks as well as bombers.

FOCKE-WULF

TA 152

- Fw 190 development ● Interceptor/fighter-bomber ● High altitude

Brilliant German designer Kurt Tank was credited with dramatic improvements to his Focke-Wulf Fw 190 fighter, producing the Ta 152 high-altitude interceptor. Tank's Ta 152 and the related Ta 153 were similar to 'long-nosed' versions of the Fw 190 but were meant to have even greater performance. It was not an easy task for a new aircraft to measure up to a predecessor that was immortal in aviation, but the Ta 152/153 were exceptional designs.

▲ *A truly exceptional aircraft, the Ta 152 might have been a highly effective weapon, but the desperate war situation led to it being used outside its intended role.*

PHOTO FILE

FOCKE-WULF TA 152

▼ **Post-war US testing**
The third production Ta 152H-0 was taken by the British after the war and passed on to the Americans. British markings have been replaced with inaccurate Luftwaffe equivalents.

▲ **British evaluation**
This Ta 152 underwent limited flight testing in the UK and is seen at a display of 'captured' German aircraft in October 1945.

▼ **Supercharged engine**
A large air inlet on the right-hand side of the nose fed the supercharger of the powerful Jumo 213EB engine. The propeller blades required very broad chord to handle the enormous power.

▲ **All-weather fighter**
Full bad-weather flying equipment equipped the three Ta 152C-0/R11 test aircraft.

◄ **Mixed ancestry**
Flying as a Ta 152H-03 in August 1944, this aircraft was rebuilt from the Fw 190 V30/U1 and was powered by a Jumo 213A-1; engine accessories were taken from an Fw 190D-9.

FACTS AND FIGURES

➤ Although the Ta 152 was a high-altitude interceptor, attack and reconnaissance versions were also designed.

➤ The Ta 152C developmental prototype first flew on 19 November 1944.

➤ The first of 20 pre-production Ta 152 fighters flew at Cottbus in October 1944.

➤ Most Ta 152s differed from the 'long-nosed' Fw 190D in having a pressurised cockpit.

➤ Trials of the Ta 152 were carried out by Erprobungskommando 152 at Rechlin.

➤ A photo-reconnaissance Ta 152 variant was never employed operationally.

High-altitude Reich defender

Two of many projects being pursued by Germany near the end of the war, the Ta 152 and Ta 153 were high-altitude versions of the Fw 190. Intended to intercept high-flying US Army Air Force bombers, they were used to safeguard bases where the newly developed jets would be stationed. The Luftwaffe rushed ahead with several versions of the Ta 152, the variants having short- and long-span wings and various sets of armament. However, all had the ability to take off quickly, climb at a phenomenal rate and intercept Allied bombers at their operating height.

This thoroughbred aircraft was difficult to master, but in the right hands it was a fantastic performer. However, the Ta 152 was not used for the role for which it had been intended. Pilots found themselves fighting at medium and even low altitude, where other fighters, including the traditional Fw 190, would have performed better. They were rarely given a chance to fight at altitude, where the Ta 152 was superior.

Above: Considered to be a heavy fighter, the Ta 152C was to have been delivered from April 1945, but the Allies overran the factories before production started.

Below: A Ta 152H-0 is prepared for delivery. Calibration of the aircraft's compass is performed on this compass-swinging platform.

Like so many of the Luftwaffe's advanced projects, the Ta 152 entered service too late and in too few numbers to alter the course of the war.

Ta 152H-1

Type: single-seat high-altitude fighter

Powerplant: one 1305-kW (1,750-hp.) Junkers Jumo 213E 12-cylinder inverted-Vee piston engine

Maximum speed: 760 km/h (471 m.p.h.) at 12,500 m (41,000 ft.)

Initial climb rate: 1050 m/min (3,445 f.p.m.)

Range: 1200 km (745 mi.)

Service ceiling: 14,800 m (48,550 ft.)

Weights: empty 3920 kg (8,624 lb.); maximum take-off 4750 kg (10,450 lb.)

Armament: one 30-mm (1.18-in.) Mk 108 cannon with 90 rounds firing through the spinner and two wing-mounted 20-mm (0.79-in.) MG 151/20 cannon with 175 rounds per gun

Dimensions:
span	14.50 m	(48 ft. 6 in.)
length	10.80 m	(35 ft. 5 in.)
height	4.00 m	(13 ft. 2 in.)
wing area	23.50 m²	(253 sq. ft.)

Water-methanol (MW 50) injection on take-off boosted power from 1305 kW (1,750 hp.) to 1529 kW (2,050 hp.). At 8000 m (26,250 ft.) the power from the 12-cylinder inverted-Vee inline engine was 1342 kW (1,800 hp.). With a large fuel capacity the Ta 152H-1 was a heavy aircraft and required a great deal of power, especially during take-off and at low level.

Ta 152H-1 pilots sat in a pressurised cockpit. World War II fighter designers did not often use this type of cockpit, since it added weight and complexity to the design. Flying the Ta 152H-1 for long periods at high altitude was stressful and the aircraft was equipped with autopilot.

TA 152H-1

'Black 14' flew with JG 301 on Defence of the Reich duties during the last few months of the war. The unit mainly flew top cover for Me 262 jet fighters during their landing and take-off cycles.

In order to counter the huge power and torque of the Jumo 213E engine and to provide adequate directional stability at high altitudes, the Ta 152 series were fitted with fins of far greater chord than the Fw 190D. This and the long-span wings caused some loss of roll rate.

As an aircraft assigned to Defence of the Reich, this machine carries brightly coloured bands. The small, inclined black bar indicates that this was the personal aircraft of a Geschwader adjutant.

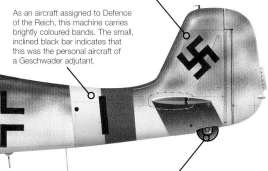

At 8000 m (26,250 ft.) the exhausts produced 2.17 kN (485 lb.) of residual thrust. This thrust was in addition to the pull of the three-bladed VS 111 propeller. The inboard tank of the left wing carried 70 litres (18.5 gal.)of MW 50.

A long, high-aspect ratio wing gave the Ta 152H-1 outstanding climb and altitude performance. Unfortunately, necessity forced the aircraft to be used at low level where Fw 190D-9s would have performed better.

Although many Fw 190 variants left their retracted main undercarriage partly exposed, that of the Ta 152H-1e was entirely enclosed by two sets of doors. The tailwheel of all models was stowed partially retracted.

Kurt Tank's warplane dynasty

■ **Fw 189 UHU:** Designed as an army co-operation and reconnaissance aircraft, the Fw 189 also flew as a night-fighter.

■ **Fw 200 CONDOR:** Developed from an outstanding airliner, the Condor became infamous in the anti-shipping role.

■ **Fw 190:** Built as a contemporary of the Hawker Typhoon, the Fw 190 developed into a series of fighters and attack aircraft.

■ **Ta 154 MOSKITO:** Tank's design genius was recognised by the adoption of the Ta prefix for later Focke-Wulf aircraft.

COMBAT DATA

CEILING

Both the Spitfire PR.Mk 19 and Ta 152H used a complicated engine supercharging system to provide additional power in the thin air encountered at high altitudes. They also had pressurised cockpits.

Ta 152 H-1 14,800 m (48,550 ft.)	SPITFIRE PR.Mk 19 13,106 m (43,165 ft.)	P-51H MUSTANG 12,680 m (41,600 ft.)

MAXIMUM SPEED

Except for the Messerschmitt Me 262 and Heinkel He 162 jets, the P-51H was the fastest production fighter of World War II. Nitrous oxide (GM 1) injection at high altitudes gave the Ta 152H an additional performance boost, while water-methanol (MW 50) injection boosted take-off performance.

Ta 152 H-1	760 km/h (471 m.p.h.)
SPITFIRE PR.Mk 19	740 km/h (459 m.p.h.)
P-51H MUSTANG	784 km/h (486 m.p.h.)

ARMAMENT

Although it carried only three guns, the Ta 152H-1 was armed with powerful cannon: the 30-mm (1.18-in.) MK 108 fired through the spinner and the MK 151s from the wings. The Spitfire relied on speed and altitude for safety in its photo-reconnaissance role.

Ta 152 H-1	1 x 30-mm (1.18-in.) cannon 2 x 20-mm (0.79-in.) cannon
SPITFIRE PR.Mk 19	none
P-51H MUSTANG	6 x 12.7-mm (.50 cal.) machine-guns

FOCKE-WULF

FW 189 UHU

● Tactical reconnaissance ● Army co-operation ● Observation post

Built in France and Czechoslovakia as well as at Focke-Wulf's Bremen factory during World War II, the Fw 189 was one of the Luftwaffe's most useful multi-role aircraft. Originally designed for tactical reconnaissance as a successor to the Hs 126, it was also used for casualty evacuation, ground support and night-fighting. In the process it earned an outstanding reputation for reliability and became popular with its pilots.

▲ The Uhu (Eagle Owl) served with distinction on the Eastern Front, its superb agility and reliable engines making it a far from easy quarry even for agile fighters.

FOCKE-WULF FW 189 UHU

▼ **Prototype Fw 189**
The Focke-Wulf Fw 189, piloted by its chief designer Kurt Tank, first flew in 1938, and was dubbed 'The Flying Eye' by the media.

▲ **Uhu trainer**
The Fw 189B was a five-seat dedicated training platform for reconnaissance pilots.

▼ **Cockpit glazing**
The Uhu had unsurpassed all-round vision from the rear, with no tail to obscure the view.

▼ **Battleproof platform**
A very stable and rugged platform, the Uhu could absorb a certain amount of heavy-calibre gunfire with little adverse effect on flight.

◄ **Assault variant**
The Fw 189C, which was never adopted for service, was an experimental assault aircraft with a tiny, heavily armoured cabin for the pilot and gunner.

◄ **Low-level reconnaissance**
The Uhu was essentially a low-altitude tactical reconnaissance aircraft and was particularly at home on the front-line fighting in support of the army.

FACTS AND FIGURES

➤ The Fw 189 first flew in June 1938, competing with the BV 141 and unsuccessful Ar 198 for orders.

➤ It was first known as the Eule (Owl) before becoming the Uhu.

➤ The Uhu was exported to the Slovakian and Hungarian air forces.

➤ The Fw 189C assault version was never ordered into production; the Luftwaffe preferred the all-new Henschel Hs 129.

➤ The Fw 189 V4 prototype carried equipment to spray mustard gas.

➤ The Fw 189D was a floatplane trainer version, but it never flew.

PROFILE

The Luftwaffe's eye in the sky

Designer Kurt Tank selected the twin-boom configuration for the Fw 189, which had the advantage of allowing different fuselage nacelles to be used in the same basic airframe.

For its basic role of tactical reconnaissance, the Fw 189A's three-man nacelle was extensively glazed and carried machine-guns in the top and rear. There was a further machine-gun in each wing, in addition to racks for a total of

eight 50-kg (110-lb.) bombs. The aircraft entered service in late 1940, and went on to equip nine long-range and 15 short-range reconnaissance Gruppen, most of which served on the Eastern Front. Among its qualities were the agility to evade fighter interception and the strength and firepower to survive if it did come under attack. Some even survived being rammed, managing to return to base with large sections of their tailfins missing.

The Fw 189B, a five-seater with an enclosed nacelle, was intended for training but only a few were built. And the two-seat 189C, which had a reduced-sized, heavily armoured nacelle and was intended for assault and close support, was rejected in favour of the cheaper Hs 129.

Late in the war a number of Fw 189s were refitted as stop-gap night-fighters flying in Scandinavia.

The Fw 189A-2 was produced in large numbers in three different countries until it was replaced in production by the Fw 189A-4 which had heavier armour and new 20-mm (0.79-in.) wingroot cannon.

The heavily glazed nacelle accommodated the pilot, navigator/observer and, in the rear, a gunner with a revolving Ikaria-powered cone turret fitted with two MG 81 7.9-mm (0.31-in.) machine-guns.

Fw 189A-2 Uhu

This A-2 Uhu served with Aufklarungsgruppe (H)/14 flying from Salzburg during 1945. The aircraft was eventually captured by US forces in the area.

Further gun armament was provided by two fixed MG 17 7.9-mm (0.31-in.) machine-guns in the wingroots and two MG 81 7.9-mm machine-guns on flexible dorsal mounts directly above the navigator's position.

The large tailplane between the twin-booms allowed a full-length elevator which made the Fw 189 surprisingly agile.

The long wings were of strong, three-spar stressed-skin construction with tapering outer panels and electronically operated, fabric-covered trailing-edge flaps. Rudders, elevator and ailerons were manually controlled.

The twin-boom layout was ideal for reconnaissance and observation missions. It also made the aircraft supremely stable, as well as agile enough to avoid enemy aircraft and anti-aircraft guns.

The powerful Argus 12-cylinder inverted-Vee engines were renowned for their reliability, and their speed enabled the Fw 189 to escape from fighters.

The tailwheel-type undercarriage was exceptionally tough and when retracted it was protected by armoured undercarriage doors. The Uhu was at home on rough airstrips.

Four ETC 50 racks, each capable of carrying two SC50 50-kg (110-lb.) anti-personnel or anti-armour bombs for the support of the ground forces fighting below, were fitted underwing. These carriers were often empty.

The tailwheel neatly retracted to port to lie within the tailplane.

SH + RK

The Luftwaffe over the battlefield

BLOHM UND VOSS BV 141: Designed to the same specification as the Fw 189, the unique BV 141 featured twin fuselages – one contained the tail and engine and the other a glazed cabin.

FIESELER Fi 156: The Storch was undoubtedly the finest air observation post of the war. Serving on all fronts, its short take-off and landing capability was a major asset.

HENSCHEL Hs 126: The Hs 126 was the aircraft that the Fw 189 was destined to replace. It first flew in 1935, but survived in service throughout World War II as a light reconnaissance aircraft/trainer.

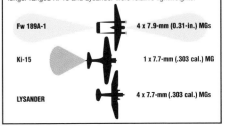

FOCKE-WULF

FW 200 CONDOR

● Long-range reconnaissance bomber ● Anti-shipping strike

Churchill called it 'the scourge of the Atlantic'. The Focke-Wulf Fw 200 Condor prowled the seaways and sank an enormous number of Allied ships, disrupting maritime operations so severely that it almost changed the course of World War II. This was an incredible achievement for an aircraft which, although gifted with rare beauty and remarkable endurance, had never been designed as a long-range bomber at all.

▲ *A crew undergo a final briefing and map check in front of their Condor. The aircraft ranged far over the Atlantic to attack Allied convoys in an attempt to starve Britain into submission.*

FOCKE-WULF FW 200 CONDOR

▲ Flying the Condor
The Fw 200's cockpit was fairly standard for a large aircraft. The type was slow and cumbersome, but did fight some slow-motion dogfights against RAF Sunderlands.

▲ French base
For much of the war the Condors operated from Bordeaux-Mérignac, flying out over the Atlantic to hunt convoys.

▼ Bomb carriage
Bombs were carried under the wings and engine nacelles.

▲ Ventral gondola
Scabbed under the belly of most Condors was this gondola. In the front was a Lofte 7D bombsight (in the strange protuberance) and an MG 131 machine-gun.

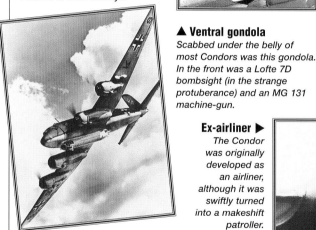

Ex-airliner ▶
The Condor was originally developed as an airliner, although it was swiftly turned into a makeshift patroller. Unfortunately, it was structurally weak, and many of the early ones broke their backs.

▲ Fighter fodder
After the early days of success, Fw 200s increasingly fell foul of shipborne fighters.

FACTS AND FIGURES

➤ The first flight of the Condor occurred after only 12 months of development.

➤ In 1938 an Fw 200 flew from Berlin to Tokyo in 42 hours 18 minutes' flying time.

➤ Two Condors each were exported to Finland and Brazil. A Japanese order for five aircraft was never filled.

➤ With fuel connections for the engines on its underside, the Condor was extremely vulnerable to anti-aircraft fire.

➤ Though Lufthansa never had more than a handful of Fw 200s, one of these flew the last wartime airline flight on 14 April 1945 from Barcelona to Berlin.

PROFILE

'The scourge of the Atlantic'

The Fw 200 Condor was intended for peaceful air commerce. It was an attractive, greyhound-like airliner, one example of which was used by Adolf Hitler as his personal transport.

But the Condor was to become famous as a warplane.

Britain depended on a transatlantic lifeline for survival, and the Luftwaffe knew that everything possible had to be done to prevent convoys from crossing the ocean with the weapons and equipment being churned out by American factories. The Condor was hastily pressed into action as a long-range maritime reconnaissance bomber. Under very difficult circumstances of extremely bad weather and near impossible navigation challenges, Condor crews fought a dramatic campaign over the Atlantic.

Co-operating with U-boat packs, the Condor overcame the handicaps of its inherently frail design and inflicted enough damage to threaten Britain's survival. But the deployment of fighters aboard escort carriers was to signal the end of the Condor's career.

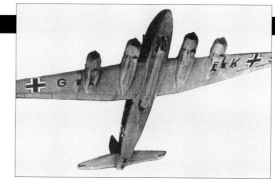

When the Wehrmacht's needs were pressing, military Condors were rushed into service as makeshift transports. They took part in the Stallingrad airlift.

Fw 200C-3 Condor

Type: seven-seat long-range maritime reconnaissance bomber

Powerplant: four 895-kW (1,200-hp.) BMW-Bramo 323 R-2 Fafnir radial engines

Maximum speed: 360 km/h (220 m.p.h.)

Range: 4400 km (2,700 mi.)

Service ceiling: 6000 m (19,000 ft.)

Weights: empty 13,000 kg (28,000 lb.); loaded 23,000 kg (51,000 lb.)

Armament: four 13-mm (0.51-in.) MG 131 machine-guns in dorsal and beam positions and one MG 131 or 20-mm (0.79-in.) MG 151 in a ventral gondola; up to 2100 kg (4,600 lb.) of bombs carried in the ventral gondola and under the wings

Dimensions:
span	32.85 m (107 ft. 9 in.)
length	23.45 m (77 ft.)
height	3.30 m (20 ft. 8 in.)
wing area	119.85 m² (1,290 sq. ft.)

Fw 200C-8 CONDOR

The Fw 200 grew from being little more than an airliner in camouflage to a fully equipped ship-killer. The Fw 200C-8/U10 was the ultimate Condor, carrying a heavy load of radar, missiles and full defensive armament.

Most Condor variants were fitted with radar to aid sea searches. Antennas were mounted in the nose and on the wings. The standard equipment was the FuG 200 Hohentwiel.

In addition to the fore and aft guns in the gondola, the Fw 200 had two dorsal positions for guns, and two firing laterally through the beam hatches.

The Condor's chief weakness was a tendency to structural failure in the rear fuselage.

The ventral gondola of the Fw 200C-8 was longer than that of the earlier variants, and had a very neat installation of the accurate bombsight. The gun at the front was the MG 131.

The Henschel Hs 293 was one of the first successful air-to-surface guided missiles. It was command guided by the bomb aimer.

Flares mounted at the back of the missile allowed the bomb aimer to follow its progress after launch. He had a joystick which transmitted control signals to the missile, which he 'flew' to the target like a model plane.

Shadowing the convoys

3 ATTACK: Condor patrol sectors were generally flown at very low level, with periodic pop-ups to about 300 m (1,000 ft.) for an orbiting radar search. If a target was detected, the Condors climbed to about 3000 m (10,000 ft.) for the bombing attack.

2 SHADOWING: The normal operating procedure for Condor units was to take off in fours, which then fanned out into parallel search paths, or sectors, covering several hundred kilometres of ocean. Once a convoy was detected, the crew could choose either to attack or to shadow.

1 REPORTING: When shadowing, the big bombers flew in circles around the convoy, all the while transmitting reports to naval headquarters and guiding U-boat wolfpacks to their quarry.

ACTION DATA

RANGE

The key to successful maritime reconnaissance is the ability to stay aloft over the ocean for a long time. With maximum fuel the Condor had a range of more than 4000 km (2,400 mi.). It could intercept an Allied convoy 1000 km (620 mi.) out into the Atlantic, and shadow it for up to 10 hours at a time. Operating in relays, the Condors would then vector U-boat wolfpacks in for the kill.

B-24 LIBERATOR 4000 km (2,485 mi.)	Fw 200 CONDOR 4400 km (2,700 mi.)	SUNDERLAND 4600 km (2,900 mi.)

FOKKER

G.1

● Heavy fighter/ground attack ● Early war service ● Luftwaffe use

A sensation at the 1936 Paris air show, the Fokker G.1 heavy fighter's twin-engined, twin-boom shape was new and innovative. The aircraft appeared to set a new standard of speed and performance. In fact, the Fokker G.1 was a transitional design, merging ageing technology of the 1930s with improved features that were to characterise World War II aircraft. Outperformed by single-seaters, the G.1 had a modest and short career.

▲ A radical design departure for Fokker, the G.1 was poised to sell well in export markets when the outbreak of war in 1939 saw the Dutch air force commandeer production in order to bolster its own G.1 units.

FOKKER G.1

▼ **Undelivered Finnish G.1B**
Upon arrival in Finland the G.1Bs were to be fitted with two Oerlikon 20-mm (0.79-in.) cannon and two 7.92-mm (0.31-in.) machine-guns. In 1939 all completed aircraft were kept by the Dutch.

▲ **On test over Schipol Airport**
Only part of the aircraft's serial number has been applied to this production G.1A.

◀ **In Luftwaffe service**
After four days of fighting, the Netherlands capitulated on 14 May 1940. At the Fokker factory the German invaders found two serviceable G.1As and a number of G.1Bs, originally destined for Finland. They were completed and transferred to Germany.

▲ **Captured G.1**
G.1B no. 348 was one of a number captured by the Luftwaffe and employed as trainers. It retains its Dutch serial number and wing markings but has gained a set of Luftwaffe insignia.

◀ **Decimated**
Outclassed by the Luftwaffe, the small force of Dutch G.1s sustained heavy casualties during the German invasion. By 14 May, the last day of operations, only five G.1s were left in service.

FACTS AND FIGURES

➤ When the Netherlands entered the war in May 1940, just 23 machine-gun-armed G.1As were in service with three units.

➤ After its Paris show appearance, the G.1 made its maiden flight on 16 March 1937.

➤ The Dutch navy was on the point of ordering G.1s when World War II began.

➤ Fokker's G.1 made use of advanced wooden construction and was a leader in this field for years after its first flight.

➤ Among planned G.1 developments was the G.2 with Mercedes DB600 engines.

➤ Sweden tested a G.1 at a speed of 644 km/h (400 m.p.h.) in the dive-bomber role.

PROFILE

Holland's heavy fighter

Originally flown with Hispano-Suiza radials, the G.1 was initially slow in development, after a mishap in which the prototype suffered brake failure and rammed a hangar at Schipol Airport on 4 July 1937.

A private venture by Fokker, the G.1 proved to be a sound design and attracted the attention of the Dutch Army Air Service. Changes were made to meet their requirements, which caused further delay, and the G.1 finally began to reach squadrons in mid-1939. As the aircraft went into Dutch service, export orders were placed by several European countries, though deliveries were not possible – war had broken out in 1939 and the Netherlands would need all the aircraft it could get.

When Germany occupied the Netherlands in May 1940, G.1s (armed with eight machine-guns or mixed cannon/machine-gun armament) made little impact against the advancing forces. The G.1s made a few bomb attacks on the invaders and shot down some German aircraft, but their own losses were high.

Germany later made use of captured aircraft as trainers. Of 62 G.1s built, none has survived.

Below: The Fokker G.1 prototype, X-2, was equipped with the 559-kW (750-hp.) Hispano-Suiza 80-02 radial engines, which failed during testing.

Above: On 5 May 1941 two Dutch workers at the German-controlled Fokker works fled to England in a G.1 while on a test flight. The aircraft was examined at the Royal Aircraft Establishment.

G.1A

Type: twin-engined heavy fighter and ground attack aircraft

Powerplant: two 619-kW (830-hp.) Bristol Mercury VIII radial piston engines

Maximum speed: 432 km/h (268 m.p.h.)

Range: 1400 km (870 mi.)

Service ceiling: 9100 m (30,000 ft.)

Weights: empty 3150 kg (6,930 lb.); gross 4400 kg (9,680 lb.)

Armament: eight 7.92-mm (0.31-in.) FN-Browning machine-guns in the nose, one flexible 7.92-mm FN-Browning machine-gun in the rear fuselage, plus up to 300 kg (660 lb.) of bombs

Dimensions:
span	16.50 m (54 ft. 2 in.)
length	11.50 m (37 ft. 9 in.)
height	3.40 m (11 ft. 2 in.)
wing area	35.70 m² (381 sq. ft.)

G.1B

No. 343 was one of a batch of 26 G.1Bs (nos 337 to 362) ordered by Finland and taken over by the Luchtvaartefdeling (Dutch air force) in April 1940. Only 12 were delivered before the German invasion.

Originally envisaged as having a mixed cannon/machine-gun armament (as planned for the smaller G.1B), production G.1As were armed with a battery of eight 7.92-mm (0.31-in.) FN-Browning machine-guns in the nose of the aircraft.

The standard G.1 cabin layout allowed a crew of two to be carried: a pilot and radio operator/rear gunner. Production aircraft allowed for a third crewman, an observer, to be accommodated.

In the glazed tailcone at the rear of the cabin, the upper panels folded inward to allow operation of the defensive machine-gun mounted on an internal horizontal bar.

Intended for export, the G.1B (originally known as 'G.1 Wasp') was 1.2 m shorter than the G.1A. Its wingspan was similarly narrowed by 0.65 m (2 ft.). Consequently, less powerful engines were used.

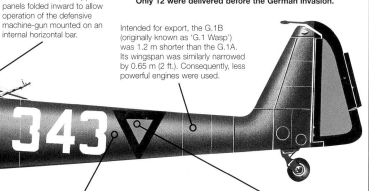

After the Hispano-Suiza radials fitted to the original G.1 prototype proved unsuitable, 619-kW (830-hp.) Bristol Mercury VIIIs were substituted on the G.1A. G.1Bs for export were powered by 559-kW (750-hp.) Pratt & Whitney Twin Wasp Juniors.

Principally a heavy fighter, the G.1 had only a modest bomb load. Bomb stowage and release equipment was fitted under the fuselage, with a capacity of 300 kg (660 lb.) on the G.1A and 400 kg (880 lb.) on the G.1B.

Had the outbreak of war not intervened, Fokker would have been able to fulfill export orders for the G.1 from Finland, Estonia and Sweden. Denmark planned to build a number under licence.

The Netherlands changed its national markings to the orange and black insignia depicted on this aircraft in October 1939, shortly after the beginning of World War II. Some captured G.1s kept these markings while flying with the Luftwaffe.

COMBAT DATA

MAXIMUM SPEED

By the time World War II had begun, the Fokker G.1A was outclassed in terms of its top speed. Even the Messerschmitt Bf 110 was considerably faster. Both aircraft were outpaced by the later de Havilland Mosquito.

G.1A	432 km/h (268 m.p.h.)
Bf 110C-4/B	560 km/h (347 m.p.h.)
MOSQUITO FB.Mk VI	583 km/h (361 m.p.h.)

RANGE

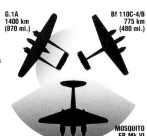

Range was an area in which the G.1 performed better than the Bf 110. However, both types were eclipsed by the long range of the Mosquito which, in fighter-bomber guise, was able to fly sorties of over 2500 km (1,600 mi.).

G.1A 1400 km (870 mi.)

Bf 110C-4/B 775 km (480 mi.)

MOSQUITO FB.Mk VI 2655 km

ARMAMENT

With half the bombload of the Bf 110 and Mosquito, the G.1A's usefulness as an attack aircraft was limited. Its eight forward-firing machine-guns were comparable to other Allied fighters, though cannon armament was to become more common later in the war.

G.1A 9 x 7.92-mm (0.31-in.) machine-guns 400-kg (880-lb.) bomb load

Bf 110C-4/B 2 x 20-mm (0.79-in.) cannon 5 x 7.92-mm (0.31-in.) machine-guns 1000-kg (2,200-lb.) bomb load

MOSQUITO FB.Mk VI 4 x 20-mm (0.79-in.) cannon 4 x 7.7-mm (.303 cal.) machine-guns 907-kg (2,000-lb.) bomb load

Fokker G.1 markings

■ **PROTOTYPE G.1** In this view, prototype X-2 is seen after being re-engined with two Pratt & Whitney Twin Wasp Juniors. X-2 was later rebuilt to G.1B standard and became aircraft no. 341 of the undelivered Finnish order.

■ **PRE-OCTOBER 1939 MARKINGS:** Aircraft no. 314, a 619-kW Bristol Mercury VIII-engined G.1A (also known as the 'G.1 Mercury'), is seen in pre-October 1939 Dutch national markings. This machine flew with either the Third or Fourth Fighter Group.

■ **LUFTWAFFE SERVICE:** As well as taking delivery of the 12 ex-Finnish G.1Bs, the Luftwaffe ordered the completion of the other 14 machines still at the Fokker factory and shipped them to Germany for use as fighter trainers.

GLOSTER

GLADIATOR

● Single-seat fighter ● Last RAF and Royal Navy biplane fighter

B iplane fighters were already on the way out when the Gladiator development of the Gloster Gauntlet was proposed in 1933, but Britain's urgent need for combat aircraft led to orders for an eventual total of 581. These included 350 Gladiator Mk IIs, which had improved equipment and three-blade metal propellers in place of the Gladiator Mk I's two-bladed wooden airscrew. All had been delivered by April 1940 and a number went into combat.

▲ The Gladiator prototype flew for the first time in September 1934 as a private venture. The Air Ministry ordered the type the following year, with 480 being delivered. The Royal Navy took 60.

PHOTO FILE

GLOSTER **GLADIATOR**

▲ Last flyer
The last surviving airworthy Gladiator is this Mk I, which belongs to the Shuttleworth Collection in Bedfordshire. Here it wears the colours of No. 247 Squadron, RAF, while they were flying defensive patrols over Plymouth.

▲ Twenty RAF squadrons
No fewer than 20 home-based RAF squadrons were equipped with the Gladiator from 1937 to 1940.

▼ Air display practice
Representing the RAF's fighter force of 1938, these tethered Gladiators practise for the 1938 Hendon air display.

Scandinavian ▶ Gladiators
The Swedish and Finnish air forces bought Gladiators in the late 1930s. These saw action early in World War II.

◀ Battle of Britain
One of the last home-based Gladiator units was No. 247 Squadron, which flew the type until late 1940 over Plymouth.

FACTS AND FIGURES

➤ One Swedish squadron fighting with the Finns claimed 12 Soviet aircraft for only three losses.

➤ Gladiators entered RAF service in 1937, the year of the first Hurricane deliveries.

➤ The last RAF Gladiators, meteorological and liaison aircraft, were retired in 1944.

➤ The Sea Gladiators that defended Malta in early June 1940 were dubbed 'Faith', 'Hope' and 'Charity' by the Maltese.

➤ Sea Gladiators had catapult points, an arrester hook and a dinghy fairing fitted.

➤ Early Mk Is had two Vickers and two Lewis 7.7-mm (.303 cal.) machine-guns.

PROFILE

The last British biplane fighter

Despite being a biplane the Gladiator saw widespread action during the early stages of World War II. However, the results only underlined the type's obsolescence. The single squadron of Gladiators in Norway and the two squadrons based in France were all but wiped out during the German invasions in May and June 1940.

Other Gladiator squadrons fought in North Africa, Greece and Palestine in 1939 and 1940. Many were flown by Australian and South African units and a few were transferred to Egypt and Iraq. Another 36, which were supplied to China, joined the war against Japan in 1938.

The Sea Gladiator variant served aboard the aircraft-carriers *Courageous, Eagle* and *Glorious* and a handful were based in Malta when Italy joined the war in June 1940. For the next month, just four aircraft were the island's only defence against the Italians.

K5200 was the Gladiator prototype. The enclosed cockpit had yet to appear, although the gun armament was fitted at an early stage.

A major improvement on the Gladiator in terms of pilot comfort was the fully enclosed cockpit, which had a rear-sliding Perspex canopy.

The forward and rear spars of the mainplanes were made of high-tensile steel of 'dumb-bell' cross-section. The wing leading edge was made of duralumin.

Gladiator Mk I

Type: single-seat interceptor

Powerplant: one 627-kW (840-hp.) Bristol Mercury Mk IX air-cooled radial engine

Maximum speed: 407 km/h (253 m.p.h.) at 4420 m (14,500 ft.)

Climb rate: 9.5 min to 6095 m (20,000 ft.)

Range: 547 km (340 mi.)

Service ceiling: 10,060 m (33,000 ft.)

Weights: empty 1565 kg (3,450 lb.); maximum take-off 2155 kg (4,751 lb.)

Armament: four 7.7-mm (.303 cal.) Browning machine-guns; two nose-mounted and two wing-mounted

Dimensions:
span	9.83 m (32 ft. 3 in.)
length	8.36 m (27 ft. 5 in.)
height	3.15 m (10 ft. 4 in.)
wing area	30.01 m² (323 sq. ft.)

The two-bladed wooden airscrew was a feature of the early Mk I Gladiators; Mk IIs were fitted with a three-bladed metal propeller.

Four fuselage- and wing-mounted 7.7-mm (.303 cal.) Browning machine-guns were fitted.

A silver dope finish was standard on RAF fighters between the wars. Often squadrons would add their individual markings to aircraft.

Behind the pilot's seat was the radio compartment, the aerials for the radio being strung between the wings and the tailfin.

Bristol's Mercury Mk IX radial engine also powered the earlier Gauntlet and other types like the twin-engined Blenheim bomber.

GLADIATOR MK I

K7985 was a Gladiator Mk I, one of a batch of 180 ordered in September 1935. Here it carries the well-known markings of No. 73 (Fighter) Squadron.

Like most fighters of the 1930s, the Gladiator was of basically metal construction with a fabric skin.

K 7985

K7985

COMBAT DATA

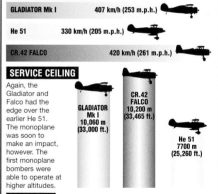

MAXIMUM SPEED

Arriving on the scene at the end of the biplane era, the Gladiator was fast for an aircraft of this type. It had an advantage over the He 51, but a lower top speed than the CR.42 which saw considerable wartime service.

GLADIATOR Mk I	407 km/h (253 m.p.h.)
He 51	330 km/h (205 m.p.h.)
CR.42 FALCO	420 km/h (261 m.p.h.)

SERVICE CEILING

Again, the Gladiator and Falco had the edge over the earlier He 51. The monoplane was soon to make an impact, however. The first monoplane bombers were able to operate at higher altitudes.

GLADIATOR Mk I 10,060 m (33,000 ft.)

CR.42 FALCO 10,200 m (33,465 ft.)

He 51 7700 m (25,260 ft.)

ARMAMENT

Four machine-guns was about the limit for the last of the biplane fighters. These had to be fuselage-mounted or fitted under the wings. On monoplanes, guns were carried inside the wing assembly; monoplane wings were thicker and had more space.

GLADIATOR Mk I 4 x 7.7-mm (.303 cal.) machine-guns

CR.42 FALCO 2 x 12.7-mm (.50 cal.) machine-guns

He 51 2 x 7.92-mm (0.31-in.) machine-guns

Gladiators around Europe

■ **FINLAND:** This Gladiator Mk II of the Suomen Ilmavoimat saw service in late 1939 and early 1940. Unlike the other Gladiator users, Finland flew its machines on the Axis side.

■ **NORWAY:** This Gladiator Mk II of the Norwegian Haerens Flyvevaben was based at Fornebeu, near Oslo, during April 1940. Ski landing gear was regularly fitted.

■ **PORTUGAL:** An important part of Portugal's airpower during World War II, this Gladiator II is shown in the markings of Esquadrilha de Caca de Base Aerea 2, flying from Ota in 1940.

GLOSTER

METEOR

● RAF's first jet fighter ● Flying bomb interceptor ● Single squadron

Even before Britain's first jet aircraft, the E.28/39, proved the practicality of this radical power source, Gloster was planning a new fighter to use the jet engine. After convincing the Air Ministry to draw up a specification (F.9/40) around their design, Gloster built a number of prototypes and by mid-1944 had equipped the first RAF jet unit, No. 616 Squadron. The intention was that the new jet would be pitted against Germany's jet fighter, the Me 262.

▲ *Entering service*
in 1944, the Meteor scored most of its victories against the high-speed V-1 flying bombs that plagued the British Isles towards the end of the war.

GLOSTER METEOR

▲ **Meteor F.Mk 1s in colour**
Contemporary colour images of wartime Meteors are rare. This photograph was taken in June 1944, at Farnborough, prior to a flight to Manston.

▲ **No. 616 re-equips**
No. 616 Squadron, RAF, was flying Spitfire Mk VIIs when it was announced that the unit was to become the RAF's first jet squadron. Here, Mk 1s and Mk 3s can be seen at RAF Manston.

▲ **Short service life**
Issued to No. 616 Squadron in July 1944, this Meteor F.Mk 1 was written off one month later after suffering a forced landing.

▼ **Clear-view canopy**
Unlike the F.9/40, the Meteor had a clear-view canopy to allow the pilot to see the rear of his aircraft.

▲ **Three different engines**
Of the three engine types fitted to F.9/40s, the Rover W.2B and Halford H.1 were centrifugal flow designs, while the Metropolitan-Vickers F.2 had an axial-flow compressor. One aircraft flew with the Metro-Vickers engines installed, but soon crashed.

FACTS AND FIGURES

➤ Among the other names suggested for the Meteor were Ace, Reaper, Scourge, Terrific, Thunderbolt and Wildfire.

➤ F.Mk 1s took part in trials to give USAAF crews experience of jet fighter tactics.

➤ When first deployed in Europe, Meteors were forbidden from flying over Germany.

➤ F.9/40 prototype, DG202/G, was later used for deck handling trials aboard HMS *Pretoria Castle*.

➤ The Halford H.1 engine was developed as the Goblin for the Vampire jet fighter.

➤ DG202, the first F.9/40, is displayed at the Aerospace Museum, Cosford.

PROFILE

RAF jet pioneer at war

Below: A Meteor F.Mk 3 is seen here just prior to touch-down. The Meteor Mk 3 benefited from improved Rolls-Royce Derwent engines.

As the first jet engines produced little thrust, Gloster was forced to design a twin-engined aircraft. As this allowed the installation of different engine types with relative ease, it was decided to test three different engines in the F.9/40 prototypes, eight of which were built.

Delays with the Rover W.2B engine (based on Frank Whittle's engine for the E.28/39 aircraft) resulted in prototype DG206/G, powered by two Halford H.1s, taking to the air first on 5 March 1943. As the other prototypes were flown, testing revealed a lack of directional stability, though these teething problems were corrected by modifications to the aircraft's tail.

On 12 January 1944, the Meteor F.Mk 1 made its first flight. This was effectively an F.9/40 powered by Rolls-Royce W.2B/23C Welland engines (Rolls having taken over development of the W.2B from Rover) and fitted with four 20-mm (0.79-in.) nose-mounted cannon.

Twelve F.Mk 1s were handed to No. 616 Squadron in July 1944 and the following month

Above: EE214/G was the fifth F.Mk 1 and was used to test a ventral fuel tank. It was scrapped in 1949.

Flying Officer Dean scored the RAF's first jet 'kill', when he downed a V-1 flying bomb.

In December, No. 616 re-equipped with the improved F.Mk 3. In 1945 the unit moved to Holland to make armed reconnaissance flights over Germany, but no Messerschmitt Me 262s were ever encountered.

Meteor F.Mk 1

Type: single-seat day fighter

Powerplant: two 7.56-kN (17,000-lb.-thrust) Rolls-Royce W.2B/23C Welland Series 1 turbojets

Maximum speed: 675 km/h (419 m.p.h.) at 3048 m (10,000 ft.)

Service ceiling: 12,192 m (40,000 ft.)

Weights: empty 3737 kg (8,221 lb.); loaded 6258 kg (13,768 lb.)

Fuel capacity: 1363 litres (360 gal.)

Armament: four Hispano 20-mm (0.79-in.) cannon in the nose

Dimensions: span 13.10 m (42 ft. 11 in.)
length 12.50 m (41 ft.)
height 3.90 m (12 ft. 9 in.)
wing area 34.70 m² (373 sq. ft.)

F.9/40

DG205/G was the fourth F.9/40 prototype and the second to fly, on 12 June 1943. It was therefore the first example to fly with W.2 engines fitted, but had only a short life, being written off in April 1944.

Among the improvements introduced in the Meteor F.Mk 3 were a sliding cockpit canopy, increased fuel capacity, new Derwent I engines, slotted air brakes and a strengthened airframe.

Like many of the Meteor variants that followed it, the F.9/40 was an all-metal, stressed-skin design. The fuselage was constructed in three sections: the front fuselage with cockpit and armament; the centre-section with the fuel tank, main landing gear, engines and air brakes; and the rear fuselage and lower fin.

To correct the directional stability problems exhibited by the F.9/40, an enlarged fin and rudder, test flown on DG 208/G, were fitted, along with flat-sided rudders and an 'acorn' fairing at the intersection of the fin and tailplane.

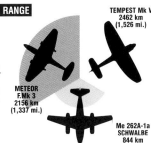

Though not fitted to the F.9/40 prototypes, four Hispano 20-mm (0.79-in.) cannon were installed in the F.Mk 1 and F.Mk 3 service variants. These were prone to jamming in early production aircraft.

DG205/G was powered by W.2 engines derived from Frank Whittle's original design for the E.28/39 pioneer jet. Five of the eight F.9/40s were so-equipped; two others had Halford H.1s, the eighth having Metro-Vickers F.2s.

Standard Fighter Command day-fighter camouflage was applied to the upper surfaces of the F.9/40s, with prototype yellow on the undersides to aid recognition. The 'P' marking in a yellow circle indicated a prototype aircraft.

The aircraft had a 'G' suffix added to its serial number to indicate that it was to have an armed guard at all times when on the ground. This was a reflection of the secret nature of jet-powered aircraft at the time of their appearance.

ACTION DATA

MAXIMUM SPEED

With its Derwent engines, the Meteor F.Mk 3 was able to exceed the top speed of the RAF's fastest piston-engined fighter, the Hawker Tempest Mk V (and tropicalised Mk VI). The Luftwaffe's Messerschmitt Me 262 was faster than both aircraft, but suffered serious engine reliability problems.

METEOR F.Mk 3	793 km/h (492 m.p.h.)
TEMPEST Mk V	685 km/h (425 m.p.h.)
Me 262A-1a SCHWALBE	869 km/h (539 m.p.h.)

OPERATIONAL RANGE

An area in which the Meteor very comfortably out-performed the Me 262 was its range. It was able to fly almost as far as the Tempest Mk V, nearly three times the German jet's range. Later Meteors carried ventral fuel tanks to increase range even further.

TEMPEST Mk V 2462 km (1,526 mi.)

METEOR F.Mk 3 2156 km (1,337 mi.)

Me 262A-1a SCHWALBE 844 km (523 mi.)

MAXIMUM TAKE-OFF WEIGHT

Though heavier than the Hawker Tempest, the Gloster Meteor had a lower maximum take-off weight than the Messerschmitt Me 262. Unlike the other two types, the Meteor was also limited to gun armament and carried no air-to-surface weapons. The Luftwaffe was forced to use its Me 262s in the ground-attack role.

METEOR F.Mk III 6033 kg (13,272 lb.)

TEMPEST Mk V 5897 kg (12,973 lb.)

Me 262A-1a SCHWALBE 6400 kg (14,080 lb.)

Early Meteor variations

■ **METEOR F.Mk 3:** For service in Europe in the final weeks before VE-Day, No. 616 Squadron's Meteor F.Mk 3s wore this overall white paint scheme during a harsh winter.

■ **'TRENT METEOR':** EE227, the eighth Meteor F.Mk 1 completed 80 hours of trials fitted with two Rolls-Royce Trents – the world's first turboprop engines.

■ **'CAMERA NOSE' Mk 3:** During planning for the still-born photo-reconnaissance version of the post-war Meteor Mk 4, Gloster fitted Mk 3 EE338 with a nose-mounted camera.

■ **'HOOKED' F.Mk 3:** With EE387, EE337 was fitted with an arrester hook for deck-landing trials aboard HMS *Implacable*. Thirty-two highly successful landings were made in all.

GRUMMAN

F4F WILDCAT

● Carrier-based fighter bomber ● Pacific War hero ● Royal Navy service

Wildcat squadrons used by the American Marines and Navy made their stand against Japan's superior Mitsubishi A6M Zero. While the Zero held the advantage in performance, the Wildcat achieved its greatness in part due to the exceptional men who flew it. As Foster Hailey of the *New York Times* said in 1943: 'The Grumman Wildcat, it is no exaggeration to say, did more than any single instrument of war to save the day in the Pacific.'

▲ *The American F4F was exported to the Royal Navy for operation aboard its carriers, and was for a while designated the Grumman Martlet until the service returned to the name Wildcat.*

GRUMMAN F4F WILDCAT

◀ **Carrier operations**
With its folding wings and catapult gear the Wildcat was a dedicated carrier fighter both with the US Navy and the Royal Navy. However, the F4F also saw action from land bases.

▲ **Grumman heritage**
The Wildcat was one of a long line of Grumman-built naval fighters, from the F3F to today's F-14 Tomcat.

▲ **Carrier battlegroup protector**
The Wildcat shared the decks of the US Navy's Pacific carriers in the early battles of the war with other classic types such as the Douglas Dauntless, Grumman Avenger and later the Vought Corsair.

Fleet Air Arm fighter ▶
The Royal Navy's first American fighter, the Wildcat was greatly respected.

◀ **Pacific warrior**
Until it started being replaced by the Hellcat from 1943, the Wildcat was the US Navy's most important fighter. This example carries the markings of fighter squadron VF-41. The red centre of the national marking was deleted from late 1942.

FACTS AND FIGURES

➤ Total production was 7825 Wildcats, including 1988 Grumman F4Fs and 5837 General Motors FMs.

➤ The Wildcat was first flown by Robert L. Hall on 2 September 1937.

➤ Fleet Air Arm Wildcats were the remnant of orders by France and Greece.

➤ A long-range reconnaissance version of the Wildcat was effective but was quickly replaced by a photo-reconnaissance F6F.

➤ Top Wildcat ace was Major John L. Smith who shot down 19 Japanese warplanes.

➤ Wildcats were also used by the Royal Canadian Air Force and US Marines.

PROFILE

Grumman's fleet defender

In the 1930s the US Navy mistakenly chose the Brewster Buffalo over the Grumman F4F Wildcat. By the 1941 Pearl Harbor attack, however, the decision was reversed: the Wildcat replaced Navy biplane fighters and battled Japanese Zeros in the Pacific. A far better fighter than the Brewster, the Wildcat did not meet the standards of the Japanese Zero but it contributed mightily to the American war effort. Lieutenant Edward 'Butch' O'Hare, flying an F4F, shot down five Japanese bombers in five minutes to become the first US Navy ace.

The Wildcat was sturdy and very manoeuvrable. It was not the easiest aircraft to fly but, once mastered, was incredibly responsive. Most Wildcats were manufactured by General Motors as the FM-2. Some went to Britain's Royal Navy, which called it the Martlet.

This portly, mid-winged fighter made a vital contribution: outnumbered and outgunned, it held the line until the most successful naval fighter in history, the Grumman F6F Hellcat, became available to turn the tide of the Pacific War.

A US Navy Wildcat drops its tailhook in order to catch the wire aboard the deck of a carrier in the Pacific.

The pilot was protected by thick armour behind the cockpit, bulletproof glass ahead and the massive engine in front of him.

All-metal vacuum operated split trailing-edge flaps were fitted.

Wing tanks contained 606 litres (158 gal.) of aviation gasoline, and were self sealing.

A rugged and powerful Wright Cyclone engine gave the F4F a good power-to-weight ratio. The two-stage blower sometimes caused problems and was replaced by a single-stage model.

The cockpit was rather cramped and visibility was not great, but the problems were resolved on Grumman's F4F replacement, the F6F Hellcat. Immediately behind the pilot was a Mk 1A liferaft.

F4F-4 WILDCAT

The F4F was heavily involved in Operation Torch in November 1942, the codename for the important Allied invasion of French North Africa.

This F4F carries early intermediate markings. The red spot has been removed from the centre of the star, but the yellow recognition circle around the roundel has yet to be applied.

The F4F was heavily armed with no less than six wing machine-guns. Although not as powerful as cannon, they were quite adequate against most Japanese opposition.

The undercarriage design was little changed from that on inter-war Grumman biplanes, with the mainwheels only half retracting to lie flat against the lower fuselage in a shallow well.

F4F-4 Wildcat

Type: single-seat carrier-based fighter

Powerplant: one 895-kW (1,200-hp.) Wright R-1830-36 Cyclone radial piston engine

Maximum speed: 512 km/h (317 m.p.h.)

Cruising speed: 249 km/h (154 m.p.h.)

Range: 1239 km (768 mi.)

Service ceiling: 12,010 m (39,400 ft.)

Weights: empty 2612 kg (5,746 lb.); maximum take-off 3607 kg (7,935 lb.)

Armament: six fixed 12.7-mm (.50 cal.) Browning air-cooled machine-guns with 240 rounds per gun plus two 45-kg (100-lb.) bombs

Dimensions:
span	11.60 m (38 ft.)
length	8.50 m (28 ft.)
height	3.60 m (12 ft.)
wing area	24.15 m² (260 sq. ft.)

COMBAT DATA

MAXIMUM SPEED

The power of engines and improved aerodynamics during the 1940s led to a consistently higher maximum speed of the F4F over its predecessor the F3F, and the F6F over the Wildcat which it replaced in US Navy squadron service.

F4F-4 WILDCAT	512 km/h (317 m.p.h.)
F3F	425 km/h (263 m.p.h.)
F6F HELLCAT	612 km/h (379 m.p.h.)

RANGE

Surprisingly, the F4F had less impressive range than the earlier F3F, due to its fuel thirsty and powerful engine and the efficiency of the F3F's wing. The F6F had greater range because of the addition of an underfuselage tank and new powerplant.

F4F-4 WILDCAT 1239 km (768 mi.)

F3F 1577 km (978 mi.)

F6F HELLCAT 1674 km (1,038 mi.)

ARMAMENT

The Wildcat introduced much improved armament over the F3F, the six Browning 12.7-mm machine-guns (retained on the later Grumman Hellcat) having long range and a hard punch.

F4F-4 WILDCAT	6 x 12.7-mm (.50 cal.) machine-guns
F6F HELLCAT	6 x 12.7-mm (.50 cal.) machine-guns
F3F	2 x 7.62-mm (.30 cal.) machine-guns

Wildcats over Wake Island

AERIAL PATROL: Flying in close formation on interception duties above the clouds, the Wake Island Wildcats did not catch sight of the attacking Japanese aircraft because of the bad weather.

AIRBASE ASSAULT: After evading the attentions of the defending F4Fs, the Japanese aircraft were free to bomb Wake's air base and destroy most of the island's 12 Wildcats before they had time to react.

REVENGE: The four Wildcats which had not been on the ground during the raid were able to attack the invading Japanese fleet, and managed to sink two destroyers.

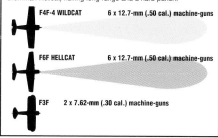

GRUMMAN

F6F HELLCAT

● Fleet carrier aircraft ● Naval strike-fighter ● Used by US Navy aces

▲ Most of the
US Navy's wartime aces notched
up their kills using the tough and manoeuvrable F6F.
Lieutenant Hanks was a Hellcat ace, shooting down
five Japanese aircraft in just one month.

Powerful and pugnacious, the Hellcat is one of the few aircraft in history which was right from the start. Designed after Pearl Harbor, the Hellcat required almost no testing or development work before being rushed into production. Swarms of these beefy, gloss-blue fighters wrested control of Pacific skies from the vaunted Japanese Zero and chalked up a record of success in air combat that has rarely been matched.

GRUMMAN F6F HELLCAT

▲ Radar goes to sea
Later Hellcats had advanced instruments such as radio altimeters and radar.

▼ Take-off flag
Lieutenant John Clarke gives the take-off signal flag to an F6F pilot. Taking off with the canopy open meant that it was easy to escape if the aircraft ditched after leaving the ship.

▲ Strike Hellcat
Hellcats served on with France after the war and saw extensive action in Indochina.

▼ Crowded decks
The US Navy's carriers carried more aircraft than could be hangared, and many Hellcats were parked on deck alongside Avengers and SBDs.

▲ Spreading wings
Like most naval fighters, the Hellcat had folding wings. They used the typical Grumman feature of swivelling back to lie each side of the fuselage.

FACTS AND FIGURES

➤ The XF6F-1 prototype made its first flight on 26 June 1942.

➤ Of 6477 aerial victories claimed by US Navy pilots during World War II, 4947 were credited to F6F Hellcat pilots.

➤ On 3 April 1944, Royal Navy Hellcats attacked the *Tirpitz* at Kaafjord, Norway.

➤ Grumman made 12,275 Hellcats at its New York plant between June 1942 and November 1945, the largest number of fighters ever produced at a single factory.

➤ F6F-3K drones gathered particles from atomic clouds during the 1946 nuclear tests at Bikini atoll.

King of the carrier fighters

The sturdy, powerful F6F Hellcat is one of the few fighters developed after the outbreak of World War II to succeed in that conflict. A big, heavy machine in an age when experts lauded small, light fighters, the Hellcat was fast enough and agile enough to become the outstanding dogfighter of the Pacific war.

Pilots also praised the strength of the F6F, which they jokingly called a product of the 'Grumman Iron Works' because they knew that sustaining damage in combat no longer meant certain death. The Hellcat could and did bring its pilot home.

This remarkable aircraft also proved its merit as a night-fighter (using early air-intercept radar)

and a reconnaissance aircraft. Britain employed the Hellcat throughout the East Indies, Malaya, Burma and in the final assault on Japan. Half a decade later, the Hellcat was all but gone from American service when the final examples were used as unmanned flying bombs – the Korean War's equivalent of today's cruise missile.

Two of the elements which won the Pacific War: the F6F Hellcat aboard an 'Essex'-class carrier.

F6F-5 Hellcat

Type: single-seat carrier-based fighter

Powerplant: one 1492-kW (2,000-hp.) Pratt & Whitney R-2800-10W Double Wasp 18-cylinder radial piston engine

Maximum speed: 620 km/h (380 m.p.h.) at medium altitude

Range: 1675 km (1,040 mi.)

Service ceiling: 11,500 m (37,500 ft.)

Weights: empty 4191 kg (9,200 lb.); loaded 6991 kg (15,400 lb.)

Armament: six 12.7-mm (.50 cal.) Browning M2 machine-guns; up to 907 kg (2,000 lb.) of bombs; six 127-mm (5-in.) rockets

Dimensions:
span	13.08 m	(42 ft. 10 in.)
length	10.23 m	(33 ft. 7 in.)
height	3.99 m	(13 ft. 1 in.)
wing area	31.03 m²	(334 sq. ft.)

F6F-5 HELLCAT

This Hellcat was flown by fighter squadron VF-27 from the light carrier USS *Princeton*, sunk during the Battle of Leyte Gulf in October 1944.

The F6F was strongly built. For added protection, it was equipped with a self-sealing fuel tank and a tough sheet of armour to protect the pilot.

The F6F was powered by the 18-cylinder Pratt & Whitney Double Wasp engine, one of the largest piston powerplants available during World War II.

This VF-27 fighter is armed for a ground-attack mission, with bombs and 127-mm high-explosive rockets.

The fin and tailplanes were built around very strong central spars. The aircraft itself was extremely strong, and could survive substantial battle damage.

Like the rest of the fighter, the undercarriage was extremely tough to withstand repeated carrier landings.

On internal fuel the F6F had a combat radius of 800 km (500 mi.), but this could be extended by the use of external tanks.

COMBAT DATA

MAXIMUM SPEED

F6F-5 HELLCAT	620 km/h (380 m.p.h.)
A6M5 ZERO	570 km/h (355 m.p.h.)
P-38J LIGHTNING	666 km/h (415 m.p.h.)

The Hellcat was not particularly fast by European standards, and it was outperformed by US land-based fighters like the P-38. But it had a significant advantage over its main rival in the Pacific, the previously all-conquering Mitsubishi Zero.

ARMAMENT

American fighters were always fairly lightly armed, especially compared to their opponents. But the USA more than made up for any inferiority by the ruggedness of its aircraft, the superior training of its pilots, and the accuracy of their shooting. The A6M5 Zero was equipped with cannon giving more deadly firepower but it lacked defensive armour.

F6F-5 HELLCAT
6 x 12.7-mm (.50 cal.) machine-guns

A6M5 ZERO
2 x 20-mm (0.79-in.) cannon
2 x 13-mm (0.51-in.) machine-guns

P-38J LIGHTNING
1 x 20-mm (0.79-in.) cannon
4 x 12.7-mm (.50 cal.) machine-guns

Battle of the Philippine Sea

Fought on 19 and 20 June 1944, the Battle of the Philippine Sea saw the final elimination of Japanese carrier air power as a factor in the Pacific war. An American invasion fleet was approaching the Mariana Islands; capture of the islands would give the USA air bases from which its bombers could strike direct at the Japanese homeland. It was the task of the Imperial Navy to stop the landings and defeat the US Pacific fleet.

FIRST MOBILE FLEET: On 15 June three fleet carriers and six light carriers sail from Japanese bases in the Philippines 800 km (500 mi.) west.

INVASION FORCE: On 11 June the American amphibious fleet approaches from the east, guarded by the massive Task Force 58 – seven battleships and no less than 15 carriers. After destroying the Japanese fighters on the islands, TF 58 moves to guard the landings from the Japanese fleet approaching from the Philippines.

HEAVY LOSSES: Japanese aircraft are shot out of the sky by F6F Hellcats. 253 Japanese fighters lost for 30 American.

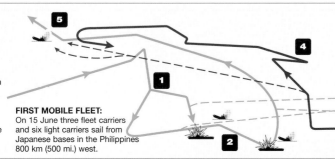

SAIPAN

TINIAN

GUAM

1. **19 JUNE** Japanese fleet divides to launch air attack
2. **19 JUNE** Carriers *Taiho* and *Shokaku* sunk by US submarines
3. **19 JUNE** Japanese air power annihilated, fleet withdraws
4. **20 JUNE** Pursuing US fleet launches air strike
5. **20 JUNE** US aircraft sink one carrier and damage three

GRUMMAN

TBF/TBM AVENGER

● Three-seat torpedo-bomber ● Battle of Midway veteran

▲ *Avengers saw their*
first combat in the Battle of Midway in June 1942.
Although their losses were high, production was
stepped up, with nearly 10,000 being built in
several variants before the war ended.

Grumman's portly TBF Avenger (built by Eastern Aircraft as the TBM) was the most important American torpedo-bomber of World War II. Big, noisy and powerful, the Avenger flew from carrier decks and spanned vast Pacific distances to attack the Japanese Navy with its torpedo or bombs. The Avenger had staying power, with many Allied nations using the type long after the war. US Navy Avengers were still on hand for transport duty in the Korean War.

GRUMMAN TBF/TBM AVENGER

▲ Royal Navy Avengers
This TBF-1 (Avenger Mk I) flew with the Fleet Air Arm's No. 846 Squadron. FAA aircraft were carrier and land based.

▲ Flying on into the 21st century
A number of Avengers have survived to be restored by enthusiasts. In service until the 1950s, some surplus aircraft were converted into water bombers and were used to fight forest fires for many years. Some of the restored aircraft are ex-fire bombers.

▲ Barrel shaped
For a single-engined aircraft the TBM was fairly big. The same engine was fitted to the B-25 Mitchell bomber.

▼ Airborne early warning
To provide early warning protection for USN carriers the TBM-3W, with its large radome, entered service after the war.

▲ Carrier-borne
A US Navy Avenger lumbers off the deck of a carrier. The bulk of Avengers were built by General Motors (Eastern Division) as Grumman was fully committed to building fighters for the Navy.

FACTS AND FIGURES

➤ US President George Bush was the youngest naval aviator when he flew Avengers in combat in the Pacific.

➤ Avenger production totalled 9839; 7546 by General Motors, the rest by Grumman.

➤ The TBF was initially called the 'Tarpon' in the Royal Navy and later the 'Avenger'.

➤ When used against submarines, Avengers destroyed or shared in the destruction of 42 U-boats.

➤ Avengers used the first high-velocity aircraft rockets (HVARs) in January 1944.

➤ Six TBFs saw action in the Battle of Midway on 4 June 1942; only one returned.

General Motors torpedo truck

Grumman Iron Works was a nickname for the company that designed the Avenger. Grumman created shipboard aircraft that were sturdy, heavy and tough. When it replaced the inadequate Douglas TBD Devastator as the US Navy's torpedo-bomber in the Pacific, the Grumman Avenger had the strength and power to do the job.

However, as Grumman was busy fulfilling large orders for fighters, the job of constructing the bulk of the Avenger order

was subcontracted to the Eastern Aircraft Division of the General Motors Corporation.

Despite a poor start at the 1942 Battle of Midway, the Avenger performed superbly through to the end of the war and, in addition to torpedo bombing, took on other roles including close air support of ground troops.

The Avenger was pleasant to fly, although spinning was prohibited. When flown with determination by a strong pilot, it could almost turn like a fighter,

hence its single, and later twin, forward-firing gun armament.

Britain (921 aircraft) and New Zealand (63) also used Avengers during the war. Canada, France, Japan and the Netherlands employed it after 1945.

Above: The Avenger's weapons bay was big enough for a torpedo or 907-kg (2,000-lb.) bomb. The prototype first flew on 1 August 1941.

Above: A Royal Navy Avenger aboard HMS Illustrious. *Thirty-three first- and second-line FAA squadrons were equipped with the Avenger, which served from numerous carriers and shore bases from Canada to the Far East.*

TBF-1 Avenger

Type: three-seat carrier-based torpedo-bomber

Powerplant: one 1268-kW (1,700-hp.) Wright R-2600-8 Cyclone 14-cylinder radial piston engine

Maximum speed: 436 km/h (270 m.p.h.) at 5030 m (15,000 ft.)

Climb rate: 435 m/min (1,425 f.p.m.)

Range: 1778 km (1,100 mi.)

Service ceiling: 6830 m (22,400 ft.)

Weights: empty 4788 kg (10,534 lb.); maximum take-off 7876 kg (17,327 lb.)

Armament: (TBF-1C) two fixed forward-firing 12.7-mm (.50 cal.) machine-guns; one 12.7-mm machine-gun in rear turret, one 7.62-mm (.30 cal.) machine-gun in ventral position; 907 kg (2,000 lb.) of bombs or one torpedo in internal bomb-bay

Dimensions:
span	16.51 m	(54 ft. 2 in.)
length	12.20 m	(40 ft.)
height	5.00 m	(16 ft. 5 in.)
wing area	45.52 m²	(490 sq. ft.)

TBM-1 (AVENGER MK II)

As well as the US Navy, Britain's Fleet Air Arm and the Royal New Zealand Air Force operated Avengers during World War II.

Power for the Avenger was supplied by Wright's big R-2600 Cyclone 14 radial engine. Three main fuel tanks were fitted with a total capacity of 1248 litres (330 gal.).

Two crewmembers sat in the long cockpit 'glasshouse': the pilot, who also fired the wing guns and released the torpedo, and the radio operator, who also manned the rear gun turret.

To ease stowage aboard aircraft-carriers the Avenger had hydraulically folding wings. The main undercarriage retracted into the wings; the rear wheel also retracted. The arrester hook was electrically operated.

Avenger Mk II serial number JZ490 was based in Britain in mid-1944 and carried the black and white identification stripes worn by Allied aircraft during the invasion of Europe.

NAVY
490

The ventral machine-gun position was occupied by the bomb-aimer. The hydraulically operated bomb-bay doors could be controlled by the bomb-aimer or the pilot.

COMBAT DATA

ARMAMENT

The Avenger was in every way an improvement over the TBD. Its gun armament was significantly greater and it could deliver twice the weight of bombs or a larger torpedo. The B6N was lightly armed.

TBD-1 DEVASTATOR
2 x 7.62-mm (.30 cal.) machine-guns
454 kg (1,000 lb.) of bombs/torpedoes

TBF-1 AVENGER
3 x 12.7-mm (.50 cal.) machine-guns
1 x 7.62-mm (.30 cal.) machine-gun
907 kg (2,000 lb.) of bombs/torpedoes

B6N TENZAN
2 x 7.7-mm (.303 cal.) machine-guns
800 kg (1,760 lb.) bombs/torpedo

MAXIMUM SPEED

The TBF had a 100 km/h (60 m.p.h.) speed advantage over the TBD. The more streamlined B6N was faster still, due to its more powerful engine and lighter weight. The B6N was intensively used in the last two years of the war, latterly as kamikaze aircraft.

TBD-1	332 km/h (206 m.p.h.)
TBF-1 AVENGER	436 km/h (270 m.p.h.)
B6N TENZAN	480 km/h (298 m.p.h.)

RANGE

With well over twice the range of the TBD, the TBF still lagged far behind the equivalent Japanese design. Range is a very important attribute for a carrier-based aircraft. The B6N's long range allowed it to strike first in a carrier battle.

TBD-1 DEVASTATOR 669 km (415 mi.)

TBF-1 AVENGER 1778 km (1,100 mi.)

B6N TENZAN 3045 km (1,890 mi.)

Post-war Avengers

■ **CANADIAN NAVY TBM-3E:** The Canadian navy was one of several to receive Avengers under the Mutual Assistance Program after World War II. Another was the former enemy, Japan.

■ **FIRE BOMBER:** As the TBF/TBM was retired by the US Navy in the 1950s, surplus aircraft found other uses. This example is one of a number used as water bombers in Canada and the US.

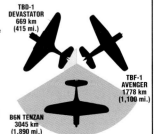

■ **CROP SPRAYER:** Another role for the civilian Avenger in Canada was that of forest or agricultural crop sprayer. In New Zealand experimental crop dusting was tried with Avengers.

HANDLEY PAGE

HALIFAX

● Heavy bomber ● Long-range maritime patroller ● Transport

A s one of the four-engined bomber types which provided the backbone of the Royal Air Force's night bombing offensive against Germany the Halifax was a vital cog in the Allied war effort. Although the Avro Lancaster grabbed the glory, its pilots and crews found the Halifax to be a superb heavy bomber with formidable striking power. It also flew a wide variety of missions, ranging from anti-submarine patrols to para-dropping agents into occupied Europe.

▲ Halifaxes served in every part of the European and Atlantic theatres. In the maritime role crews like this ranged far over the ocean, protecting convoys from the U-boat threat.

HANDLEY PAGE HALIFAX

▲ Cargo master
The Halifax Mk VIII transport variant, distinguished by its lack of gun turrets and its bulging belly, could carry 3600 kg (7,920 lb.) of freight.

▲ Merlin cargo
Although designed to carry bombs of up to 1800 kg (3,690 lb.), the bomb-bay could hold more unusual loads, like this engine.

▲ Night bird
The black undersides were designed to hide the aircraft from searchlights when night-bombing. Although overshadowed by the Lancaster, the Halifax was an effective combat aircraft.

▲ Caught in the glare
Silhouetted against the glare of target indicator flares, a Halifax drops its bombs on a V-weapon site. The bomb-run was the most dangerous part of the mission.

◀ Defensive formation
Even when it kept to a tight defensive formation, the Halifax's gun turrets could not defend it effectively enough by day. Most bombing missions by the aircraft were at night.

FACTS AND FIGURES

➤ First flight of a Halifax prototype was on 25 October 1939.

➤ In addition to Bomber Command, the Halifax was flown by RAF Coastal Command for anti-submarine and other maritime duties.

➤ 6178 Halifaxes were built, but not one survives fully intact today.

➤ Because of its great hauling capacity, the Halifax was used as a freighter and transport by the RAF and civil users.

➤ The almost-complete wreckage of a Halifax bomber was retrieved from Lake Hoklingen, Norway, in 1973.

➤ The Halifax was the first aircraft to carry H2S radar-bombing equipment.

PROFILE

Handley Page's great all-rounder

The Halifax Mk III introduced the Bristol Hercules radial engine, an extended-span wing, new tailfins and a long glazed nose without a gun turret. The enhanced performance endeared it to crews.

Its reputation has been overshadowed to some extent by its great contemporary, the Lancaster. But at its peak the Handley Page Halifax equipped 34 squadrons of RAF Bomber Command, and in 75,532 sorties over Europe between 1941 and 1945 the type dropped 231,263 tonnes (227,609 tons) of bombs.

It was in some respects the best aircraft in its class, gifted with great bomb-carrying capacity, toughness and the strength to survive when hit.

The Halifax was also the most versatile RAF heavy bomber. Remembered for nocturnal raids over Europe, the Halifax took on many duties, including pathfinder, ambulance, freighter, glider-tug, personal transport and maritime reconnaissance aircraft.

The Halifax offered as much protection as feasible, but flying this bomber was a dangerous business, especially during the bloody campaign over Berlin (November 1943–March 1944), which cost the RAF 1,000 aircraft to the barrage of anti-aircraft artillery and swarms of Luftwaffe night-fighters encountered on every sortie. Every man in a Halifax crew shared a bond. Some of the most courageous pilots were those who brought the Halifax home burning and crippled from battle damage – to a safe landing.

Halifax B.Mk III

Type: seven-seat long-range heavy bomber; also troop transport and long-range anti-submarine aircraft

Powerplant: four 1204-kW (1,613-hp.) Bristol Hercules XVI 14-cylinder radial piston engines

Maximum speed: 500 km/h (281 m.p.h.)

Service ceiling: 7315 m (24,000 ft.)

Range: 2000 km (1,240 mi.) with maximum bombload

Weights: empty 17,345 kg (38,159 lb.); loaded 29,484 kg (64,865 lb.)

Armament: nine 7.7-mm (.303 cal.) machine-guns in nose and quad dorsal and tail turrets, plus up to 5897 kg (13,200 lb.) of bombs

Dimensions:
span	31.75 m (104 ft.)
length	21.82 m (72 ft.)
height	6.32 m (21 ft.)
wing area	118.45 m² (1,275 sq. ft.)

Although a co-pilot's seat was fitted, Halifaxes were, like Lancasters, flown by a single pilot.

The twin-fin tail was a desirable feature, as more than one Halifax crew was forced to fly home with half the tail unit shot away.

HALIFAX B.MK I

Halifax L9530 was one of the very first production aircraft, which was delivered to the RAF's No. 76 Squadron in the winter of 1940–41.

The 'acorn' on top of the fuselage housed a rotating radio-direction-finding antenna.

The B.Mk I had gun positions in the beam windows. Later versions were equipped with two- or four-gun dorsal turrets.

The original small tailfins seen here were later replaced by larger square surfaces.

Early Halifaxes were fitted with a two-gun nose turret. This was replaced in later variants by a streamlined Perspex moulding which created much less drag.

Although intended to be a twin-engined bomber, early examples were powered by four Rolls-Royce Merlins.

The capacious bomb-bay could carry almost 6000 kg (13,200 lb.) of bombs of up to 1800 kg (4,000 lb.) in size, and was later adapted to carry cargo.

All Halifax bombers carried a four-gun tail turret to counter German night-fighters, which generally attacked from astern.

COMBAT DATA

MAXIMUM SPEED

The original Halifax was underpowered with four Merlins, and could be fairly sluggish with a heavy load. Mk IIIs were equipped with powerful Bristol Hercules radial engines, which transformed the bomber into one of the fastest aircraft in its class.

HALIFAX B.Mk III	500 km/h (310 m.p.h.)
B-17D	462 km/h (286 m.p.h.)
LANCASTER B.Mk I	460 km/h (285 m.p.h.)

MAXIMUM BOMBLOAD

British bombers generally carried near-capacity bombloads on operations. American bombers rarely used their full lifting capacity, and a typical load for the B-17 was usually about 2500 kg (5,500 lb.).

HALIFAX B.Mk III	5897 kg (12,973 lb.)
B-17D	5800 kg (12,760 lb.)
LANCASTER B.Mk I	6350 kg (13,970 lb.)

RANGE

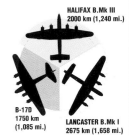

Most Western four-engined bombers had the range to carry a heavy weapons load from bases in England to attack targets as far away as east Prussia or the oilfields in Romania. Losses to unescorted bombers could be great, however, as they braved the heavily defended skies over the Reich. The RAF bombers main defence was operating in darkness.

HALIFAX B.Mk III 2000 km (1,240 mi.)

B-17D 1750 km (1,085 mi.)

LANCASTER B.Mk I 2675 km (1,658 mi.)

Night bombers raid the Reich

MISSION LAUNCHED: RAF bomber raids were extremely complex operations. Up to 1000 heavy aircraft would take off from fields all over eastern England, crossing the coast of Europe in several streams. Late in the war they were accompanied by aircraft equipped with electronic countermeasures equipment, as well as heavily armed Mosquito night-fighters, to counter the fierce German defences.

HAMBURG

THE RUHR

MUNICH

SPOOF RAIDS: Bombers would appear to be heading for any one of a number of widely dispersed cities, forcing the Luftwaffe's defences to be divided.

THE REAL TARGET: At a pre-determined point the bomber streams converged, aiming to be over the primary target almost simultaneously, overwhelming the defences and giving a greater chance of survival.

MULTIPLE THREAT: Defenders were faced with an overwhelming threat coming from differing directions at differing heights. Precision planning was essential to prevent collision. By the end of the war a 1000-bomber raid took only minutes to unload its deadly cargo, compared to the hours it had taken three years earlier.

HAWKER

HURRICANE MK II/IV

● Fighter-bomber ● Cannon and rocket armament ● Anti-tank role

▲ Fighter-bomber
Hurricane Mk IIs and IVs remained in production in Britain and Canada for the duration of World War II, serving with home-based and overseas RAF squadrons.

British fighter development during World War II, like that of the other combatants, centred on improvements in engine power output and armament firepower. Hawker's Hurricane was typical in this respect. Although outclassed as an interceptor by 1941, the Rolls-Royce Merlin-powered Hurricane, armed with cannon and rockets, went on to serve as a valuable fighter-bomber in Europe, the Far East and North Africa.

HAWKER HURRICANE MK II/IV

Mk IIC night intruder ▶
No. 247 'China-British' Squadron was one of five RAF squadrons equipped with cannon-armed Mk IICs for raids over France and the Low Countries.

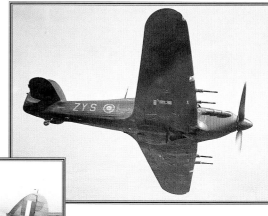

▼ Twelve-gun 'Hurribomber'
Armed with twelve 7.7-mm (.303 cal.) Browning machine-guns and able to be fitted with racks for two 227-kg (500-lb.) bombs, the Mk IIB was the first dedicated attack Hurricane.

▼ Rocket projectiles
Although more often associated with the Hawker Typhoon, the 76.2-mm, 27-kg (60-In.) rocket projectile was pioneered on the Mk IV.

◀ Anti-tank Mk II
With two 40-mm (1.57-in.) 'S' cannon, the Mk IID was a formidable anti-armour aircraft. The first unit equipped, No. 6 Squadron, RAF, was appropriately known as the 'Flying Can Openers'.

3rd TAF, India 1944 ▶
Seen in a muddy Assam, India during the monsoon season of 1944, this Mk IIC attached to the Third Tactical Air Force has a Vokes tropical air filter fitted under its nose and twin 200-litre (53-gal.) drop tanks under its wings.

FACTS AND FIGURES

➤ Early 20-mm (0.79-in.) cannon-equipped Mk IICs were tested operationally during the Battle of Britain by No. 151 Squadron.

➤ No. 6 Squadron was the RAF's last Hurricane unit, retaining Mk IVs until 1946.

➤ The last Hurricane built, PZ865, is a Mk IIC and remains airworthy with the RAF.

➤ Canadian Hurricane production included the Mk XII – a Mk II with varied armament and a Packard Merlin engine.

➤ The stillborn Mk III was a proposal for a Packard Merlin-engined Hurricane.

➤ Russia, Turkey, Ireland, Egypt and India used Hurricane Mk IIs during World War II.

'Hurribombers' and tank-busters

Merlin XXs were first fitted to a Hurricane Mk I in 1940. The re-engined fighter immediately demonstrated a 32 km/h (20 m.p.h.) speed improvement over the Mk I and entered production as the Mk IIA. It was soon joined by the Mk IIB with 12 7.7-mm (.303 cal.) machine-guns. During 1941 Mk IIs began fighter and later fighter-bomber sweeps over France, the latter armed with up to 454 kg (1,000 lb.) of bombs. Other units performed

'Channel Stop' anti-shipping patrols. In autumn 1941, Mk IIAs and IIBs were sent to the Eastern Front. With the emphasis moving toward the Hurricane as a ground attacker, new armament (four 20-mm/0.79-in. cannon) was introduced. From April, the Mk IIC entered day-fighter service; from August, night-fighter units were also equipped. From late 1941, the Mk IID was available, primarily as an anti-tank aircraft armed with two Vickers 40-mm (1.57-in.) cannon. They proved

effective both in Burma and the Western Desert.

In 1943, on the Mk IV, a 'universal' wing was introduced for adaptation in the field. Mk IVs carried 40-mm (1.57-in.) cannon, drop tanks, or two 113-kg (250-lb.) or 227-kg (500-lb.) bombs. Extra armour was also fitted. It was the Mk IVs, entering service in 1943, that pioneered the use of 27-kg (60-lb.) rocket armament in the RAF.

Persia ordered Hurricanes in 1939, but their delivery was delayed until after World War II. This two-seat Mk IIC trainer was among them.

Four 20-mm (0.79-in.) Hispano or Oerlikon cannon were the most common armament fitted to Mk IIs. The 'universal' wing of the Mk IV was not able to carry four cannon.

In May 1942 the first Mk IICs arrived in India and Ceylon. By June the following year, 16 squadrons in India, northern Burma and Ceylon were equipped. By 1944, this number had reached 29, seven of which were IAF units. No. 1 Squadron, IAF, had a secondary tactical reconnaissance role, its Mk IICs carrying a wing-mounted camera.

Late production Mk IIAs and all Mk IIs built subsequently were 17.8 cm (7 in.) longer than the Mk I, to accommodate an extra fuselage bay for an enlarged engine coolant tank.

KZ352 is finished in the RAF's so-called 'SEAC' (Southeast Asia Air Command) camouflage scheme of grey and olive drab with two-tone blue roundels, as used in the Far East.

The addition of a two-stage supercharger boosted the power of the Rolls-Royce Merlin XX initially to 884 kW (1,185 hp.) and later 954 kW (1,620 hp.). Hurricane Mk IVs were fitted with a 1208-kW Merlin 23 or 27. Unusually, this aircraft did not have a Vokes air filter fitted.

HURRICANE Mk IIC

The Indian Air Force used about 300 Hurricane Mk IIBs, IICs, IIDs and IVs during World War II. KZ352 was with No. 1 Squadron, IAF, in 1944.

Unlike contemporaries such as the Spitfire, the Hurricane had a fabric-covered rear fuselage, which it retained throughout its production history.

Hurricane Mk IIC

Type: fighter and fighter-bomber

Powerplant: one 954-kW (1,280-hp.) Rolls-Royce Merlin XX liquid-cooled piston engine

Maximum speed: 541 km/h (335 m.p.h.) 'clean'

Initial climb rate: 6100 m (20,000 ft.) in 9.1 min

Range: 740 km (460 mi.) 'clean'; 1480 km (920 mi.) with two 200-litre (53-gal.) drop tanks

Service ceiling: 10,850 m (35,600 ft.)

Weights: empty 2631 kg (5,788 lb.); loaded 3674 kg (8,083 lb.)

Armament: four Hispano or Oerlikon 20-mm (0.79-in.) cannon and underwing racks for two 113-kg (250-lb.) or 227-kg (500-lb.) bombs

Dimensions:
span	12.19 m	(40 ft.)
length	9.75 m	(32 ft.)
height	3.99 m	(13 ft. 1 in.)
wing area	23.92 m²	(257 sq. ft.)

COMBAT DATA

POWER

The relatively modest power of the Hurricane is illustrated by this comparison with the Hawker Typhoon and a ground-attack variant of the Focke-Wulf Fw 190. All three types were originally conceived as fighters.

HURRICANE Mk IIB 954 kW (1,280 hp.)

TYPHOON Mk IB 1626 kW (2,180 hp.)

Fw 190F-3/R1 1268 kW (1,700 hp.)

RANGE

Hurricanes were able to undertake missions over reasonable distances with their 772-km (480-mi.) range. The Typhoon was marginally more capable in this respect, and the Fw 190 was quite 'short-legged' by comparison.

HURRICANE Mk IIB 772 km (480 mi.)

TYPHOON Mk IB 821 km (510 mi.)

Fw 190F-3/R1 531 km (330 mi.)

Ground-attack armament

40-mm (1.57-in.) CANNON: Mk IIDs sported twin 40-mm (1.57-in.) Vickers 'S' cannon, each with 15 rounds of ammunition, as well as two 7.7-mm (.303 cal.) machine-guns for sighting purposes. The cannon, and extra armour added a performance penalty.

ROCKET PROJECTILES: 'Universal' wings fitted to the Mk IV (originally designated Mk IIE) allowed the carriage of eight 27-kg (60-lb.), 76.2-mm (3-in.) rocket projectiles. Extra armour was also fitted to protect the aircraft's Merlin 27 engine, which was optimised for low-level operations in high temperatures.

UNDERWING STORES: The most-produced Hurricane, the Mk IIC, featured four 20-mm (0.79-in.) cannon and a variety of underwing stores.

BOMBS AND FUEL TANKS: Mk IIC stores included two 200-litre (53-gal.) drop tanks or two 113-kg (240-lb.) or 227-kg (500-lb.) bombs. Ground-attack Hurricanes sometimes carried asymmetric loads, mixing, for example, four rockets and a fuel tank.

HAWKER

TEMPEST

● Strong and powerful ● Flying bomb destroyer ● Last piston fighter

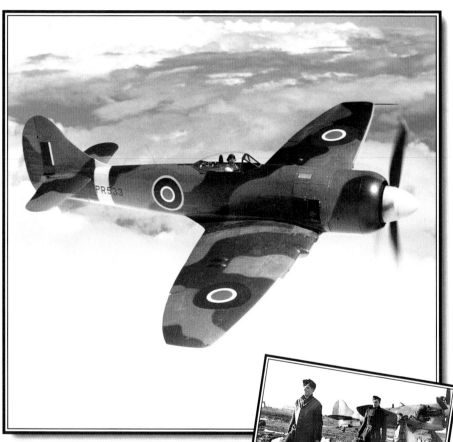

The Hawker Tempest was a big, powerful fighter developed to follow the better-known Typhoon. With a huge engine, 'bubble' canopy and high performance, the Tempest proved to be a tremendous weapon for the Allies in the war in Europe. This fine fighter took on many challenges, but is best remembered for intercepting and shooting down V-1 'flying bombs' that were launched against England in 1944 and 1945.

▲ The Hawker Tempest Mk V (above) was the last RAF fighter aircraft to enter service before the end of World War II. The Centaurus-powered Tempest Mk II (main picture) was intended for operations in the Far East against the Japanese, but the war ended before the aircraft were ready.

HAWKER TEMPEST

▼ Tempest Mk II
The Bristol Centaurus-powered Tempest Mk II never saw service in World War II, but served in the Far East after the war.

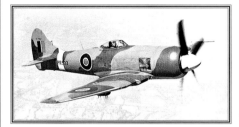

▲ Powerful fighter
The Tempest's Centaurus engine made it the most powerful single-engined fighter of the time. It served principally with the Far East Air Force.

▲ Tropicalised Tempest
This Mk VI was a tropicalised version of the Mk V with the Sabre V engine and a bigger radiator.

Thin wing ▶
A new, thin, elliptical, laminar flow wing was produced for the Tempest. Sydney Camm, the designer, said he only designed this wing shape because of the RAF's fixation with the success of the Spitfire.

▲ Tempest production
The first version of the Tempest, the Mk V, was equipped with four 20-mm (0.79-in.) Hispano guns and had provision for rockets or bombs under its wings.

FACTS AND FIGURES

➤ Top-scoring Tempest pilot was D. C. Fairbanks, an American in the RAF, credited with 11 air-to-air victories.

➤ The first Tempest to fly, a Mk V, was converted from a Typhoon.

➤ Tempests remained in service with the RAF as target tugs until July 1955.

➤ Tempests destroyed 240 Luftwaffe planes, including 80 Messerschmitt Bf 109s and 115 Focke-Wulf Fw 190s.

➤ One Tempest pilot is credited with shooting down over 60 V-1 buzz-bombs.

➤ Total production of the Tempest fighter was more than 1400 aircraft.

RAF's flying bomb destroyer

The Hawker Tempest began on engineers' drawing boards as an improvement of the famous Typhoon with a different wing design and more power. An early flight test report by Royal Air Force pilots called the Tempest 'a manoeuvrable and pleasant aircraft to fly, with no major handling faults'. It was a robust and powerful fighter and at low altitudes it was up to 70 km/h (45 m.p.h.) faster than the Luftwaffe's Messerschmitt Bf 109 or Focke-Wulf Fw 190. In combat, pilots found that the Tempest was able to take devastating hits from gunfire and still remain in the air.

Tempests began service in April 1944 and were active during the build-up to the Normandy invasion two months later. Pitted against the V-1 flying bomb, Tempest pilots were credited with shooting down 638 of the RAF's total of 1771 destroyed. Tempests supported the Allied advance across Europe and fought the Messerschmitt Me 262 jet fighter successfully, shooting down at least 11.

After the war Tempest Vs continued in service with British Air Force of Occupation (BAFO) squadrons until they were replaced by Tempest Mk IIs and Vampires. The tropicalised, more powerful Tempest Mk VI was also operated by the RAF in the Middle East. Centaurus-powered Tempest Mk IIs entered service in 1946 and were flown by squadrons based in Germany, Hong Kong, India and Malaya until they were replaced by Hornets in 1951. The Indian and Pakistan air forces also flew Tempest Mk IIs.

Above: During 1944-45 RAF Tempest Mk Vs were successfully engaged in ground attack, train busting, destroying V-1s and supporting the Allied assault through Belgium and Holland.

Left: These Tempest Mk V Series 2s flew in trials with the RAF's Central Fighter Establishment at West Raynham in 1945. The nearest Tempest has eight lengthened rocket rails fitted under the wings.

Tempest Mk V

Type: single-seat fighter and fighter-bomber

Powerplant: one 1766-kW (2,366-hp.) Bristol Centaurus Mk V 24-cylinder piston engine (Mk II); one 1626-kW (2,180-hp.) Napier Sabre IIA/B 24-cylinder 'H' piston engine (Mk V)

Maximum speed: 686 km/h (425 m.p.h.) at 5640 m (18,500 ft.)

Range: 1191 km (740 mi.)

Service ceiling: 11,125 m (36,500 ft.)

Weights: empty 4082 kg (8,980 lb.); maximum take-off 6142 kg (13,512 lb.)

Armament: four 20-mm (0.79-in.) cannon, plus two 227-kg (500-lb.) or two 454-kg (1,000-lb.) bombs or eight 27-kg (60-lb.) rocket projectiles

Dimensions:
span	12.50 m	(41 ft.)
length	10.26 m	(34 ft.)
height	4.90 m	(16 ft.)
wing area	28.06 m²	(302 sq. ft.)

TEMPEST MK VI

The RAF's last and most powerful wartime piston-engined fighter and effective ground-attack aircraft, the Tempest Mk VI was also used against the V-1 flying bombs.

The forward fuselage housed the powerplant. The fuel tank had detachable metal panels.

Protection was good, with a bulletproof windscreen and single-piece bubble canopy that could be jettisoned. Armour plating was fitted forward and aft of the pilot.

The forward fuselage was formed from a rectangular rigid-braced tubular structure. The rear fuselage was a monocoque structure with oval shaped frames, longitudinal stringers and stressed skin.

This Tempest Mk VI was flown by No. 213 Squadron, based at Shallufa near to the Suez Canal. It carried the squadron's hornet emblem on its fin.

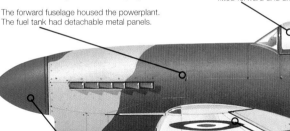

U●AK NX245

The four-bladed de Havilland Hydromatic constant speed propeller was fixed to a large spinner.

Four 20-mm (0.79-in.) Hispano Mk V cannon were carried in the wings, firing outside of the propeller arc. Provision was made for two 227-kg (500-lb.) or two 454-kg (1,000-lb.) bombs or eight rocket projectiles under the wings.

The Tempest's tail was a cantilever all-metal tail unit with a dorsal fin extension. Tailplane and fin were stress skin covered, but the rudder was fabric-covered. All control surfaces had trim tabs.

COMBAT DATA

MAXIMUM SPEED

Tempests were very fast. They were capable of catching V-1 flying bombs in a dive, and some shot down Me 262s. Many pilots flew the Tempest close to the sound barrier in long dives.

TEMPEST Mk V	686 km/h (425 m.p.h.)
Fw 190D-9	627 km/h (389 m.p.h.)
P-47 THUNDERBOLT	689 km/h (450 m.p.h.)

ARMAMENT

Four cannon armament was standard on British fighters by 1944. The large 20-mm (0.79-in.) shells were far more effective than bullets. A pair of bombs or eight rockets could also be carried.

4 x 20-mm (0.79-in) cannon	
TEMPEST Mk V	plus 2 x 454-kg (1,000-lb.) bombs
2 x 20-mm (0.79-in.) cannon	
Fw 190D-9	plus 2 x 13-mm (0.51-in.) MGs, 1 x 500-kg (1,100-lb.) bomb
8 x 12.7-mm (.50 cal.) MGs	
P-47 THUNDERBOLT	plus 1 x 1134-kg (3,600-lb.) bomb

CLIMB RATE

With its powerful engine and superb wing design, the Tempest was a superb climber. The heavy Thunderbolt was inferior to the Fw 190 in climb, but could easily outdive its German rival.

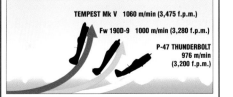

TEMPEST Mk V	1060 m/min (3,475 f.p.m.)
Fw 190D-9	1000 m/min (3,280 f.p.m.)
P-47 THUNDERBOLT	976 m/min (3,200 f.p.m.)

Doodle-bug defender

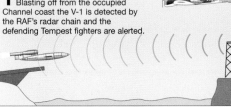

1 FLYING-BOMB LAUNCHED: Blasting off from the occupied Channel coast the V-1 is detected by the RAF's radar chain and the defending Tempest fighters are alerted.

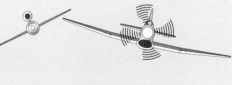

2 RACE TO DESTRUCTION: Making use of altitude, the Tempest dives in to attack the flying bomb before it reaches its city target.

3 KNOCK OUT BLOW TO V-1: An effective method of bringing down a V-1 was for the Tempest to fly alongside the bomb and destabilise it using its wingtip.

HAWKER

TYPHOON

● Lethal low-level ground attacker ● Rocket-armed train-buster

A n interceptor that failed, the Hawker Typhoon was nearly cancelled before it blossomed into the finest close-support aircraft of World War II. With its pugnacious snub nose, four long-barrelled cannon and whining Sabre engine, the big fighter-bomber wreaked havoc on its foes. Ranging far and wide over the battlefields of north-west Europe, swarms of Typhoons made an indelible mark on the history of warfare.

▲ The Typhoon
was designed as an interceptor,
but made its name as a high-speed, low-level strike aircraft. It was one of the Allies' most important anti-tank weapons.

HAWKER TYPHOON

▼ **Brute power**
The massive radiator for the Napier Sabre engine gave the Typhoon a very brutal appearance.

▲ **Tornado prototype**
The Typhoon was designed in parallel with the Rolls-Royce Vulture-powered Tornado.

▼ **Chunky**
The compact, strong design of the Typhoon resembled the Fw 190 from certain angles, which caused more than one 'friendly fire' incident with Spitfires.

▲ **Tail problem**
The Typhoon was almost cancelled because at first it suffered tail flutter problems that caused several crashes.

'Bomb- ▶
phoon'
Bomb-armed Typhoons were known as 'Bombphoons', and were very effective ground-attackers.

FACTS AND FIGURES

➤ The Typhoon prototype made its maiden flight on 24 February 1940.

➤ The Typhoon, nicknamed the 'Tiffy', did not reach its first operational squadron until September 1941.

➤ The Tornado was a similar aircraft with a different, endlessly troublesome engine.

➤ The only surviving Typhoon, retrieved from the USA, is on display in the RAF Museum at Hendon, north London.

➤ The Typhoon shot down 246 Luftwaffe aircraft during European fighting.

➤ The top-scoring Typhoon 'ace' was J. R. Baldwin, with 15 aerial victories.

PROFILE

Hawker's tank-buster supreme

Although it first flew in 1940, the Hawker Typhoon did not come into its own until much later in the war. Rushed into service in 1941 as an Fw 190 destroyer, the Typhoon was fast enough to do the job but was not as agile as its foe, and its engine was plagued by reliability problems.

But as a low-level close-support machine, the Typhoon was supreme. It was a superb gun platform, and could carry

and deliver with precision a heavy load of bombs or air-to-surface rockets.

The climax of the Typhoon's career came in the third week of August 1944 when all of the surviving German forces in northern France – 5th Panzer Army, 7th Army and Panzer Group 'Eberbach' – were caught in a trap near Falaise. Typhoons, mainly from the RAF's No. 83 Group, unleashed rockets, cannon shells and bombs until

hardly one German vehicle was capable of movement.

Once the war was over, the Typhoon's lack of reliability meant that the type was rapidly taken out of service. Only one Typhoon survives intact today.

Rocket-armed Typhoons were one of the most powerful weapons in the Allied inventory after D-Day, making life very difficult for German armoured forces fighting in France.

Originally carrying 12 Browning 7.7-mm (.303 cal.) machine-guns, the Typhoon was soon equipped as standard with a harder-hitting fit of four 20-mm (0.79-in.) Hispano cannon and eight 27-kg (60-lb.) rockets.

Typhoon Mk IB

Type: single-seat fighter-bomber

Powerplant: one 1626-kW (2,180-hp.) Napier Sabre IIA inline piston engine

Maximum speed: 664 km/h (413 m.p.h.) at 6000 m (19,685 ft.)

Range: 975 km (606 mi.); 1500 km (932 mi.) with drop-tanks

Service ceiling: 10,700 m (35,100 ft.)

Weights: empty 3992 kg (8,800 lb.); loaded 6010 kg (13,250 lb.)

Armament: four 20-mm (0.79-in.) Hispano cannon each with 140 rounds; two bombs of up to 454 kg (1,000 lb.) each; numerous other combinations including eight or 12 27-kg (60-lb.) rockets or two 205-litre (45-gal.) drop-tanks

Dimensions: span 12.67 m (41 ft. 7 in.)
length 9.73 m (31 ft. 11 in.)
height 4.52 m (14 ft. 10 in.)
wing area 25.90 m² (279 sq. ft.)

TYPHOON MK IB

Typhoons were crucial to the Allied advance through France in 1944. The squadrons deployed there were part of the 2nd Allied Tactical Air Force.

The Typhoon was much improved as a combat aircraft when a sliding bubble canopy was installed.

All Allied aircraft were painted with large 'invasion stripes' just before the invasion of France in June 1944.

Typhoon pilots were well protected, with a bulletproof canopy, a huge engine in front of them and superb armour plate behind.

The Napier Sabre was a hugely powerful engine, but suffered from chronic problems at first, with engine life as low as 20 hours.

The Typhoon had a wide-track undercarriage, which made it a safe aircraft to use on rough tactical airstrips.

The Typhoon wing was a very solid structure, allowing the aircraft to carry large bombs and to make power dives at almost 800 km/h (500 m.p.h.).

The early tail problems of the Typhoon were cured by the fitting of 'fish plates' to strengthen the structure.

COMBAT DATA

MAXIMUM SPEED

The Typhoon had a good turn of speed and could just outrun the Fw 190, especially at low level. Early P-47s were of similar power and speed to the Typhoon, but continuous development was to see the massive American fighter leap ahead.

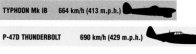

TYPHOON Mk IB	664 km/h (413 m.p.h.)
P-47D THUNDERBOLT	690 km/h (429 m.p.h.)
Fw 190A	654 km/h (406 m.p.h.)

RANGE

Both the Typhoon and the Fw 190 were designed as interceptors and were used tactically. The P-47 was specifically designed to escort bombers, and had much greater range.

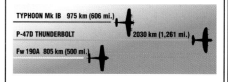

TYPHOON Mk IB	975 km (606 mi.)
P-47D THUNDERBOLT	2030 km (1,261 mi.)
Fw 190A	805 km (500 mi.)

ARMAMENT

The Typhoon's four-cannon armament was far more powerful than the P-47's machine-guns, and almost as potent as the standard fit on the Fw 190. However, the German fighter was often modified to carry a pair of hard-hitting 30-mm (1.18-in.) cannon.

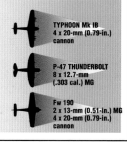

TYPHOON Mk IB 4 x 20-mm (0.79-in.) cannon

P-47 THUNDERBOLT 8 x 12.7-mm (.303 cal.) MG

Fw 190 2 x 13-mm (0.51-in.) MG 4 x 20-mm (0.79-in.) cannon

Typhoons on call

CLOSE SUPPORT: Blockhouses were capable of delaying an advance, and the Typhoon was often called upon to demolish them with 454-kg (1,000-lb.) high-explosive bombs.

'CAB RANK': Developed by the British Desert Air Force in North Africa, the 'cab ranks' were patrols of fully-armed Typhoons orbiting over the battlefield, on call to give immediate assistance to ground units in need of air support.

TANK-BUSTER: A single Pzkpfw VI 'Tiger' tank could, and often did, hold up an entire Allied armoured advance in Normandy. A single salvo of eight 27-kg (60-lb.) rockets from a Typhoon had the explosive power of a destroyer broadside, and was enough to remove the problem.

HEINKEL

HE 111

● Medium bomber ● Torpedo-bomber ● Transport

L ike the Luftwaffe, the military purpose of the He 111 was at first a secret: it was a high-speed airliner that could be converted into a bomber. This twin-engine, low-wing aircraft with its glazed nose and elliptical wing was the muscle of Germany's bomber force during the hard-fought Battle of Britain, and even though obsolete it kept on bombing until the war's final days.

▲ *The Heinkel He 111*
flew on every front in World War II, from the Arctic to the desert. It first saw combat in the Spanish Civil War, and was still in action as the Third Reich crumbled into ruin.

HEINKEL HE 111

▲ **First of many**
Although the He 111 entered service with Lufthansa in 1936, this ostensible high-speed airliner was actually designed to be a bomber.

▲ **Glazed nose**
The transparent nose area gave excellent visibility to both the gunner and bomb-aimer, but was very vulnerable to gunfire.

◀ **Balloon buster**
This huge framework was an attempt to deflect barrage balloon cables, but it was too cumbersome and reduced speed.

Survivor ▶
Ability to survive huge battle damage was one of the He 111's greatest assets.

▼ **Rocket assist**
For operations from rough fields or at very heavy take-off weights, He 111s could be, and often were, equipped with disposable rockets.

▲ **Over the Thames**
He 111s attacked London in large numbers in 1940. After being beaten off by day, they were switched to night raids.

FACTS AND FIGURES

➤ The prototype for the He 111 series first flew at Marienehe on 24 February 1934.

➤ He 111s served with the Condor Legion during the Spanish Civil War in 1937.

➤ He 111s made very successful attacks on the Bristol and Supermarine factories during the Battle of Britain.

➤ Heinkel He 111s destroyed 43 American B-17s and 15 P-51s at Poltava airfield, Russia, on 21 June 1944.

➤ More than 7300 Heinkel He 111s were built before and during the war.

➤ Spanish He 111s with British Merlin engines were built by CASA after the war.

Mainstay of the Luftwaffe's bomber force

Obsolescent at the start of World War II, and testimony to Germany's mistake in not developing four-engine bombers, the He 111 was nevertheless an effective strike machine. From the Spanish Civil War via the London Blitz and on through every Luftwaffe campaign until the end of 1944, this reliable machine provided the backbone of Germany's air power.

Although considered quite advanced when introduced as a pseudo-airliner, the 'Spaten' – so called because of the spade-like shape of the characteristic Heinkel elliptical wing – quickly became outmoded. But it was tough and serviceable, and the Luftwaffe never really managed to find a replacement.

But the spectacle of He 111 bomber formations pressing through swarms of Allied fighters is just part of the story: the He 111 attacked ships with torpedoes and the first guided missiles, towed gliders, dropped secret agents, transported VIPs, and hauled high-value cargoes.

Many special versions were produced for experimental purposes. One in particular was noteworthy, carrying and launching the Fieseler Fi 103 (V-1) flying bomb from beneath the starboard wing.

The crew could all see each other in the He 111, which in spite of increased vulnerability was considered a good morale feature by German designers. The He 111 was able to accommodate extra armour and defensive weaponry, unlike the Dornier Do 17.

He 111H-16

Type: four-/five-seat medium bomber

Powerplant: two 1006-kW (1,350-hp.) Junkers Jumo 211F-2 inline piston engines

Maximum speed: 435 km/h (270 m.p.h.) at 6000 m (20,000 ft.) (light load)

Range: 1950 km (1,200 mi.)

Service ceiling: 8500 m (28,000 ft.)

Weights: empty 8680 kg (19,096 lb.); loaded 14,000 kg (30,800 lb.)

Armament: one 20-mm (0.79-in.) cannon, one 13-mm (0.51-in.) and up to nine 7.92-mm (0.31-in.) machine-guns, plus provision for up to 3307 kg (7,275 lb.) of bombs carried internally and externally

Dimensions:
span	22.60 m	(74 ft. 1 in.)
length	16.40 m	(53 ft. 9 in.)
height	4.00 m	(13 ft. 1 in.)
wing area	86.50 m²	(931 sq. ft.)

The bomb-aimer lay on a horizontal pad, looking down at the target. The excellent forward view was especially useful when making torpedo attacks.

A large fuel tank with a capacity of 700 litres (182 gal.) was contained in the inner section of the wing.

The pilot sat on the left of the cabin, with a folding seat for the bombardier to his right. A gangway between the bomb racks led to the rear compartment, which housed the gunners and radio operator.

HE 111H-16

The He 111H was the major production variant of the bomber, being produced in at least 23 official variants and in innumerable field modified forms. It served in many different roles, including bombing, torpedo-carrying, transport and glider towing.

The long, broad dihedral wing was lightly loaded, and gave the He 111 pleasant, stable flying characteristics allied to the ability to carry large loads.

The He 111's rugged undercarriage left plenty of clearance to carry large weapons externally, even over rough forward airfields.

The entire fuselage and tail section was of metal construction, with metal skinning. The He 111 could just about fly with one elevator entirely shot away.

Despite the presence of a nose gun, Allied fighter pilots soon found that the way to attack the He 111 was from the front, where there was no cockpit armour.

The ventral gondola mounted a single machine-gun and was horribly vulnerable to attack from below. It was known as the 'Sterbebett' (Deathbed) to its occupants.

COMBAT DATA

MAXIMUM SPEED

Designed as an airliner, with a streamlined shape, the He 111 was as fast as most service fighters when introduced. With its contemporaries, however, it was quickly outclassed by the new generation of monoplane fighters.

He 111H-16	435 km/h (270 m.p.h.)
B-25 MITCHELL	438 km/h (272 m.p.h.)
WELLINGTON	411 km/h (255 m.p.h.)

RANGE

The Luftwaffe's primary mission was to support the Wehrmacht, so the He 111 was designed for tactical rather than strategic missions. It had a fairly good range nevertheless, although it could not match a long-range bomber like the Wellington.

He 111H-16	WELLINGTON
1950 km (1,200 mi.)	2480 km (1,488 mi.)

B-25 MITCHELL
2170 km (1,345 mi.)

INTERNAL BOMBLOAD

Both the Heinkel and the Wellington put bombload in front of defensive armament. The B-25, however, had a light bombload, as it relied on its defensive armament and high speed to survive.

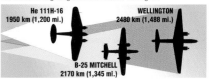

WELLINGTON	B-25 MITCHELL
2040 kg (4,488 lb.)	1360 kg (2,992 lb.)

He 111H-16
2500 kg (5,500 lb.)

History of a classic warplane

■ PROTOTYPE: Used by Lufthansa for mail flights and to carry four passengers, the He 111 was never a commercial proposition as an airliner in the pre-war years.

■ COMBAT DEBUT: In 1937, Kampfgruppe 88 of the Legion Condor took the He 111 into action with great success during the Spanish Civil War.

■ LUFTWAFFE WORKHORSE: The He 111P and the later He 111H series were the backbone of Germany's bomber force in World War II, taking part in all theatres of the war.

■ SPECIAL PURPOSE: He 111s were modified for many roles. The double-fuselage 'Zwilling' was developed as a tug for the Luftwaffe's giant gliders.

■ SURVIVORS: Some 236 Rolls-Royce Merlin-powered He 111s were built in Spain after the war, serving into the 1960s as transports and trainers.

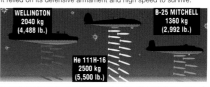

HEINKEL

HE 162 SALAMANDER

● Wooden construction ● Single-seat 'Volksjäger'

Heinkel rushed the design of the He 162 Salamander in an attempt to develop a mass-produced fighter that would stem the tide of Allied bombers over the Reich. One of the first operational jet aircraft, the He 162 was a sound concept but suffered from structural and aerodynamic problems as a result of its hasty introduction. This was a tricky and difficult aircraft to fly, and few saw any combat action before the end of hostilities.

▲ Novice pilots, with training only on gliders, were to have flown the He 162, and would have completed their training in combat. The Salamander was an interesting concept, but it was doomed to fail.

HEINKEL HE 162 SALAMANDER

▲ Underground production
US units advancing on Magdeburg found a massive production facility for the He 162 in abandoned salt mines. Several of the jets were near completion.

▲ Post-war testing
Large numbers of former Luftwaffe aircraft, including He 162s, were captured by the Allies and tested in Britain and the United States.

▼ Narrow track
A very narrow undercarriage, combined with the heavy, dorsally mounted engine, would have made ground handling tricky.

▲ Perfectly preserved
Several He 162s survive in museums. This aircraft is finished in the colours of II/Jagdgeschwader 1, which became part of Einsatz-Gruppe I/JG 1.

Tail prop ▶
Parked aircraft, especially those with their guns removed, tended to fall back onto their tails, and therefore a tail prop was used to prevent damage.

FACTS AND FIGURES

➤ The prototype He 162 made its first flight on 6 December 1944 but was lost in a mishap four days later.

➤ A Gruppe equipped with 50 He 162 fighters was formed at Leck on 4 May 1945.

➤ More than 270 He 162s were completed and 800 unfinished aircraft were captured.

➤ Heinkel's jet was one of the first aircraft to use an ejection seat for emergency escape by the pilot.

➤ Plans were in existence to build 5000 He 162s per month.

➤ Loss of the prototype in December 1944 was due to the break-up of the right wing.

PROFILE

Luftwaffe's last line of defence

Designed, developed and built in an extraordinarily short time, the Heinkel He 162 was first flown as the pressures of war closed in on Germany. The prototype was in the air just 38 days after detail drawings were issued to the factory.

An attractive and potentially useful fighter, the He 162 was plagued by problems resulting from its over-hasty development. This single-seat, single-engined warplane was supposed to be a 'people's fighter', devoid of frills, inexpensive to manufacture and easy to use. In fact it proved to be extremely difficult to fly. Wartime leaders had hoped that pilots with little or no experience could be recruited and trained quickly to fly the aircraft, but the He 162 could be fatally difficult, even in the hands of experienced fighter aces with hundreds of hours in the Messerschmitt Bf 109 or Focke-Wulf Fw 190. One pilot called the He 162 'totally unforgiving', but spoke of the jet as a pleasure to fly in favourable circumstances.

The programme, and not the aircraft, was called the Salamander and designer Ernst Heinkel called the jet the 'Swallow'. The He 162 became operational but no reports of actual combat were ever confirmed.

Photographed during a high-speed pass, this He 162 underwent tests in Britain. One aircraft was destroyed in a fatal crash.

Mounting the BMW 003 engine above the fuselage made the aircraft unstable in pitch, which made it very difficult to fly.

A cartridge-actuated ejection seat provided an escape route for the pilot. Leaving the aircraft by the conventional means of bailing out with a parachute would have been impossible with the jet intake behind and above the cockpit.

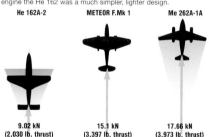

He 162A-2

Type: single-seat jet fighter

Powerplant: one BMW 003E-1 axial-flow turbojet engine rated at 7.80 kN (1,755 lb. thrust) for take-off and 9.02 kN (2,030 lb. thrust) for maximum bursts of up to 30 seconds

Maximum speed: 890 km/h (490 m.p.h.) at sea level

Range: 620 km (384 mi.)

Service ceiling: 12,010 m (39,400 ft.)

Weights: empty 1663 kg (3,659 lb.); empty equipped 1758 kg (3,868 lb.); loaded 2805 kg (6,171 lb.)

Armament: two 20-mm (0.79-in.) MG 151 cannon in forward fuselage

Dimensions:
span	7.20 m	(23 ft. 7 in.)
length	9.05 m	(29 ft. 8 in.)
height	2.60 m	(8 ft. 6 in.)
wing area	11.20 m²	(121 sq. ft.)

HE 162A-2

This aircraft was captured by the British at Leck. It had previously served with 3. Staffel, Einsatz-Gruppe I/JG 1 and was the personal aircraft of the Staffelkapitän.

A one-piece canopy and windscreen glazing gave the pilot an exceptional view. The raised position of the cockpit glazing was similar to that of modern fighters.

An unusually narrow main undercarriage was fitted to the He 162. This resulted from there being no room for the structure in the wings, and therefore all systems had to be accommodated in the narrow, cramped fuselage.

Oberleutnant Erich Demuth had 16 kill markings on the tail of his He 162, all gained in other types.

A single MG 151 cannon was mounted in a recess on either side of the lower forward fuselage. By good fortune, Heinkel had chosen a configuration which avoided engine gun-gas ingestion problems.

Aerodynamic problems led to the adoption of turned down wingtips. The small wings were mostly of wood, with light alloy flaps. Much of the wooden wing, tail and undercarriage door structure was of adhesively bonded wood and after an undercarriage door had broken away in flight, it was discovered that acid in the adhesive was corroding the wood.

COMBAT DATA

THRUST

Both the Meteor and Me 262 employed twin engines to overcome the low thrust available from early turbojets. Fitted with only one engine the He 162 was a much simpler, lighter design.

He 162A-2	METEOR F.Mk 1	Me 262-1A
9.02 kN (2,030 lb. thrust)	15.1 kN (3,397 lb. thrust)	17.66 kN (3,973 lb. thrust)

MAXIMUM SPEED

Due to its streamlined fuselage and small size the He 162 was a fast aircraft, especially compared to Britain's first operational jet fighter, the Gloster Meteor. The speed shown is for maximum engine power.

He 162A-2	890 km/h (521 m.p.h.)
METEOR F.Mk 1	668 km/h (414 m.p.h.)
Me 262A-1A	869 km/h (540 m.p.h.)

ARMAMENT

Early jets relied on their speed for surprise attacks, with armament limited by the need to save weight to maintain performance. The Me 262 was the most successful design and had powerful weapons.

He 162A-2 2 x 20-mm (0.79-in.) cannon	METEOR F.Mk 1 4 x 20-mm (0.79-in.) cannon	Me 262A-1A 4 x 30-mm (1.18-in.) cannon 12 x rockets

German jet developments

ARADO Ar 234 BLITZ: Ar 234s saw some operational service, mostly in the reconnaissance role, and proved to be immune to interception by Allied fighters. However, they suffered from short engine life and servicibility problems.

GOTHA Go 229 (HORTEN Ho IX): Gotha developed the radical Ho IX tailless glider as the Go 229 jet-powered fighter. Tests showed the aircraft had exceptional handling, but the war ended before production aircraft were completed.

HEINKEL He 280: Having lost out in the competition with the exceptional Me 262, examples of this single-seat, twin-jet interceptor were used as research aircraft and included a version with a V-tail.

MESSERSCHMITT P.1101: Although failing to fly before the end of the war, the P.1101 was a highly advanced aircraft which indicated Germany's lead in jet aircraft design. It was used by the US as the basis of the Bell X-5.

HEINKEL

HE 177 GREIF

● Maritime strike aircraft ● Heavy bomber ● Guided-missile launcher

Germany's only wartime heavy bomber, the He 177 was also one of its most troublesome aircraft. It was designed to use two pairs of engines, each driving a single propeller, to have three remotely controlled gun positions. Predicted performance figures included a top speed of 550 km/h (341 m.p.h.) and a range of 6700 km (4,150 mi.) with a 1000-kg (2,200-lb.) bombload, but the He 177 was never completely successful in service.

▲ As a heavy bomber the Greif was used only to a limited extent and it is best remembered as an anti-shipping aircraft equipped with guided air-to-surface missiles, torpedoes and bombs.

PHOTO FILE

HEINKEL HE 177 GREIF

▼ Tricky take-off
Engine fires were the most serious threat faced by He 177 crews, but take-off could also be difficult. Any slight imbalance in power output between left and right engines resulted in a vicious tail swing.

▲ Came to grief
Of 35 He 177A-0 aircraft built, 25 were destroyed in accidents or fires. At least seven crashed while taking off.

Greif bomber ▶
This He 177A-5/R2 belonged to 6. Staffel, Kampfgeschwader 100, and was used on bombing missions during May 1944. It was based at Toulouse-Blagnac and is seen fitted with Hs 293 and Fritz X launching racks.

◀ Atlantic reconnaissance
During the spring of 1944 He 177A-5/R6s began flying attack and reconnaissance missions over the Atlantic. This aircraft belonged to II./KG 40.

Special variants ▶
Several special versions of the He 177 were built, including this aircraft with an unusual bulged and glazed nose. A further variant, the V38, based on the A-5, was possibly intended as a delivery platform for a German nuclear bomb.

FACTS AND FIGURES

➤ On its first flight the V1 prototype proved to be slow with insufficient range, but it showed no other problems.

➤ V2, the second prototype, broke-up in flight; V4 and V5 were also lost.

➤ Arado built five of the He 177A-0 pre-production aircraft.

➤ Production of the improved He 177A-3 was planned at 70 aircraft per month but only five per month were completed.

➤ A-3/R7 and A-5 aircraft could launch the LT 50 glider torpedo.

➤ I./KG 50 flew some He 177A-1s, with MK 101 cannon, for flak suppression duties.

Heinkel's fiery Greif

Things started to go wrong at an early stage in the He 177's development. First the advanced cooling system for the twin engine installations was abandoned in favour of bigger radiators. This increased drag, however, and so more fuel was needed and the fuselage had to be strengthened, which made the aircraft heavier and reduced performance.

Then the remotely-controlled defensive armament was replaced by manned gun positions, adding more weight. And to meet the requirement for 60° diving attacks, further strengthening was required, which increased the weight still further.

Many prototypes were lost during test flights as a result of structural failure or engine fires. In service, take-offs proved tricky and led to several more accidents. More operational aircraft were lost to engine fires than to combat.

Attempts to cure the aircraft's faults were never successful. Even so, more than 1000 of the various models were built. In 1943/44 three were converted to prototypes of the He 277, with four separate engines each driving its own propeller, and

Above: Early production aircraft had full-span flaps which extended below the ailerons. From the A-3 onwards, these aileron flaps were abandoned.

Right: Combining two DB 601 engines to produce the DB 606 unit produced a high degree of complexity in the He 177. This was magnified by the way the engine was installed, which made it prone to fire.

a single prototype of the improved four-propeller He 274 was completed by Farman in France and flown in December 1945.

He 177A-5/R2 Greif

Type: heavy bomber, reconnaissance and anti-shipping aircraft

Powerplant: two 2200-kW (2,950-hp.) Daimler-Benz DB 610 24-cylinder liquid-cooled engines

Maximum speed: 488 km/h (303 m.p.h.) at 6100 m (20,000 ft.)

Initial climb rate: 190 m/min (623 f.p.m.) at sea level

Range: 5500 km (3,400 mi.) with two Hs 293 missiles

Service ceiling: 8000 m (26,250 ft.)

Weights: empty 16,800 kg (39,960 lb.); maximum take-off 31,000 kg (68,200 lb.)

Armament: two 20-mm (0.79-in.) cannon, three 7.9-mm (0.31-in.) and three 13-mm (0.51-in.) machine-guns, up to 1000 kg (2,200 lb.) in the bomb bay plus two missiles under the wings

Dimensions:
span	31.44 m	(103 ft. 2 in.)
length	22.00 m	(72 ft. 2 in.)
height	6.39 m	(20 ft. 11 in.)
wing area	102.00 m²	(1,098 sq. ft.)

HE 177A-5/R2 GREIF

Tasked with anti-ship duties this aircraft was based at Bordeaux-Mérignac with 4. Staffel, II Gruppe, Kampfgeschwader 100, during 1944.

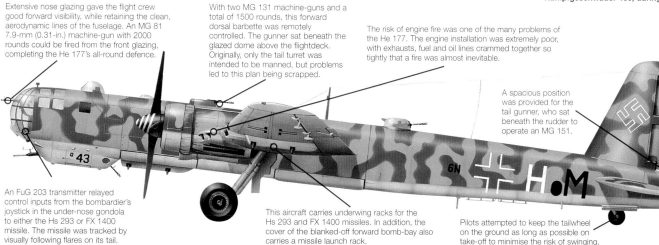

Extensive nose glazing gave the flight crew good forward visibility, while retaining the clean, aerodynamic lines of the fuselage. An MG 81 7.9-mm (0.31-in.) machine-gun with 2000 rounds could be fired from the front glazing, completing the He 177's all-round defence.

With two MG 131 machine-guns and a total of 1500 rounds, this forward dorsal barbette was remotely controlled. The gunner sat beneath the glazed dome above the flightdeck. Originally, only the tail turret was intended to be manned, but problems led to this plan being scrapped.

The risk of engine fire was one of the many problems of the He 177. The engine installation was extremely poor, with exhausts, fuel and oil lines crammed together so tightly that a fire was almost inevitable.

A spacious position was provided for the tail gunner, who sat beneath the rudder to operate an MG 151.

An FuG 203 transmitter relayed control inputs from the bombardier's joystick in the under-nose gondola to either the Hs 293 or FX 1400 missile. The missile was tracked by visually following flares on its tail.

This aircraft carries underwing racks for the Hs 293 and FX 1400 missiles. In addition, the cover of the blanked-off forward bomb-bay also carries a missile launch rack.

Pilots attempted to keep the tailwheel on the ground as long as possible on take-off to minimise the risk of swinging.

COMBAT DATA

MAXIMUM SPEED

From the outset the He 177, with its streamlined airframe, was designed to be very fast. Although it never achieved its design speed, it was still faster than contemporary heavy bombers.

He 177A-5/R2 GREIF	488 km/h (303 m.p.h.)
LIBERATOR GR.Mk VI	467 km/h (290 m.p.h.)
Fw 200C-3/U4 CONDOR	360 km/h (223 m.p.h.)

RANGE

Offering significantly greater range than other similar designs, the He 177 would have made an exceptional bomber and maritime aircraft had it proved reliable. Official requirements called for even greater range, but modifications and problems made the aircraft heavier and less efficient than intended.

He 177A-5/R2 GREIF 5500 km (3,400 mi.)

LIBERATOR GR.Mk VI 3380 km (3,100 mi.)

Fw 200C-3/U4 CONDOR 3560 km (2,200 mi.)

ARMAMENT

As a legacy of its heavy bomber design, the He 177A-5/R2 was able to carry a large anti-ship warload, including guided missiles and advanced torpedoes. Defensive armament was also heavy.

He 177A-5/R2 GREIF
3 x 7.9-mm machine-guns
3 x 13-mm (0.51-in.) machine-guns
2 x 20-mm (0.79-in.) cannon
2 x Hs 293 missiles
1000-kg (2,200-lb.) bombload

LIBERATOR GR.Mk VI
10 x 11.7-mm machine-guns
2268-kg (5,000-lb.) bombload

Fw 200C-3/U4 CONDOR
4 x 13-mm (0.51-in.) machine-guns
1 x 20-mm (0.79-in.) cannon
2100-kg (4,600-lb.) bombload

Greif in action

ANTI-SHIP ATTACKS: Attacking from a distance of 10 to 15 km, the He 177 was able to use radio-controlled Hs 293 and FX 1400 missiles, in addition to Fritz X glide-bombs and torpedoes.

OPERATION 'STEINBOCK': In the early weeks of 1944 the Luftwaffe initiated a series of revenge attacks on London. Experienced He 177 crews climbed to 9000 metres and attacked in a shallow dive at 700 km/h, avoiding interception by fighters.

TRANSPORT OVER RUSSIA: German forces besieged near Stalingrad were gallantly supplied by a small number of He 177s acting as transport aircraft. The cost to Greif crews was high, however, with many falling to Soviet fighters.

HEINKEL

HE 219 UHU

● Radar-equipped night-fighter ● Mosquito hunter

It could have been the best combat aircraft of World War II, but the Heinkel He 219 Uhu suffered from misjudgements by the German high command which never used it to its best effect. Conceived as a multi-purpose warplane, it saw service only as a heavily armed night-fighter. It was one of the few Luftwaffe aircraft which stood any chance of intercepting the fast-flying British Mosquito.

▲ Had it been available in numbers to replace slower aircraft like the Ju 88, the He 219 might have made a difference to the Luftwaffe's fierce night-time struggle with the bombers of the Royal Air Force.

HEINKEL HE 219 UHU

▲ Captured test plane
The RAF evaluated the He 219 after many were captured in 1945. The aircraft was received enthusiastically by Allied pilots, who were very impressed with its high performance and the novel ejection seat.

▲ Radar nose
The prominent aerials in the nose were part of the Lichtenstein FuG 220 radar, which was far more effective than previous sets. The secret of the FuG 220 was revealed after one was captured when a straying Ju 88 landed by accident in Britain.

▲ Heinkel graveyard
Heinkel produced 296 He 219s, far too few to make a difference to the eventual outcome of the war.

▼ Touching down
The He 219 was easy to land; ace pilot Major Werner Streib managed a landing without flaps.

▲ From prototype to night warrior ▼
The He 219 VI prototype demonstrated excellent performance from the start. Only radar and guns were needed to turn a test aircraft into one of the finest night-fighters of the war.

FACTS AND FIGURES

➤ The He 219 was one of the few aircraft which could catch the fast and agile de Havilland Mosquito.

➤ The Heinkel He 219 prototype first took to the air on 15 November 1942.

➤ The He 219 won a fly-off against the Dornier Do 217N and Junkers Ju 88S.

➤ Due to the priority assigned to jets and single-engine fighters, the Luftwaffe halted He 219 production in May 1944.

➤ Some He 219 variants had a knockout armament of eight heavy cannon.

➤ Final production of the He 219 was 296 aircraft, with some built from spares.

PROFILE

Heinkel's night stalker

Many features of the He 219 were at the outer edge of technology. It was the Luftwaffe's first operational aircraft with tricycle landing gear – criticised by some staff officers as 'this unnecessary American innovation'. It was also one of the first warplanes to be equipped with ejection seats, and the first to use them in combat.

Derived from Heinkel's P.1060 fighter-bomber proposal,

which attracted only lukewarm support in Berlin, the all-metal, shoulder-wing He 219 seated its pilot and navigator back-to-back. It was a practical, sensible design and performed well, but bitter opposition, led by Generalfeldmarschall Erhard Milch who favoured the Junkers Ju 188, delayed production.

As a result of squabbling, the He 219 was late reaching service. But this fighter showed its capabilities on 11/12 June 1943 when a mission led by

Major Werner Streib shot down five RAF Lancasters. The He 219 had some limited success in combat, but built in larger numbers it might have had a dramatic impact on the war.

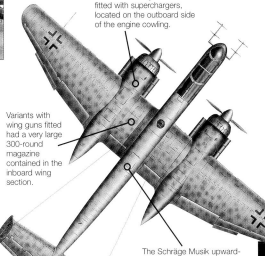

The combination of a slim fuselage and two very powerful engines was a recipe for a good fighter. The He 219 had the advantage over its rivals by being a dedicated design rather than a conversion from another role.

The DB 603 engines were fitted with superchargers, located on the outboard side of the engine cowling.

Variants with wing guns fitted had a very large 300-round magazine contained in the inboard wing section.

The Schräge Musik upward-firing cannon installation allowed the He 219 to attack from below, which was a blind spot for most night bombers.

He 219A-7/R1 Uhu

Type: two-seat night-fighter

Powerplant: two 1417-kW (1,900-hp.) Daimler-Benz DB 603G piston engines

Maximum speed: 670 km/h (415 m.p.h.)

Cruising speed: 630 km/h (390 m.p.h.)

Range: 2000 km (1,240 mi.)

Service ceiling: 12,200 m (40,000 ft.)

Weights: empty 11,200 kg (24,640 lb.); loaded 15,300 kg (33,660 lb.)

Armament: two upward firing 30-mm (1.18-in.) MK 108, two 30-mm (1.18-in.) MK 108 in wingroots, two 20-mm (0.79-in.) MG 151/20 and two 30-mm (1.18-in.) MK 103 cannon in ventral tray

Dimensions:
span	18.50 m (60 ft. 8 in.)
length	15.54 m (51 ft.)
height	4.10 m (13 ft. 6 in.)
wing area	44.50 m² (479 sq. ft.)

HE 219A-7/R2 UHU

This aircraft was flown by Hauptmann Paul Forster, a member of Stab I/NJG 1 based at Münster in the summer of 1944.

The bulletproof front windscreen had hot-air demisting and screen wipers.

Most He 219s carried the bulk of their armament in a ventral tray, but other locations included Schräge Musik cannon in the rear fuselage and wingroot-mounted guns.

The He 217A-7/R4 had a tail warning radar system to inform the crew of impending attacks by the much-feared Mosquito night-fighter.

G9 BA

With the cockpit far forward of the engines and guns, the noise and flash of exhausts and gun muzzle blast were not a problem for the crew.

A tricycle undercarriage was not just the gimmick some senior officers said it was. Landing a damaged aircraft at night was much easier than with a more conventional tail dragger.

The He 219's three fuel tanks were located in the fuselage. The tanks were self-sealing and well protected.

The He 219R3 had a single machine-gun in the tail, but this was abandoned in subsequent versions. Experiments with guns in the engine nacelles were also tried, without much success.

COMBAT DATA

MAXIMUM SPEED

The He 219 was very fast – it could even outpace the Mosquito, which very few German aircraft had been able to do. But it was probably less agile than the British fighter, although it could easily outfight the very large and somewhat clumsy American Black Widow, which had appeared over Europe late in 1944.

P-61 BLACK WIDOW	600 km/h (372 m.p.h.)
He 219A-7/R1 UHU	670 km/h (415 m.p.h.)
MOSQUITO NF.Mk XII	660 km/h (409 m.p.h.)

RANGE

The Heinkel He 219 had one great advantage over its opponents. It was operating over home territory, and did not need the range of the Allied aircraft. However, it could fly far enough to follow the British bomber streams all the way home, acting as intruders over airfields in Britain.

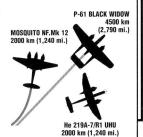

P-61 BLACK WIDOW 4500 km (2,790 mi.)

MOSQUITO NF.Mk 12 2000 km (1,240 mi.)

He 219A-7/R1 UHU 2000 km (1,240 mi.)

ARMAMENT

The Heinkel carried a phenomenally heavy cannon fit, with four cannon in a belly tray, two in the wing roots, and two upwards-firing in the rear fuselage. The Mosquito and P-61 had much lighter armament, although their four cannon still made them formidable opponents.

P-61 BLACK WIDOW 4 x 20-mm (0.79-in.) cannon 4 x 12.7-mm (.303 cal.) MGs

MOSQUITO NF.Mk XII 4 x 20-mm (0.79-in.) cannon

He 219A-7/R1 UHU 2 x upward firing 30-mm (1.18-in.) cannon, 4 x 30-mm (1.18-in.) cannon, 2 x 20-mm (0.79-in.) forward firing cannon

Interception at night

1 DETECTION: Incoming British bomber raids were detected by the extensive network of Würzburg and Freya radars.

2 ALARM: Raid data was fed to night-fighter units, who took off and were vectored onto target by ground controllers.

3 AIRBORNE INTERCEPT: The fighter's own radar was effective from about three km (two miles), and the radar operator controlled the last stage of the intercept.

4 SURPRISE ATTACK: Most British bombers had a blind spot beneath the belly, so the ideal night-fighter attack meant flying in formation and shooting with upward-pointing cannon.

HENSCHEL

Hs 123

● Dive-bomber ● Close support ● High combat survivability

▲ Pilots appreciated the Hs 123's ability to absorb combat damage when operating just above the heads of enemy troops. The aircraft excelled in the dive-bombing and ground-attack roles.

Dive-bombers were an essential element of the German Blitzkrieg concept of warfare. Therefore, in 1933, Henschel was asked to design an interim machine for use until the Ju 87 was ready for service. Although regarded as obsolete by the late-1930s, the Hs 123 proved to be a rugged and reliable close-support aircraft. After being scheduled for retirement in mid-1940, it fought on for another four years until the last examples were lost in action.

PHOTO FILE

HENSCHEL Hs 123

▲ **Building for war**
A partially assembled Hs 123A demonstrates the nine-cylinder BMW engine, before the cowling has been fitted.

▲ **Close-support units**
Wearing the badge of the Infanterie-Sturmabzeichen, this Hs 123A has the standard weapon load of four 50-kg (110-lb.) bombs.

▲ **Further developments**
In 1938 Henschel flew the Hs 123 V5 prototype. Powered by a 716-kW (960-hp.) BMW 123K radial, the aircraft was the prototype for the cancelled Hs 123B.

▲ **Spanish Civil War**
Five Hs 123A-1s were evaluated with great success in combat over Spain from early 1937.

Upper wing failures ▶
After two prototypes shed their upper wings in flight, stronger centre-section struts were fitted.

FACTS AND FIGURES

➤ The Luftwaffe high command intended to use the Hs 123 to establish the dive-bomber units ready for the Ju 87.

➤ Fieseler submitted its Fi 98 design but lost out to the superior Hs 123.

➤ Almost no bracing was used between the wing and the fuselage on the prototypes.

➤ Over Spain the Hs 123 was so impressive that the Spanish bought all five aircraft and ordered a further 11.

➤ During flight tests the Hs 123 demonstrated its ability to pull out of near-vertical dives.

➤ Many military people wanted the Hs 123 put back into production during 1943.

PROFILE

Attacking across Europe

This exceptional dive-bomber and close-support machine was a sesquiplane, or 'one-and-a-half-wing' aircraft, rather than a true biplane. With its strut-braced wings, fixed undercarriage and two-bladed propeller, the Hs 123 proved itself in the Spanish Civil War. It demonstrated that it could be extremely effective in the close-support role, operating in the thick of the fighting and surviving multiple direct hits.

Nevertheless, production ended in 1938 and there

was only one Hs 123 Gruppe in service by the time of the invasion of Poland in September 1939. This unit achieved such remarkable results, both in Poland and again during the invasion of France in May 1940, that it was still flying its old biplanes during the May 1941 invasion of Russia.

On the Eastern Front the

Above: An extremely broad chord and smooth cowling distinguished the first prototype Hs 123 V1.

Hs 123 again proved its worth as a close-support aircraft and, as a result, additional units were formed using retired aircraft. There was even a move to resume production in 1943, but the tooling had been destroyed.

Above: Demonstrating a three-colour splinter camouflage scheme, this Hs 123A-1 flies without the armoured headrest.

Hs 123A-1

Type: dive-bomber and close-support aircraft

Powerplant: one 649-kW (870-hp.) BMW 132Dc nine-cylinder air-cooled radial engine

Maximum speed: 341 km/h (211 m.p.h.) at 1200 m (3,900 ft.)

Initial climb rate: 900 m/min (2,950 f.p.m.) at sea level

Range: 860 km (533 mi.)

Service ceiling: 9000 m (29,500 ft.)

Weights: empty 1505 kg (3,311 lb.); normal loaded 2217 kg (4,877 lb.)

Armament: two 7.9-mm (0.31-in.) MG 17 machine-guns in forward fuselage plus two 20-mm (0.79-in.) MG FF cannon or up to four 50-kg (110-lb.) bombs under wings

Dimensions:
span	10.50 m (34 ft. 5 in.)
length	8.33 m (27 ft. 4 in.)
height	3.22 m (10 ft. 6 in.)
wing area	24.85 m² (267 sq. ft.)

Hs 123A-1

This early machine was based at Fürstenfeldbruck, with 7./Stukageschwader 165 'Immelmann', during October 1937. Later aircraft adopted the armoured headrest tested on the Hs 123 V6 prototype.

Most in-service Hs 123s flew with the headrest and fairing in place. Some may have used a sliding cockpit hood, as trialled on the Hs 123 V6. The first aircraft were also delivered with a crutch beneath the fuselage for launching an SC250 bomb, but in service this was usually replaced by an auxiliary fuel tank.

In the immediate pre-war period, German military aircraft had their tail swastikas painted on a red band. This was similar to the markings used on civilian aircraft and was an attempt at making the Luftwaffe's new military machines look like civilian aircraft to foreign observers.

Only the Hs 123 V1 flew with the smooth cowling. All production Hs 123s had a cowling with 18 fairings covering the engine valves. Twin exhaust pipes protruded from the rear of the cowling on both sides.

During wet weather, especially on the Eastern Front, the Hs 123 was kept operational by removing the spats, preventing mud from clogging the wheels.

Although the tailwheel was fixed, it was very neatly faired with a spat and partial trouser fairing. Many of the features of the Hs 123 appeared to be outdated, but several aircraft were returned to the front line once their abilities had been realised.

COMBAT DATA

MAXIMUM SPEED

Heinkel's He 50A was the Luftwaffe's first operational dive-bomber and served on into World War II, gradually being replaced by the Hs 123. The Hs 123 was only marginally slower than the Skua.

Hs 123A-1	341 km/h (211 m.p.h.)
SKUA Mk II	362 km/h (224 m.p.h.)
He 50A	235 km/h (146 m.p.h.)

RANGE

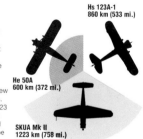

Blackburn's Skua monoplane offered greater range than the Hs 123A-1, but was larger and of similar vintage. The Skua was carrier-based, however, while the Hs 123 flew from forward strips. This gave the Hs 123 a quick turnaround time which allowed more missions to be flown per day.

Hs 123A-1 860 km (533 mi.)

He 50A 600 km (372 mi.)

SKUA Mk II 1223 km (758 mi.)

ARMAMENT

With its secondary fighter role, the Skua carried more offensive machine-guns. It also carried a greater bombload but could not offer the versatility of the Hs 123 in combat.

Hs 123A-1	2 x 7.9-mm machine-guns 200-kg (440-lb.) bombload
SKUA Mk II	5 x 7.7-mm (.303 cal.) machine-guns 227-kg (500-lb.) bombload
He 50A	1 x 7.9-mm (0.31-in.) machine-gun 250-kg (550-lb.) bombload

World War II biplanes

■ **FIAT CR.42:** Italy flew a large number of these biplane fighters at the beginning of the war. Some early missions were flown over the UK.

■ **GLOSTER GLADIATOR:** Representing the last and ultimate development of the Gloster biplane fighter, the Gladiator fought gallantly.

■ **HEINKEL He 60:** By early-1940 this shipboard reconnaissance floatplane had been largely withdrawn, but reappeared in 1941.

■ **POLIKARPOV I-153:** When the USSR was attacked in June 1941, most of its fighter strength consisted of I-153s.

HENSCHEL

Hs 126

● Battlefield reconnaissance ● Short takeoff ● Glider tug

Henschel's 126 was based on an earlier company design for an army co-operation and short-range reconnaissance aircraft. The Hs 122 had proved its ability to operate from short strips and at low airspeeds, but was too slow. With a more powerful engine and refined wings to improve performance, the resulting Hs 126 became the Luftwaffe's standard tactical reconnaissance aircraft in the early years of World War II.

▲ Design of the Hs 126 included a high-lift parasol wing, which gave the aircraft excellent short- and rough-field performance. Access to the cockpit was via a ladder on the fuselage side.

PHOTO FILE

HENSCHEL Hs 126

▼ Photo reconnaissance
Over the battlefield, the Hs 126 was the aerial eyes of the Wehrmacht. Leaning over the side of the fuselage a gunner photographs enemy positions.

▲ Desert campaign
The Hs 126 participated in all German theaters of operation up until 1942. In North Africa, they were used extensively for spotting Allied positions.

Pre-war production ▶
Production Hs 126A-1s line up at Henschel's Schönefeld factory field in 1938 prior to delivery to the Luftwaffe. Later in the year six were sent to Spain for service with the Légion Condor.

▼ High-lift wing
The Hs 126's parasol wing provided excellent lift, allowing the aircraft to operate from short strips close to the front line. Large flaps allowed the Hs 126 to land and take off at low speeds.

▲ Open cockpit
Unusual for German aircraft of the period, the Hs 126 featured an open rear cockpit. Although this was not a problem in North Africa, it was unpleasant during the harsh Russian winter.

FACTS AND FIGURES

➤ The Hs 126 was developed from the Hs 122, which was powered by a Rolls-Royce Kestrel engine.

➤ The prototype Hs 126 first flew in the autumn of 1936.

➤ As well as reconnaissance, the Hs 126 also strafed and bombed enemy positions.

➤ During the invasion of Russia in June 1941, no fewer than 48 Staffeln were equipped with Hs 126B-1s.

➤ From 1942, many Hs 126s were relegated to glider-towing duties.

➤ Late in the war, Hs 126s were employed as night harassment aircraft.

Eyes of the Wehrmacht

As well as providing the right combination of performance and handling characteristics, the Hs 126 was well equipped for its role. The sliding canopy over the cockpit incorporated deflector panels to shield the observer's gun from slipstream, while a bay in the rear fuselage could carry cameras or ten 10-kg (22-lb.) bombs. Deliveries to the Luftwaffe started in the spring of 1938, and in September 1939 a total of 13 tactical reconnaissance squadrons operating the Hs 126 took part in the invasion of Poland. They were used for ground attack, as well as reconnaissance missions, and with little opposition their losses were light.

By mid 1940 over the Western Front, life was growing harder for the Hs 126. Production ended in January 1941 as deliveries of its replacement, the Fw 189, got under way. Most of the operational units had been transferred to the Eastern Front by June 1942, though one squadron operated the Hs 126 in North Africa.

Although it was used mainly as a glider tug after mid 1942, the Hs 126 was also used to equip several units specializing in night-time, close-support operations.

Above: Armed with a single 50-kg (110-lb.) bomb fitted to an optional fuselage side rack, an Hs 126 prepares for takeoff. This example flew highly successful combat evaluation sorties in Spain.

Left: At low level over the battlefield, the Hs 126 was in a dangerous environment. It could, however, take considerable battle damage and survive.

Hs 126B-1

Type: two-seat tactical reconnaissance aircraft

Powerplant: one 671-kW (900-hp.) BMW Bramo Fafnir 323 nine-cylinder air-cooled radial engine

Maximum speed: 354 km/h (220 m.p.h.) at 3050 m (10,000 ft.)

Climb rate: 3.5 minutes to 600 m (1,968 ft.)

Endurance: 2 hours 15 minutes

Service ceiling: 8200 m (26,900 ft.)

Weapons: Two 7.92-mm (0.31-in.) machine guns, one in forward fuselage and one in rear cockpit; 10 x 10-kg (22-lb.) and one 50-kg (110-lb.) bombs.

Weights: empty 4,470 lb.); loaded 3270 kg (7,209 lb.)

Dimensions:
Span	14.50 m (47 ft. 7 in.)
Length	10.85 m (35 ft. 7 in.)
Height	3.73 m (12 ft. 3 in.)
Wing area	31.59 m² (340 sq. ft.)

Hs 126A-1

As well as serving on the Eastern and Western Fronts and in the Mediterranean, the Hs 126 also saw extensive service in North Africa. This example flew with the Fliegerführer Afrika Unit during July 1941.

The Hs 126 owed its responsive, yet docile handling to its parasol wing, developed by Henschel's chief designer Friedrich Nicolaus.

Developed from the Hs 122, the Hs 126 incorporated several improvements, including a canopy over the pilot to give protection from the elements.

The camouflage scheme and the white band around the fuselage were typical markings for Hs 126s operating in the North African theater.

Armament comprised one forward-firing 7.92-mm (0.31-in.) MG 17 machine gun, plus one similar weapon on a trainable mounting in the rear cockpit.

Power for the first production version, the Hs 126A-1, was provided by a BMW 132Dc radial engine. The later Hs 126B-1 was fitted with the more powerful Bramo 323 engine.

The cantilever main undercarriage featured long struts, giving the aircraft a pronounced 'nose high' appearance on the ground. Wheel spats could be fitted to reduce drag.

The back-seat crewmember operated a topographic camera, a hand-held camera and a 7.92-mm (0.31-in.) machine gun from his open-cockpit position.

A Zeiss Rb topographic camera is situated in a bay behind the gunner/observer, which he operated from his position.

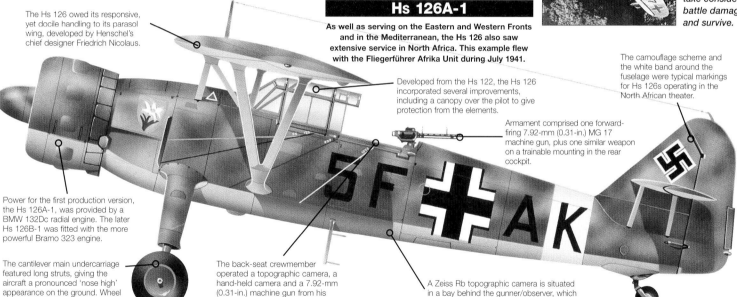

Battlefield spotters of World War II

■ **POLIKARPOV U-2:** The U-2 was used in a number of roles by Soviet forces, including battlefield reconnaissance and ground attack.

■ **WESTLAND LYSANDER:** More than 1600 Lysanders were built and flew many roles during World War II, including army co-operation.

■ **MITSUBISHI Ki-51 'SONIA':** This Japanese tactical reconnaissance aircraft also flew ground-attack missions during World War II.

■ **FOCKE-WULF Fw 189 UHU:** Designed to replace the Hs 126, the Fw 189 was a success, especially over the Eastern Front.

ACTION DATA

SPEED

The Hs 126 was the slowest of the types, although all three relied more on escort fighters or camouflage to escape enemy fighters rather than speed. The more powerful Ki-51 was a later design, but was still easy prey for fighter aircraft.

Hs 126B-1	354 km/h (220 m.p.h.)
LYSANDER Mk I	367 km/h (228 m.p.h.)
Ki-51 "SONIA"	425 km/h (264 m.p.h.)

WEAPONS

All three types carried armament for self-defense and for attacking targets of opportunity on the ground. The observer in each aircraft would use a trainable machine gun to ward off enemy fighters.

Hs 126B-1	2 x 7.9-mm (0.31-in.) machine guns
LYSANDER Mk I	4 x 7.7-mm (.303 cal.) machine guns
Ki-51 'SONIA'	3 x 7.7-mm (.303 cal.) machine guns

POWER

All three aircraft have a similar amount of horse power at their disposal. The slightly larger engine in the Ki-51 allowed it to climb quicker and possess a higher top speed. The power in the engines gave the Lysander and Hs 126 a very short take-off run.

Hs 126B-1	LYSANDER Mk I	Ki-51 'SONIA'
671 KW (900 hp.)	664 kW (890 hp.)	700 kW (940 hp.)

HENSCHEL

Hs 129

● Anti-tank aircraft ● Poor serviceability ● Heavily armoured

Designed in 1938, the Hs 129 was the only aircraft of World War II to be designed from the outset explicitly for destroying hostile armour. Its angular shape and small cross-section made the aircraft look aggressive, and its powerful cannon could penetrate any tank's armour. However, the type suffered from a protracted development and the problems of lack of power and unreliability from its twin engines were never fully solved.

▲ To keep the risk of damage by small arms fire to a minimum, the Hs 129 was designed to have a small cross-sectional area. This resulted in a small and very cramped cockpit.

HENSCHEL Hs 129

▼ Tank buster
To provide a hard-hitting weapon for use against Soviet tanks, the Hs 129B-3/Wa was developed with a 75-mm Pak 40 gun.

▲ Allied evaluation
Captured in North Africa, this Hs 129B was flown to the United States for evaluation. It carries the 'Foreign Equipment' registration FE-4600.

◀ Final sorties
As the Allies advanced, a lack of spares and fuel resulted in many Hs 129s being abandoned. By the spring of 1945, very few remained in service.

▼ Desert service
Arriving in North Africa at the end of 1942, the Hs 129B encountered serious reliability problems. Its twin Gnome-Rhône engines were prone to seizure and the aircraft were rapidly withdrawn to Tripoli for overhaul.

▲ Early engines
The pre-production Hs 129A-0s were fitted with Argus engines. They were found to be underpowered and were assigned to a training unit.

FACTS AND FIGURES

➤ In mid-1938 Henschel received orders to build three Hs 129 prototypes, the first of which flew in March 1939.

➤ The Hs 129 cockpit was so cramped that many pilots could not fit in it.

➤ When production ended in September 1944, 871 Hs 129s had been built.

➤ An Hs 129 was tested with the SG 113A weapon which fired tubes containing explosive triggered by light-sensitive cells.

➤ The Hs 129B-3/Wa's 75-mm (2.95-in.) Pak 40 gun could destroy a tank with one shell.

➤ After a *coup* in 1944, Romanian Air Corps Hs 129s were used against Germany.

Eastern Front tank destroyer

In 1937 the Technische Amt issued a specification for a cannon-armed close-support aircraft, small in size but heavily armoured. The final competing aircraft were the Focke-Wulf Fw 189 and the Hs 129. Both aircraft performed particularly badly in tests, showing sluggish performance, and the Hs 129's cramped cockpit was unpopular.

The Hs 129 eventually won, not because it was superior but because it cost about two-thirds as much as the other type, and was smaller. Eight pre-production

Hs 129A-0s with Argus As 410A-1 engines were tested, but it soon became obvious that the aircraft was under-powered. Henschel's chief engineer set about designing a new larger version with Gnome-Rhône engines.

The resulting Hs 129B was a great improvement. The cockpit was modified with larger areas of armoured glass, giving better vision and superior protection.

After the invasion of the Soviet Union in June 1941, it became obvious that the Hs 129B would be an essential weapon, but poor

engine reliability and production problems lowered confidence in the aircraft. When introduced to North Africa in 1942 the first Hs 129 unit suffered engine problems caused by sand ingestion, and was evacuated with no serviceable aircraft.

Various improvements incorporated into the Hs 129B-2 finally resulted in some success against Soviet armour, but by the spring of 1945 few remained in service.

Early production Hs 129B-2s featured a central nose aperture for an Rb 24 automatic camera.

Two small diagonal white stripes on each wing were used by the pilot as guides for adjusting the ailerons and flaps.

Hs 129B-2/R2

Seen in Eastern Front markings, this Hs 129 served with 8./Schlachtgeschwader (Assault Group) in June 1943. Red was not used in the markings to avoid confusion with the enemy.

The Hs 129's cockpit was very cramped owing to the triangular shape of the forward fuselage. The gunsight was mounted outside the cockpit and the engine instruments were located on the engine nacelles.

Hs 129s possessed an impressive internal gun armament of two 20-mm (0.79-in.) cannon in the upper fuselage sides and two 7.9-mm (0.31-in.) machine-guns mounted in the wingroots.

The blue code markings denote that this aircraft was from II. Gruppe. All German combat aircraft on the Eastern Front carried yellow theatre bands.

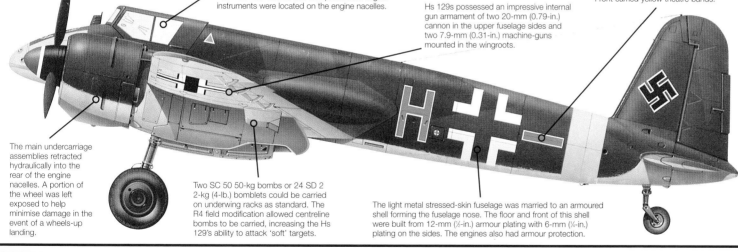

The main undercarriage assemblies retracted hydraulically into the rear of the engine nacelles. A portion of the wheel was left exposed to help minimise damage in the event of a wheels-up landing.

Two SC 50 50-kg bombs or 24 SD 2 2-kg (4-lb.) bomblets could be carried on underwing racks as standard. The R4 field modification allowed centreline bombs to be carried, increasing the Hs 129's ability to attack 'soft' targets.

The light metal stressed-skin fuselage was married to an armoured shell forming the fuselage nose. The floor and front of this shell were built from 12-mm (½-in.) armour plating with 6-mm (¼-in.) plating on the sides. The engines also had armour protection.

COMBAT DATA

MAXIMUM SPEED

The Hs 129 was regarded as being underpowered, and this is reflected in its top speed, which was actually inferior to the earlier Ju 87 design. The Hurricane Mk IID, which the RAF used as a tank buster in North Africa, was basically a fighter design and possessed superior performance.

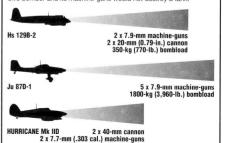

Hs 129B-2 407 km/h (252 m.p.h.)

Ju 87D-1 410 km/h (254 m.p.h.)

HURRICANE Mk IID 518 km/h (321 m.p.h.)

ARMAMENT

Both the Hs 129B-2 and the Hurricane Mk IID were designed as tank busters and their primary weapon was a powerful cannon whose shells could penetrate a tank's armour. The Hs 129 could also carry bombs for use against 'soft' targets. The Ju 87 was designed as a dive bomber and its machine-guns would not destroy a tank.

Hs 129B-2 2 x 7.9-mm machine-guns / 2 x 20-mm (0.79-in.) cannon / 350-kg (770-lb.) bombload

Ju 87D-1 5 x 7.9-mm machine-guns / 1800-kg (3,960-lb.) bombload

HURRICANE Mk IID 2 x 40-mm cannon / 2 x 7.7-mm (.303 cal.) machine-guns

Hs 129 colours and variants

Hs 129B-1: This aircraft belonging to 4./Sch.G.2 was delivered in September 1942 and served in Poland before adopting this colour scheme for operations in North Africa.

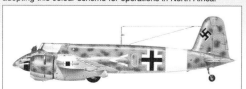

Hs 129B-2/R2: Incorporating many improvements over the B-1, this B-2 wears temporary winter camouflage for operations against Soviet tanks on the Eastern Front.

Hs 129B-3/Wa: This version was factory-fitted with the very powerful 75-mm cannon. Two Eastern Front units operated the B-3/Wa in the winter of 1944/45.

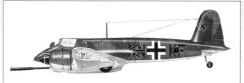

ILYUSHIN

IL-2/10 SHTURMOVIK

● Eastern Front 'flying tank' ● Anti-armour ground-attack specialist

The Shturmovik – an armoured attack warplane – is a uniquely Russian concept. The Ilyushin Il-2 entered service in 1941, only months before the German invasion of the Soviet Union. Ilyushin began designing the aircraft by fitting armour around a pilot and engine, and then thinking about the aerodynamics. The Il-2 and the developed Il-10 were used on a vast scale and proved to be devastating ground-attack weapons. The Shturmovik became a legend to the Soviet public, who saw it as an instrument of salvation and cheered its successes in battle.

▲ The Soviet Il-2 was an effective weapon in World War II. Like most Soviet equipment, it was unsophisticated, but extremely rugged. Heavily-armed and armoured, it was built in greater numbers than any other warplane.

ILYUSHIN IL-2/10 SHTURMOVIK

Shturmovik ▶ expert
Ilyushin Il-2s were used by Allied units fighting on the Eastern Front. Lieutenant Cheben of the 3rd Air Regiment flew an Il-2 with the Czech division, fighting through the Ukraine in 1944.

▲ Mass produced
Production of Il-2s was made a top priority. Demand was so high that major modifications were deliberately discouraged.

▲ Strike formation
Il-2s flew in huge formations, forming a large 'circle of death' to attack. This allowed them to keep a target area under constant fire.

▲ Lethal harvest
Casualties among Il-2 squadrons were always high. The aircraft had good protection, but their low-level role was extremely perilous.

Korean warrior ▶
The Shturmovik's career did not end in 1945. It was used against UN troops in Korea, but often fell victim to more modern Western fighters.

FACTS AND FIGURES

➤ In 1941/42 an experimental Il-2 powered by an M-82 radial engine was tested, but it was not manufactured.

➤ At one stage, production of Il-2s reached more than 1000 aircraft per month.

➤ German soldiers in the Soviet Union called the Il-2 the 'Black Death'.

➤ A dual-control Il-2 capable of carrying torpedoes was built in small numbers for the Soviet navy.

➤ Il-2s were sometimes flown by women pilots in the Soviet air force.

➤ A few Il-2s were converted to two-seat tandem trainers for flight instruction.

PROFILE

Stalin's flying battle tank

An incredible 36,000 Il-2 Shturmoviks were manufactured, making this the most numerous military aircraft in history. The Il-2 was called a 'flying tank', because it was heavily armoured and had great firepower from its cannon and rockets.

A low-wing metal craft with wood in the aft fuselage, the Il-2 began as a single-seater. At first production difficulties plagued

its builders. Premier Josef Stalin cabled factory workers saying, 'The Red Army needs the Il-2 as it needs air and bread.' Though handicapped by the war, Soviet industry rose to the occasion.

In February 1942 a two-seat Il-2 was introduced. This had a rear gunner under an extended canopy. Production versions appeared at the Front, while single-seaters were converted in the field.

The Il-2 could carry 1200 kg (2,640 lb.) of bombs over a distance of 400 km (250 mi.), and was agile enough to give attacking fighters a good run for their money.

Even more potent was the Il-10 Shturmovik, which arrived just as the war was ending. The aircraft saw extensive action in Korea with the Communist forces.

Czechoslovakia built large numbers of Il-10 aircraft, under the name Avia B.33. They served into the late 1950s, as did the Soviet-built machines supplied to Poland. Both countries used the Il-2 in the last year of the war.

IL-10 SHTURMOVIK

The Ilyushin Il-10 served with the Soviet Tactical Air Force on the Eastern Front in Poland in 1945. A development of the Il-2, the Il-10 had an uprated engine and an enclosed rear gunner's cockpit.

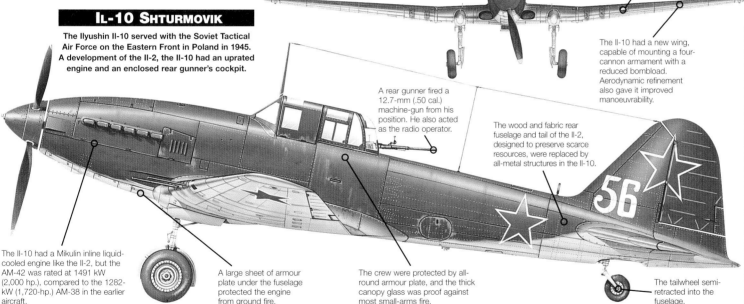

Both the Il-2 and Il-10 used a three-bladed variable-pitch propeller.

The 20-mm (0.79-in.) VYa cannon were later replaced by more powerful NS 23-mm (0.9-in.) weapons.

The Il-10 had a new wing, capable of mounting a four-cannon armament with a reduced bombload. Aerodynamic refinement also gave it improved manoeuvrability.

A rear gunner fired a 12.7-mm (.50 cal.) machine-gun from his position. He also acted as the radio operator.

The wood and fabric rear fuselage and tail of the Il-2, designed to preserve scarce resources, were replaced by all-metal structures in the Il-10.

The Il-10 had a Mikulin inline liquid-cooled engine like the Il-2, but the AM-42 was rated at 1491 kW (2,000 hp.), compared to the 1282-kW (1,720-hp.) AM-38 in the earlier aircraft.

A large sheet of armour plate under the fuselage protected the engine from ground fire.

The crew were protected by all-round armour plate, and the thick canopy glass was proof against most small-arms fire.

The tailwheel semi-retracted into the fuselage.

Il-2M3 Shturmovik

Type: one-/two-seat armoured close-support aircraft

Powerplant: one 1282-kW (1,720-hp.) Mikulin AM-38F piston engine

Maximum speed: 430 km/h (267 m.p.h.) at 6700 m (22,000 ft.)

Range: 600 km (375 mi.)

Service ceiling: 9700 m (31,825 ft.); 6500 m (21,320 ft.) with bombload

Weights: empty 3250 kg (7,150 lb.); loaded 5872 kg (12,920 lb.)

Armament: two 20-mm (0.79-in.) and/or two 37-mm (1.47-in.) cannon in wings and one manually-aimed 12.7-mm (.50 cal.) machine-gun in rear cockpit, plus 600 kg (1,320 lb.) of bombs, or eight RS-82 or four RS-132 rockets under outer wing

Dimensions:
span	14.60 m	(48 ft.)
length	11.65 m	(38 ft.)
height	3.40 m	(11 ft.)
wing area	38.50 m²	(414 sq. ft.)

COMBAT DATA

MAXIMUM SPEED

Ground-attack fighters required protection more than ultimate performance, and the heavy weapons and armour plate carried by aircraft like the Ilyushin Il-2 and Henschel Hs 129 meant that they were not very fast. The Shturmovik was nevertheless quite an agile machine.

Il-2M3 SHTURMOVIK	430 km/h (267 m.p.h.)
Ju 87D STUKA	400 km/h (250 m.p.h.)
Hs 129	410 km/h (255 m.p.h.)

BOMBLOAD

The famous Stuka was originally designed as a bomber rather than a ground-attacker, and so could carry a heavier weapons load then either of the two armour-plated aircraft. These generally carried large numbers of small armour-piercing or anti-personnel weapons.

Il-2M3 SHTURMOVIK	Ju 87D STUKA	Hs 129
600 kg (1,300 lb.)	1800 kg (3,960 lb.)	250 kg (550 lb.)

ARMAMENT

Destroying a tank calls for a powerful gun, and the standard 37-mm (1.47-in.) calibre weapons on the Eastern Front could penetrate the thin top or rear armour of most tanks. However, the Shturmovik needed bombs or rockets to deal with the immensely well-protected Panthers and Tigers which Germany fielded after the battle of Kursk in 1943.

Il-2M3 SHTURMOVIK
2 x 37-mm (1.47-in.) cannon
2 x 20-mm (0.79-in.) cannon

Ju 87D STUKA
2 x 37-mm (1.47-in.) cannon

Hs 129
1 x 37-mm (1.47-in.) cannon up to 4 x 20-mm (0.79-in.) cannon, 2 x 7.92-mm (0.31-in.) machine-guns

Shturmovik on the Eastern Front

GERMANY INVADES: Many of the German tanks in Operation Barbarossa, the great invasion of Russia in 1941, were surprisingly light. The Shturmovik could deal with the thin armour of a Pzkpfw II or III with cannon fire or small bombs and rockets.

HARDER TARGETS: As German tanks got bigger and vehicles such as the Pzkpfw IV were given extra armour, the Shturmovik needed larger and more sophisticated bombs and rockets to deal with them.

THE ULTIMATE CHALLENGE: To destroy the Pzkpfw V Panther which equipped the Wehrmacht at the end of the war, Shturmoviks needed to attack with large RS-132 rockets or PTAB armour-piercing bombs.

ILYUSHIN

IL-4

● Medium bomber ● Major redesign ● Torpedo-bomber

Ilyushin's Il-4 was a redesigned version of the DB-3. Instead of the earlier model's nose turret, the Il-4 had a glazed nose with a simple machine-gun mounting. Two more guns, one in a turret and one firing through lower hatches, were carried in the aft fuselage and an internal bay could hold 1000 kg (2,200 lb.) of bombs. First flown in January 1940 and redesigned from DB-3F to Il-4 in March 1942, the aircraft had a new streamlined shape and simplified structure.

▲ By 1943 Soviet forces were much better organised. These Il-4s have been prepared for another mission by the groundcrew and the chief engineer confirms that the aircraft are ready to fly.

ILYUSHIN IL-4

▼ **Rapid production**
By 1944 Soviet industry was producing aircraft at a rapid rate. Eventually, 5256 Il-4s were built.

▲ **Bombing Berlin**
When the Soviet Union entered World War II DB-3Bs of the ADD (Long-Range Aviation) made some of the earliest attacks on Berlin. This DB-3B was captured and then operated by the Finnish air force against the Soviet Red Army.

▲ **Record attempt**
The prototype DB-3 crash-landed on Miscou Island after covering 8000 km (4,960 mi.) in an attempt to fly from Moscow to New York non-stop. Here one of the crew rests on a life raft.

▲ **Salvaging aircraft**
As the Germans invaded western Russia, materials became scarce. Vital equipment was salvaged from damaged aircraft.

◄ **Forward firepower**
The Il-4 had a completely revised nose which housed the navigator/bombardier. The nose-mounted ShKAS machine-gun was mounted on a universal joint.

FACTS AND FIGURES

➤ The Il-4 was developed from the DB-3, which set several world altitude records during the late 1930s.

➤ Improved production meant that the Il-4 took half the time to build of the DB-3.

➤ Captured DB-3s and Il-4s were used by Finland against Soviet forces.

➤ The DB-3F (Il-4) showed very impressive performance in State Acceptance Trials which were completed in June 1939.

➤ Most Il-4s were fitted with a cleat for towing A-7 or G-11 gliders.

➤ Many Il-4s were converted post-war for cargo or geophysical survey work.

PROFILE

Russia's superb wartime bomber

The Il-4 became the workhorse of the Soviet long-range and naval aviation units. With a full load of fuel it could carry an internal load of ten 100-kg (220-lb.) bombs more than 3500 km (2,450 mi.) at 270 km/h (167 m.p.h.). Three 500-kg (1,100-lb.) bombs could be carried under the wings and fuselage over shorter ranges, and a maximum 2500-kg (5,500-lb.) bombload could be loaded for short-range tactical missions.

In its naval version it could be loaded with at least one torpedo.

Improvements during production run included replacing the M-87A engines with M-88s. Wood was used instead of light metal alloys wherever possible, and 12.7-mm (.50 cal.) machine-guns became standard. More than 5000 Il-4s had been built by the time production ended in 1944.

In August 1941, 15 Il-4s mounted the first Soviet raid on Berlin, which caused minor damage. The type also saw extensive service on the German Eastern Front attacking supply lines and strategic targets.

As well as for their primary missions, Il-4s were also used for transport, glider towing and strategic reconnaissance (with a camera in the bomb-bay). Some naval aircraft remained in service until 1949, and NATO designated the type 'Bob'.

Left: With good range and speed, a respectable bombload and effective armament, the Il-4 was one of the best Soviet bombers.

Above: As a result of a shortage of metal after the German invasion, the outer wing panels, cockpit floor and tailcone had to be made from wood.

Il-4

Type: long-range bomber and torpedo-bomber

Powerplant: two 820-kW (1,100-hp.) Tumanskii M-88B 14-cylinder air-cooled radial engines

Maximum speed: 420 km/h (230 m.p.h.) at 6000 m (19,700 ft.)

Climb rate: 5000 m (16,400 ft.) in 12 min

Combat radius: 1510 km (936 mi.)

Range: 3585 km (2,220 mi.) with maximum fuel

Service ceiling: 9400 m (30,850 ft.)

Weights: empty 5800 kg (12,760 lb.); maximum take-off 10,300 kg (22,660 lb.)

Armament: three machine-guns plus up to 2500 kg (5,512 lb.) of bombs or one torpedo

Dimensions:
span	21.44 m	(70 ft. 4 in.)
length	14.80 m	(48 ft. 6 in.)
height	4.20 m	(13 ft. 9 in.)
wing area	66.70 m²	(718 sq. ft.)

The most noticeable design change from the DB-3B was the more streamlined, fully-glazed nose. The gunner, firing a 7.62-mm (.30 cal.) or 12.7-mm (.50 cal.) machine-gun or a 20-mm (0.79-in.) cannon, sat in front of the navigator/bombardier.

A shortage of metal meant the cockpit floor was made of wood. Equipment included a radio compass, automatic pilot and a de-icing system. All crewmembers were protected by 6-mm or 9-mm (¼ or ⅓ in.) thick armour plating.

The Ilyushin dorsal power turret could be fitted with either a UBT 12.7-mm (0.5 cal.) machine-gun or the ShVAK 20-mm (0.79-in.) cannon. These gave good protection from attack from above or behind.

The fixed ventral machine-gun ring fitted to the DB-3B was replaced by a much more complex semi-retractable mount on the Il-4. This gave greater protection against attack from below.

Power for the Il-4 came from two Tumanskii M-88B radial engines with direct fuel injection. In 1942 the propellers were changed to a fully-feathering type.

The Il-4 had all-metal wings. However, most aircraft built in 1942 had wooden wing spars because of a shortage of light alloy metals.

Compared to the earlier DB-3, the fuselage was simplified to make production easier. The bomb-bay could hold up to 2700 kg (5,940 lb.) of bombs or mines. Alternatively, low-level or high-level torpedoes could be carried.

IL-4

This Red Air Force Il-4 belonged to an unidentified bombardirovoshchnaya aviatsionnyi polk (bomber regiment) operating over the Eastern Front in 1944.

COMBAT DATA

MAXIMUM SPEED

For an aircraft of its type the Il-4 had a good top speed of around 430 km/h (267 m.p.h.), marginally more than that of the He 111. With its better range and load-carrying ability, the Il-4 was perhaps the better suited of the three types to the tactical bombing role.

Il-4	430 km/h (267 m.p.h.)
He 111H-13	370 km/h (230 m.p.h.)
A-20G HAVOC	510 km/h (317 m.p.h.)

RANGE

Range was a particular strength of the Il-4, and it was able to reach Berlin from well inside the Soviet Union. The shorter-ranged A-20 was used for tactical missions. Heinkel He 111s were always hampered by their short range.

Il-4	3585 km (2,220 mi.)
He 111H-13	1950 km (1,209 mi.)
A-20G HAVOC	1754 km (1,087 mi.)

ARMAMENT

The USAAF's A-20G had a formidable set of nose-mounted guns, which were ideal for ground strafing. Both the He 111 and Il-4 had better bomb-carrying ability, being able to carry about 2.5 tons.

Il-4	1 x 12.7-mm (.50 cal.) machine-gun, 2 x 7.62-mm (.30 cal.) machine-guns, 2500-kg (5,940-lb.) bombload
He 111H-13	1 x 20-mm (0.79-in.) cannon, 1 x 13-mm (0.51-in.) cannon, 7 x 7.9-mm (0.31-in.) machine-guns, 2500-kg (5,500-lb.) bombload
A-20G	9 x 12.7-mm (.50 cal.) machine-guns, 1364-kg (3,000-lb.) bombload

Ilyushin twin-engined bombers

■ **DB-3B:** The forerunner of the Il-4, the DB-3B proved to be vulnerable to enemy fighters as it was not as well armed or as fast as its successor. This is a captured Finnish example.

■ **Il-28 'BEAGLE':** As the primary Soviet bomber during the first few years of the Cold War, the Il-28 was an important aircraft. Built in large numbers, the 'Beagle' is still in limited service in China.

■ **Il-54 'BLOWLAMP':** Only one example of this supersonic bomber was constructed. Aerodynamic difficulties on take-off caused major problems and the project was cancelled in 1957.

JUNKERS

JU 52/3M

● Tri-motor transport ● World War II fame ● Nicknamed 'Tante Ju'

L uftwaffe personnel bestowed the name 'Tante Ju' ('Aunt Ju') upon Hugo Junkers' three-engine transport design as a gesture of faith in the slow, but strong and reliable aircraft. Ju 52/3ms formed the backbone of German airlift capability throughout World War II, delivering thousands of troops and tons of supplies to European theatres. Suffering heavy losses, it was often the strength of the aircraft that carried it through a mission.

▲ Troop-carrying and parachuting were major roles for the Ju 52/3m. It made possible some of the earliest and most daring paratroop raids of the war and served postwar in several countries.

JUNKERS JU 52/3M

◀ Flying to Crete
Float-equipped Ju 52/3ms were active in Norway and the Mediterranean. Access to the aircraft was gained via a ladder.

Under attack ▶
A Ju 52/3m under Allied attack in North Africa. Losses on the ground and to Allied fighters were high.

▼ Parachuting from 'Tante Ju'
Paratroops leap from a Luftwaffe Ju 52/3m. Note the static line attached to the soldier's parachute and the low altitude.

▲ Float-equipped
The floats fitted to some Ju 52s would have decreased its slow top speed even more. This aircraft taxies on one engine.

▲ North Africa 1941
Luftwaffe Ju 52/3ms prepare for a supply dropping sortie in support of the Afrika Korps.

FACTS AND FIGURES

➤ In all, 4835 Ju 52/3ms are said to have been built in Germany; on VE-Day fewer than 50 were airworthy.

➤ As an airliner the Ju 52/3m flew in 28 countries from the UK to Uruguay.

➤ Postwar, 400 aircraft were built in France and 170 in Spain.

➤ In just three months, 22,399 tonnes (22,045 tons) of supplies were airlifted to six divisions of troops trapped at Demyansk.

➤ Three Ju 52/3ms were flown by the Swiss Fliegertruppe until the early 1980s.

➤ At 10,476 kg (23,100 lb.) a Ju 52/3m lifted off at 109 km/h (68 m.p.h.) in just 350 m (1,150 ft.).

PROFILE

'Tante Ju': the Luftwaffe's 'Aunt'

First flown in April 1932, the Junkers Ju 52/3m was the culmination of Junkers' vast experience in building single-engine civil transports of all-metal construction with their characteristic load-bearing, corrugated skin.

Originally a single-engine design, the Ju 52/3m was intended primarily as a freighter. Deutsche Lufthansa took delivery of 230, equipped as airliners; many were exported. From 1932 the covert establishment of the Luftwaffe was

beginning and in 1934 the first military version, the Ju 52/3mg3e bomber appeared. Ju 52s seldom, if ever, performed in this role during World War II (though a number had in the Spanish Civil War). The type will be remembered as a transport.

Active from the first days of the Blitzkrieg on Poland, the aircraft flew in every European theater in a number of versions, though, with two exceptions, these differed only in detail.

The float-equipped Ju 52/3m Wasser alighted on fjords during

the Norwegian campaign to disembark troops and equipment, while the Ju 52/3m(MS) was fitted with energized dural hoops, which were used to explode Allied mines.

Tactical transport remained its primary role, however, a role in which the lumbering 'Tante Ju' suffered huge losses, but served widely and with distinction.

Left: Ju 52/3ms were the Luftwaffe's primary means of deploying paratroops, in the same way the Douglas C-47 was the Allies' main transport aircraft.

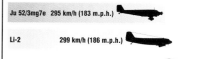

Above: Minesweeping sorties had to be flown at low level and were therefore extremely hazardous.

JU 52/3MG7E

1Z+LK served with 2.Staffel, KGzbV 1, based at Milos in Greece, in May 1941 immediately prior to the invasion of Crete. A fleet of 493 Ju 52/3ms was assembled for these landings.

A three-member crew sat in a cockpit that was elevated above cabin level. In the cabin 18 passengers could be seated, or with seats removed a large amount of cargo could be carried.

Three BMW 132T-2 engines powered the Ju 52/3m. Those on the wings were angled outward slightly, to make control easier in the event of a single wing engine failure. Wings and fuselage became characteristically exhaust stained.

Many Junkers designs of the period featured flaps and ailerons that hung behind the main wing. The ailerons could drop at low speed, complimenting the flaps for STOL.

A small glass windshield protected the gunner from the slipstream while he operated the dorsally mounted 7.92-mm (0.31-in.) MG 15 machine gun.

Mechanical controls on the Ju 52/3m worked by chain links and pulleys. The control lines for the tail surfaces ran beneath the cabin floor.

The corrugated duralumin skin of the Ju 52 was load-bearing and therefore immensely strong, without a weight penalty. This type of construction was a feature of many early airliners.

Ju 52/3m in many theaters

MINESWEEPING IN FINLAND: This Ju 52/3mg6e flew from Malmi with the Minensuchgruppe, minesweeping over the Gulf of Finland during the winter of 1943–44.

IN THE MEDITERRANEAN: This Ju 52/3mg6e, with an unusual gun turret fitted above the flight deck, was based in Italy in 1942. White markings indicate the Mediterranean theatre.

ON THE RUSSIAN FRONT: Wearing a water-soluble temporary white camouflage, this Ju 52/3m was active on the Russian front in the winter of 1942/43, supplying ground troops.

Ju 52/3mg7e

Type: 18-seat military transport

Powerplant: three 619-kW (830-hp.) BMW 132T-2 nine-cylinder air-cooled radial engines

Maximum speed: 295 km/h (183 m.p.h.) at sea level

Initial climb rate: 208m/min (682 f.p.m.)

Service ceiling: 5500 m (18,050 ft.)

Weapons: typically three 7.92-mm (0.31-in.) machine gun, one in dorsal position and two mounted to fire abeam through the side windows

Weights: empty 6546 kg (14,432 lb.); max 10,493 kg (23,133 lb.)

Dimensions:
span 29.24 m (95 ft. 11 in.)
length 18.80 m (61 ft. 8 in.)
height 4.50 m (14 ft. 9 in.)
wing area 110.46 m² (1,189 sq. ft.)

ACTION DATA

SPEED

The slow maximum speed of the Ju 52/3m left it vulnerable, with crews relying on its rugged construction for their safety. The Li-2, a Russian-built C-47, was slower than the American-built version.

Ju 52/3mg7e 295 km/h (183 m.p.h.)

Li-2 299 km/h (186 m.p.h.)

C-47A SKYTRAIN 481 km/h (299 m.p.h.)

RANGE

While range is an important quality for any transport, these aircraft were more often involved in tactical operations where cargo or troop capacity over shorter distances was most important.

Ju 52/3mg7e 1287 km (800 mi.)

Li-2 2492 km (1,550 mi.)

C-47A SKYTRAIN 2414 km (1,500 mi.)

POWER

Three engines gave the Ju 52/3m a significant safety advantage in the event of a single engine failure. The additional power also allowed excellent load carrying abilities and combined with the wing design to give exceptional STOL performance.

Ju 52/3mg7e
3 x 619 kW
(830 hp.)

Li-2
2 x 746 kW
(1,000 hp.)

C-47A SKYTRAIN
2 x 895 kW
(1,200 hp.)

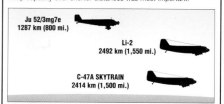

JUNKERS
Ju 86

● Spanish Civil War ● Poor visibility ● High-altitude bomber

As the Luftwaffe secretly expanded during the 1930s, the German air ministry (RLM) and the national airline, Deutsche Lufthansa (DLH), collaborated in preparing a specification for a dual-purpose medium bomber for the Luftwaffe and a 10-seat transport for Lufthansa's high-speed routes. Heinkel and Junkers were asked to prepare designs to meet this demanding specification. They were, respectively, the He 111 and Ju 86.

▲ Criticism from
pilots resulted in Junkers modifying the cockpit area of the Ju 86, but accidents still occurred during ground operations. Swedish examples served until 1956.

JUNKERS Ju 86

English raider ▶
One of the specialised variants was the high altitude Ju 86P-1, used to raid Britain. They achieved little success, although were a nuisance to RAF fighters.

▲ Pilot vision
One unimpressive aspect of the Ju 86 was the extremely poor visibility from the cockpit. It led to numerous accidents while aircraft were taxiing or landing.

▲ Airline service
Although designed for combat operations, a limited number of Ju 86s saw service as airliners. After World War II some Ju 86s remained in service as cargo haulers with the Swedish air force until the 1950s.

▲ Lufthansa operations
Prior to the outbreak of World War II, Ju 86s were flown as high-speed airliners by the German airline. Later, the aircraft were operated by the Luftwaffe.

Nose over ▶
This Ju 86 crashed while attempting to land on a snow-covered Eastern Front airfield.

FACTS AND FIGURES

➤ During the siege of Stalingrad, Ju 86 trainers airlifted supplies to the trapped German soldiers; 40 Ju 86s were lost.

➤ A few Ju 86 bombers served on the Eastern Front in September 1943.

➤ The Hungarian air force employed Ju 86s against Soviet targets until mid-1944.

➤ Ju 86 airliners delivered to South African Airways were impressed by the South African air force for training duties.

➤ Sweden operated Ju 86 transports, built by Saab, into the 1950s.

➤ Junkers developed the Ju 86P into the Ju 86R, but it was too late to see service.

Junkers goes to war

Heinkel's He 111 was produced to the same specification as the Ju 86 and served throughout World War II. The Ju 86, on the other hand, was obsolete by 1939. The Ju 86 was a twin-engined, low-wing monoplane of stressed-skin construction, powered by two Junkers Jumo diesel engines.

On 4 November 1934, the first Ju 86 (V1) bomber took to the air. Early flights revealed stability problems which were cured by a new wing and in 1936 Ju 86A-1 bombers entered

Luftwaffe service. DLH took delivery of Ju 86B-0s about the same time.

Five Ju 86D-1s (with modified tail cones to cure persistent control problems) were evaluated by the Condor Legion. Weaknesses of the Jumo diesel were confirmed and the Ju 86E-1 entered service in 1937 with BMW 132 radials.

Meanwhile, Junkers was developing the Ju 86 as a high-altitude reconnaissance/bomber. The Ju 86P prototype, with supercharged Jumo 207s and a

pressurised cabin, first flew in February 1940.

Prototypes flew unchallenged on high altitude sorties over Britain in the summer of 1940. Ju 86Ps (converted from Ju 86Ds) were later active over the Soviet Union also.

Above: Though an advanced bomber for its day, the Ju 86 in Luftwaffe service was found to be unreliable.

Below: Early operations by the Luftwaffe utilised massed formations of bombers working in concert with ground forces.

Ju 86D-1

Type: four-seat medium bomber

Powerplant: two 447-kW (600-hp.) Jumo 205C-4 six-cylinder diesel engines

Maximum speed: 325 km/h (202 m.p.h.) at 3000 m (9,850 ft.)

Cruising speed: 285 km/h (177 m.p.h.) at 3500 m (11,485 ft.)

Range: 1500 km (932 mi.)

Service ceiling: 5900 m (19,360 ft.)

Weights: empty 5150 kg (11,354 lb.); maximum take-off 8200 kg (18,078 lb.)

Armament: three 7.92-mm (0.31-in.) machine-guns in the nose, dorsal and ventral positions, plus a bomb load of 800 kg (1,764 lb.)

Dimensions:
span 22.50 m (73 ft. 10 in.)
length 17.87 m (58 ft. 8 in.)
height 5.06 m (16 ft. 7 in.)
wing area 82.00 m² (883 sq. ft.)

Pilots complained about the lack of visibility from the cockpit of the Ju 86, and many examples were damaged in landing accidents when pilots lost sight of the ground on approach.

Though featuring a number of design innovations, the Ju 86 was hindered by the poor performance of its engines. When war broke out the aircraft was quickly replaced in front-line service, although high-altitude examples remained in reconnaissance roles.

Ju 86D

The Ju 86 was originally developed as an airliner for Lufthansa, in an effort to hide its military potential. Though eventually outclassed, the Ju 86 paved the way for the He 111 and Ju 88.

Displaying a large swastika on its tail surfaces, this Ju 86 is shown in early World War II colours. The need to camouflage the aircraft against attack from enemy fighters led to the adoption of a much more sombre colour scheme.

Junkers received some export orders for military models with alternative powerplants. Sweden acquired three aircraft fitted with Pratt & Whitney Hornet radial engines. Other variants were powered by Polish-built Bristol Pegasus engines.

A retractable gondola was positioned on the underside of the fuselage. Mounted on this was a single machine-gun, operated by a member of the bomber's crew. Speed was reduced while the gun was deployed.

COMBAT DATA

MAXIMUM SPEED

Junkers was one of the main suppliers of bombers for the Luftwaffe. Constant advances in aviation technology meant that their aircraft improved in performance.

Ju 86D-1 — 325 km/h (202 m.p.h.)
Ju 88A — 440 km/h (273 m.p.h.)
Ju 188D-2 — 539 km/h (335 m.p.h.)

MAXIMUM RANGE

Recognising that it would need to attack targets at a greater distance, the Luftwaffe requested a more modern design than the Ju 86. The Ju 88 became one of the principal bombers of the wartime Luftwaffe.

Ju 86D-1 — 1500 km (932 mi.)
Ju 88A — 1800 km (1,118 mi.)
Ju 188D-2 — 3395 km (2,110 mi.)

SERVICE CEILING

More powerful engines gave aircraft the ability to operate from a higher altitude and elude enemy fighters. One variant of the Ju 86 was specially adapted for the high-flying reconnaissance role. The later Ju 188 could reach double the altitude of the standard Ju 86.

Ju 86D-1 — 5900 m (19,360 ft.)
Ju 88A — 8200 m (26,900 ft.)
Ju 188D-2 — 10,000 m (32,800 ft.)

Junkers wartime designs

■ **Ju 52:** The 'Tante Ju' was the Luftwaffe's primary transport aircraft in 1939. A host of variants were later produced. This view shows a specialised mine counter-measures version that saw limited service.

■ **Ju 87:** Developed as a ground attack aircraft, the 'Stuka' was used extensively during the early stages of the war. Later, the design proved extremely vulnerable to enemy fighters.

■ **Ju 88:** Developed to replace the Ju 86, the Ju 88 was used extensively by the Luftwaffe. A number of specialised variants were produced, including night-fighters.

JUNKERS

JU 87 'STUKA'

● Dive-bomber ● Anti-tank aircraft ● Ship attack

Few memories of war have endured more than the high-pitched scream of the Junkers Ju 87 'Stuka' swooping to strike its prey with claws of gunfire and bomb blast. This dive-bomber made its reputation during the Polish campaign, where it excelled at close support of ground troops. The Ju 87 fought on every front between 1939 and 1945. Adaptable and cheap, the 'Stuka' became a potent anti-tank machine on the Eastern Front.

▲ The 'Stuka' acted as a long-ranged artillery piece for the advancing Wehrmacht. Able to operate from fields just behind the front line, it could decimate a target holding up the advance in minutes.

JUNKERS JU 87 'STUKA'

▲ Carrier strike
Ju 87Rs operating in the Mediterranean caused the Royal Navy many casualties, severely damaging the aircraft carrier HMS Illustrious.

Gunfighter ▶
In the hands of experts like Hans-Ulrich Rudel, the Ju 87G was lethal to tanks, but it was also very vulnerable to fighters.

▲ Lucky escape
This rear gunner was lucky to have survived this damage, the result of a close battle with Russian fighters.

▼ Death in the desert
'Stukas' performed well in support of the Afrika Korps, particularly in bombing Tobruk. When the RAF regained air superiority, however, the 'Stuka' was very vulnerable.

▲ Winter skier
Skis were more use than wheels when the 'Stuka' fought in Russia. By 1943 the type was being replaced by the Fw 190 in the close-support role.

FACTS AND FIGURES

➤ The prototype 'Stuka' flew in the spring of 1935, powered by a 477-kW (640-hp.) Rolls-Royce Kestrel engine.

➤ The last of more than 5700 Ju 87s delivered in September 1944.

➤ Hans-Ulrich Rudel destroyed over 500 Soviet tanks while flying the Ju 87G.

➤ The Ju 87 was fitted with a device to pull the aircraft out of a steep dive even if the pilot blacked out and lost control.

➤ A batch of naval Ju 87s was built for use aboard the aircraft-carrier Graf Zeppelin.

➤ The 'Stuka' was used by Bulgaria, Hungary, Italy, Romania and Slovakia.

Blitzkrieg dive-bomber

Designed to work closely with the Wehrmacht, the Ju 87 could attack with deadly accuracy, acting as a kind of highly mobile artillery. Swarming down on Poland, Norway, France and the Low Countries, the 'Stuka' (from the word *Sturzkampfflugzeug*, or dive-bomber) left a trail of devastation and struck terror even in the hearts of seasoned combat troops.

The Ju 87's invincible reputation took a hammering, however, when it came up against Hurricanes and Spitfires in the Battle of Britain. The distinctive aircraft with its gull wings and fixed landing gear proved slow and highly vulnerable to modern fighter opposition.

Even so, it remained a rugged and reliable machine, and was used extensively on the Eastern Front. The Ju 87 destroyed more tanks than any aircraft except for Russia's Ilyushin Il-2 Sturmovik.

From 1939, every Ju 87 was made by Weser at Tempelhof. Improvements to the 'Stuka' saw it gaining more power and better protection, but it was never to overcome its vulnerability to fighters.

Below: The 'Stuka' was a good ground-attack aircraft, but its success was totally dependent on having air cover. Enemy fighters found the Ju 87 very easy prey as it lacked armament and speed.

Above: The Ju 87's gun packs were a powerful weapon, but the drag further reduced the aircraft's speed.

Ju 87D-1 'Stuka'

Type: two-seat dive-bomber/attack aircraft

Powerplant: one 1051-kW (1,410-hp.) Junkers Jumo 211J-1 12-cylinder inverted Vee piston engine

Maximum speed: 410 km/h (254 m.p.h.) at 3840 m (12,600 ft.)

Range: 1535 km (950 mi.)

Service ceiling: 7290 m (23,910 ft.)

Weights: empty equipped 3900 kg (8,580 lb.); maximum take-off 6600 kg (14,520 lb.)

Armament: 7.92-mm (0.31-in.) MG 17 machine-guns in wings and two 7.92-mm MG 81Z guns in rear cockpit, plus up to 1800 kg (3,960 lb.) of bombs beneath fuselage, or alternate underfuselage/underwing loads

Dimensions:
span	13.80 m	(45 ft.)
length	11.50 m	(38 ft.)
height	3.90 m	(13 ft.)
wing area	31.90 m²	(343 sq. ft.)

The Ju 87 was also armed with two forward-firing cannon or machine-guns, which were useful in suppressing return fire from the ground.

The 'Stuka' featured a cranked-wing design so that the undercarriage could be short and strong while having enough room to carry a large bomb under the fuselage.

Ju 87G 'Stuka'

This 'Stuka' was flown by SG.3 in the USSR during spring 1944, commanded by Major Theo Nordmann. He flew over 1200 combat missions in Ju 87s.

Defensive armament was one or two machine-guns, usually insufficient to ward off fighters.

The original tail was a twin-fin arrangement, but this was replaced by a single fin after the early prototypes.

The Ju 87G was powered by the Junkers Jumo 211 engine. The marking on the cowling is a 'kill' badge. The Jumo also powered the Ju 88 and Heinkel 111.

The cannon were modified 37-mm (1.47-in.) Flak 18 guns. In the hands of an expert like Theo Nordmann the Ju 87's fire was lethal.

The 'Stuka' was designed for mass production, with the fuselage being made in two halves joined along the aircraft's centreline by a metal frame.

1 OVERHEAD: The 'Stuka' began its attack by flying straight and level until it was nearly over the target.

2 ROLL AND PULL: Just short of the target the pilot performed a half roll and then pulled back on the stick, putting the aircraft in a near vertical dive.

3 STEEP AND PULL: During the dive the pilot used his ailerons to keep the aircraft aligned on the target. The divebrakes automatically set up the dive at the correct angle.

4 SIREN SCREAM: A wind-driven siren was mounted on the undercarriage leg, releasing a terrifying wail during the dive to heighten the psychological effect of the attack.

Dive-bombing attack

PRECISION STRIKE: Dive-bombing is lethally accurate. The pilots would begin a dive from about 2000 m (6,000 ft.) or less, releasing their bombs from as low as 300 m (900 ft.). Diving at an angle of between 60° and vertical, the pilot looked down at exactly where the bomb would hit. Because of this, 'Stuka' crews often dropped a bomb within a few metres of their target, or even scored direct hits. The final pull-out from the dive was a vulnerable moment.

5 AUTOMATIC PULL-OUT: With the bombs released, an automatic recovery system pulled the 'Stuka' out of its near-vertical dive. The system used a contact altimeter and was activated by the pilot by means of a stick-mounted knob. Pull-out was usually accomplished at 6g.

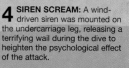

JUNKERS

Ju 88

● Fast bomber ● Night-fighter ● Multi-role aircraft

▲ *Luftwaffe crews liked the Ju 88A because of its toughness and speed. As enemy fighters became faster, the aircraft mounted more guns and armour. As a heavy fighter, it also carried large cannon.*

The Junkers Ju 88A was one of the most versatile warplanes in history. No match for a fighter in a dogfight, it could nevertheless perform just about every other military mission. Ju 88s were employed as bombers, escort fighters, night-fighters, tank busters, torpedo-bombers, transports and reconnaissance platforms, and in many other roles. Fast, tough and reliable, by the middle of World War II it had become the Luftwaffe's most important tactical bomber.

JUNKERS Ju 88

▲**Shipping attack**
Formations of Ju 88 bombers wreaked havoc among Allied convoys, from the Mediterranean to the Arctic.

◀**Field maintenance**
Although complex, field maintenance still had to be carried out on the Ju 88. Ground crews were expected to be able to change engines anywhere, from the Steppes to the desert.

▼ **Close quarters**
The crew were tightly grouped in the Ju 88: good for morale, but it made them more vulnerable when the aircraft was shot at. Even so, Ju 88s were tough and often survived fighter attacks.

▲ **Flying bomb**
War-weary Ju 88s were used as Mistel flying bombs. The pilot sat in the fighter, flying both aircraft. He aimed the explosive-packed bomber at the target before separating and escaping.

▼ **'Schnell' bomber**
Unlike their night-fighter colleagues, bomber crews did not have enough firepower. The high speed of the Ju 88A was its main defence.

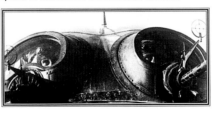

Taxiing out ▶
The glazed nose of the Ju 88A gave the crew an excellent view, essential for accurate bombing. However, as with all bombers with this feature, it proved very vulnerable to head-on fighter attacks.

FACTS AND FIGURES

➤ **The Ju 88A prototype first flew on 21 December 1936.**

➤ **The fifth Ju 88A set a 1000-km (620-mi.) closed-circuit record in March 1939, carrying a 2000-kg (4,100-lb.) payload at a speed of 517 km/h (320 m.p.h.).**

➤ **A Ju 88A was used as a flying testbed for one of the first jet engines.**

➤ **The ultimate Ju 88S bombers had a top speed of more than 600 km/h (370 m.p.h.).**

➤ **Total production of bomber and reconnaissance versions of the Ju 88 is estimated at 10,774.**

PROFILE

Mainstay of the Luftwaffe

Brought into service after the invasion of Poland, the Ju 88 was one of the few bombers used in Germany's attack on Britain which stood much chance of getting away from a fighter. But the Ju 88 was more than a survivor. Fighting in all conditions from the desert to the Arctic, it proved itself in combat roles as diverse as reconnaissance and night-fighting.

Even when Germany had all but lost the war, Ju 88 bombers were still flying lone-wolf raids against English cities. Endurance, performance and a wealth of new electronic gadgetry made fighter and bomber variants of the Ju 88 tremendously successful.

In its ability to fly and fight, the Ju 88 was the best ship in its class. Most Ju 88s had a four-man crew in a cramped flight compartment, more men than needed in a craft of this size. Even three-man versions were far from comfortable, but the Ju 88 had plenty of power and was responsive enough in almost any situation.

The Ju 88A-V7 was yet another special version. The prototype of the Ju 88 fighter, it was later converted as a high-speed communications aircraft.

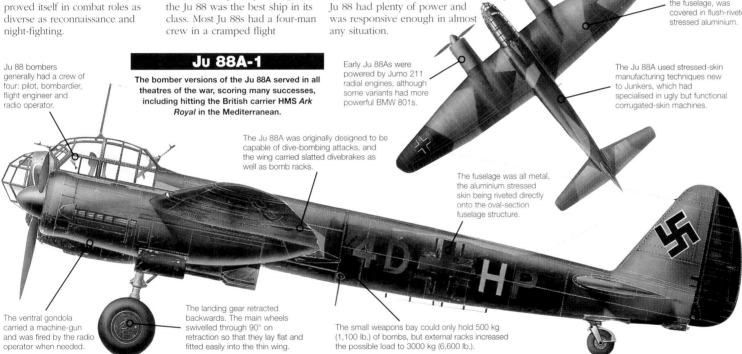

Ju 88A-1

The bomber versions of the Ju 88A served in all theatres of the war, scoring many successes, including hitting the British carrier HMS *Ark Royal* in the Mediterranean.

Ju 88 bombers generally had a crew of four: pilot, bombardier, flight engineer and radio operator.

The Ju 88A was originally designed to be capable of dive-bombing attacks, and the wing carried slatted divebrakes as well as bomb racks.

Early Ju 88As were powered by Jumo 211 radial engines, although some variants had more powerful BMW 801s.

The fuselage was all metal, the aluminium stressed skin being riveted directly onto the oval-section fuselage structure.

The wing had two main spars and, like the fuselage, was covered in flush-riveted stressed aluminium.

The Ju 88A used stressed-skin manufacturing techniques new to Junkers, which had specialised in ugly but functional corrugated-skin machines.

The ventral gondola carried a machine-gun and was fired by the radio operator when needed.

The landing gear retracted backwards. The main wheels swivelled through 90° on retraction so that they lay flat and fitted easily into the thin wing.

The small weapons bay could only hold 500 kg (1,100 lb.) of bombs, but external racks increased the possible load to 3000 kg (6,600 lb.).

Arctic attack

The Allied convoys taking badly-needed supplies to Russia ran a gauntlet of attacks. One of the most effective weapons in the Luftwaffe's armoury was the torpedo-armed Ju 88. Based at airfields in northern Norway, Ju 88s sank thousands of tons of British shipping in icy-cold Arctic waters.

■ **TORPEDO BOMBING:** (Right) The Ju 88s of Kampfgeschwader 30 mounted mass attacks on convoys, with as many as 12 aircraft flying in line abreast releasing torpedoes.

■ **NORTHERN CONVOYS:** (Left) The convoy route to Russia took Allied merchant ships into the high Arctic. In summer, the midnight sun north of the Arctic Circle meant that they were vulnerable to air attack 24 hours a day.

Ju 88A-4

Type: four-seat medium- and dive-bomber

Powerplant: two 1000-kW (1,200-hp.) Junkers Jumo 211J 12-cylinder liquid-cooled engines

Maximum speed: 440 km/h (280 m.p.h.)

Range: 1800 km (1,200 mi.)

Service ceiling: 8200 m (27,000 ft.)

Weight: empty 8000 kg (17,600 lb.); loaded 14,000 kg (31,000 lb.)

Armament: two 13-mm (0.51-in.) machine-guns, four 7.92-mm (0.31-in.) machine-guns and 3000 kg (6,600 lb.) of bombs

Dimensions:
span	20.13 m	(60 ft. 3 in.)
length	14.40 m	(47 ft. 1 in.)
height	4.85 m	(17 ft. 6 in.)
wing area	54.50 m²	(587 sq. ft.)

COMBAT DATA

MAXIMUM SPEED

Ju 88A-4	440 km/h (280 m.p.h.)
B-25C MITCHELL	460 km/h (286 m.p.h.)
G4M1 'BETTY'	428 km/h (264 m.p.h.)

Although considered very fast when first flown, the twin-engined bombers in development at the start of World War II were soon outclassed by new generations of fighters. They still managed a fair turn of speed, however.

RANGE

Ju 88A-4
1800 km
(1,200 mi.)

B-25C MITCHELL
2400 km (1,500 mi.)

G4M1 'BETTY'
5000 km
(3,100 mi.)

Japanese bombers were designed for operations across the vast reaches of the Pacific, while German machines were designed to support the army, never being too far from a forward operating base.

DEFENSIVE ARMAMENT

Ju 88A-4	B-25C MITCHELL	G4M1 'BETTY'
2 x 13-mm (0.51-in.) MGs	4 x 12.7-mm (.50 cal.) MGs	1 x 20-mm (0.79-in.) cannon
4 x 7.92-mm (0.31-in.) MGs	3 x 7.62-mm (.30 cal.) MGs	3 x 7.7-mm (.303 cal.) MGs

All the bombers which relied on speed as a defence were found wanting when this proved not to be enough. With its crew in close proximity in a very small cabin, it was particularly difficult to up-gun the Ju 88.

JUNKERS

Ju 188

- High-altitude reconnaissance bomber ● Ju 88 development

Germany's air ministry (RLM) issued the 'Bomber B' requirement for a twin-engined replacement for the the He 111 and Ju 88 in 1939. Junkers' candidate was the Ju 288, a radical development of its earlier bomber design that was making its mark in the early years of the war in Europe. However, by late 1942, the ill-fated Ju 288 design was hopelessly delayed, leaving the Lutfwaffe with a need to urgently fill the bomber requirement. This paved the way for the more conventional Ju 188.

▲ *A victim of the success of the Ju 88, the Ju 188 failed to be produced in sufficient numbers to have a significant effect on the Luftwaffe's fortunes. In fact, this was potentially a very effective aircraft, preferred by crews for its superior handling at high weights, its only real weakness being a lack of armament.*

JUNKERS Ju 188

Captured Ju 388 high-altitude bomber ▶
This Ju 388K-0, captured in 1945, was extensively tested by the British Royal Aircraft Establishment until it was placed on display in 1948.

▼ SNCASE-built Ju 188
Based on a BMW 801-powered Ju 188F-1 reconnaissance variant, this is the third example of about a dozen Ju 188Es and Fs built by SNCASE for the French Aéronavale after 1945. Employed as the service's chief land-based bombers, these aircraft joined 30 ex-Luftwaffe Ju 188s.

▲ Reconnaissance Ju 188F-1
Over half the Ju 188s completed were for reconnaissance duties. Ju 188s were able to make better use of the power of the BMW 801 and Jumo 213 than was the Ju 88.

◀ Abandoned by retreating Luftwaffe
This was the sad fate of many unserviceable Ju 188s, caught by the advancing Allies. If not wrecked by retreating Germans, they were 'shot-up' by the Allied armies.

Torpedo-bomber with Hohentwiel radar ▶
Sporting the distinctive arrays associated with the FuG 200 maritime search radar, this Ju 188E-2 torpedo-bomber also has the starboard fuselage bulge housing torpedo steering adjustment gear.

FACTS AND FIGURES

- ➤ At least 30 ex-Luftwaffe and 12 SNCASE-built Ju 188Es and Fs were used by the the French Aéronavale after World War II.

- ➤ Ju 188s gained a reputation with crews for good handling.

- ➤ Ju 188R was a night-fighter version that failed to progress past evaluation.

- ➤ Fast high-altitude intruder Ju 188S and reconnaissance Ju 188T variants were proposed, giving rise to the Ju 388.

- ➤ At least one Ju 188E was converted to a fast staff transport for senior personnel.

- ➤ A remotely-controlled tail barbette was trialled in a Ju 188C, but was inaccurate.

Ju 88 successor with unrealised potential

Official development of the Ju 88 had been effectively frozen for more than three years, although Junkers had continued trials with the Ju 88E-0 on a low-priority basis.

The first true Ju 188 (Ju 188 V1) was the Ju 88 prototype V44, a Ju 88E airframe with a new dorsal turret and 13-mm (0.51-in.) machine-gun, extended wingtips and a square tail fin. By January 1943, a second aircraft, Ju 188 V2, was under test. Production aircraft would be powered by Jumo 213 in-line or BMW 801 radial engines.

On 18 August 1943, French-based Ju 188s flew their first sortie, pathfinding for a bombing raid over northern England. By the end of 1943, 283 had been accepted by the Luftwaffe. In January 1944, 188s took part in Operation *Steinbock*, Germany's retaliatory 400-bomber raid on London.

The BMW-engined Ju 188Es (some of which were fitted with dive brakes) and Jumo-powered Ju 188As (which also sported a dorsal cannon in place of the machine-gun, and MW50 engine power boosting) were the initial variants – medium bombers with a 3000-kg (6,600-lb.) bombload.

However, 570 of the 1076 Ju 188s built were 188D and F reconnaissance marks. Some were fitted with FuG 200 radar for the maritime role, these aircraft seeing action in Russia and Scandinavia, often in concert with Ju 188A-3 and E-2 torpedo-bombers.

Ju 188D-2s of 1.(F)/124 at Kirkenes in Arctic Norway. The nearest aircraft appears to have had its FuG 200 Hohentwiel *radar removed.*

Ju 188D-2

Serving with 1.Fernaufklärungsgruppe 124 at Kirkenes, Norway, was one of 17 Stafflen equipped with Ju 188D and F reconnaissance versions. 1.(F)/124 often provided sighting reports for III./KG 26 Ju 188A-3 torpedo-bombers.

Ju 188D-2

Type: maritime reconnaissance/strike aircraft

Powerplant: two 1268-kW (1,700-hp.) (for take-off; 1671 kW/2,240 hp. with MW50 injection) Junkers Jumo 213A-1 12-cylinder inline engines

Maximum speed: 539 km/h (334 m.p.h.) at 6096 m (20,000 ft.)

Range: 3395 km (2,100 mi.) at 6096 m (20,000 ft.) with drop tanks

Service ceiling: 10,000 m (32,800 ft.)

Weights: empty 9900 kg (21,780 lb.); maximum loaded 15,195 kg (33,430 lb.)

Armament: one 20-mm (0.79-in.) MG 151 cannon in dorsal turret; one 13-mm (0.51-in.) MG 131 machine-gun in the rear cockpit; one 7.9-mm (0.31-in.) MG 81z twin machine-gun in ventral step, plus various camera fits for day and night missions.

Dimensions:
span	22.00 m (72 ft. 2 in.)
length	14.95 m (49 ft.)
height	4.44 m (14 ft. 7 in.)
wing area	56.00 m² (603 sq. ft.)

Luftwaffe Ju 188s suffered throughout World War II from a lack of defensive armament, the extreme rear of the aircraft being perhaps the most vulnerable. On reconnaissance variants, the redundant bomb bay could be fitted with an extra fuel tank.

MW50 methanol-water injection for the engines and extended wing tips gave improved altitude performance. Initially, the latter feature led to the aircraft being confused with the RAF's Mosquito.

Four hardpoints under the wing centre-section, available for two torpedoes on the Ju 188A-3 and E-2 variants, were often fitted with external fuel tanks on reconnaissance machines.

Unlike the four-man medium bomber variants, the Ju 188D-2 had only three crew – pilot, flight engineer and radar/wireless operator. The forward-firing 20-mm (0.79-in.) MG 151 cannon was also deleted from the cockpit. Intended for the maritime role, the Ju 188D-2 and BMW 801-engined Ju 188F-2 were equipped with FuG 200 search radar.

From the outset, the RLM demanded that the Ju 188 be able to accept either Jumo 213 liquid-cooled 12-cylinder or BMW 801 14-cylinder radial engine assemblies, or 'power eggs', interchangeably on the production line, minimising the effect of fluctuations in engine availability.

This aircraft carries a pale blue-grey *Wellenmüster* sprayed over the standard green camouflage scheme. *Balkenkrauz* and *Hakenkreuz* national markings are applied in outline form.

COMBAT DATA

MAXIMUM SPEED AT ALTITUDE

Though endowed with good high-altitude speed, the Ju 188D-2 was still no match for the RAF's de Havilland Mosquito. However, the Arado Ar 234 reconnaissance jet was unbeatable.

Ju 188D-2	539 km/h (334 m.p.h.)
Ar 234B-2/b	742 km/h (460 m.p.h.)
MOSQUITO PR.Mk 34	684 km/h (424 m.p.h.)

RANGE

PR Mosquitos had excellent range performance, to match their speed. Although fast, the Ar 234 was, like other early jet designs, short on range. All three designs were also developed in the long-range bombing role.

Ju 188D-2	3395 km (2,100 mi.)
Ar 234B-2/b	1630 km (1,000 mi.)
MOSQUITO PR.Mk 34	5633 km (3,500 mi.)

Junkers Ju 88 bomber family

Ju 88: There were few roles for which the Luftwaffe's Ju 88s were not adapted during World War II. More than 14,500 were built and carried out many tasks from bombing to tank-busting and night-fighting. The prototype flew in 1936.

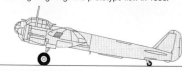

Ju 288: The RLM's 'Bomber B' requirement called for a medium bomber able to take a 4000-kg (8,800 lb.) load at 600 km/h (370 m.p.h.) to Britain from anywhere in France or Norway. Unlike the Ju 188, 388 and 488, the ill-fated 288 was an entirely new design.

Ju 388: A high-altitude reconnaissance and bomber development of the Ju 188, the Ju 388 featured a pressurised cockpit section and boosted engines. Ju 388K bombers had a tail gun barbette. None entered service.

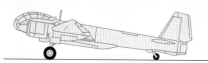

Ju 488: By 1944, the Luftwaffe was still without a reliable strategic bomber. Junkers suggested the quick production of the four-engined Ju 488 using existing tooling and components from the Ju 188, 288 and 388. None had flown by VE-Day.

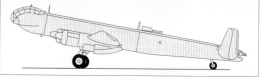

JUNKERS

Ju 90/290

● Airliner derivative ● Long-range maritime patrol ● Transport

PHOTO FILE

JUNKERS Ju 90/290

▲ Germany's largest
The Ju 390 V2 was the second of only two aircraft completed, and remains the largest conventional aircraft to be built in Germany.

▲ US missile launcher
This rare Ju 290A-7 was evaluated in America after the war. The variant introduced a glazed nose and the ability to launch guided anti-ship missiles.

▲ Henschel 293 and Fritz X
If more Ju 290A-7s, with their Henschel Hs 293, 294 and Fritz X missiles and Hohentwiel radar, had been delivered, they would have made a powerful anti-shipping force.

▲ Airliner origins – Ju 90 V1
With World War II imminent, Junkers was not allowed to use the strategically important Jumo 211 or DB 600 engines that had been tested on the prototypes.

Transport to maritime reconnaissance ▶
Defensive armament was introduced on the Ju 90 V8, which led to development of the Ju 90 V11. This was redesignated the Ju 290 V1.

After its Ju 89 bomber was cancelled, Junkers was keen to gain something from the effort expended on the aircraft. By mating a new fuselage with the Ju 89's wings, a new transport aircraft, known as the Ju 90, was produced. Further development of this design led to the Ju 290 maritime reconnaissance aircraft and, ultimately, to the giant, six-engined Ju 390 which flew to within 20 km (12 mi.) of the US coast.

▲ *Both the Ju 290 and Ju 90 gave good service with the Luftwaffe, at a time when the force was stretched to its limits and suitable aircraft were in desperately short supply.*

FACTS AND FIGURES

➤ **D-AALU, the first Ju 90 V1 prototype, was lost in an accident during February 1938; V3 was lost later that year.**

➤ **Two Ju 290A-0s and five Ju 290A-1s were used in the relief of Stalingrad.**

➤ **Operations over the Atlantic began with 1./FAGr 5 on 15 October 1943.**

➤ **South African Airways aircraft would have been powered by Pratt & Whitney Twin Wasp engines.**

➤ **Three Ju 290A-5s, stripped of equipment, were used on transport missions to Japan.**

➤ **The Ju 290A-6 may have carried escaping Nazi leaders to Spain in April 1945.**

PROFILE

Junkers giant on patrol

Lufthansa ordered eight Ju 90s and South African Airways a further two aircraft, but all were impressed into Luftwaffe squadrons. In 1940 work started on a new version, designated Ju 290, which was bigger than the original. It was to be built in both transport and maritime reconnaissance versions.

The Ju 290A-0 and A-1 transport aircraft were immediately put into service since the Luftwaffe was desperately short of transport capacity. The A-2 to A-5 variants were maritime reconnaissance models, and the A-6 was intended as a transport for the personal use of Adolf Hitler. The A-7 and A-8 were to be missile-armed anti-ship aircraft.

About 40 Ju 290s were built, nearly half of them by Letov in Czechoslovakia. Maritime versions were based in southwest France and used to locate Atlantic convoys for the German U-boats. The Ju 290A-6 was completed as a 50-seat VIP transport. It flew to Barcelona in April 1945 and later served with the Spanish air force until the mid-1950s. Ju 290B, D and E bomber variants, the C transport/reconnaissance aircraft and the MS mine-clearer were all abandoned during the final years of the war.

Eleven Ju 290A-5s were built, making this the most common sub-type. The antennas of the Hohentwiel system can be clearly seen on the nose of this aircraft.

Ju 290A-5

Type: long-range maritime reconnaissance aircraft

Powerplant: four 1268-kW (1,700-hp.) BMW 801D 14-cylinder air-cooled radial engines

Maximum speed: 440 km/h (273 m.p.h.) at 5800 m (19,000 ft.)

Initial climb rate: 1850 m (6,070 ft.) in 9.8 min

Range: 6150 km (3,813 mi.)

Service ceiling: 6000 m (19,700 ft.)

Weights: normal loaded 40,970 kg (90,134 lb.); maximum take-off 44,970 kg (98,934 lb.)

Armament: one 20-mm (0.79-in.) MG 151 cannon in each of two dorsal turrets, the tail position, each waist position and the ventral gondola, plus one 13-mm (0.51-in.) machine-gun in the rear of the gondola

Dimensions:
span	42.00 m	(137 ft. 8 in.)
length	28.64 m	(93 ft. 11 in.)
height	6.83 m	(22 ft. 5 in.)
wing area	203.6 m²	(2,213 sq. ft.)

Ju 290A-5

Fernaufklärungsgruppe 5, with its force of no greater than 20 aircraft flying from Mont-de-Marsan, France, in 1944, constantly struggled to fulfil its commitments.

Restricted to low-powered engines, Junkers set about redesigning the Ju 90 to give improved performance using the available power. New features were incorporated into the Ju 90 V4, an aircraft which also introduced the twin-wheel undercarriage and Trapoklappe ramp of the Ju 290.

The Ju 90, with its BMW 123 radials, had been underpowered, and so the Ju 290 was fitted with the 1268-kW (1,700 hp.) BMW 801D.

Being a large, heavy aircraft, the Ju 290 required a substantial undercarriage. When the Ju 390 was produced by adding extra sections to the wings and fuselage of the Ju 290, two extra main undercarriage units were added.

All aircraft from the Ju 90 V11 onwards had these distinctive angular fins. New windows and a redesigned wing were also introduced on this aircraft.

Using its nose-mounted FuG 200 search radar, the A-5 was able to detect a convoy at a distance of 80 km (50 mi.) from an altitude of 500 m (1,650 ft.), or at 100 km (60 mi.) from 1000 m (3,300 ft.). The aircraft would remain on station until it was relieved by another Ju 290.

The otherwise vulnerable underside of the aircraft was protected by a single, forwards-firing MG 151 cannon and a rearwards-firing MG 131 machine-gun. Both were mounted in the ventral gondola, which was offset to port.

All Ju 290A series aircraft retained the Trapoklappe. This was a hydraulically actuated ramp set into the underside of the rear fuselage. It could be opened in flight for paratrooping and was able to lift the aircraft into a horizontal position for easy loading when on the ground.

A multitude of roles

■ **Ju 90B-1:** Two or three of the 10 production Ju 90B-1 airliners, in spurious Iraqi markings, were used by the Luftwaffe to ferry personnel and equipment to Iraq. Before the war the aircraft had belonged to Lufthansa.

■ **Ju 290A-5:** Typical of the most numerous variant, this A-5 shows the type's powerful defensive armament, which was improved as a result of operational experience with the A-4. The A-5 also introduced armour protection and fuel-dumping facilities.

■ **Ju 290A-6:** By 1945 all surviving Ju 290s were being used for agent-dropping and clandestine transport missions by KG 200. The single A-6, which was designed as a personal transport for Hitler, was in fact only used by this unit.

COMBAT DATA

RANGE

The Ju 290's very long range was principal among the aircraft's excellent qualities. In addition to giving the aircraft a useful transport capability, long range also allowed crews to stay on station for extended periods at considerable distances from base when directing U-boats on to a convoy.

PB4Y-1 LIBERATOR
4764 km (3,207 mi.)

Ju 290A-5
6150 km (3,813 mi.)

Fw 200C-3/44
3560 km (2,953 mi.)

KAWANISHI

H6K 'MAVIS'

● Maritime reconnaissance/bomber ● Long range ● Transport

It was a Japanese navy need for an aircraft which could cover the vast expanses of the Pacific that inspired Kawanishi to design the 'Mavis'. Powered by four engines, the H6K, first flown in July 1936, was one of the most reliable and efficient of the flying-boats used by Japan during World War II. It also had a very long range and an endurance of more than 24 hours, making it ideally suited to long overwater missions.

▲ Although the 'Mavis' was undoubtedly one of the finest World War II flying-boats, it was notoriously difficult to service. Large platforms were erected by engineers for engine maintenance.

KAWANISHI H6K 'MAVIS'

▼ **Allied evaluation**
Many Japanese aircraft were captured as the Allies overran Japanese bases in the Pacific. This H6K flew with the Allied Technical Air Intelligence Unit (ATAIU) which tested the capabilities of enemy types.

▲ **Early introduction**
In 1938 the first H6K1s entered service with the Imperial Japanese Navy after 18 months of flying and sea trials with four prototypes.

◀ **Transport version**
Code-named 'Tillie' by the Allies, the H6K4-L was a transport version with additional cabin windows. Armament was removed and sleeping berths were provided.

▼ **Offensive armament**
In the attack role, the H6K could carry two 800-kg (1,760 lb.) torpedoes or up to 1000 kg (2,200 lb.) of bombs attached to the wing-supporting struts.

▲ **Series prototype**
Originally named the Kawanishi Navy Experimental 9-Shi Large-size Flying-Boat, the 'Mavis' prototype was first flown on 14 July 1936, with test pilot Katsuji Kondo at the controls.

FACTS AND FIGURES

➤ Powered by four Nakajima Hikari engines, the prototype first flew in 1936 after three years of design work.

➤ The H6K was regarded as a success during the Sino-Japanese War of 1938–39.

➤ Total production of the H6K reached 215, of which 127 were H6K4s.

➤ As well as for maritime patrol, H6K4s were used against land targets in the Dutch East Indies during 1942.

➤ Transport versions were fitted with mail, cargo and passenger compartments.

➤ H6Ks were vulnerable to fighters as they lacked self-sealing fuel tanks and armour.

Reconnaissance for the Imperial Fleet

The initial production model of the 'Mavis', the H6K2, had a powered turret with a single machine-gun on top of the rear fuselage, plus manually operated guns in the nose and tail. The 10 built were delivered to the Japanese navy in 1939, but were subsequently converted for use as transports.

The main version was the H6K4, which had two blisters for machine-guns on the sides of the forward fuselage. There were 66 of this model in service at the time of the attack on Pearl Harbor, and during the Japanese conquests of early 1942 they were used widely both for bombing and maritime patrol.

In 1942 the H6K5 introduced 969.4-kW (1,300-hp.) engines, but by this time the 'Mavis' was proving too vulnerable to Allied fighters, and its H8K replacement, the fastest flying-boat of the war, was already in production.

Altogether, 215 H6Ks were built before production ended in 1943. They included some 18 transports used by the Kaiyo (Ocean) division of Greater Japan Air Lines until 1945. A few survivors were used by the republican Indonesian air force during the post-war fight for independence and the civil war which followed.

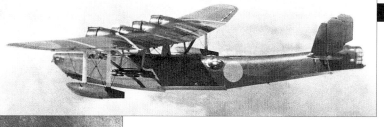

Above: The final maritime reconnaissance version was the H6K5. Fitted with more powerful Mitsubishi Kinsei 53 radial engines, this version had a turret housing a 7.7-mm (.303 cal.) machine-gun aft of the flight deck.

Left: As Allied fighters improved during the course of the Pacific War, the lumbering H6Ks became easy targets. This example was downed in 1944 by Lieutenant John D. Keeling of VB-109, US Naval Reserve.

H6K5 'MAVIS'

As the final production version, the H6K5 was fitted with more powerful engines and improved armament. This example is seen in standard Imperial Japanese Navy colours.

H6K4 'Mavis'

Type: long-range reconnaissance, bomber or transport flying-boat

Powerplant: four 745.7-kW (1,000-hp.) Mitsubishi Kinsei 43 14-cylinder radial engines

Maximum speed: 340 km/h (211 m.p.h.) at 4000 m (13,125 ft.)

Climb rate: 5000 m (16,400 ft.) in 13 min 31 sec

Range: 6080 km (3,778 mi.)

Service ceiling: 9610 m (31,530 ft.)

Weights: 21,545 kg (47,499 lb.) maximum take-off

Armament: four 7.7-mm (.303 cal.) machine guns (one each in nose, dorsal and fuselage-side mountings) plus one 20-mm (0.79-in.) cannon in tail; two 800-kg (1,760-lb.) torpedoes or 1000 kg (2,200 lb.) of bombs

Dimensions:
span	40.00 m (131 ft. 3 in.)
length	25.63 m (84 ft. 1 in.)
height	6.27 m (20 ft. 7 in.)
wing area	170.00 m² (1,830 sq. ft.)

Replacing the bow gun position, a turret containing a 7.7-mm (.303 cal.) machine-gun was added immediately aft of the flight deck. This position protected the aircraft from attack from above or head-on.

The final production versions were powered by Kinsei 51 or 53 radials which were 224 kW (300 hp.) more powerful than earlier versions.

Offensive armament was mounted on the parallel wing supporting struts and consisted of bombs or two torpedoes. The beam blisters on each side of the fuselage each contained a single, hand-held 7.7-mm (.303 cal.) Type 92 machine-gun.

After studying the American Sikorsky S-42, Kawanishi designed the H6K with a slender two-step hull. The parasol wing was mounted above the fuselage and a stabilising float was fitted to each wing.

The tail turret had a large glazed section giving the gunner good visibility. Armament comprised a hand-held 20-mm (0.79-in.) Type 99 Model 1 cannon.

In earlier versions of the 'Mavis' a 7.7-mm (.303 cal.) hand-held Type 92 machine-gun was mounted in an open bow position. This was removed in the H6K5 but observation windows remained.

After the first test flight the forward step of the hull was moved 50 cm (20 in.) rearwards. This modification was successful and the H6K had the best water-handling characteristics of any World War II flying-boat.

COMBAT DATA

RANGE

All three of these types were respected for their highly impressive range and endurance. The H6K was capable of remaining aloft for 24 hours and crew fatigue was often the limiting factor, rather than the endurance of the aircraft. Long range was especially important in order to cover the vast area of the Pacific theatre.

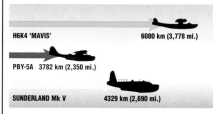

H6K4 'MAVIS'   6080 km (3,778 mi.)

PBY-5A   3782 km (2,350 mi.)

SUNDERLAND Mk V   4329 km (2,690 mi.)

Kawanishi Seaplanes

■ **E7K 'ALF':** Flying anti-submarine, convoy escort and reconnaissance patrols in 1941-43, many E7K2s ended up in *kamikaze* attacks.

■ **E8K:** Designed in 1933 as a reconnaissance seaplane, the E8K lacked manoeuvrability and lost out to the Nakajima E8N1 biplane.

■ **E15K SHIUN 'NORM':** Repeated failures of the float assemblies were the main downfall of the Shiun (Violet Cloud). Only 15 were built.

■ **N1K KYOFU 'REX':** An ambitious design, the N1K suffered from a protracted development and only 97 of these floatplane fighters were built.

KAWANISHI

H8K 'EMILY'

● Long-range flying-boat ● Maritime patrol bomber

Given the allied reporting name of 'Emily', the Kawanishi H8K was one of the most outstanding and advanced flying-boats to be built during World War II. Heavily armed and armoured, it had a very long range and flew superbly. Yet it was a complex machine, and the 167 examples built never fully replaced the Sikorsky-influenced H6K 'Mavis' with which the Imperial Japanese Navy had been equipped at the start of World War II.

▲ *The H8K was similar to Britain's Short Sunderland in layout and role, but although the Sunderland was better known, the Japanese aircraft had superior performance. It was also far better than its Kawanishi predecessor, the H6K.*

KAWANISHI **H8K 'EMILY'**

▲ Float trials
The initial trials of the H8K showed some flaws in handling on water, but performance was otherwise very good and it was ordered into production.

Under attack ▶
This 'Emily' was shot up by an A-26 over Saipan in 1944. It made a hurried forced landing after the port inner engine caught fire.

▲ Transport
The H8K was turned into a transport capable of carrying up to 64 passengers. Mitsubishi MK4Q engines were installed and armament was reduced.

▲ High power
The main advantage of the H8K over the H6K was the amount of power. Top speed was markedly higher, and take-offs were shorter and much easier.

◀ Hitting the sea
Attacking even a stricken 'Emily' like this could be a hazardous business because of its heavy defensive armament of 20-mm (0.79-in.) cannon.

FACTS AND FIGURES

➤ The H8K prototype flew for the first time in January 1941.

➤ The first operational mission took place in 1942, when two aircraft set off from Wake Island to bomb Pearl Harbor.

➤ An H8K trials version was built with retractable floats and dorsal turret.

➤ Radar-equipped H8Ks sank at least three American submarines north of the Philippines in 1945.

➤ As a VIP transport the H8K could seat 29 passengers in great comfort.

➤ The 'Emily' could fly further than any other operational flying-boat of the war.

PROFILE

A floating flying fortress

The H8K prototype was first flown in 1941. It was designed to meet a 1938 requirement for a four-engined maritime reconnaissance flying-boat superior in all respects to the British Sunderland, then the best in the world. After modification improved the initially poor water handling qualities, the type was put into production as the Navy Type 2 Flying Boat Model 11. With armour protection, self-sealing fuel tanks, an armament that included 20-mm (0.79-in.) cannon and a maximum speed of over 430 km/h (267 m.p.h.), it represented a great advance over previous types. The further improved H8K2 had more power, greater speed and its armament increased to five 20-mm (0.79-in.) cannon and four 7.7-mm (.303 cal.) machine-guns. This made it unquestionably one of the toughest opponents faced by the Allies in the Pacific. It was also one of the first Japanese aircraft to be fitted with anti-surface vessel radar, and achieved some success against American submarines late in the war.

Above: With an empire stretching across thousands of kilometres of the Pacific, the Japanese needed good flying-boats urgently. This need became acute when American naval supremacy began to deny Japanese shipping access to the sea lanes.

Left: Equipped with radar, the 'Emily' was one of the few serious threats to the US Navy submarines which were strangling Japan's seaborne lifelines.

H8K2 'Emily'

Type: long-range maritime reconnaissance flying-boat

Powerplant: four 1380-kW (1,850 hp.) Mitsubishi Kasei 22 14-cylinder radial piston engines

Maximum speed: 467 km/h (290 m.p.h.)

Range: 7180 km (4,461 mi.)

Service ceiling: 8760 m (28,740 ft.)

Weights: empty 18,380 kg (40,520 lb.); loaded 32,500 kg (71,650 lb.)

Armament: 20-mm (0.79-in.) cannon in bow, dorsal, tail turrets and on each beam; four 7.7-mm (.303 cal.) machine-guns from beam hatches; up to 2000 kg (4,400 lb.) of bombs or two 800-kg (1,760-lb.) torpedoes

Dimensions:
span	38.00 m (124 ft. 8 in.)
length	28.13 m (92 ft. 3 in.)
height	9.15 m (30 ft.)
wing area	106.00 m² (1,141 sq. ft.)

H8K2 'EMILY'

The H8K2 was the major production version of the 'Emily', with 112 boats being completed and entering service between 1942 and 1944.

Unlike many Japanese aircraft, the H8K had excellent armour protection for the crew.

Prototypes were powered by the Mitsubishi Mars MK4A engine, but later aircraft used the 1380-kW (1,850 hp.) MK4Q engine, driving Hamilton propellers.

The wing structure was all-metal, with a metal covering. The wing had slight dihedral for enhanced stability during long patrols.

The dorsal turret was powered and mounted a single 20-mm (0.79-in.) cannon.

Normally flown with a crew of 10, the H8K's capacious fuselage could hold up to 64 passengers.

The nose gunner operated a 20-mm (0.79-in.) cannon from his position, which was retained in the H8K transport.

The bulk fuel tanks in the hull were self-sealing and had a carbon dioxide fire suppression system.

The tail gunner operated a 20-mm (0.79-in.) cannon from the rear turret.

COMBAT DATA

CRUISING SPEED

Flying-boats are not the most streamlined of machines, and none of the really heavy examples was particularly fast. The specification for the H8K called for it to be able to outperform the British Sunderland, which it did. Both cruised faster than the massive German Bv 222.

H8K 'EMILY'	295 km/h (183 m.p.h.)
SUNDERLAND	285 km/h (177 m.p.h.)
Bv 222 WIKING	250 km/h (155 m.p.h.)

RANGE

Maritime reconnaissance requires the aircraft to stay in the air for long periods. The H8K was designed to operate over the vast expanses of the Pacific, and had a considerably longer range than its rivals. It could remain on patrol for an entire day and night, the only limiting factor being the endurance of the crew.

H8K 'EMILY' 7180 km (4,461 mi.)

Bv 222 WIKING 6000 km (3,728 mi.)

SUNDERLAND 4700 km (2,920 mi.)

DEFENSIVE ARMAMENT

The Short Sunderland was not an easy target in a fight and was nicknamed 'the Flying Porcupine' by the Luftwaffe. But the British aircraft's armament paled in comparison with that of the H8K. It took strong nerves on the part of an American fighter pilot to get in close to the 'Emily', with its powerful all-round armament of 20-mm (0.79-in.) cannon.

H8K 'EMILY' 5 x 20-mm (0.79-in.) cannon 4 x 7.7-mm (.303 cal.) MGs

SUNDERLAND 8 x 7.7-mm (.303 cal.) MGs

Bv 222 WIKING 3 x 20-mm (0.79-in.) cannon 5 x 13-mm (0.51-in.) MGs

Giants of the oceans

■ SHORT SUNDERLAND: Smaller and slower than the 'Emily', the British Sunderland performed a similar function and amassed a superb combat record.

■ BLOHM & VOSS Bv 222 WIKING: The huge six-engined Wiking served from the north of Norway to the Mediterranean. It carried huge loads, but was vulnerable to Allied fighters.

■ LATÉCOÈRE 631: This elegant flying-boat was completed in occupied France and was immediately confiscated by the Germans. After the war it flew Atlantic passenger routes.

■ CONSOLIDATED PB2Y CORONADO: Reliable but sluggish, the Coronado was used by the US Navy as a long-range patroller, 44-seat transport and ambulance.

■ MARTIN JRM MARS: Ordered in 1938, only five examples of the US Navy's largest flying-boat were built. They were used from the end of the war as long-range cargo transports.

KAWASAKI

KI-61 HIEN 'TONY'

● Single-seat fighter ● Liquid-cooled engine ● More than 3000 built

One of the better-looking fighters of World War II, the Kawasaki Ki-61 Hien (Swallow) was initially developed under the guidance of a German engineer and was powered by the Daimler-Benz DB 601A in-line piston engine. Japan produced this powerplant under licence from its designers, and called it the Kawasaki Ha-40. The Hien reached units in the Pacific from 1942 and served until Japan collapsed in 1945.

▲ The Ki-61 Hien did not face any real challenge until the P-51 Mustang appeared in the Pacific. Up until this time Allied pilots suffered at the hands of the Japanese in this high-performance machine.

KAWASAKI KI-61 HIEN 'TONY'

▼ Improved Ki-61-II
With its larger engine and airframe changes, the initially troublesome Ki-61-II eventually entered production in September 1944.

▲ Camouflage schemes
Ki-61s wore a variety of camouflage patterns and high-visibility unit markings.

◀ Nationalist Chinese Hien
This Ki-61 was one of a number of Japanese aircraft to fall into Nationalist Chinese hands.

▼ Home defence units
Although most Ki-61s served in Japan, others saw combat in New Guinea, Rabaul and the Philippines.

▲ Three-bladed propeller
Both the Ki-61-I and Ki-61-II were fitted with a three-bladed, constant-speed propeller, in common with the Bf 109.

Training School Hiens ▶
These Ki-61-Ias are seen at the Akeno Fighter Training School. Some Ki-61-Ias were equipped with two 20-mm (0.79-in.) cannon.

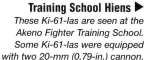

FACTS AND FIGURES

➤ When production ended in 1945, a total of 3078 Kawasaki Ki-61 'Tony' fighters had been manufactured.

➤ The prototype Ki-61 was completed in December 1941.

➤ Ki-61-I KAIc production at Kagamigahara peaked at 254 per month in July 1944.

➤ The radial-engined Ki-100 was developed after the factory which produced the Ki-61-II's engine was bombed.

➤ There were several proposals for advanced Ki-61 versions, but none was built.

➤ An improved Ki-61-III mock-up was built, but the Ki-100 was put into production.

PROFILE

Japan's only in-line-engined fighter

Americans in the Pacific often filed reports stating they had come up against Japanese pilots flying the Messerschmitt Bf 109 fighter. In fact, Japan never flew the Bf 109 operationally. The fighter in question was the Kawasaki Ki-61 Hien fighter, codenamed 'Tony' by the Allies. The Hien was a superb fighter of Japanese design and powered by a Japanese-built Daimler-Benz engine as fitted to the Messerschmitt.

A clean, streamlined, fast and manoeuvrable aircraft, the Ki-61

was the only liquid-cooled fighter to enter service with the Japanese air arms during World War II. The Hien scored many aerial victories against the Allies, and it also pioneered the use of armour and self-sealing fuel tanks that had been so useful in Europe.

Ironically, the engine that made the 'Tony' possible was also its biggest limitation. The licence-built Daimler DB 601A powerplant had little potential for further development. An attempt was made to improve the Ki-61 as the Ki-61-II, with an Ha-140

engine, but teething problems delayed its introduction. Thus, although the 'Tony' had an important role in the war, it never achieved the fame of the A6M 'Zero'.

Below: The Ki-61-I was unable to match the American B-29's service ceiling and was outclassed by its P-51.

Above: After trials, an early production Hien was test-flown against a captured P-40E and an imported Bf 109E. The Ki-61 was the superior performer.

Ki-61-I KAIc HIEN 'TONY'

This aircraft flew with the HQ Chutai, 244th Sentai, based at Chofu, Tokyo, during 1944/45. By the end of World War II 13 Sentais were equipped with the Ki-61, mainly in the defence of the Japanese mainland.

Ki-61-I KAIc Hien 'Tony'

Type: single-seat fighter

Powerplant: one 880-kW (1,180-hp.) Kawasaki Ha-40 inverted-vee piston engine

Maximum speed: 590 km/h (366 m.p.h.) at 4260 m (14,000 ft.)

Climb rate: 7 minutes to 5000 m (16,400 ft.)

Range: 580 km (360 mi.)

Service ceiling: 10,000 m (33,000 ft.)

Weights: empty 2630 kg (5,786 lb.); maximum take-off 3470 kg (7,634 lb.)

Armament: two 20-mm (0.79-in.) Ho-5 cannon in the nose and 12.7-mm (.50 cal.) Type 1 (Ho-103)

Dimensions:
span	12.00 m (36 ft. 4 in.)
length	8.94 m (29 ft. 4 in.)
height	3.70 m (12 ft. 2 in.)
wing area	20.00 m² (215 sq. ft.)

Daimler-Benz's DB 601 inverted-vee, 12-cylinder, liquid-cooled engine that had powered the early Messerschmitt Bf 109 was licence-built by Kawasaki as the Ha-40. The first example was in operation by mid-1941.

After the Ki-61-I entered production, the factory immediately started development of a more powerful Ki-61-II with a 1118-kW (1,500-hp.) Ha-140 engine, an improved version of the Ha-40. This proved to be unreliable, as the crankshaft was prone to breakage.

The Ki-61-II featured improvements to the airframe, including a redesigned cockpit canopy and enlarged wings to enhance manoeuvrability at altitude. However, test-flights revealed handling problems.

The Hien's fuel capacity (one fuselage tank behind the cockpit able to carry 165 litres/44 gal.) could be augmented by fitting a 200-litre (53-gal.) drop-tank under each wing.

The Ki-61 did not have a gun fitted in the propeller hub, but was equipped with two machine-guns mounted above the nose and firing through the propeller.

The oil cooler radiator was positioned under the main wings, in a similar manner to that of the P-51 Mustang.

To reduce drag, the earliest Ki-61s had a retractable tailwheel. In later models, in order to simplify production, a fixed tail wheel was fitted.

Japanese warplanes with inline powerplants

AICHI M6A SEIRAN: Intended as a submarine-borne attack aircraft, the M6A was almost operational when war ended in 1945.

KAWASAKI Ki-32: The last Japanese army bomber powered by a liquid-cooled engine, the Ki-32 took part in the bombing of Hong Kong.

KAWASAKI Ki-60: Kawasaki was instructed to build two designs for the licence-built DB 601 engine. Only three of this heavy fighter were built.

YOKOSUKA D4Y SUISEI: This two-seat dive-bomber initially saw service as a reconnaissance aircraft because of its speed.

COMBAT DATA

MAXIMUM SPEED

While the Ki-61 was a high-performance machine that presented a major challenge to Allied fighters in 1943, the P-51 and P-38 were both superior and outclassed the Hien later in the war. If the Ki-61-II had not been trouble-plagued, the tables may have been turned.

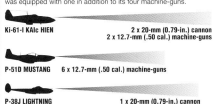

Ki-61-I KAIc HIEN	590 km/h (366 m.p.h.)
P-51D MUSTANG	716 km/h (437 m.p.h.)
P-38J LIGHTNING	666 km/h (413 m.p.h.)

ARMAMENT

Japanese fighter designers benefited from German advances in fighter armament, utilising 20-mm (0.79-in.) cannon in the Ki-61. The USAAF was slow to fit cannon to its aircraft, although the Lightning was equipped with one in addition to its four machine-guns.

Ki-61-I KAIc HIEN	2 x 20-mm (0.79-in.) cannon 2 x 12.7-mm (.50 cal.) machine-guns
P-51D MUSTANG	6 x 12.7-mm (.50 cal.) machine-guns
P-38J LIGHTNING	1 x 20-mm (0.79-in.) cannon 4 x 12.7-mm (.50 cal.) machine-guns

RANGE

Without auxilliary fuel the range of the Ki-61-I KAIc Hien was much less than that of contemporary US aircraft. Drop-tanks could be fitted to the Hien and, although these improved range, they reduced its top speed by 80 km/h (50 m.p.h.).

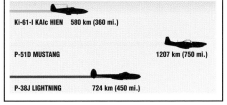

Ki-61-I KAIc HIEN	580 km (360 mi.)
P-51D MUSTANG	1207 km (750 mi.)
P-38J LIGHTNING	724 km (450 mi.)

LAVOCHKIN

LaGG-3

● Wooden fighter ● More than 6000 built ● Early Soviet defender

▲ During the early stages of the Luftwaffe onslaught, the good reputation of the LaGG-3 owed more to its rugged construction and the courage of its pilots than to its design as a fighter.

Designed by a new bureau and rushed into production as World War II was getting under way, the LaGG-3 was an improved version of Lavochkin's original LaGG-1. Although they had many shortcomings, the urgent need for new fighters meant that around 300 LaGG-3s were in service by the time Germany invaded the Soviet Union in June 1941. And by the time production ended just over a year later a further 6000 had been delivered.

LAVOCHKIN LaGG-3

▲ **Early Lavochkin**
The basic design of the LaGG-3 was progressively improved in production, with later aircraft having retractable tailwheels and heavier armament.

▲ **Flying the LaGG-3**
Reports vary with regard to the flying qualities of the LaGG-3. Some sources suggest it was as dangerous to its pilots as it was to the enemy.

▲ **Finnish LaGG**
Wearing Finnish markings, this LaGG-3 was probably captured after landing in Finland during World War II.

◄ **LaGGs abroad**
Another captured aircraft, this machine was flown in Japanese markings. Japan and the Soviet Union shared a long-running territorial dispute.

Finnish inspection ►
At least two LaGG-3s were flown in Finland, since this aircraft does not have the leading-edge slats of the machine shown above right.

FACTS AND FIGURES

➤ Designers Lavochkin, Gorbunov and Gudkov used the initial letters of their names to produce the LaGG designation.

➤ Both the LaGG-1 and LaGG-3 were constructed of wood.

➤ The LaGG-3 was intended as a stop-gap fighter, but 6528 were built.

➤ The I-22 prototype of the LaGG-1 was later modified as the I-301 prototype of the LaGG-3.

➤ Late versions of the LaGG-3 were able to carry drop-tanks.

➤ Lavochkin developed the La-5 from an M-82-powered version of the LaGG-3.

PROFILE

Long-serving Soviet stop-gap

First flown as the I-22 in March 1939, the LaGG-1 was built largely of wood and armed with a 23-mm (0.9-in.) cannon plus two 12.7-mm (0.5 cal.) machine-guns in the nose. It proved short on performance, range and manoeuvrability and was difficult to control.

The need for a new fighter was urgent, however, and so the LaGG-1 was fitted with lighter weapons, had its control system improved and had additional fuel tanks installed to produce the

LaGG-3. This aircraft still suffered from a lack of power and had a very poor view from the cockpit.

Most units equipped with the type suffered heavy losses and the pressure of war meant that few of the improvements proposed were actually carried out. Instead, the heavier weapons of the LaGG-1 were often fitted so that the LaGG-3 could be used for close support missions against ground targets.

Modifications included three aircraft fitted with 37-mm

Soviet forces relied heavily on the LaGG-3, flying it against far superior enemy fighters until the introduction of more advanced Soviet fighter designs.

(1.47-in.) cannon and one with a 1230-kW M-10A engine. But it was the installation of the M-82 air-cooled radial to produce the La-5 that finally turned Lavochkin's design into a worthwhile fighter.

Both the LaGG-1 and -3 were poorly armed and tricky to fly. It was an air force joke that LaGG actually stood for *lakirovannii garantirovannii grob* – Russian for 'guaranteed varnished coffin'.

Lavochkin retained the best features of the LaGG-3 in subsequent designs. The tail and wing surfaces of the La-5 and -7, for example, owed much to the earlier fighter.

LaGG-3

Type: single-seat fighter

Powerplant: one 925-kW (1,240-hp.) Klimov M-105PF-1 liquid-cooled V-12 engine

Maximum speed: 560 km/h (348 m.p.h.) at 5000 m (16,400 ft.)

Climb rate: 5.85 min to 5000 m (16,400 ft.)

Range: 650 km (404 mi.)

Service ceiling: 9600 m (31,500 ft.)

Weights: empty 2620 kg (5,776 lb.); maximum take-off 3280 kg (7,231 lb.)

Armament: one 20-mm (0.79-in.) cannon and two 12.7-mm (.50 cal.) machine-guns, plus six 82-mm (3.2-in.) rockets or two 100-kg (220-lb.) bombs

Dimensions: span 9.80 m (32 ft. 2 in.)
length 8.90 m (29 ft. 2 in.)
height 3.30 m (14 ft. 5 in.)
wing area 17.50 m² (188 sq. ft.)

LaGG-3

This LaGG-3 was assigned to an IAP (Independent Air Regiment) of the VVS KBF (Red Banner Baltic Fleet Air Force). It was shot down over Finland in March 1942.

LaGG-3 armament varied considerably, according to mission. Typically, a LaGG-3 was armed with a single ShVAK cannon (with 120 rounds) firing through the propeller hub and two 12.7-mm (.50 cal.) BS machine-guns, each with 220 rounds, mounted above the engine.

The only parts of the LaGG-3's structure which were not made from wood were the control surfaces, which were light alloy with fabric covering, and the flaps, which were all-metal to avoid damage.

A Hucks starter could be used for starting the engine via the shaft in the propeller spinner.

Both the LaGG-1 and -3 were powered by a Klimov M-105P in-line V-12 liquid-cooled piston engine. The LaGG-3's M-105PF developed 157 kW (210 hp.) more power and drove an improved propeller.

The birch plywood skinning was both impregnated and bonded with phenolformaldehyde resin. Radical at the time, this wood-bonding technique is now widely used.

Rare among contemporary monoplane fighters in not having metal stressed-skin construction, the LaGG-3 was built almost entirely of wood. Diagonal strips of plywood were bonded onto its internal wooden structure.

COMBAT DATA

MAXIMUM SPEED

With extensive Spanish Civil War combat experience and continuous development, the Messerschmitt Bf 109E-7 could outperform most contemporary fighters.

LaGG-3 — **560 km/h (348 m.p.h.)**
Bf 109E-7 — **578 km/h (358 m.p.h.)**
HURRICANE Mk IA — **515 km/h (319 m.p.h.)**

ARMAMENT

Although the Hurricane Mk IA lacked the cannon armament of its rivals, its eight reliable machine-guns packed a devastating punch and marked a revolution in aircraft armament design. LaGG-3 armament often varied, even between aircraft of the same unit.

LaGG-3 — 1 x 20-mm (0.79-in.) cannon, 2 x 12.7-mm (.50 cal.) MGs
Bf 109E-7 — 1 x 20-mm (0.79-in.) cannon, 4 x 7.9-mm (0.31-in.) MGs
HURRICANE Mk IA — 8 x 7.7-mm (.50 cal.) MGs

POWER

Even with its powerful engine the LaGG-3 offered a poor rate of climb and was generally inferior to all other Soviet fighters. It was also largely outclassed by Luftwaffe fighters.

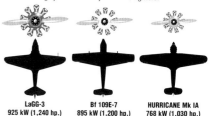

LaGG-3 925 kW (1,240 hp.) | Bf 109E-7 895 kW (1,200 hp.) | HURRICANE Mk IA 768 kW (1,030 hp.)

Soviet World War II monoplane fighters

■ **LAVOCHKIN La-7:** Working on his own, Lavochkin produced the highly successful La-7, based on the LaGG-3 with a radial engine.

■ **LAVOCHKIN La-9:** Arriving late in the war, the La-9 was a truly exceptional fighter and several continued to serve after the war.

■ **MIKOYAN GUREVICH MiG-3:** Though an improvement over the earlier MiG-1, the MiG-3 was still no match for Luftwaffe fighters.

■ **POLIKARPOV I-16:** About 4000 I-16s fought against the Luftwaffe. Hopelessly obsolete, they were often used in deliberate ramming attacks.

LAVOCHKIN

LA-5 AND LA-7

● Soviet dogfighter ● Wooden construction ● Flown by aces

Developed from the disappointing LaGG-3, the Lavochkin La-5 was one of the great fighters of World War II. It shared the earlier machine's wooden construction, but the new radial engine gave it vastly superior performance. The La-5 and its successors were amongst the best dogfighters of the war, especially at low level, and were flown by most leading Soviet pilots including Ivan Kozhedub, the Allied 'ace of aces'.

▲ The La-5 inspired confidence in those who flew it. Pavel Kocfelda of the Ist Fighter Regiment of the Red air force christened his personal machine 'Rene'.

PHOTO FILE

LAVOCHKIN LA-5 AND LA-7

Simple cockpit ▶
The 'Lavochka' was basic, with a rough finish. There was no cockpit heating and the instruments and radios were often very poor, but it handled like a dream.

▲ Ready for battle
The La-5 was simply and ruggedly constructed. Its structure was mostly built from wood rather than scarce light aircraft alloys.

▼ On the ground
The La-5 was superb in the air, but it had bad manners on the ground. Landings were usually a bouncy, prolonged business.

Forced down ▶
The Lavochkin's basic construction was easy to repair after minor accidents like this.

▼ Rugged radial
The La-5's excellent radial engine and wooden bonded construction were ideal for service in Russia. Complex aircraft with tricky liquid-cooled engines like the Spitfires supplied by Britain proved harder to maintain in the field.

▲ Tactical hideout
The rapid advance across Russia in 1944 meant that the La-5 was usually based in remote strips. Russian airmen always hid their aircraft well.

FACTS AND FIGURES

➤ Lavochkins were very successful at the battle of Kursk, where they escorted Il-2 Shturmovik rocket-firing tank-busters.

➤ About 12,000 radial-engine Lavochkin fighters were manufactured.

➤ The La-11, the last piston Lavochkin, still served with Communist forces in 1960.

➤ The La-5 was flown by the highest-scoring Allied ace, Ivan Kozhedub, who scored 62 kills against the Luftwaffe.

➤ The La-5 wing structure was made of plastic bonded wood veneer strips.

➤ A volunteer unit of Czech pilots fought with the Red air force using the La-5.

PROFILE

Wooden warrior of the Eastern Front

As the Soviet armies reeled back from the German invasion of 1941, there were frantic demands for the Soviet air force to be re-equipped with modern fighters. In October 1941, Semyon Lavochkin began work on an improved version of the heavy LaGG-3 fighter. The ensuing La-5, equipped with a powerful radial engine and cut-down rear fuselage, entered production in July 1942, and more than 1000 were built by the end of the year.

The first large-scale use of the La-5 came in 1942 over Stalingrad. Here, and at Kursk the following year, it proved to be a ferocious dogfighter, especially at low level. The lightweight La-5FN appeared that year, and was flown by many top Soviet aces.

The La-7 of 1944 had more power and many minor improvements, making it one of the most effective fighters of the war.

The La-5 had excellent low-speed handling, assisted by the automatic slats on the leading edges of the wings, which are shown here in the operating position.

LA-5FN

This lightweight variant of the La-5 was used by hero of the Soviet Union P.J. Linkholetov, who shot down 25 enemy aircraft in 1944.

The basic wing construction was made of birch wood, cross-grained and impregnated with a resin mixture and covered in plywood.

The La-5 control surfaces were of fabric-covered light alloy construction, and were paired with large flaps. With a low wing loading, the La-5 had an exceptionally fast rate of roll.

Twin 20-mm (0.79-in.) cannon were mounted above the engine, and were synchronised to fire through the propeller disc.

Most La-5s wore the brown and green paint scheme, but winter white was also used, sometimes topped with dramatic red arrows and Cyrillic slogans.

The elevator and rudder were among the few metal parts, having an alloy frame and fabric covering.

The success of the Lavochkin series owed much to its ability to accept ever bigger engines. The later La-7's Shvetsov radial produced 1500 kW (2,000 hp.). These engines performed best at an altitude of around 2000 m (6,000 ft.).

Five self-sealing fuel tanks were contained in each wing. The two outer tanks were generally left empty, as their weight when filled limited manoeuvrability.

This Cyrillic slogan translates as 'for Vasek and Zhora'.

The retractable tailwheel often proved unreliable.

Lavochkin development

■ **LaGG-3:** Developed by Lavochkin, Gorbunov and Gudkov in 1940, the LaGG was fast and reasonably agile, but it was a sluggish climber and pilots complained of very heavy controls.

■ **LAVOCHKIN La-5:** Fitting a more powerful radial engine to the LaGG-3 led to marginally increased drag, but much greater power meant that the La-5 gained more than 50 km/h (30 m.p.h.) in speed.

■ **LAVOCHKIN La-7:** More power and lower drag meant that the La-7 of 1944 had a top speed of 680 km/h (422 m.p.h.). This is the La-7 in which Ivan Kozhedub achieved the last of his 62 victories.

La-5FN

Type: interceptor fighter

Powerplant: one 1231-kW (1,650-hp.) Shvetsov M-82FN (ASh-82FN) radial piston engine

Maximum speed: 650 km/h (403 m.p.h.)

Climb rate: 5 minutes to 5000 m (16,000 ft.)

Range: 765 km (475 mi.)

Service ceiling: 11,000 m (36,000 ft.)

Weights: empty 2605 kg (5,737 lb.); loaded 3360 kg (7,932 lb.)

Armament: two or three 20-mm (0.79-in.) ShVAK or 23-mm (0.9-in.) NS cannon plus provision for 158 kg (350 lb.) of bombs or four 82-mm (3-in.) rockets underwing

Dimensions:
span	9.80 m	(32 ft.)
length	8.67 m	(28 ft.)
height	2.54 m	(8 ft.)
wing area	17.59 m²	(189 sq. ft.)

COMBAT DATA

MAXIMUM SPEED

The La-5 was considerably faster than the Messerschmitt Bf 109 at all levels below 6000 m (20,000 ft.), but the German fighter was better at high altitude. However, since combat on the Eastern Front was at low level, this was no real disadvantage to Russian pilots.

La-5FN	650 km/h (403 m.p.h.)
Bf 109G-6	620 km/h (384 m.p.h.)
P-39	612 km/h (379 m.p.h.)

SERVICE CEILING

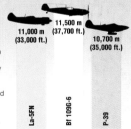

Although the Lavochkin and the American-supplied Bell P-39 each had a reasonable service ceiling, neither was much good at extreme altitude. The P-39 was particularly bad, but like the Lavochkin it generally fought at lower levels, and both Soviet-operated fighters achieved considerable success.

La-5FN	Bf 109G-6	P-39
11,000 m (33,000 ft.)	11,500 m (37,700 ft.)	10,700 m (35,000 ft.)

ARMAMENT

The Lavochkin was relatively lightly armed, but this did not stop it becoming a highly successful dogfighter. The P-39 had a particularly heavy but slow-firing gun, which doubled as an effective ground-attack weapon. The Messerschmitt's standard armament was often heavily augmented by field conversions.

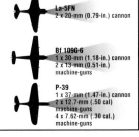

La-5FN
2 x 20-mm (0.79-in.) cannon

Bf 109G-6
1 x 30-mm (1.18-in.) cannon
2 x 13-mm (0.51-in.) machine-guns

P-39
1 x 37-mm (1.47-in.) cannon
2 x 12.7-mm (.50 cal) machine-guns
4 x 7.62-mm (.30 cal.) machine-guns

LOCKHEED

P-38 LIGHTNING

● Twin-engine fighter ● Flown by top aces

Many believe the Lockheed P-38 Lightning was the finest American fighter of World War II. The twin-boomed P-38 was fast, heavily-armed and extremely versatile. While it had trouble matching single-engine fighters like the Messerschmitt 109 and Focke-Wulf 190, the Lightning was very manoeuvrable for such a big machine, and in capable hands it could hold its own. The P-38 more than held its own in the South West Pacific, where the aircraft was flown by Major Richard I. Bong and Major Thomas B. McGuire, America's top-scoring aces of all time.

▲ Lieutenant Murray J. Shubin was just one of the many aces to succeed in a Lightning. Shubin gained five kills in an hour in his P-38, which he named after his Australian girlfriend.

LOCKHEED P-38 LIGHTNING

▼ **Photo fighter**
The F-5 reconnaissance Lightning performed dangerous lone missions without any armament.

▲ **Napalm attack**
Lightnings blast Japanese positions with napalm bombs near the Ipoh Dam in the Philippine Islands.

Night Lightning ▶
The P-38M was one of the fastest night-fighters of the war, despite the added weight of radar and a second crewmember.

◀ **Clothes line**
The Lightning served throughout the Solomons. It performed many tasks, including drying the clothes of 13th Air Force pilots!

Caught napping ▶
It wasn't all victories; this sad remnant of a P-38 at Tacloban was the result of Japanese bombing during the 1944 struggle for Leyte.

▲ **Outdoor factory**
Lightnings were built in the California sun while the Lockheed production line was modernised.

FACTS AND FIGURES

➤ The P-38 Lightning prototype made its first flight on 27 January 1939.

➤ The Lightning produced for the Royal Air Force was at first named the Atlanta.

➤ Experimental Lightning variants included the high-altitude XP-49 and XP-58 Chain Lightning bomber escort.

➤ To overcome tail buffeting in early P-38s, an aluminium fillet was added to the wingroot.

➤ F-4 and F-5 photo-gathering Lightnings were among the best reconnaissance aircraft of the war.

➤ Production of all versions of this great Lockheed fighter totalled 9924 aircraft.

PROFILE

The fork-tailed devil in the sky

A s late as 1944, when Mustangs were sweeping the skies clear of foes, a poll in flying classes showed that student pilots' 'most wanted' aircraft was the Lockheed P-38 Lightning, the design of which dated back to 1937.

The P-38 was rugged and versatile, and because of its low-drag aerodynamic shape and heavy weight it accelerated to high speeds faster than any previous warplane. A potent

fighter and a superb fighter-bomber, it also flew as a night-fighter, reconnaissance aircraft, ambulance, torpedo-bomber and target tug.

More than 100 US Army squadrons flew the P-38, which was produced in at least two-dozen versions. In the Pacific, P-38 pilots carried out the long-range intercept mission which downed and killed Japan's Admiral Isoroku Yamamoto, a planner of the Pearl Harbor

attack. In the Mediterranean, Luftwaffe pilots showed respect for the Lightning by calling it *der gabelschwanz Teufel* (the fork-tailed devil).

The ultimate P-38L model was flown by Dick Bong and Tommy McGuire, who with 40 and 38 victories, respectively, were the most successful American fighter pilots in history.

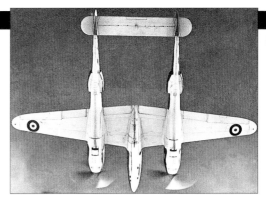

RAF Lightnings were early aircraft with low-rated engines, and had all the faults and none of the advantages of later machines. They were not popular with British pilots.

P-38L Lightning

Type: single-seat fighter and fighter-bomber

Powerplant: two turbo-charged 1194-kW (1,600-hp.) Allison V-1710-111/113 in-line piston engines

Maximum speed: 666 km/h (414 m.p.h.) at 7620 m (25,000 ft.)

Range: 765 km (475 mi.) on internal fuel

Service ceiling: 13,400 m (44,000 ft.)

Weights: empty 5806 kg (12,800 lb.); loaded 9798 kg (21,600 lb.)

Armament: one 20-mm (0.79-in.) cannon and four 12.7-mm (.50 cal.) machine-guns, plus up to 1450 kg (3,197 lb.) of ordnance – usually two 454-kg (1,000-lb.) or 726-kg (1,600-lb.) bombs or 10 127-mm (5-in.) rocket projectiles under wings

Dimensions:
span	15.85 m	(52 ft.)
length	11.53 m	(37 ft. 10 in.)
height	3.00 m	(9 ft. 10 in.)
wing area	30.42 m²	(327 sq. ft.)

One 20-mm (0.79-in.) cannon and four heavy machine-guns concentrated in the nose made the P-38 one of the hardest-hitting American fighters of the war. The battery of guns was also very useful in the ground-attack role.

P-38J LIGHTNING

This Lockheed P-38J served with the 55th Fighter Squadron at Kingscliffe, Northamptonshire, and flew fighter escort for 8th Air Force bombers over Germany.

Unlike British twin-engine aircraft such as the Mosquito, the P-38 was built with 'handed' engines turning in opposite directions. This eliminated engine torque reaction, making take-off extremely simple.

Early Lightnings were notoriously uncomfortable, having a cramped cockpit that lacked proper heating. The first attempts at flying at high altitude resulted in pilots getting frostbite.

328430

N·KI

The turbo-charged Allison in-line engines were never the P-38's best feature, being prone to over-heating.

The Lightning's nosewheel undercarriage was a very welcome new feature for pilots. It made engine maintenance easy for the engineers, as well as reducing accidents on take-off and landing.

Turbo-charged engines with boom-mounted radiators gave the P-38 superb high-altitude performance. Early examples for Britain were delivered without turbos, which virtually crippled the aircraft as a fighting machine.

Early Lightning prototypes suffered severe buffeting around the tail from the airflow over the wings, but this was cured in production versions.

COMBAT DATA

MAXIMUM SPEED

The P-38 was the first American Army Air Force fighter capable of more than 650 km/h. Its sensational high-altitude performance remained a feature of the type throughout its career, along with its superb climbing and diving ability.

P-38L LIGHTNING	666 km/h (414 m.p.h.)
A6M6 ZERO	557 km/h (346 m.p.h.)
Bf 109G	620 km/h (385 m.p.h.)

SERVICE CEILING

The P-38's twin turbo-charged engines gave it superb high-altitude performance, and at heights over 8000 metres it was one of the best fighters in the world. At medium altitudes, however, the big fighter had less of an advantage, and could get into trouble against more agile German or Japanese machines which could out-turn the P-38L.

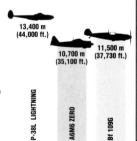

		13,400 m (44,000 ft.)
10,700 m (35,100 ft.)	11,500 m (37,730 ft.)	

P-38L LIGHTNING — A6M6 ZERO — Bf 109G

ARMAMENT

Although on paper the P-38 had lighter armament than most of its opponents, the concentration of guns in the nose allowed it to bring an immense amount of fire to bear on targets at all ranges. Lightnings were known to 'saw Zeros in half' with a long burst of fire.

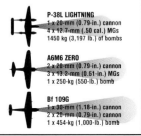

P-38L LIGHTNING
1 x 20-mm (0.79-in.) cannon
4 x 12.7-mm (.50 cal.) MGs
1450 kg (3,197 lb.) of bombs

A6M6 ZERO
2 x 20-mm (0.79-in.) cannon
3 x 13.2-mm (0.51-in.) MGs
1 x 250-kg (550-lb.) bomb

Bf 109G
1 x 30-mm (1.18-in.) cannon
2 x 20-mm (0.79-in.) cannon
1 x 454-kg (1,000-lb.) bomb

The Lightning's prey

■ **KAWANISHI N1K2:** Developed from a floatplane, the N1K2 was one of the most manoeuvrable fighters ever, let down by unreliable engines.

■ **MITSUBISHI A6M ZERO:** The great Japanese fighter was far more agile than the Lightning, but it was considerably slower.

■ **MITSUBISHI G4M:** The Japanese navy's main bomber proved horribly vulnerable to being set ablaze by the P-38's concentrated firepower.

■ **NAKAJIMA Ki-43:** The Japanese army's equivalent of the Zero was regularly shot down by Lightning pilots in the South West Pacific.

■ **NAKAJIMA Ki-84:** This was the best Japanese fighter of the war. Although slower, in competent hands it could sometimes outfly the Lightning.

LOCKHEED

P-80 SHOOTING STAR

● Jet fighter ● European deployment ● Test flying

I n 1944 the US Army Air Force began gunnery trials in Nevada with the Lockheed P-80 Shooting Star; this design promised to revolutionise air warfare. The P-80 was the first fully operational type in the US to have a jet engine – an innovation already familiar to German and British scientists. The US rushed four P-80s to Europe – two each to England and Italy – and they were hours from entering combat when World War II ended.

▲ Proudly wearing
the Lockheed emblem on its nose, the P-80 Shooting Star was equipped with six forward-firing machine-guns, a typical armament fit for fighters of the era.

PHOTO FILE

LOCKHEED P-80 SHOOTING STAR

▼ Graceful lines
Before the addition of wingtip tanks and essential service equipment, the Shooting Star was one of the most elegant aircraft ever produced by Lockheed. Pilots marvelled at the design.

▲ Fighter testing
Known as Lulu Belle, this P-80 was flown against the conventionally powered fighters of the period to explore jet tactics.

▲ Future potential
With large test markings displayed on its fuselage, this particular P-80 undertook a series of developmental flights to try out future jet fighter equipment.

▲ Service entry
Seen high over California's foothills, this P-80A was assigned to the 412th Fighter Group at March Field in late 1945.

◄ Lakebed landings
Early flights were performed from the Muroc range in California, and made use of the many dry lakebeds.

FACTS AND FIGURES

➤ The Shooting Star was designed from the start to be the United States Army Air Force's first operational jet fighter.

➤ One of the first examples of the P-80 was completed in just 143 days.

➤ Early aircraft were given names like The Grey Ghost and Silver Ghost.

➤ Lockheed hoped to deliver 450 Shooting Stars per month during World War II, but this was never accomplished.

➤ Richard Ira Bong, America's highest-scoring ace, was killed testing a P-80.

➤ Many pilots found it hard to adjust to the new demands of jet flying.

PROFILE

Shooting for success

Work on the P-80 began in 1943 when famous engineer Clarence L. ('Kelly') Johnson persuaded his bosses at Lockheed to attempt to build the USAAF's first operational jet fighter in just 180 days. They actually completed the pace-setting first P-80 in 143 days.

The P-80 was a clean design with straight wings and tail surfaces, and a tricycle landing gear. Air intakes positioned on the lower fuselage forward of the wing leading edge fed the British-designed de Havilland H.1B turbojet, which was replaced in production examples by the Allison/General Electric I-40 (J33).

Many pilots with propeller experience took to the jet-powered P-80 with enormous enthusiasm. An ambitious programme progressed toward the goal of getting the Shooting Star into combat. Several P-80s were lost in tragic mishaps, but the aircraft performed well, and the USAAF moved rapidly to finalise the configuration of this fighter and to develop a photo-reconnaissance version. Had World War II lasted weeks longer, it is certain that the P-80 Shooting Star would have done battle with the top fighters developed by the Axis, including Germany's much-vaunted Messerschmitt Me 262.

Above: After completing extensive test work, this Shooting Star was restored by ex-Lockheed employees.

Below: Having just completed another test flight, an early P-80 is seen parked on one of Muroc's dry lakebeds. A major debrief followed each flight.

XP-80 Shooting Star

Type: single-seat jet fighter

Powerplant: one 10.9-kN (2,450-lb.-thrust) de Havilland H.1B Goblin turbojet

Maximum speed: 808 km/h (557 m.p.h.); cruising speed 692 km/h (429 m.p.h.)

Initial climb rate: 914 m/min (3,000 f.p.m.) from sea level

Range: 1609 km (1,000 mi.)

Service ceiling: 12,497 m (41,000 ft.)

Weights: empty 2852 kg (6,274 lb.); maximum take-off 4498 kg (9,896 lb.)

Armament: six 12.7-mm (.50 cal.) nose-mounted machine-guns

Dimensions:
span	11.27 m (36 ft. 11 in.)
length	10.00 m (32 ft. 9 in.)
height	3.12 m (10 ft. 3 in.)
wing area	22.29 m² (240 sq. ft.)

RF-80A SHOOTING STAR

Many early model Shooting Stars were built for, or converted to, the photo-reconnaissance role. This example saw service in Korea, where the aircraft operated with an escort of fighters.

The pilot enjoyed exceptional visibility through a teardrop sliding canopy. The cockpits of reconnaissance versions differed very little from fighter variants. The only additions were camera switches, film counters and blinker lights to replace the K-14 gunsight.

Despite the early success of the Shooting Star, it was quickly overshadowed by more advanced designs from rival manufacturers. The type was retained for second-line duties, in which the Shooting Stars remained for a number of years until fatigue problems caused their withdrawal.

Though the aircraft were initially flown in their peacetime natural colour scheme, some RF-80s adopted olive-drab upper surfaces when they went to war in Korea. Despite this the retention of the large 'buzz' numbers compromised the end result.

US AIR FORCE
485467

FT-467

An enlarged forward section housed the reconnaissance camera suite. Access to the camera bay installation was by way of an upward-hinging nose section. Camera film could be replaced in a few minutes by experienced personnel.

Mounted low on either side of the fuselage were the small intakes. They were prone to ingesting foreign objects when the aircraft operated from semi-prepared runways.

To answer requests from USAF pilots for additional range, wingtip tanks were installed on the Shooting Star. They varied in size, and later models were fitted with additional fuel tanks under the wings.

A red fuselage band was painted on all early Shooting Stars. This denoted the turbine position within the engine. At this point the rear fuselage could be removed to allow maintenance personnel access to the engine.

FIGHTING JETS

BRITISH FIGHTERS: Entering service with the Royal Air Force in late 1944, the Gloster Meteor (pictured above) saw limited use, often on ground attack duties. After the end of World War II, a host of specialised variants were introduced into service, such as night-fighters, target-tugs and tactical photo-reconnaissance models. Widely exported to European and Middle Eastern countries, the Meteor remained in limited service until the late 1970s when it was finally replaced by more modern types. The Meteor had the distinction of being the first jet fighter in RAF service.

GERMAN GENESIS: Widely regarded as the best fighter of World War II, the Messerschmitt Me 262 was introduced into (limited) operational service before its rivals. Allied pilots found the Me 262 had remarkable agility and was able to outperform anything the Americans or British could offer. Hampered by a dwindling fuel supply, the Germans initially used the aircraft as a light bomber before pilots saw the full potential of the fighter. After the end of hostilities, Allied pilots flight-tested the aircraft and were thoroughly impressed. It had only limited post-war service, but the aircraft's design influenced fighter design for years to come. Other variants constructed were two-seat trainers, night-fighters, and precision attack bombers which were equipped with a glazed nose-section for an additional crew member.

Lockheed's adaptable lady

T-33 SHOOTING STAR: Developed into a highly successful trainer, the T-33 is operated by a number of countries. It provides the first experience of jet flight for many pilots.

XF-90: Offered to the USAF as a potential long-range bomber escort, the XF-90 was not successful and eventually lost out to the two-seat McDonnell F-101 Voodoo.

F-94C STARFIRE: A specialised variant of the T-33 was developed to intercept intruders at night. Fitted with an improved radar, the aircraft saw much service with the USAF.

LOCKHEED

PV-1 VENTURA/PV-2 HARPOON

● Light bomber/maritime patroller ● Built to an RAF requirement

Although designed to an RAF requirement for a light bomber, the Ventura was found to be more suitable for maritime patrol duties. When the US Navy took over ASW duties in spring 1942, it ordered the PV-1.

Its initial sorties as a light bomber with the RAF were not a success, but in the maritime role the Ventura proved invaluable. Impressed by this performance, the US Navy adopted the type as the PV-1 for Pacific service. A major redesign to increase range and load-carrying ability resulted in the PV-2 Harpoon. After war service, surplus aircraft flew with several air forces, while others were converted to crop sprayers and executive transports.

LOCKHEED PV-1 VENTURA/PV-2 HARPOON

◀ RAF Ventura Mk II
The RAF took delivery of 394 Ventura light bombers, which entered service in 1942. By 1943 all were with Coastal Command units.

▼ Post-war conversions
Harpoons were among a number of wartime aircraft converted into executive transports after 1945.

▼ North Atlantic livery
This all-white colour scheme was usually used over the North Atlantic and made the black rubber de-icer boots very prominent. The underwing tanks carried 587 litres (150 gal.) each and bomb-bay tanks increased range further.

▼ Improved war load
Successive versions of the Ventura carried between 1134 kg (2,495 lb.) and 1362 kg (2,994 lb.) of weapons. The Harpoon increased this to 1816 kg (3,990 lb.) internally, with an extra 454 kg (1,000 lb.) under each wing.

▼ Post-war Reserve PV-2
This Harpoon, seen in post-war markings, has had its undernose 12.7-mm (.50 cal.) guns removed.

FACTS AND FIGURES

➤ The first Marine Corps night-fighter unit, VMF(N)-531, scored its first kill with a radar-equipped PV-1 in November 1943.

➤ A failure as an RAF bomber, all Venturas went to Coastal Command in 1943.

➤ PV-2 Harpoons saw limited war service, being phased out by the US Navy in 1948.

➤ On Christmas Eve 1943, a No. 1 Squadron, RNZAF, Ventura crew shot down three Japanese 'Zero' fighters.

➤ Venturas built on British contract and taken over by the US Navy were PV-3s.

➤ US Marine Corps PV-1 night-fighters had six forward-firing guns and British AI radar.

Lodestars in Allied uniforms

Pleased with the Hudson, the British Air Ministry was interested in Lockheed's proposal to modify the Lodestar in a similar way, as a replacement for both the Hudson (in the maritime reconnaissance role) and the Bristol Blenheim light/medium bomber.

The Ventura, as it was to be known, was larger than the Hudson, with more powerful engines, improved armament and a greater load-carrying capability. Large numbers went to the RAF, RAAF, RNZAF and SAAF. A few were retained by the USAAF for over-water patrols as B-34 and B-37 Lexingtons.

From 1942 the US Navy took over all ASW work from the army and obtained 1600 PV-1s. The improved PV-2 Harpoon followed, with major design changes to optimise it for the maritime role.

War surplus PV-1s and -2s were used after the war for a variety of roles. Some have been restored by warbird enthusiasts.

The Harpoon was a major redesign of the Ventura to optimise it for maritime patrol. It had longer span wings to improve take-off performance with a full fuel load and enlarged vertical tail surfaces.

Initial PV-2 operations revealed a serious wing wrinkling problem. Attempts to solve this by reducing the span failed and a complete wing redesign was required, which slowed down production.

The Harpoon differed from the Ventura in almost every detail except for small sections of the fuselage, inboard wing ribs and engine cowlings.

PV-2 HARPOON

This PV-2 wears the markings of US Navy Patrol Bomber Squadron VPB-142 based in the Marianas Islands in 1945. Wartime deliveries to Allied air arms included five to the Brazilian air force and four to the RNZAF.

As a maritime patrol bomber the PV-2 had a crew of four or five, comprising a pilot, navigator/bomb aimer, radio operator/gunner and turret gunner. When operated solely as a patrol aircraft a fifth crewmember was carried.

This PV-2 carried eight 127-mm high-velocity aerial rockets (HVAR) below the wings as well as two 587-litre (150-gal.) drop-tanks. An internal bomb-bay held up to 1816 kg (3,990 lb.) of bombs.

Armament consisted of eight 12.7-mm (.50 cal.) machine-guns, including three in an undernose pack, two above the nose, two in a dorsal turret and one in the ventral position.

Harpoons (and most Venturas) were fitted with two Pratt & Whitney R-2800 Double Wasps, each rated at 1491 kW (2,000 hp.). These engines were also fitted to the Vought F4U and Douglas A-26.

PV-1 Ventura

Type: twin-engined maritime patrol/bomber

Powerplant: two 1491-kW (2,000-hp.) Pratt & Whitney R-2800-31 Double Wasp radial engines

Maximum speed: 518 km/h (321 m.p.h.) at 4205 m (13,800 ft.)

Maximum range: 2670 km (1,650 mi.)

Service ceiling: 8015 m (26,300 ft.)

Weights: empty 9161 kg (20,154 lb.); maximum take-off 15,422 kg (33,924 lb.)

Armament: two 12.7-mm (.50 cal.) machine-guns each in nose and dorsal turret, two 7.62-mm (.30 cal.) machine-guns in ventral position, plus six 227-kg (500-lb.) bombs or one torpedo in bomb-bay and up to two 454-kg (1,000-lb.) bombs under the wings

Dimensions:

span	19.96 m	(65 ft. 6 in.)
length	15.77 m	(51 ft. 8 in.)
height	3.63 m	(11 ft. 10 in.)
wing area	63.73 m²	(686 sq. ft.)

COMBAT DATA

MAXIMUM SPEED

Based on the civil Lodestar, the Ventura was a relatively fast warplane, even with a typical weapon load aboard. The G4M 'Betty' first flew in 1939 and suffered at the hands of Allied fighters. Both the 'Betty' and Warwick were purpose-designed military aircraft.

PV-1 VENTURA	518 km/h (321 m.p.h.)
G4M2 'BETTY'	438 km/h (272 m.p.h.)
WARWICK B.Mk II	483 km/h (300 m.p.h.)

MAXIMUM RANGE

Although its speed was good, the range of the PV-1 Ventura could not match that of the 'Betty' naval bomber. To boost its range the Ventura could carry internal bomb-bay tanks and external drop-tanks under the wings. Because they were larger aircraft, the 'Betty' and Warwick had greater internal capacities.

PV-1 VENTURA 2670 km (1,650 mi.)

WARWICK B.Mk II 4575 km (2,837 mi.)

G4M2 'BETTY' 6059 km (3,756 mi.)

INTERNAL BOMBLOAD

Although it was a bigger aircraft than the PV-1, the G4M had a limited load capacity. The Warwick carried over two and a half tonnes of bombs and was intended as a replacement for the Wellington in the maritime reconnaissance role.

PV-1 VENTURA 1362 kg (2,994 lb.)

G4M2 'BETTY' 1000 kg (2,200 lb.)

WARWICK B.Mk II 2608 kg (5,738 lb.)

Disaster over Amsterdam

1 **OPERATION 'RAMROD 16':** On 3 May 1943 twelve Venturas of No. 487 Squadron, a New Zealand-manned unit, set off on a daylight raid on Amsterdam. At 4.43 p.m. Squadron Leader Leonard Trent led his squadron skywards towards Amsterdam.

2 **GERMAN WOLFPACK:** Unknown to the Ventura force, two crack Luftwaffe fighter units were alerted to the raid. The Venturas lumbered into the trap and most were ripped to shreds by the 70 enemy fighters.

3 **LONE SURVIVOR:** Trent continued the bomb run with five remaining Venturas. Four of these were shot down, but Trent managed to release his bombs over the target before being shot down himself. He was awarded the Victoria Cross for his bravery.

LOCKHEED

HUDSON

● Maritime patrol ● Anti-submarine ● Light bomber transport

One of the few combat aircraft to have been developed from a civil transport, the Lockheed Hudson maritime patrol bomber (and navigator trainer) owes its basic design to the Lockheed Model 14 Super Electra of the late 1930s. The Hudson was a smooth-handling and popular aircraft which never quite had the performance needed in warfare. Nevertheless, it made a fine contribution to the Allies' war effort.

▲ Converted airliners often made rather indifferent warplanes, but the Hudson was an immediate success. Orders for it from Britain made Lockheed a big name in America's aircraft industry.

LOCKHEED HUDSON

▼ Rockets and radar
For anti-submarine patrol work, the Hudson was fitted with eight rockets and simple radar.

▲ Airliner lines
The Hudson's airliner heritage made it a good warplane. The capacious but sleek fuselage gave the aircraft long range and high speed, and the broad wings made it very stable in flight.

▲ Lifeboat carrier
Hudsons also saved lives. This aircraft from No. 123 Squadron, Royal Canadian Air Force, carried a large lifeboat under the fuselage, which could be dropped to survivors at the scene of a disaster.

▲ American patrol
This immaculate Hudson, with the pre-1942 American markings and British camouflage, was one of the first A-29s repossessed by America.

◀ Hudson down
The crew walked away from this mishap in a Hudson Mk VI, which has a radio direction-finding loop aerial.

FACTS AND FIGURES

➤ A Hudson directed British naval forces to the German prison ship *Altmark* in February 1940.

➤ The prototype for the Hudson made its maiden flight on 10 December 1938.

➤ A single Hudson was used by the Sperry Gyroscope Company as a test aircraft.

➤ No. 280 Squadron, RAF, was the first to use Hudsons to drop airborne lifeboats over the North Sea in 1943.

➤ Some Hudsons were based in Manaos, Brazil, to patrol the South Atlantic.

➤ A total of 2941 Hudsons had been built when production ended in May 1943.

PROFILE

Airliner turned patrol bomber

Based on the Super Electra civil transport, the Hudson was the first American-built aircraft to fly with the Royal Air Force during World War II. The airframe was instantly recognisable as a modified Electra, with more powerful engines, gun armament and internal bomb-bay. This bomber was rushed into production to meet Britain's requirement for a maritime patrol aircraft and navigation trainer. Search-and-rescue Hudsons were also built, with a lifeboat stored under the fuselage.

After its early success in British use, the Hudson was employed by the US Army Air Forces in A-28 and A-29 attack variants, and as the AT-18 advanced trainer. The US Navy adopted the Hudson as a patrol bomber, and called it the PBO.

US Navy Hudsons sank two U-boats on 15 March 1942. This was the first of several such successes in combat. An A-29 sank the German submarine U-701 on 7 July 1942.

Hudsons were used by many Allied air forces, including the Soviet Union and South Africa. The aircraft continued to serve faithfully in support roles up until the end of the war.

Above: This highly polished Hudson is an AT-18 gunnery trainer. These aircraft allowed trainee gunners to fire shots realistically from the turrets in peacetime conditions.

Right: In US Army Air Force service, the A-28 and A-29 series was never officially known as the Hudson, reflecting the fact that the aircraft was first and foremost designed to serve the RAF.

Hudson Mk I

Type: maritime patrol-bomber

Powerplant: two 820-kW (1,100-hp.) Wright GR-1820-G-102A radial piston engines

Maximum speed: 396 km/h (245 m.p.h.) at 1980 m (6,500 ft.)

Range: 3154 km (1,955 mi.)

Service ceiling: 7620 m (25,000 ft.)

Weights: empty 5275 kg (11,605 lb.); maximum take-off 7938 kg (17,464 lb.)

Armament: two 7.62-mm (.30 cal.) forward-firing machine-guns and two similar weapons in a dorsal turret, plus up to 635 kg (1,400 lb.) of bombs or depth charges in internal bomb-bay

Dimensions:
span	19.96 m (65 ft.)
length	13.51 m (44 ft.)
height	3.61 m (12 ft.)
wing area	51.19 m² (551 sq. ft.)

HUDSON MK V

This Lockheed Hudson Mk V served with No. 48 Squadron of the Royal Air Force Coastal Command, based at Stornoway in the Outer Hebrides during 1941. Its main tasks were patrol and air-sea rescue.

The upper surface of the fuselage contained a Perspex astrodome for visual observation, a large aerial mast with cables to the horizontal tailfin and a bullet-shaped fairing for the D/F loop antenna.

The Hudson's Boulton Paul dorsal turret provided good visibility and two hard-hitting 7.62-mm (.30 cal.) machine-guns.

The RAF's Hudson had provision for two forward-firing fixed machine-guns in the upper fuselage, ahead of the pilot.

Standard accommodation was for a crew of four: pilot, navigator, bomb-aimer and radio operator.

The Hudson's fuselage was very similar to the Super Electra airliner it was developed from. The lower fuselage, however, contained a large bomb-bay with provision for up to 635 kg (1,400 lb.) of offensive weapons or rescue life-rafts.

The large internal space could be converted into a troop transport or for VIP work.

The tail unit featured twin vertical fins and rudders, enabling the gunner (generally the radio operator) to have an almost completely clear field of vision and the ability to engage fighters flying behind him.

Coastal Command patrollers

■ **BRISTOL BEAUFORT:** Coastal Command's standard torpedo-bomber from 1940 to 1943, the prototype first flew in 1938.

■ **ARMSTRONG WHITWORTH WHITLEY:** Outmoded as bombers, Whitleys were the first to carry ASV.Mk II radar in Coastal Command.

■ **CONSOLIDATED LIBERATOR:** Late-model B-24s were used as VLR (very-long-range) patrol aircraft hunting for German U-boats.

■ **VICKERS WARWICK:** An enlarged variant of the famous Wellington, in the anti-submarine role the Warwick was just too late for war service.

COMBAT DATA

MAXIMUM SPEED

Flying-boats, carrying the extra weight of a strong hull, tend to have a lower top speed than equivalent landplanes. The Hudson design was based on that of a small airliner and had a fairly good speed compared to its contemporaries.

HUDSON Mk IIIA	407 km/h (252 m.p.h.)
PBY-5A CATALINA	288 km/h (179 m.p.h.)
BV 138C-1	275 km/h (170 m.p.h.)

RANGE

To take advantage of the ability to land on water, flying-boats tend to have a good range performance. This also allows longer periods on patrol. Both the Catalina and BV 138 were renowned for range, especially compared to the Hudson.

HUDSON Mk IIIA 2494 km (1,546 mi.)

BV 138C-1 5000 km (3,100 mi.)

PBY-5A CATALINA 4096 km (2,540 mi.)

BOMBLOAD

In the anti-submarine role the Catalina was a great threat to the U-boat because of its armament capacity. For its size the Hudson was also well-equipped, hauling a similar load to the BV 138.

HUDSON Mk IIIA 726 kg (1,600 lb.)

PBY-5A CATALINA 1814 kg (3,990 lb.)

BV 138C-1 300 kg (660 lb.)

MACCHI

MC.200 SAETTA

● Monoplane fighter ● Entered service 1939 ● Co-belligerent service

As holder of the world speed, height and distance records in the late 1930s, the Regia Aeronautica (Italian air force) was perhaps blind to the fact that its service aircraft were lagging behind in terms of performance. During the Spanish Civil War, the success of Italian fighter and bomber types reinforced the air force's view of their aircraft. Consequently, the Macchi MC.200 was obsolete as soon as it entered service in 1939.

▲ *Best known for its exploits in North Africa, the MC.200 was well-suited to desert operations, with its structural strength and short take-off run. Hurricanes and P-40s were its opponents.*

MACCHI MC.200 SAETTA

▲ **Eastern Front**
From August 1941 until the spring of 1942, 51 Italian MC.200s of 22º Gruppo and later 21º Gruppo operated over Russia, mainly on air-to-ground sorties.

▲ **Defending Rome, 1940**
This early production MC.200 of 371ª Squadriglia, 22º Gruppo, was based at Campino near Rome.

▼ **Allied service**
After the Italian surrender, the Aeronautica Cobelligerante del Sud (Southern Co-belligerent Air Force) operated around 23 MC.200s.

▲ **Pre-war markings**
Green, white and red stripes on this Saetta's tail were typical of the markings carried by the aircraft prior to Italy joining the fighting in 1940.

Off the production line ▶
This aircraft was among the last batch of MC.200s built by Macchi. The fully enclosed cockpit was a feature of only the earliest production examples; Regia Aeronautica pilots preferred the traditional open cockpit to which they were accustomed.

FACTS AND FIGURES

➤ The only Macchi MC.200s operated by the Allies were used as trainers by the co-belligerent air force.

➤ Eastern Front MC.200s flew over 6300 sorties; 88 Soviet aircraft were downed.

➤ Denmark ordered 12 MC.200s, but they were cancelled after the German invasion.

➤ Macchi developed a version with a new fuselage and engine, the MC.201, but it did not proceed beyond one prototype.

➤ MC.200 fighter-bombers fitted with bomb shackles were designated MC.200CBs.

➤ During raids on Malta in 1940, MC.200s escorted Luftwaffe Ju 87 dive-bombers.

PROFILE

Italy's under-powered Lightning

Below: This Regia Aeronautica Saetta is in the company of a tri-motored Italian bomber and a Romanian-built IAR.80 monoplane fighter. MC.200s saw service on the Eastern Front where they scored a number of victories.

Known as the Saetta (Lightning), the MC.200 flew in prototype form for the first time on 24 December 1937. A cantilever, low-wing monoplane of all-metal construction (apart from fabric-covered control surfaces), the Macchi fighter had a retractable tail wheel and an enclosed cockpit. Pilots liked its light controls and all-round manoeuvrability. The design's main weak point was its 649-kW (870-hp.) Fiat A.74 RC.38 radial engine, which bestowed a top speed of just 502 km/h (312 m.p.h.) at 4500 m (14,800 ft.).

Fighter development in the late 1930s had moved on rapidly, resulting in aircraft like the Bf 109 and Spitfire. They were powered by in-line, liquid-cooled engines that offered more power and greater streamlining, and thus much higher speeds.

The MC.200's armament of two machine-guns was also inadequate – even when it was doubled to four in later aircraft.

Entering service in October 1939, Saettas numbered 150 when Italy entered World War II in June 1940. Their first combat

Above: MC.200AS was the designation of aircraft fitted with dust filters for North African service.

came in the autumn, when Lightnings escorted bombers attacking Malta. Action over Greece and Yugoslavia followed; a few served on the Eastern Front during 1941–42. However, it was in the deserts of North Africa that the type saw the most use.

MC.200 Saetta

Type: single-seat fighter/fighter-bomber

Powerplant: one 649-kW (870-hp.) Fiat A.74 RC.38 radial piston engine

Maximum speed: 502 km/h (312 m.p.h.) at 4500 m (14,800 ft.)

Range: 870 km (541 m.p.h.) with auxiliary fuel

Service ceiling: 8900 m (29,200 ft.)

Weights: empty 1895 kg (4,178 lb.); maximum take-off 2590 kg (5,710 lb.)

Armament: two fuselage-mounted Breda-SAFAT 12.7-mm (.50 cal.) machine-guns (and two wing-mounted Breda-SAFAT 7.7-mm (.303 cal.) machine-guns on later aircraft), plus up to 294 kg (648 lb.) of bombs on field-modified aircraft

Dimensions:
span	10.58 m	(34 ft. 9 in.)
length	8.19 m	(26 ft. 10 in.)
height	3.50 m	(11 ft. 6 in.)
wing area	16.80 m²	(181 sq. ft.)

MC.200 SAETTA

This aircraft was among those of 90ª Squadriglia, 10º Gruppo, 4º Stormo at Crotone, Sicily in 1941. The squadron's emblem, a red elephant, was painted below the cockpit.

Regia Aeronautica pilots disliked the MC.200's original enclosed cockpit. Macchi redesigned the canopy, this semi-enclosed design being the result. Still unimpressed, some pilots discarded the side panels to improve visibility.

4º Stormo's famous 'Cavallino Rampante' emblem was applied to their aircraft on a white fuselage band. Regia Aeronautica aircraft were among the most colourfully adorned of the war.

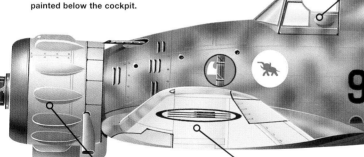

Given Macchi's success with in-line engines in its Schneider Trophy-winning aircraft, the choice of a radial design for its new generation of fighters was surprising. Fiat's 14-cylinder A.74 radial powered the MC.200, as it did the Fiat CR.42 biplane fighter and G.50 monoplane.

Initially, the MC.200 was fitted with just two 12.7-mm (.50 cal.) Breda-SAFAT machine-guns mounted above and behind the engine. This armament fit was later doubled to four, with the addition of a gun in each wing, though the aircraft was still seriously under-armed by the standards of the day.

The MC.200's semi-monocoque fuselage structure and wings were all-metal save for fabric-covered control surfaces. Field modifications included the fitting of underwing hardpoints for two 147-kg (325-lb.) bombs or fuel tanks. Ground strafing and offensive sweeps became major roles for the Saetta as it became increasingly vulnerable in the fighter role.

ACTION DATA

MAXIMUM SPEED

Faster than its contemporary, the Fiat G.50, the Macchi 200 was nevertheless still on the slow side and could not match the performance of the superb Spitfire or Messerschmitt Bf 109.

MC.200	502 km/h (312 m.p.h.)
KITTYHAWK Mk IV	552 km/h (343 m.p.h.)
G.50	472 km/h (293 m.p.h.)

POWER

A major problem with the Saetta was its lack of power. Producing just 649 kW, the Fiat A74 hardly made the MC.200 a super-fighter, and it proved extremely vulnerable to attack. Like the Kittyhawk and the G.50, it was more suitable as a fighter-bomber.

MC.200	KITTYHAWK Mk IV	G.50
649 kW (870 hp.)	895 kW (1,200 hp.)	626 kW (840 hp.)

ARMAMENT

None of these aircraft was known for its hard-hitting armament, though later versions of the Kittyhawk had six guns. A lack of heavy armament was yet another drawback of the Saetta, and battle experience showed that both it and the G.50 were obsolete.

MC.200	2 x 12.7-mm (.50 cal.) machine-guns / 2 x 7.7-mm (.303 cal.) machine-guns
KITTYHAWK Mk IV	6 x 12.7-mm (.50 cal.) machine-guns / 680-kg (1,5000 lb.) bombload
G.50	2 x 12.7-mm (.50 cal.) machine-guns

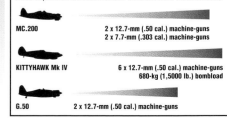

Fighters in North Africa

■ **CURTISS TOMAHAWK:** Members of the American P-40 family served the RAF in large numbers in North Africa. No. 112 Squadron became famous for its sharkmouth markings.

■ **FIAT G.50:** Powered by the same Fiat radial as the MC.200 – and bearing a strong resemblance to that aircraft – the G.50 served as a fighter-bomber in the North African campaign.

■ **HAWKER HURRICANE:** Gradually outmoded as interceptors, Hurricanes became bombers and 'tank-busters'. For the latter role Mk IVs were fitted with 40-mm (1.57-in.) cannon.

■ **MACCHI MC.202 FOLGORE:** The best fighter to serve with the Regia Aeronautica in large numbers during World War II, the Folgore (Thunderbolt) entered service in Libya in 1941.

MACCHI

M.C.202 AND M.C.205V

● Italy's finest dogfighter ● Tactical fighter-bomber

▲ Before the war, Macchi produced some of the world's fastest record breakers, and that experience was put to good use in the company's fine series of wartime fighters.

The Macchi M.C.202 Folgore (Thunderbolt) was among the most beautiful fighters to fly with wartime Axis forces, reflecting the aerodynamic flair of designer Mario Castoldi – the genius behind most Macchi warplanes. Building upon the M.C.200 Saetta (Lightning) but offering cleaner lines and more power, the M.C.202 was rushed into production and fought from 1941 onwards. To many, this was the best Italian fighter of the war.

MACCHI **M.C.202** AND **M.C.205V**

▼ Nose down
A little too hard on the brakes on a desert airstrip, and the result was a broken propeller.

▲ Alfa power
The Alfa Romeo RA.1000 was one of the finest aero engines which Italy built. Many other Italian fighters were underpowered.

◄ Sleek lines
Italian fighters were, like the early Soviet MiG fighters, reliant on light weight and clean lines. Fitted with neat inline engines for their speed, they emphasised agility at the expense of armament.

Smashed Veltro ►
This M.C.205V crashed in 1986, after being lovingly restored. Examples of the aircraft are now rare, as few survived the war.

▲ Inside
The M.C.202 had a small cockpit with modern, well laid out instruments and controls.

FACTS AND FIGURES

➤ The Folgore traces its heritage in part to the Macchi floatplanes that competed in the Schneider Trophy Races.

➤ The first flight of a Folgore took place on 10 August 1940.

➤ About 1500 M.C.202s were built, including 393 built by Macchi.

➤ Although agile, the M.C.202 was slower than the Bf 109 and the Spitfire.

➤ A specialised fighter-bomber version, the M.C.202CB, carried two 320-kg (700-lb.) bombs.

➤ A restored Macchi M.C.202 is displayed in the US National Air & Space Museum.

PROFILE

Italy's finest wartime fighter

Following Italy's military campaigns in East Africa, the Regia Aeronautica re-equipped with the Saetta (recognised by its radial engine) and later the M.C.202 Folgore and M.C.205V Veltro (Greyhound). Of the trio, the Folgore was the most pleasing to the eye. It introduced a new fuselage and improved engine but retained the tail unit, landing gear and similar wings to the Saetta.

Manufactured by Macchi, Breda and SAI-Ambrosini alongside the Saetta, the graceful Folgore was propelled by a German Daimler-Benz DB 601A-1 engine until a licence-built Alfa Romeo version became available. It had a dramatically better performance than its Saetta ancestor, but Italy was under bombardment and its aero industry could not produce enough engines. MC.202 Folgores began

fighting in Libya in November 1941 and on the Eastern Front in September 1942. Italian pilots regarded the Folgore as an excellent combat aircraft, and many fought superbly in it. It could easily outfly Hurricanes and P-40s in the desert, and was a match for the famous Spitfire.

The M.C.205 Veltro was the ultimate Macchi fighter. With great agility, adequate speed and, in its final version at least, a powerful cannon armament, the Castoldi design team had produced a fighter to match the best produced in Britain, Germany or America.

M.C.202 Folgore

Type: single-seat fighter/fighter-bomber

Powerplant: one 876-kW (1,175-hp.) Alfa Romeo RA.1000 RC 41-I Monsone inverted V-12 piston engine (licence-built Daimler-Benz DB 601)

Maximum speed: 596 km/h (370 m.p.h.) at 4570 m (15,000 ft.)

Range: 765 km (272 mi.)

Service ceiling: 11,500 m (37,700 ft.)

Weights: empty 2350 kg (5,170 lb.); loaded 3010 kg (6,620 lb.)

Armament: two 12.7-mm (.50 cal.) machine-guns in engine cowling

Dimensions:
span	10.58 m	(34 ft. 8 in.)
length	8.85 m	(63 ft. 9 in.)
height	3.04 m	(10 ft.)
wing area	16.80 m²	(181 sq. ft.)

The tail unit was a metal monocoque unit with fabric-covered moving control surfaces. The tailwheel was retractable.

The Macchi design showed its racing heritage with a very thin wing. Cannon armament had to be fitted beneath later M.C.202s' wings rather than in them.

M.C.202

This MC.202 Folgore served with 22° Gruppo, 369° Squadriglia, based at Capodichino, Naples. The sparrow badge on the white band was the wing emblem, and '369' was the number of the squadron.

Its long nose meant that the M.C.202 was difficult to taxi on the ground, even though it was stunning in the air.

The fuselage and wing were of all-metal construction, with fabric covering for the moveable control surfaces.

A large sheet of armour protected the pilot – not always a feature of Italian fighters.

The secret of the M.C.202's success was in its engine, the German DB 601, built under licence as the Alfa RA.1000. The engine radiator was located underneath the engine, which drove a three-bladed variable-pitch airscrew.

The wing featured interconnected flaps and slats. When the pilot selected flap down, the ailerons also lowered, giving a more efficient wing at low airspeeds. The flaps were also hydraulically operated.

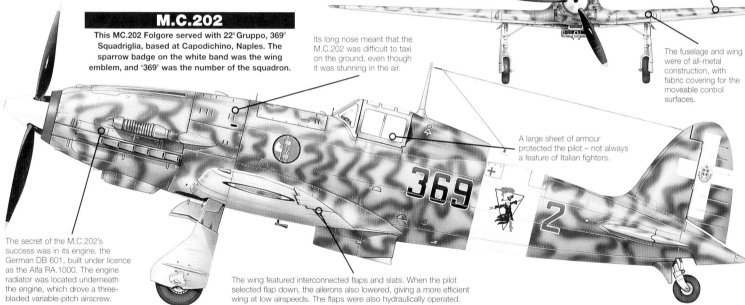

COMBAT DATA

MAXIMUM SPEED

Although the Macchi was faster than previous Italian fighters, it could not quite match the speeds possible in the Allied fighters which it faced in North Africa. But the difference was marginal, and its fine handling meant that it was better than a P-40 and a match for the Spitfire.

M.C.202 FOLGORE	595 km/h
SPITFIRE Mk V	602 km/h
P-40N WARHAWK	609 km/h

SERVICE CEILING

The Macchi could climb fairly high, just being able to outperform the standard Spitfire, and easily outstripping those assigned to the desert campaign with 'low-blown' engines. On paper the P-40 could fly even higher, but this was not its best altitude, and it was sluggish and difficult to manoeuvre.

M.C.202 FOLGORE 11,500 m (37,700 ft.)	SPITFIRE Mk V 11,300 m (37,000 ft.)	P-40N WARHAWK 11,600 m (38,000 ft.)

ARMAMENT

Armament was a major weakness in Italian fighters. The M.C.202 was originally designed with only two guns at a time when British fighters were carrying eight and German fighters were armed with cannon. Later examples of the Macchi fighter were fitted with cannon under the wings, but increased drag meant lower performance.

M.C.202 FOLGORE 2 x 12.7-mm (.50 cal.) MGs, 2 x 7.7-mm (.303 cal.) MGs

SPITFIRE Mk V 2x 20-mm (0.79-in.) cannon, 4 x 7.7-mm (.303 cal.) MGs

P-40N WARHAWK 6 x 12.7-mm (.50 cal.) MGs

Macchi fighter development

■ **M.C.200 SAETTA:** Light and extremely agile, the radial-engined M.C.202 with which Italy began the war was at a disadvantage when confronting British fighters like the Spitfire.

■ **M.C.202 FOLGORE:** Fitting a Daimler-Benz DB 601 engine into a Saetta airframe transformed the Macchi fighter into a much more capable machine, which fought with distinction in Africa.

■ **M.C.205 VELTRO:** The powerful DB 605 kept Macchi fighters competitive, but poor industrial performance meant that only 262 Veltros were produced before the Italian armistice.

MARTIN

167 MARYLAND/187 BALTIMORE

● Desert operations ● Export only ● Reconnaissance

I n the late 1930s the Glenn L. Martin Company created the Maryland for the US Army (later selling it to France) and the Baltimore for Britain's RAF. Both were twin-engined light bombers with a modest bombload, defensive armament and performance that compared poorly with modern fighters like the Supermarine Spitfire and the Messerschmitt Bf 109. Although they were solidly designed aircraft, they were not advanced enough for World War II.

▲ All 400 Baltimores initially ordered by the RAF were sent to Egypt to help the Allied effort against Rommel's 1942 offensive. Escorted by Curtiss Kittyhawks, they excelled in the Battle of El Alamein.

PHOTO FILE

MARTIN 167 MARYLAND/187 BALTIMORE

▲ Maryland prototype
The prototype first flew on 13 March 1939 and was given the designation XA-22. It lost out to the Douglas A-20 in the US Army competition.

▲ Narrow fuselage
The Baltimore's narrow fuselage prevented the crew from moving about and stretching on long trips.

British Marylands ▶
Both the RAF and Royal Navy operated Marylands in the long-range reconnaissance role.

◀ Advancing through Italy
An RAF Baltimore Mk III drops its load over the railway station and sidings at Sulmona in northern Italy. British and South African Baltimores fought throughout the Italian campaign.

Turkish delight ▶
A number of Baltimores were supplied to Turkey during the later stages of World War II under the Lend-Lease arrangement. This is an ex-RAF aircraft.

FACTS AND FIGURES

➤ Martin built 496 Maryland bombers, all but one for France; many of these were transferred to the RAF and Royal Navy.

➤ The Maryland was produced at what was the USA's largest aircraft factory in 1939.

➤ More than 20 Baltimores were lost during delivery by sea to Great Britain.

➤ In all, 1,575 Baltimores were built – more than any Martin aircraft except for the B-26 Marauder (5266).

➤ The Baltimore cost $120,000, compared with $78,000 for a B-26 Marauder.

➤ After the war a Baltimore was used by the US Navy to test experimental airfoils.

PROFILE

Distinguished desert bomber

The Maryland was designed by Martin engineer James S. McDonnell, who later gave his name to the McDonnell Douglas Corporation. It was tested by the US Army as the XA-22 and performed better than attack bombers put forward by other manufacturers. The Army withheld a production contract, however, and the Maryland was exported instead to France. The first Marylands left the factory on 2 September 1939, the day before France and Britain declared war on Germany. They had little impact on the conflict, however.

The Maryland led to the Baltimore, which was known by the US Army as the A-30. Built to satisfy British requirements, the Baltimore was a somewhat more formidable attack bomber that was used extensively in North African fighting at El Alamein in June 1942. The Baltimore also achieved moderate success in Italy later in the war.

The last Baltimores served with the RAF in Kenya, performing aerial mapping and locust control duties until 1948.

Above: Ordered before the prototype had even flown, France received 140 Marylands. A number of them served with the Free French forces until 1943.

Right: No. 13 Squadron re-equipped with the Baltimore in December 1943, and spent the next 10 months on day and night operations in northern Italy.

Baltimore Mk IV

Type: four-seat light bomber (Martin 187 Baltimore)

Powerplant: two 1238-kW (1,660-hp.) Wright R-2600-19 Cyclone 14 radial piston engines

Maximum speed: 491 km/h (304 m.p.h.) at 3505 m (11,500 ft.)

Range: 1741 km (1,080 mi.)

Service ceiling: 7100 m (23,300 ft.)

Weights: empty 7013 kg (15,429 lb.); maximum take-off 10,251 kg (22,550 lb.)

Armament: four 7.7-mm (.303 cal.) wing-mounted machine-guns, two or four similar guns in ventral position and provision for four 7.62-mm (.30 cal.) machine-guns in fixed, rear-firing position, plus a bombload of up to 907 kg (2,000 lb.)

Dimensions:
span	18.69 m (61 ft. 4 in.)
length	14.78 m (48 ft. 6 in.)
height	5.41 m (17 ft. 9 in.)
wing area	50.03 m² (538 sq. ft.)

BALTIMORE MK V

This example flew with No. 232 Wing, comprising Nos 55 and 223 Squadrons, of the North-west African Tactical Air Force in the Italian campaign during 1944.

With the narrow fuselage, communication between crewmembers was difficult. If the pilot was injured it was almost impossible for anyone else to reach the controls.

Early versions of the Baltimore had only poor protection from the mid-upper gun position. This made the aircraft extremely vulnerable to attacks from above and behind. The problem was solved in the Mk III with the introduction of a Boulton-Paul hydraulically-operated turret containing four Browning 7.7-mm (.303 cal.) machine-guns.

With a distinctive curved rudder and a low-mounted tailplane, the Baltimore had responsive controls which were necessary for a single pilot on long-range operations.

The rear fuselage was virtually a boom carrying the tail unit. The Baltimore featured a much deeper front fuselage than the Maryland.

Originally powered by two Wright R-2600-19 engines, the more powerful Mk V was fitted with two 1268-kW (1,700-hp.) R-2600-29 radials. These improved speed and climb performance.

Up to 907 kg (2,000 lb.) of bombs could be carried in the Baltimore's bomb-bay. The aircraft could bomb very accurately and on some occasions dropped bombs from more than 3000 m (12,000 ft.) on targets situated only 700 m (2,300 ft.) from Allied troops.

Much of the Baltimore's design was based on its predecessor, the Maryland. Its all-metal wing was practically identical and was similarly mounted in the low-mid position.

All Baltimores delivered to the RAF served in the Mediterranean theatre and were painted in a brown/sand desert camouflage scheme.

COMBAT DATA

CRUISING SPEED

Although the Baltimore had more powerful engines than the Maryland, they had similar top speeds. The Maryland actually cruised faster than the Baltimore, thanks to its more aerodynamically streamlined shape. Both were slower than the Boston, however.

BALTIMORE Mk IV	362 km/h (224 m.p.h.)
MARYLAND Mk I	399 km/h (247 m.p.h.)
BOSTON Mk III	402 km/h (249 m.p.h.)

POWER

The Boston and Baltimore had a distinct power advantage over the Maryland. This allowed them to carry more defensive armament and gave them a better rate of climb.

BALTIMORE Mk IV	MARYLAND Mk I	BOSTON Mk III
2476 kW (3,320 hp.)	1566 kW (2,100 hp.)	2386 kW (3,200 hp.)

ARMAMENT

Later marks of the Baltimore had heavy defensive armament and could put up a stubborn defence against enemy fighters. The Maryland had poor defence against attack from behind. All three types carried a similar bombload.

BALTIMORE Mk IV 8 x 7.7-mm (.303 cal.) machine-guns 4 x 7.62-mm (.30 cal.) machine-guns, 907-kg (2,000-lb.) bombload

MARYLAND Mk I 4 x 7.62-mm (.30 cal.) machine-guns 2 x 7.7-mm (.303 cal.) machine-guns, 907-kg (2,000-lb.) bombload

BOSTON Mk III 7 x 7.7-mm (.303 cal.) machine-guns 4 x 20-mm (0.79-in.) cannon, 907-kg (2,000-lb.) bombload

RAF Lend-Lease bombers

■ BOEING FORTRESS: Of 125 Lend-Lease Fortresses delivered to the RAF, 19 were Mk IIs (equivalent to the B-17F). Most were used by Coastal Command for maritime reconnaissance.

■ CONSOLIDATED LIBERATOR: Famous for helping to close the U-boat 'gap' in the middle of the Atlantic, Liberators also served with Bomber Command and in the Middle and Far East.

■ MARTIN MARAUDER: Around 525 Marauders were delivered to the RAF and SAAF under the Lend-Lease arrangement. They were used exclusively in the Mediterranean theatre.

■ NORTH AMERICAN MITCHELL: The Mitchell proved to be a capable close-support bomber for the RAF when operating with the 2nd Tactical Air Force during the Allied advances of 1944/45.

MARTIN

B-26 MARAUDER

● Very fast ● Difficult to fly ● USAAF's most potent medium bomber

During World War II the Martin B-26 Marauder was considered a 'hot' ship – high-powered, unforgiving and risky to fly. But in spite of unflattering nicknames like 'Widowmaker' and 'Flying Coffin', the Marauder was not as dangerous as was widely believed. In fact, it was a potent warplane – a silvery sleek bullet of a medium bomber which could carry a respectable bombload and outrun the opposition.

▲ Designed in 1939 for the US Army Air Corps, the sleek, fast, twin-engined Martin Model 179 Marauder was ordered straight into production without a prototype or trials.

MARTIN B-26 MARAUDER

▲ Streamlined for speed
The B-26 was designed with a very sleek, circular section fuselage, curving to the nose and tail cones. The cockpit windscreen was streamlined, and the wing was designed for speed rather than lift.

◀ Fast targets
Some Marauders were stripped of their armour and used as high-speed target tugs and trainers by the US Air Force and Navy.

▲ Medium bombload
A stick of 114-kg (250-lb) bombs falls from the internal bomb-bay of a raiding B-26. The aircraft could carry a rather modest total weight of 2359 kg (5,200 lb.).

▼ Tactical bomber
Flying with the US 9th Air Force from May 1943, the B-26 quickly became the hardest-worked Allied daylight medium bomber over Europe.

▲ Shot down
As crews got used to the B-26's performance it became less vulnerable. By VE Day it had the lowest loss rate of any US bomber in Europe.

FACTS AND FIGURES

➤ The first flight of the B-26 took place at the Martin factory in November 1940.

➤ B-26s began service with the 22nd Bomb Group in Australia just after Pearl Harbor.

➤ Future American president Lyndon B. Johnson received a Silver Star for a Marauder mission in New Guinea.

➤ During an attack on Ijmuiden, Holland, in May 1943, an entire group of 10 B-26s was shot down by fighters, flak and collisions.

➤ The price of a B-26 was $261,000 in 1940, which had reduced to $192,000 by 1944.

➤ Of the 5157 Marauders built, 522 were supplied to the Royal Air Force.

PROFILE

The flying torpedo

The Martin Marauder went straight into production, the first aircraft to fly being a service model and not a prototype. It made an immediate impact, rumour giving the new medium bomber an (exaggerated) top speed of almost 600 km/h (370 m.p.h.), faster than most fighters then in service. Its engines were in streamlined nacelles underslung from a shoulder-mounted wing, enhancing the image of the Marauder as a silvery 'Flying Torpedo'.

Although employed to good effect for conventional and torpedo bombing, the Marauder never made its mark in the Pacific theatre where the more conventional, less challenging B-25 Mitchell was preferred.

In Europe the story was very different, with B-26s joining US squadrons in 1942. The initial deployment by the 319th Bomb Group was trouble-plagued. The Marauder landed at 210 km/h (130 m.p.h.) and could betray an unskilled pilot. But the B-26 soon made its mark over the continent, proving to be a rugged, accurate and extremely hard-hitting tactical weapon. Following their success in covering the invasion of Normandy, Marauders again proved successful in attacking the heavily defended German V-1 flying bomb launch sites during 1944.

When it entered service the B-26 had the highest wing loading of any aircraft in the USAAF. The high-set, short-span wing and two large, powerful engines optimised it for high speed rather than bombload or handling.

The 525 Marauders that flew with the RAF and the South African air force replaced Blenheims in the Mediterranean theatre.

B-26B Marauder

Type: seven-seat medium day-bomber

Powerplant: two 1432-kW (1,920-hp.) Pratt & Whitney R-2800-43 Double Wasp radial piston engines

Maximum speed: 454 km/h (317 m.p.h.) at 4570 m (15,000 ft.)

Climb rate: to 4600 m (15,000 ft.) in 13 minutes

Range: 1851 km (1,148 mi.) with 1361 kg (2,994 lb.) of bombs

Service ceiling: 6400 m (23,500 ft.)

Weights: empty 10,886 kg (23,950 lb.); normal take-off 16,783 kg (36,923 lb.)

Armament: up to eight 12.7-mm (.50 cal.) machine-guns with 3950 rounds of ammunition, plus a maximum internal bombload of 2359 kg (5,170 lb.)

Dimensions:
span late models 21.64 m (71 ft.)
early models 19.12 m (63 ft.)
length 17.75 m (58 ft.)
height 6.55 m (21 ft.)
wing area 61.13 m² (679 sq. ft.)

B-26C MARAUDER

This B-26C, nicknamed 'Baby Bumps II', was flown by the 557th Squadron of the 98th Wing based at Chipping Ongar.

As a medium bomber the B-26 crew varied from five to seven. One gunner manually operated the nose machine-guns and others the electrically-operated dorsal turret, tail turret and the manually aimed waist guns.

When it entered service the Marauder had the highest wing loading of any USAAF aircraft. This gave it high take-off and landing speeds, which caused problems for inexperienced pilots.

In order to save weight, the Marauder's flying control surfaces (rudder, elevators and ailerons) were wooden ribbed and covered with doped fabric.

In order to improve handling performance on take-off and landing, the B-26's fin and rudder was extended and the wing span was increased.

The B-26C had a heavier armament and more powerful engines than the major production version, the B-26B, that preceded it.

The B-26 was powered by two 1432-kW (1,920-hp.) Pratt & Whitney R-2800-43 piston engines, which drove large four-blade propellers.

The engine nacelles housed the large, single wheels of the tricycle undercarriage. All three units had single strut legs, the nosewheel retracting rearwards into the lower fuselage below the cockpit.

This B-26 carries the black and white invasion stripes applied at the time of the Normandy landings of June 1944. It is in standard USAAF colours with the KS code letters of the 557th Squadron.

COMBAT DATA

ARMAMENT

The B-26's defensive armament was better than its German and Japanese contemporaries. Having both fixed and mobile guns in the nose, dorsal and tail turrets, together with rear side-window guns, it had an all-round arc of fire.

Ju 88A-4
3000 kg of bombs
4 x 7.92-mm
(0.31-in.) MGs

B-26B MARAUDER
2359 kg of bombs
8 x 12.7-mm
(.50 cal.) MGs

Ki-49-IIA 'Helen'
1000 kg of bombs
5 x 7.7-mm
(.50 cal.) MGs
1 x 20-mm
(0.79-in.) cannon

Medium bombers: the rivals

■ **JUNKERS Ju 88:** One of the Luftwaffe's main bombers, the Ju 88 was designed as a medium-range tactical aircraft that was also used as a dive-bomber and night-fighter. It was nearly 100 km/h (60 m.p.h.) slower than the B-26, but could carry nearly double the weight of bombs. Total production of the Ju 88 was about 15,000.

■ **MITSUBISHI Ki-67 HIRYU 'PEGGY':** This Japanese army Type 4 was the country's fastest medium-range bomber of the war, with a top speed of 537 km/h, nearly 100 km/h (60 m.p.h.) greater than that of the B-26. The penalty for this was a small bombload of just 800 kg (1,760 lb.). Only 698 Ki-67s were built before the war ended.

■ **NORTH AMERICAN B-25 MITCHELL:** The USAAF's 'gull-wing' B-25 was developed at the same time as the Marauder. It carried a smaller bombload, was a good deal slower, but was more rugged and relatively easy to fly. Nearly twice as many B-25s were built (9816) than B-26s (5157).

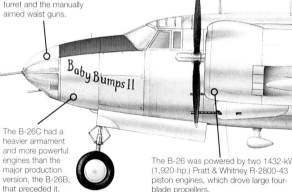

MARTIN

PBM MARINER

● Flying boat ● Amphibian ● Anti-submarine and SAR aircraft

One of the truly great flying boats of all time, the Martin PBM Mariner was produced in seaplane and amphibian versions. It was the most important naval aircraft in its class during World War II. Largely used as a replacement for the Consolidated PBY Catalina, which was perhaps the only better-known flying boat, the big, sturdy PBM Mariner served in every combat theatre. Many other countries used the Mariner well into the 1950s.

▲ The amphibious capabilities of the later Mariner versions made them versatile aircraft. The high-mounted engines, search radar and gull wing were distinctive features.

MARTIN PBM MARINER

▲ **Search and rescue**
Used in the search and rescue role after World War II, the Mariner served on into the 1950s with the US Coast Guard and US Navy.

▼ **Onto the ocean**
Launched from a slipway at NAS Norfolk, Virginia, this Mariner is being prepared for a mission in late 1942. The aircraft is armed with eight machine guns.

▲ **Rocket assistance**
Rockets fixed to the fuselage sides helped heavily loaded aircraft get airborne. Drag from the water was a serious problem.

▼ **Full power**
The two huge Wright Cyclone engines haul the Mariner into the air on another long-range patrol mission.

Search radar ▶
Radar allowed the Mariner to hunt for submarines and ships. Later it was useful in the search and rescue role, operating far out to sea.

FACTS AND FIGURES

➤ The prototype for the Mariner series completed its maiden flight on 18 February 1939.

➤ British Mariners were returned to the US without seeing operational service.

➤ Seven PBMs sank the submarine U-615 near Aruba on 6 August 1943.

➤ The Navy first used RATO (rocket-assisted take-off) boosters to fly a stranded PBM off the Colorado river.

➤ A 3/8 scale model of the Mariner was flown before the prototype PBM flew.

➤ The Martin 162-A scale model was manned and had Chevrolet engines.

PROFILE

US Navy patrol flying boat

The Mariner was designed in 1937 when the US Navy wanted a new patrol flying boat. The big, gull-wing Mariner was sturdy and tough, and featured weapons bays in its engine nacelles.

The pilots and crew of the Mariner had tremendous confidence in a ship that had been optimized to give them the strongest chance of surviving combat and getting home safely. There were numerous combat actions in which the PBM Mariner excelled, beginning on

30 June 1942, when a crew headed by Lieutenant Richard E. Schreder sank the German submarine U-158 near Bermuda. Exactly a dozen U-boats had been sent to the bottom of the sea by Mariners by the time the war ended.

In the Pacific, Mariners fought just about everywhere, but were particularly active at Saipan and in the liberation of the Philippines. In the post-war era, Mariners took part in atomic weapons tests in the Pacific and fought in the 1950–53 Korean

War. Production of the Mariner ceased in 1949, but the aircraft remained a mainstay of the US Coast Guard for many years.

Below: The Royal Air Force received 27 Mariners. Fitted with British equipment, they were never used operationally and were returned to the United States.

Above: Although the Mariner could reach an altitude of 6095 m (20,000 ft.), patrols were normally flown at low level. Attacks on submarines were made at wave-top height using bombs and depth charges.

PBM-3D Mariner

Type: seven- or eight-seat patrol flying boat

Powerplant: two 1417-kW (1,900-hp.) Wright R-2600-22 Cyclone radial piston engines

Maximum speed: 338 km/h (210 m.p.h.) at 520 m (1,700 ft.)

Cruising speed: 303 km/h (188 m.p.h.) at 520 m (1,700 ft.)

Ceiling: 6095 m (20,000 ft.)

Combat radius: 1162 km (722 mi.)

Range: 3597 km (2,235 mi.)

Weights: empty 15,017 kg (33,106 lb.); maximum take-off 26,253 kg (57,878 lb.)

Weapons: eight 12.7-mm (.50 cal.) machine guns in nose, dorsal turrets, waist and tail; plus up to 1,646 lb.) of bombs, torpedoes or depth charges

Dimensions:
span 35.97 m (118 ft.)
length 24.38 m (80 ft.)
height 8.23 m (27 ft.)
wing area 130.71 m² (1,407 sq. ft.)

PBM-5 Mariner

The PBM-5 variant was used post-war by the US Navy and Coast Guard, mainly in the search and rescue role. This aircraft carries a Pacific theatre paint scheme.

The two Wright R-2600 engines were mounted high on the gull wings to keep the propellers clear of corrosive saltwater spray.

A fixed float under each wing kept the wingtips clear of the water and allowed a stable take-off and landing in rough seas.

The prototype mounted its twin fins and rudders on horizontal tailplanes. Those on production aircraft were angled upward, keeping them in line with the inboard section of the wings.

The large search radar was enclosed by a streamlined fairing, mounted above and behind the cockpit.

The large engine nacelles were each able to carry up to 1,811 kg (3,993 lb.) of bombs, depth charges or air-dropped rescue equipment.

Nose, dorsal and tail turrets contained a total of six 12.7-mm (.50 cal.) machine guns. These were supplemented by two more guns in the waist positions.

The boat-shaped underside was the key to easy operations from any large area of water. Early aircraft had retractable wing floats, while the PBM-5 was amphibious, with retractable wheeled landing gear.

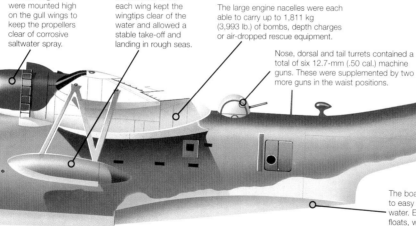

ACTION DATA

WEAPONS

Carrying a heavier bombload, the Mariner was designed to replace the smaller Catalina. Although it carried fewer bombs, the Sunderland had more defensive guns.

SUNDERLAND GR.Mk 5 463-kg (1,021-lb.) bombload 10 x 7.62-mm (.30 cal.) machine guns

PBM-5A MARINER 1654-kg (3,646-lb.) bombload 8 x 12.7-mm (.50 cal.) machine guns

PBY-5A CATALINA 374-kg (824-lb.) bombload 1 x 12.7-mm (.50 cal.) machine gun 3 x 7.7-mm (.303 cal.) machine guns

RANGE

The Catalina was renowned for its excellent range. The Mariner comes a close second and both aircraft beat the Sunderland by almost 1000 km (620 mi.).

PBY-5A CATALINA 3774 km (2,345 mi.)

PBM-5A MARINER 3597 km (2,235 mi.)

SUNDERLAND GR.Mk 5 2482 km (1,766 mi.)

MAXIMUM TAKE-OFF WEIGHT

The Sunderland and Mariner are closely matched in weight. In the Mariner, however, far more of this weight consists of fuel and weapons. The lighter Catalina, although very successful, would have been more difficult to handle on open sea.

PBY-5A CATALINA 16,033 kg (35,347 lb.)

PBM-5A MARINER 26,218 kg (57,800 lb.)

SUNDERLAND GR.Mk 5 26,253 kg (57,878 lb.)

U.S. Navy patrol aircraft

■ **LOCKHEED PV-2 HARPOON:** Developed from the Lodestar airliner, the PV-2 was a well-armed coastal patrol aircraft.

■ **CONSOLIDATED PBY CATALINA:** Hugely successful, the Catalina served throughout World War II in the long-range patrol mission.

■ **CONSOLIDATED PB4Y-2 PRIVATEER:** This was a long-range patrol version of the B-24 Liberator developed for the Navy.

■ **CONSOLIDATED PB2Y CORONADO:** Similar in size to the PBM, the PB2Y carried a heavier bomb load and had more power.

MESSERSCHMITT

BF 109

● 'Emil' in combat ● Bomber escort ● Fighter-bomber missions

H aving seen extensive service during the Spanish Civil War, early-model Bf 109s had given way to the Bf 109E by the spring of 1940. The Bf 109E series offered superior diving performance and various armament options, including the common layout of two cannon plus two machine-guns. The result was a highly effective fighter, but the operational circumstances of the Battle of Britain meant the odds were stacked heavily against it.

▲ Conditions were harsh for all the combatants during the Battle of Britain. The Bf 109 stood up well to outdoor servicing in makeshift canvas hangars at forward airstrips.

MESSERSCHMITT BF 109

▼ **Early action**
Crews soon applied dark mottling to cover the light blue sides of their aircraft.

▲ **Captive evaluation**
Several Bf 109Es fell into Allied hands before, during and after the Battle of Britain. This machine was tested by American analysts.

▼ **Out of combat**
This downed III./JG 26 aircraft shows the yellow nose colours which were used in the initial stages of the battle as a recognition feature.

▼ **Ace Galland**
By 24 September 1940 the rudder of Adolf Galland's aircraft had 40 kill markings applied.

◄ **Post-Battle honours**
By the end of the Battle of Britain, Werner Mölders had racked up an impressive score, as indicated by the rudder of his Bf 109. Like Galland, Mölders had led a unit during the Spanish Civil War.

FACTS AND FIGURES

➤ Bf 109E-4 pilot Franz von Werra was the only German to escape a Western Allied prisoner of war camp and get home.

➤ Early Bf 109Es had arrived in Spain by the very end of 1938.

➤ A Bf 109E captured by the French was lost in a collision with a Hawk 75A.

➤ Captured Bf 109s were flown by the Royal Air Force in mock combat against Hurricanes and Spitfires.

➤ Cooling and vibration problems made the engine-mounted cannon troublesome.

➤ Late in the Battle, the Bf 109E-7 version introduced a 300-litre drop tank.

Messerschmitts over Britain

By the time Germany launched its Eagle Day attack on Britain in August 1940, Bf 109Es (commonly known as 'Emils') had for a month been escorting bombers in attacks against coastal targets and shipping from bases in occupied France.

The German fighter pilots knew that their aircraft had an edge in performance over the British Hurricanes and Spitfires, and their twin cannon had proved highly effective. But when they were forced to escort the Luftwaffe's bombers further inland, they began to lose their initial advantage.

As long as they were allowed to cross the Channel at altitudes of around 9000 m (29,000 ft.) and engage the British fighters in open combat, the 'Emils' more than held their own. Tied to the bomber formations, though, they lost their independence and, before the introduction of the drop-tank-equipped Bf 109E-7, they could spend no more than 30 minutes over England.

Their pilots faced other disadvantages. British radar could detect the approaching formations, giving the RAF's fighters a tactical advantage. All missions involved long overwater flights, and the strain on the Luftwaffe fighter force proved too much. In September the Luftwaffe switched its efforts to night raids on London.

As a source of great curiosity for the people of Eastbourne, this crashed 'Emil' is representative of the hundreds of aircraft lost by both sides during the Battle.

Bf 109E-3

Type: single-seat fighter

Powerplant: one 876-kW (1,175-hp.) Daimler-Benz DB 601A liquid-cooled inverted V-12 engine

Maximum speed: 560 km/h (347 m.p.h.) at 4440 m (14,500 ft.)

Initial climb rate: 1000 m/min (3,300 f.p.m.)

Range: 660 km (410 mi.)

Service ceiling: 10,500 m (34,400 ft.)

Weights: empty 1900 kg (4,180 lb.); maximum take-off 2665 kg (5,863 lb.)

Armament: one engine-mounted 20-mm (0.79-in.) MG FF cannon and four 7.9-mm (0.31-in.) MG 17 machine-guns

Dimensions:
span	9.87 m (32 ft. 4 in.)
length	8.64 m (28 ft. 4 in.)
height	2.50 m (8 ft. 3 in.)
wing area	16.40 m² (176 sq. ft.)

Bf 109 pilots were accommodated in a small cockpit with poor forward view through the armoured windscreen. The cockpit's small dimensions allowed frontal area to be kept to a minimum, however.

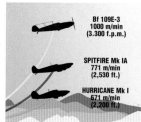

Bf 109E-4

Flown by Major Helmut Wick during October 1940 while he was Gruppenkommandeur of I./JG 2, this aircraft was based at Beaumont-le-Roger, France.

A 7.9-mm (0.31-in.) MG 17 machine-gun, synchronised to fire through the propeller, was mounted behind each of the troughs above the forward fuselage.

A combination of initial air superiority and their long operational deployments allowed Luftwaffe fighter pilots to amass large scores. Shown here with 44 kills, Wick was to score 55 with this aircraft before it was shot down on 28 November 1940.

Even though the main landing gear was widely splayed, the Bf 109 still had a very narrow track. This meant that, like the Spitfire, the aircraft was tricky to handle on the ground.

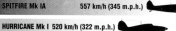

Easily distinguished from earlier Bf 109s by its lack of undernose radiator, the Bf 109E series introduced the DB 601 engine. The smaller undernose fairing housed an oil cooler.

A red 'R' on a white shield was proudly worn beneath the cockpit. This referred to Jagdgeschwader (JG) 2's heritage as the 'Richthofen' Geschwader. The marking was only worn during the early stages of the war.

A distinguishing feature of all early Bf 109s, up to and including the 'Emils', were the struts bracing each tailplane. They were deleted from the Bf 109F onwards; that type entered service with JG 2 from March 1941.

COMBAT DATA

MAXIMUM SPEED

Faster than the Spitfire IA, the Bf 109E-3 was easily a match for the more numerous Hurricane Mk I. Rapid development work was necessary to give the Spitfire a new-found superiority over the Bf 109E-3.

Bf 109E-3	560 km/h (347 m.p.h.)
SPITFIRE Mk IA	557 km/h (345 m.p.h.)
HURRICANE Mk I	520 km/h (322 m.p.h.)

CLIMB RATE

A high rate of climb often allowed the Bf 109E-3 to get away from trouble or to climb above its adversaries for a high-speed, diving attack, a tactic which became impossible once the aircraft had been tasked with bomber escort.

Bf 109E-3 1000 m/min (3.300 f.p.m.)

SPITFIRE Mk IA 771 m/min (2,530 ft.)

HURRICANE Mk I 671 m/min (2,200 ft.)

ARMAMENT

Although they had a greater number of weapons, the British fighters with their machine-guns did not have the power or destructive capacity of the German cannon.

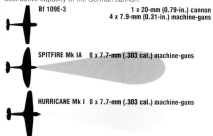

Bf 109E-3 — 1 x 20-mm (0.79-in.) cannon / 4 x 7.9-mm (0.31-in.) machine-guns

SPITFIRE Mk IA — 8 x 7.7-mm (.303 cal.) machine-guns

HURRICANE Mk I — 8 x 7.7-mm (.303 cal.) machine-guns

Battle of Britain aces

■ **BALTHASAR:** Having fought gallantly with the Condor Legion in Spain, Wilhelm Balthasar flew throughout the Battle of Britain, but was killed in 1941 when his Bf 109F shed a wing in combat.

■ **BÄR:** A veteran of the Battle of Britain and several other campaigns, Heinz Bär performed the difficult task of introducing the Heinkel He 162 into service early in 1945.

■ **GALLAND:** Wearing his personal Mickey Mouse badge and the S-marking of JG 26, Adolf Galland's BF 109s, an E-3 and later this E-4, allowed him to score 40 victories by 24 September 1940.

MESSERSCHMITT

BF 110

● 'Destroyer' fighter ● Night-fighter ● Fighter-bomber

▲ Firepower
The powerful cannon and machine-gun nose was lethal to ground targets and made short work of enemy bombers.

▲ Desert destroyer
A Bf 110 kicks up sand as it departs its desert base in north Africa. Its powerful armament was effective in the tank-busting role.

▼ Air supremacy
Operating over France in June 1940, the Bf 110s of ZG 52 were free to carry out attacks on enemy airfields with near impunity.

▲ Photo mission
Bf 110s flew a variety of missions. This Libyan-based example is being loaded with reconnaissance cameras.

Bomber buster ▶
Rocket-armed Bf 110s were potent bomber-destroyers, but were almost helpless against Allied escort fighters.

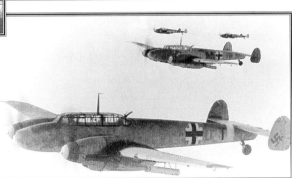

Messerschmitt's Bf 110 was one of the Luftwaffe's great hopes at the start of World War II, but the twin-engined Zerstörer (destroyer) proved hopelessly vulnerable to single-engined fighter opposition during the Battle of Britain. Nevertheless, it was fast and heavily armed, and as the war progressed proved to be a solid fighting machine as a long-range fighter and fighter-bomber, as a bomber-destroyer and as a night-fighter.

▲ Like so many
wartime German aircraft, the Bf 110 was a good design that was kept in service too long because its replacement (the Me 210) was a failure. It was still in production when the war ended.

FACTS AND FIGURES

➤ During the invasions of Poland and France, Bf 110s operated with great success in support of the Wehrmacht.

➤ The Bf 110 also saw service on bombing and reconnaissance missions.

➤ The prototype Bf 110 made its maiden flight on 12 May 1936.

➤ In addition to its guns, the Bf 110 could carry 1250 kg (2,750 lb.) of bombs or rockets on underfuselage racks.

➤ The Bf 110 was used by Rudolf Hess to fly to Britain in 1941.

➤ When production ended in March 1945, about 6050 Bf 110s had been built.

The Zerstörer fighter

The Bf 110 was without peer when it entered service in 1938 as a long-range heavy 'destroyer' fighter for the Luftwaffe. Development had been protracted due to problems with its DB 601 engines, but the Bf 110 was in action in time for the 1939 Polish campaign. That year, the Messerschmitt confirmed its worth as a 'bomber-destroyer' by shooting down nine of 22 RAF Wellington medium

bombers on a single mission.

This twin-tailed, tailwheel-equipped fighter was rakish and nimble for its size and weight. Pilots found it adequate in combat, although interior space and outside vision left a little to be desired.

Even with a back-seat gunner, however, the Bf 110 could never cope with single-engine fighters, whether early Hurricanes or late P-51D Mustangs. But as a radar-

equipped night interceptor, facing only bombers, the Bf 110 was capable of wreaking immense destruction. Even in this role, however, the Bf 110 was outclassed by later warplanes, but it pioneered nocturnal fighting with radar and air-to-air rockets.

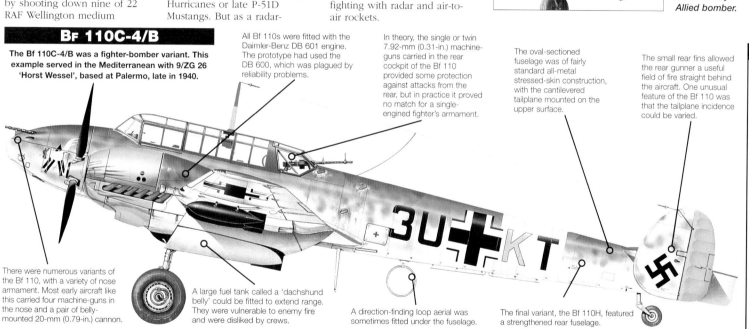

Tactical air support was another role the Bf 110 was increasingly called on to perform as the war went on. This Bf 110, flying over Russia, carries the distinctive 'wasp' nose art of S.KG 210.

The main strength of the Bf 110 was its ability to accept armament such as the Bk 3.7 cannon. A single hit from this weapon was usually certain death to any Allied bomber.

Bf 110C-4/B

Type: two-seat fighter-bomber/reconnaissance fighter

Powerplant: two 895-kW (1,200-hp.) Daimler-Benz DB 601N inverted V-12 piston engines

Maximum speed: 562 km/h (348 m.p.h.) at 7000 m (22,960 ft.)

Range: 850 km (527 mi.)

Service ceiling: 10,000 m (33,000 ft.)

Weights: empty 4500 kg (9,900 lb.); loaded 7000 kg (15,400 lb.)

Armament: two 20-mm (0.79-in.) Oerlikon MG FF cannon in belly and four 7.92-mm (0.31-in.) MG 17 machine-guns in nose; one 7.92-mm MG 15 machine-gun in rear cockpit; racks for four 250-kg (550-lb.) bombs under centre section

Dimensions:
span	16.25 m (53 ft.)
length	12.10 m (40 ft.)
height	3.50 m (11 ft.)
wing area	39.40 m² (424 sq. ft.)

Bf 110C-4/B

The Bf 110C-4/B was a fighter-bomber variant. This example served in the Mediterranean with 9/ZG 26 'Horst Wessel', based at Palermo, late in 1940.

All Bf 110s were fitted with the Daimler-Benz DB 601 engine. The prototype had used the DB 600, which was plagued by reliability problems.

In theory, the single or twin 7.92-mm (0.31-in.) machine-guns carried in the rear cockpit of the Bf 110 provided some protection against attacks from the rear, but in practice it proved no match for a single-engined fighter's armament.

The oval-sectioned fuselage was of fairly standard all-metal stressed-skin construction, with the cantilevered tailplane mounted on the upper surface.

The small rear fins allowed the rear gunner a useful field of fire straight behind the aircraft. One unusual feature of the Bf 110 was that the tailplane incidence could be varied.

There were numerous variants of the Bf 110, with a variety of nose armament. Most early aircraft like this carried four machine-guns in the nose and a pair of belly-mounted 20-mm (0.79-in.) cannon.

A large fuel tank called a 'dachshund belly' could be fitted to extend range. They were vulnerable to enemy fire and were disliked by crews.

A direction-finding loop aerial was sometimes fitted under the fuselage.

The final variant, the Bf 110H, featured a strengthened rear fuselage.

COMBAT DATA

MAXIMUM SPEED

Many nations developed twin-engined heavy fighters before World War II, and the various designs reflected different philosophies. The Bf 110 was much faster than the similar French Potez design, but could not match the smaller and lighter single-seat Westland Whirlwind.

Bf 110C	562 km/h (348 m.p.h.)
WHIRLWIND Mk I	580 km/h (360 m.p.h.)
POTEZ 63	440 km/h

RANGE

The Bf 110 was designed as a long-range fighter, and by contemporary German standards in the 1930s it had a fair performance. But it could not fly as far as its rivals, possibly because most German aircraft of the time were designed primarily for close support of the Wehrmacht.

Bf 110C	850 km (527 mi.)
WHIRLWIND Mk I	1300 km (800 mi.)
POTEZ 63	1500 km (930 mi.)

ARMAMENT

The Bf 110 had a powerful all-round armament, supplemented by the ability to carry a one-ton bombload. Later in the war, the aircraft proved capable of being significantly up-gunned, carrying 30-mm (1.18-in.) cannon or even 37-mm (1.47-in.) anti-tank guns.

Bf 110C	2 x 20-mm (0.79-in.) cannon 4 x 7.92-mm (0.31-in.) MGs 1 or 2 x 7.92-mm MGs in rear cockpit 1000 kg (2,200 lb.) of bombs
WHIRLWIND MK I	4 x 20-mm (0.79-in.) cannon 454 kg (1,000 lb.) of bombs
POTEZ 63	6 x 7.5-mm (0.3-in.) MGs 2 x 7.5-mm (0.3-in.) MGs in rear cockpit 600 kg (1,320 lb.) of bombs

Messerschmitt's Zerstörer rivals

■ **HENSCHEL Hs 124:** Designed to meet the original Kampfzerstörer (bomber-destroyer) specification of 1934, the Henschel was a large, heavy and mediocre machine.

■ **FOCKE-WULF Fw 57:** Even larger than the Henschel, the Focke-Wulf Kampfzerstörer was grossly underpowered, and could not match the Bf 110's performance.

■ **MESSERSCHMITT Bf 162:** Based on the Bf 110, the Bf 162 featured an enlarged fuselage and was designed as a high-speed bomber. It was used for research.

■ **JUNKERS Ju 88:** Germany's premier 'Schnellbomber' was so agile that it was easy to convert as a heavy fighter, and was vastly more capable than the original Zerstörers.

■ **FOCKE-WULF Fw 187:** A superb performer which was faster than the Bf 109 single-seter, the Fw 187 was the victim of official indifference and never entered service.

MESSERSCHMITT

ME 262

● Pioneering jet fighter ● Revolutionised aircraft design

▲ The Me 262 pilot had under his control the world's first operational jet warplane. Had it been built earlier, it could have had a major impact on the course of the war.

During World War II the Me 262 was a high point of German scientific achievement. This shark-like craft with its epoch-making jet engines and potent firepower might have swept Allied bombers from the skies, had it been used properly. With the Me 262, Messerschmitt gave pilots a superb fighting machine for which the Allies had no equal, and a revolutionary portent of the future.

MESSERSCHMITT ME 262

▼ **Precision bomber**
This trials aircraft had a position in the nose for a bomb-aimer, who lay face-down and peered through the glazed nose.

▲ **Night-fighter**
They could have been the best night-fighters of the war, but fewer than a dozen Me 262B-1a/U1s got into service. They had radar in the nose and a second crew member to operate the equipment.

◀ **Air-to-air fighter**
At full speed and altitude, nothing could catch the Me 262, but it was clumsy at low speeds and was vulnerable while landing and taking off: many were shot down by Allied fighters patrolling the Me 262 bases for returning jets.

Fighter or bomber? ▼
The Me 262 was designed as a fighter, but Hitler's insistence on it being a bomber is often believed to have impeded deliveries. In truth, it was the slow supply of engines which limited supply.

▼ **First jet flight**
Me 262 V3 first flew on jet power on 18 July 1942. It had a tailwheel, and when it landed unburned fuel ignited when the aircraft touched down.

FACTS AND FIGURES

➤ From March 1944 to April 1945, the Luftwaffe received 1433 Me 262s.

➤ As a bomber the Me 262, with two 227- or 454-kg (500- or 1,000-lb.) bombs, had little impact on advancing Allied armies.

➤ An awesome Mauser 50-mm MK 214 cannon mounted on two Me 262A-1/U4 test ships was not used operationally.

➤ Five new Me 262s built by entrepreneurs in Texas, using American J85 engines, will begin flying in 1997.

➤ Though the Me 262 was a joy to fly at full power, it was sluggish and awkward at lower speeds.

➤ Me 262 two-seaters performed training and night-fighting duties.

PROFILE

Germany's wonder jet

One of Germany's finest fighter pilots, Major Walter Nowotny, formed the Kommando Nowotny in late 1944 to combat Allied bombers and their fighter escorts. The result set off alarm bells in the USAAF. The graceful, potent Me 262 was easily the fastest fighter in the world: with guns and unguided R4M rockets, this fighter of the future had the potential to knock down Flying Fortresses almost with impunity. It was only the destruction of Germany's

industry by massive Allied raids that slowed the production of this incredible aircraft.

Other pilots flew the Me 262 as a bomber, a decision which may have squandered many of the technical advances offered by this new kind of warplane.

Too late and not always used in the best way, the Me 262 frightened the Allies but could not alter the outcome of the war. Afterwards, Allied experts studied the airframe and engine and determined that the

An operational Me 262A takes off from its base at Lechfeld. In the spring of 1945 the Me 262 scored many victories over Allied aircraft.

Messerschmitt Me 262 was years ahead of fighters of other nations. Its secrets helped the Americans, Russians and British to develop more advanced jet engines and airframes to the magic of Mach 1 and beyond over the ensuing years.

The prototype of the Me 262 first flew as a tail-dragger. However, this caused problems on take-off, so the Messerschmitt engineers revamped their design and operational aircraft came equipped with a nosewheel.

Me 262A-2

Type: single-seat air superiority fighter

Powerplant: two 8.82-kN (1,980-lb.-thrust) Junkers Jumo 004B-1, -2 or -3 axial-flow turbojets

Maximum speed: 870 km/h (540 m.p.h.)

Range: 1050 km (650 mi.) at 9000 m (30,000 ft.)

Service ceiling: 11,450 m (37,500 ft.)

Weights: empty 3800 kg (8,738 lb.); maximum 6400 kg (14,110 lb.)

Armament: four 30-mm (1.18-in.) Rheinmetall-Borsig MK 108A-3 cannon with 100 rounds for the upper pair and 80 rounds for the lower pair; 12 R4M air-to-air rockets; two 226-kg (500-lb.) bombs or one 452-kg (1,000-lb.) bomb

Dimensions:
span 12.50 m (40 ft. 11 in.)
length 10.58 m (34 ft. 9 in.)
height 3.83 m (12 ft. 7 in.)
wing area 21.73 m² (234 sq. ft.)

Handling and control of the Me 262 was surprisingly good, but it tended to snake at high speed, making accurate gun-firing difficult. If an engine failed at low speed (a common occurrence) the results were usually catastrophic.

ME 262 'SCHWALBE'

Beautifully sleek for its time, the Me 262 also had acceptable handling qualities and blistering performance. Its one disadvantage was its sluggishness and lack of manoeuvrability in the airfield circuit.

Visibility from the Me 262's cockpit was considerably better than from the preceding Bf 109 piston-engined fighter, thanks to a relatively unobstructed canopy.

500491

7

Fighter Me 262s carried a heavy punch in the form of four 30-mm (1.18-in.) MK 108 cannon in the forward fuselage. Twelve R4M unguided air-to-air rockets could be carried under the wings.

The Me 262 was powered by a pair of Junkers Jumo 004B-1 turbojets, each giving about 9 kN (1,900 lb. thrust). These early engines had a life of only 25 hours, and needed major overhaul every 10 hours.

The Me 262's fuselage was of all-metal monocoque construction. The wings, tailplane and fin were also all-metal, and each had a moderate sweepback on the leading edge only.

COMBAT DATA

MAXIMUM SPEED

Me 262A-1	870 km/h (540 m.p.h.)
METEOR Mk III	700 km/h (435 m.p.h.)
P-80 SHOOTING STAR	898 km/h (556 m.p.h.)

The Me 262 was considerably faster than its contemporary, the Gloster Meteor, and was almost as fast as America's Lockheed P-80 Shooting Star, which only became operational in the last week of conflict. However, early jet fighters had poor acceleration at low speeds.

SERVICE CEILING

Jet engines are much more efficient at high altitude than piston-engine-driven propellers, and all the early jets had considerably better high-altitude performance than other fighters of the day.

Me 262 11,450 m (37,500 ft.)
METEOR Mk III 12,250 m (40,200 ft.)
P-80 SHOOTING STAR 13,715 m (45,000 ft.)

ARMAMENT

The Me 262 was designed primarily as a bomber-destroyer, and was very heavily armed for the purpose, as well as cannon they could also carry unguided rockets. The Meteor was also cannon-armed, although less powerfully than the German jet. Like most American fighters of the period, the P-80 was underarmed by European standards carrying only machine-guns.

Me 262 4 x 30-mm (1.18-in.) cannon

METEOR Mk III 4 x 20-mm (0.79-in.) cannon

P-80 6 x 12.7-mm (.50 cal.) machine-guns

The first jets

■ **HEINKEL He 178:** One of the most important aircraft in history, the He 178 was the first aircraft to fly under jet power, on 27 August 1939, paving the way for jet-powered fighters.

■ **HEINKEL He 280:** Heinkel flew the world's first twin jet in May 1941. Completely outclassing all piston-engined fighters, its development was stopped in favour of the Me 262.

■ **GLOSTER E28/39:** Britain had been ahead of Germany in engine design thanks to pioneer Frank Whittle, but due to official indifference the first British jet did not fly until 15 May 1941.

■ **GLOSTER METEOR:** Although it first flew in March 1943, nine months after the Me 262, the Meteor became operational a week before the Messerschmitt, in July 1944.

187

MESSERSCHMITT

ME 323 GIGANT

● Giant glider ● Multi-engine transport ● Huge cargo loads

A real weightlifter, the Me 321 Gigant was a huge glider intended for an invasion of England. With up to six engines, it became the Me 323 transport to get soldiers and equipment into battle areas. It had the perfect name: this incredible flying machine was one of the largest World War II aircraft, and had astonishing carrying capacity. But it was slow, and easy prey for fighters.

▲ In spite of its fragile-looking steel tube and canvas construction, the Me 323 Gigant carried some of the heaviest payloads of World War II.

MESSERSCHMITT ME 323 GIGANT

◀ **Outsize cargo carrier**
The Gigant was one of the largest aircraft of its time. Even with the power of six engines it was a poor performer, and very hard to fly.

Monster glider ▶
The unpowered Me 321 glider was designed to carry heavy equipment and artillery for airborne troops. But it was so big that finding a suitable glider tug was a problem.

▲ **Keeping the giant flying**
Servicing the Gigant was a problem. Its six engines were more than 5 m (16 ft 5 in.) off the ground, so special work vehicles were developed to allow maintenance engineers access. But these were only available at airfields where the Gigants were based.

▼ **Easy prey**
The Gigant was slow and sluggish, and was easy meat for long-range fighters. Many were shot down over the Mediterranean as they tried to bring supplies to the beleaguered Afrika Korps.

▲ **Power for the giant glider**
The Gigant was never a viable proposition as a glider, so Messerschmitt decided to produce a powered variant using French-built Gnome-Rhône engines. These were in production in Vichy France and were available in some numbers.

FACTS AND FIGURES

➤ Rocket boosters were needed to get a loaded Gigant into the sky.

➤ One Me 323 evacuated 220 soldiers from North Africa to Italy – 140 in the cargo compartment and 80 inside its wings!

➤ A weapons carrier Me 323 carried 11 automatic cannon and a crew of 17 men.

➤ The Gigant's cockpit was as high as a third-storey window.

➤ Me 323s saw service from the ice on the Eastern Front to the heat of the desert.

➤ The Gigant introduced many features now standard on cargo aircraft, including clamshell loading doors and high wings.

PROFILE

Messerschmitt's monster weight lifter

Germany dominated the world in the design of gliders, and the Gigant proved it. The Me 321 was so huge that a special aircraft had to be developed as a tow ship. To carry soldiers and vehicles into a combat landing zone, a real mammoth was needed, and the Gigant filled the bill.

The powered version, the Messerschmitt Me 323, was so big it required six engines. As a glider and as an aircraft, the Gigant carried three vehicles or 200 combat troops with equipment. The clamshell nose door and the ability to 'roll-on, roll-off' cargoes was a futuristic idea adopted on big transports today.

Size and capacity were not enough. The Me 323 Gigant was very slow and, even with gun turrets, almost unable to defend itself. Made of fabric-covered steel tubes, the Gigant was nevertheless immensely strong and Allied fighters sometimes expended their ammunition without downing the lumbering giant. This remarkable aircraft succeeded only in regions where it did not have to face Allied warplanes.

Left: Key to the Gigant's ability was its huge cargo capacity. Its outsize fuselage could hold loads of up to 20 tons.

Even with six engines, it was an effort to get the Gigant into the air. The Luftwaffe had a lot of experience with assisted take-off, however, and using rockets enabled the Me 323 to lift heavy loads into the air with relative ease.

Me 323E Gigant

Type: heavy general-purpose transport

Powerplant: six 850-kW (1,140-hp.) Gnome-Rhône 14N 48/49 radial air-cooled engines

Maximum speed: 253 km/h (157 m.p.h.) at 1500 m (4,900 ft.)

Range: 1100 km (682 mi.)

Service ceiling: 4500 m (18,730 ft.)

Weights: empty 29,060 kg (69,932 lb.); loaded 45,000 kg (99,000 lb.)

Armament: one 20-mm (0.79-in.) cannon in each of two turrets (one on each wing), two 13-mm (0.51-in.) machine-guns in nose doors, and five 13-mm machine-guns firing from the flight deck

Dimensions:
span	55.00 m (180 ft.)
length	28.50 m (93 ft.)
height	9.60 m (31 ft.)
wing area	300 m² (3,228 sq. ft.)

Gigants were powered by French Gnome-Rhône radial engines, which were available in large numbers after the fall of France.

Armament varied greatly, but most Gigants carried five machine-guns in the flight deck, together with mounts for five or six infantry machine-guns in beam windows. More guns were added in the field.

The Me 323 had the then-novel feature of clamshell nose doors, which allowed vehicles to be rolled directly into the capacious cargo hold.

The low bed of the cargo hold and the wide-opening front doors made it simple to load outsize cargoes. This effective feature has been copied many times since the 1940s.

ME 323E-2 GIGANT

Fitted with a Mediterranean white theatre band this Me 323 was rushed into service on the Eastern Front serving with 1 Gruppe, Transportgeschwader 54, late in 1943.

Early gliders took off with jettisonable main wheels, landing on skids. The powered version had a pioneering multi-wheeled undercarriage for use on rough fields.

Structure of the Gigant was brutally simple: a strong framework of steel tubes mated with wooden-framed wings, and covered in fabric.

The Gigant was difficult to fly, since flaps and rudders required very high control forces to operate.

WEAPONS DATA

ME 323E-2/WT

In an attempt to provide protection against fighters, one Me 323 was heavily armed to serve as escort to other Gigants.

The Waffenträger carried 11 MG 151 cannon. Added to the machine-guns fired from the beam windows, they made the Me 323WT one of the most heavily armed aircraft ever flown.

Beam gun positions were protected by 90 mm (3½ in.) of armoured glass and 20 mm (¾ in.) of steel plate.

The Waffenträger concept was never really put to the test: extensive trials showed that conventional escort fighters provided more effective protection.

Gigant cargo loads

■ **TROOP CARRIER:**
At a time when most tactical transport aircraft could carry about 20 troops the Gigant could seat 120, three or four abreast on two decks. During the evacuation of North Africa Gigants were pushed to their limits. The lack of transport aircraft forced them to carry up to 200 troops, some in the wings.

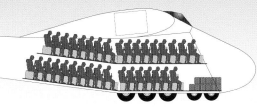

■ **ARTILLERY CARRIER:** Gigant was the only aircraft which could carry an artillery piece, its tractor and its crew in a single load. Gigant's large nose doors meant that it could also carry trucks, fuel bowsers, ambulances or other assorted cargo up to 20 tons with a minimum of preparation.

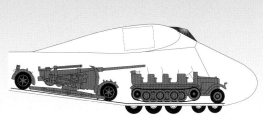

MIKOYAN-GUREVICH

MiG-1 AND MiG-3

● Interceptor fighter ● First of the MiGs ● Tactical reconnaissance

▲ The MiG-3 was a fast fighter but had poor handling and light armament. At the time of the invasion in 1941, over a third of the Soviet fighter force was equipped with MiG-1 and MiG-3 fighters.

I f they had not used the scarce Mikulin AM-35 engine, the MiG-1 and MiG-3 fighters might have served the USSR for much longer than they actually did. Unusually for wartime Soviet fighters, they performed better at altitude than at low level, and for this reason were often used as high-flying reconnaissance aircraft. More importantly, these warplanes launched the Mikoyan-Gurevich design bureau, the first to bear the immortal MiG name.

PHOTO FILE

MIKOYAN-GUREVICH MiG-1 AND MiG-3

▼ Radial engine
The I-211 was an attempt to match a radial M-82 engine to a MiG-3 airframe. It proved successful, but by this time the rival La-5 was in mass production and required these radial engines.

▲ First service
Many Soviet fighter units were still converting to the MiG-3 as war struck the USSR. These pilots of 12 GvIAP are swearing allegiance to the flag.

◄ Victim of the Luftwaffe
Below 5000 metres, the MiG-3 was inferior to the Bf 109 and Fw 190, and many were downed by the Luftwaffe in 1941. The machine-guns on top of the engine cowling have been exposed in this crashed aircraft.

▼ Caught on the ground
Because the Soviets hoped to contain German forces in the western USSR, many MiGs were based in this area. Consequently, hundreds were destroyed in the initial assault in June 1941. A final batch of 50 were built in 1942 from old spare parts.

◄ Design genius
Artem Mikoyan was half of the design team that produced the MiG fighters. Between 1940 and 1970, this outspoken and open-minded Armenian was the inspiration behind some of the world's finest fighters.

FACTS AND FIGURES

➤ Pilots of the 401st Fighter Squadron, one of the first MiG-3 units, included test pilot and fighter ace Stepan Surprun.

➤ A. N. Yekatov first flew the I-200 prototype for the MiG-1 on 5 April 1940.

➤ MiG tried the AM-39 engine in a revised MiG-3 airframe, called the I-231.

➤ Alexandr Pokryshkin gained his first kill, a Bf 109E of Jagdgeschwader 77, on 23 June 1941 while flying a MiG-3.

➤ The rear fuselage skin was made of Bakelite plywood bonded with glue.

➤ Test pilot Yekatov was killed in a MiG-3 when the supercharger exploded.

Genesis of the MiG fighters

MiG's first fighters were capable machines that fell foul of the requirement for an inline engine. The basic design was fairly capable, and the prototype (I-200), powered by a Mikulin AM-35 engine, was the equal of a Spitfire or early Bf 109.

The urgent demand for modern fighters to replace the Polikarpov I-16 set production going in 1940, despite some early handling problems. The first units were operational by the time of the invasion in 1941.

The weakness of the MiG-3 was that it shared the Mikulin AM-35 engine with Ilyushin's Il-2 Shturmovik. Stalin and his generals decreed that the Il-2 had absolute priority, and sent threatening telegrams to factory managers who continued to produce MiGs instead of Il-2s. Consequently, production was terminated in 1942, after only 3120 aircraft had been built.

Attempts to fit radial engines proved unsuccessful as they only added to the MiG's unforgiving reputation. This resulted in many MiGs being promptly replaced by Yak and Lavochkin fighters.

Despite its failure, the MiG proved useful in combat, giving a good account of itself when fighting above heights of 5000 metres. At lower altitudes, where much of the fighting took place, it was not quite the equal of the Fw 190 or Bf 109F.

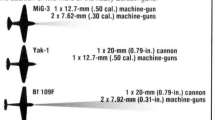

Left: By the time of the German invasion in June 1941, 13 fighter units had been fully equipped with the MiG-3.

Below: Demand for modern fighters was such that the I-200 prototype was built in just 100 days from first drawings.

MiG-3

Type: single-seat fighter

Powerplant: one 1007-kW (1,350-hp.) Mikulin AM-35A V-12 piston engine

Maximum speed: 640 km/h (397 m.p.h.) at 7800 m (25,600 ft.)

Range: 1195 km (743 mi.)

Service ceiling: 12,000 m (39,400 ft.)

Weights: empty 2595 kg (5,709 lb.); maximum take-off 3350 kg (7,370 lb.)

Armament: one 12.7-mm (.50 cal.) Beresin and two 7.62-mm (.30 cal.) ShKAS machine-guns, plus up to 200 kg (440 lb.) of bombs or six RS-82 rocket projectiles on underwing racks

Dimensions:
span	10.20 m	(33 ft. 9 in.)
length	8.25 m	(20 ft. 9 in.)
height	3.50 m	(11 ft. 6 in.)
wing area	17.44 m²	(188 sq. ft.)

MiG-3

Between December 1940 and December 1941, just over 3100 MiG-3s were built. The badge on this aircraft reads 'for the motherland'.

In the long nose section the Mikulin AM-35 engine with two 110-litre (29-gal.) fuel tanks was fitted. The MiG-3 had a second oil cooler and improved engine cooling compared to the MiG-1. The engine was quite heavy, at 830 kg (1,826 lb.) compared to the Bf 109's DB 601 of 575 kg (1,265 lb.). The exhaust pipes were made of EYa1-TL-1 heat-resistant steel.

All armament was grouped above the engine. It consisted of a UBS 12.7-mm machine-gun with 300 rounds and two 7.62-mm ShKAS machine-guns with 375 rounds each.

Like most Soviet aircraft the MiG-3 had a very austere cockpit fit, with only 13 instruments and no radio. The pilot sighted his weapons through a PBP-1 gunsight.

ЗА РОДИНУ

The engine drove a 3-m (10-ft.) diameter VISh-22Ye propeller made of a magnesium alloy known as electron.

Although the forward fuselage was made of steel tubing with an alloy stressed skin, the rear fuselage consisted of four pine longerons with a 0.5-mm (⅟₅₀-in.) plywood and calico skin.

COMBAT DATA

ARMAMENT

Perhaps the biggest failure of the MiG-3 was its weak armament. The weight of a salvo from the MiG was more than doubled with the addition of two more of the heavy Beresin guns.

MiG-3 1 x 12.7-mm (.50 cal.) machine-gun
2 x 7.62-mm (.30 cal.) machine-guns

Yak-1 1 x 20-mm (0.79-in.) cannon
1 x 12.7-mm (.50 cal.) machine-gun

Bf 109F 1 x 20-mm (0.79-in.) cannon
2 x 7.92-mm (0.31-in.) machine-guns

MAXIMUM SPEED

Supercharging the engine and the MiG's beautiful streamlined shape gave it very high speed, but without the AM-35 the MiG was useless, and no replacement engine was forthcoming.

MiG-3 628 km/h (397 m.p.h.)

Yak-1 531 km/h (329 m.p.h.)

Bf 109F 589 km/h (365 m.p.h.)

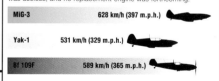

CEILING

Another benefit of the supercharger was the MiG's high ceiling. Performance at altitude was so good that German pilots always avoided combat with MiGs above an altitude of 5000 m (16,000 ft.). The reconnaissance MiGs were very hard to catch.

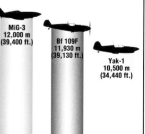

MiG-3
12,000 m
(39,400 ft.)

Bf 109F
11,930 m
(39,130 ft.)

Yak-1
10,500 m
(34,440 ft.)

Exploits of the MiG aces

ALEXANDR LUBOV: A pilot of the crack 16th Guards Polk, Lubov was never afraid to attack against superior odds. On one occasion, he flew his MiG-3 against a force of six Bf 109s, destroying two in seconds.

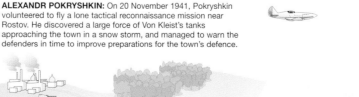

ALEXANDR POKRYSHKIN: On 20 November 1941, Pokryshkin volunteered to fly a lone tactical reconnaissance mission near Rostov. He discovered a large force of Von Kleist's tanks approaching the town in a snow storm, and managed to warn the defenders in time to improve preparations for the town's defence.

MITSUBISHI
A5M 'CLAUDE'

● Naval fighter ● Open cockpit ● Successful in China

▲ Pilots of the 'Claude' had to face the elements as it was the last Japanese naval fighter to be fitted with an open cockpit. However, they did have an exceptional field-of-view.

When it entered service at the beginning of 1937, the A5M 'Claude' represented a giant leap forwards in carrier-based fighters. Replacing antiquated biplane aircraft, it was the fastest naval fighter in the world and would remain so for almost two years. The A5M was the dominant fighter in the Sino-Japanese conflict, and built up an enviable reputation for strength and agility. By 1942, however, A5Ms were relegated to training duties.

MITSUBISHI **A5M 'CLAUDE'**

▲ **Action over China**
With superior training and high morale, pilots flying A5M2s devastated the Chinese air force, including its faster Polikarpov I-16s.

▲ **Long-legged 'Claude'**
To improve effective range the A5M4 was fitted with a 160-litre ventral drop-tank, which gave increased patrol endurance.

Dominant fighter ▶
When the 12 and 13 Kokutais entered the Sino-Japanese war in 1937, the A5M2 quickly gained complete air superiority.

▼ **A5M1 roll-out**
With its sleek lines and a flush-rivetted aluminium stressed-skin covering, this was the first A5M from the Sasebo Naval Factory. A total of 1094 'Claudes' had been built when production ended in 1940.

▲ **Small but strong**
After early handling problems were solved the A5M was a joy to fly, although landing accidents still occurred on rough strips. The 'Claude' could take considerable battle damage; one aircraft made it home despite losing a third of its port wing.

FACTS AND FIGURES

➤ Originally called the Ka-14, the 'Claude' easily exceeded the demands of the strict naval 9-Shi specification.

➤ The aircraft first flew at Kagamigahara on 4 February 1935.

➤ The first A5M aerial victories were three Curtiss Hawks of the Chinese air force.

➤ Seven A5M pilots became aces in the Sino-Japanese conflict; Lt Tetsuzo Iwamoto was the top ace with 14 'kills'.

➤ After May 1942 remaining A5Ms were relegated to training duties in Japan.

➤ A number of A5Ms ended their days in kamikaze attacks on Allied shipping.

PROFILE

Champion fighter over China

Despite decimating supposedly superior Chinese opposition in 1938, the A5M and the other rapid advances in Japanese aviation went largely unnoticed in the West. By the time Japan entered World War II the 'Claude' was being replaced by the superb A6M 'Zero', but it continued to serve in secondary roles throughout the war.

The strict 9-Shi specification of 1934 requested a fighter that was small enough to fit on an aircraft-carrier, but which was fast and manoeuvrable. Mitsubishi proposed the Ka-14, and production commenced with the A5M1, which proved in operations that the Japanese had a world-beating fighter. Development led to the more powerful A5M2 and A5M4 which were very impressive in the Sino-Japanese War.

Carrier-based A5M4s saw action at the start of World War II in Malaya and the Dutch East Indies. However, many A5Ms were used for last-ditch kamikaze raids in 1945.

A5M4 'CLAUDE'

Based on the aircraft-carrier *Soryu* during the blockade of the East China Sea in November 1939, this A5M4 was flown by Lieutenant Tamotsu, leader of the *Soryu* fighter element.

Work on a two-seat advanced trainer version, designated A5M4-K, began in 1940. A turn-over pylon was fitted between the cockpits to improve safety.

Two 7.7-mm (.303 cal.) Type 89 machine-guns were the standard armament for all operational versions of the 'Claude' except the A5M1a which had two 20-mm (0.79-in.) Oerlikon cannon.

To replace the biplane fighters in service, Mitsubishi's team designed the A5M as a low-wing gull monoplane.

The 'Claude' had an open cockpit. The pilot often had a gunsight extending from the centre of the windshield.

Japanese fighters were generally colourfully decorated in their squadron markings. Many aircraft were funded by public subscription and carried the inscription 'Hokokugo' (patriotism).

The Nakajima Kotobuki 41 KAI nine-cylinder radial engine drove a three-bladed propeller. To improve forward visibility from the cockpit a NACA (National Advisory Committee for Aeronautics) cowling with cooling flaps was fitted.

As the Chinese retreated beyond the range of the A5M2, the A5M4 was developed with a 160-litre (42-gal.) drop-tank.

At the design stage great attention was given to minimising the cross-section of the airframe to reduce drag. The metal structure was covered in an aluminium stressed skin.

A5M4 'Claude'

Type: single-seat carrier-borne fighter

Powerplant: one 529-kW (710-hp.) Nakajima Kotobuki 41 nine-cylinder air-cooled radial engine

Maximum speed: 440 km/h (270 m.p.h.)

Initial climb rate: 3000 m (9,800 ft.) in 3 min 35 sec

Range: 1200 km (750 mi.)

Service ceiling: 9800 m (32,200 ft.)

Weights: empty 1216 kg (2,675 lb.); maximum take-off 1705 kg (3,751 lb.)

Armament: two 7.7-mm (.303 cal.) Type 89 machine-guns fitted in the upper fuselage, plus two 30-kg (66-lb.) bombs

Dimensions:
span	11.00 m	(36 ft. 1 in.)
length	7.57 m	(24 ft. 10 in.)
height	3.27 m	(10 ft. 9 in.)
wing area	17.80 m²	(192 sq. ft.)

COMBAT DATA

MAXIMUM SPEED

When it entered service the A5M was the fastest naval fighter in the world. However, by the time of the Sino-Japanese War it had been overtaken by land-based fighters such as the I-16 and D.XXI.

A5M4 'CLAUDE'	440 km/h (270 m.p.h.)
I-16 TYPE 24	490 km/h (304 m.p.h.)
D.XXI	460 km/h (258 m.p.h.)

ARMAMENT

One of the major deficiencies of the A5M was its lack of firepower. By the mid to late 1930s most fighters had four, six or even eight machine-guns, which were much more destructive than two.

A5M4 'CLAUDE' 2 x 7.7-mm (.303 cal.) machine-guns 60-kg (132-lb.) bombload

I-16 TYPE 24 4 x 7.62-mm (.30 cal.) machine-guns 200-kg (440-lb.) bombload

D.XXI 4 x 7.9-mm (0.31-in.) machine-guns

RANGE

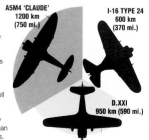

With its ventral drop-tank the 'Claude', like its replacement the A6M 'Zero', had far superior range over its contemporaries. This allowed it to harass opponents deep into enemy territory, as well as mounting patrols of great endurance. Land planes generally required less range than their naval equivalents.

A5M4 'CLAUDE' 1200 km (750 mi.)

I-16 TYPE 24 600 km (370 mi.)

D.XXI 950 km (590 mi.)

'Claude' colour schemes

TRAINING SQUADRONS: After the B-25 Doolittle raid on mainland Japan in April 1942, training aircraft were camouflaged with dark green upper surfaces and orange underneath.

14 KOKUTAI: Typical of the colour schemes worn by aircraft of the 14 Kokutai operating from China, this particular A5M4 was flown by Lieutenant Motonari Suho from Wichow Island in 1940.

SORYU AIRCRAFT-CARRIER: The 'W' prefix on the fin of this A5M4 clearly identifies it as being from the aircraft-carrier *Soryu*. The black auxiliary tank and fuselage bands were not standard.

MITSUBISHI

A6M ZERO

● Carrier fighter ● Highly agile dogfighter

▲ The A6M Zero in the hands of the highly trained pilots of the Imperial Japanese Navy could match any fighter in the world in the first two years of the Pacific war.

When Imperial Japanese forces burst like a tidal wave across the Pacific in December 1941, they were spearheaded by the amazing Mitsubishi Zero. It was not new even then, but Western experts had shrugged off reports that Japan possessed a world-class warplane. No American fighter matched the Zero in firepower, agility or range, and in the early stages of the war it was absolutely dominant.

MITSUBISHI A6M ZERO

▲ **Wonder fighter**
The Zero gained a reputation as an invincible opponent in the first two years of the Pacific war. Very much a 'pilot's aeroplane', it was one of the most agile aircraft ever built.

▲ **Range and performance**
With a drop-tank, the lightly-built Zero's combat endurance was an astonishing eight hours. Early versions had a range of more than 3000 km (1,900 mi.).

▲ **Pearl Harbor attack**
Zeroes aboard the carrier Shokaku prepare to take off as Japan launches the surprise attack on Pearl Harbor which marked the start of World War II in the Pacific.

▲ **Floatplane fighter**
The Zero's excellent range and adaptable airframe made it a successful seaplane fighter. It was given the codename 'Rufe'.

◄ **Jungle relic**
The remnants of a Zero lie rotting on a jungle airstrip. Such aircraft were still being discovered in remote Pacific islands as late as the 1970s, often in fair condition.

FACTS AND FIGURES

➤ The Reisen or 'zero fighter', named for the Japanese year 2600 (1940), was called 'Hamp' and 'Zeke' by the Allies.

➤ Early Sakae radial engines were superb, but quality declined sharply in the war.

➤ More Zeroes were manufactured than any other Japanese aircraft of the war.

➤ Of 125 Zeroes which participated in the 7 December 1941 raid on Pearl Harbor, only nine failed to return.

➤ More Zeroes were used in kamikaze attacks than any other Japanese aircraft.

➤ Only two airworthy Zeroes out of the 10,499 built exist today.

From Pearl Harbor to kamikaze

The A6M1 prototype flew on 1 April 1939. Built to an exacting Imperial Navy specification, it performed better than almost any fighter in the world in every area except speed.

The notion that Japan could produce a superb combat craft was so alien to the West that ordinary fighters like the Nakajima Ki-43 'Oscar' were mistakenly called 'Zeroes' and overestimated by besieged Americans. Colonel Claire Chennault's 'Flying Tigers' in China never saw a Zero but their combat reports fuelled growing alarm as the Japanese navy swept across the Pacific with squadrons of the real thing: the A6M, designed by Mitsubishi's Jiro Horikoshi.

The early successes of the Zero were due in part to its light weight, power, armament and manoeuvrability – but also partly to its brilliant and courageous pilots, many of whom fell along the way and proved difficult to replace.

The initial success was not to last for long. Within two years, Japan's adversaries developed new warplanes like the hard-hitting Grumman F6F Hellcat, while only minor improvements were made to the Zero. The tide turned, Japan's situation deteriorated, and in the end, as defeat closed in, this great fighter was reduced to the role of kamikaze – suicide – aircraft.

A6M3 Zero

Type: single-seat carrier-based fighter-bomber

Powerplant: one 843-kW (1,130-hp.) Nakajima NK1F Sakae 21 radial engine

Maximum speed: 565 km/h (350 m.p.h.)

Range: 1800km (1,200 mi.) with drop-tank

Service ceiling: 11,740 m (38,500 ft.)

Weights: empty 1876 kg (4,000 lb.); loaded 2733 kg (6,025 lb.)

Armament: two 7.7-mm (.303 cal.) machine-guns with 600 rounds above the engine and two 20-mm (0.79-in.) Type 99 cannon with 100 rounds each in the wings, plus two 60-kg (130-lb.) bombs under wings (suicide mission, one 250-kg/550-lb. bomb)

Dimensions:
span	11.00 m	(36 ft. 1 in.)
length	9.12 m	(29 ft. 11 in.)
height	3.60 m	(11 ft. 6 in.)
wing area	21.30 m²	(230 sq. ft.)

A6M5c ZERO

By the end of 1943 the original Zero was being outfought by new American fighters. The improved A6M5 was introduced to try to close the gap, and was built in greater numbers than any other model.

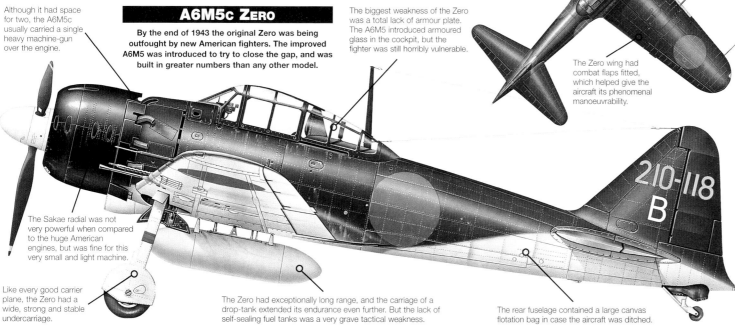

Although it had space for two, the A6M5c usually carried a single heavy machine-gun over the engine.

The Sakae radial was not very powerful when compared to the huge American engines, but was fine for this very small and light machine.

Like every good carrier plane, the Zero had a wide, strong and stable undercarriage.

The Zero had exceptionally long range, and the carriage of a drop-tank extended its endurance even further. But the lack of self-sealing fuel tanks was a very grave tactical weakness.

The biggest weakness of the Zero was a total lack of armour plate. The A6M5 introduced armoured glass in the cockpit, but the fighter was still horribly vulnerable.

The Zero wing had combat flaps fitted, which helped give the aircraft its phenomenal manoeuvrability.

Zeroes had three fuel tanks, one in each wingroot and a fuselage tank just in front of the pilot. This usually meant death for the pilot if a bullet hit the aircraft.

The A6M5c carried a 20-mm (0.79-in.) cannon inboard and a 13.2-mm heavy machine-gun outboard in each wing.

The rear fuselage contained a large canvas flotation bag in case the aircraft was ditched.

COMBAT DATA

RANGE

The Zero's light weight and highly efficient engine meant that it had a longer range than almost any other single-seat fighter of World War II. This made it ideally suited to the long-range war over the Pacific, but less suited to actual combat, where the lack of protection made it vulnerable to enemy fire.

P-40C WARHAWK 975 km (605 mi.)

A6M2 ZERO 3110 km (1,900 mi.)

F6F-1 HELLCAT 1750 km (1,080 mi.)

CLIMB RATE

One rule which successful American pilots followed was to never get into a dogfight with a Zero. At low speeds the lightly-built Japanese machine could easily out-turn its heavier American opponents, and in the early days of the war it could climb twice as fast as heavy machines like the Curtiss P-40.

A6M2 ZERO 1370 m/min (4,500 f.p.m.)

F6F-1 HELLCAT 990 m/min (3,200 f.p.m.)

P-40C WARHAWK 750 m/min (2,400 f.p.m.)

ARMAMENT

Although the Zero's designers sacrificed protection to save weight, they decided from the very beginning to equip their nimble fighter with heavy cannon. Although slow-firing, these hard-hitting weapons gave the Zero a decided advantage over American fighters armed only with machine-guns.

A6M2 ZERO 2 x 20-mm (0.79-in.) cannon 2 x 7.7-mm (.303 cal.) machine guns

P-40C WARHAWK 6 x 12.7-mm (.50 cal.) machine guns

F6F-1 HELLCAT 6 x 12.7-mm (.50 cal.) machine gun

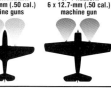

Attack on Pearl Harbor

DRAGGED INTO THE WAR: The Japanese assault came as a complete surprise to the American Pacific Fleet. At 6 a.m. on the morning of 7 December 1941, Zero fighters took off from the six aircraft-carriers of Japan's First Air Fleet, followed by Aichi 'Val' dive-bombers and Nakajima 'Kate' torpedo-bombers. Their destination: Pearl Harbor.

FIRST WAVE

Wheeler
Kaneohe
Bellows
Ewa
Hickam
Pearl Harbor

FIRST WAVE: The first wave reached Oahu at 7.53 a.m. The fighters and dive-bombers concentrated on Wheeler Field, Bellows Field and Kaneohe, while level bombers and torpedo-bombers hit Pearl Harbor and the airfields on Ford Island, Ewa and Hickam Field.

SECOND WAVE

Wheeler
Kaneohe
Ford Island
Hickam

SECOND WAVE: Taking off at 7.15, the second wave arrived 30 minutes after the end of the first attack. The main bulk of the attack concentrated on port facilities and the battleships at Ford Island, although some fighters and bombers diverted to make further strikes at airfields.

MITSUBISHI
G4M 'BETTY'

● Bomber ● Missile carrier ● Transport

▲ Mitsubishi's G4M was a very modern design when it appeared in 1941, and it was modified considerably with extra guns, more powerful engines and propellers and a laminar-flow wing.

Mitsubishi's G4M 'Betty' bomber made its name by sinking two battleships in a day in 1941. Although the 'Betty' was not a perfect design, lacking in protection, this twin-engine warplane had respectable performance and bomb-carrying capacity. This much admired aircraft was the backbone of Japan's bomber force all the way through to the end of World War II, by which time it was used for carrying missiles.

MITSUBISHI G4M 'BETTY'

▼ **Best bomber**
For all its faults, the G4M was one of the best bombers Japan owned, and was built in larger numbers than any other Japanese bomber.

▲ **Glazed nose**
The distinct glazed nose housed a 7.7-mm (.303 cal.) machine-gun and the bomb-aimer's seat. The nose also contained anti-surface vessel radar in a small number of modified 'Bettys'.

Long range ▼
For duties in Japan's vast Pacific empire, the G4M had exceptional range.

▲ **Dorsal turret**
In an effort to increase defence, the G4M2 was fitted with a dorsal gun turret containing a 20-mm (0.79-in.) Type 99 cannon. The gunner reached the weapon by standing on a platform inside the fuselage.

▼ **Dead 'Betty'**
Like many Japanese aircraft, the G4M had long range but little armour protection. It did not take much attention from enemy fighters to destroy one.

▲ **More power**
Another improvement to the G4M2 was to fit bigger engines with four-bladed propellers, namely the Kasei 21 radial with water injection.

FACTS AND FIGURES

➤ In April 1943, P-38s downed a 'Betty' carrying Admiral Yamamoto, killing Japan's top commander.

➤ The prototype G4M bomber first took to the skies on 23 October 1939.

➤ Though primarily a bomber, the G4M existed in trainer and transport versions.

➤ The first mission to launch Okha missiles from G4Ms was a disaster, as all were shot down before releasing the weapon.

➤ In 1944 many G4M bombers were converted to carry Okha suicide aircraft.

➤ G4Ms helped sink the British battleships Prince of Wales and Repulse.

PROFILE

Bombing with the 'Betty'

The G4M was a sound design, but too much was asked of it, especially at the end of the war. It was very successful during early operations in China.

Nicknamed 'Betty' by the Allies, this bomber did not have enough defensive armament and was susceptible to a fiery doom if its fuel was ignited. Some American pilots called the G4M the 'flying cigarette lighter'. Even so, Japan threw 2000 Mitsubishi G4Ms into the Pacific battle. The practical qualities of this aircraft, including its reliability and long range, frequently overcame its shortcomings, leaving a trail of

destruction in its wake.

Designed in 1937 and becoming operational in 1940, the 'Betty' had an unremarkable record with the Japanese army, but became one of the strongest weapons in Japan's naval force. Manufactured in greater numbers than any other Japanese aircraft, the G4M achieved considerable success in long-range bombing duties.

Mitsubishi engineers improved the 'Betty' as the war progressed, adding a better

tailgun and other features, but even though pilots liked the aircraft it was a creature of the past, not the future. Ironically, after years of war, the G4M's final duty was to carry the Japanese surrender delegation to the island of Ie Shima four days after the fighting ended.

G4M2 'Betty'

Type: twin-engined seven-seat land-based naval medium-bomber

Powerplant: two 1343-kW Mitsubishi Kasei 25 radial engines

Maximum speed: 438 km/h (270 m.p.h.) at 4600 m (15,000 ft.)

Climb rate: 32 minutes to 8000 m (26,250 ft.)

Range: 4335 km (2,694 mi.)

Weights: empty 8160 kg (17,952 lb.); loaded 12,500 kg (27,500 lb.)

Armament: one 20-mm (0.79-in.) cannon in tail, two 7.92-mm (0.31-in.) machine-guns in nose and one in each beam position; 1000 kg (2,200 lb.) of bombs or one 800-kg (1,760-lb.) torpedo

Dimensions:
span	25.00 m	(82 ft.)
length	20.00 m	(66 ft.)
height	6.00 m	(20 ft.)
wing area	78.12 m²	(841 sq. ft.)

The two pilots sat side-by-side in the cockpit, which had an emergency roof escape hatch. The navigator sat below and to the rear.

Kiro Honjo, the G4M designer, had envisaged a longer span wing for greater range, but for structural strength he eventually decided on this design with four fuel tanks in the leading edge of the wings.

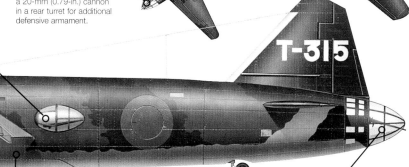

G4M 'BETTY'

This G4M Model 11 served on the Rabaul front in 1942 with the first Chutai of the Takao Kokutai, which suffered very heavy losses in action. This model does not have the dorsal turret of the G4M2.

Early 'Bettys' had distinct blisters on the fuselage sides for the waist gunners, who each operated a 7.7-mm (.303 cal.) machine-gun. These were deleted in the G4M2 in favour of a further gun position with 20-mm (0.79-in.) cannon.

The low-set tailplane was aerodynamically very clean and had a glass tailcone for a rearwards observer. Later versions possessed a 20-mm (0.79-in.) cannon in a rear turret for additional defensive armament.

T-315

Kasei 21 two-row radial engines were fitted to the early G4Ms, followed by Kasei 25s in the G4M2.

Unusually, the G4M bomb-bay did not have conventional hinged doors but fixed ones which could be removed before a mission to accommodate the weapon load.

The tail gunner's position gave the fuselage its distinct cigar shape. It also housed a 20-mm (0.79-in.) Type 99 cannon with a 60-round ammunition drum.

ACTION DATA

MAXIMUM SPEED

The G4M was a fast, twin-engined bomber that could outrun many fighters at the start of the war. However, with the introduction of newer fighters, such as the F6F Hellcat and P-51 Mustang, lightly armed G4Ms became easy prey.

G4M2 'BETTY'	438 km/h (270 m.p.h.)
WELLINGTON	378 km/h (230 m.p.h.)
He 111H	365 km/h (225 m.p.h.)

BOMBLOAD

The Wellington could carry more than twice the weight of bombs of its two contemporaries. The G4M sacrificed a heavy bombload for increased speed and range. By 1943 all three of these aircraft were outclassed by the massive British and American four-engined bombers of the war.

G4M2 'BETTY'	WELLINGTON	He 111H
1000 kg (2,200 lb.)	2041 kg (4,490 lb.)	1000 kg (2,200 lb.)

RANGE

Designed for operations over the vast areas of the Pacific Ocean, G4Ms possessed excellent range allowing them to strike far from their bases. Both the Wellington and He 111 operated in the more confined European theatre and therefore did not need such long reach. Later in the war long-range versions of the Wellington were used for maritime patrol and strike.

G4M2 'BETTY' 4334 km (2,694 mi.)

WELLINGTON 2500 km (1,550 mi.)

He 111H 1950 km (1,200 mi.)

Japanese bombers of World War II

■ **MITSUBISHI G3M:** Also possessing very long range, the G3M was used in the attacks on HMS *Prince of Wales* and *Repulse*. Most G3Ms were used for secondary roles by 1945.

■ **MITSUBISHI Ki-21:** Another medium-bomber design that was approaching obsolescence, the Ki-21 was used on suicide commando attacks on US bases in 1944.

■ **NAKAJIMA Ki-49:** Codenamed 'Helen' by the Allies, the Ki-49 featured a good defensive armament and fuel protection, but carried only a light bombload over a fairly short range.

■ **MITSUBISHI Ki-67:** Produced at the end of the war, the Ki-67 was a fast design with good armament. By the time it was in production massive American air raids hindered delivery.

MORANE-SAULNIER

M.S.406

● Interceptor ● Used by Finland ● Also built in Switzerland

French experts developed the M.S.406 while the Messerschmitt Bf 109 was entering service in Germany. Unfortunately, the Morane-Saulnier aircraft looked better than it flew. It lacked power and was never the equal of the Bf 109. After suffering heavy losses in France, the M.S.406 was relegated to serving with a single unit of the Vichy air force. Ironically, M.S.406s with Russian engines were used with some success by Finland's air force.

▲ This Finnish M.S.406 is seen next to a captured Soviet Yak-1, its opponent which provided the Klimov engines which the Finns fitted in their Morane-Saulnier aircraft.

PHOTO FILE

MORANE-SAULNIER M.S.406

▲ Prototype test
This M.S.405, forerunner to the M.S.406, was used for early trials. Pilots liked the aircraft, but immediately recognised the limitations of its design.

▲ Colonial base
Many M.S.406s were deployed to North Africa before the German invasion of France and saw no action. A few French aces, such as Robert Wuilliame, downed aircraft over France, usually Ju 87 Stukas.

▲ Nose in the grass
The majority of the M.S.406s that fought ended up like this aircraft. Although some gained kills, tangling with a Messerschmitt was a dangerous occupation.

▼ Swiss defender
Switzerland built almost 290 of the EFW D-3800 fighter, based closely on the M.S.406 airframe.

▲ Lebanese gold
France deployed the M.S.406 to its Middle Eastern bases in March 1940. This aircraft of G.C.1/7, number 805, was off-loaded in Beirut by the seaplane carrier Commandant Teste. The M.S.406 had little more success here than in Europe.

FACTS AND FIGURES

➤ Only 572 of the planned 1,000 M.S.406s had been delivered to the French air arm when the war began.

➤ Switzerland manufactured 289 fighters in two models based on the M.S.406.

➤ The first production M.S.406 flew on 24 January 1939.

➤ On the first day of the Battle of France 37 M.S.406s were destroyed by the Luftwaffe on the ground.

➤ The limited production run of the M.S.406 occupied three factories over 14 months.

➤ Some French aircraft ended up in Finland and Croatia during the occupation.

France's failed fighter

Developed from the M.S.405 of 1934, the M.S.406 was a sleek monoplane but had features which were soon out of date, including a braced tailplane and significant fabric construction.

Although the aircraft was well-behaved in the hands of a capable pilot and was not difficult to fly, it lacked power for the aerial combat that was to become routine in the 1940s. During the first year of the war, the M.S.406 claimed 175 kills but for the loss of over 400 of its kind.

Versions of the M.S.406 for China, Lithuania and Yugoslavia were never delivered, although others flew with Finland and Switzerland. The Vichy French regime kept some of these planes flying, but by then it was too late for the M.S.406 to mount the effective defence for which it had been intended. Germany gave the captured French aircraft to its Croat and Finnish allies, and the Finns made the M.S.406 a success by installing the powerful 820-kW (1,100-hp.) Klimov engine. With this powerplant the aircraft proved quite successful, and served until the end of the war.

Above: The pre-production M.S.405 was produced as a testbed for the mass-produced M.S.406 fighter.

Below: Poland was one of several customers that ordered the M.S.406 but did not receive it in time. It was then used by the French air force.

M.S.406C-1

Type: single-engine fighter

Powerplant: one 641-kW (860-hp.) Hispano-Suiza 12Y-31 V-12 piston engine

Maximum speed: 485 km/h (300 m.p.h.) at 5000 m (16,500 ft.)

Range: 1100 km (680 mi.)

Service ceiling: 9400 m (31,000 ft.)

Weights: empty 1900 kg (4,180 lb.); maximum take-off 2470 kg (5,434 lb.)

Armament: one engine-mounted 20-mm (0.79-in.) cannon firing through propeller hub and two wing-mounted 7.5-mm (0.3-in.) machine-guns

Dimensions:
span	10.60 m	(23 ft. 9 in.)
length	8.15 m	(26 ft. 9 in.)
height	2.80 m	(9 ft. 3 in.)
wing area	16.00 m²	(172 sq. ft.)

M.S.406C

The most numerous fighter in service with the Armée de l'Air in 1940, only half of the 1000 M.S.406s ordered reached the squadrons. By the end of July 1940, 400 of these had fallen to the Luftwaffe.

One of the best features was the engine-mounted 20-mm (0.79-in.) Hispano cannon, which fired through the propeller hub.

The tubular gunsight in front of the cockpit was a throwback to the 1930s.

The majority of the rear fuselage was fabric-covered. The tailplane had large bracing struts for support.

Most of the failings of the M.S.406 were caused by lack of power from the Hispano-Suiza 12Y engine. When Finland replaced this with the Klimov powerplant the resultant aircraft (known as Morko Moraani) was greatly improved.

Secondary armament of two 7.5-mm (0.3-in.) machine-guns was housed in the wings. These fired outside the propeller disc.

Early M.S.406s had only a tailskid, but later aircraft were fitted with a retractable tailwheel.

COMBAT DATA

MAXIMUM SPEED

French fighters of 1939 were slower than their German and British contemporaries. Although the D.520 was deemed adequate, taking on a Bf 109 in an M.S.406 or a Bloch 152 was disastrous.

M.S.406C-1	485 km/h (300 m.p.h.)
D.520	535 km/h (331 m.p.h.)
BLOCH 152	482 km/h (298 m.p.h.)

ARMAMENT

With only a single cannon and two machine-guns the M.S.406 was underarmed. The D.520, however, had superior firepower and could match the Bf 109 in weaponry during 1940.

M.S.406C-1	1 x 20-mm (0.79-in.) cannon / 2 x 7.5-mm (0.3-in.) MGs
D.520	1 x 20-mm (0.79-in.) cannon / 4 x 7.5-mm (0.3-in.) MGs
BLOCH 152	2 x 20-mm (0.79-in.) cannon / 2 x 7.5-mm (0.3-in.) MGs

RANGE

The French warplanes of the period had relatively small, but economical, engines. The Hispano-Suiza 12Y gave the M.S.406 excellent range allowing it to dogfight for longer than its opponents.

BLOCH 152 955 km (592 mi.)

D.520 890 km (552 mi.)

M.S.406C-1 1100 km (680 mi.)

French fighters in 1940

■ **BLOCH 152:** Another design that reflected the sorry state of French aircraft design in the 1930s, it was difficult for the Bloch 152 to catch a Dornier 17, let alone a Bf 109.

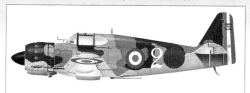

■ **CURTISS HAWK:** Purchased from America, the Curtiss 75 claimed some victories against the Luftwaffe, but was inferior to the Bf 109; many French Hawks were given to Finland by Germany.

■ **DEWOITINE 520:** The best fighter available to France in 1940, the D.520 was only in service with a few units. Unlike the M.S.406, it could take on the Bf 109 with a reasonable chance of success.

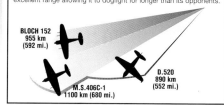

NAKAJIMA

KI-43 HAYABUSA 'OSCAR'

● Interceptor ● Air defence ● Kamikaze aircraft

Named Hayabusa (peregrine falcon) by the Japanese army, the Ki-43 was ordered in December 1937 as a replacement for the Ki-27 'Nate'. The aircraft had a retracting undercarriage, but its performance was not much better than that of the earlier fighter. Even so, the Hayabusa was more than a match for the Allied fighters in the early stages of the Pacific War, and in terms of numbers it became the Imperial Army's most important fighter.

▲ The Hayabusa might not have been produced if the Japanese army had adopted the superior Mitsubishi A6M, but the rivalry with the navy meant that the service had to have its own fighter despite the inferiority of the design.

▲ PHOTO FILE

NAKAJIMA KI-43 HAYABUSA 'OSCAR'

▼ **Big wing**
The prototype Hayabusa had poor manoeuvrability, so a new wing was designed with increased area and combat flaps. This gave the aircraft an excellent ceiling as well as improved agility.

▲ **On test**
The Allies tested a Hayabusa and discovered its lack of armour protection and limited armament. In many ways the Ki-43 was a poor performer, but it could outmanoeuvre most Allied fighters.

▼ **Fighter mission**
Most Ki-43s were used on fighter missions in a vain attempt to stop American bomber raids, but by 1944 a shortage of other aircraft meant that it was used for ground-attack duties.

▲ **Hucks starter**
Like many fighter aircraft of the day, the Hayabusa required mechanical starting. The Sakae radial engine was one of the plane's best features.

More guns ▶
In an attempt to give the Hayabusa more effective firepower, it was fitted with two 20-mm (0.79-in.) cannon but still lacked punch.

FACTS AND FIGURES

➤ Hayabusas were used in theatres of war as far apart as Burma, China, Japan, the Philippine Islands and Thailand.

➤ The Ki-43-IIIb interceptor with cannon armament never entered service.

➤ By 1945 Hayabusas were often used as kamikaze aircraft on suicide missions.

➤ The Hayabusa was designed to replace Nakajima's own Ki-27 to a specification from the Imperial Japanese army.

➤ Production of the Ki-43 totalled 5,919, including 3239 by Nakajima.

➤ When it entered service the Ki-43 was said to be the army's most agile fighter.

PROFILE

Japan's peregrine falcon

W ith a top speed of less than 500 km/h (310 m.p.h.) and armed with only a pair of light 7.7-mm (.303 cal.) machine-guns, the Ki-43-I-Hei was almost obsolete by the time it entered service in 1941. It was highly agile, though, and the 40 in service by December of that year faced little opposition during the invasions of Burma and Malaya.

More powerful engines improved performance, however, and the Ki-43-II-Ko was used

widely as a fighter-bomber, carrying a 250-kg (550-lb.) bomb under each wing. In September 1943 the Allies captured several damaged 'Oscars' on an airfield in New Guinea. They were able to build a complete example from the wreckage, and after testing it they worked out how to counter its outstanding low-speed manoeuvrability.

But its replacement, the P-51 Mustang-beating Ki-84, was late, and the more powerful Ki-43-III-Ko had to remain in production

until the end of the war. Nearly 6000 Ki-43s had been completed by then, and the Hayabusa was still in widespread service, even though it was clearly outclassed by the modern fighters it faced. One of the Hayabusa's last roles was as a kamikaze aircraft, frequently loaded up with underwing bombs for additional effect.

Although it was a capable performer in 1941, the Hayabusa was not in the same league as later Allied fighters and losses were very high in 1944.

KI-43 HAYABUSA 'OSCAR'

Built between 1939 and 1945, the Ki-43 was the most numerous fighter in Japanese army service. By 1945 most aircraft had been withdrawn to the home islands for defence against daylight B-29 bomber raids.

The Hayabusa was powered by a Nakajima 14-cylinder air-cooled radial engine. The final interceptor variant would have used the Ha-112 version of this engine if it had ever been put into production.

Unlike most single-seat Japanese fighters, the Ki-43 had some cockpit armour and fuel tank protection.

The Ki-43 was superseded in production by the Ki-43-IIa. This featured a Ha-115 engine and additional pilot armour, as well as innovative self-sealing fuel tanks.

The wing hardpoints were repositioned in the Ki-43-IIb, as some early aircraft had taken off their own propellers when dropping their bombload.

The main armament was two 12.7-mm (.50 cal.) machine-guns in the wings. This had originally been two 7.7-mm (.303 cal.) weapons, later changed to one 7.7-mm and one 12.7-mm gun in the Ki-43-1b variant.

A pair of fuel tanks could be fitted under the wings to extend the Hayabusa's impressive range.

Two underwing 250-kg (550-lb.) bombs could be carried for ground attack or kamikaze missions.

Combat flaps were fitted to the wings to enhance turning performance in a dogfight.

The Japanese forces frequently painted their fighters with gaudy unit markings, like the red lightning strikes on the tail of this aircraft and the blue spinner and stripes shown in the plan view.

Ki-43IIb Hayabusa 'Oscar'

Type: single-seat land-based radial-engined interceptor fighter

Powerplant: one 858-kW (1,150-hp.) Nakajima Ha-115 radial piston engine

Maximum speed: 530 km/h (329 m.p.h.)

Climb rate: 5000 m (16,400 ft.) in 5.8 min

Maximum range: 1760 km (1,090 mi.)

Service ceiling: 11,200 m (36,750 ft.)

Weights: empty 1910 kg (4,202 lb.); loaded 2925 kg (6,435 lb.)

Armament: two 12.7-mm (.50 cal.) machine-guns and up to two 250-kg (550-lb.) bombs underwing

Dimensions:
span	10.84 m	(35 ft. 6 in.)
length	8.92 m	(29 ft. 3 in.)
height	3.27 m	(10 ft. 9 in.)
wing area	21.40 m²	(230 sq. ft.)

COMBAT DATA

MAXIMUM SPEED

The lightweight Ki-43 had a good power-to-weight ratio, making it one of the best performers in its class. Although quicker than the less aerodynamic MC.200, the Ki-43 was slower than the big P-40.

Ki-43IIb HAYABUSA — 530 km/h (329 m.p.h.)

MC.200 — 502 km/h (311 m.p.h.)

P-40N WARHAWK — 552 km/h (378 m.p.h.)

SERVICE CEILING

In terms of altitude, the Ki-43 was superior to both the P-40 and MC.200. However, by the time the American Hellcat and Mustang were on the scene it was firepower and agility that counted most.

Ki-43IIb HAYABUSA 11,200 m (36,750 ft.)

MC.200 SAETTA 8900 m (29,200 ft.)

P-40N WARHAWK 9450 m (38,000 ft.)

FIXED ARMAMENT

The small Ki-43 was let down by its light armament, especially when compared to the Italian MC.200 and the P-40N, which are in a class of their own. However, the Ki-43 could carry additional bombs.

Ki-43IIb HAYABUSA 2 x 12.7-mm (.50 cal.) machine-guns

MC.200 2 x 12.7-mm (.50 cal.) and 2 x 7.7-mm (.303 cal.) machine-guns

P-40N WARHAWK 6 x 12.7-mm (.50 cal.) machine-guns

Nakajima fighters

■ **Ki-27 'NATE':** Production of the pre-war vintage Ki-27 ended in 1942, after nearly 4000 had been delivered. For most of the war it served only in less-important theatres and as a trainer.

■ **Ki-44 SHOKI 'TOJO':** Nakajima began designing the Ki-44 immediately after the Ki-43, and the new machine featured an uprated engine, and increased manoeuvrability and top speed.

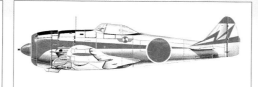

■ **Ki-84 HAYATE 'FRANK':** Entering service late in the war, the Ki-84 was superior to the P-51H Mustang and P-47N Thunderbolt. It was deployed in small numbers, however, so its impact was reduced.

NAKAJIMA

KI-84 'FRANK'

● Single-seat fighter/fighter-bomber ● Agile defender of Japan

No fighter ace of World War II was deadlier than the pilot of the powerful Nakajima Ki-84 Hayate ('gale' – nicknamed 'Frank' by the Allies). One of the few entirely new fighters developed by Japan once hostilities were under way, the potent Ki-84 climbed faster and was more manoeuvrable than the American P-51D Mustang and P-47N Thunderbolt. Unfortunately for Japan, this impressive warplane came too late to turn the tide.

▲ *The Ki-84 was by many accounts Japan's best fighter of World War II. Adding performance to the extreme agility of earlier Japanese fighters, it was an immensely potent war machine. But for Japan it was too little, too late.*

PHOTO FILE

NAKAJIMA KI-84 'FRANK'

▲ Raw pilots
The Ki-84 might have performed better if Japan had better pilots, but many of the experts had been killed in the early war years.

Wasted potential ▶
Poor reliability and Allied air superiority meant that most Ki-84s undeservedly ended up as scrap metal on Pacific Islands.

▲ Powerful performer
With a large engine and a four-bladed propeller, the Ki-84 was in the same league as the large Allied designs that it faced. It also maintained the startling manoeuvrability of earlier Japanese fighters.

▼ American 'Frank'
The US Technical Air Intelligence Command evaluated the Ki-84 after the war, prompting admiration from American test pilots. One Ki-84 was rebuilt in the USA in 1963, and was eventually returned to its homeland in 1973.

▲ Air defender
The Ki-84 ended up flying desperate defence missions against B-29 bombers attacking the Japanese homeland. This was less than ideal for the Ki-84, which performed better at low altitudes.

FACTS AND FIGURES

➤ Delivery of 373 Ki-84s in December 1944 marked the highest monthly production rate for any Japanese army fighter.

➤ Nakajima and Mansyu delivered 3382 Ki-84s in 17 months.

➤ Three Ki-106 all-wood fighters based on the 'Frank' design were built.

➤ The Ki-113 with strengthened structure and the Ki-116 with a lightweight engine were 'one-off' experimental Hayates.

➤ The planned Ki-117 interceptor version never reached service.

➤ Although slower, the 'Frank' could outmanoeuvre late-model Mustangs.

PROFILE

Japan's greatest fighter

Given the codename 'Frank' by the Allies, the Nakajima Ki-84 Hayate entered service in the summer of 1944. Had it come earlier, this excellent warplane would have posed serious problems for them: it was clearly the best Japanese fighter to serve in large numbers.

The prototype flew at Ojima in April 1943, and was rushed into service while the Allies pursued their relentless advance toward the Japanese home islands. In early clashes in the Philippines the 'Frank' proved a superior combatant, but was outnumbered from the start.

Production aircraft were plagued by inferior workmanship. Fuel and hydraulic problems were never fully solved but the Ki-84 performed effectively anyway, proving a fierce opponent in the final battle for Okinawa. Later models used wooden rear fuselage, fittings and wingtips to conserve strategic materials, but performance remained superb, an impression confirmed by American tests conducted after the war.

By the close of the conflict, underground factories were being readied to produce 200 Ki-84s per month.

The Ki-84 was a dangerous opponent against even the latest Allied types. When pitted against Curtiss P-40s in China and slower US Navy Hellcats, it proved deadly.

Ki-84-Ia 'Frank'

Type: single-seat interceptor fighter/fighter-bomber

Powerplant: one 1416-kW (1,900-hp.) Nakajima Ha-45-23 18-cylinder radial piston engine

Maximum speed: 631 km/h (391 m.p.h.) at 6120 m (20,000 ft.)

Range: 2168 km (1,350 mi.)

Service ceiling: 10,500 m (34,500 ft.)

Weights: empty 2660 kg (5,830 lb.); loaded 3890 kg (8,558 lb.)

Armament: two 12.7-mm (.50 cal.) Ho-103 synchronised nose machine-guns and two wing-mounted 20-mm (0.79-in.) Ho-5 cannon (later models had four cannon), plus underwing racks for two 250-kg bombs or two 190-litre (50-gal.) drop-tanks

Dimensions:
span	11.24 m (36 ft. 10 in.)
length	9.92 m (32 ft. 6 in.)
height	3.39 m (11 ft. 1 in.)
wing area	21.00 m² (226 sq. ft.)

KI-84-IA 'FRANK'

This 'Frank' was a home defence fighter serving with the 74th Sentai at Naruhatsu, Japan, in the summer of 1945.

The four-bladed propeller was a constant-speed electrically-operated variable-pitch unit.

The main fuselage tank carried up to 217 litres (60 gal.) of fuel. The provision of self-sealing tanks was a major improvement for Japanese fighters.

The bubble canopy gave the Ki-84's pilot superb all-round combat visibility.

A long-wing version of the Ki-84 was planned to counter high-flying B-29 bombers, but it never saw combat.

A pair of 190-litre (50-gal.) fuel tanks could be carried under the wings. The internal wing tanks had a capacity of 173 litres (45 gal.).

The handling of the Ki-84 was almost faultless, although test pilots complained that the elevators felt heavy at high speed and the rudder felt mushy at low speed.

The radio was fitted in a bay behind the cockpit, which had a large sheet of armour protecting the pilot's back.

The Ha-45-23 radial proved more reliable than previous Japanese engines. Later variants were turbo-supercharged.

The bomber-destroyer Ki-84-Ic variant carried a pair of 30-mm (1.18-in.) cannon mounted in the wingroots.

The white panel behind the national markings indicated a 'home defence' aircraft.

COMBAT DATA

MAXIMUM SPEED

Although the Ki-84 was faster than most other Japanese fighters, it could not match its American opponents for sheer speed. But at combat speeds it could accelerate very quickly, and its agility was superior.

Ki-84-Ia	631 km/h (391 m.p.h.)
P-51D MUSTANG	700 km/h (438 m.p.h.)
P-38J LIGHTNING	666 km/h (412 m.p.h.)

CLIMB RATE

The Japanese army and navy both emphasised climbing ability in their fighter specifications, and the Ki-84 was no exception. It could outclimb faster and more powerful types such as the P-51 Mustang and the P-38 Lightning.

- Ki-84-Ia 'FRANK' 1100 m/min (3,600 f.p.m.)
- P-51D MUSTANG 1000 m/min (3,280 f.p.m.)
- P-38J LIGHTNING 870 m/min (2,854 f.p.m.)

SERVICE CEILING

If the Ki-84 had a weakness, it was in its lack of ability at high altitude. That was no problem early in the war when its design was fixed, but by the end of the conflict bombers like the B-29 routinely operated at high altitudes that the 'Frank', with its radial engine, struggled to reach.

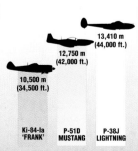

- Ki-84-Ia 'FRANK' 10,500 m (34,500 ft.)
- P-51D MUSTANG 12,750 m (42,000 ft.)
- P-38J LIGHTNING 13,410 m (44,000 ft.)

Defending Japan's home islands

■ NAKAJIMA Ki-44 'TOJO': The first Japanese fighter designed as an interceptor, the Ki-44's limited manoeuvrability made it unpopular when introduced in 1940. But late in the war it was to prove reasonably effective against high-level bombers.

■ KAWASAKI Ki-61 'TONY': The Ki-61 was powered by a Japanese copy of the German DB 601 inline engine. It was a capable fighter in the Messerschmitt Bf 109 mould, but maintenance problems meant that it could not be relied upon.

■ MITSUBISHI J2M 'JACK': Designed by the team which produced the Zero, the Raiden was a very different machine. An out-and-out interceptor it climbed fast and was heavily armed, but like most late-war Japanese fighters it was unreliable.

NORTH AMERICAN
B-25 MITCHELL

● Medium bomber ● Devastating low-level attacker ● Gunship

R ushing in at low level with guns blazing, this twin-engine medium bomber was the most fearsome sight of World War II. The North American B-25 Mitchell sent bombs screaming earthward from high in the sky, but it also attacked with speed and surprise down on the deck, strafing ships and troops with its lethal nose guns. The B-25 was a hard-hitter, a superb weapon, and a great aircraft.

▲ After the USAAF, the Royal Air Force was the most important B-25 user, taking 910 of nearly 10,000 built. Russia was also given 870 aircraft for the war on the Eastern Front.

NORTH AMERICAN B-25 MITCHELL

▼ **Long-lived B-25**
Mitchells fought in all theatres, including Italy, where this famous B-25 racked up an incredible 103 missions in a theatre in which air and ground defences were fierce.

▲ **Low-level gunship**
When the USAAF realised that most B-25 missions were at low level, they took out the bombardier and replaced him with a battery of guns in the nose and on the fuselage sides.

◀ **Mitchell with a message**
This B-25 carries the rousing legend 'Finito Benito, next Hirohito' along its wings – a reference to the defeat of the Italian dictator and the anticipated battle for Japan.

▼ **Shipping strikes**
In the Far East the B-25s were used to devastating effect against Japanese shipping, their low-level attacks being accurate and deadly.

▲ **Parachute bomber**
Attacking airfields at low level was no easy task because standard bombs would explode beneath the aircraft. Using bombs on parachutes allowed the B-25 to escape the blast.

FACTS AND FIGURES

➤ The Mitchell's American combat debut came on Christmas Eve 1941, when a B-25 sank a Japanese submarine.

➤ In the early years of the war, the B-25 was faster in a dive than many fighters.

➤ Mitchells often skip-bombed, bouncing bombs from low level across the water.

➤ The bombardier was not needed at low level, so many Mitchells were fitted with solid noses bristling with guns.

➤ A B-25H sank a Japanese destroyer with just seven shots from its 75-mm (2.95-in.) cannon.

➤ Mitchells were still flying as multi-engine trainers in the 1950s.

PROFILE

First of the gunships

The first bomber from North American, the graceful and deadly B-25 was named after the outspoken champion of US air power, General 'Billy' Mitchell. The B-25 is best remembered for the April 1942 bombing of Tokyo led by Lieutenant Colonel James Doolittle, which was launched from the carrier *Hornet*. At the time, the Allies were being defeated in the Pacific and this first strike on Japanese soil boosted American morale.

The Mitchell bomber fought all over the world. Pilots praised its speed, brute strength and quick control response. Some Mitchells carried nose 75-mm (2.95-in.) cannons to increase their firepower during low-level raids on Japanese shipping.

Mitchells flew with the Marines in tough Pacific fighting and were called PBJs. The B-25 also flew with a dozen other nations in Russia, North Africa and throughout Europe. It was frightening to be on the receiving end of a B-25 attack, but to the Allies the aircraft was a great warrior and a triumph of weaponry.

With a hard-hitting 75-mm (2.95-in.) cannon in the lower left fuselage, the B-25H was one of the most heavily armed aircraft of World War II.

The B-25's best-known exploit was the daring raid in April 1942 when Lt Col Jimmy Doolittle led 16 Mitchells from the deck of USS Hornet *on the first strike against the Japanese mainland.*

B-25H Mitchell

Type: five-seat medium bomber

Powerplant: two 1268-kW (1,700-hp.) Wright R-2600-92 Cyclone 14-cylinder radial piston engines

Maximum speed: early versions 500 km/h (275 m.p.h.); armed and armoured aircraft (typically) 438 km/h (240 m.p.h.) at 4000 m (13,125 ft.)

Range: 2200 km (1,300 mi.) with bombload

Service ceiling: 7375 m (23,800 ft.)

Weights: empty 8836 kg (19,400 lb.); loaded 15,876 kg (36,000 lb.)

Armament: one 75-mm (2.95-in.) cannon or up to 16 x 12.7-mm (.50 cal.) machine-guns, plus eight 127-mm (5-in.) rocket projectiles and up to 1360 kg (3,000 lb.) of bombs

Dimensions:
span	20.60 m (67 ft. 7 in.)
length	16.13 m (51 ft.)
height	4.98 m (15 ft. 9 in.)
wing area	56.67 m² (610 sq. ft.)

All but the first few Mitchells had this characteristic 'inverted gull' wing. This modification made the B-25 much more manoeuvrable than when it had a standard straight wing.

B-25J 'BETTY'S DREAM'

'Betty's Dream' flew in the south-west Pacific with the famed 499th Bomb Squadron, otherwise known as the 'Bats Outa Hell'. The whole front-end was adorned with a massive bat figure with teeth and wings.

The dorsal turret was used as protection against fighters, but could be locked forwards to add extra weight to the nose guns.

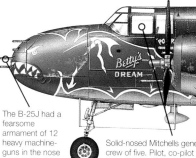

The B-25J had a fearsome armament of 12 heavy machine-guns in the nose and on the sides of the fuselage.

Solid-nosed Mitchells generally flew with a crew of five. Pilot, co-pilot and gunner occupied the flight deck, while two more gunners manned the waist and tail guns.

Quite apart from the heavy gun armament, the B-25 could also lift 1360 kg (3,000 lb.) of bombs in its two vertical bomb-bays.

The crew boarded the aircraft through hatches in the lower fuselage.

By far the most colourful of all the wartime Mitchells were those assigned to the 345th Bomb Group (Medium), which flew this solid-nosed B-25J in the Far East. The group was known as the 'Air Apaches', and its aircraft carried a large Indian's head on their tails.

M43 227-kg (500-lb.) General-Purpose Bomb

American GP bombs were generally of thin case construction, giving a high-explosive filling-to-weight ratio of around 51 per cent. There were two fuses, in the nose and tail.

The B-25 carried a maximum bombload of 1360 kg (3,000 lb.) internally, increased by underwing racks in some models to 2360 kg (5,000 lb.). A 907-kg (2,000-lb.) weapon could be carried, but four 227-kg (500-lb.) or two 454-kg (1,000-lb.) bombs were more usual.

3 GETTING CLEAR: At the last minute the aircraft lifted up and over the ship, an instant before the bomb hit.

Skip-bombing in the Pacific

Leading on from trials with a B-17, the USAAF honed the concept of skip-bombing to a fine art with the B-25.

2 FLAK SUPPRESSION: After bomb release the Mitchell continued its run towards the ship, with up to 14 guns blazing to keep Japanese heads down.

1 BOMB RUN: Releasing the bomb at low level and high speed caused it to bounce or 'skip' across the water, greatly increasing its range and accuracy against ship targets.

NORTH AMERICAN

P-51D MUSTANG

● Long-range escort fighter ● Most Allied kills ● 281 Mustang aces

▲ One of the great Mustang heroes, Major Don Gentile, with his favourite machine 'Shangri-La' during 1943. He made 15 kills in Mustangs – half of them in one month!

As the bombers of the Eighth Air Force fought their way deep into Hitler's German heartland, it was the Mustang that cleared the skies of Luftwaffe fighters. No other combat airplane of the war could fly as high, go as far and fight as hard as the mighty Mustang. In the skilled hands of young USAAF pilots, it took on all comers and accounted for more kills than any other Allied aircraft.

NORTH AMERICAN P-51D MUSTANG

◀ **All the way!**
With underwing tanks, Mustangs had enough range to be able to escort their charges more than 1200 km (746 m.p.h.) to the target and were agile enough to beat all comers when they got there.

▼ **High flyer**
The Mustang's phenomenal range and performance made it ideal for escorting high-flying B-29s across the vast Pacific.

◀ **Mud movers**
The Mustang's hard-hitting and accurate guns made it an excellent ground-attack aircraft, which could also deliver air-to-ground rockets or bombs.

Powerpack ▶
The early Mustang was transformed into a superb high-level fighter by the British-designed, Packard-built Rolls-Royce Merlin engine, which could deliver 1186 kW (1,590 hp.).

▼ **Flying veterans**
The Mustang's impeccable handling characteristics, bubble canopy and performance make it a popular rich man's toy; many of them are still flying. This example even carries a passenger!

FACTS AND FIGURES

➤ Ordered by the British, the prototype Mustang was proposed, designed, built and flown in an incredible 117 days.

➤ That initial aircraft was the first of 15,586 examples of the P-51 produced.

➤ The Mustang was flown by 11 Allied air forces in addition to the USAAF.

➤ A total of 281 Allied Mustang pilots were to qualify as 'Aces', with five or more kills.

➤ The P-51H was, at 760 km/h (472 m.p.h.), one of the fastest piston-engined fighters.

➤ In October 1944, Mustang pilot Lieutenant Urban L. Drew managed the astonishing feat of shooting down two Me 262 jets.

PROFILE

Top Gun to the bomber force

Faced with imminent invasion in 1939 and desperately short of fighters, the Royal Air Force asked North American Aviation to produce urgently the existing but obsolete P-40 Warhawk. But instead the company designed, built and flew a new airplane in just 117 days – the Mustang.

Using an existing Allison engine and the latest laminar-flow wing, the new fighter immediately went into service with the RAF. In December 1941 America joined the war, and it too needed good fighters fast. So the USAAF took the basic RAF Mustang, re-armed it with four machine-guns, and added an uprated engine. It was a good performer, but couldn't operate well alongside the high-flying long-range bomber.

By 1944 the aircraft used the Rolls-Royce Merlin engine, had a new bubble cockpit and

Mustangs were flown by more aces than any other Allied fighter. Their prey even included the Me 262 jet.

increased firepower to six 12.7-mm (.50 cal.) machine-guns. It was now the best fighter in the war and fought superbly in all theatres, as fighter, fighter-bomber and reconnaissance platform. It was loved by its aircrews, and no fewer than 281 Mustang pilots became aces by scoring five kills apiece.

P-51D Mustang

Type: single-seat long-range escort fighter, fighter-bomber

Powerplant: one 1186-kW (1,590-hp.) Packard V-1650-7 (US-built Rolls-Royce Merlin 61) inverted-vee 12-cylinder inline water-cooled piston engine

Maximum speed: 716 km/h (445 m.p.h.) at 7620 m (25,000 ft.)

Combat radius: 525 km (326 mi.) on internal fuel; 1210 km (752 mi.) with two 491-litre (108-gal.) tanks

Service ceiling: 12,770 m (41,900 ft.)

Weights: empty 3232 kg (7,125 lb.); loaded 5265 kg (11,607 lb.)

Armament: six 12.7-mm (.50 cal.) Browning machine-guns in wings; two 227-kg (500-lb.) bombs or eight 75-mm rockets in place of long-range drop-tanks

Dimensions:
span	11.29 m (37 ft.)
length	9.83 m (32 ft. 3 in.)
height	3.71 m (12 ft. 2 in.)
wing area	21.83 m² (235 sq. ft.)

The low-drag laminar-flow wing was largely responsible for the Mustang's combination of agility and long-range capability, and accommodated six 12.7-mm (.50 cal.) machine-guns.

P-51K MUSTANG 'NOOKY BOOKY IV'

This shortened propeller version of the P-51D was flown by Major Leonard 'Kit' Carson (left) of the 362nd Fighter Squadron, based at Leiston, Suffolk, during 1944. Carson was one of the top-scoring Mustang aces, with 18½ air-to-air victories.

The bubble canopy and cut-down rear fuselage of the P-51D gave the pilot an unsurpassed all-round view.

MAJ. KIT CARSON

Nooky Booky IV

G4 ★ C

411622

The P-51 was transformed by the adoption of the Merlin engine. The original Allison engine delivered plenty of power at low altitude, but was disappointing at higher altitude.

Even without optional underwing fuel tanks, the Mustang had a good radius of action: with tanks fitted it could escort bombers all the way to Berlin. These tanks could be jettisoned if the Mustang had to engage in manoeuvring combat.

Despite having an inline, liquid-cooled engine and a prominent and vulnerable ventral (underfuselage) radiator, the P-51D was remarkably tolerant of battle damage.

Initially painted with olive drab camouflaged top surfaces, paint was soon stripped off to save weight, and the bare skin was highly polished to reduce drag.

COMBAT DATA

RANGE

400 km (249 mi.) SPITFIRE Mk IX
580 km (360 mi.) P-47D THUNDERBOLT
1207 km (750 mi.) P-51D MUSTANG

The Mustang's combat radius was better than that of any other Allied fighter, and could stretch to Berlin.

MAXIMUM SPEED

Bf 109G	623 km/h (387 m.p.h.)
P-47D THUNDERBOLT	708 km/h (440 m.p.h.)
P-51D MUSTANG	716 km/h (445 m.p.h.)

The P-51D's clean, low-drag airframe and powerful Merlin engine endowed it with superb performance.

ARMAMENT

The P-51D packed a powerful punch, its fast-firing 12.7-mm (.50 cal.) calibre machine-guns proving deadly against enemy fighter targets, although they lacked the stopping power of a 20- or 30-mm cannon.

P-51D MUSTANG
6 x 12.7-mm (.50 cal.) machine-guns

Bf 109G
1 x 30-mm (1.18-in.) cannon in the spinner, 2 x 13-mm (0.51-in.) machine-guns in the nose
2 x 20/30-mm cannon underwing

SPITFIRE Mk IX
4 x 7.7-mm (.50 cal.) machine-guns
2 x 20-mm (0.79-in.) Hispano cannon

Mustang: the all-the-way escort fighter

■ **THE BOMBERS:** Eighth Air Force bombers left their British bases an hour ahead of the Mustangs, escorted in the first part of the mission by shorter-ranged P-38s and P-47s.

■ **HAND OVER:** The faster Mustangs would catch the formation over the Dutch/German border, where they would relieve the P-47 and the Thunderbolts high above the B-17s.

■ **ESCORT:** Some fighters flew close escort. Their nearness boosted the morale of the bomber crews, who had been so severely mauled over Germany the year before.

■ **DOGFIGHTER:** The Mustang had more than long range. It was fast and it was a ferocious dogfighter, as the pilot of this Messerschmitt Bf 109G shot down by a P-51 discovered to his cost.

■ **CONTROL OF THE SKIES:** It was the appearance of swarms of these graceful fighters in the skies over Germany that was to signal the death knell of the Luftwaffe.

NORTHROP

P-61 BLACK WIDOW

● **Enormous but agile** ● **Powerful** ● **Complex fighter**

Northrop's P-61 Black Widow was a creature of the night. This large, powerful, twin-engined craft was the first American combat plane designed from the beginning as a night-fighter and optimised for air-to-air combat during the nocturnal hours. Beneath its slick coat of black paint, the P-61 proved itself a deadly foe in the dark, invisibly approaching Japanese aircraft and blasting them from the sky.

▲ *Long in development, the P-61 only saw service in the last year of the war. It was the biggest, heaviest and most powerful night-fighter of the war, but was also agile and fast.*

PHOTO FILE

NORTHROP P-61 BLACK WIDOW

◄ **Heavily armed**
The P-61's dorsal barbette was fitted with four 12.7-mm (.50 cal.) Colt-Browning M-2 machine-guns. In addition, it had four 20-mm (0.79-in.) cannon in the fuselage.

▲ **Pacific theatre**
Ten squadrons of Black Widows operated in the Central Pacific theatre as the standard USAAF night-fighter from June 1944.

Slow development ►
The original XP-61 prototype was flown on 26 May 1942 with most of its features mocked-up while awaiting the real parts.

▲ **Good night-fighter**
Once the strict initial flight limitations were lifted, P-61s became highly regarded.

Long range ►
This P-61B carries four drop-tanks, which increased fuel capacity by 4692 litres (1,110 gal.) and provided for an impressive range.

FACTS AND FIGURES

➤ On 26 May 1942 famous test pilot Vance Breese flew the P-61 on its first flight.

➤ On 6 July 1944, the P-61 racked up its first air-to-air victory, a Japanese Mitsubishi G4M 'Betty' bomber.

➤ Production of the Black Widow totalled 706 aircraft of all variants.

➤ P-61 Black Widows shot down nine German V-1 'buzz' bombs.

➤ Design and development of the P-61's SCR-720 search radar involved 172,000 man-hours of work.

➤ Three P-61 pilots became aces, with two of them including kills flying other types.

PROFILE

Killer of the night

The P-61 Black Widow was the largest, heaviest and most powerful fighter of World War II. It resulted from efforts by designer Jack Northrop to create a night-fighter able to use air-to-air radar to destroy enemy warplanes after dark.

The Black Widow was deceptively agile, and challenged and defeated smaller fighters. More than a twin-engine, twin-boomed aircraft of great size and strength, the Black Widow was truly a fighter, and it produced an impressive number of air-to-air kills.

The Black Widow looked like a strange, menacing machine. In fact, it was easy to fly and responsive to the touch. The unusual cockpit layout placed the radarman/forward gunner above and behind the pilot (the third crewman was behind both), and pilots disliked having the propellers in line with their cockpit position. But

This XF-15A conversion of a P-61C was the second Black Widow adapted for the photographic reconnaissance role, fitted with six cameras in the lengthened nose. It had a long, clear-view canopy over the tandem cockpits. Only 36 F-15As were built, although 175 were ordered.

once P-61s reached night-fighter squadrons in Europe and the Pacific in 1944, they achieved an impressive combat record.

P-61B BLACK WIDOW

The Northrop P-61 Black Widow was the first USAAF night-fighter designed for this role. This aircraft was called 'Time's a'Wastin' and was one of the most famous Black Widows of the Pacific theatre.

The nose-mounted SCR-720 radar scanner was covered by a painted dielectric nose cone.

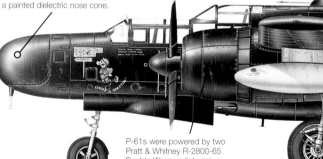

P-61s were powered by two Pratt & Whitney R-2800-65 Double Wasp radial engines, powering Curtiss Electric propellers.

Additional firepower was provided by a General Electric dorsal barbette with four 12.7-mm (.50 cal.) Colt-Browning machine-guns, each with 560 rounds.

Twin tailbooms extended aft from the engine nacelles. The fins were built integral with the tailbooms and the tailplane was located between the fins. The crew of three was housed in the large central pod.

The all-metal, shoulder-mounted wing had a broad chord and straight leading edge. It had a span of 20.11 m (66 ft.) and a wing area of 61.53 m² (662 sq. ft.), giving a low wing loading and agile performance.

Underwing drop-tanks extended the P-61's range to 2172 km (1.350 mi.).

The unique twin-boom configuration housed a crew of three in a large pod mounted onto a sturdy centre section. The fuselage nacelle also housed the radar and most of the armament.

Built as an early P-61B, 'Time's a'Wastin' was one of only two of the first 200 P-61Bs that retained the dorsal barbette. This was not revived until buffeting problems from the guns were solved.

P-61B Black Widow

Type: three-seat night-fighter

Powerplant: two 1491-kW (2,000-hp.) Pratt & Whitney R-2800-65 Double Wasp 18-cylinder radial engines

Maximum speed: 589 km/h (365 m.p.h.) at 6096 m (20,000 ft.)

Range: 1513 km (940 mi.) (2172 km/1,350 mi. with drop tanks)

Service ceiling: 12,445 m (40,800 ft.)

Weights: empty 9654 kg (21,239 lb.); loaded 13,471 kg (29,636 lb.); maximum overload 16,420 kg (36,124 lb.)

Armament: four 20-mm (0.79-in.) M-2 cannon each with 200 rounds; dorsal barbette with four 12.7-mm (.50 cal.) machine-guns each with 560 rounds; pylons for 454 kg (1,000 lb.) of bombs, rockets or other weapons

Dimensions:
span	20.11 m	(66 ft.)
length	15.11 m	(50 ft.)
height	4.47 m	(15 ft.)
wing area	61.53 m²	(662 sq. ft.)

COMBAT DATA

MAXIMUM SPEED

The bigger and much heavier Black Widow was only slightly slower than the nimble Rolls-Royce Merlin-engined Mosquito night-fighter variant. The Ki-45 was appreciably slower.

P-61B BLACK WIDOW — 589 km/h (365 m.p.h.)
MOSQUITO NF.Mk II — 595 km/h (370 m.p.h.)
Ki-45 'NICK' — 547 km/h (340 m.p.h.)

ARMAMENT

After development problems had been cured, the P-61B was equipped with four cannon and four powerful machine-guns, giving it superb firepower. The Ki-45 had a 37-mm (1.47-in.) fixed forward-firing cannon which was a very powerful weapon, but had a slow rate of fire.

P-61B BLACK WIDOW — 4 x 20-mm (0.79-in.) cannon 4 x 12.7-mm (.50 cal.) MGs

MOSQUITO NF.Mk II — 4 x 20-mm (0.79-in.) cannon 4 x 7.7-mm (.50 cal.) MGs

Ki-45 'NICK' — 2 x 20-mm (0.79-in.) cannon, 1 x 37-mm (1.47-in.) cannon 1 x 7.92-mm (0.31-in.) MGs

RANGE

The maximum range achieved by the Mosquito when fitted with two underwing drop-tanks was 2993 km (1,856 mi.), some 25 per cent greater than the P-61B with its four additional tanks. The ranges were similar on internal tanks only. The Ki-45 had the shortest range of the three night-fighters.

Ki-45 'NICK' — 2000 km (1,240 mi.)
P-61B BLACK WIDOW — 2172 km (1,350 mi.)
MOSQUITO NF.Mk II — 2993 km (1,856 mi.)

Twin-engined night-fighters

DE HAVILLAND MOSQUITO NF.Mk II: The Mosquito night-fighter was developed throughout the war, the first NF.Mk IIs entering service in March 1942. Later versions had the same SCR-720 radar as the P-61, but were less heavily armed.

JUNKERS Ju 88G-7B: The Luftwaffe's definitive night-fighter, the Ju 88G entered service in the summer of 1944, becoming Germany's night fighter by the end of the war. It was used effectively for home defence in the final months.

KAWASAKI Ki-45 'NICK': The Japanese contemporary of the P-61, the Ki-45 Model C had good speed and performance but failed to receive its centimetric nose radar. It was successful against B-29s for home defence during the last year of the war.

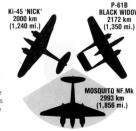

PETLYAKOV

PE-2

● Dive-bomber ● Tactical reconnaissance ● Heavy fighter

Second in importance only to the Tupolev Tu-2 for its wartime role, the Petlyakov Pe-2 was a superb Russian light bomber. It was actually a close Soviet counterpart to Britain's de Havilland Mosquito, although the Mosquito was constructed of wood and the Pe-2 of metal. Designed as a high-altitude fighter, the Pe-2 entered service as a tactical support dive-bomber, proving a huge success in a role it was not intended for.

▲ *In common with the majority of the best twin-engined multi-role aircraft of the 1940s, the Pe-2 was designed as a long-range fighter like the Bf 110 but spent most of the war in tactical air support.*

PHOTO FILE

PETLYAKOV PE-2

Defensive formation ▶
Fighter escort was a rare luxury for Soviet fighter-bombers, with Pe-2 pilots relying on mutual protection. The ventral gun can be seen on the nearest Pe-2.

▲ **Reconnaissance patrol**
A special Pe-2R variant was built for long-range reconnaissance. It had no divebrakes or bombs, but carried extra fuel and three BS machine-guns.

▼ **Dive-bomber**
For its new found dive-bombing role the Pe-2 was fitted with special automatic divebrakes.

▼ **Polish squadron**
In 1945 units of the new Polish army began receiving Pe-2s, which assisted in the liberation of the country. This is a 'UT' trainer version, with a second cockpit positioned behind the standing pilot.

▲ **Equipment testbed**
The versatility of the Pe-2 meant that it was used for trials of a large amount of new equipment being tested, such as ejection seats. The RD-1 rocket motor and special heavy cannon were also tested.

FACTS AND FIGURES

➤ In the late-1950s, many years after it was in service, the Pe-2 was given the NATO codename 'Buck'.

➤ The prototype Pe-2 series first appeared in the 1940 May Day flypast.

➤ The Pe-2Sh was a ground-attack version with oblique-firing gun batteries.

➤ On 12 January 1942 a test Pe-2 caught fire and all on board, including bureau chief Vladimir M. Petlyakov, were killed.

➤ Prototype Pe-2 versions were built for long-range bombing and as fighters.

➤ Post-war experimental versions used rocket engines and German pulse-jets.

PROFILE

Fighter turned dive-bomber

Soviet designer Vladimir M. Petlyakov is really known for only one aeroplane, but his Pe-2 was such a success that it assures immortality. First conceived as a high-altitude fighter, the Pe-2 was ordered into production as a light bomber in 1940.

The Pe-2 became the backbone of the Soviet light bomber force after Germany invaded Russia in 1941. Flying with wheels, or skis in the severe Russian winter, Pe-2 pilots

used the speed and flexibility of this twin-engine aircraft to fly bombing missions and carry out reconnaissance duties.

Usually the Pe-2 was fast enough to evade fighters if challenged, but when lightly loaded it was manoeuvrable enough to fight any Bf 109 or Fw 190 that caught up. In fact, because the Pe-2 was so nimble, its two gunners had the ride of their lives in the midst of battle.

Although the demand for attack aircraft gave the Pe-2

a new role, some fighter versions were still completed, such as the Pe-2VI high-altitude fighter. The majority of the 11,400 aircraft built were used in support of the Red Army.

Above: Although designed to fight at high altitude, the Pe-2 usually operated below 3000 metres, and often very much lower than that.

Below: Bombs away – a formation release their weapons together at medium altitude. The Red air force seldom had much success with these tactics, preferring low-level strikes.

Pe-2

Type: three-seat bomber

Powerplant: two 939-kW (1,260-hp.) Klimov VK-105PF 12-cylinder piston engines

Maximum speed: 449 km/h (278 m.p.h.)

Range: 1315 km (815 mi.)

Service ceiling: 8800 m (28,900 ft.)

Weights: empty 6200 kg (13,640 lb.); maximum 8520 kg (18,744 lb.)

Armament: four 100-kg (220-lb.) bombs in bay plus two in rear of engine; four 250-kg (550-lb.) bombs under centre section; two forward-firing 7.62-mm (.30 cal.) ShKAS machine-guns; MV-3 dorsal turret with single 12.7-mm (.50 cal.) UBT; one ShKAS in ventral position plus one at rear beam

Dimensions:
span	17.11 m (56 ft. 2 in.)
length	12.78 m (41 ft. 11 in.)
height	3.42 m (11 ft. 3 in.)
wing area	40.50 m² (436 sq. ft.)

PE-2

One of the finest twin-engined aircraft of the war, over 11,400 Pe-2s were built and served as light bombers and reconnaissance aircraft.

The radio operator, seated in the cockpit back-to-back with the pilot, could get into the prone bomb-aiming position in the nose by crawling under the pilot's seat.

Eleven fuel tanks were installed in the wings and fuselage, feeding small header tanks above each engine. Inert exhaust gases were fed to the tanks as a fire-suppressant measure.

The wide track undercarriage gave good stability for operating from rough Russian airstrips. However, the aircraft had a notorious reputation for bouncing heavily on landing.

The Pe-2 was powered by two VK-105 12-cylinder Vee liquid-cooled engines with electrically-driven two-speed superchargers.

Defence was provided by a rear gunner, who fired a hand-held gun in the cockpit as well as the ventral weapon. The gunner would also call out the movements of enemy fighters to the other crewmembers.

The twin-fin tail allowed the gunner a good field of fire, as well as allowing the pilot some measure of control authority if one fin was shot off.

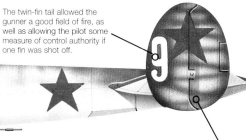

The cockpit was well laid-out, offering an excellent view for the crew. High-altitude variants had special pressurised cabins.

Offensive armament was carried in an internal bomb-bay and on external racks inboard of the engine nacelles. Normal load was four FAB-100 bombs in the bomb-bay and one in each nacelle, with four FAB-250s under the wings.

The ventral rear gun was sighted by a periscope and controlled remotely. It was of more use for strafing overflown targets than fighting off a determined fighter attack.

The tail section was constructed of metal alloy with fabric-covered tabbed control surfaces.

COMBAT DATA

MAXIMUM SPEED

Although slower than a Mosquito or Bf 110, the Pe-2 was still capable of shaking off a fighter attack, and was faster than the RAF's Blenheims and the Luftwaffe's Ju 88 bombers.

Pe-2	449 km/h (278 m.p.h.)
Bf 110C	560 km/h (347 m.p.h.)
MOSQUITO B.Mk XVI	668 km/h (471 m.p.h.)

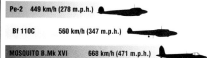

SERVICE CEILING

Although designed as a high-altitude fighter, the Pe-2 had an inferior ceiling to the Mosquito and Bf 110. This mattered little, as most Pe-2s carried out attacks from very low level.

MOSQUITO B.Mk XVI	12,192 m (37,500 ft.)
Bf 110C	10,000 m (35,000 ft.)
Pe-2	8800 m (28,900 ft.)

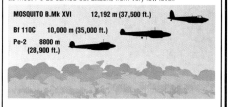

BOMBLOAD

The Pe-2 had a hefty bombload, but generally carried a large number of small bombs. The Mosquito had a smaller bombload which it generally used for precision attacks.

Pe-2	MOSQUITO B.Mk XVI	Bf 110C
3000 kg (6,600 lb.) of bombs	1814 kg (3,000 lb.) of bombs	1000 kg (2,200 lb.) of bombs

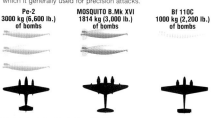

Twin-engined fighter-bombers

■ **DE HAVILLAND MOSQUITO:** Capable of outrunning most fighters of its day, the all-wooden Mosquito was one of the finest aircraft of the war. It was used in the fighter-bomber, reconnaissance, night-fighter and pathfinder roles.

■ **LOCKHEED P-38 LIGHTNING:** Originally a high-altitude long-range fighter like the Pe-2, the P-38 was eventually found to be better suited to low-level attack and reconnaissance missions but also flew the early escort missions over Germany.

■ **MESSERSCHMITT Bf 110:** Designed specifically as a heavy fighter, the Bf 110 was also used as a light bomber, a night-fighter equipped with Schräge Musik cannon and radar, and for daylight air defence duties armed with air-to-air rockets.

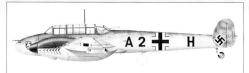

POLIKARPOV

I-15/I-153

● Fighter biplane ● Fought in Spain and China ● Highly manoeuvrable

▲ Polikarpov fighters fought with distinction in the late 1930s, taking on aircraft like the CR.32 and Ki-27.
The I-15 was so manoeuvrable that it broke records, turning through 360° in only eight seconds. The design formed the basis of the later I-16 monoplane.

Designed by Polikarpov while he was in prison, the biplane I-15 'Chaika' (Seagull) was involved in many air battles in the 1930s from Mongolia to Spain. The aircraft was continually improved; the final I-153 was one of the most capable biplane fighters ever built. Displaying excellent manoeuvrability, the I-15 was still in service in large numbers in 1941, by which time it had been rendered obsolete.

POLIKARPOV I-15/I-153

▲ **Still fighting**
The I-153 was still in action as late as 1943 dropping light bombs in the close support role. The type was flown by aces Grigory Rechkalov and Alexander Klubov before they flew MiG-3s.

▼ **Hidden in the woods**
The Soviets were masters of camouflage, but that did not save these I-15s from destruction in 1941. Luftwaffe fighters decimated the Soviet biplanes.

◀ **Fighting the invader**
Finland's forces used 14 captured 'Chaikas' fitted with German radios and Browning machine-guns. With the advantage of having better pilots and the fact that they were often mistaken as friendly, the Finns wrought havoc against the Soviets.

▼ **Starting up**
These bomb-armed 'Chaikas' are being started up by trucks using a Hucks starter.

▲ **Spanish tour**
The 'Chaika' was the main Republican fighter in the Spanish Civil War, fighting Nationalist Fiat CR.32s. The two types were closely matched, although the I-15 had better firepower.

FACTS AND FIGURES

➤ More than 550 I-15s were supplied to the Spanish Republicans; they were known as 'Chato' (flat nose) to their opponents.

➤ I-153s were cleared to fire six RS-82 underwing rockets for ground attack.

➤ The 'Chaika' was flown by the Spanish ace Miguel Zamudio in the Civil War.

➤ A single I-15 variant was produced with rubber-sealed pressurised cockpits for high-altitude work.

➤ Two I-152s were rebuilt as 'Shturmovik' dedicated ground-attack prototypes.

➤ In October 1940 an I-153/DM-4 reached 440 km/h (274 m.p.h.) in a ramjet test flight.

PROFILE

Dogfighting in the 'Seagull'

When he designed a replacement for the earlier I-5, Polikarpov retained the biplane formula but created a gull-wing shape, leading to the nickname Seagull. Early versions were powered by an American Wright Cyclone engine driving a Russian propeller. First flown in 1933, the aircraft displayed astonishing agility.

The 'Chaika' gained its nickname from the distinct shape of its upper wing. Many pilots disliked the gull-wing, saying the view was worse.

Production began in 1934 and the armament was doubled to four guns with a high reserve of ammunition. The I-15 had an active combat life, fighting the Japanese at the battle of Khalkin Gol and in China. The aircraft also served the Republican cause in Spain, and fought on both sides in the Finnish campaign in 1940.

The Soviets tried to prolong the life of the I-15 with various improvements, such as revised cowlings and more powerful engines, for the I-15bis, I-152 and I-153 models. Even with turbocharged engines, however, the performance was not vastly improved, and Polikarpov turned to the monoplane I-16 which was very similar. Over 1000 'Chaikas' were still in service with the USSR in 1941.

Above: The bizarre I-153/DM-4 was an experimental version used to test ramjet-assisted propulsion.

Left: Fitting a Cyclone engine in such a short airframe gave the I-15 its distinctive portly lines. The Soviet M-62 engine was used in the I-153 version.

I-15

Type: single-seat radial-engined biplane fighter and ground-attack aircraft

Powerplant: one 528-kW (708-hp.) Wright Cyclone F-3 radial piston engine

Maximum speed: 367 km/h (228 m.p.h.) at 3000 m (9,840 ft.)

Initial climb rate: over 900 m/min (2,953 f.p.m.)

Combat radius: 550 km (342 mi.)

Service ceiling: 9800 m (32,150 ft.)

Weights: empty 1130 kg (2,491 lb.); loaded 1390 kg (3,064 lb.)

Armament: four PV-1 7.62-mm (.30 cal.) machine-guns with 3000 rounds; provision for four 20-kg (44-lb.) bombs or (I-153) six rockets

Dimensions: span 9.75 m (32 ft.)
length 6.10 m (20 ft. 1 in.)
height 2.19 m (7 ft. 2 in.)
wing area 23.55 m² (253 sq. ft.)

I-15

One of the most successful biplane fighters ever, the I-15 was the main Spanish Republican fighter.

At an early stage in its production, the I-15 was equipped with seat armour. PV-1 guns were fitted in the fuselage sides in addition to the pair in original versions.

The multicoloured tail was the emblem of the Spanish Republican air force. The black cross of the Nationalists was later painted over this.

Such was the demand for the I-15 that the first examples had the original American engines, but most had Russian licence-built M-25 versions of the Wright Cyclone.

One outstanding feature was the undercarriage legs; the lower portion slid up and down inside the upper portion through an internal slot to provide wheel suspension.

The fuselage was constructed of KhMA gas-welded tube with light-alloy removable skin panels forwards of the windscreen and fabric covering behind.

COMBAT DATA

MAXIMUM SPEED

By the end of the 1930s fighters were approaching the feasible maximum speeds for biplane design. Even the first all-metal monoplane fighters which were entering service were at least as fast.

I-15	367 km/h (228 m.p.h.)
CR.32	375 km/h (233 m.p.h.)
GLADIATOR Mk I	410 km/h (255 m.p.h.)

ARMAMENT

Four-gun armament was a vital improvement in the last biplane fighters, as a lethal shot was less easy to attain due to the increasing speed and armour protection of enemy aircraft.

I-15 — 4 x 7.62-mm (.30 cal.) machine-guns
CR.32 — 2 x 7.7-mm (.303 cal.) machine-guns
GLADIATOR Mk I — 4 x 7.7-mm (.303 cal.) machine-guns

SERVICE CEILING

The I-15 had a good climb rate and ceiling, and against a CR.32 pilots often had the edge in diving and climbing. With its pressurised cockpit the I-152GK could routinely operate at high altitudes.

I-15 9800 m (32,150 ft.)
CR.32 8800 m (28,900 ft.)
GLADIATOR Mk I 10,060 m (33,000 ft.)

'Chaikas' at war

OUTSMARTING THE JAPANESE: During the Sino-Japanese War, which began in 1937, Chinese Nationalists flew their manoeuvrable I-15s against more advanced Japanese fighters.

WITH REPUBLICAN FORCES: Spanish Republican forces equipped with I-15s came up against Nationalist and Condor Legion fighters from Germany during the Spanish Civil War.

CAPTURED CHAIKAS: During World War II, Finland used 14 captured examples fitted with Browning guns and German radio to bomb Soviet positions.

POLIKARPOV

I-16

● Early monoplane fighter ● Spanish war veteran ● Dogfighter

W hen Hitler invaded the USSR in 1941, the open-cockpit I-16 was the most numerous fighter In service with the Soviet. Designed to replace biplane fighters, the I-16 was a fast machine when it first appeared in 1934, and was the first low-wing cantilever monoplane with a retractable undercarriage. It is best remembered for fighting with government forces in Spain and China against desperate odds, and facing the invasion of the USSR.

▲ *Polikarpov's I-16 was something of a compromise design, accepted into service for all its faults in an attempt to match rival designs that outperformed the earlier (biplane) I-15 in Spain. This I-16 is shown at Jerez airfield in Spain prior to acceptance by the Republican 22 Rgt.*

POLIKARPOV I-16

▲ Fighting for the enemy
During the war with Finland, numerous I-16s were captured by the Finns and restored to use against their former owners. This example is a Type 12 with a tubular sight in the windshield. Soviet I-16 pilots had a hard time flying against Finnish pilots.

▲ Ski champion
For operations in the ferocious Russian winter, the I-16 was often fitted with skis. These could be retracted to lie flat against the wing in flight.

Fighting fly ▶
Known as 'Mukha' (Russian for fly) in Spain the I-16 was the best Government fighter aircraft.

▼ Spanish warrior
Nationalist forces inherited the I-16s previously used by the Republican side in Spain's civil war.

◀ No more flying
Hundreds of I-16s were destroyed in June 1941, when the Luftwaffe attacked Soviet airfields. Even those that took off in time were soon shot down.

FACTS AND FIGURES

➤ Although outmoded by 1941, the I-16 equipped about 65 per cent of the Soviet fighter force when the Germans invaded.

➤ The I-16 was the first monoplane fighter to enter service in 1935.

➤ Production of the I-16 exceeded 8000 single- and two-seat examples.

➤ I-16 ace Grigori Ravchenko shot down three Japanese aircraft in China and later led an I-16 unit with success in Mongolia.

➤ The I-16 type 5 SPB was a fast dive-bomber variant with special dive brakes.

➤ At least one I-16P was tested with a powerful four-cannon installation.

PROFILE

Dogfighting in the mighty 'fly'

Polikarpov began planning a successor to the biplane I-15 series while he was in a Soviet labor camp. In 1933, he designed a rival monoplane to the ANT-31, and the result was the I-16, with its wooden fuselage and metal wing. First prototypes used Soviet M-22 engines, but by 1934 licence-built Wright Cyclone engines were

fitted, giving a dramatic increase in performance and making the I-16 one of the fastest machines of its day. Although hard to fly, the Soviet forces ordered thousands of them.

The I-16 really made its mark in the Spanish Civil War, where government forces pitted the I-16 against the Fascists. The I-16 was built under license there by

Hispano-Suiza. In China, Soviet I-16s flew well in overwhelming air battles with Japanese pilots, repeating this again in 1939 in battles on the Manchurian border. Huge numbers of I-16s were destroyed in the invasion of the USSR, but the aircraft remained in service until 1943, by which time it was obviously obsolete.

Flying the I-16 called for considerable skill, because it was prone to stalling and spinning, stability was marginal and the aircraft would easily drop a wing if the pilot allowed speed to bleed off during landing. Without trimmers to take back pressure forces off the controls, it was exhausting to fly.

I-16

Type: single-seat interceptor fighter

Powerplant: one 578-kW (775-hp.) Shvetsov M-25 air-cooled radial

Maximum speed: 489 km/h (304 m.p.h.)

Service ceiling: 8268 m (27,125 ft.)

Weights: empty 1347 kg (2,970 lb.); loaded 1711 kg (3,773 lb.)

Armament: four 7.62-mm (.30 cal.) Shpital'ny-Komaritsky ShKAS machine guns in upper fuselage and wings; up to six RS-82 rocket projectiles, six Der-31 bomb containers or two 100-kg (220-lb.) bombs (I-16P); and two 20-mm (0.79-in.) ShVAK cannon in wings

Dimensions:
span	9.14 m	(30 ft.)
length	5.79 m	(19 ft.)
height	2.44 m	(8 ft.)
wing area	14.49 m²	(156 sq. ft.)

I-16 (TYPE-17)

The Type-17 variant carried two ShKAS machine guns and two ShVAK cannon and was the first version to fire RS-82 rockets. Many saw action against Japanese forces in August 1939.

Best feature of the I-16 was its armament of two ShVAK cannon in the wings. Two ShKAS machine guns were carried in the upper fuselage.

Foreign pilots often complained about the narrow cockpit with its folding sidewall exit. The lack of trim tabs meant that constant stick and rudder forces had to be suffered by the pilot. After the type 4, thick rear armor, over 6mm (¼ in.), was fitted.

Early I-16s were powered by Wright Cyclone radials imported and built under license, driving Hamilton two-pitch propellers. After the type 6, I-16s used M-25A engines, later types having M-62 and M-63 engines with superchargers.

Undercarriage retraction was another failing of the early I-16. It took no less than 44 progressively harder turns of a crank to raise the gear, which often jammed half way when lowered. Pilots were even issued cable shears to free jammed undercarriages.

Slogans painted on aircraft were much loved by Soviet pilots. This one reads 'For the USSR'.

The tail structure was made of D6 alloy with a fabric covering for lightness. There was no counterweighted or aerodynamic balancing, making the controls rather heavy.

ACTION DATA

SPEED

The first generation of monoplane fighters that began to appear in the early 1930s had a significant speed advantage over their biplane rivals. The Ki-27 and I-16 were evenly matched.

I-16	489 km/h (304 m.p.h.)
P-26	377 km/h (234 m.p.h.)
Ki-27	468 km/h (291 m.p.h.)

RANGE

Fighters of the 1930s had notoriously short range. Designed to operate close to their bases, they traded extra fuel capacity for speed and agility. All three had similar ranges.

I-16	599 km (372 mi.)
P-26	579 km (360 mi.)
Ki-27	624 km (388 mi.)

WEAPONS

The P-26 and the Ki-27 possessed the standard fighter armament of the time consisting of two machine guns. The I-16 was one of the few more heavily armed fighters with four machine guns.

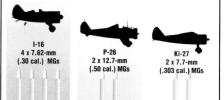

I-16	P-26	Ki-27
4 x 7.62-mm (.30 cal.) MGs	2 x 12.7-mm (.50 cal.) MGs	2 x 7.7-mm (.303 cal.) MGs

Fighters in the Spanish Civil War

■ **Bf 109B:** The finest fighter of the war, the Bf 109 totally outclassed machines like the I-16 and earlier biplanes.

■ **HAWKER FURY:** Supplied to the Government side, the Fury was an obsolete design that performed adequately.

■ **POLIKARPOV I-15:** Predecessor to the I-16, 550 biplane I-15s were used in Spain with some success against Fiat CR.32s.

POLIKARPOV

Po-2/U-2

● Multiple variants ● Massive production ● Built pre- and post-war

▲ Having been built in massive numbers in the Soviet Union and in Poland between 1948 and 1953, it is not surprising that examples of this tough, versatile biplane remain airworthy.

Designed originally as a trainer to replace the U-1 Soviet-built version of the Avro 504, the U-2 and its derivatives were produced from 1928 until 1944. Production was resumed after World War II, when thousands more were built in Poland. Designated 'Mule' by NATO in 1954, Russian troops nicknamed the aircraft 'Kukuruzhnik' ('corn-cutter'). In 1944 the U-2's designation was changed to Po-2 in recognition of Polikarpov's role in its creation.

POLIKARPOV Po-2/U-2

◀ **Preserved Polikarpov**
Wearing the markings of the former Yugoslavia, this Po-2 has been displayed at air shows in France.

▼ **Soviet service**
Serving in a multitude of roles, the Po-2/U-2 was highly respected by Soviet forces.

▲ **Wartime trainer**
When it first flew in 1928 as a basic trainer design, the U-2 already appeared obsolete. Its simple structure proved to be the basis for success, however.

◀ **Civilian roles**
This aircraft, wearing CCCP codes, represents one of the many thousands of civilian Po-2/U-2s used in roles as diverse as training, transport (with open and enclosed cabins), crop-dusting and flying ambulance.

Still flying ▶
A strong cross-axle undercarriage unit with comprehensive shock-absorbing gave good airfield handling. The U-2 was originally designed with interchangeable, rectangular wing panels for ease of maintenance and repair, but this resulted in very poor flight characteristics.

FACTS AND FIGURES

➤ Deliveries of the Po-2 began in 1928 and by the time of the 1941 German invasion 13,000 had been built.

➤ U-2s flew low-level, night-time nuisance raids against German forces.

➤ An incredible 80 different factory-built variants of the U-2 were produced.

➤ Continuing its nuisance raider role, the Po-2 flew 'bed-check Charlie' raids against UN positions in the Korean War.

➤ A Po-2SKF variant could carry two stretcher patients in underwing pods.

➤ One experimental aircraft was tested with a 'butterfly' tail.

PROFILE

Prolific Polikarpov

A great number of variants of the Po-2/U-2 have been identified. Military versions were used for training, observation and light attack, as close-support aircraft with rockets and bombs, and as black-painted night-bombers carrying two 100-kg (220-lb.) bombs. Two aircraft were even equipped with transmitters and loudspeakers for psychological warfare.

Several ambulance versions were produced. The first carried a single stretcher and attendant, but later medevac models had an enclosed rear cockpit for two stretchers. Another variant carried a cylindrical container for a stretcher on each lower wing.

One of the first non-military uses was crop-dusting, and large numbers were built for this task both before and after the war. A tank for chemicals replaced the rear cockpit. There were other versions with three seats, some of which had enclosed cabins, and one 1944 model had five seats for military liaison.

There was also a series of floatplane versions, including one fitted with a 537-kW (720-hp.) Wright Cyclone engine, which set new altitude records for seaplanes in 1937, as well as many one-off and experimental conversions.

Left: Polish-built aircraft had the basic designation CSS-13, but like their Soviet equivalents they were produced in many forms, often with different designations.

Above: Although it was widely used and often modified, the U-2 airframe remained largely unchanged. Features such as the tailskid were retained throughout the extended production run.

U-2VS

Type: trainer and multi-purpose biplane

Powerplant: one 75-kW (100-hp.) M-11 five-cylinder air-cooled radial engine

Maximum speed: 156 km/h (97 m.p.h.) at sea level

Landing speed: 69 km/h (43 m.p.h.)

Service ceiling: 4000 m (13,000 ft.)

Range: 400 km (250 mi.)

Weights: empty 635 kg (1,397 lb.); loaded 890 kg (1,958 lb.)

Armament: (U-2LSh) one 7.7-mm (.303 cal.) ShKAS machine-gun on a ring mounting over the rear cockpit and racks for up to 120 kg (260 lb.) of bombs and four RS-82 rockets

Dimensions:
span	11.40 m	(37 ft. 5 in.)
length	8.17 m	(26 ft. 9 in.)
height	3.10 m	(10 ft. 2 in.)
wing area	33.15 m²	(357 sq. ft.)

U-2LSH

Soviet forces flew these aircraft in a light Shturmovik role. Many pre-war aircraft were modified for these light-attack duties and saw action from 1941 onwards. Flying at low level, they were very successful.

No attempt was made to streamline or protect the engine installation. This seems to have caused few problems since the engine remained uncowled on most variants.

Having rejected the original wing design, Polikarpov adopted this more conventional staggered wing layout. A single set of interplane struts braced the wings on each side, making this a single-bay biplane.

This ring-mounted 7.7-mm (.303 cal.) ShKAS machine-gun gave the U-2LSh a limited self-defence and ground strafing capability.

A large, tall rudder of broad chord was typical of the Po-2/U-2. Like all of the control surfaces, it was linked to the cockpit controls by a series of cables.

A windscreen was provided for the pilot and rear-seat occupant, in this case a gunner. Some aircraft were given enclosed cabins, with the Po-2ShS accommodating the pilot and three passengers.

Ailerons were fitted to each wing, with the upper and lower surfaces on each side connected by cables. The tips of the lower wings were protected in the event of a rough landing by underwing skids.

Cables running along the fuselage side connected the elevators to the control column and the rudder to the pedals. One aircraft was built with all the controls connected to the control column.

ACTION DATA

MAXIMUM SPEED

With its comparatively low power, the U-2VS could not match its Western equivalents for speed. No alternative to the U-2 existed, however, and its performance was adequate for a range of roles.

U-2VS	156 km/h (97 m.p.h.)
DH.82C TIGER MOTH	172 km/h (107 m.p.h.)
PT-3A	164 km/h (102 m.p.h.)

POWER

Most variants of the Po-2 used the M-11 engine which produced a maximum of 75 kW (100 hp.). The standard trainer version illustrated in no way improved by the installation of a 149-kW (200-hp.) M-48.

U-2VS	DH.82C TIGER MOTH	PT-3A
75 kW (100 hp.)	108 kW (145 hp.)	164 kW (220 hp.)

NUMBER BUILT

A truly astounding 33,000 Po-2/U-2s were built, making this one of the largest production runs in the history of aviation. The most widely-built west European contemporary, the Tiger Moth, reached barely a quarter of this total.

U-2VS	33,000
DH.82C TIGER MOTH	8000
PT-3A	300

World War II trainers

■ **AVRO TUTOR:** Used by the RAF as a basic trainer during World War II, the Tutor wore the standard yellow training colour scheme.

■ **BOEING STEARMAN KAYDETT:** Built in huge numbers, the Kaydett provided basic training for US Army and Navy pilots throughout the war.

■ **BÜCKER Bü 131 JUNGMANN:** This aerobatic trainer was used to teach many of the Luftwaffe's best pilots the art of flying.

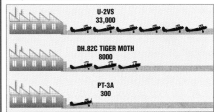

■ **NIHON TYPE 93 K5Y1:** The two-seat K5Y1 was among a number of Japanese aircraft used to train naval pilots.

POTEZ

25

● More than 4000 built ● General-purpose biplane ● Numerous variants

Built in large numbers and used by the air forces of more than 20 countries, the Potez 25 was developed from the earlier models 15S and 24, and flew for the first time early in 1925. During the following 10 years more than 4000 were built, several hundred of them under licence for export customers, in over a dozen different versions. The Potez's career with the French air force ended in the mid-1930s, but some served elsewhere into the 1940s.

▲ In addition to its military applications, the Potez 25 found useful employment as a mail plane in South America during the 1930s. Aéropostale and its associated companies made regular mail flights, frequently taking the aircraft on hazardous routes over the Andes with considerable loads.

POTEZ 25

▲ Swiss 25 A.2
This Potez 25 A.2 observation aircraft was powered by a Lorraine-Dietrich 12Eb liquid-cooled engine.

▲ Potez 25 'Jupiter'
Switzerland operated a mixture of aircraft with liquid- and air-cooled engines. This aircraft has a 313-kW (420-hp.) Gnome-Rhône 9Ac Jupiter radial installed.

▲ Unequal-span wings
A common feature of all 25s was the design's unequal span mainplanes. Tail shapes varied; the Salmson radial-engined machines had an extended rudder.

▲ Salmson engine
A distinctively shaped engine cowling was a feature of the 388-kW (520-hp.) Salmson radial-powered Potez 25 versions.

Clean lines ▶
The clean lines of the 25 are evident in this view, though they are spoilt slightly by the radial engine.

FACTS AND FIGURES

➤ Licence production was undertaken in factories in Poland, Yugoslavia, Romania and Portugal.

➤ Apart from Potez, ANF Les Mureaux and Hanriot built 25s in France.

➤ China employed Potez 25s in action against the Japanese.

➤ A dozen countries, including the Soviet Union, took delivery of Potez 25s for test purposes.

➤ Ethiopian 25s saw action against the invading Italian troops in 1935.

➤ Civil-operated 25s were used by Hanriot and Caudron flying schools in France.

PROFILE

Widely used French design

Below: This Potez 25 TOE was among 2,270 examples of this general-purpose variant built. They were designed for colonial use but many saw home service with the French air force.

Basic models of the Potez 25 built for the French Armée de l'Air were the A.2 reconnaissance aircraft, the B.2 bomber and the TOE for operations in overseas theatres. The B.2's bombload consisted of 12 12-kg (26-lb.) or four 50-kg (110-lb.) bombs under the fuselage, plus six 12-kg (26-lb.) bombs under the wings.

There were also civil derivatives of the aircraft. Some were used to carry mail in South America, and two were built with metal fuselages and extra fuel tanks as part of an unsuccessful attempt to make the first non-stop flight from Paris to New York. Designated 25-O (for Océan), they were designed to jettison their undercarriage after take-off and land on a strengthened skid on the underside of the fuselage. The 25H was a floatplane variant built in two forms, one with a large central float, the other with twin floats. Many engine types, both in-line and radial, were used

Above: Like its other aircraft, Switzerland's large fleet of French-built Potez 25s was long-serving, the last flying until 1940.

with power ratings in the 298- to 447-kW (400- to 600-hp.) range. Other operators were the air arms of Afghanistan, Algeria, Argentina, Brazil, China, Estonia, Ethiopia, Finland, Guatemala, Indo-China, Japan, Madagascar, Morocco, Poland, Portugal, Romania, Switzerland, Turkey, Uruguay, the USSR, and Yugoslavia.

25 A.2

During the Gran Chaco War of 1932-35, this aircraft operated from Isla Poi with 2º Escuadrón de Reconocimiento y Bombardeo, Paraguayan air force. In this conflict Paraguay disputed the sovereignty of Chaco Boreal with neighbouring Bolivia.

25 TOE

Type: two-seat general-purpose biplane

Powerplant: one 335-kW (450-hp.) Lorraine-Dietrich 12Eb liquid-cooled piston engine

Maximum speed: 208 km/h (129 m.p.h.) at sea level

Range: 1260 km (783 mi.)

Service ceiling: 5800 m (19,000 ft.)

Weights: empty equipped 1510 kg (3,329 lb.); maximum take-off 2500 kg (5,512 lb.)

Armament: one fixed forward-firing 7.7-mm (.303 cal.) Vickers machine-gun and two 7.7-mm Vickers machine-guns on trainable single mounting in observer's cockpit, plus 200 kg (440 lb.) of bombs

Dimensions:
span	14.14 m (46 ft. 5 in.)
length	9.10 m (29 ft. 10 in.)
height	3.67 m (12 ft.)
wing area	47.00 m² (506 sq. ft.)

A variety of engine types was fitted to Potez 25s, to drive a wooden fixed-pitch propeller.

Pilot and observer were accommodated close together in tandem cockpits beneath a cut-out in the trailing edge of the upper wing centre-section.

Twin Lewis 7.7-mm (.303 cal.) machine-guns was mounted on a TO 7 ring in the observer's cockpit. Another was fixed to fire forward.

Designed by Louis Coroller, the Potez 25 was derived from the Potez 24 A.2-category fighter aircraft.

Potez 25s were fitted with a new cross-axle landing gear with specially designed shock absorbers. The undercarriage wheels were formed with metal spokes and fitted with rubber tyres.

Bombloads of around 200 kg (440 lb.) could be carried by the Potez 25 on underfuselage racks, further enhancing the type's versatility. The 25 B.2 variant was specifically designed for the role.

A refined 25 prototype was flown for the first time from the new Méaulte factory in early 1925.

COMBAT DATA

MAXIMUM SPEED

Compared to other general-purpose types of the inter-war period, the Potez 25 had a good top speed. With a bombload this would be considerably reduced.

25 TOE	208 km/h (129 m.p.h.)
WAPITI Mk IIA	217 km/h (135 m.p.h.)
IIIF Mk IV	193 km/h (120 m.p.h.)

POWER

Engines of varying power were fitted to Potez 25s, the 25 TOE having a Lorraine rated at 335 kW. Westland's Wapiti had a larger engine, while that of the Fairey IIIF was of a similar rating.

25 TOE 335 kW (450 hp.)	WAPITI Mk IIA 373 kW (500 hp.)	IIIF Mk IV 339 kW (455 hp.)

RANGE

The Potez 25's range figure fell between those of the Fairey IIIF and Westland Wapiti. The Wapiti was a modest performer at 579 km (360 mi.), while the Fairey type was designed for maritime patrols over long distances of almost 2500 km (1,550 mi.) (though this would be considerably reduced with a full weapons load).

25 TOE 1260 km (783 mi.)

WAPITI Mk IIA 579 km (360 mi.)

IIIF Mk IV 2446 km (1,520 mi.)

Aircraft of the Chaco War

BREDA Ba.44: This transport design, bearing a remarkable resemblance to the de Havilland DH.84, served the Paraguayan forces.

FIAT CR.30: A small number of these Italian biplane fighters served with the Paraguayan air force, opposing Bolivian Curtiss Hawk IAs.

CURTISS TYPE 18T: Designed for the US Navy, one example of this two-seat triplane was imported by Bolivia in 1919.

JUNKERS W.34: Transport aircraft like this one were converted to bombers by the Bolivian air force. Many pilots were mercenaries.

PZL

P.11

● Interceptor fighter ● Light attack ● Poland's last line of defence

● lthough heavily outnumbered by superior fighters, Polish air force pilots flying P.11s and P.7s put up a heroic resistance during the German invasion of their country in September 1939. By then their fighters, among the fastest in the world a few years earlier, were slower than any of the opposing machines except for the Hs 126 and Ju 87. Yet they scored the first Allied aerial victories of World War II, and shot down 126 German aircraft.

▲ The P.11 fell in large numbers to the superior German fighters, but scored an impressive number of kills for such a dated machine, thanks to the aggression of its pilots.

PZL P.11

◀ **Revolutionary design**
At a time when others were still using biplane wings, Poland's Zygmunt Pulawski pioneered the gull-wing monoplane fighter.

◀ **Imported engines**
The P.11 first flew with a French Gnôme-Rhône radial engine, later replaced by a licence-built British Mercury VIS.

▲ **Poland's defender**
At the time of the German invasion in 1939 the obsolete P.11 made up the majority of the small Polish air arm. In battle they were outclassed.

▼ **P.11 exported**
The tough P.11 fighter was used by several smaller air forces, notably the Romanians whose aircraft fought against the Allies.

▲ **Gallant defeat**
Poland's 128 P.11s were arranged into six defence regiments, who fought bravely against the invading German forces in 1939. They lost a total of 46 aircraft in the first three days of the short conflict.

FACTS AND FIGURES

➤ Romania produced 120 of its own P.11f version, which went on to fight with the German Luftwaffe.

➤ The prototype PZL P.11 first flew in September 1931.

➤ The first production variant, the two-gun P.11b, entered service in 1935.

➤ A total of 50 P.11b models with indigenous engines and instruments were exported to Romania.

➤ In all, a total of 330 PZL P.11s of all types had been built when production ended.

➤ Three hundred of the improved P.24 series were made solely for export.

PROFILE

Poland's gull-winged defender

The P.11's distinctive gull wing helped it to set new standards of performance in the age of biplane fighters. The wing was intended to partner a V-type engine, but after being used on a series of prototypes it was combined with a radial engine on the production P.7 and its successor, the P.11.

The P.11a had a 373-kW (500-hp.) Bristol Mercury engine and two fuselage-mounted machine-guns. It was followed by the more powerful P.11c, which carried an extra machine-gun in each wing. The P.11c's top speed of 390 km/h (242 m.p.h.) was impressive in the early 1930s. By 1939, though, its two-blade propeller, open cockpit and fixed undercarriage were clearly outmoded.

Romania bought 50 P.11bs, with Romanian engines and instruments, and IAR in Bucharest built 120 P.11fs.

These participated in the war against the Soviet Union. The 12 squadrons of Polish P.11s claimed the destruction of 126 Luftwaffe aircraft in 1939, losing 114 of their own aircraft.

The P.11c model was by far the most modern fighter asset available to the Poles in any number. It was comparable to the British Gloster Gladiator or German Heinkel 51, and although it was less heavily armed it featured a more advanced monoplane wing.

P.11c

Type: single-seat monoplane interceptor and light-attack fighter

Powerplant: one 373-kW (500-hp.) Skoda-built Bristol Mercury VIS.2 radial piston engine

Maximum speed: 390 km/h (242 m.p.h.) at 5500 m (18,000 ft.)

Initial climb rate: 5000 m (16,400 ft.) in 6 min

Combat radius: maximum loaded range 700 km (435 mi.)

Service ceiling: 8000 m (26,250 ft.)

Weights: maximum take-off weight 1800 kg (3,960 lb.)

Armament: two 7.7-mm (.303 cal.) machine-guns

Dimensions: span 10.72 m (35 ft. 2 in.)
length 7.55 m (24 ft. 9 in.)
height 2.85 m (9 ft. 4 in.)

The P.11c was equipped with two KM Wz33 machine-guns in the forward fuselage sides and light bombs under each wing.

The single pilot sat in a modestly sized cockpit. This did not have a canopy, was unarmoured and had only a small windscreen.

Of sturdy construction and using primitive cable controls, the P.11 could survive a fair degree of gunfire.

P.11c

This aircraft wears the markings of No. 113 'Owls' Squadron, Polish Air Force. The aircraft was used by the 1st Air Regiment, during the invasion of September 1939.

Power came from a Skoda-built Bristol Mercury VIS.2 radial piston engine.

The undercarriage was fixed, but the double bracing and heavy-duty wheels made it exceptionally strong.

Its high parasol wing was revolutionary for the time and enabled the aircraft to outmanoeuvre, if not outrun, the less agile aircraft of the German invasion, notably the Dornier Do 17, Junkers Ju 87 Stuka and the Henschel Hs 126.

The P.11 shown here carries the colourful unit markings of No. 113 Squadron: a black owl on either side of the fuselage. Four weeks into the fighting P.11 squadrons were instructed to paint over the markings to reduce the planes' visibility.

A simple spring-loaded tail skid was fitted.

COMBAT DATA

ARMAMENT

As speeds increased in the late 1930s designers realised that more firepower was needed, as pilots would only have a target in their sights for a few seconds. Earlier twin-gun designs like the P.11 and He 51 were replaced by four- or six-gun types.

P.11C	2 x 7.7-mm (.303 cal.) MGs
He 51	2 x 7.92-mm (0.31-in.) MGs
GLADIATOR	4 x 7.7-mm (.303 cal.) MGs

MAXIMUM SPEED

Although the P.11 was a fast aircraft compared to most of the biplanes of its day, it presented little problem for the monoplanes that appeared soon after, like Germany's Bf 109 which were 50 per cent faster.

P.11C	390 km/h (242 m.p.h.)
He 51	330 km/h (205 m.p.h.)
GLADIATOR	410 km/h (254 m.p.h.)

SERVICE CEILING

The P.11 could outclimb most biplane fighters, but compared to its adversary, the Bf 109 monoplane with its fuel injection and more advanced airframe, it was a poor performer and an easy victim.

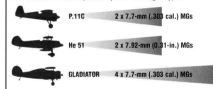

Poland's air force in the 1930s

ANSALDO BALILLA A-1: An Italian design built under licence, the Balilla was used by both sides during the Russo-Polish war.

PZL P.37 LOS: This bomber was the best aircraft used by Poland in the war. Romania operated the P.37 against the Soviet Union.

BREGUET 19: This multi-role French design was used by many air forces in Europe, including the Spanish republican air force.

PZL P.23 KARAS: This single-engined army co-operation aircraft was heavily committed during the invasion of 1939.

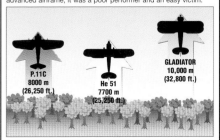

P.11C
8000 m
(26,250 ft.)

He 51
7700 m
(25,250 ft.)

GLADIATOR
10,000 m
(32,800 ft.)

REGGIANE

RE.2001/5

● German power ● Built in small numbers ● Late-war fighter

T hough Reggiane attempted to address the worst of the Re.2000's weaknesses – its lack of power – by introducing an in-line engine, the change made little impact. The Re.2001's performance was hardly improved and engine supplies were limited. The ultimate member of the family – the Re.2005 Sagittario – was one of the finest Italian fighter designs of World War II, but was built in only small numbers.

▲ *Disappointing*
performance by the Re.2000 led to the marriage of the Daimler-Benz DB.601 to the Falco airframe. The result was an improvement over its predecessor.

REGGIANE RE.2001/5

▼ **One-off**
One Re.2001 was fitted with a Fraschinin Delta IV engine. Performance was even worse than that of other Falcos.

▲ **Good handling**
Only 252 Re.2001s were built, though a handful did see combat over Malta in 1942. They proved to be extremely agile against the Allied fighters.

▼ **Last and best**
Having little in common with the Falco II, the Re.2005 Sagittario was truly outstanding and was arguably the best Italian fighter of the war. Only a handful ever became operational.

▲ **Falcons by night**
Most numerous of all variants was the Re.2001CN night-fighter. This featured a 20-mm (0.79-in.) cannon under each wing and was designed to confront the Allies' nocturnal bombing raids over northern Italy.

Low production ▶
Of the 48 Sagittarios actually completed, the majority ended up in the hands of the 22º Gruppo de Cacci, which was tasked with the defence of Rome and Naples during the last months of the war in Europe. A further 300 were almost completed.

FACTS AND FIGURES

➤ Proposed Re.2001 versions included a two-seat trainer, tank-buster and torpedo-fighter.

➤ Of the 252 Re.2001s built, 150 were completed as Re.2001CN night-fighters.

➤ Towards the war's end in Italy, plans were advanced for an all-wooden Re.2001.

➤ Reggiane planned to build a 730-km/h Re.2005R with a centrifugal compressor powered by an additional piston engine.

➤ After Italy surrendered, the Co-Belligerent Air Force continued to operate Re.2001s.

➤ Two Re.2001s were fitted with arrester hooks for deck-landing trials.

PROFILE

In-line Falcons and Archers

Left: Only the wing of the Re.2001 was retained, the fuselage being extensively redesigned.

Without doubt an excellent design, the Re.2000 Falco was underpowered. The Piaggio radial fitted to the first example developed just 649 kW (870 hp.), providing a top speed of only 529 km/h (328 m.p.h.). Believing that an in-line engine would improve top speed, Reggiane next developed the Re.2001, known as the Falco II.

This was fitted with a licence-built Daimler-Benz DB.601A-1 (Alfa Romeo RA.1000 RC.41-1a Monsonie) rated at 876 kW

(1,175 hp.). However, its maximum speed was just 542 km/h (336 m.p.h.). Re.2001s entered the war with the Regia Aeronautica over Malta in 1942. Only 252 were built, for most RA.1000 engines were earmarked for Macchi M.C.202 production.

The second in-line Re.2000 variant was the last of the line – the Re.2005 Sagitarrio (Archer). It retained the basic configuration of earlier aircraft, but was considerably redesigned, with outward-retracting undercarriage and a licence-built DB.605A-1

Right: A few Sagittarios took part in the defence of Bucharest and Berlin alongside the Luftwaffe.

engine (the Fiat RA.1050 R.C.58 Tifone) rated at 1100 kW (1,475 hp.). Only 48 of these 630-km/h (390-m.p.h.) aircraft were completed before Italy's collapse, seeing combat during the defence of Sicily, Naples and Rome. A few later served in the defence of Bucharest and Berlin.

Re.2005 Sagitarrio

Type: single-seat fighter/fighter-bomber

Powerplant: one 1100-kW (1,475-hp.) Fiat RA.1050 R.C Tifone (Daimler-Benz DB.605A-1) in-line liquid-cooled piston engine

Maximum speed: 630 km/h (390 m.p.h.)

Range: 1250 km (775 mi.)

Service ceiling: 12,000 m (39,400 ft.)

Weights: empty 2600 kg (5,720 lb.); loaded 3560 kg (7,832 lb.)

Armament: three Mauser MG 151 20-mm (0.79-in.) cannon, one engine- and two wing-mounted, plus two 12.7-mm (.50 cal.) machine-guns with 350 rounds, and up to 630 kg (1,390 lb.) of bombs

Dimensions:
span	11.00 m	(36 ft. 1 in.)
length	8.73 m	(28 ft. 8 in.)
height	3.15 m	(10 ft. 4 in.)
wing area	20.40 m²	(220 sq. ft.)

RE.2001 FALCO II

Wearing an interesting colour scheme, this Re.2001 was on the strength of the 82ª Squadriglia, 21⁰ Gruppo, 51⁰ Stormo of the Co-Belligerent Air Force, based at Puglia towards the end of 1943.

Compared to Allied fighters such as the Spitfire and P-51, the cockpit of the Falco II was cramped and visibility was rather poor.

All Re.2000 series fighters were cantilever stressed-skin monoplanes. The basic airframe bore a strong resemblance to the Seversky P-35. This was no coincidence, as the chief engineers of the design, Alessio and Longhi, had worked for Seversky prior to World War II.

A very broad fin made the Re.2000 series instantly recognisable and contributed significantly to its excellent handling.

Powering the Falco II was a 12-cylinder Alfa Romeo RA.1000. Essentially a copy of the DB.601, this engine offered only a slight performance gain over the Piaggio P.XI radial of the earlier Re.2000.

Most Re.2001s were built as night-fighters and were fitted with a 20-mm (0.79-in.) cannon under each wing, mounted in a gondola. They proved quite effective against medium- and heavy-bombers.

A feature unique to the Re.2001 variant was the fixed tailwheel. Both the radial-engined Falco and the later Re.2005 Sagitarrio featured fully-retractable tailwheels.

COMBAT DATA

MAXIMUM SPEED

Both the Bf 109K and Re.2005 were powered by essentially the same engine, but superior aerodynamics made the Italian machine discernably quicker. Neither was a match for the Spitfire, however.

Re.2005 — 630 km/h (390 m.p.h.)
Bf 109K-4 — 608 km/h (377 m.p.h.)
SPITFIRE FR.Mk XIVe — 721 km/h (447 m.p.h.)

RANGE

Throughout World War II, short range remained the Achilles heel of the Spitfire and Bf 109. Italian fighters, in particular late-war types such as the Re.2005, had much greater endurance and could loiter for longer periods.

Re.2005 SAGITTARIO 1250 km (775 mi.)
Bf 109K-4 573 km (355 mi.)
SPITFIRE FR.Mk XIVe 845 km (525 mi.)

ARMAMENT

Armed with two and three 20-mm (0.79-in.) cannon respectively, both the Spitfire and Sagitarrio were formidable opponents in battle; despite their heavy armament, they retained excellent agility.

Re.2005 SAGITTARIO
3 x 20-mm (0.79-in.) cannon, 2 x 12.7-mm (.50 cal.) machine-guns

Bf 109K-4
1 x 30-mm (1.18-in.) cannon, 2 x 15-mm (0.59-in.) machine-guns

SPITFIRE FR.Mk XIVe
2 x 20-mm (0.79-in.) cannon, 2 x 12.7-mm (.50 cal.) machine-guns

Falcos in service with the Regia Aeronautica

■ **REGGIANE Re.2000:** Prior to the Armistice, Regia Aeronautica aircraft wore distinctive white recognition bands.

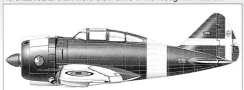

■ **REGGIANE Re.2001 2⁰ GRUPPO:** Among the last Falco IIs fighting with the Regia Aeronautica were those of 2⁰ Gruppo.

■ **REGGIANE Re.2001 22⁰ GRUPPO:** Painted in the standard dark green, this Falco II served with one of the most famous units.

REPUBLIC

P-47D/M/N THUNDERBOLT

● Tactical fighter-bomber ● Long-range escort ● Train-buster

More Republic P-47 Thunderbolts were built than any other US fighter. The 'Jug', named for its bulky shape, was a monster of a machine, yet it was fast and manoeuvrable. The pilot had enormous power at his fingertips and knew that if his aircraft was hit by gunfire, he had an excellent chance of getting home safely. From the early XP-47B to the final P-47N, the 'T-bolt' was a real winner.

▲ While the P-47 will always be remembered as an escort fighter, the beefy warplane was perhaps even more effective as a fighter-bomber.

REPUBLIC P-47D/M/N THUNDERBOLT

▼ Pacific island-hopper
Two Thunderbolts power into the air from a temporary coral air strip on a Pacific island. P-47s were employed in every theatre of the war, flying air-to-air and air-to-ground missions.

Rocket launcher ▶
Tube-launched rockets were a fearsome addition to the Thunderbolt's armoury. The fighters decimated German armour in France in 1944 using this weapon, flying precision low-level attack missions.

▲ Air superiority
The P-47N was the ultimate Thunderbolt. It had an immensely powerful engine which made it the fastest piston-engined fighter in the world, and had increased fuel capacity to enable it to accompany B-29 bombers over the Pacific.

▼ Crash and burn
Thunderbolts were famed for their enormous strength and ability to survive damage, but this aircraft did not fly again after crash-landing.

▲ French dive-bomber
France was one of many countries that used the P-47 into the 1950s. The aircraft were used as dive-bombers in French Indochina, often dropping napalm tanks.

FACTS AND FIGURES

➤ The first Thunderbolt was the XP-47B, which flew on 6 May 1941.

➤ According to designer Alexander Kartveli, the layout of the P-47 was drawn on the back of an envelope at a meeting in 1940.

➤ 15,683 Thunderbolts were built between 1940 and 1945, with more 'D' models than any other aircraft sub-type in history.

➤ With a fully loaded weight of 9390 kg, a late-model P-47N was heavier than a bombed-up Dornier Do 17 bomber.

➤ On 5 August 1944, a specially prepared Thunderbolt attained a speed of 811 km/h (504 m.p.h.), a record for WWII fighters.

➤ 'Jugs' flew over 500,000 combat sorties between March 1943 and August 1945.

PROFILE

Biggest, fastest and meanest

Never beautiful like the Spitfire, not as agile as the Bf 109, nor as long-legged as the P-51 Mustang, the big Republic P-47 Thunderbolt nevertheless was one of the most successful and best-loved fighters of all time. With its huge R-2800 engine driving a colossal 3.71-m (12-ft.) propeller, the Thunderbolt was well suited to long-distance

escort operations. With its ability to haul bombs and absorb punishment, it was equally well suited to ground attack.

The P-47 is remembered for ranging over European skies, where aces like those of Colonel Hubert 'Hub' Zemke's 56th Fighter Group valiantly fought the Luftwaffe. But the 'Jug' was widely used elsewhere. Among

Allied forces during World War II, Thunderbolts were flown by the Brazilian, British, French, Mexican and Russian pilots. The long-range P-47N fought in the Pacific, where it was a potent weapon against the Japanese. Another service variant was the 'hot-rod' P-47M, which was quickly produced in the summer of 1944 to counter the V-1 flying bombs.

The P-47 was an excellent fighter, but gained its legendary reputation flying hard-hitting ground-attack missions.

P-47D Thunderbolt

Type: single-seat fighter and fighter-bomber

Powerplant: one 1715-kW (2,535-hp.) Pratt & Whitney R-2800-59 Double Wasp 18-cylinder radial engine

Maximum speed: 697 km/h (430 m.p.h.)

Range: 3000 km (1,860 mi.) with drop-tanks

Service ceiling: 13,000 m (42,000 ft.)

Weight: empty 4853 kg (10,660 lb.); loaded 7938 kg (17,500 lb.); later versions: loaded 9390 kg (20,700 lb.)

Armament: eight 12.7-mm (.50 cal.) Browning M2 machine-guns with 267 to 500 rounds; plus provision for maximum external load of 1134 kg (2,500 lb.) including bombs, napalm or eight rockets

Dimensions: span 12.42 m (40 ft. 9 in.)
length 11.02 m (36 ft. 2 in.)
height 4.30 m (14 ft. 2 in.)
wing area 27.87 m² (300 sq. ft.)

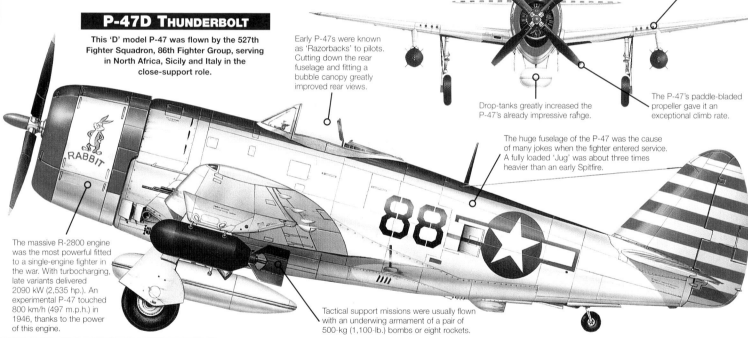

P-47D THUNDERBOLT

This 'D' model P-47 was flown by the 527th Fighter Squadron, 86th Fighter Group, serving in North Africa, Sicily and Italy in the close-support role.

Early P-47s were known as 'Razorbacks' to pilots. Cutting down the rear fuselage and fitting a bubble canopy greatly improved rear views.

Thunderbolts were fitted with eight 12.7-mm (50-cal.) machine-guns. Although lightly gunned by British or German standards, they proved highly effective.

Drop-tanks greatly increased the P-47's already impressive range.

The P-47's paddle-bladed propeller gave it an exceptional climb rate.

The huge fuselage of the P-47 was the cause of many jokes when the fighter entered service. A fully loaded 'Jug' was about three times heavier than an early Spitfire.

The massive R-2800 engine was the most powerful fitted to a single-engine fighter in the war. With turbocharging, late variants delivered 2090 kW (2,535 hp.). An experimental P-47 touched 800 km/h (497 m.p.h.) in 1946, thanks to the power of this engine.

Tactical support missions were usually flown with an underwing armament of a pair of 500-kg (1,100-lb.) bombs or eight rockets.

COMBAT DATA

MAXIMUM SPEED

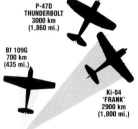

Bf 109G — 690 km/h (428 m.p.h.)
P-47D THUNDERBOLT — 697 km/h (430 m.p.h.)
Ki-84 — 624 km/h (388 m.p.h.)

The P-47D was introduced in 1943, and immediately proved itself at least as fast as anything else in the sky in Europe, until the advent of the powered Me 163 Komet rocket in 1944. It had considerably greater performance than the best of its Pacific opposition, although Japanese aircraft like the Nakajima Ki-84 'Frank' were much more agile.

RANGE

Nothing could be more striking than the difference between fighters intended for a close-range European war, such as the Bf 109, and those like the P-47 and the Ki-84, whose designers had the vast operational distances of the Pacific in mind. It was the Thunderbolt's range which made it such a capable escort fighter.

P-47D THUNDERBOLT 3000 km (1,860 mi.)
Bf 109G 700 km (435 mi.)
Ki-84 'FRANK' 2900 km (1,800 mi.)

SERVICE CEILING

American bombers were designed to attack from high altitude, so American fighters had to be equally capable at great heights. The P-47's immensely powerful Double Wasp engine pulled the 'T-bolt' higher than most of its rivals. The Messerschmitt was also good near its slightly lower altitude limits, but Japanese fighters simply could not compete.

Ki-84 'FRANK' 10,500 m (34,400 ft.)
Bf 109G 11,600 m (38,000 ft.)
P-47D THUNDERBOLT 13,000 m (42,000 ft.)

All-the-way bomber escort

The P-47 Thunderbolt and the P-51 Mustang changed the war in the air. American bombers could now attack anywhere in the Reich, secure in the knowledge that they were being escorted all the way.

TEAMWORK DEFENCE: The P-47 originally lacked the range to go all the way to Berlin with the bombers. It was used to protect the B-17s and B-24s on the outward and homeward legs of the flight, handing over responsibility to the long-range P-51 for the central portion of the mission.

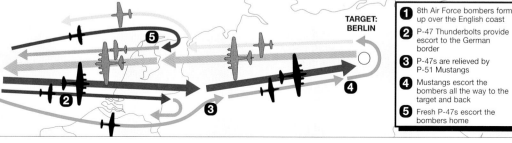

TARGET: BERLIN

1 8th Air Force bombers form up over the English coast
2 P-47 Thunderbolts provide escort to the German border
3 P-47s are relieved by P-51 Mustangs
4 Mustangs escort the bombers all the way to the target and back
5 Fresh P-47s escort the bombers home

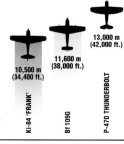

SAVOIA-MARCHETTI

S.M.79 SPARVIERO

● Bomber ● Torpedo aircraft ● Three-engined design

W ith its robust tri-motor shape and extensive fabric covering, the Savoia-Marchetti S.M.79 Sparviero was very much a creature of the 1930s. Designed for a long-distance air race, it became famous as Italy's most successful bomber. Contrary to wartime propaganda, its British and American foes found the Sparviero an effective and very tough adversary that proved difficult to shoot down.

▲ The Sparviero crews of the Regia Aeronautica and Aerosiluranti were Italy's best, delivering highly effective blows against British shipping in the Mediterranean in daring torpedo attacks.

SAVOIA-MARCHETTI S.M.79 SPARVIERO

◄ **Spanish Sparviero**
The Aviazione Legionara of the Italian air force took the S.M.79 into combat during the Spanish Civil War. Against the meagre fighter opposition of the Republican forces, it did well.

Record breaker ►
Civil S.M.79s took the first three places in the 1937 Istres-Damascus-Paris race, beating the 'MacRobertson' race winner, the DH.88 Comet, into fourth place.

▲ **Luftwaffe prize**
After the Armistice in 1943, the Luftwaffe took over all the S.M.79s using them mainly as transport aircraft.

Three engines ►
Italy's lack of suitable powerplants led to the three-engined configuration, which aided survival in combat conditions.

◄ **Gunner's view**
Looking back at another S.M.79 in close formation, the forward-mounted machine-gun bulge above the cockpit is clearly visible. This unusual feature earned the S.M.79 the nickname 'Il Gobbo' ('The Hunchback').

FACTS AND FIGURES

➤ The prototype S.M.79, built as a commercial airliner, made its first flight in October 1934.

➤ The first S.M.79 made a record flight from Milan to Rome in June 1935.

➤ Production of the S.M.79 totalled 1,330 in Italy and about 80 in Romania.

➤ Sparvieri sank four British destroyers and damaged a battleship and three carriers.

➤ When Italy surrendered, 36 airworthy S.M.79s survived at Capodichino, Littoria, Pisa and Siena; most flew again.

➤ Three surviving S.M.79s were sold as transports to the Lebanon in 1950.

Three-engined 'Hunchback'

Before war clouds loomed, Italy's brilliant Alessandro Marchetti proposed the high-speed, eight-passenger S.M.79 for an England–Australia air race. Too late for this event, the S.M.79 racked up other long-distance records. A twin-engine 'no-frills' version was quite advanced when delivered to Romania (which also produced it), Brazil and Iraq.

Italian pilots flew S.M.79 bombers with success in the Spanish Civil War, and they were to repeat the success in World War II. Well-armed and carrying a respectable payload, the S.M.79 made plenty of trouble for the Allies. Given Italy's reputation in torpedo warfare, the Sparviero (Sparrow) inevitably served as a potent torpedo bomber.

The Sparviero was a great aircraft which never reached full potential because Allied bombing of Italy disrupted supplies and production. Ethyl injection improved the performance of the Sparviero's engines but wore them out, leaving most of them unserviceable by the time the Allies invaded Sicily in 1943. A few Sparvieri survived the war as transports, but this was an aircraft whose time came and went quickly.

In the course of the Mediterranean air–sea war, Sparvieri severely damaged the battleship HMS Malaya and the carriers HMS Indomitable, Victorious and Argus. Successful pilots such as Cimicchi, Di Bella and Melley together with Capitano Buscaglia, commanding the 132° Gruppo, became national heroes in Italy.

The crew had access to each other in the S.M.79. This, and good armour protection, made the aircraft popular in service.

The S.M.79 had a wooden wing structure with a fabric covering, with all the trailing edge consisting of flaps and ailerons and the leading edge having Handley Page slots.

S.M.79-I Sparviero

Type: four-/five-crew medium bomber and torpedo-bomber

Powerplant: three 582-kW (780-hp.) Alfa Romeo 126 RC.34 nine-cylinder air-cooled radial piston engines

Maximum speed: 430 km/h (267 m.p.h.) at 4000 m (13,000 ft.)

Range: 1900 km (1,178 mi.)

Service ceiling: 6500 m (21,000 ft.)

Weights: empty 6800 kg (14,960 lb.); loaded 10,500 kg (23,100 lb.)

Armament: one 12.7-mm (.50 cal.) machine-gun firing forward over the cabin roof, 12.7-mm guns in dorsal and ventral positions, one 7.7-mm (.303 cal.) machine-gun for beam defence, plus five 250-kg (550-lb.) bombs or one 45-cm (18-in.) naval torpedo

Dimensions:
span	21.20 m (69 ft. 6 in.)
length	15.60 m (51 ft. 2 in.)
height	4.60 m (15 ft.)
wing area	61.70 m² (664 sq. ft.)

S.M.79 SPARVIERO

The S.M.79 served Italy throughout the war in the bombing, transport and torpedo attack roles. Sparvieri fought in the Balkans and North Africa as well as the Mediterranean.

The SM.79 was no easy meat for attacking fighters, with thick armour in the cockpit.

205-1

Performance of the S.M.79 was much improved when the Alfa Romeo radials were replaced by more powerful Piaggio radials.

The wireless operator doubled as a rear gunner. His position gave a good field of fire for the Breda 12.7-mm (.50 cal.) machine-gun.

All of the S.M.79's bombs were contained in its internal fuselage bomb-bay. Torpedoes were mounted under the fuselage.

Because the nose was occupied by an engine, the S.M.79's bomb-aimer occupied the front of the ventral gondola. A rearward-firing machine-gun was added to all military aircraft after the prototype.

The tail unit was constructed of tubular steel, covered in fabric. Its unusual curved outline and the three-engined layout made the Sparviero easy to recognise.

COMBAT DATA

MAXIMUM SPEED

S.M.79-I SPARVIERO	430 km/h (267 m.p.h.)
WELLINGTON	378 km/h (234 m.p.h.)
He 111	365 km/h (226 m.p.h.)

Designed from the outset as a racing machine, the Sparviero showed a good turn of speed and was considerably faster than its British and German contemporaries. It could even outpace fighters when it first flew, but it was no match for the new generation of monoplane fighters which were soon to appear.

RANGE

The monoplane bombers of the mid-1930s were far more capable than their biplane predecessors. Their lower-drag airframes and more efficient engines meant that they could travel much further on a load of fuel, greatly increasing strike ranges.

S.M.79-I SPARVIERO	1900 km (1,178 mi.)
WELLINGTON	2500 km (1,550 mi.)
He 111	1950 km (1,209 mi.)

ARMAMENT

S.M.79-I SPARVIERO	WELLINGTON	He 111
3 x 12.7-mm (.50 cal.) MGs, 1 x 7.7-mm (.303 cal.) MG 1250 kg (2,750 lb.) of bombs	8 x 7.7-mm (.303 cal.) MGs 2000 kg (4,400 lb.) of bombs	1 x 20-mm (0.79-in.) cannon, 1 x 13-mm (0.51-in.) MG, 3 x 7.92-mm (0.31-in.) MG 1000 kg (2,200 lb.) of bombs

The Sparviero was a good compromise between speed and bombload, but its defensive armament was not as good as it might have been.

Savoia-Marchetti's Sparviero family

■ **PROTOTYPE:** Although not completed in time to take part in the air race for which it was designed, the prototype S.M.79 flew for the first time in October 1934.

■ **BOMBERS:** The second prototype was completed as a bomber, and from 1936 the aircraft saw service in the Spanish Civil War with the Stormi Bombardamento Veloce.

■ **TWIN ENGINES:** Twin-engined Sparviero achieved some export success, being sold to Iraq, among other nations. Licence-built Romanian aircraft saw action in Russia.

■ **MARITIME BOMBER:** The S.M.79 was a fast and stable low-level striker and, armed with torpedoes, achieved considerable success against the British in the Mediterranean.

■ **THE LAST SPARVIERO:** Upgraded with more powerful Piaggio engines, the ultimate S.M.79 was entering service just as the Armistice of 1943 took Italy out of World War II.

SHORT

STIRLING

● RAF heavy bomber ● Glider tug ● Paratroop carrier

▲ The Stirling stands tall on its stalky undercarriage designed to improve take-off performance with a full bombload. Its usefulness was limited by the size of bombs it could carry in its bomb-bay.

Short's Stirling is one of the unsung heroes of the war. This large aircraft was Britain's first four-engine monoplane bomber to enter service. It became a stalwart of the night bombing campaign over Europe, even though it was never given as much credit as the better known Lancaster and Halifax. First entering service with No. 7 Squadron in February 1941, the Stirling flew on Bomber Command's major raids until September 1944.

SHORT STIRLING

▲ **Limited ceiling**
With a top speed of 435 km/h (269 m.p.h.) and a maximum all-up weight of 31,751 kg (69,938 lb.), the Stirling was handicapped by its low service ceiling.

▲ **Bombing-up**
Stirling Mk I of No. 7 Squadron, the first unit to equip with the heavy bomber, receives its load of bombs.

▲ **Short-span wings**
The Stirling's wing span was limited so that it could fit into RAF hangars. This gave a very low aspect ratio wing and the need for a stalky undercarriage.

▼ **MacRobert's Reply**
This Short Stirling Mk 1 of No. XV Squadron was named 'MacRobert's Reply' in honour of Lady MacRobert's sons when it was delivered to the RAF in 1941. It is painted matt-black for night bombing.

▲ **Mass production**
The RAF received a grand total of 2,374 Stirlings comprising four marks – I, III and IV (bombers) and the Mk V transport. They were built at three factories, with most produced by Short & Harland in Belfast.

FACTS AND FIGURES

➤ No. 7 Squadron became the RAF's first four-engined bomber squadron when it received Stirlings in August 1940.

➤ The prototype Stirling flew on 14 May 1939, but was destroyed on landing.

➤ In total, 162 Stirlings were built as transport aircraft.

➤ An advantage of the Stirling's internal layout was the absence of a wing spar to impede crew movement.

➤ The last bombing raid by Stirlings was on 8 September 1944 against Le Havre.

➤ Stirlings played a major part in the D-Day landings as glider tugs and for air supply.

PROFILE

Short's lofty Stirling bomber

A bulky, four-engine bomber, the Stirling was especially heavy for its tailwheel landing gear. It became an important participant in the war over the European continent.

The Stirling has been called the 'ugly duckling' of Royal Air Force bombers, and is deemed by many not to have reached its full potential. Facing flak and fighters, many Stirling crews feared their plane was a firetrap. This negative reputation was exaggerated: many crewmembers had great confidence in what was, in most respects, a fine aircraft.

After bloody battles on bombing sorties against ferociously defended targets, from early 1944 the Stirling's primary role changed to glider tug and transport.

Towing troop-carrying gliders, Stirlings had an important role in the Normandy invasion. Thereafter, Stirlings hauled gliders for the failed airborne operations at Arnhem and the March 1945 crossing of the Rhine.

By March 1946, most Stirling squadrons had been disbanded or had converted to other aircraft and the last Stirling was retired from Royal Air Force service.

Stirlings were operated by 11

Bomber Command squadrons, made 18,440 sorties, dropping 28,268 tonnes (27,821 tons) of bombs and laid about 20,000 mines. Of the 2369 production Stirlings, 769 were lost, including 641 in action. During 1947 two dozen Stirling Mk Vs were converted as cargo and passenger aircraft for a Belgian operator.

Above: With its long, narrow fuselage bomb-bay that was divided into four sections, the Stirling was not able to carry a worthwhile bombload on very long-range missions.

Right: The Stirling V was a dedicated transport version with no armament. The first was flown for the first time in August 1944, and entered service in January 1945 with Transport Command.

Stirling B.Mk III

Type: seven-place heavy bomber with a crew of seven or eight

Powerplant: four 1230-kW (1,650-hp.) Bristol Hercules VI or XVI radial piston engines

Maximum speed: 435 km/h (270 m.p.h.) at 4420 m (14,500 ft.)

Range: 950 km (590 mi.)

Service ceiling: 5180 m (17,000 ft.)

Weights: empty 19,595 kg (43,109 lb.); maximum take-off 31,751 kg (69,938 lb.)

Armament: eight 7.7-mm (.303 cal.) Browning machine-guns in Frazer-Nash FN.5A nose turret (two), FN.7A dorsal turret (two) and FN.20A tail turret (four), plus up to 6350 kg (14,000 lb.) of bombs

Dimensions:
span	30.20 m (99 ft.)
length	26.59 m (87 ft. 3 in.)
height	6.93 m (22 ft. 9 in.)
wing area	135.63 m² (1,482 sq. ft.)

STIRLING MK I

This Stirling Mk I of No. 7 Squadron Pathfinder Force, fitted with top secret H2S radar, attacked Hamburg on 30/31 January 1943.

The Stirling was powered by four 1230-kW (1,650-hp.) Bristol Hercules 14-cylinder air-cooled sleeve-valve radial engines driving three-bladed de Havilland constant-speed propellers. It contained self-sealing fuel tanks within the wing spar trusses.

Armament consisted of two 7.7-mm (.303 cal.) Browning machine-guns in the nose (FN.5) and dorsal (FN.50) turrets and four 7.7-mm Browning machine-guns in the FN.20A rear turret.

The centre section above the bomb-bay was braced to allow the crew to pass through. Aft of the centre section were the main flare chutes and a walkway through to the tail turret. Crew entered via a door on the port side.

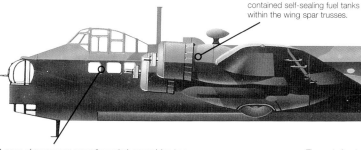

A crew of seven was normally carried, comprising two pilots, navigator/bomb-aimer, front gunner/wireless operator, two air gunners and a flight engineer/air gunner.

The main fuselage bomb-bay was 13 metres long and divided into six cells by longitudinal girders with arched members, each section with a hinged door. Also internal bomb racks inboard of the engine nacelles.

The tail unit was of cantilever construction with the single fin and rudder and tailplane of similar shape and size. It was based on the previous Empire flying-boat design.

COMBAT DATA

MAXIMUM SPEED

One feature of the Stirling that did not endear it to its crews was its lack of speed. Pilots preferred Lancasters and Halifaxes as they had an edge in performance that often proved vital.

STIRLING B.Mk III	435 km/h (270 m.p.h.)
B-17F FLYING FORTRESS	475 km/h (295 m.p.h.)
HALIFAX B.Mk III	454 km/h (281 m.p.h.)

BOMBLOAD

The Stirling could carry a slightly smaller bombload than the Halifax, which was one reason why it was more suitable for transport duties. The B-17F was a far more powerful bomber.

B-17F FLYING FORTRESS	7983 kg (17,600 lb.)
STIRLING B.Mk III	6350 kg (14,000 lb.)
HALIFAX B.Mk III	6577 kg (14,500 lb.)

ARMAMENT

Like most British bombers, the Stirling had good power turrets. These 7.7-mm machine-guns were no answer to the Ju 88's 20-mm (0.79-in.) cannon and there was no protection from fighters below.

STIRLING B.Mk III	8 x 7.7-mm (.303 cal.) machine-guns
B-17F FLYING FORTRESS	12 x 12.7-mm (.50 cal.) machine-guns
HALIFAX B.Mk III	9 x 7.7-mm (.303 cal.) machine-guns

Four-engined RAF bombers

■ **HANDLEY PAGE HALIFAX:** Powered by the same Bristol Hercules engines, the Halifax B.Mk III was faster than the Stirling, had a higher service ceiling, carried more bombs and had better defensive armament.

■ **AVRO LANCASTER:** With its four Rolls-Royce Merlin 24 engines, unrestricted bomb-bay carrying 8165-kg (17,963-lb.) bombs, good service ceiling and huge range, the Lancaster was superior to the Stirling and Halifax in most respects.

■ **CONSOLIDATED LIBERATOR:** The American B-24 was flown by RAF Bomber and Coastal Commands. Although it had a better performance than the British bombers it carried a significantly smaller bombload.

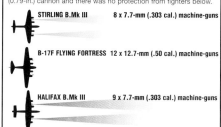

SHORT

SUNDERLAND

● Maritime patrol ● Anti-submarine ● Long-range flying-boat

Derived from the pre-war Empire flying-boat, the Sunderland became a legend in World War II as the main patrol flying-boat of British Commonwealth forces. It was tough and reliable, performing just about any maritime task including U-boat hunting, air-sea rescue and transport. Adversaries found the Sunderland a prickly customer and nicknamed it 'The Flying Porcupine'.

▲ The rugged Sunderland was one of the finest flying-boats of the war. Its vital role in fighting the U-boat blockade around Britain made it one of the most important weapons in the RAF's arsenal.

SHORT SUNDERLAND

▲ Maritime heritage
Short Brothers' expertise in flying-boat design was perfected with 'Empire'-type boats before the war. The Sunderland first flew in October 1937, and the type was operational by 1938.

▼ Run ashore
The Sunderland, as a flying-boat, had no undercarriage. Repair work on land meant that it had to be beached on a landing trolley and fitted on chocks.

▲ Coastal patrol
Sunderlands operated from some of the most remote areas in Europe and Asia. The crew had the comfort of knowing that they could always land on the sea if the engines failed.

▲ In the hull
The huge interior allowed space for weapon and flare stowage, crew rest areas, a galley, radio and radar, and plenty of fuel.

▲ Depth-charged
This attack in the Bay of Biscay in 1943 sent a U-boat to the bottom. Radar-equipped Sunderlands forced U-boats to cross the bay submerged.

◄ On the slipway
The addition of radar to the Sunderland Mk II was a key turning point in the war against the U-boats, giving Royal Air Force Coastal Command the ability to hunt by day or by night. This new Mk II was the first built by Shorts in Belfast. The four radar aerials are visible along the aircraft's spine.

FACTS AND FIGURES

➤ The prototype Sunderland made its maiden flight from the River Medway on 16 October 1937.

➤ One Sunderland won a battle with eight Ju 88 fighters, shooting down two.

➤ The Sunderland was the first flying-boat to have power-operated gun turrets.

➤ Shorts produced 721 Sunderlands between 1937 and 1945, and 17 Royal Air Force squadrons flew them.

➤ Sunderlands delivered 4877 tonnes (4,800 tons) of supplies during the Berlin Airlift.

➤ France was the last country to fly military Sunderlands, retiring them in 1960.

PROFILE

The flying porcupine

When the Short Sunderland entered service in 1938, this big seaplane gave the RAF the endurance for gruelling 20-hour patrols. During the war Sunderlands undertook many dangerous missions, including evacuating Crete by making trips with up to 82 armed passengers plus a 10-man crew. As the war progressed, improved Sunderlands introduced search radar with huge antennas atop

the rear fuselage; no other aircraft was more capable at stalking and attacking U-boats.

The Sunderland carried bombs and depth charges internally, then cranked them out on underwing pylons when preparing to attack. Its gunners could rake the deck of an enemy submarine, preventing its crew from manning their own weapons.

Some Sunderlands became stripped, high-speed transports for British Overseas Airways

Corporation. During the 1948 Berlin Airlift Sunderlands lifted almost five million kilograms of freight flying hazardous mercy missions.

The final Sunderland introduced Pratt & Whitney R-1890-90B Twin Wasp engines to replace the reliable but somewhat underpowered Pegasus. This impressive aircraft remained the standard RAF ocean flying-boat until its retirement in 1959.

Sunderland Mk III

Type: long-range reconnaissance and anti-submarine flying-boat

Powerplant: four 794-kW (1,064-hp.) Bristol Pegasus XVIII nine-cylinder radial piston engines

Maximum speed: 341 km/h (211 m.p.h.)

Range: 4828 km (2,993 mi.)

Service ceiling: 5300 m (17,930 ft.)

Weights: empty 15,663 kg (34,459 lb.); loaded 26,308 kg (57,878 lb.)

Armament: eight 7.7-mm (.303 cal.) Browning machine-guns in nose, dorsal and quad tail turrets; some fitted with four fixed forward-firing 7.7-mm and twin 12.7-mm (.50 cal.) Brownings in waist; 2250 kg (4,950 lb.) of bombs, depth charges, mines or pyrotechnics

Dimensions:
span	34.38 m (113 ft.)
length	26.01 m (85 ft.)
height	9.79 m (32 ft.)
wing area	138.14 m² (1,486 sq. ft.)

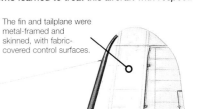

On land, the Sunderland looked clumsy and heavy. But its performance in the air surprised many enemy pilots, who learned to treat this aircraft with respect.

SUNDERLAND Mk III

This Sunderland Mk III is seen in the markings of No. 228 Squadron RAF during its deployment to the Mediterranean in 1940 and 1941.

The powered Frazer-Nash nose turret mounted two 7.7-mm (.303 cal.) machine-guns. It could be retracted into the nose.

Most Sunderlands were powered by Bristol Pegasus nine-cylinder radial engines, replaced in the final variant by more powerful Pratt & Whitney R-1890 14-cylinder radials.

The mid-upper turret replaced the single hand-held guns fired from beam windows of the Mk I.

The aft section of the fuselage contained the crew's quarters, bomb stowage and galley area.

The aerials of the ASV Mk II surface-search radar were mounted on the upper fuselage.

The fin and tailplane were metal-framed and skinned, with fabric-covered control surfaces.

The rear gunner's turret mounted four 7.7-mm (.303 cal.) machine-guns. Unlike tail gunners in other aircraft, he had easy access to the main hull.

Royal Air Force flying-boats of the 1930s

■ **SHORT SINGAPORE Mk III:** Developed from the Singapore Mk I of 1926, the Singapore Mk III patrol boat served from 1935 to 1941. With a speed of 230 km/h (143 m.p.h.), it could carry a tonne of bombs over a range of 1600 km (994 mi.).

■ **SUPERMARINE STRANRAER:** The last of Supermarine's classic series of biplane flying-boats, the twin-engined Stranraer was operational from December 1936 to 1940. Smaller than the Singapore, it had a 454-kg (1,000-lb.) bombload.

■ **SARO LONDON:** Ordered to a 1931 maritime reconnaissance requirement, the London was Britain's last front-line biplane, serving in home waters and the Mediterranean until late 1941. It had a range of 2800 km (1,736 mi.).

COMBAT DATA

ENDURANCE

Although it served all over the world, the Sunderland's main area of operations was the Atlantic, where it partnered the American-built Catalina and where its great German rival was the Focke-Wulf Fw 200 Condor. All three aircraft were well suited to maritime patrol, where the prime performance requirement was to be able to monitor large areas of ocean for extremely long periods of time.

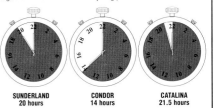

SUNDERLAND 20 hours	CONDOR 14 hours	CATALINA 21.5 hours

SUKHOI

Su-2

● Close-support bomber ● Heavy losses ● Wooden construction

▲ Many of the 500 Su-2s that were hastily constructed to provide the Soviet air force with a close-support bomber were lost in the first few months of Operation Barbarossa. A large number, like this example, were damaged on the ground and could not be repaired before being taken by advancing German soldiers.

A long with Germany, Great Britain and the USA, in the mid-1930s the Soviet Union saw the need to develop a multi-purpose tactical bomber. The resulting Su-2 never achieved the air superiority enjoyed by the Germans and suffered terrible losses at the hands of Messerschmitt Bf 109 and Focke-Wulf 190 fighters. These losses resulted in the Su-2's premature relegation to second-line tasks in 1942.

SUKHOI Su-2

▲ Sukhoi on skis
For winter operations in the snow and ice that cover much of Russia during the winter, the Su-2w/M-82 could be fitted with non-retractable skis.

▲ Molotov production
Production of the Su-2w/M-82, also referred to as the Su-4, was based in the town of Molotov.

High attrition ▶
Because of the heavy losses suffered, only one Su-2 (mostly replica parts) survives today at Monino, Moscow.

▼ Heavy losses
Even when fitted with the more powerful M-88 engine, the Su-2's performance was inadequate. Losses to German fighters were prohibitively high.

▲ German onslaught
As the German forces rapidly advanced through western Russia during the summer of 1941, many Soviet aircraft were destroyed or damaged on the ground, such as this hastily camouflaged Su-2.

FACTS AND FIGURES

➤ Three factories – Kharkov, Tananrog and Aircraft Factory No. 207 near Moscow – built production Su-2s (BB-1s).

➤ Fifteen Soviet air regiments operated the Su-2 during World War II.

➤ During 1941, several Su-2s were pressed into emergency action as fighters.

➤ In September 1941, Yekaterina Zelenko, flying an Su-2, made the only ramming attack in history by a female pilot.

➤ A camera located in a special photo turret could be fitted on the starboard side.

➤ The BB-1 designation stood for *Blizhny Bombardirovshick* (short-range bomber).

First Sukhoi to see combat

Pavel Osipovich Sukhoi was undoubtedly one of the greatest Soviet aircraft designers of all time. However, his first design to see combat, the Su-2, suffered greatly at the hands of German fighters in 1941 and 1942.

Developed from the ANT-51, the first production Su-2 (then designated BB-1) flew in April 1940 and, by September 1941, five aircraft were being produced every day. With its two-man crew, cockpit armour and robust, mainly wooden construction, the aircraft was initially successful, carrying out short-range bombing, reconnaissance and artillery-spotting missions in the first weeks of the German invasion. However, once the Su-2 encountered the Bf 109 fighters, losses rapidly began to mount.

Desperate fighting in 1942, when some Su-2s were converted into makeshift fighters, resulted in severe attrition rates. By the end of the year, the surviving Su-2s had been withdrawn and assigned to second-line duties.

Throughout the Su-2's service life, a number of different variants were produced, including a version carrying eight unguided rockets, and the more powerful Su-4 with an M-82 engine.

Below: This ski-equipped Su-2 is fitted with a removable machine-gun, attached to the rear-fuselage escape hatch.

Above: Built only in prototype form, the aerodynamically improved ShB strike bomber was based on the Su-2. Its modifications enhanced performance.

Su-2 (BB-1)

Type: two-seat armed close-support bomber and reconnaissance aircraft

Powerplant: one 820.3-kW (1,100-hp.) Tumanskii M-88B radial piston engine

Maximum speed: 455 km/h (282 m.p.h.)

Climb rate: 4000 m (13,120 ft.) in 8 min

Range: 850 km (525 mi.)

Service ceiling: 8900 m (29,200 ft.)

Weights: empty 2875 kg (6,325 lb.); maximum take-off 4150 kg (9,130 lb.)

Armament: up to four 7.62-mm (.30 cal.) ShKAS machine-guns in wings and one 7.62-mm ShKAS machine-gun in turret, plus up to 600 kg (1,320 lb.) of bombs

Dimensions:
span	14.30 m	(46 ft. 11 in.)
length	10.25 m	(33 ft. 8 in.)
height	3.94 m	(12 ft. 11 in.)
wing area	29.00 m²	(312 sq. ft.)

Su-2 (BB-1)

Like many Soviet combat aircraft flying over snow-covered terrain, this example was camouflaged by being painted white. Production of Su-2s reached 889.

Power was provided by the 14-cylinder M-88B radial engine. A three-bladed VISh-23 variable-pitch propeller was usually fitted.

A raised sliding canopy covered the pilot. Cockpit heat was fed through to the pilot's seat via a special pipeline running along the starboard side of the fuselage.

The navigator/gunner was covered by a canopy comprising both a fixed and hinged section. He was protected by 9-mm (⅓-in.) armour located in the front and bottom of the seat.

The monocoque fuselage was of all-wood construction with a load-bearing skin. Four main spars supported 20 frames with associated stringers.

The all-metal horizontal stabiliser was designed in two pieces for ease of assembly. The fin was of wooden construction.

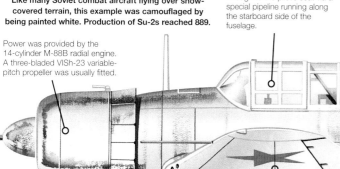

The cantilever, two-spar wing was of all-metal construction. The outer sections were flush-riveted to reduce drag. Up to 250 kg (550 lb.) of bombs could be carried beneath the wings.

Ordnance was attached on bomb racks within the fuselage bomb bay. Bombs, each ranging from 8 to 100 kg (18 to 220 lb.) (up to a maximum of 600 kg/882 lb.), could be carried.

An emergency escape hatch made from a Duralumin sheet was positioned underneath the rear fuselage. If necessary, a gun mount could be fitted to the hatch to provide some protection from the rear.

COMBAT DATA

ARMAMENT

Although the Su-2 could carry a heavy bombload, its poor defensive firepower made it easy prey for enemy fighters. The Il-2 was the best Soviet ground-attack aircraft of World War II.

Su-2 5 x 7.62-mm (.30 cal.) machine-guns 1000-kg (2,200-lb.) bombload

A-24 2 x 12.7-mm (.50 cal.) machine-guns 2 x 7.62-mm (.30 cal.) machine-guns, 544-kg (1,200-lb.) bombload

Il-2m3(Mod) 1 x 12.7-mm (.50 cal.) machine-gun, 2 x 7.7-mm (.303 cal.) machine-guns, 2 x 20-mm (0.79-in.) cannon, 600-kg (1,320-lb.) bombload

POWER

The A-24 and Su-2 had a similar level of power, but the A-24's lighter weight gave it an edge in performance. The more powerful Il-2 was built in huge numbers by the Soviet Union.

Su-2 820.3 kW (1,100 hp.)   **A-24** 746 kW (1,000 hp.)   **Il-2m3(Mod)** 1320 kW (1,770 hp.)

RANGE

Based on the naval SBD dive-bomber, the A-24 had the reach of a naval aircraft, although such a range was unnecessary on close-support bombing missions. Although the Il-2 had a limited range, it was more than adequate for operations close to the front line. The range of the Su-2 was easily sufficient.

Su-2 850 km (525 mi.)

A-24 2092 km (1,300 mi.)

Il-2m3(Mod) 600 km (370 mi.)

Early Sukhoi designs

■ **Su-3:** The high-altitude Su-1/Su-3 fighters were the first designs to bear Sukhoi's name. Despite excellent performance, they were not put into production because of the unreliable turbochargers.

■ **Su-5:** Designed as an interceptor, the Su-5 featured a piston/jet engine combination. Although able to reach a speed of 793 km/h (492 m.p.h.), it was abandoned in 1945 in favour of pure-jet designs.

■ **Su-6:** The Su-6 was superior to the Il-2/Il-10 Shturmovik in most respects, but was not selected for production as a ground-attack aircraft. The programme ended in 1944.

■ **Su-8:** This superb attack aircraft never entered production despite having the heaviest forward firepower of any World War II aircraft. It also handled very well.

SUPERMARINE

SPITFIRE MK I-V

● Air defence interceptor ● Tactical fighter-bomber

▲ No. 303 (Polish) Squadron notch up their 178th kill. Many RAF Spitfire squadrons were crewed by foreign pilots, including Czechs, French, Belgians and the famous American Eagle squadron.

The Spitfire is the most famous British aircraft of all time. Although less numerous than the Hawker Hurricane during the Battle of Britain, it is nevertheless remembered as the sleek, thoroughbred fighting machine that turned the tide during that campaign. The Spitfire is among the fastest and most manoeuvrable fighters of World War II, and served in every combat theatre.

SUPERMARINE SPITFIRE MK I-V

Flying to fight ▼
Pilots loved the Spitfire cockpit, which was roomy and had an excellent view. The sliding canopy was later replaced by a bubble canopy.

▶ Instant recognition
The Spitfire's performance was in part due to its efficient and beautiful elliptical wing.

▼ Prototype
The first Spitfire to fly had a twin-bladed propeller and a tailskid. Its Merlin engine had only half the power of the massive Griffon engines of later Spitfires.

In the factory ▶
Spitfires were hand-built by craftsmen, but took up to three times as long to assemble as their main adversary, the fearsome German Messerschmitt Bf 109.

▼ Rhubarb patrols
After the Battle of Britain, Spitfires were sent on patrols over France known as 'rhubarb' missions, to attack such opportune targets as trains or convoys.

▲ Tactical air strike
Armed with a pair of 110-kg (243-lb.) bombs, the Spitfire was a very useful fighter-bomber, serving with distinction in North Africa and Europe. The weapon load was doubled in the later Spitfires, and could also include eight rocket projectiles.

FACTS AND FIGURES

➤ The Spitfire prototype made its initial flight on 5 March 1936.

➤ More than 600 Spitfires were flown by the US Army Air Force during World War II.

➤ The Spitfire will always be compared to its adversary, the Messerschmitt Bf 109; both were among the best of their day.

➤ By 1941 Spitfires were being fitted with cannon in place of machine-guns.

➤ Spitfires intended for low-level combat had 'clipped' wings for extra agility.

➤ 22,890 Spitfires and Seafires were built between 1936 and 1947. Merlin engines powered 20,017 of them.

PROFILE

Victorious in the Battle of Britain

Supermarine designer Reginald Mitchell created a small, graceful fighter with elliptical wing and eight guns in the wings, able to fire without being hindered by the propeller. The immortal Spitfire thus became not merely one of the best-performing fighters of all time, but also one of the best-looking. Although never a long-ranged aircraft, the Spitfire was a champion in an air-to-air duel. Spitfires were routinely dived at velocities approaching the speed of sound, faster than any of the German jets.

Merlin engines were used in the early versions of the Spitfire, later supplanted by the more powerful Griffon. Late Spitfires introduced a bubble canopy which made one of history's most beautiful aircraft even more appealing. The carrier-based Seafire, derived from the Spitfire Mk V, made a vital contribution to British naval air power until new American carrier fighters appeared later in the war. The Spitfire also found a new role as a tactical fighter-bomber.

Few airworthy Spitfires survive; those that do are the stars of any air show at which they appear.

Spitfire Mk VA

Type: single-seat fighter/interceptor

Powerplant: one 1103-kW (1,440-hp.) Rolls-Royce Merlin 45 Vee piston engine

Maximum speed: 594 km/h (374 m.p.h.) at 5945 m (13,000 ft.)

Range: 1827 km (1,135 mi.)

Service ceiling: 11,125 m (37,000 ft.)

Weights: empty 2267 kg (5,000 lb.); loaded 2911 kg (6,400 lb.)

Armament: eight 7.7-mm (.303 cal.) Browning machine-guns with 350 rounds per gun

Dimensions:
span	11.23 m (36 ft. 10 in.)
length	9.12 m (29 ft. 11 in.)
height	3.02 m (11 ft. 5 in.)
wing area	22.48 m² (242 sq. ft.)

The ejector exhaust stubs were designed to add thrust to the Spitfire's propellers: designers claimed they added 5 km/h (3 m.p.h.) to the fighter's maximum speed.

The Spitfire's instantly identifiable elliptical wing combined low drag with huge strength.

Mk I Spitfires were armed with eight 7.7-mm (.303 cal.) Browning machine-guns in the wings, but in later models some or all of the guns were replaced by two or four 20-mm (0.79-in.) cannon.

The radio aerial ran from a mast behind the cockpit to the top of the tailfin.

SPITFIRE MK IA

The Mk I Spitfire was introduced in May 1938, and fought in the desperate battles over Britain and France in 1940. Production of Mk Is ceased in 1941, when cannon-armed versions were introduced.

Behind the cockpit was a thick sheet of armour, fitted as a result of early air battles over France. Pilots were very glad to have it.

The Spitfire's success owed much to its engine. The Rolls-Royce Merlin was constantly modified to give more power, keeping it ahead of the Fw 190 and Bf 109. Power almost doubled during the war years.

One weakness in the Spitfire, which it shared with the Bf 109, was its narrow-track outward-retracting undercarriage. This made it prone to accidents on the ground or on carrier decks.

While not as effective as the teardrop hoods which later became standard, the bulged cockpit canopy gave the Spitfire pilot much better visibility than his German counterpart in the Bf 109.

The prototype Spitfire was equipped with a tailskid, which was replaced by a castoring tailwheel in the production Mk I.

COMBAT DATA

MAXIMUM SPEED

The Spitfire and the Bf 109 were comparable in performance: the Spitfire was fractionally quicker at some altitudes, while the Messerschmitt was faster in a dive. The Hurricane was considerably slower than the other two fighters, but was very tough and manoeuvrable.

SPITFIRE Mk I	580 km/h (360 m.p.h.)
Bf 109E	570 km/h (354 m.p.h.)
HURRICANE Mk I	511 km/h (318 m.p.h.)

ARMAMENT

The standard British fighter armament of eight machine-guns was considered heavy before the war. But although they could pump out a lot of ammunition, the machine-guns were not as effective as the heavy cannon carried by German fighters.

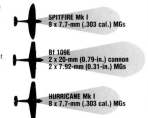

SPITFIRE Mk I 8 x 7.7-mm (.303 cal.) MGs

Bf 109E 2 x 20-mm (0.79-in.) cannon 2 x 7.92-mm (0.31-in.) MGs

HURRICANE Mk I 8 x 7.7-mm (.303 cal.) MGs

CEILING

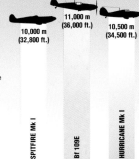

The Messerschmitt's engine had direct fuel injection, which gave it an advantage over the Spitfire at high altitudes. But for much of the Battle of Britain that advantage was negated by the need for the German fighter to stay down and protect the bombers. The Bf 109's ceiling advantage was important when tackling US daylight raids from 1942.

SPITFIRE Mk I 11,000 m (36,000 ft.)
Bf 109E 10,000 m (32,800 ft.)
HURRICANE Mk I 10,500 m (34,500 ft.)

Defence of the Kingdom

SECTOR CONTROL: RAF fighters were controlled from centralised nerve centres. These collated all information from radar stations, observers and fighters in contact with the enemy. They assigned units to deal with specific threats, ensuring the most efficient use of scarce fighter resources.

CHAIN HOME DEFENCE RADAR: A chain of radar stations along the south and east coasts ensured that no air raid approached undetected.

INCOMING AIR RAIDS: German aircraft were often detected by radar as they formed up over their French bases, so that by the time they had crossed the Channel the RAF's fighters were already in the air and in a position to intercept.

TAYLORCRAFT

AUSTER SERIES

● Battlefield observation ● Communications ● D-Day veteran

O riginally designed pre-war in the USA as lightplanes for the growing civilian private pilot market, the Auster series provided some of Britain's most important light observation aircraft of World War II. Although the Auster was slow and appeared old-fashioned, it was an ideal mount for artillery spotting and provided the pilots with an excellent field of view. It was also agile enough to dodge enemy fighters and operate from tiny grass airstrips.

▲ *The Auster Mk I-V series was built in large numbers and served in every combat theatre, throughout the war, with the RAF's Air Observation Post (AOP) Squadrons.*

TAYLORCRAFT AUSTER SERIES

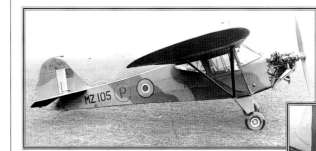

▼ **Basic interior**
Inside, the Auster Mk IV variant was spartan to say the least. The flying controls were mounted on the left side. This example carries a wireless system in place of the right-hand seat.

▲ **Powerplant exposed!**
One of the only two Auster Mk IIs built sits with its engine cowling removed, revealing the compact Lycoming engine.

High-mounted wing ▶
In common with other light observation aircraft, the Auster series featured a single high-mounted wing, which provided an unobstructed view of the ground and generated tremendous lift.

◀ **Built tough**
Knowing that these little observation machines would spend most of their lives operating from primitive airstrips out in the open, Taylorcraft kept the design very simple and made it strong.

Enter the Auster Mk III ▶
Looking externally very similar to the Cirrus Minor-powered Auster Mk I, the Mark III variant differed in being fitted with a 97-kW (130-hp.) Gipsy Major. This was one of the most widely produced of the early Auster variants with 470 examples built.

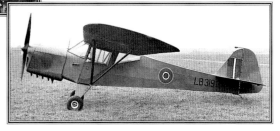

FACTS AND FIGURES

➤ In 1938 Taylorcraft Aeroplanes (England) Ltd was established to build the parent company's light aircraft under licence.

➤ Austers played an important part during the Allied invasion of France in 1944.

➤ Only one unit, No. 656 Squadron, operated the Auster in the Far East.

➤ Only two examples of the Auster Mk II were built, because of a severe shortage of American Lycoming engines.

➤ Experiments with a floatplane version, the Auster Mk V, were conducted in 1945.

➤ Austers were used for air photography duties in the closing stages of the war.

PROFILE

Supreme artillery spotter

Following on from the success of the Taylorcraft series of lightplanes in the USA, licence production was established at Thurmaston, in Leicestershire, under the name of Taylorcraft Aeroplanes (England) Ltd.

Several civilian variants were produced and with the outbreak of World War II these were evaluated for the airborne observation role. The Taylorcraft Plus C was selected for production under the military designation Auster Mk I.

The suitability of the aircraft was quickly appreciated and the design was developed into the Mk III. Powered by a 97-kW Gipsy Major I engine, 470 of this version were produced.

Next major production variant was the Mk IV which was fitted with an American Lycoming O-290 engine and had a larger cabin to accommodate a third seat. The most common wartime Auster was the Mk V, which introduced blind-flying instrumentation and other improvements. About 800 of this variant were built.

Auster series aircraft gave invaluable service in North Africa and, later in the war, in southern and northern Europe. At their peak, Austers equipped 19 squadrons, often using their remarkable short-field performance to operate very close to the front line.

Left: Outward visibility was not particularly good on the early Auster variants, especially to the side and rear.

Above: MZ 105 was one of the prototype Auster Mk IIs and illustrates the unique snub-nose profile of this rare variant.

Auster Mk V

Type: light liaison and observation/reconnaissance aircraft

Powerplant: one 97-kW (130-hp.) Lycoming O-290-3 horizontally opposed four-cylinder engine

Maximum speed: 209 km/h (130 m.p.h.)

Maximum cruising speed: 180 km/h (112 m.p.h.)

Range: 402 km (250 mi.)

Service ceiling: 5639 m (18,500 ft.)

Weights: empty 499 kg (1,098 lb.); loaded 839 kg (1,846 lb.)

Accommodation: one pilot and observer, sitting side by side

Dimensions:	span	10.97 m (36 ft.)
	length	6.83 m (22 ft. 5 in.)
	height	2.44 m (8 ft.)
	wing area	15.51 m² (167 sq. ft.)

The engine was enclosed underneath two upward-lifting hatches for easy maintenance with the minimum of equipment in the field.

The high-set wing was fitted with large-trailing edge flaps allowing for an extremely low speed, this was particularly useful during missions when targets on the ground needed to be observed and recorded.

A large rudder allowed the Auster exceptional turning ability when operating at low speed. Positioned above this was a mass balancing weight.

AUSTER MK IV

Operating near the front line of every major battlefield in Europe, the Auster allowed Allied commanders to observe enemy movements. This camouflaged example was in operation after the D-Day landings.

Because of the requirement to operate from rough landing strips the Auster had large wheels and tyres. Specialised variants were equipped with skis or floats for operations from snow-covered airfields or lakes.

Enclosed in a fully glazed cockpit, the pilot and his observer were afforded excellent visibility from the Auster. The rear of the cockpit could be utilised for urgent cargo if required for particular flights.

COMBAT DATA

MAXIMUM SPEED

Though equipped with a rather low-powered engine, the Auster was faster than Germany's Fieseler Storch. Because of its reasonable speed the Auster was often used for courier duties.

AUSTER Mk V	209 km/h (130 m.p.h.)
Fi 156C-2 STORCH	175 km/h (108 m.p.h.)
O-49 VIGILANT	196 km/h (122 m.p.h.)

RANGE

The ability to fly great distances for observation purposes was a requirement for all light reconnaissance aircraft. The Auster compared favourably to the German Storch but offered slightly less range than the American Stinson Vigilant.

AUSTER Mk V 402 km (250 mi.)

Fi 156C-2 STORCH 385 km (240 mi.)

O-49 VIGILANT 451 km (280 mi.)

MAXIMUM TAKE-OFF WEIGHT

Its low take-off weight helped the Auster to operate from small forest clearings or similar front-line locations and respond quickly when a reconnaissance or artillery spotting mission was needed.

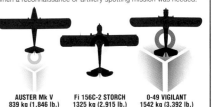

AUSTER Mk V 839 kg (1,846 lb.)

Fi 156C-2 STORCH 1325 kg (2,915 lb.)

O-49 VIGILANT 1542 kg (3,392 lb.)

British military light aircraft

■ **DE HAVILLAND DH. 82 TIGER MOTH:** One of the most famous British aircraft of all time, the Tiger Moth served as the RAF's basic trainer from February 1932 and was finally retired as late as 1955.

■ **MILES M.38 MESSENGER:** Evaluated as a potential three-seat observation aircraft, the distinctive Messenger was never adopted by the RAF, but was successful on the civilian market.

■ **PERCIVAL PRENTICE T.MK 1:** Incorporating many features learned during the war, the Prentice T.Mk 1 was a far more powerful and advanced training aircraft, though it did not enter service until 1947.

TUPOLEV

TB-3

● TB-1 successor ● First modern four-engined bomber

I n 1926 the Tupolev design bureau, under Vladimir Petliakov, was given the task of designing the world's first monoplane bomber with engines mounted on the leading edge of the wing. So challenging was the project that the aircraft did not fly until 1930. What finally emerged was the ANT-6, a tremendously capable long-range bomber. It entered VVS (Soviet air force) service in 1932 as the TB-3. It was truly an aircraft ahead of its time.

▲ At the time of its first flight, nothing like the ANT-6 had ever been seen before. It proved to be a tough and reliable aircraft, though early variants suffered from weak engines.

TUPOLEV TB-3

▼ Air force assets
Introduction of the TB-3 significantly improved the capabilities of the VVS (Soviet air force). These bombers were among the first Soviet aircraft employed to drop paratroops.

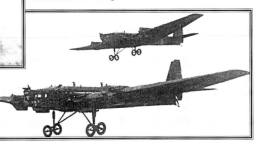

▲ Tupolevs at the North Pole
Two ANT-6s (as civilian TB-3s were known) were used as support aircraft on a survey party to find a suitable base for an Arctic expedition.

▼ World renown
During its early years, the giant Tupolev earned international recognition because of its size.

▼ Heavyweight bomber
Early tests illustrated the need to beef up the structure and production machines were very heavy by the standards of the time.

▲ Ahead of its time
Even by the mid-1930s few aircraft were capable of matching the capabilities of the TB-3.

FACTS AND FIGURES

➤ When tests were conducted on the first production TB-3, it was found to be 1000 kg (2,200 lb.) heavier than the prototype.

➤ Nine aircraft embarked upon a series of goodwill flights over the summer of 1935.

➤ A single TB-3 was used as a mother ship for Zveno (link) trials with I-16 fighters.

➤ In September 1936 pilot A Yumashev set an international altitude record, reaching 8116 m with a five-ton load in a TB-3.

➤ Sadly, no TB-3s still exist. All had been scrapped by the mid-1950s.

➤ An ANT-6, SSSR-N169 flew on the last pre-war Soviet Polar expedition in 1941.

238

Soviet bombers come of age

Taking to the air for the first time on 22 December 1930, the ANT-6 at first seemed little more than a scaled up Tupolev TB-1. True, it did retain many features of the older design, including the landing gear, engines and propellers, but it was destined to be of far greater importance.

A massive production programme was instigated and the first ANT-6s (TB-3s) began to roll off the assembly lines in 1930, with deliveries to the VVS beginning soon after. Amazingly

few problems were met, although early aircraft were fitted with unreliable Mikulin M17 engines and had poor build quality. Once these problems had been rectified, the TB-3 proved itself to be the most modern and capable bomber in the world and did more than any other aircraft to give the Soviet Union a long-range strike capability.

Besides bombing, TB-3s were also used for paratroop drops, and the unorthodox Zveno (link) experiments, in which the aircraft acted as

mother ship for Polikarpov I-5 and I-16 fighters.

By the late 1930s the aircraft were approaching obsolescence and began to be withdrawn from service, though a handful were still active by the outbreak of World War II in 1939.

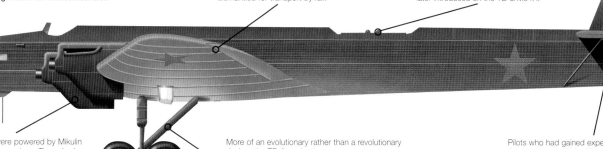

Above: Zveno experiments were conducted for several years. The combination actually saw combat, attacking a bridge in August 1941.

Right: A logical step from the earlier TB-1, the TB-3 truly established the Soviet Union as a major builder of heavy bombers. Later versions, with M-34 engines, were able to reach speeds of 288 km/h (179 m.p.h.).

TB-3/M34R

Type: five-seat long-range bomber and transport aircraft

Powerplant: four 615-kW (825-hp.) Mikulin M-34 water cooled in-line V-12 piston engines

Maximum speed: 288 km/h (179 m.p.h.)

Initial climb rate: 227 m/min (745 f.p.m.)

Maximum operating radius: 960 km (595 mi.)

Normal range: 1400 km (868 mi.)

Service ceiling: 7740 m (25,400 ft.)

Weights: empty 12,585 kg (27,687 lb.); loaded 18,877 kg (61,917 lb.)

Armament: six DA machine guns, in pairs

Dimensions:
span	41.85 m	(137 ft. 3 in.)
length	25.10 m	(82 ft. 4 in.)
height	5.60 m	(18 ft. 4 in.)
wing area	234.50 m²	(2,523 sq. ft.)

TB-3/M34

This machine is an M34 variant, which featured more powerful engines with revised cooling, including repositioned radiators, and a slightly redesigned forward fuselage with a gondola for the bombardier.

The wing, one of the largest built up to that time, was based extensively on that used for the TB-1. It was built in five sections, all of which could be conveniently dismantled for transport by rail.

Armament was also similar to that of the earlier TB-1 with twin batteries of DA machine guns mounted in the nose and two mounted in tandem in the rear fuselage. A tail turret was later introduced on the TB-3/M34R.

Early aircraft were powered by Mikulin M17 V12 in-line engines. These had a complex cooling system and were prone to overheating. They were later replaced by more powerful M34s which featured Allison superchargers.

More of an evolutionary rather than a revolutionary design, the TB-3 retained many proven components of the TB-1, including the landing gear. To cope with the extra weight of the four-engined aircraft, the oleos were strengthened and tandem tyres fitted on bogies.

Pilots who had gained experience on TB-1s, found the new bomber little different and the TB-3 also retained some traits of its predecessor, notably the heavy handling. The elevators were especially hard work, and in-flight vibration could be quite severe, especially towards the rear of the aircraft.

ACTION DATA

MAXIMUM SPEED

With more power available from its four engines, the TB-3 was faster than its predecessor, but was still heavy and lumbering. Later aircraft such as the Hendon were more advanced and faster.

TB-3/M-17	226 km/h (140 m.p.h.)
TB-1	178 km/h (110 m.p.h.)
HENDON	249 km/h (154 m.p.h.)

SERVICE CEILING

During the late 1920s, few aircraft were capable of reaching the same altitude as the TB-3. The Hendon was conceived later and although it could climb to 6553 m, it did not prove successful in RAF service.

TB-3/M-17	TB-1	HENDON
5100 m (16,700 ft.)	4830 m (15,800 ft.)	6553 m (21,500 ft.)

BOMBLOAD

Operational TB-3s could carry more bombs than any other aircraft during their heyday and set several records for altitude with a full bombload. A major drawback of inter-war British bombers such as the Hendon was their inability to carry substantial bombloads.

TB-3/M-17	2000 kg (4,400 lb.)
TB-1	1000 kg (2,200 lb.)
HENDON	753 kg (1,660 lb.)

Soviet bombers of World War II

■ **TUPOLEV TU-2R 'BAT':** A twin-engined attack bomber and reconnaissance aircraft, the Tu-2 entered service in 1944.

■ **TUPOLEV SB-2:** Built in huge numbers, the SB-2 was one of the most numerous Soviet aircraft of World War II.

■ **ILYUSHIN IL-4:** Know initially as the DB-3F, this was one of Ilyushin's most successful designs in the bureau's early years.

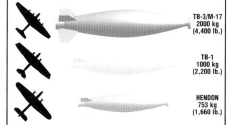

TUPOLEV

Tu-2

● Medium bomber ● Ground and torpedo-attack ● Reconnaissance

TUPOLEV Tu-2

▲ Crew accommodation
The pilot, radio operator/gunner and bombardier/navigator were accommodated forward of the wing.

▲ UTB trainer
Designed by P.O.Sukhoi, the UTB was a simplified and lighter Tu-2 airframe with lower powered engines. The Polish air force had 100 delivered.

▲ Jet testbed
A Tu-2 was fitted with a Russian version of the Rolls-Royce Nene 1 turbojet engine for flight test development work as the Tu-2N.

▲ Tu-2 Paravan
Two aircraft had a giant 6-m (20-ft.) probe on the nose. This carried wires attached to the wingtips, where cable cutters were installed to cut balloon cables.

▲ Fighter prototype
This much modified variant, the ANT-63P, was a heavily armed fighter first flown in December 1946. It had provision for radar.

◄ Special service
With a GAZ-67B cross country vehicle in its bomb-bay, this Tu-2 was used for special missions.

Few great aircraft have been designed in a prison cell. Andrei Tupolev was ordered to produce a versatile aircraft 'better than the Luftwaffe's Ju 88' on his drawing board in the Butyrkii prison. He did just that. The Tupolev Tu-2 family was one of the most varied and successful aircraft of World War II. It remained in production until 1948, by which time 2527 had been delivered for service.

▲ With its exceptionally aerodynamic design and inherent versatility, the Tu-2 gave long and distinguished service to the Soviet air force and was widely exported.

FACTS AND FIGURES

➤ Designed for tactical attack, the Tu-2 was also an effective dive-bomber, torpedo bomber and armored strike fighter.

➤ The first prototype was flown on 29 January 1941, but production was slow.

➤ Tu-2s first went to the front line in November 1942 and were well received.

➤ With two forward-firing 20-mm (0.79-in.) cannon, the Tu-2 proved to be an effective fighter when attacking bombers from the rear.

➤ Only 1111 were built during the war with 1416 more built post-war.

➤ Tu-2s served in Bulgaria, China, Hungary, North Korea, Poland and Romania.

PROFILE

Tupolev's tactical masterpiece

By mid-1938 Tupolev had a full team of designers and engineers working for him. All were held prisoner by the Soviet authorities and none could have imagined the excellence of the design they were producing.

After a number of delays, the ANT-58 design, which was to become the Tu-2, was finally approved on 1 March 1940. Unfortunately, the prototype had to wait until 1941 before its engines were ready, but when it eventually flew on 29 January 1941, it proved to be an

exceptional performer in every respect. Further testing refined the aircraft and it entered series production in 1943. The first machines went into combat in the spring of 1944.

Such was its success that Tupolev and his team were released from prison and Tupolev himself was awarded the Stalin Prize. Continuous development, mostly centred on

the engine installations, resulted in the Tu-2 remaining a viable combat aircraft in the post-war era and it was produced in quantity until 1948.

Late production Tu-2Ss had four-blade propellers, more powerful engines and equipment improvements. Given the NATO codename 'Bat', it saw combat in the Korean War and served with Communist air forces until the late 1950s.

Tupolev Tu-2S

Type: multi-role medium bomber

Powerplant: two 1380-kW (1,850-hp.) Shvetsov ASh-82FN 14-cylinder radial piston engines

Maximum speed: 546 km/h (339 m.p.h.) at 5395 m (17,700 ft.)

Initial climb rate: 9.5 min to 5000 m (16,400 ft.)

Range: 1400 km (870 mi.)

Service ceiling: 9500 m (31,170 ft.)

Weights: empty 7458 kg (16,443 lb.); maximum take-off 11,336 kg (24,992 lb.)

Armament: two 20-mm (0.79-in.) ShVAK cannon; three 12.7-mm (.50 cal.) UBT machine guns; and up to 3084 kg (6,800 lb.) of bombs

Dimensions:
span	18.85 m	(61 ft. 10 in.)
length	13.79 m	(45 ft. 3 in.)
height	4.55 m	(14 ft. 11 in.)
wing area	48.77 m²	(525 sq. ft.)

TUPOLEV TU-2S

This aircraft is typical of Soviet Tu-2s. Pilots were impressed by the aircraft's handling, which was said to be fighter-like. Such was the success of the airframe that several postwar versions were built.

A tall radio mast was mounted on the left side above the bullet-proof windscreen. Wires ran to the port fin and down to the left side of the nose.

The aircraft was aerodynamically outstanding, due to the low drag, stiff sandwich wing skins and flush riveting. It had detachable wingtips.

Giving the Tu-2 good ground clearance, the stalky main landing gear retracted to the rear, as did the single tailwheel. The fuselage nose was plywood with a near conical shape. The pilot sat high above the nose had a good forward view, even while on the ground.

The high-mounted, fixed, fabric-covered tailplane had an eight degree dihedral with balanced, trim-tabbed elevators. The oval-shaped twin fins and rudders remained standard on all variants.

Two 1,850-hp. ASh-82FN 14-cylinder radial piston engines powered the Tu-2S. Some had enlarged carburetor intakes and shorter exhausts.

Armament comprised two 20-mm (0.79-in.) ShVAK cannon in the wing roots and three single 12.7-mm (.50 cal.) UBT guns, aimed by three crewmembers: one behind the pilot, another in a ventral turret and the third in a dorsal turret, all rearward facing.

ACTION DATA

SPEED
Tupolev paid great attention to the aerodynamic qualities of the Tu-2. This resulted in an impressive top speed, and the aircraft remained fast even with the addition of more equipment.

Tu-2S — 547 km/h (339 m.p.h.)
Ju 88A-4 — 468 km/h (291 m.p.h.)
B-25J — 438 km/h (272 m.p.h.)

WEAPONS
The Tu-2S carried a much heavier bomb load than its major contemporaries. The North American B-25J was optimized as a ground-attack aircraft with heavy forward fire-power.

Tu-2S — 3 x 12.7-mm (.50 cal.) machine guns, 2 x 20-mm (0.79-in.) cannon, 4000-kg (8,800-lb.) bombload

Ju 88A-4 — 3 x 7.92-mm (0.31-in.) machine guns, 2 x 20-mm (0.79-in.) cannon, 2000-kg (4,400-lb.) bombload

B-25J MITCHELL — 18 x 12.7-mm (.50 cal.) machine guns, 1358-kg (2,994-lb.) bombload

RANGE
As one of the great Soviet combat aircraft of World War II, the Tu-2S also offered good range and was on a par with its American rival. The Junkers Ju 88A-4 was used in the long-range role, but had been designed for medium range. It was not as versatile as the Tu-2S.

Tu-2S 1400 km (870 mi.)
Ju 88A-4 2728 km (1,695 mi.)
B-25J MITCHELL 2173 km (1,350 mi.)

Soviet twin bombers

■ **ILYUSHIN Il-4:** With its 2694-kg (5,940-lb.) bomb load and 3581-km (2,225-mi.) range, the Il-4 was a useful medium- to long-range bomber. It was not as versatile as the Tu-2.

■ **PETLYAKOV Pe-2:** A range of Pe-2 variants was built, serving as light- and dive-bombers and ground attack aircraft. The Pe-2m bomber had a maximum bomb load of 2000 kg (4,400 lb.).

■ **POLIKARPOV NB, T:** An exceptionally advanced night-bomber, the NB, T was designed under mysterious circumstances and never entered series production.

■ **TUPOLEV SB-2:** One of the most important bombers of the 1930s, the SB-2 was developed from the ANT-20. The aircraft was still in production at the beginning of World War II.

VICKERS
WELLINGTON

● Medium bomber ● U-boat destroyer ● Mine hunter

Affectionately nicknamed 'Wimpey' after a wartime cartoon character, the Wellington was one of the most popular aircraft used by RAF Bomber Command. Designed to deliver bombs over medium ranges, its twin-engined performance prevented the Wellington from reaching targets deep in Germany. It was ultimately employed in many other roles throughout World War II, including anti-submarine warfare and mine hunting.

▲ *Wellingtons made the first RAF attacks on German targets in 1939 and were the mainstay of Royal Air Force Bomber Command until the advent of the four-engined heavy bombers. It was the first bomber type to drop the 4000-lb. (1814-kg) 'blockbuster' bomb, in 1941.*

VICKERS WELLINGTON

▲ Six crewmembers
Wellington bombers carried a crew of six. The wireless operator manned a machine-gun position if the aircraft was attacked.

▲ Night camouflage
Bomber Command Wellingtons had a matt-black fuselage and lower surfaces.

Geodetic strength ▶
The Wellington's designer, Barnes Wallis, devised the immensely strong geodetic structure which was unique to the Wellington and the earlier Vickers Wellesley light bomber.

▲ Flying testbeds
The Wellington served as a test aircraft for various types of new equipment. One series of trials involved mounting a Vickers 40-mm (1.57-in.) gun in a dorsal turret and replacing the single fin by two smaller ones to ensure adequate rudder control.

◀ Various engines
Wellingtons were fitted with a number of different types of engine, including the Bristol Hercules, Bristol Pegasus, Pratt & Whitney Twin Wasp and Rolls-Royce Merlin. The aircraft in this photograph contains a Hercules engine.

FACTS AND FIGURES

➤ The Wellington prototype, the Vickers Type 271, first flew as an unarmed prototype on 15 June 1936.

➤ Coastal Command Wellingtons sank or damaged 51 U-boats during the war.

➤ Wellingtons were built in 16 marks and 11,461 were completed by 1945.

➤ Special high-flying Wellingtons (Mks V and VI) fitted with a pressure cabin reached an altitude of 11600 m (38,000 ft.).

➤ The last Wellingtons in RAF service were withdrawn in 1953.

➤ Wellingtons equipped no less than 57 Royal Air Force squadrons.

PROFILE

Barnes Wallis' 'Wimpey'

Built on the then-advanced principle of aerodynamic construction known as geodetic (inherently self-supporting), the Wellington prototype was the brain-child of Dr Barnes Wallis, later to win fame for his 'Dam Buster' bouncing bomb.

The Wellington's long wartime service showed that the 'basket weave' method of interlaced metal sections bolted together for high strength was very sound. This often enabled 'Wimpeys' to return to base with huge holes torn in them by flak and fighter attack. Wellingtons were first used as day-bombers, but their vulnerability was exposed in several disastrous raids.

After British night bombing passed to larger aircraft such as the Lancaster and Halifax in 1943, Wellingtons saw sterling service with Coastal Command as maritime reconnaissance aircraft. A number became successful U-boat hunters by both day and night. Sometimes fitted with Leigh Lights to illuminate submarines, the aircraft carried a fearsome array of depth charges and bombs to destroy them. One of the Wellington's most unusual roles was to destroy magnetic mines. The aircraft were fitted with a huge metal ring that released echoes powerful enough to trigger the mines, enabling aircrew to 'sweep' ports and coastal waters sown with such weapons. After the war the Wellington was used as a crew trainer.

More than 600 Wellingtons were involved in the first 1000 bomber raid of the war, which targeted Cologne on the night of 30/31 May 1942. In all, 1042 aircraft took part in the raid.

The only Victoria Cross awarded to a Wellington crewmember was won by a New Zealander, Sergeant J. A. Ward, flying as second pilot with No. 75 Squadron, RAF, after he climbed onto the aircraft's wing to put out an engine fire.

WELLINGTON B.Mk IC

R1492 was one of 2,685 Vickers Wellington B.Mk IC bombers constructed. It was delivered to an Operational Training Unit from Vickers' Chester factory in 1941.

Training versions of the Wellington often had their machine-gun armament removed and the nose turret faired over. Operational aircraft had two 7.7-mm (.303 cal.) guns in the turret.

Unlike other RAF types, especially those designed later in the war, all Wellington's were built by the company which designed the aircraft. Vickers used three factories at Weybridge, Chester and Blackpool.

Lacking a dorsal turret, the Wellington was somewhat vulnerable to attacks from the beam. Some aircraft had an improvised gun armament in the beam to remedy this.

The Bristol Hercules was a reliable and efficient engine that was able to survive considerable battle damage. Rolls-Royce Merlins were tried as an alternative powerplant in the Wellington Mk II.

Early Wellington B. Mk I aircraft required modification to carry the 1814-kg (4,000-lb.) 'blockbuster' bomb.

Early examples of the Wellington bomber were fitted with a 'dustbin' machine-gun turret which was lowered amidships when required.

The rear gunner was armed with four 7.7-mm (.303 cal.) Browning machine-guns, and many Wellington gunners shot down Bf 109s that strayed too close.

COMBAT DATA

MAXIMUM SPEED

For a medium-bomber the Wellington was very fast by pre-war standards, but fighter design evolved rapidly as the war began and the Wellington could not outrun fighters. The G4M had a higher speed, but lacked the Wellington's armour and power turrets.

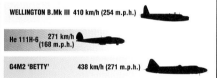

WELLINGTON B.Mk III 410 km/h (254 m.p.h.)

He 111H-6 271 km/h (168 m.p.h.)

G4M2 'BETTY' 438 km/h (271 m.p.h.)

ARMAMENT

RAF bombers were well armed by contemporary standards, and the Wellington carried a fair bombload and defensive armament. Despite its gun armament, it was vulnerable to enemy fighters.

G4M2 'BETTY'
3 x 7.7-mm (.303 cal.) MGs
2 x 20-mm (0.79-in.) cannon
1000 kg (2,200 lb.) of bombs

He 111H-6
1 x 13-mm (0.51-in.) MG
2 x 7.2-mm (0.28-in.) MGs
2 x 7.9-mm (0.31-in.) MGs
1 x 20-mm (0.79-in.) cannon
2000 kg (4,400 lb.) of bombs

WELLINGTON B.Mk III
8 x 7.7-mm (.303 cal.) MGs
2041 kg (4,500 lb.) of bombs

RANGE

Wellingtons had a reasonable range. Japanese aircraft had to fly over long distances in the Pacific and had greater range, gained at the expense of armour and offensive load.

WELLINGTON B.Mk III
2478 km (1,535 mi.)

G4M2 'BETTY'
6059 km (3,757 mi.)

He 111H-6
1950 km (1,209 mi.)

Leigh Light Wellington versus the U-boat

RADAR SEARCH: RAF Coastal Command used Wellingtons and other aircraft equipped with ASV (Air-to-Surface Vessel) radar and the Leigh Light to harass the German U-boat fleet.

TARGET DETECTION: Once the target had been found using the ASV radar and was within a suitable range the Leigh Light was triggered to illuminate the surfaced U-boat. This allowed an accurate attack to be made using depth charges.

SUCCESSFUL ATTACK: The first Leigh Light attack on a submarine was made in June 1942, with the first successful attack taking place on 6 July.

VOUGHT
F4U CORSAIR

● Carrier fighter ● Potent ground-attacker ● Dominant in the Pacific

Vought's F4U Corsair was one of the finest fighters ever built. At first thought too powerful to fly from carrier decks, the Corsair weaved a path of destruction in battle after battle during World War II, totally outclassing the much-feared Japanese Zero. With its instantly recognisable gull-wing shape and its great speed and firepower, the Corsair was still coming off the production line in 1953, one of the last of the great piston-engined fighters.

▲ Flying in May 1940, the XF4U-1 was the smallest possible airframe mated with the most powerful engine then available. It was the first of more than 12,500 Corsairs built over the following 13 years.

VOUGHT F4U CORSAIR

▲ Gull wing
The kinked wing allowed short landing gear to be fitted while lifting the huge propeller clear of the deck.

▲ Into the air
With a self-generated vapour trail spiralling around the propeller, a radar-equipped F4U night-fighter runs down the deck of a 'Midway'-class aircraft-carrier.

◀ Raw power
The massive 18-cylinder Pratt & Whitney Double Wasp radial engine was the key to the Corsair's superb performance.

▼ Super performer
From its earliest test flights in 1940, the Corsair showed that it could exceed 650 km/h (400 m.p.h.) in a straight line. This was faster than any other American aircraft, a unique achievement for a naval fighter designed for carrier operations.

▲ Pacific killer
Superb as a dogfighter or ground-attack platform the Corsair helped the Allies sweep through the western Pacific in 1944-45.

FACTS AND FIGURES

➤ The F4U's propeller was one-third larger than that of the Messerschmitt Bf 109.

➤ The final F4U-7 Corsair was delivered to France in 1953, just as the last attack Corsairs were reaching the US Marines.

➤ The 'ultimate' Corsair was the Goodyear F2G, fitted with a P&W R-4360 engine delivering 2685 kW (3,600 hp.) of power.

➤ Charles Lindbergh demonstrated Corsair tactics during a Pacific tour in 1943.

➤ A US Navy Corsair night-fighter pilot was the only Allied ace of the Korean War who did not fly the F-86 Sabre.

➤ Except for Yugoslavia's S-49 and Spain's Ha 1112, the 12,571 Corsairs were the last piston fighters produced.

PROFILE

The mighty Corsair

As the Corsair's place as a fighter was taken by jets, the tough Vought warbird was turned into a highly effective ground-attack machine.

The fighter which took shape on designer Rex Beisel's drawing board in 1938 was a monster. The prototype Vought F4U Corsair, flown on 29 May 1940, was the heaviest shipborne fighter built to that time. It was tough, fast and very manoeuvrable, but early pilots encountered handling problems at low speeds, and the restricted view made carrier landing very tricky. As a result, the first Corsairs in combat were flown with enormous success by land-based Marines.

Modified with a raised seat and bulged canopy, Corsairs were flying from British carriers in 1943 and from US Navy carriers by 1944, and racked up an impressive score of aerial victories against Japan's best fighters. Corsairs using bombs and rockets paved the way for the final battles at Iwo Jima and Okinawa. The Royal Navy also used the Corsair to great effect in the Pacific, attacking Japanese oil refineries and airfields.

Vought's remarkable fighter, also manufactured by Brewster and Goodyear, was still an important component in US naval air power during the Korean War. One Corsair even shot down a MiG-15 jet fighter.

The most instantly recognisable feature of the Corsair was its inverted gull wing. In addition to giving the huge propeller extra ground clearance, it also ensured that the wing met the fuselage at right-angles, causing minimum interference drag.

Early Corsairs had the standard American fighter armament of six 12.7-mm (.50 cal.) machine-guns. Later variants carried four cannon.

F4U-1A CORSAIR

This aircraft was flown by Lieutenant Ira C. Kepford, the US Navy's leading ace in 1944. He was one of 15 aces from VF-17, the first Navy Corsair squadron.

Much of the Corsair's long nose was occupied by a single self-sealing fuel tank holding 896 litres (237 gal.).

Structure of the Corsair was conventional all-metal, although extensive spot welding rather than riveting gave it a very smooth skin.

The 18-cylinder Pratt & Whitney Double Wasp engine drove a three-bladed Hamilton Standard propeller. At 4.04 m (13 ft.) across, it was easily the biggest fitted to a fighter of the time.

The cockpit was set well back along the fuselage. Visibility ahead and down was poor, which contributed to the type's early carrier landing problems.

F4U-1A Corsair

Type: single-seat, carrier-operable fighter-bomber

Powerplant: one 1492-kW (2,000-hp.) Pratt & Whitney R-2800-8 Double Wasp 18-cylinder radial piston engine

Maximum speed: 671 km/h (417 m.p.h.) at 6605 m (20,000 ft.)

Range: 1650 km (1,010 mi.)

Service ceiling: 11,247 m (37,000 ft.)

Weights: empty 4074 kg (9,000 lb.); loaded 6350 kg (14,000 lb.)

Armament: six 12.7-mm (.50 cal.) Browning M2 machine-guns with 400 rounds (outboard) and 375 rounds (inboard) per gun; up to 1800 kg (4,000 lb.) of bombs or rockets

Dimensions:
span	12.49 m	(41 ft.)
length	10.16 m	(33 ft. 5 in.)
height	4.90 m	(15 ft. 1 in.)
wing area	29.17 m²	(314 sq. ft.)

COMBAT DATA

MAXIMUM SPEED

The Corsair remained one of the fastest fighters of the war. Far superior to hasty improvisations like the Seafire, it was also much faster than late-war Japanese interceptors like the Raiden, which had been designed to try to match American fighter performance.

F4U-1A CORSAIR	671 km/h (417 m.p.h.)
J2M RAIDEN	612 km/h (380 m.p.h.)
SEAFIRE Mk III	570 km/h (354 m.p.h.)

RANGE

Air warfare at sea is generally fought at longer ranges than on land, especially when the sea is the Pacific Ocean. Aircraft designed for Pacific operations generally had far greater range than those like the Seafire, which were intended for more confined areas of operation.

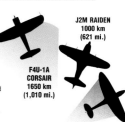

J2M RAIDEN 1000 km (621 mi.)

F4U-1A CORSAIR 1650 km (1,010 mi.)

SEAFIRE Mk III 750 km (470 mi.)

ARMAMENT

The Corsair carried a heavy bombload at great speed. It was more lightly armed than some of its contemporaries, although superior American pilot training meant that this was not too much of a handicap during a dogfight. The big '50-calibre' machine-gun still packed quite a punch, with the ability to sink small warships.

F4U-1A CORSAIR 6 x 12.7-mm (.50 cal.) machine-guns 1800 kg (4,000 lb.) of bombs

J2M RAIDEN 2 x 20-mm (0.79-in.) cannon 2 x 7.7-mm (.303 cal.) machine-guns

SEAFIRE Mk III 2 x 20-mm (0.79-in.) cannon 4 x 7.7-mm (.303 cal.) machine-guns 227 kg (500 lb.) of bombs

A combat record second to none

■ **1943 – FIRST COMBAT:** The first F4U users were the Marines of Guadalcanal's 'Cactus Air Force', who revelled in its speed and power.

■ **1944 – AIR SUPERIORITY:** Going to sea with the US Navy in early 1944, the Corsair established domination over Japanese fighters.

■ **1945 – NIGHT-FIGHTER:** By the end of WWII, night-fighting Corsairs carried airborne intercept radar with a wing-mounted antenna.

■ **1951 – ATTACK BOMBER:** With rockets and up to 2000 kg (4,400 lb.) of bombs, the Corsair was a mainstay of US Korean War attack capability.

VOUGHT

SB2U VINDICATOR

● US Navy scout-bomber ● Pacific 1942 ● Royal Navy trainer

Built in 1935, while the service still favoured biplanes, Vought's SB2U Vindicator was the US Navy's first monoplane scout bomber. This two-seat, all-metal combat plane was a step forward in the 1930s, but by the time World War II began it was inferior to other fighting machines in its class. Vulnerable to fighter attack, the SB2U actually saw relatively little combat service, although it performed admirably in the training role.

▲ *The Battle of Midway of 1942 was one of the few engagements in which the Vindicator saw combat in World War II. Its lack of performance against fighters like the Japanese Zero meant it was replaced by the Douglas SBD Dauntless.*

VOUGHT SB2U VINDICATOR

◀ **Improved variants**
Carrying bright pre-war markings, nine SB2Us formate. Later versions carried more fuel, armament and armour.

▲ **Prototype**
This is the first XSB2U-1 seen shortly after completion. The Vindicator was relatively lightly constructed compared to later dive-bomber types.

▲ **Fleet Air Arm Chesapeake**
The V-156 proved unsuitable for the Royal Navy's escort carriers due to its long take-off run, and was relegated to a land-based training role.

▲ **Based aboard USS Saratoga**
These three SB2U-1s are seen on 23 May 1939 in the full markings of bomber squadron VB-3.

◀ **SB2U-3 of VS-1**
The US Navy did not officially adopt the name Vindicator until the SB2U-3 version was delivered.

FACTS AND FIGURES

➤ In 1936, tests at Anacostia Naval Station, Washington, showed the SB2U to be superior to its SB3U biplane competitor.

➤ The prototype for the SB2U series made its maiden flight on 4 January 1936.

➤ The first SB2Us went to US Navy unit VB-3 from 20 December 1937.

➤ Captured French V-156s are reputed to have been used to bomb Dover, although this was never confirmed.

➤ Two Marine Corps squadrons flew Vindicators in action in the Pacific.

➤ In 1939 a single SB2U-1 had floats added and flew as a seaplane XSB2U-3.

PROFILE

Diving pioneer monoplane

Configured much like other scout and torpedo-bombers of the 1930s, the Vought SB2U Vindicator was designed to fly from aircraft-carrier decks. However, once in the air it lacked the speed, manoeuvrability or defensive armament to survive against the nimble, single-seat fighters emerging in the late 1930s.

In the mid-1930s, it took the US Navy many months to choose the Vindicator in preference to a competing biplane design. Once production Vindicators began to emerge

from Vought Sikorsky's Stratford, Connecticut, factory in 1937, it was very clear that the monoplane was the wave of the future. Designers kept improving the Vindicator. Even so, it was at best only an equal for the Navy's other scout bomber of the era, the Douglas SBD Dauntless. US Navy and Marine Corps SB2Us were active against the Japanese in the Pacific, including the Battle of Midway, during World War II, but were soon replaced by other types.

Vought built and delivered 24 of 40 planned aircraft to France

under the designation V-156. Some of these fell into German hands after the French capitulated. Fifty more, called Chesapeakes, went to the British Fleet Air Arm, which used them in an operational training role serving with two squadrons.

Left: Bomber squadron VB-3 'Top Hatters' equipped with SB2U-1s in 1939. The squadron was still active in 1990, serving in the Gulf War as fighter squadron VF-14 with F-14 Tomcats.

Above: In 1938 France's naval air service ordered the SB2U under the Vought company designation V-156-F3.

SB2U-3 Vindicator

Type: carrier-based scout/bomber

Powerplant: one 615-kW (825-hp.) Pratt & Whitney R-1535-02 Twin Wasp Junior radial piston engine

Maximum speed: 391 km/h (242 m.p.h.) at 2895 m (9,500 ft.)

Range: 1802 km (1,117 mi.)

Service ceiling: 7195 m (23,600 ft.)

Weights: empty 2556 kg (5,623 lb.); loaded 4273 kg (9,400 lb.)

Armament: two 12.7-mm (.50 cal.) machine-guns (one forward-firing and one in rear cockpit), plus up to 454 kg (1,000 lb.) of bombs

Dimensions:
span	12.80 m	(42 ft.)
length	10.36 m	(34 ft.)
height	3.12 m	(10 ft. 3 in.)
wing area	28.33 m²	(305 sq. ft.)

CHESAPEAKE MK I

In Royal Navy service the Vought V-156 was known as the Chesapeake. AL924 was one of 50 V-156-B1s ordered, and the first entered service in 1941 with No. 811 Squadron at Lee-on-Solent.

Pratt & Whitney's R-1535 Twin Wasp Junior engine powered the SB2U and V-156. This drove a two-bladed metal propeller.

The Chesapeake had provision for four forward-firing machine-guns in the wings, with a further free-mounted gun in the rear cockpit. American SB2U-3s had one forward- and one aft-firing 12.7-mm (.50 cal.) machine-gun.

A Fleet Air Arm three-tone grey colour scheme was applied to the Chesapeake. This aircraft also carries early-style national markings as displayed at the start of World War II.

ROYAL NAVY AL924

A 'trapeze' below the cockpit was fitted to a bomb on the centreline pylon. This pulled the bomb downwards and clear of the aircraft.

The undercarriage on the Vindicator retracted to the rear and rotated through 90°, with the wheels fitting into a recessed bay in each wing.

Maximum ordnance load for Fleet Air Arm Chesapeakes was 680 kg (1,500 lb.) of bombs: either three 227-kg (500-lb.) bombs or a dozen 53-kg (117-lb.) bombs. US Navy Vindicators were restricted to 454 kg (1,000 lb.) of bombs.

The arrester hook can be seen in the retracted position on this aircraft. The arrester gear on British aircraft was of a different design to the American.

COMBAT DATA

BOMBLOAD

Even though it was an improvement over that of the SBU-1, the bombload carried by the Vindicator was still inferior to that of the Dauntless, the Navy's main wartime scout/bomber.

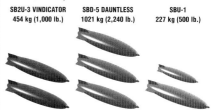

SB2U-3 VINDICATOR	SBD-5 DAUNTLESS	SBU-1
454 kg (1,000 lb.)	1021 kg (2,240 lb.)	227 kg (500 lb.)

MAXIMUM SPEED

Top speed performance of the Dauntless was only marginally better than that of the Vindicator. However, other more marked performance improvements made the SBD the superior aircraft.

SB2U-3 VINDICATOR	391 km/h (242 m.p.h.)
SBD-5 DAUNTLESS	406 km/h (251 m.p.h.)
SBU-1	330 km/h (198 m.p.h.)

ENGINE POWER

Power ratings climbed steadily to take advantage of better engines. SBDs introduced a significantly more powerful engine which improved flight performance and load-carrying capability.

SB2U-3 VINDICATOR	SBD-5 DAUNTLESS	SBU-1
615 kW (825 hp.)	895 kW (1,200 hp.)	522 kW (700 hp.)

Naval dive-bombers of World War II

■ **AICHI D3A:** Known as 'Val' to the Allies, the D3A was a major participant in the Pearl Harbor attack of 1941. Over 1400 were built.

■ **DOUGLAS SBD DAUNTLESS:** Entering service in 1940, the SBD served with the Navy and Marine Corps, and replaced the SB2U.

■ **FAIREY BARRACUDA:** First flown in 1940, this aircraft was employed as a dive-bomber by the Royal Navy in the Atlantic and the Pacific.

■ **JUNKERS Ju 87:** The Ju 87C-1 variant of the 'Stuka' was intended for the German carrier *Graf Zeppelin* before construction was halted.

WESTLAND

LYSANDER

● Army co-operation ● Clandestine spyplane ● Air–sea rescue

When Westland created its most famous aircraft, the immortal Lysander, in 1935, no one dreamed that this high-winged craft would fly into occupied territory, at night, on secret missions vital to the outcome of World War II. The Lysander introduced STOL (short take-off and landing) capability, crucial to today's military, long before the term was coined. As a flagship for spying missions behind the lines, it had no equal.

▲ *With a wide range of speed, short-field take-off and landing capability and a strong undercarriage, the Lysander was well suited to clandestine flights into the fields of Belgium, France and Holland.*

WESTLAND LYSANDER

▲ Field operations
The winter of 1939/40 was very difficult for the Army co-operation Lysanders in France. Wheel covers were removed to prevent the mud from clogging the inside of the spats when flying from fields.

▲ Air-sea rescue
Lysanders were flown by RAF air-sea rescue squadrons. The Mk IIIA had a good range and slow-flying qualities for dropping dinghies to aircrew in the sea.

▼ Easy access
Almost all of the starboard side of the Lysander's fuselage panels could be removed for inspection and access to internal equipment.

◀ Ground attack
The first Lysander had a 20-mm (0.79-in.) Oerlikon cannon mounted above each of the wheel fairings for a possible army ground-attack support role.

Gunner down ▶
The first production Lysander, nicknamed 'The Pregnant Perch', was fitted with a ventral gun position with two cannon for strafing trials. Here it has come to grief after suffering engine failure.

FACTS AND FIGURES

➤ The prototype for the Lysander series made its first flight on 15 June 1936.

➤ First entering RAF service in May 1938, the Lysander went on to fly with more than 30 squadrons during World War II.

➤ Total production of all models of the Lysander was 1652 aircraft.

➤ Lysanders saw service in Burma, Egypt, Greece, India and Palestine.

➤ A total of 225 Lysanders were manufactured by National Steel Car Corporation of Canada.

➤ A remarkable 21 Lysanders survive today as display aircraft or in flying condition.

PROFILE

Westland's Lysander spyplane

The Westland Lysander entered service in 1938 and served throughout the war. A versatile, solid performer useful for a wide range of duties, the aircraft earned a special place in history for its ability to land in unbelievably short spaces and drop off, or retrieve, secret agents working far behind enemy lines. The Lysander's broad wing and huge flight surfaces enabled it to land in unpaved fields, often with as little as 200 m (650 ft.) of taxi space. This was a treacherous job for its pilot – in many ways, riskier than the more glamorous task of flying fighters – but these covert missions were of paramount importance.

The Lysander is best-remembered for its use by confidential agents of British Intelligence and of the American Office of Strategic Services, but it also carried out many other tasks. Although less than ideal as an observation craft, the Lysander carried out reconnaissance missions and served as a spotter for Allied warplanes and artillery. Some aircraft functioned as VIP transports at battlefields where paved runways were unavailable. The Lysander made a unique contribution to World War II.

Right: RAF Lysander Mk IIIAs completed over 400 special operations between August 1941 and December 1944. They supplied the Resistance and flew agents in and out.

Above: This Lysander wears the markings of the Finnish air force early in 1940. Nine aircraft were obtained for Army co-operation duties, being fitted with removable stub winglets/bomb racks on each undercarriage leg for up to six 9-kg high-explosive bombs.

LYSANDER MK II

The high-winged Westland Lysander is most famous for its many night missions into mainland Europe, using its short take-off and landing capabilities to maximum advantage.

Lysander Mk IIIs were powered by a nine-cylinder Bristol Mercury XX air-cooled radial engine, developing 649 kW (870 hp.) at 4160 m (13,653 ft.). It had a front edge exhaust collector ring.

The pilot sat high in the cockpit, which took him level, and in front of, the wing leading edge. It had transparent sliding roof and deep glazed side windows.

The high wing was a distinctive shape with a single main spar. Leading-edge slats were positioned along the full span, in two sections. Handley-Page flaps were fitted between the elevators and the fuselage.

The all-metal framed fin and rudder was fabric covered. The tailplane was metal-framed and covered, although the elevators had fabric covering.

The propeller was a three-bladed, pitch-controllable de Havilland type with a medium-sized spinner. A Rotax electric engine starter was normally fitted.

The main fixed landing gear was machined aluminium alloy, bent into shape, with Dowty internally sprung wheels.

The front fuselage consisted of square, light-alloy tubing, while the rear fuselage was welded steel tube. It was covered by fabric over wooden stringers with detachable metal panels.

The non-retractable Dunlop 'Ecta' tailwheel was fully castoring. A message hook could be provided at the rear.

Lysander Mk III

Type: army co-operation aircraft

Powerplant: one 649-kW (870-hp.) Bristol Mercury XX radial piston engine

Maximum speed: 341 km/h (211 m.p.h.) at 1525 m (5,000 ft.)

Range: 966 km (600 mi.)

Service ceiling: 6655 m (21,800 ft.)

Weights: empty 1980 kg (4,356 lb.); maximum take-off 2866 kg (6,305 lb.)

Armament: four 7.7-mm (.303 cal.) Browning machine-guns (one in each wheel spat and two on trainable mount in rear cockpit); up to 227 kg (500 lb.) of flares, rocket projectiles or bombs

Dimensions:
span	15.24 m	(50 ft.)
length	9.30 m	(30 ft. 6 in.)
height	4.42 m	(14 ft. 6 in.)
wing area	24.15 m²	(260 sq. ft.)

Clandestine mission

1 UNARMED: Using dead-reckoning the pilot flies his black-painted Lysander by moonlight to a secret landing site in France. It is identified by coded torch flashes.

2 FIELD LANDING: With only portable lights marking the strip the pilot makes a steep approach and a short field landing.

3 RAPID PICK-UP: In real danger of discovery the pilot releases a rope ladder from the side of the cockpit and the agent climbs quickly into the Lysander.

4 SHORT TAKE-OFF: Now much heavier, with an extra person on board, the pilot has to take-off from the field and clear obstacles, before setting course back home.

COMBAT DATA

ARMAMENT

The Lysander carried more defensive armament and a higher bombload than either the Henschel Hs 126 or the Fieseler Fi 156 Storch. For self-defence it had two pairs of Browning machine-guns, compared with the Hs 126's two singles and just one gun fitted to the Storch. Lysanders could also carry over 200 kg (500 lb.) of bombs while the Henschel only manage half that weight.

Fi-156 STORCH
1 x 7.9-mm (0.31-in.) MGs

LYSANDER Mk III
4 x 7.7-mm (.303 cal.) MGs

Hs 126
2 x 7.9-mm (0.31-in.) MGs

WESTLAND

WHIRLWIND

- Long-range fighter ● Ground attack ● Heavily armed

A sound design let down by unreliable engines, the Whirlwind was a bold attempt to give the RAF a fighter with greater range than single-engined types. With four cannon grouped in the nose, it was able to bring a heavy weight of fire to bear on ground targets. Only two squadrons were issued with Whirlwinds, but the aircraft was greatly appreciated by its pilots. If it had been fitted with better engines, the Whirlwind's career might have taken a different turn.

▲ Although designed as a fighter, the Whirlwind was a very capable light-bomber. On anti-shipping patrols in the Channel or attacking German airfields in northern France the Whirlwind proved a success. The squadrons even developed a dive-bombing technique for the aircraft, achieving good results against the E-boats.

WESTLAND WHIRLWIND

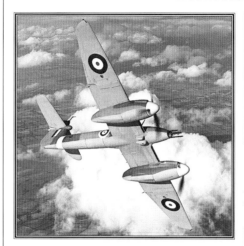

▲ Low-level striker
Carrying bombs on the wing pylons, Whirlwinds made low-level dashes across the Channel before attacking German-held airfields. The success of these missions depended on the element of surprise.

▲ Capable dogfighter
With good speed and excellent handling the Whirlwind could match the Bf 109 in a dogfight. They notched up a number of kills in 1942.

▲ Production problems
Deliveries of Whirlwinds from the Westland factory were painfully slow due to a shortage of engines.

▲ Powerful punch
The Whirlwind was fitted with four 20-mm (0.79-in.) cannon, making it the most powerfully armed fighter in the RAF. However, early problems with these reduced serviceability and a mixed armament may have been a better option.

▲ Fast fighter
The key to the Whirlwind's impressive performance was its highly streamlined shape.

FACTS AND FIGURES

- ➤ The Whirlwind was the first single-seat twin-engined fighter to enter RAF service.

- ➤ The Whirlwind was so secret that the first public mention of it in Britain was in a German magazine article.

- ➤ In August 1941 Whirlwinds escorted a force of Blenheims all the way to Cologne.

- ➤ Whirlwind production ran to 112 aircraft before the final service delivery to the RAF was made in December 1941.

- ➤ Bomb-laden Whirlwinds were usually nicknamed 'Whirlibombers' by pilots.

- ➤ Whirlwinds attacked the *Scharnhorst* and *Gneisenau* battleships in February 1941.

PROFILE

Westland's wonder

During the early part of World War II, Britain was very short of twin-engined fighters with the endurance to fly operational sorties across the English Channel and attack targets well inside occupied France. The Westland Whirlwind seemed to be the answer.

Entering service with No. 263 Squadron in December 1940, the Whirlwind was well armed for the ground-attack role and few pilots had ever seen such a concentrated weight of fire from four closely grouped 20-mm (0.79-in.) cannon.

The main problem was the engines, which were sometimes quite a liability. The Rolls-Royce Peregrine gave trouble both on the ground and in the air and the decision was taken – after No. 137 Squadron had also received Whirlwinds in September 1941 – not to develop it further. Installation of better engines would have meant a major and time-consuming redesign, and in view of the steady availability of Beaufighters and Mosquitoes, the Whirlwind became one of the war's potential outstanding aircraft that had to be left on the sidelines.

Before it was withdrawn, however, the Whirlwind gave a good account of itself on cross-Channel fighter operations. This attractive twin made short work of German ground targets, E-boats and other enemy shipping. Bombs supplemented the Whirlwind's cannon and for a time, the two squadrons were the scourge of the Germans.

Above: Despite the engine problems, No. 263 Squadron achieved some success with the Whirlwind. A profitable month was August 1941, when they destroyed four Bf 109s and an E-boat.

Left: If the Whirlwind had been fitted with the superlative Merlin engine it could have been a great fighter with a top speed of 680 km/h (422 m.p.h.). Unfortunately, the Merlin was needed for the single-engined fighters and the heavy bombers.

Whirlwind Mk I

Type: single-seat fighter/fighter-bomber

Powerplant: two 660-kW (885-hp.) Rolls-Royce Peregrine liquid-cooled piston engines

Maximum speed: 580 km/h (360 m.p.h.)

Range: 1290 km (800 mi.)

Service ceiling: 9144 m (30,000 ft.)

Weights: empty 3770 kg (8,294 lb.); loaded 5166 kg (11,365 lb.)

Armament: four 20-mm (0.79-in.) Hispano cannon in fuselage nose, plus up to 454 kg (1,000 lb.) of bombs under wings

Dimensions:
span	13.72 m (45 ft.)
length	9.98 m (32 ft. 9 in.)
height	3.52 m (11 ft. 6 in.)
wing area	23.22 m² (250 sq. ft.)

WHIRLWIND MK I

Deliveries of the Whirlwind began in June 1940 when the first machine was delivered to No. 263 Squadron. This machine also served with No. 263 Squadron in the winter of 1941/42 from Charmy Down.

The Whirlwind carried its armament in the nose. It was heavily armed for the early stages of the war with four 20-mm (0.79-in.) cannon.

The single-seat cockpit bulged high above the fuselage giving the pilot excellent visibility.

This aircraft carries the markings of No. 263 Squadron. The only other squadron to fly the Whirlwind operationally was No. 137 which flew anti-shipping sorties.

The tailplane was mounted mid-way up the tall tailfin, which gave the Whirlwind good stability. This was especially useful when dive-bombing.

Despite being an excellent design with superb low-altitude performance, the Whirlwind was never built in large numbers. The main reason was the unreliability of its Rolls-Royce Peregrine engines.

The Whirlwind's rudder extended to the bottom of the fin, allowing the pilot to line up the aircraft very accurately during a bomb run.

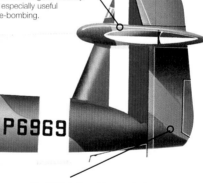

COMBAT DATA

MAXIMUM SPEED

At the start of the war the Whirlwind was the fastest twin-engined fighter in the world. The later P-38 was exceptionally fast and proved the equal of most single-engined fighters.

WHIRLWIND Mk I — 580 km/h (360 m.p.h.)
P-38 LIGHTNING — 666 km/h (413 m.p.h.)
Bf 110C — 560 km/h (347 m.p.h.)

RANGE

Designed from the start as a long-range fighter, the Whirlwind could escort the early British bombing raids well inside enemy territory. The P-38 could double its range by carrying drop-tanks.

WHIRLWIND Mk I — 1290 km (800 mi.)
P-38 LIGHTNING — 724 km (450 mi.)
Bf 110C — 775 km (480 mi.)

ARMAMENT

The Whirlwind was very heavily armed for RAF fighters of the time, but it experienced some problems with its cannon. German aircraft were always well armed and the Bf 110 was no exception.

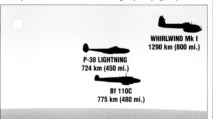

WHIRLWIND Mk I — 4 x 20-mm (0.79-in.) cannon
P-38 LIGHTNING — 1 x 20-mm (0.79-in.) cannon, 4 x 12.7-mm (.50 cal.) MGs
Bf 110C — 2 x 20-mm (0.79-in.) cannon, 5 x 7.92-mm (0.31-in.) MGs

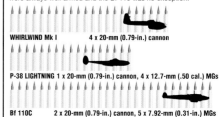

Twin-engine day-fighters of World War II

LOCKHEED P-38 LIGHTNING: The P-38 was particularly effective as a long-range fighter in the Pacific War. P-38s were credited with more Japanese aircraft than any other type.

MESSERSCHMITT Bf 110C: At the start of World War II the Bf 110 was Germany's primary long-range fighter. It performed well in Poland and France, but suffered in the Battle of Britain.

PETLYAKOV Pe-2: Often referred to as the 'Russian Mosquito', the Pe-2 was a versatile combat aircraft. The interceptor version was fast and heavily armed.

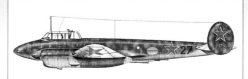

YAKOVLEV

YAK-1 & YAK-7

● Fighter ● Ground attack ● Trainer

irst of the modern Yak fighters, the Yak-1 came into service just in time to meet the German invasion in 1941. Agile and fast, the Yak was the best of the new Soviet fighters and could equal a Bf 109 or Fw 190 in a dogfight, in addition to being a useful ground attacker. The Yak-7, originally designed as a trainer, was hastily converted for fighter duties. Both aircraft evolved into better designs, the later Yak-3 and Yak-9.

▲ These Soviet pilots on the Kharkov front shot down 15 enemy aircraft in a week in May 1942. The Yaks gave the USSR air superiority after the appalling defeats inflicted in 1941.

PHOTO FILE

YAKOVLEV YAK-1 & YAK-7

◀ **Ramjet Yak**
The DM-4S ramjet engine was tested on a few Yak-7UTI trainers. Despite the success of the trials, the system was not adopted for operational use.

▼ **Best of the Yaks**
Finest of the Yak-1s was the Yak-1M, which soon evolved into the Yak-3. Reduced weight helped give agility, although oil cooling was problematic.

▲ **Trainer variant**
Best of the trainers was the Yak-7V with a fixed undercarriage and full dual controls, but no armament, radio or self-sealing fuel tanks.

◀ **Enemy colours**
This Yak-7 was seized by the Germans and tested. Most German pilots thought the Yak rather crude and simple, but respected its combat performance.

Mass production ▶
More than 8700 Yak-1s and 6300 Yak-7s were produced in total. Yaks were by far the most important fighters in the Soviet arsenal.

FACTS AND FIGURES

➤ Test pilot Piontkovskii was killed in January 1940 while flying the prototype, which had manufacturing defects.

➤ Naval aviation units of the Black Sea Fleet used the Yak-1 over Crimea.

➤ The Yak-7DI long-range fighter version ultimately became the Yak-9.

➤ Female ace Lilya Litvak claimed 13 victims in a year of flying the Yak-1 over Rostov and Stalingrad.

➤ The 728th Polk replaced its old I-16s with Yak-7Bs only in mid-1943.

➤ Stepan Suprun was made a Hero of the Soviet Union for test flying the Yak-1.

PROFILE

First of the new Yak fighters

Yak began the project for a single-seat lightweight fighter before the war, and the prototype I-26 first flew in January 1940. Emphasis was on the use of cheap materials (using composite wooden skins and fabric covering) and integral armament, with a nose-mounted cannon. The aircraft showed immediate promise, and was rushed into production even before trials were complete. By March 1942, the Yak-1 was being produced in a lightened form for increased agility.

The acute shortage of fighters meant that the trainer Yak-7 was converted to combat use, including artillery spotting and fighter duties. The aircraft was also fitted with rockets for ground attack and tank-busting, and cameras for reconnaissance. The Yak-7R even mounted a rocket engine in the tail. Best of the Yak-1s was the Yak-1M, which was quickly redesignated the Yak-3. This aircraft gave its pilots a much improved field of vision, and was one of the war's most agile fighters.

The early Yaks were a vital stopgap between obsolete designs like the I-16 and the excellent later Yaks and Lavochkin La-5s with which the Soviet Union won the air war on the Eastern Front.

Left: The prototype I-26 proved to be a winner immediately. Few modifications were made to the production fighter, the main ones being a strengthened wing and better armour protection. The prototype was known as the Krasavyets (Beauty).

Right: The Yak-1M was a far better dog-fighter, thanks to its new wing, bubble canopy and new gunsight.

Yak-1

Type: single-seat fighter and fighter-bomber

Powerplant: one 782-kW (1,050-hp.) Klimov M-105 V-12 liquid-cooled engine

Maximum speed: 530 km/h (329 m.p.h.)

Initial climb rate: 7 min to 5000 m (16,400 ft.)

Turning time: 360° in 17.6 sec

Range: 700 km (435 mi.)

Service ceiling: 9000 m (29,500 ft.)

Weights: empty 2550 kg (5,610 lb.); loaded 3130 kg (6,886 lb.)

Armament: 1 x 20-mm (0.79-in.) ShVAK cannon, one or two ShKAS 12.7-mm (.50 cal.) machine-guns; wing racks could carry six RS-82 rockets

Dimensions:
span 10.00 m (32 ft. 10 in.)
length 8.48 m (27 ft. 9 in.)
wing area 17.15 m² (185 sq. ft.)

YAK-1M

The ultimate Yak-1, the Yak-1M was soon to become the Yak-3, the most feared foe of Luftwaffe pilots at low level. First flown on 20 September 1943, the Yak-1M's fuel tanks were fitted with a nitrogen fire-suppression system.

One of the biggest improvements to the Yak-1M was the upgraded jettisonable hood, which gave all-round vision and was less prone to jamming than those of the first models. A sheet of 9-mm (⅜-in.) back armour protected the pilot from enemy fire.

A slogan painted on the fuselage was a common feature of Soviet fighters. This one reads: 'To the pilot of the Stalingrad front B.N. Yeremin, from the farmers of Stakhanov collective farm'. Wooden bonded skin materials were cheaper than aluminium, and easier to repair after combat damage.

Летчику Сталинградского фронта
Гвардии Майору тов Еремину Б.Н.
От колхозника колхоза „Стаханова„
тов Головатова

Armament comprised a single 20-mm (0.79-in.) ShA-20M cannon firing through the spinner (replacing the heavier ShVAK of earlier Yak-1s) and two UBS 12.7-mm (.50 cal.) machine-guns in the upper fuselage.

The Yak-1M used the all-metal wing fitted to the Yak-9, which could be more easily replaced in the field. Oil coolers were mounted in the wingroots.

The radiator was cooled by air from a long ventral intake. The 30-kg (66-lb.) central fuselage fuel tank supplemented two larger wing tanks.

Another improvement to the Yak-1M was the addition of an elevator mass balance to lighten control forces. The rear fuselage skin was 2-mm (⅛-in.) plywood. The tailwheel retracted, unlike that of the early Yak-1s.

Wartime Russian interceptors

■ **La-5:** Almost as agile as the Yak-3, the La-5 was relatively lightly armed and had fuselage skins made of wooden composite. It was produced in vast numbers, and updated variants like the La-7 and La-9 flew in Korea.

■ **MiG-3:** Very fast and possessing excellent high-altitude performance, the MiG-3 was doomed to a short life by its need for the AM-35 engines used by the Il-2 Shturmovik attack aircraft, which was deemed by Stalin to have production priority.

■ **Yak-9D:** Filling the need for a long-range escort fighter, the Yak-9 proved the equal of the Bf 109G and Fw 190D. This was also the most numerous of the 37,000 Yaks produced in the war; some were flown by the French Normandie-Niemen squadron.

COMBAT DATA

MAXIMUM SPEED

The Yak-1 was slower than most of its adversaries, mainly because of its higher drag. However, its agility more than made up for its lack of all-out speed, and most combat occurred at low level where the Yak was at least as good as its German adversaries.

YAK-1 530 km/h (329 m.p.h.)

Bf 109F 624 km/h (387 m.p.h.)

HURRICANE Mk IIB 541 km/h (335 m.p.h.)

SERVICE CEILING

Most Soviet fighters performed best at low level, and the Yak was no exception. German pilots were even ordered to avoid combat with the later Yak-3 at heights below 5000 m. The rival MiG-3, however, flew better than the Yak at altitude.

HURRICANE Mk IIB 10,850 m (35,600 ft.)

Bf 109F 10,668 m (35,000 ft.)

YAK-1 9000 m (29,500 ft.)

RANGE

The Yak achieved its performance and agility at the expense of reduced fuel capacity. Since Soviet fighters usually flew from bases close to the front line, this was not a problem. The Yak-9 was fitted with long-range fuel tanks.

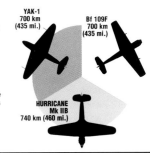

YAK-1 700 km (435 mi.)

Bf 109F 700 km (435 mi.)

HURRICANE Mk IIB 740 km (460 mi.)

YAKOVLEV

YAK-9

● Dogfighter supreme ● Long range ● Soviet fighter

▲ *Widely regarded as the most important fighter of the Great Patriotic War, the Yak-9 was the mount of many of the top-scoring Soviet aces of World War II.*

Based on the Yak-7, the Yak-9 had metal wing spars to make room for additional fuel. Deliveries started in August 1942, and by October the type was in action at Stalingrad. The new fighter proved popular with its pilots, despite its limited armament of one 20-mm (0.79-in.) cannon and a single 12.7-mm (.50 cal.) machine-gun. By mid-1944 there were more Yak-9s in Soviet service than all other fighters put together, and the final variant fought in the Korean War.

PHOTO FILE

YAKOVLEV YAK-9

▼ **Proven design**
Although its makers studied British and German fighter designs, the Yak-9 relied on the proven layout of wooden wings with a welded steel fuselage.

▲ **Constant combat**
Having been produced in larger numbers than any other Russian fighter, the Yak-9 saw continuous action against German Fw 190s and Bf 109s and always gave an excellent account of itself.

Russia's defender ▶
Lined-up on a grass airfield, rows of Yak-9s wait for the signal to attack the German army in another of the great battles which took place on the Eastern Front.

▲ **Source of pride**
Preserved Yak-9s are displayed throughout the former Warsaw Pact countries as a reminder of the war.

Feared foe ▶
German pilots were given orders to avoid combat with any Yakovlev fighter fitted with an air scoop because of the superior handling of such designs in a dogfight.

FACTS AND FIGURES

➤ A variant of the Yak-9 was fitted with a 37-mm (1.47-in.) cannon which, on firing, made the aircraft pitch up violently.

➤ The 'D' variant was developed to meet a request for a fighter with more range.

➤ By 1944 the Yak-9 outnumbered all other fighters in the Soviet air force.

➤ Yakovlev developed a long-range courier variant, stripped of all excess weight, for use over the battlefield.

➤ A batch of aircraft was supplied to Bulgaria in late 1944.

➤ One aircraft factory produced 20 Yak-9 fighters per day.

PROFILE

Fighter of the Eastern Front

Compared with the earlier Yak-7B, the Yak-9 had a retractable tailwheel and just a single 12.7-mm (.50 cal.) machine-gun in the forward fuselage, where the previous model had two. The cockpit was moved slightly aft and the radiator was moved forward, but otherwise it was externally similar. However, there were frequent later modifications to meet operational requirements.

The Yak-9D had fuel capacity increased to 650 litres (172 gal.)

and was powered by a 1014-kW (1,360-hp.) M-105PF-3 engine, while the -9DD had its fuel capacity increased to 880 litres (233 gal.) for operations over Romania and Yugoslavia. The -9T carried a 37-mm (1.47-in.) cannon for anti-tank missions.

A more radical change was the all-metal Yak-9U, which flew for the first time early in 1943. Powered by a 1230-kW (1,650-hp.) engine, it was capable of 670 km/h (415 m.p.h.), but development was delayed by

the loss of the prototype on an early test flight and it did not become operational until late 1944.

The all-weather Yak-9P did not appear until after the war. It was to be Yakovlev's last piston-engined fighter, and it was exported to several Soviet-allied countries.

The immense pride in what was achieved with the Yak-9 is demonstrated by the numerous preserved examples displayed at various military installations in Russia.

YAK-9D

This Yak-9 was one of those equipping the Free French Normandie-Niemen regiments in 1944; this example survived until the end of the war.

A feature of the Free French aircraft was the spinner painted in the three colours of the French flag.

Despite its intended role as a fighter, the Yak-9D carried no armament in its wings. These were of a mainly wooden construction with later variants incorporating metal ribbing.

Yak-9D

Type: single-seat long-range fighter/ground attack aircraft

Powerplant: one 940-kW (1,260-hp.) Klimov VK-105PF-1 liquid-cooled piston engine

Maximum speed: 533 km/h (330 m.p.h.) at sea level; 597 km/h (370 m.p.h.) at 3650 m (12,000 ft.)

Range: 1360 km (843 mi.); operational range 1329 km (824 mi.)

Service ceiling: 10,000 m (33,000 ft.)

Weights: empty 2420 kg (5,324 lb.); maximum take-off 3115 kg (6,850 lb.)

Armament: one 20-mm (0.79-in.) ShVAK cannon mounted in the spinner; one 12.7-mm (.50 cal.) machine-gun installed in the engine cowling

Dimensions:
span	9.74 m	(31 ft. 11 in.)
length	8.50 m	(27 ft. 10 in.)
height	2.60 m	(8 ft. 6 in.)
wing area	17.15 m²	(185 sq. ft.)

Positioned in the nose spinner was the 20-mm (0.79-in.) ShVAK cannon with 120 rounds of ammunition; to the right of this on the upper cowling was a single 12.7-mm (.50 cal.) machine gun, supplied with 200 rounds.

Visibility for the pilot from the Yak-9 cockpit was exceptional, especially when later variants were produced with a cut-down rear fuselage allowing the pilot all-round vision.

Many colour schemes were used by the front-line Soviet fighter squadrons; this example displays the summer camouflage. In winter a rough coat of white would be applied over the entire aircraft.

After the enlargement of the oil tank a larger oil cooler was installed in the nose of the aircraft. German fighter pilots were ordered by their superiors not to engage in combat with Soviet fighters with this feature.

The wide track undercarriage of the Yak-9 was adopted from earlier Yakovlev fighters. This allowed the aircraft to operate from rough fields alongside the advancing Soviet army. Very few landing accidents were encountered with the aircraft.

COMBAT DATA

MAXIMUM SPEED

Though not the fastest of the Russian fighters of World War II (that was Lavochkin's La-5FN), the Yak-9D was able to compete and win in dogfights with German fighters. The advent of the Fw 190D to the theatre saw the Russian fighters pushed to their limit.

Yak-9D	597 km/h (370 m.p.h.)
La-5FN	648 km/h (402 m.p.h.)
MiG-3	640 km/h (397 m.p.h.)

OPERATIONAL RANGE

In response to requests from the Russian army for a fighter with more range, the Yakovlev design team incorporated additional fuel tanks in the wings into the design. This development allowed the Yak-9D to perform better for strike missions than both the MiG-3 and La-5FN.

Yak-9D 1329 km (824 mi.)

La-5FN 764 km (474 mi.)

MiG-3 1195 km (740 mi.)

TAKE-OFF WEIGHT

The take-off weight of the Yak-9D was surprisingly small compared to other similar Soviet fighters. Both the MiG-3 and La-5FN were more often used in the ground-attack role, while the Yaks provided air cover and performed air interception duties.

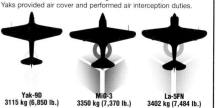

Yak-9D 3115 kg (6,850 lb.)

MiG-3 3350 kg (7,370 lb.)

La-5FN 3402 kg (7,484 lb.)

Stalin's air power

■ **MIG-3:** Developed from the MiG-1 the MiG-3 was found to have extremely poor performance and was quickly relegated to secondary tasks in 1942.

■ **Pe-2:** The most outstanding tactical bomber of World War II, this versatile twin-engined aircraft continued to serve with the Soviet air force after the war.

■ **P-39 AIRACOBRA:** Offered to the Soviet air force under the terms of the Lend-Lease agreement, the P-39 was used as a ground attack aircraft.

INDEX

594035